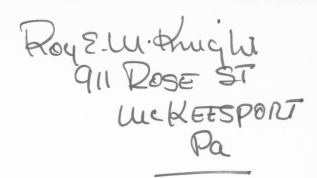

**Prentice-Hall
Industrial Relations and Personnel Series**

*DALE YODER, Editor*

BELCHER—*Wage and Salary Administration, 2nd ed.*
BELLOWS—*Psychology of Personnel in Business and Industry, 3rd ed.*
BELLOWS, GILSON, AND ODIORNE—*Executive Skills*
BRINKER—*Social Security*
DAVEY—*Contemporary Collective Bargaining, 2nd ed.*
DUBIN—*Human Relations in Administration, 3rd ed.*
DUBIN—*Working Union-Management Relations*
ECKER, MACRAE, OUELLETTE, AND TELFORD—*Handbook for Supervisors*
GOMBERG—*A Trade Union Analysis of Time Study, 2nd ed.*
LINDBERG—*Cases in Personnel Administration*
MAHONEY—*Building the Executive Team*
OTIS AND LEUKERT—*Job Evaluation, 2nd ed.*
PFIFFNER AND FELS—*The Supervision of Personnel, 3rd ed.*
SHARTLE—*Executive Performance and Leadership*
SHARTLE—*Occupational Information, 3rd ed.*
SHOSTAK AND GOMBERG—*Blue-Collar World*
STONE AND KENDALL—*Effective Personnel Selection Procedures*
THOMPSON—*Personnel Management for Supervisors, 2nd ed.*
TOLLES—*Origins of Modern Wage Theories*
YODER—*Personnel Management and Industrial Relations, 5th ed.*
YODER—*Personnel Principles and Policies, 2nd ed.*

third edition

# HUMAN RELATIONS IN ADMINISTRATION

## with Readings

## ROBERT DUBIN

*Research Professor, Department of
Sociology, University of Oregon*

PRENTICE HALL, INC., Englewood Cliffs, N.J.

*Library of Congress
Catalog Card No.: 68–28328*

Current Printing (last digit):

10 9 8 7 6 5 4 3 2 1

Printed in the United States of America


PRENTICE-HALL INTERNATIONAL, INC., *London*
PRENTICE-HALL OF AUSTRALIA, PTY. LTD., *Sydney*
PRENTICE-HALL OF CANADA, LTD., *Toronto*
PRENTICE-HALL OF INDIA PRIVATE, LTD., *New Delhi*
PRENTICE-HALL OF JAPAN, INC., *Tokyo*

# Preface to Third Edition

When the first edition of this book was published
seventeen years ago, it was designed to give a behavioral science focus to the new field that was later
to be called organization theory. The second edition
added more of the behavioral science theory and
research as it developed. This latest edition continues
in the same tradition, and strengthens it.

Contemporary developments in organization theory
have specialized two aspects of this field. The first is
decision theory with its emphasis on the structure of
decision making about a single problem. Still in its
infancy is normative decision making which is concerned with the ordering of decisions about multiple
and interrelated problems. This is, of course, where
the human relations of decision making enters, for
most organization decisions involve solving several
related problems in the same decision. This more
complex feature of many organizational decisions was
emphasized in the two earlier editions of this volume
and continues to receive similar emphasis in this
edition.

A second major development in organization theory
has been the growing sophistication of ideas about
motivation and the ways in which individuals fit themselves into group enterprises. The disciplines of industrial psychology and industrial psychiatry, and
what has recently been labelled industrial social
psychology, all emphasize the *intra*-personal motives
for behavior, and reactions to situations. Human relations, as the title of this volume suggests, deals with

*inter*-personal relations. The theory and analysis of this book, therefore, supplements psychological approaches. Major developments in the behavioral sciences have been in precisely this direction. *Human Relations in Administration*, consequently, is a book which carries forward the developments in *all* of the behavioral sciences and applies them to the administration of organizations.

The specific changes in this third edition over the previous edition include the following major modifications.

(1) There have been thirty-one new selections added to the text. Most of these deal with empirical studies of business behavior and provide further substantiation for the theoretical conclusions contained in this volume.

(2) Eighteen selections included in the second edition have been removed from this new edition. Those items dropped have either been replaced by a more up-to-date empirical treatment of the subject or they have been theoretical statements for which we now have some sort of research base which has been substituted.

(3) An entirely new chapter entitled "Leadership and Productivity" has been added to draw attention specifically to a critical issue in the area of human relations in administration. This chapter is the final one in the section on Administrative Action.

(4) As with the previous editions, the chapter introductions and the introductory statements to the individual selections have often been rewritten to insure the greatest possible clarity and integration of the text as a whole.

(5) As with the two previous editions, special attention has been given to maintaining unity in this volume. The earlier editions emphasized the development of coherent theory of human relations in administration and this theory has been further amplified and substantiated in this latest edition.

(6) Some of the readings which had previously been employed have been further edited to insure that they made their point as concisely as possible.

Your attention is called to the fact that the cases included in the previous editions have been deleted. This is done in order to make room for enlarged substantive chapters. It is also done in recognition of the fact that the number of cases in all fields of administration has vastly increased since the first edition. Many professors will want to continue to employ cases, and even those previously included in this volume. The publisher has therefore graciously granted to any user of this new edition of *Human Relations in Administration*, the right to reproduce and use the cases of the earlier edition in supplementing the present volume. The copyright restriction on the cases is not waived covering reproduction of the cases for any purpose other than use in conjunction with a course of instruction employing the present edition.

The "organizational revolution" has made necessary an increasing knowledge of administration for more and more present and future administrators. This volume contributes to this knowledge of administration an integrated and balanced picture in which management and behavioral science theory and research have been effectively joined. It is hoped that the new generation of managers and administrators who will include this volume as part of their education will benefit as much as did their predecessors.

## Note to the Reader

The individual readings and selections of this volume are tied together by the introductory notes. Each broad section has its own introduction; each chapter is introduced with a statement of its purpose and content; and each selection is introduced with a summary of its contents. Each of these linking statements points out the connections for what you are reading and the rest of the volume.

It is therefore suggested that you be sure to read the initial statements as well as the substantive selections. The two are intimately related and should be read together to gain the fullest measure of benefit in using this volume.

R. D.

# Preface to Second Edition

Since the publication of the first edition of this book a decade ago, a name has been given to designate the broad area of which human relations in administration are a part. That name is "organization theory."

For recent students of the subject it might appear that the newness of the name is an indication that the subject is also of recent origin. It is perhaps more accurate to say that naming this field of inquiry resulted from intensive analytical concentration by specialists on the facts of administration, and from the need to give a distinctive title to their endeavors. The "classic" organization theory had its roots in the writings of Aristotle and Plato; was given detailed attention by Machiavelli in *The Prince* in the 16th century; assumed its modern dress in the early work of Frederick W. Taylor with his development of scientific management at the beginning of the 20th century; and reached a level of high analytical sophistication in the last decade with the appearance of such representative works as March and Simon, *Organizations* (1958); Haire, *Modern Organization Theory* (1959); and the founding of new journals like *Administrative Science Quarterly* (1956) and *Management Science* (1954). The field of inquiry is ancient, but it is only within our generation that specialized attention has been focused upon it.

The leadership of organized human groups can be summarized as the administration of four basic resources necessary for their functioning: men, materials, machines, and money. The management of each of these basic resources has already become specialized. This volume deals with the human resources of organizations, and the human relations involved in their administration. The subject matter of our attention is coordinate with the administration of materials, machines, and money.

This new edition retains the broad theoretical framework of the original volume. The framework continues to prove viable and productive of useful insights about human administration.

The specific revisions in the new edition include:

(1) Reorganizing the order of chapters and regrouping them into analytically consistent units represented by the six parts of the text. This provides a smooth developmental use of concepts, moving from a broad frame of reference, through detailed analysis of administrative personnel and basic administrative relationships, to actual administrative behavior and the environments of administrative action.

(2) Deleting two chapters, portions of whose contents have been combined with other chapters.

(3) Adding a new chapter, "Organization and Society," to round out the consideration of the environments surrounding the administrator.

(4) Replacing fifteen reading selections with twenty-five new ones. In the selection of new readings particular emphasis has been placed on adding empirical studies that provide a strong reality referent for the theory of each chapter.

(5) Presenting enough new material on the theoretical controversies about human relations to give the reader a real awareness of the fact that our theoretical models are constantly evolving as research penetrates more deeply into the facts of human administration. We do have established knowledge, but with that has also come an awareness of what we still do not know for sure. Every serious student of administration should be sensitive to the balance between knowledge and ignorance so that his own outlook will remain open-minded.

(6) Rewriting many of the chapter introductions and discussions of the readings as well as adding new overviews for each part in order to further improve the connectedness of the text.

The cases in Part VII have not been changed from the first edition. Since their first publication, a broad range of case materials has become readily available for instructional use. In particular, the Intercollegiate Case Clearing House (Soldiers Field, Boston 63, Massachusetts) periodically publishes the *Intercollegiate Bibliography: Cases in Business Administration*, which lists and describes hundreds of cases in print and available at a very nominal fee from that agency. Cases emphasizing governmental administration are published by the Inter-University Case Program, whose catalog may be secured from the University of Alabama Press, Drawer 2877, University, Alabama. Our cases have been retained in the volume for the continued use of those professors who have found them valuable. [The cases have been deleted from the Third edition.]

The first edition was widely used in the education of persons whose

future careers involve administration of the human resources of organizations. The volume proved useful in the curricula of business administration,
public administration, engineering administration, hospital administration,
recreational administration, and institutional management, as well as in such
disciplines as sociology and social anthropology with their focus on social
organization. It is hoped that this second edition will have continuing usefulness in these and related areas.

R. D.

# Preface to First Edition

This book deals with an exceedingly difficult and complex subject. We all know that there is nothing simple about individual human behavior. When men join together into groups, new complexities are introduced. A structuring of interaction between people results. New dimensions of interaction and sentiment are created. A host of new kinds of relationships between people, between groups, and with physical objects comes into play.

Is there some possibility that the nature of this thing called human organization is so complex as to defy understanding? I think not. The state of our knowledge about the formal organizations of society has reached the point where we have both systematic knowledge and reinforcing insights. It should be possible to distill out of the fund of human knowledge a system of principles—theory, if you will—about human organizations. I firmly believe, furthermore, that this theory would have the utmost practical value to men of affairs.

This book is organized around two approaches to learning. For the student, still relatively inexperienced about the ways people behave in organizations, a long series of cases of actual organizational behavior is included. [Deleted from the Third edition.] These cases should provide him with inductive insights into the nature of organizations. For the individual who has already had considerable experience in organizations, the first part of the book should serve to arrange his insights into a systematic body of principles. For both, the combination of experience (from direct contact or through these cases) and theory should establish a mature foundation for knowledge about and successful participation in the many organized groups around which their lives will center. In fact, life is inextricably interwoven with the organizations of which one is a part. No one can afford not to make a serious attempt to understand human behavior in organizations.

The whole of this book is based upon the conviction that theory is practical. There are those who say that administration or organized group action is an art. There are those who insist that the human relations of administration is most certainly an art. My only reply must be this—read this book. See if the theoretical insights are artistic in character. I think not.

This book is grounded in research. It is my conviction that theory that is not significantly related to research is but a prelude to knowledge, not the handmaiden of action. Well-grounded theory gives us the basis for meaningful and appropriate action. On the other hand, we must distinguish between theory and application. The market is flooded today with books that tell specifically what to do under this, that, or the other circumstance. None of them is grounded in fundamental theory. The result is that there are as many rules for "good human relations" as there are different human relations situations. Can you keep a card file of 500 "human relations" rules in your head? (I have counted that many separate rules in the books.) The answer is No. But you can keep a fundamental theory in your head, because good theory is basically simple. It summarizes and classifies thousands of historically unique events in coordinated and significantly interrelated categories.

This, then, is not a "cook book." It does not contain 10 rules for this and 14 steps for that. Such rules are the height of impracticability. They confuse rather than enlighten. This is especially true when one becomes the slave of the rules, when one thinks only of the rules and not of the situations to which they are supposed to apply, how they are to apply, what they are to accomplish, or why they accomplish it. In short, in being rule-oriented, there is real danger of behaving pathologically in relation to the rules. (The meaning of this will be seen in Chapter 7.)

This book was written for the general reader, not for my academic colleagues. In assembling the readings, and in laying out the theoretical structure of which they are a part, I have purposely followed the practice of asking: Does this make sense, and how can it be most readily understood? My colleagues are sophisticated men and would, perhaps, have preferred a more esoteric language. But language is a means to understanding, not an end in itself.

I am particularly happy to be able to present the theory of human relations of administration in the form of readings. It means that the knowledge in this field is cumulative. It means that we can add bits and parts and get a coordinated whole. This is not just a set of readings, covering, in encyclopedic form, every last aspect of the human relations of administration. It is intended as a consistent and integrated treatment of the subject. There is constant interplay and feed-back among all the parts of the theory. It would, of course, have been possible to write the book in textbook form, relegating the authors to footnotes. But I welcome the opportunity to give the fullest measure of recognition to the men who have constructed or contributed to the theory of human relations of administration. There is no better way to do this than by quoting their very words.

The debt owed to the men who have contributed to one's education and insights is seldom fully perceived. To the men whose thoughts are here quoted must be extended the thanks of a grateful student. To their publishers go thanks for permission to reprint, which is acknowledged individually at the beginning of each selection. Professors Louis Wirth and Everett C. Hughes of the University of Chicago were the first to arouse the author's deep interest in the study of human organization. Dean Austin Grimshaw of the University of Washington College of Business Administration was responsible, when in charge of the Management Division at the University of Illinois, for inviting me to teach a course on "Problems of Administration and Organization" in the College of Commerce and Business Administration. His continued encouragement led to the collection of the cases contained in this book. The intellectual curiosity of the students in "Problems" and in a graduate seminar in sociology on "Theory of Social Groups" provided the immediate stimulus for developing the theoretical portion of this book. A small grant of funds from the Business Management Service of the University of Illinois facilitated the collection of some case material. Professor Merten J. Mandeville has taught many of the cases in this book and has been helpful with suggestions for their final form. Many individuals in numerous organizations have contributed their time, experience, and insights to the case materials. For obvious reasons they must go unnamed.

A special debt is owed to Professor Herbert Blumer for providing a long-time stimulus to the study of human behavior.

I can, of course, shift responsibility for the contents of this volume to others only where they are the named authors of selections.

R. D.

# Table of Contents

## part 1
**ADMINISTRATIVE PERSPECTIVES**    1

### 1. Education for Executives

Introduction    3

Changing Character of American Business    5
*Robert A. Gordon* and *James E. Howell*

Basic Elements in the Practice of Business    9
*Robert A. Gordon* and *James E. Howell*

Managerial Education—Soviet Style    16
*Raymond A. Bauer* and *Barbara Tschirwa*

Education for Executives    19
*Chester I. Barnard*

## part 2
**ORGANIZATIONS**    27

### 2. Organization as a Social System

Introduction    29

Significance of Organizations    31
*James G. March* and *Herbert A. Simon*

Administration of Organizations    34
*Peter B. Hammond, Robert W. Hawkes, Buford H. Junker, James D. Thompson,* and *Arthur Tuden*

Organization as a Resource    37
*Frederick Harbison*

The Organization Environment    44
*Robert Dubin*

## 3. Motivation in Organizations

Introduction    49

Motivation of Organization Activities    53
*Robert Dubin*

Social Handles of the Pay-Cup    60
*Whiting Williams*

Incentives for Work    63
*Robert Dubin*

Necessary vs. Voluntary Behavior    72
*Robert Dubin*


## 4. Organization and the Person

Introduction    77

Personal vs. Organizational Goals    80
*Chris Argyris*

Person and Organization    90
*Robert Dubin*

Personality-Versus-Organization Hypothesis    93
*George Strauss*


## 5. Informal Groups:    Structure and Processes

Introduction    104

Types of Work Teams    108
*Elton Mayo* and *George F. F. Lombard*

Informal Work Groups and the Formal Organization    110
*Leonard R. Sayles*

Organization Goals and Primary Groups    115
*Edward A. Shils*

Social Structure of the Whole Organization: The Restaurant    119
*William Foote Whyte*


# part 3

## ADMINISTRATIVE PERSONNEL    127


## 6. Organization Office

Introduction    129

Professionalization of Business Leadership    131
*Robert A. Gordon*

Cross-Cultural Comparisons of Managerial Offices    137
*Frederick Harbison* and *Charles A. Myers*

**7. Administrative Systems—Bureaucracy**

      Introduction   144

      Technical Characteristics of a Bureaucracy   147
         *Robert Dubin*

      The Efficiency of Bureaucratic Administration   152
         *Robert Dubin*

      The Nature and Sources of Pathological Bureaucratic
      Behavior   155
         *Robert K. Merton*

      Bureaucratic Problems in Business Organizations   159
         *Marshall E. Dimock* and *Howard K. Hyde*

**8. Executives**

      Introduction   163

      Current Opinions about Qualifications for Success in
      Business   164
         *Robert A. Gordon* and *James E. Howell*

      Executive Careers in Business   170
         *Robert A. Gordon* and *James E. Howell*

      Managerial Behaviors   179
         *Robert Dubin*

      Conflict in the Executive Suite   185
         *Ross Stagner*

**9. Specialists**

      Introduction   190

      The Administrator's Objectives and Staff Specialists   193
         *Fritz J. Roethlisberger*

      Specialists and the Ignorance of Nonspecialists   195
         *Wilbert E. Moore* and *Melvin M. Tumin*

      Limited Perspective of Staff Specialists   197
         *Robert K. Merton*

      The Management Consultant   201
         *Modern Industry*

      Staff and Line Relationships—A Study of Conflicts   202
         *Melville Dalton*

      Specialists and Work-Flow Frictions:  A Case Study of
      Purchasing Agents   214
         *George Strauss*

      Scientists as Employees in Industry   219
         *Simon Marcson*

## 10. Supervisors

Introduction    222

The Foreman:    "Man In The Middle"    223
*Fritz J. Roethlisberger*

The Changing Role of the Working Supervisor    232
*George Strauss*

The Behavior of Foremen    243
*Robert Dubin*

Executives and Supervisors:    Self-views and Views of Each Other    248
*Charles H. Coates* and *Roland J. Pellegrin*


## part 4

### ADMINISTRATIVE RELATIONSHIPS    253


## 11. Power

Introduction    255

Types of Power    257
*Herbert Goldhammer* and *Edward A. Shils*

Power In Identical Organizations    263
*James D. Thompson*

Power of Subordinates in Complex Organizations    272
*David Mechanic*


## 12. Authority

Introduction    278

Authority    279
*Herbert A. Simon*

Managers, Staff Experts and Authority    286
*Amitai Etzioni*

The Horizontal Dimension of Interaction    291
*Henry A. Landsberger* and *Frank B. Miller*

Authority, Bureaucracy, and Leadership    294
*Robert Dubin*

Authority and Privilege Pay    297
*Robert Dubin*


## 13. Status

Introduction    300

Functions of Status Systems in Formal Organizations    302
*Chester I. Barnard*

Clothing and the Man at Work    315
   *William H. Form* and *Gregory P. Stone*

Power Pay, Authority Pay, and Status Pay    317
   *Robert Dubin*

## part 5
### ADMINISTRATIVE ACTION    321

## 14. Communication

Introduction    322

Communication and Symbols    324
   *Fritz J. Roethlisberger*

The Executive's Environment is Verbal    325
   *Fritz J. Roethlisberger*

Shared Knowledge and Teamwork    328
   *Herbert A. Simon*

Authority and Communications to Subordinates    330
   *Tom Burns*

Communication and Decision-Making    332
   *Marvin D. Dunnette*

The Reciprocal Perception of Communication    339
   *Theodore D. Weinshall*

Non-Verbal Communication on the Job    342
   *Martin Meissner*

Informal Communication and the "Grapevine"    345
   *Herbert A. Simon*

## 15. Decision-Making

Introduction    347

Decision-making in Organizations    348
   *Chester I. Barnard*

Limitations on Decision-making    355
   *Robert Tannenbaum*

Imperatives Affecting Profit and Price Decisions    360
   *Robert A. Gordon*

Imperatives Affecting Industrial Relations Decisions    367
   *Robert Dubin*

"Muddling Through"—Science or Inertia    372
   *Yehezkel Dror*

How Useful are "Scientific" Tools of Management?    375
   *Edward F. R. Hearle*

Sharing Decision-making with Subordinates    379
   *Robert Tannenbaum* and *Fred Massarik*

## 16. Leadership

Introduction    385

Functions of Organizational Leadership    388
*Philip Selznick*

Dilemmas of Leadership in the Democratic Process    390
*Chester I. Barnard*

Strengthening Leadership—Cooptation    395
*Philip Selznick*

Ambition, Mobility, and Sponsorship    397
*Everett C. Hughes*

Leadership and Executive Subordination    400
*Tom Burns* and *G. M. Stalker*


## 17. Subordination

Introduction    406

Upward Orientation Toward Superiors    407
*Robert Dubin*

Subordination    409
*Georg Simmel*

Reaction to Subordination    412
*Henri de Man*

Administrative Compliance and Initiative    414
*Reinhard Bendix*


## 18. Control

Introduction    421

The Administrator's Control Functions    422
*Fritz J. Roethlisberger*

A Theory of Non-Financial Controls in Small Enterprises    425
*Dale Henning*

Rules, Standards, and Rationality    427
*Dickson Reck*

The Inspectors and the Foreman    431
*Harold E. Kubly*

Control Evasion at the Managerial Level    433
*Robert Dubin*

Use and Misuse of Efficiency Controls    437
*Frank J. Jasinski*


## 19. Leadership and Productivity

Introduction    443

What Productivity Is    445
*General Electric Relations Services*

Supervision and Productivity    449
*Robert Dubin*


## part 6

### INTERNAL AND EXTERNAL ENVIRONMENT    465

## 20. Technology

Introduction    467

The Pace of Technological Change    468
*National Commission on Technology, Automation, and Economic Progress*

Technology and Production    471
*Robert Dubin*

Automations Effect on Skill Levels    478
*Richard C. Wilcock*

Technology, Collaboration, and Morale    481
*William J. Goode* and *Irving Fowler*

## 21. Organizational Fictions

Introduction    488

Fictions    489
*Morris R. Cohen*

Organization Fictions    493
*Robert Dubin*

The Office Caste System    499
*Harrison R. Johnson*

## 22. Organization and Society

Introduction    502

Public Opinion and Institutional Change    503
*Robert Dubin*

The Manager's "Structure of Living" and Outside Intervention    507
*Neil W. Chamberlain*

Social Responsibilities of Businessmen    509
*Howard R. Bowen*

Local Business and Labor Leadership    517
*William H. Form* and *Warren L. Sauer*

Industry and Social Values    524
*Robert Dubin*

## Index    529

# part 1

# ADMINISTRATIVE

# PERSPECTIVES

This book is particularly designed for readers who want to know more about the complex business of running organizations. That means we are both involved in the process of education. It is especially appropriate, therefore, that the volume open with a consideration of education for executives. ᶰ~

In order to achieve an education in a particular area we need to know: (1) the characteristics of the portion of reality about which we are seeking knowledge; and (2) a useful way for orienting thinking in order to maximize the amount and value of the knowledge to be gained. One important way to achieve these twin goals in understanding administration is to answer the question: "What kind of education makes a good executive?"

In examining this question attention is directed at two primary issues. We first want to find out something about the general characteristics of the organizations whose administration is the subject matter of our study. We then turn to a consideration of the frame of reference which seems best suited to making executives sensitive to what they are doing, and why, so that they may be most effective in performing their functions. This leads to a consideration of the broad values by which components of the education of executives are ordered, from important to trivial, as they contribute to effective performance.

**OVERVIEW**

The issue of values and frame of reference is raised specifically again in the concluding chapter of the book when we consider the relationships between organiza-

*1*

tions and the society in which they operate. We begin this volume, then, by examining the valuable knowledge that will make the administrator most effective *inside* his organization as an executive. We close the book by turning attention to the administrator's functions *outside* his organization in relating it to the society of which it is a part.

# 1

# Education for Executives

You and I will agree that executives need education. We will also agree that this education needs to be extensive in areas covered, and intensive in the depth of coverage. Beyond these agreements there may be many points of argument about how to achieve both breadth and depth in the education of executives.[1]

We can well begin by asking: "What are the products of an education?" It seems to me that there are two general outcomes of useful education. First, *the educated man possesses a set of values with its accompanying frame of reference.* Second, *a fund of knowledge about an area of reality is acquired by the educated man.*

The value system of an educated executive can be sensed by drawing a contrast with the beliefs of an ignorant (not stupid) man. The educated man is likely to value truth, the ignorant man to accept convenience and expediency. With education, a man develops humility and a desire to know more; the ignorant man,

---

[1]Two recent inquiries have been directed at the education of business executives. Both pose the problem of the contrast between breadth and depth in the education of businessmen— between general education and specialization. It is my belief that this is not the choice faced by business education. Executives need both general knowledge *and* special knowledge. What is really much more difficult than choosing between these alternatives is to satisfy both. See: R. A. Gordon and J. E. Howell, *Higher Education for Business* (New York: Columbia University Press, 1959); and Frank Pierson *et al., The Education of American Businessmen* (New York: Mc-Graw-Hill Book Company, 1959).

in T. S. Eliot's words, is "one of the low on whom assurance sits, as a silk hat on a Bradford millionaire." A man with education displays constructive imagination—the ability to reach beyond present knowledge by keeping in touch with the known; the uneducated man merely builds castles in the air. Education develops a sense of relativity, a realization that things have an order of importance, and skill in discovering what this order is; ignorance breeds dogmatism by insisting that whatever is being done now is the best and most important thing to do. The educated man avoids glittering generalities; the ignorant man is most likely to traffic in them. These are several of the contrasting value preferences of educated men *vs.* ignorant men.

There follows from the preferred values a frame of reference for the educated executive. As Barnard so aptly states in his contribution to this chapter, "A need of the executive of the future is for broad interests and wide imagination and understanding." This means among other things a readiness to go beyond a "tool" approach to education; a willingness to develop individual intellectual abilities as the personal means for being a competent administrator; and a desire to understand the operating world of an organization. In short, the frame of reference of the educated executive most conducive to his efficient and effective performance includes valuing knowledge, insight, and understanding.

Accepting the frame of reference, we then have to inquire about the bodies of knowledge whose mastery marks the educated and effective executive. There are as many areas of detailed knowledge as there are types of operating problems of an organization whose daily solution is the con-

stant concern of administrators. This book deals with one such area—*the means by which human cooperation is built and sustained in getting accomplished the work of any organization.* This volume is lengthy and deals with a number of complex problems of human social systems. It is an attempt to give depth to knowledge, insight, and understanding about human relations in administration.

We should not confuse depth of knowledge with detailed information. Depth of knowledge requires a "big picture" into which the detailed parts can be fitted meaningfully. A broad theory of administration is a "big picture"; an encyclopedia of administrative practices is merely an unorganized collection of detailed information to which an alphabetical index is the only guide. This book features a comprehensive administrative theory; the footnote references suggest the supporting detailed information. We should add at once that this is not the only possible comprehensive theory of human administration. An understanding of it, however, should provide a foundation of knowledge with which to build a better theory, or to decide why alternative theories should be preferred. Whichever of the three possible outcomes is yours (that you like the content of this volume, that you can improve on it, or that you find other "big pictures" make more sense), reading this volume is designed to contribute to the education of executives.

The administration of business organizations is more widely understood than administration in any other kind of formal organization. Businesses also employ the largest single body of executives in our society. For these reasons most of the analysis in this book deals with business.

The first selection by Gordon and

Howell underscores some of the broad developments in our society which mold the character of business organizations. It pictures an organizational environment in which change is one of the central features. From this, the conclusion is drawn that the executives who run such organizations have to be aware of the dynamic environments in which they operate, and need a set of values and a frame of reference from which are generated matching dynamic administrative skills. The areas of business decision are then dealt with by the same authors in the second article with a view to suggesting some of the skills required in administrative behavior. In the concluding selection in this chapter, Barnard, writing fifteen years earlier, sets forth with remarkable foresight some important ideas about the content of education for executives. He particularly emphasizes knowledge about the human factors in administration—the special province of this book.

---

## CHANGING CHARACTER OF AMERICAN BUSINESS

*Robert A. Gordon* and *James E. Howell**

We should like to say a bit more about the important trends that have been "professionalizing" the practice of business. While numerous observers have commented on them, further consideration of these developments may suggest some of the kinds of education college students contemplating careers in business are likely to need. Since these trends will not soon be reversed, they also tell us something about the kind of environment in which businessmen will have to operate in the years ahead.

1. As business firms have grown in size, increasing emphasis is being placed on organizational problems. There has been an enormous increase in the importance of the administrative function. The process of decision-making has been diffused, greatly increasing the need for coordination and planning within the enterprise.

2. With the separation of ownership and management in the large firm, business leadership has largely been taken over by salaried executives. Capital or family connection is no longer necessary for a top position in business. For success in large-scale business, a "college degree has become more important than great wealth, and easier to obtain."[1]

3. The accelerating tempo of scientific and technological change is having a profound effect upon the practice of management. Businessmen increasingly need some technical background so that they can communicate with scientists and engineers. Long-range planning becomes more difficult but at the same time more essential. Increasing flexibility, of organization and of mind, is needed to permit rapid adjustment

*From *Higher Education for Business* (New York: Columbia University Press, 1959) pp. 13–17. Used with the gracious consent of the authors.

[1] Mabel Newcomer, *The Big Business Executive* (1955), p. 146.

to new situations. "Automation" in the factory, data processing equipment, and the like are revolutionizing production methods and office procedures, radically changing the composition of manpower demands, and increasing "the need for intellect and skill among all who plan, produce, operate, and maintain the process."[2] "If all these changes in industry are bewildering for the operative, they throw even more problems of adjustment onto the shoulders of the manager. Indeed, one of the most pressing of contemporary needs is to produce a sufficient number of enterprising and competent leaders of industry and society, capable of facing up to the demands of the increasingly complex and science-based economy which we are now entering."[3]

4. Related to these developments in engineering and the physical sciences has been, since the days of Frederick Taylor, a growing scientific attitude toward management problems. At first confined to production management in a narrow sense, the scientific attitude has now spread to all aspects of management activities. At the same time, there has been a concomitant growth of usable knowledge in the social sciences and in statistics that is providing an increasingly substantial basis for rational decision-making. The new "management sciences" are still in their infancy, but in a broader sense management science is increasingly being practiced

in the various functional areas of business.

5. While today's "other-directed" world may, as Riesman and Whyte suggest, be increasing the pressure for group conformity, it is also true that there has been a growing emphasis on the role of the individual in organizations. Instead of being taken as given, the individual and his contribution to the organization have become variables which are related to other variables that students in the field of human relations attempt to analyze and that "human-relations engineers" attempt to manipulate in the interest of organizational harmony and higher output. Skill in human relations has become an essential ingredient of effective management. This new emphasis on the psychological needs of the individual and on his capacity to influence his organizational environment is certain to become even stronger in the future than it is now.

6. There is growing need for highly trained staff specialists, as well as for administrators to coordinate the work of such specialists. The complexities and ramifying activities of modern large-scale business create a dilemma. Specialization, which is essential in today's large complex organizations, is coming to rest on an increasingly technical and rapidly changing body of knowledge that derives from the physical and social sciences and from mathematics and statistics. On the other hand, the need for the broader kind of administrative abilities, particularly in the upper levels of management, is also becoming more urgent. There is a growing recognition that the solution to this dilemma is to be found in training which emphasizes

[2]Cf. National Education Association, *Manpower and Education* (1956), p. 22.

[3]Alexander King, "Management as a Technology," *Impact of Science on Society*, VIII (June, 1957), 70. See also H. J. Leavitt and T. L. Whisler, "Management in the 1980's," *Harvard Business Review*, XXXVI (November-December, 1958), 41–48.

both the fundamental disciplines and the development of problem-solving ability and flexibility of mind. The need for training in the relevant basic disciplines and for a high level of analytical and problem-solving ability will certainly continue to grow.[4] In addition, business itself is taking increasing responsibility for meeting its specialized training needs, both by intra-company educational programs and by sending its employees back to school for special courses.

7. The increasing complexity of the firm's external environment has steadily added to the difficulties of the businessman's task. This is by now a familiar story: the increase in the power of organized labor and the steady upward pressure on wages; the expanding role of government; the Cold War and the precarious state of international relations; changes in the distribution of political and economic power and in the climate of public opinion; and so on.

As a result of these changes, the social responsibilities of the businessman are greater and more complex than they once were. The business manager, particularly in the larger firm, possesses great power for good or harm, and public opinion demands that this power be exercised with responsibility, even though the goals to be served are not always clearly dis-cerned or generally agreed upon. In this respect, the large corporation, directed by salaried managers but owned for the most part by passive stockholders, presents grave problems with which we have only begun to grapple. Our legal institutions still impose on the executive (at least implicitly) the primary obligation of seeking maximum profits for his firm and his stockholders. He is also under increasing pressure from a variety of groups to further their particular sets of interests. Cutting across these pressures is the growing demand that the business leader adopt broad social criteria, aimed at benefiting the weaker groups in the economy and society at large. To these goals we must add the personal goals of the business leader himself and of his subordinates. In an economic world that lacks the automatic regulation which the classical economists' concept of perfect competition was supposed to provide, the business executive must try to reconcile these partially conflicting goals, a task which may well be impossible.[5] In any event, the task calls for men of broad knowledge and sensitive perception, with a well-developed philosophy and set of ethical values, and with the ungrudging willingness to accept the responsibilities inevitably associated with the possession of power.[6]

---

[4]In a similar fashion, the engineering schools are now finding that fundamental training in mathematics, physics, and the theoretical aspects of engineering carry an engineer further in coping with new and difficult problems than does a detailed familiarity with the details of current engineering practice. See, for example, R. B. Adler, "Science and Engineering Education," *Journal of Engineering*, XLVII (October, 1956), 121–28.

[5]Cf. R. A. Gordon, *Business Leadership in the Large Corporation* (1945), pp. 340–42; A. A. Berle, Jr., *The 20th Century Capitalist Revolution* (1954), particularly p. 181; and F. X. Sutton *et al.*, *The American Business Creed* (1956), p. 358.

[6]Cf. J. A. Bowie, *Education for Business Management* (1930), particularly pp. 10–11. For a general discussion of some of the issues raised in this paragraph, see Bowen, *Social Responsibilities of the Businessman;* Berle, *The 20th Century Capitalist Revolution;* and Sutton *et al.*, *The American Business Creed.*

It can be taken for granted that the trends described in the preceding paragraphs will continue in the years ahead and that they will be reinforced by other kinds of change which can as yet be imperfectly foreseen. Today's student who will be tomorrow's businessman must be flexible of mind and adaptable to change. He needs not so much a specialized knowledge of present business practice as the qualities of mind and the kinds of basic knowledge that will permit him to understand and adapt himself to the kind of world in which he will live and work in the years ahead.

While it has been the large corporation that has been emphasized in this discussion, much of what has been said applies to the small firm also. The rational and scientific approach is needed in firms of small and moderate size as well as in the largest concerns. Indeed, the approach is even more necessary in the small concern if the competitive advantage in favor of the great corporation is not to increase still further. . . .

It would seem, then, that American businessmen would benefit from a professional-type education. They should be able to do a better job, for their firms and for society at large, with the right sort of education—if we can determine what the "right sort" is. . . .

We have, in the preceding paragraphs, put our stress on education for *business* careers. . . . But the educational needs of businessmen are not radically different from those of the administrators of other types of organizations. Organizational skill, problem-solving ability, imagination and foresight, a rational approach to the use of resources under the control of the organization, breadth of perspective, and a sense of social responsibility are qualities that are needed in all types of organizations—for example, in labor unions, government agencies, hospitals, and the military services. . . .

---

The sweeping picture we have just gained of the changing character of American business emphasizes organizational and human relations problems. "Skill in human relations has become an essential ingredient of effective management" declare the authors. This is to be understood in the broadest sense to include the knowledge and skills necessary to administer not only the interactions among the people o. ᵔrganizations, but also the relationships between organization members and environmental factors, like technology, which affect human behavior.

It is sometimes comforting, and certainly easy, to fall into the trap of making the world center on a single idea. It would be misleading to assert that all of administration is basically human relations. There are other important aspects of the work of administrators that involve considerations in addition to human relations. We need to have some sense of balance about the various dimensions of the practice of management so that we can put human relations in perspective. We must give full value for the critical importance of human relations in effective administration. We must also recognize that human relations are not the total picture.

The next discussion presents a balanced picture of the elements involved in organization management. The well-rounded executive understands *all* the elements that enter into his decisions and actions. He also can recognize human relations problems and assign relative importance to them as he carries out his daily work. A balanced perspective is an essential ingredient of executive practice. The mastery of the human aspects of organizations contributes to this balanced perspective.

---

## BASIC ELEMENTS IN THE PRACTICE OF BUSINESS

*Robert A. Gordon* and *James E. Howell**

We shall be concerned with what constitutes business competence and with how such competence can be developed through formal education. Business competence rests upon the possession of some combination of skills, i.e., of some array of knowledge combined with the ability to use it. The nature of the needed skills depends, obviously, on the kinds of problems with which businessmen must deal—on what it is that constitutes the practice of business.

In this connection, several aspects of the structure and functioning of the business firm need to be emphasized. First, the business firm is an *organization.* Second, the firm operates in an *environment* to which it is tied by both *market* (i.e., buying and selling) and *nonmarket* relationships. Third, within this environment and continuously adjusting to it, the firm is engaged in procuring and combining the services of men, money, and physical resources in order to create something for sale. If a primary objective of the organization is to make a profit from these activities, it is a business enterprise, even though it will have also other important objectives. If we eliminate the profit objective and the consequent need to generate sales revenues in excess of costs, the elements listed above will apply to all organizations, the more so as they engage in strictly economic activities.

With respect to each of these aspects of business, it is essential to emphasize the additional element of *change.* The model of the business world we are drawing is a dynamic one. The firm's organizational problems and needs are continually changing; change is the most important characteristic of the market and nonmarket environment in which it operates; the decisions involved in combining economic resources for the purpose of production and sale must continuously take account of changes which have already occurred or are anticipated. The businessman creates change and must adjust to change. He lives in an uncertain world that is in part of his own making.

· · ·

### ORGANIZATION ASPECTS

First, the firm is an organization. It is a "system of consciously coordinat-

*From *Higher Education for Business* (New York: Columbia University Press, 1959), pp. 61–69. Used with the gracious consent of the authors.

ed personal activities."[1] The successful functioning of any organization implies the planned and conscious coordination of the efforts of a group of persons toward a common set of goals. . . .

It is worth pausing for a moment to compare the role which organizational problems play in business with that which they play in the other fields for which the universities offer professional training. In the attention that must be paid to the organizational factor, business resembles military leadership, the church, and various other forms of institutional administration, private and public. It resembles much less medicine and even law and engineering. Although they all encounter administrative problems in varying degrees, doctors, lawyers, and engineers tend to concentrate their attention on the substantive aspects of their practice. It is different with the typical businessman. He must "manage" a set of economic variables, but within an organizational context that helps to determine the choices available to him and how he selects among the alternatives. The decisions he makes are affected by the fact that he operates within a system of consciously coordinated activities.[2]

Thus business education must concern itself with two kinds of professional preparation. It must provide the knowledge and skills to deal with substantive problems of finance, production, and the like. It must also seek to develop the organizational knowledge and skills that are needed. . . .

Let us review briefly some of the kinds of organizational problems the businessman (or anyone concerned with administrative problems) must face. These problems affect the businessman at all levels, but he becomes more conscious of them as he rises in the organizational hierarchy.

The successful functioning of an organization implies the setting of organizational goals and the reconciliation of these goals with the changing demands of the environment and with the goals of subordinate groups and individuals within the enterprise.[3] It also implies the establishment of administrative relationships, including the assignment of authority and responsibility and the development of a system of communications so that the need for action can be recognized, alternatives evaluated, orders transmitted, and the implementation of decisions controlled. Since organizations imply cooperative effort and hierarchical relationships, there must be supervision and personal leadership, including the recruitment, training, and development of personnel. As most writers on the subject have pointed out, the achievement of objectives through organizations re-

---

[1]C. I. Barnard, *The Functions of the Executive* (1938), p. 72. As one authority has put it, "the term *organization* refers to the complex pattern of communications and other relations in a group of human beings. This pattern provides to each member of the group much of the information, assumptions, goals, and attitudes that enter into his decisions, and provides him also with a set of stable and comprehensible expectations as to what the other members of the group are doing and how they will react to what he says and does." H. A. Simon, *Administrative Behavior*, 2nd ed. (1957), p. xvi. Cf. also J. G. March and H. A. Simon, *Organizations* (1958), chap. 1.

[2]In the need to deal with other human

beings as individuals, business does have some resemblance to law and medicine, but not to engineering.

[3]See, for example, J. D. Thompson and W. J. McEwen, "Organizational Goals and Environment: Goal-Setting as an Interaction Process." *American Sociological Review*, XXIII (February, 1958), 23–31.

quires that there be planned coordination of the efforts of individuals. An adequate system of communication is as essential to the organization as the nervous system is to the human body. And since the cooperators in organizations are human beings, the element of "human relations"—of inducing loyalty to and identification with the organization and its goals—becomes an essential element in the efficient functioning of any organization.

Organizational behavior takes place in a world characterized by change and uncertainty. To be viable, organizations must be able to cope with uncertainty. They must be able to generate the information needed to identify changes in their environment and to predict future change. They must be flexible enough to adapt to both internal and external change. They should be able not only to adjust to perceived changes in their environment, but also to plan and initiate new types of activity—in short, to innovate.[4]

All this implies that the businessman needs some grounding in such knowledge as we have regarding how human beings function in organizations, the conditions necessary to secure continuously effective action within organizations, and the problems that arise when one attempts, in the face of change and uncertainty, to make and to implement rational decisions within organizations.[5] The

organizational factor suggests also that the businessman needs not merely certain kinds of knowledge or understanding, but also such types of skills as administrative skill in planning the design of organizational relationships, skill in devising communication systems and in communicating, and skill in eliciting cooperation from colleagues and subordinates. . . .

## THE NONMARKET ENVIRONMENT

. . . The business firm, like any organization, operates within a set of environmental influences. There is continuous interaction between the firm and the various parts of its environment, and, taking all enterprises together, economic history is the record of this interaction. Let us concern ourselves first with what earlier we called the non-market environment.

This aspect of the business environment includes all those external influences which do not involve the firm's buying and selling relationships. The elements of this environment are almost too numerous to list: for example, the legal and political framework within which business must operate, the aggregate of economic influences which determine the level of national income and employment and the way in which these change with the passage of time, the whole field of international developments, and the development of science and tech-

---

[4]For some discussion of the dynamic aspects of organizational behavior, see, for example, March and Simon, *Organizations,* chaps. 6–7.

[5]Argument exists among the experts as to whether there is a systematic and clearly delineated body of knowledge which can be called "organization theory," or whether what we have are merely scraps of knowledge and hypotheses from the various "behavioral sciences," lacking the integration which would make of them a separate and

self-contained body of knowledge. The argument regarding this issue has not been particularly fruitful. What is clear is that here is a range of problems of great importance to the businessman, that these problems must be dealt with in one way or another, and that from a variety of sources we are in the process of developing a greater understanding of the nature of these problems and how they affect the "substantive" decisions that business operations entail.

nology, which for many firms becomes the dominating force determining what they produce and the technical processes they utilize. A variety of pressures from private groups also is a part of the nonmarket environment, and these pressures exert themselves not merely through prices and the terms of contracts. Thus the influence of such groups as labor unions, farm groups, trade associations, and banks affects the way in which the firm carries on its business and the kinds of decisions which are made within the firm. Perhaps even more important is the intangible something we call the climate of opinion, both the widespread social attitudes that comprise present public opinion and the ideas of individuals and groups that will shape the public opinion of the future.

There are two points to stress about the relations between business firms and their environment. One is the fact of mutual interaction. The environment helps to determine the alternatives on the basis of which business decisions are made and also affects the value systems which supply the criteria for choosing among these alternatives. At the same time, business firms, individually and particularly collectively, react upon their environment. It is this fact that makes it so important for businessmen to bring a keen sense of social responsibility to their jobs. More than economic effects ensue from their decisions. Business activity affects government policy in a variety of ways. It helps to determine the conditions of community living; it has been largely responsible for the kind of urban civilization in which we live; it helps to shape the intellectual and moral tone of the times.[6]

Another important aspect of the interrelations between business and its environment is that these relations are continuously changing, evolving out of the past into a future that can be but vaguely foreseen. Change and uncertainty are the very essence of the businessman's life. . . .

All this suggests something about the kinds of knowledge and abilities required of the businessmen. To cope with a continuously changing nonmarket environment he needs breadth of knowledge, a sense of historical perspective, and flexibility of mind. He needs also to have a sensitive and sophisticated appreciation of the role which business does and can play in our kind of society. All this implies some familiarity with the more relevant branches of history and perhaps philosophy, and some knowledge of the social sciences, particularly economics, political science, and sociology. Implied also is some appreciation of the nature and significance of scientific and technological developments. The acquisition of knowledge in these different areas ought to bring a sense of historical perspective, contribute to flexibility of mind, and help to develop a sense of responsibility to the larger society of which the businessman is a part.

## THE MARKET ENVIRONMENT

The business firm operates in a market as well as a nonmarket environment. This is the third element in our conceptual scheme. Human, financial, and physical resources are acquired in markets, and the terms on which these resources are made available are set in these markets. The economist's factors of production must be procured before they can be combined into something which the firm

[6]See, in this connection, F. X. Sutton *et al.*, *The American Business Creed* (1956).

will attempt to sell. How much it can sell, and on what terms, will also be determined in a set of markets.

Thus the business enterprise is surrounded by an environment of market as well as nonmarket influences. Here also are mutual interaction and continuous change. The individual firm is affected by, and in turn has an effect on, the markets in which it operates, the more so the larger it is in relation to the market. Conditions in these markets are continually changing, thereby making highly uncertain the future consequences of present action and creating the need for prompt and frequent adjustment.

The critical importance of the market environment calls for both general and specialized knowledge. There are some types of knowledge about the market environment that probably all businessmen should have. They need some analytical tools which will give them a start in understanding in a general way how any kind of market functions.[7] They also need a broad familiarity with the kinds of institutional arrangements under which goods and services (including labor and money) are bought or hired. Furthermore, a great deal of specialized knowledge about particular markets is required, depending on the things a particular firm buys and sells and on the division of labor within any given enterprise. Thus there will be specialists in finance, in personnel and industrial relations, in purchasing, and in marketing. Insofar as this specialized knowledge involves knowledge of immutable facts and command of particular analytical

[7]Such understanding rests in part, but only in part, on economics. The other social sciences, particularly those called "the behavioral sciences," are also very much involved. See, for example, the recent advanced text by Wroe Alderson, *Marketing Behavior and Executive Action* (1957).

skills, it can profitably be acquired through formal education. But much of it involves a mastery of detail which is continually changing and must be acquired through actual experience.

## ECONOMIC MANAGEMENT

Knowledge of markets is closely related to the fourth element in our conceptual scheme, which for brevity we can call economic management. The firm must manage the resources it procures, combine them, and arrange for the sale of what it produces. Economic management in this sense has several aspects.

First, there is the need to procure and to conserve each of the types of resources used: labor, money, and physical resources. While the term "conserve" may seem awkward in this context, it accurately describes what is involved in much of financial management, in the management of raw materials and work in process, in the maintenance of physical equipment, and in personnel management.

There is, secondly, the job of "production," of planning the systematic combination of labor and materials with the help of plant to create the final utilities which the firm intends to sell. "The "conservation" of labor, materials, and plant goes on very largely during the act of production; thus there is an extremely close relation, both in practice and in business education, between these functions.

The last aspect of economic management involves sale of the final product. This is the larger part of the so-called marketing function. Here the business firm is concerned with decisions as to what and how much can be sold and by what means. Since the viability of a business enterprise depends on its ability to secure a continuous stream of sales receipts which exceed its costs by a satisfactory margin, the marketing function will naturally be heavily stressed. Obviously, also, this aspect of (internal) economic management must depend heavily on knowledge of the (external) market environment.

Efficient economic management requires the identification, weighing, and choice of relevant alternatives. It also requires some guarantee that decisions, once made, will be properly implemented. Hence there must be an "information system" which will yield data as a basis for both decision-making and for evaluating the results of decisions already made. Statistics, accounting, and techniques of interpretation and analysis based on numerical data are essential tools in the kinds of economic management we are now discussing. All managers require some working familiarity with these subjects. In addition, there is the need for specialized technicians capable of generating the necessary information in its most useful form, and capable also of analyzing it to extract the kinds of information the decision makers need for planning and control. These informational and analytical tools, however, are of no help unless there is a logical system of analysis to use in the evaluation of alternatives. The logical system most relevant here is that of formal economics. Some ability to work with economic criteria and some knowledge of basic economic relationships, however acquired, are essential for the various kinds of "functional management" and for the overall management which integrates these functions from the point of view of the enterprise as a whole.

Economic management requires both general and particular skills and general and particular kinds of knowledge. There is need for general problem-solving ability and skill in the use of analytical tools, especially those derived from accounting, statistics, and economics. There is also need for more particularized kinds of knowledge dealing with the various functions of business and their interrelationships. Needed also are the kinds of technical knowledge which the natural sciences and engineering provide. Depending on its size and internal organizational relationships, the firm will need both generalists and specialists. The specialists may be concerned with any one of the aspects of economic management mentioned earlier, and, within any one of these aspects, may concentrate on the management of a particular kind of economic resource, such as labor, plant, or financial resources.

Economic management obviously requires also some familiarity with the other elements in our conceptual scheme. For instance, marketing or financial decisions are made in an organizational context; they must also take into account the pressures which impinge on the firm from its market and nonmarket environment. Economic management must, of course, be particularly sensitive to the market environment. This helps to explain why, in dealing with the various "functional" areas of economic management, business schools frequently deal with the "managerial" and the external market aspects together. For example, the same course may deal with "financial management" and the operation of the money and capital markets.

This discussion of economic management must of course be interpreted in a dynamic context. The management of economic resources takes place in a continually changing environment. It must try to anticipate a future that can be but imperfectly foreseen. It must not only react to past and current change but also try to anticipate future change. Imagination, the ability to make decisions on the basis of incomplete information, and a semi-intuitive skill in anticipating the future all have to be combined with the kinds of knowledge we have described.

Some recapitulation may be useful at this point. The practice of business at what might be called a professional level centers around the making of decisions about economic variables in an organizational context and within a market and nonmarket environment that is continuously changing. Such decision-making has both a "line" and a "staff" aspect. Decision-making implies not only the final act of choice and the exercise of authority to insure that the decision is carried out. It involves also the compiling, processing, and interpretation of information which permits the listing and evaluation of the alternatives from which a choice can be made. Thus "staff work" is an integral part of business administration and is the only kind of work in which a good many men in business will engage.

Business decision-making is becoming increasingly rational and, in this sense, "scientific." But, in view of the complex and continuously changing environment within which business operates, complete rationality is impossible. Decisions must be made on the basis of incomplete information and in the face of goals which may to some degree conflict. Therefore, decision-making in business requires a generous helping of "judgment." By this we mean the ability to sense what is relevant and to grasp intuitively what cannot be formulated precisely —in brief, a feel for what is possible.

---

We can often understand a problem in our own society better by examining the solution to the same problem in a different society. The training of Soviet industrial managers differs greatly from the training of ours, for example. The following description is accurate as of the late '50's and shows the widespread concern with purely technical training. There is contemporary evidence from research in industrial sociology now under way in Poland and Yugoslavia that these socialist countries are very concerned about human relations in administration. Perhaps this may now be true in the Soviet Union as well.

---

## MANAGERIAL EDUCATION—SOVIET STYLE

*Raymond A. Bauer* and *Barbara Tschirwa**

Despite gross differences in political and economic organization, both the United States and the Soviet Union are societies based upon large-scale industry. Tasks of economic administration are more similar than might be assumed from the fact that one economy is socialist and the other capitalist. True, some functions such as marketing and finance are largely, although not entirely, taken up by the government bureaucracy. Other functions of management are somewhat differently distributed in the Soviet and American economies. But the manager of a Soviet factory or collective farm faces tasks much like those of the head of any productive enterprise.[1] The administration of the Soviet economy has been the object of considerable study in this country, but little is known about the *training which managerial personnel receives for the specifically administrative role.*

The substance of this article is based upon a review of the available printed sources in the country (by B. T.) and upon visits in the fall of 1957 (by R. B.) to several Soviet factories and about a half-dozen institutions of higher education which train persons who ultimately occupy the various managerial and administrative jobs in the Soviet economy. . . .

Four major categories of top Soviet managers and/or economic administrators may be distinguished: managers of and administrators in industrial enterprises, managers of and administrators in collective and state farms, bureaucrats in the government economic apparatus, and members of the Party apparatus. Our attention was focused primarily on the training of administrators in industrial enterprises and secondarily on bureaucrats in the government apparatus. Even in the industrial enterprises members of the Party apparatus occupy important administrative posts. The Secretary of the factory Party committees, for example, may, and in fact is enjoined to, intervene even in the technological affairs of the factory. However, information on the training of such personnel in Party schools proved very difficult to secure.

Soviet managers of major enterprises are predominantly engineers by training. The director of one engineering institute estimated that the pro-

*Reprinted by permission of the authors from: Raymond A. Bauer and Barbara Tschirwa, "The 'Illiberal' Education of Soviet Managers," *Prod*, 1:3–6 (July 1958).

[1] It is ordinarily assumed that the marketing function is totally absent in Soviet enterprises. But in some instances it may take on real proportions, as in the case of the kolkhoz mentioned below: "I was there recently . . . and examined the sources of the kolkhoz' income. . . . They live off a few profitable items—garlic, hemp, strawberries. And they know how to sell their goods. . . . It appears that the kolkhoz maintains in various cities a complete staff of agents for buying and selling everything they come across. They bought horses in the Stavropol area, drove them to the Tatar regions, sold them at three times the original price, and earned on this operation 200,000 rubles. In Kazakhstan they bought rams, traded Moldavian wine in Kharkov, and Kuban rice in Leningrad. . . ." (*Novy mir*, No. 5, 1956, p. 44. Cited in H. Achminow, "The Theoretical Foundation of the Transition to Communism and the Nationalization of the Kolkhozes." *Bulletin*, Institute for the Study of the U.S.S.R., Vol. V, No. 3, March, 1958, p. 14.)

portion of factory managers who were engineers was "easily" over 90%. In light of our other sources of information, this estimate seems generally reasonable although possibly on the high side. Characteristically, the graduate Soviet engineer will go directly into a production job and take on increasing administrative responsibility as his abilities develop and are recognized. Although the importance of administrative skills is acknowledged in the running of Soviet enterprises, one can find little in the engineering curriculum designed to prepare the student for the administrative tasks which will probably be his once he leaves his school.[2] Soviet engineering training is more narrowly technical than our own. The student will get perhaps two courses in economics. One of these, on the economy of the particular industry for which the student is training, has been added in the past few years in explicit recognition of the administrative responsibilities which fall to the lot of Soviet engineers. Some official sources suggest that this addition was specifically an anticipation of the decentralization of the economy.

One (or a half) course in "the organization of work" will be the closest approximation to specific training for management. This course smacks very much of American "scientific management" of a few decades ago. It deals with time and motion studies, the setting of production norms and wage incentives, the optimum placing of men and machines, etc.

To the extent that practical experience can develop administrative skills and an administrative point of view,

the training of Soviet engineering students is designed to give them that experience. At several stages in the engineering curriculum the student is sent to work in some productive enterprise. He is required, furthermore, to write a thesis in which, among other things, he demonstrates his practical knowledge of the industry into which he will go. Moreover, a very large proportion—over half—of Soviet engineers receive their formal education *via* evening or correspondence courses while working full time. Finally, the policy for admission to institutions of higher education has recently been revised to give preference to students who have worked for two years after graduation from secondary school.

The graduate Soviet engineer emerges from school with a thorough technical training and with a fair amount of practical job experience. He has none of the "broadening" background in the liberal arts or the social sciences that is found in our engineering curricula. (Soviet educators are talking about "broadening" the curriculum, but this would involve introducing more general technical and scientific subjects.) Finally, he has very little in the way of specific course work to prepare him to assume administrative responsibility.

What happens on the job? In conversations with factory officials it was patently clear that the newly graduated engineer is scrutinized closely for evidence of administrative ability and promoted to responsible posts as he displays that ability. What is done to develop such abilities is less clear. Supervisors apparently give their juniors personal tutelage, but we have not succeeded in getting concrete examples of how this is done. "Working with people" is granted as an essential characteristic of an administrator. But when Soviet informants were

[2]For descriptions of technical training see Nicholas DeWitt, *Soviet Professional Manpower*, National Science Foundation, 1955; and Alexander Korol, *Soviet Education for Science and Technology* (Technology Press and John Wiley & Sons, Inc., 1957).

asked how this skill was developed in those persons who were deficient, they answered either that Soviet youths learned this skill by "social work"—chiefly in the Young Communist League—or that superiors would "talk to" juniors who were deficient in such respects.

There are institutes and training courses for the post-graduate "perfecting of engineers." Typically a "comer" will be encouraged to enroll in such a course—usually an evening or correspondence course—and the successful passing of the course is the preface to appointment to an important managerial job. But the "perfection of engineers" consists of further technical training, with perhaps a course in economics and organization of work thrown in. There are also advanced conferences for engineering and management personnel, but such conferences—insofar as we could ascertain—are concerned with technical problems and none have any resemblance to our own management training programs.

In sum, the formal training for Soviet industrial administrators is almost exclusively technical. In fact, when asked for the characteristics looked for in a person to be advanced to an administrative post, Soviet officials uniformly answered, "First, technical ability." This phenomenon cannot be dismissed lightly by the observation that the job of a Soviet factory manager is different from that of the head of a large American enterprise. Probably throughout the structure of the Soviet enterprise the demand for technical competence is proportion-

ately greater than in an American enterprise. However, the need for administrative skill is apparent and acknowledged (although the lack of talented persons is not).

The other category of economic administrator to which we gave attention was the functionary in the economic bureaucracy: the planner and controller of the Soviet economic effort. Here the picture was much the same as for the manager of the industrial enterprise. Future bureaucrats are trained in institutes of applied economics. While the heads of such institutes state very firmly that their students become administrators and *not* technicians, they receive little or no direct training for administration *per se*. Like the student engineer, however, they are given "practical experience" in the course of the curriculum.

It would be difficult to contend that lack of specific training for administration has had a disastrous effect on the Soviet economy. However, it would be equally difficult to conclude that the Soviet experience casts doubt on American concern with administrative skills and management training. Despite its extraordinary successes the Soviet economy has been marked by characteristic weaknesses in the effective motivation and coordination of human effort and ingenuity, and in the delegation of responsibility that, in turn, can increase economic efficiency. It is our opinion that the Soviet economy has now passed into the phase in which administrative skills, as we understand them, will become increasingly important.

---

We now come back to our basic focus of attention on the human relations of administration. In the fol-

lowing selection Chester I. Barnard examines the goals of education for executives as these goals are derived from the functions performed by executives. It is well to underscore the starting point from which Barnard proceeds. He asserts:". . . human relations are the essence of managerial, employee, public, and political relations; and in most cases, these rather than science, technology, law and finance are the central areas of the executive functions."

Barnard's ideas are distilled from his distinguished career as an executive of many different types of organizations. He rose to become president of the New Jersey Bell Telephone Company. He served as State Director of the New Jersey Relief Administration during the Depression. He was national president of the USO during World War II. He later became president of the Carnegie Corporation, which makes vast contributions of funds for research and human

betterment. Here is a man who wrote the classic *Functions of the Executive* and pursued successive or concurrent careers in a business organization, as a government official, as director of a vast social service organization, and as top executive of a philanthropic institution. This varied experience as an executive coupled with Barnard's analytical turn of mind make his ideas about education for executives forward-looking long after he first presented them.

With this concluding selection we now have a "big picture" of the realm of administration and a set of values, or frame of reference, for understanding the main features of administrative action. We have set the stage for the succeeding .detailed consideration of the human relations of administration.

---

## EDUCATION FOR EXECUTIVES

*Chester I. Barnard**

In considering the problems of education for executives I shall not undertake to discuss either curriculums or pedagogical methods or their results. I prefer, instead, to limit my statement to what I think executives need, whether or not these needs may be met through formal educational means; and I restrict myself to a few points which I consider inadequately understood or much under-emphasized. . . .

*From "Education for Executives," *The Journal of Business,* 18:175–182 Oct., 1945). Used by permission of The University of Chicago Press.

I shall focus my thought on executives of the future; for the changes that are going on, whether in production or in distribution, in public affairs or in education, are in the direction of a much closer formal integration of social activity as a whole than has heretofore obtained. In my judgment this calls for more emphasis on the topics I shall present than I would have been inclined to give them heretofore.

One further preliminary remark: It is, I suppose, obvious to everyone who thinks about it that the most that can be accomplished in education for executives before they undertake work in the world of affairs is a preliminary training and discipline, an initial orientation, and a very limited amount of knowledge. . . . However, in conjunction with the instruction given in educational institutions, it seems to me that it should be persistently repeated that, even as to the subjects being taught, only a beginning can be made and that one of the most important functions thereby performed is to help the student to learn how to continue to educate himself.

I

A need of the executive of the future is for broad interests and wide imagination and understanding. Whether or not narrowness of interest has limited present-day executives in their contribution to the general society which impinges on all their immediate activities and has also thereby restricted the performance of their direct duties is a matter of opinion. At any rate, nothing can be done about them now. However, there is a narrow-mindedness associated with the concentration heretofore deemed indispensable. In the future it would seriously limit the capacity of men to serve effectively both in the major and in the intermediate executive positions of large and small organizations. The emphasis I am placing here is upon the so-called humanities and also upon science as a part of general education. It is an emphasis that applies not merely to instruction in the schools but also to pursuits after graduation. I hope it needs no argument that persons occupying positions of leadership in the community need an understanding of what goes on in the world and of the nature of the interests served by and underlying its activities. . . .

I fear this brief statement might appear as merely a courteous gesture in favor of general education, pleasing to that part of the academic world more directly concerned and consonant with the prevailing sentiments of educated men. I wish to demonstrate that what I have said is more than that and is not a reflection of the moment. About twenty years ago, an associate and I, who were general officers of a large organization, believed that we should try by some positive means to reduce the narrowness of view and interest that we thought afflicted too many of the men of the upper supervisory organization, limiting their flexibility and adaptability. Most of the several hundred men concerned were college graduates in either engineering or liberal arts but had been out of school in most cases fifteen years or more. We decided to subject them to a course of lectures and reading, requiring six full-time, though not consecutive, weeks. We enlisted the aid of Joseph H. Willits, the dean of the Wharton School, University of Pennsylvania, to manage the course. With a single exception no subject was given having anything directly to do with the business. The exception was the practice and philosophy of accounting, which every educated individual should know about. . . .

II

A second need of the executive of the future is that of superior strictly intellectual capacities. This is superficially in contradiction to what I have said on other occasions and to what I shall later say here. There is no doubt in my mind that training in the more logical disciplines tends to foreclose the minds of many to the proper appreciation of human beings. Nevertheless, for executives, as well as for many others, the world of the future is one of complex technologies and intricate techniques that cannot be adequately comprehended for practical working purposes except by formal and conscious intellectual processes. To understand the formal aspects of a complex organization; to analyze formal relationships between organizations; to deal appropriately with combinations of technological, economic, financial, social and legal elements; and to explain them to others so manifestly call for ability in making accurate distinctions, in classification, in logical reasoning and analysis, that the point requires no argument. This means that the student needs rigorous training in subjects of intellectual difficulty, thereby, to provide himself with the tools and the mental habits for dealing with certain classes of important problems that can be handled effectively only by the use of such tools.

III

Rigorous training in subjects intellectually difficult and, indeed, a large part of formal education, as I have already suggested, create a strong bias in many individuals against understanding in the field of human relations. The need of such understanding is of first importance to the executive; for human relations are the essence of managerial, employee, public, and political relations; and, in most cases, these rather than science, technology, law or finance are the central areas of the executive functions.

The need of understanding in the field of human relations would justify long discussion. I shall confine myself to three points. . . . The first I would stress is the need of inculcating an ap-

preciation of the importance and of the inevitability of nonlogical behavior on the part of human beings. So-called intellectuals seem disposed greatly to underestimate the importance of nonlogical behavior; and many, forgetting what the psychologists make so clear, will not recognize that it is inevitable and constitutes a large part of the behavior of any human being whatsoever. This leads to an attitude of deprecation and condescension toward those not intellectually adept, at least on the verbal level. The disposition is to characterize them as stupid, dumb, and animal-like. No proper appreciation of the individual human being or of the nature of our society seems possible to those who have such an attitude. . . . I need not elaborate the point further except to repeat that the kind of bias referred to seems to me to prevent the necessary understanding of social behavior.

Next, I think an adequate understanding in the field of human relations involves instruction as to the nature of general social systems. I am aware that, in their present state, sociology, social anthropology, and social psychology, particularly as sciences as distinct from philosophic disciplines, have been subject to much criticism. I hope I may be forgiven if I say that I believe a good deal of conflicting bunk has been taught in these fields. This argues for improvement and development, not against teaching what can be taught. . . . There is in my opinion much that is valuable to be taught about general social systems; but for the present, at least, it might well be presented to the young student not so much as science but rather as something much better than any common-sense understanding of the world he lives in can be.

My last suggestion with respect to understanding in the field of human relations is that there should be instruction about formal organizations as organic and evolving systems. I am aware that at the present time our formal knowledge, as distinct from our "know how," of such organizations is tentative and limited. The fact remains, however, that no one is an executive, as distinct from a mere leader, except in formal organizations. The fact also is that already a good deal can be taught about such specific social systems.

In this connection I should like to make clear my reason for emphasis upon formal organizations as *organic* and *evolving* social systems. It is that we persistently think about such systems in terms of mechanical, rather than biological, analogy. Our widespread use of mechanical and electrical systems makes this convenient. It results in regarding an organization as static and fixed, like a machine, instead of something that is living, that has grown up, and that is ever progressing or regressing with changing states of equilibrium of the human forces involved.

I wish to make sure that you understand my point and see its importance. To this end I shall relate an experience and give a hypothetical illustration that would have been appropriate on that occasion.

There is an institution known as the Conference of Science, Philosophy, and Religion which has met for several days in the fall for the last five years. . . . Its members are theologians, philosophers, scholars, and scientists, and an occasional businessman, trying to make sense to each other with respect to fundamental problems of modern society. Two years ago world organization was the central interest. . . . It quickly appeared that a large part of the audience was com-

pletely convinced that (1) if a good scheme of organization were worked out on paper and (2) if men competent to fill the respective positions were recruited, then (3) we would have a working, or at least a workable, organization. I strongly protested the validity of any such idea; but my view was obviously not acceptable to those present, except for a few sociologists, historians, and jurists. Most of the audience seemed unable to believe that workable organizations cannot be created in that way. Many of you will recall the testimony of an Army officer of the General Staff before a congressional committee some time ago to the effect that it was feasible to train an individual to be a soldier in comparatively few weeks, but it took much longer to create an effective division of such soldiers. That is a statement I would expect any experienced executive to accept at once.

The illustration that I thought of too late which would at least have made my point clear, if not acceptable, is as follows:

Suppose an enemy should drop a highly selective lethal gas on New Jersey that destroyed only the entire management organization of the New Jersey Bell Telephone Company (except the president, who has to be retained as a nucleus of a new organization). Now the scheme of organization of Bell Telephone companies is nearly standard. The New Jersey company is about one twentieth or one twenty-fifth of the whole system, so that, with some straining, it would in principle be feasible immediately to replace lost personnel by borrowing men from other companies. The replacing persons would know the formal organization, they would know the relations of all others relevant to their work, and each would possess adequate and tested technical competence for his position. How long would such an organization be able to function effectively? I would guess not more than twelve hours, especially without the sanctions of military discipline. Why? First, and most obviously, because no one would know the local conditions and how to interpret the changes in the environment to which the organization has constantly to adjust. Less obvious but much more important would be the inability of the men reliably to understand each other or to understand the employees or to be understood by them. In ordinary human relations the same words in the same context often have different meanings when uttered by different individuals. We understand people easily through our experience with them, which teaches us their special uses of words, the meaning of intonation and gestures, whether they are matter of fact or emotional, given to exaggeration or understatement, are reliable or unreliable, are reticent or voluble, and many other subtle characteristics of communication. Without the confidence that accompanies this kind of understanding, reticence, hesitation, indecision, delay, error, and panic ensue. "Know your people" is nearly as important as "know your language" in the communication upon which organized effort depends. The difficulty of communication on matters of concrete action between individuals who have not known each other is a matter of common experience, but its significance with respect to organization seems to be forgotten because the organizations we know have, in fact, developed usually through long periods. At a given time nearly everyone has habitual relationships with most of those with whom he needs to communicate regularly.

## IV

The discussion of approaches to understanding human relations leads to considering the need of appreciating the importance of persuasion in human affairs. This requires emphasis because a good many people of excellent intellectual development seem to regard persuasion as something undignified or as necessarily unethical, whether it relates to the selling of useful ideas or to changing harmful attitudes. In part, no doubt, this goes back to the failure to appreciate the importance and the inevitability of nonlogical behavior. Effective persuasion itself often involves also intrinsically nonlogical processes.

If the need of appreciating the importance of persuasion in human affairs is accepted, it leads to emphasis in education upon the development in the individual of the arts of expression, though not necessarily logical statement, in writing, oral exposition, and even public speaking, though not oratory. Certainly, one of the most important limitations, as well as one of the pre-eminently important difficulties of the modern executive, is the inability adequately in writing or in conference or in addressing substantial bodies of people to express intelligibly the facts with respect to complex situations of which he alone may have an understanding. In my estimation, society is suffering a good deal from this fact, for it is subjected to a barrage of expert verbalizers who do not know what they are talking about but are convincing to the uninformed because they talk about it very well. . . .

Another aspect of this subject on which I would lay emphasis is much more difficult. It will be increasingly required of the executive to translate or transform thinking on one level into that of another. The common-sense way to say this is that executives have to learn to think not only in the terms which are most convenient and appropriate from their own point of view but also in the terms of other men and from their points of view. Most people most of the time find it practically convenient to think in terms of simple cause and effect, but many of us some of the time in connection with our more complex problems have to think (often "feel" is more appropriate than "think") in terms of complex interdependencies in which no simple cause-and-effect logic is accurate or even intelligible. This calls for transformation in exposition from one type of logical process, best exemplified in mathematics, to another type which I have sometimes called "strategic reasoning." Strategic reasoning involves picking out a single factor and operating on it alone so that the effect may be said to be caused by the change in that factor. In this kind of reasoning of the everyday world the assumption is that all other things remain equal and that for all practical purposes there is only one effect. Whether this is true or not in any particular situation can usually be found out only from experience and not by reasoning. The analogy I have found illuminating is this: Although we know that a molecule of water is composed of two atoms of hydrogen and one of oxygen, nothing that we know of the properties of either hydrogen or oxygen would suggest the properties, except weight, either physical or chemical, of water. In everyday affairs, there are innumerable situations whose characteristics are not explainable by the most thorough analysis. More and more, responsible people are dealing with the situations in which the change of one factor changes many others and there is not only potentially one effect which may be desirable but others which may be undesirable. So far as I am aware, adequate attention is not being given to the dilemma in which many executives are thereby being placed. . . .

V

I come now to my final topic, which is the need of understanding which constitutes rational behavior toward the unknown and the unknowable. Unfortunately, not only the processes of education but habitual behavior and customary understandings persistently obscure the extent to which we live and act in a world of unknowns and of unknowables. Textbooks are written about what is known, not about what is unknown. We are overwhelmed by the enormous amount of factual and conceptual or theoretical knowledge which is available to us, because it far exceeds the possibility of being acquired by any human being. Indeed, the propaganda for science puts all its emphasis on the known, and only rarely does a scientist in general popular discussion emphasize the unknown. . . .

I believe it is desirable in teaching to give courageous emphasis to the practical fact that we often have to act without sufficient knowledge and that there is much that is literally unknowable. I am speaking now not in a philosophic sense but in the practical sense, that much knowledge, even if potentially procurable, at least cannot be obtained in time for use. I recently illustrated this from my experience as president of the United Service Organizations, where much of the information needed with respect to the activities of this far-flung organization would be at least three months old before it could reach headquarters, and much actually known was secret and could not be obtained or used. But decisions had to be made nevertheless.

The significance of this can be more generally stated as a need for understanding the distinction between calculable and incalculable risks. A calculable risk, as I use the term, is one in which it is approximately feasible to state that out of a collection of cases or events a certain percentage will have certain characteristics without its being possible to know of which specific cases this will be so. This is true of insured risks. The principles are applicable in actual management in a good many fields for which commercial insurance is not available. Now it seems obvious that there are many risks which are in this sense quite incalculable—indeed, specifically, they may not be known or recognized. In this connection I would emphasize that the treatises I have seen on risk and uncertainty, unfortunately from the point of view of these remarks, proceed on the assumption that facts as to the present and the past are adequately known and that the risks and uncertainties are exclusively of the future. The point I would emphasize is that executives, though they frequently act as if to deny this, are almost always lacking in adequate knowledge as to the present conditions and are unable to recover the facts of the past in many respects. Hence, the greatest of all their risks is the appraisal of the present situation, for it is only on that appraisal that it is possible at all to construct an estimate of the uncertain future.

No doubt it is apparent to you that some men are very good and others are very poor in behavior appropriate to the uncertainties. In common parlance, some are good at not getting out on a bad limb or in not sticking out their chins where there is no need or no purpose to be served thereby. Where there cannot be adequate knowledge, there is still place for wisdom. I suspect that practical people have learned patterns of behavior that generally meet such situations and that if there can be no teaching on this subject, at least at an early stage people can be taught that this is the kind of world in which they will behave.

And finally, in this same connection, emphasis should be placed upon the fact that most behavior of social groups is automatic or autonomic. I mean by this that what occurs is not directed from above but is the "spontaneous" result of interaction between people. What this means in practice is that people may be conditioned (by training, education, and many other methods) so that they collectively behave in what we regard as an appropriate way. When proper account is taken of this method, the executive may delegate authority with considerable confidence in areas where he could not have sufficient knowledge to permit giving specific orders even if it were otherwise practical to issue them. This is probably the most effective of all organization methods of dealing with the relevant facts, which, as a whole, are unknown and, indeed, unknowable by any individual executive.

# part 2

# ORGANIZATIONS

It is one of the central features of an industrial society that most of its productive work is carried out in organizations. There is a real discontinuity in our complex society between the places where we work for a living, and the places where we find our recreation, social activities, and family life. Our productive labor is, almost without exception, carried out in some kind of organization as owner, manager, or employee. This contrasts sharply with the daily round of life in primitive societies where work, play, and general social life are continuously intermingled.

What are the unique features of special-purpose organizations for the production of goods and services? The answer to this question must be our starting point for placing in context the human relations of administration. Administration means the broad coordination of the activities of people inside some organized group. The characteristics of such groups undoubtedly determine at least a part of what we do as members of them.

**OVERVIEW**

A group like a business firm has some obvious formal features. These include: (1) a limited purpose (produce particular kinds of goods or services); (2) capital assets and physical properties; (3) systematic ways of accomplishing its purposes (the production, clerical and sales technologies); (4) established ways for dealing with the economic and social world in which it operates (customers, clients, suppliers, regulatory bodies); (5) an organizational structure and an internal division of labor; and (6) a variety of mechanisms for insuring its continuity (securing and

27

holding onto finances, customers, clients, employees, supplies, and so forth). These formal properties of the organization establish its boundaries so that it is possible to say where the XYZ Company begins and ends, or what constitutes the organization called the Happy Valley School System, for example.

Knowing the boundaries of an organization is important for several reasons. *First,* it tells us the domain over which *affairs are administered* for and on behalf of the organization. *Second,* we are able to *determine the personnel component* which holds membership in the organization. *Third,* we can *follow out the consequences of decisions* made in the organization because the organization can be viewed as a closed system in which decisions about change have limited and discernable internal consequences.

When we turn attention to the human aspects of administration, certain special problems come into view. The human actor, unlike a piece of machinery or a dollar of credit available for expenditure, has social needs that must be satisfied to stimulate a personal contribution to the enterprise. It is precisely these social needs which call special attention to the aspects of formal organizations which can satisfy or frustrate these needs. Our interest in organizations in this section is focused principally on those features which have something to do with relating people to organizations through their membership in it.

We will follow two lines of inquiry. (1) Attention will center on some of the broad features of behavior of people in organized groups—their cooperative efforts in joint enterprises where there is some recognition by members that they are associated for common purposes. We will look at this problem from two standpoints: (A) the ways people become linked to a large-scale organization like a whole company; and (B) the attachments people develop to small, face to face groups that are components of a large-scale organization. This provides a general view of the *social systems* within which organized human action takes place. Chapters 2 and 6 give primary attention to this issue. (2) We will also consider the various ways in which the individual's needs and organizational requirements are meshed, or at least kept from conflicting to the detriment of productive contribution to the enterprise. This is the general topic of *motivation* and *incentives* dealt with in Chapters 3 and 4.

To summarize, we need some notion of the kinds of group activities in which human affairs have to be administered as a starting point for understanding human relations in administration. This is a unique area of analysis solely because the human actor is motivated in his behavior, and therefore, when he cooperates in a group undertaking there has to be some articulation of individual needs and group goals and operations. As a minimum, Part 2 is designed to sensitize you to the nature of the problems arising when people have to act continuously in concert. Beyond a sensitivity to the problems, there also will be found here some substantive ideas, or principles, about how the individual becomes an effective organization member.

# 2

# Organization as a

# Social System

In a frame of reference for understanding organization behavior we have to reach a middle ground between viewing the organization as an all-powerful molder of its members, and thinking of the individual member as being wholly free to pursue private goals while holding membership. Both positions have some truth in them, but neither is wholly accurate. The formal organization *does* mold its members. The individual *is* able to exercise some choice in achieving his private goals as a member of an organization. How both of these seemingly contradictory ends can be attained is partly determined by the characteristics of an organization as a social system.

We start by thinking of an organization as complete and more or less self-contained. That unit, be it a business, an army, a government bureau, or a church has limited objectives and implements them by organizing the activities of its members. This organization of the activities of people for specific purposes is what we mean here by social organization.

Organizing people into a productive unity is a complex task. We can note two broad aspects of this task. First and simplest is the design of the formal structure of the organization. This is revealed in the organization chart and in the procedures and work flow diagrams of daily operations. The formal structure is further brought into view by the specialized names given to departments and divisions which reveal their unique functions. The operation of standing and temporary committees and the location of "authorizing

**INTRODUCTION**

29

approval" tell us something about the structure and processes of coordination used to hold separate activities together. Finally, the flow of orders and communications reveals the structure of authority within which organization decisions are made. These are some of the more obvious *formal* features of organizations that require no special skill or insight to understand.

The second aspect of achieving productive unity in an organization deals with the person and personality of its members. People are not machines. They strive and are motivated. They react to their environment and especially to each other in that environment. They can turn on their best efforts on behalf of their organization, or can, with equal enthusiasm, turn strenuous activity toward thwarting organization purposes. There is no particular "set" that can be given to people's motives or actions in the same way that we can "program" a machine to do one thing and only that as long as we wish. Human actors resist being "programmed" beyond fairly simple levels of behavior. It is the degree to which behavior can be "programmed" on the one hand, and the reasons it escapes confinement on the other that constitute the central analytical problem for the study of human relations. An older theory of administration, appropriately called the "machine theory," started with the assumption that the member of an organization was essentially a physiological unit. Each person could be made to do his part, and only his part, in the organization up to the limits of his physiological capacity. From this view flowed two consequences.

*First,* in the era of so-called scientific management, means were developed to standardize and measure job tasks with the end in view of selecting the "one best method" and inculcating it through training the "operative." Accompanying these developments of motion and time study, job description, and industrial engineering, came "human engineering" with its emphasis on selecting out individuals possessing the best fit with job requirements, and modifying job content to the average physiological capacities of people. The machine model of human beings literally treated the employee as a rather imperfect physiological machine in designing and carrying out organization policies.

*Second,* a broad consequence of the "machine theory" of organization was to turn administrative attention to the manipulation of formal organization in the solution of operating problems. Thus, if an organization became too big (judged so largely because costly errors in operation began to be discovered) under centralized control, decentralization was viewed as the appropriate remedy. Or, if decisions seemed to become too weighty to be entrusted to a single man, then groups of men, called committees, were substituted as the decisional unit. Or, if the number and variety of specialized operations became too bewildering for a single supervisor to grasp, then delegation of authority and responsibility was accepted as the remedy for this situation. These examples suggest that some modification of the formal organization is viewed as the cure for organizational ills.

A large body of literature and administrative thinking still accepts the machine theory of administration, and its two general consequences we have just examined. It would be absurd to argue that formal organization structure is immaterial to organization effectiveness, and we certainly do not propose to make this contention. It can even be readily conceded that for some problems of organization behavior, the machine theory of administration provides a highly useful model from which to make decisions.

It is not necessary to slay the dragon of the machine theory in order to win the rewards of understanding organization behavior. Our aim is to supplement the machine theory at the points most needed—when we turn administrative attention to decisions about or affecting people as organization members.

In this chapter particular attention is paid to the difference between the organization as blueprinted—as it is intended to appear formally, and as

it actually is. The difference can be accounted for by the modifications introduced into the strictly formal expectations of behavior, by the people who do the work of organizations.

The first selection of this chapter emphasizes the importance of organizations for human life in our complex society. At the same time two distinguishing features of organizations are underscored: they "are assemblages of interacting human beings and they are the largest assemblages that have anything resembling a central coordinative system." We call this central coordinative system *Management*. An understanding of the human problems of administrations begins with these insights.

## SIGNIFICANCE OF ORGANIZATIONS

*James G. March* and *Herbert A. Simon**

But why are organizations important? A superficial answer is that organizations are important because people spend so much of their time in them. The working force—that is to say, the bulk of the adult population—spends more than a <u>third</u> of its waking hours in the organizations by which it is employed. The life of the child takes place to almost an equal extent in the environment of the school organization; and an uncountable host of other organizations, mostly voluntary, account for a large chunk of the leisure time of child and adult alike. In our society, preschool

*From *Organizations* (New York, 1959), pp. 2–4. Copyright by John Wiley & Sons and used by permission.

children and nonworking housewives are the only large groups of persons whose behavior is not substantially "organizational."

The ubiquitousness of organizations is not their sole or principal claim for attention. As social scientists we are interested in explaining human behavior. Taking the viewpoint of the social psychologist, we are interested in what influences impinge upon the individual human being from his environment and how he responds to these influences. For most people formal organizations represent a major part of the environment. Moreover, we would expect organizations to have an even more significant effect upon behavior than is suggested merely by looking at the time budget as we have done above. If we wished to sum up in a single quality the distinctive characteristics of influence processes in organizations, as contrasted with many other influence processes of our society, we would point to the *specificity* of the former as contrasted with the *diffuseness* of the latter.

A concrete example will help to point up the contrast we have in mind. Compare rumor transmission with the transmission of a customer order through a manufacturing company. Rumor transmission is truly a process of diffusion. Seldom does a rumor move outward along a single channel; indeed, in most cases it would soon die if it did not spread out broadly from its original source. The customer order, on the other hand, is transmitted along definite channels, and usually relatively few of them, to specific destinations. We do not wish to imply that there is *no* selectivity in the transmission of rumors, or *no* uncertainty in the destination of formal organizational communications. There certainly is a great deal of both. But the difference in degree in the specificity of channels between the two cases is striking.

Not only are organizational communications characteristically specific with respect to the channels they follow, but they also exhibit a high degree of specificity with respect to content. Here there is a strong contrast between organizational communications and communications through mass media. The audiences to whom newspapers and radio address themselves possess no common technical vocabulary; there is no subject about which they have any shared special knowledge; there is no good way of predicting what they will be thinking about when the mass communication reaches them. In principle at least, the recipient of an organizational communication is at the opposite pole. A great deal is known about his special abilities and characteristics. This knowledge is gained from considerable past experience with him and from a detailed knowledge of the work environment in which he operates.

When a mass medium exerts influence or attempts to give instruction, its messages are usually of the simplest variety—"go to your corner druggist now, and . . ."—and its appeals are to widely shared motivations. Organizational instructions, on the contrary, frequently contain great detail; often motivation can be assumed. Not only can organization communication be detailed, but it can be cryptic, relying on a highly developed and precise common technical language understood by both sender and recipient. Again we do not wish to imply any contrast of black and white, which would clearly be contrary to fact, but only to point to characteristic differences of degree that are large in magnitude and highly significant.

The great specificity that characterizes communications in organizations can be described in a slightly different way, using the sociological concept of *role*. Roles in organizations, as contrasted with many of the other roles that individuals fill, tend to be highly elaborated, relatively stable, and defined to a considerable extent in explicit and even written terms. Not only is the role defined for the individual who occupies it, but it is known in considerable detail to others in the organization who have occasion to deal with him. Hence, the environment of other persons that surrounds each member of an organization tends to become a highly stable and predictable one. It is this predictability, together with certain related structural features of organization to be discussed presently, that accounts for the ability of organizations to deal in a coordinated way with their environments.

The high degree of coordination of organization behavior can be illustrated by comparing coordination in organizations with the coordination that takes place in economic markets. To be sure, markets often exhibit considerable stability and predictability. A seller can bring his goods into the market with a fair notion of the total quantity that will be supplied and the prices at which goods will be exchanged. But he does not know in advance who specifically will be the buyer of his wares or at what precise price. Transactions that take place within organizations, far more than in markets, are preplanned and precoordinated. The automobile engine division knows exactly how many engine blocks to put into production—

not because it has made a forecast of the market, but because its production plan has been coordinated with the plans for producing completed automobiles in other departments of the company.

A biological analogy is apt here, if we do not take it literally or too seriously. Organizations are assemblages of interacting human beings and they are the largest assemblages in our society that have anything resembling a central coordinative system. Let us grant that these coordinative systems are not developed nearly to the extent of the central nervous system in higher biological organisms—that organizations are more earthworm than ape. Nevertheless, the high specificity of structure and coordination within organizations—as contrasted with the diffuse and variable relations *among* organizations and among unorganized individuals—marks off the individual organization as a sociological unit comparable in significance to the individual organism in biology.

---

We next turn attention to a more detailed consideration of what we mean by administration. By first examining four basic characteristics of organizations, the authors are able to derive three minimum requirements served by administration. The science of administration rests on the ability to develop principles governing administrative action in fulfilling these three requirements.

It should be noted that the authors are careful to designate the requirements as minimum, rather than inclusive. They are here concerned with

finding the irreducible starting points for defining administrative functions. We have already seen, particularly in Barnard's contribution to Chapter 1, that there are other requirements of organization served by administration. We will also find additional administrative functions set forth in succeeding chapters. We must begin by adding things up, one at a time; the most fundamental starting point consists in finding the irreducible requirements of organization that are satisfied by the administrative actions of its management.

## ADMINISTRATION OF ORGANIZATIONS

*Peter B. Hammond, Robert W. Hawkes, Buford H. Junker,*
*James D. Thompson, and Arthur Tuden**

What we seek is a valid set of generalizations which will offer a more precise description of administration and ultimately facilitate the prediction of administrative events in unknown but conceivable circumstances. Only as this goal is approached can the science of administration make significant contributions to the art of administration, as the sciences of medicine have contributed to its practice.

Although the goal may be distant, important beginnings have been made by those who sense inadequacies in administrative law, "scientific management," human relations, and the insights of practical administrators. The useful contributions from those sources must not be overlooked, but we look to the social, behavioral, and newer sciences for basic building blocks for the future.

Now, instead of a universally valid theory, there is a growing variety of part-theories[1]—of business administration, public administration, hospital administration, educational administration, and other administrations—and many scholars insist that the similarities among these are insignificant. . . .

### SCOPE AND FOCUS OF ADMINISTRATION

Until administration is better understood it is not likely to be defined

with much agreement or confidence. On the other hand, until it is defined the organization of relevant data remains difficult. Therefore, a tentative working definition is essential. The definition presented here will focus on what administration *does* rather than what it *is*. . . .

There seems to be reasonable consensus that administration is found in governments, armies, corporations, hospitals, prisons, school systems, universities, trade unions, churches, and philanthropic foundations. Few would insist, on the other hand, that administration is an important phenomenon in mobs, crowds, or publics.[2]

Although many societies make use of administration in certain spheres of activity such as government, it is rarely contended that societies as such are administrative organizations.[3]

If not all collectivities exhibit administration, what are the distinguish-

*Reprinted from *Comparative Studies in Administration,* edited by James D. Thompson *et al.* (Pittsburgh: University of Pittsburgh Press, 1959), pp. 3–8. Used by permission of the University of Pittsburgh Press.

[1]For a more detailed statement of this

point see E. H. Litchfield, "Notes on a General Theory of Administration," *Administrative Science Quarterly,* 1:3–29, (June, 1956).

[2]Governmental administration may be very much involved, however, in police activities directed toward *controlling* mobs or crowds, or *serving* publics.

[3]Further study may reveal empirical contradictions to these distinctions. Royal families, for example, may reveal closer similarity to the administered organization than to the typical family of the society; and in certain cultures the kinship group may also reveal a large element of administration. Absolute monarchies or totalitarian governments may be interpreted as attempts to make government and society coterminous, and to the extent that such attempts are successful the society may be considered an administered organization. Certainly in modern warfare, this situation is approached.

ing characteristics which allow us to point to certain ones as clearly having administration and others as not having it? How does the hospital or the corporation differ from the mob? What is behind the distinction between armies and crowds? How do we differentiate a trade union from a society or a family?

In seeking to answer these questions, we have identified four characteristics among those collectivities which clearly have administration. Their enumeration follows:

1. *Administered organizations exhibit sustained collective action.* They are not based on *ad hoc* activities, but on continued efforts having recognized results. They maintain identity long enough to become points of reference for those not physically in their presence; and if they exist only for weeks or days, they usually are considered failures.[4] Crowds or mobs, however, usually disband in a matter of hours or days. If they persist, it is through their conversion into permanent administered organizations.

2. *Administered organizations are integral parts of a larger system.* As systems they are not self-sufficient or self-maintaining. However many are the goals of administered groups, and however varied are the activities performed in them, they do not meet all of their requirements to persist as self sufficient collectivities. Administered organizations do not depend, for ex-

ample, on biological processes within the membership as the primary means of membership replacement. In this the administered organization is distinguished not only from the society but also from the family, both of which are persistent, species-maintaining collectivities.

3. *Administered organizations have specialized, delimited goals.* The objectives or purposes of the collectivity may change from time to time, and vary in degree of explicitness, but both members and nonmembers understand that corporations, trade unions, hospitals, and schools have different, if occasionally overlapping,[5] roles in the society.

4. *Administered organizations are dependent upon interchange with the larger system.* Requiring sustenance but being limited in their spheres of activity, administered organizations must receive inputs from and in turn discharge outputs to the larger system.

Thus, by a process of elimination we have narrowed the search for administration to certain kinds of collectivities: those which exhibit sustained activity; are part of a larger system; have specialized purposes; and are dependent upon interchange with the larger system. This tells us *where* to look for administration, but it does not tell us *what* to look for, since by this definition any and all activity in

---

[4]This generalization rests on inadequate empirical evidence. In emergency situations, such as community disaster, the crowd or public may become organized and administered only for the duration of the emergency. There is some justification, however, for thinking that usually this organization is created by an amalgamation or coordination of previously-existing administered organizations. There is also the often-noted tendency for specific-purpose organizations to identify new goals, rather than to disband, when original goals have been attained.

[5]The overlapping of organizational roles in a dynamic society results in much confusion among the several part theories of administration. Does industrial administration include hospital administration when a union builds and operates hospitals? Does educational administration become public administration when the school is a government unit, ecclesiastical administration when the church operates the school, and business administration when the corporation activates an educational program for its members? These kinds of confusion underscore the need for a more general science of administration.

such collectivities might be considered administrative activity. Again it is necessary, given the present state of our knowledge, to rely on "common sense" as a basis for distinguishing administrative from other kinds of activity in administered organizations. . . .

The problem, from our point of view, becomes one of distinguishing administrative from other kinds of activity in administered organizations—*without* declaring *a priori* that it is behavior performed by incumbents of certain kinds of fixed positions in the organization. The question of who contributes what to administration must remain an empirical question at this point.

Few would argue that the nurse's taking of a temperature is administrative behavior in the hospital, although in the vernacular, she "administers" sedatives. It is seldom said that the soldier's firing of a rifle is administrative behavior in the army. The bolt-turner on a factory assembly line is not conceived of as an administrator. But we are trapped if we attempt to describe the common characteristics of those organizational activities in terms of their *location* in a hierarchy. The fact that these activities are performed by those at the end of a chain of command, if this is so, is not the important criterion which leads to their classification as non-administrative. . . .

Thus, administrative activity may be defined as activity related to the creation, maintenance, or operation of an organization as an organization.

### ORGANIZATION REQUIREMENTS AND ADMINISTRATIVE FUNCTIONS

The characteristics which . . . distinguish . . . administered organiza-tions from other types of collectivities facilitate at least a minimum statement of organizational requirements and provide the basis for hypothesizing the following functions of administration:

1. *Structuring of the organization as an administrative function.* If such organizations must exhibit sustained rather than *ad hoc* activity, it follows that the actions of their component parts must be patterned and controlled, rather than random. While custom, convention, and habit provide a basis for common action, administered organizations must channel and modify such activity in order to meet their specific needs.

2. *Definition of purpose as an administrative function.* If administered organizations have delimited, specialized purposes, it follows that these purposes must be selected and articulated. Organizational goals do not spring automatically out of the collective performance of non-administrative tasks. In a dynamic context goals do not remain obvious, but mechanisms for their evaluation, reflection, implementation, and periodic revision must be institutionalized. . . . The definition of purposes is a function of administration.

3. *Management of the organization-environment exchange system as a function of administration.* Some of the necessary exchanges between the organizations and the environment occur in the performance of non-administrative activities; but the very essence of organization is task specialization, which calls for coordination. Hence the management of the system of exchange between an organization and its environment becomes primarily a function of administration. At a minimum this applies to the ac-

quisition and disbursement, from and to the larger system (a) of legitimation or authority; (b) of personnel; (c) of tools, equipment, or other facilities; and (d) of a medium of exchange.

In recapitulation, we have identified the administered organization by four characteristics which distinguish it from other collectivities. From those characteristics we have derived three minimum requirements of such organizations as organizations, and have said that the functions of administration are to provide for the satisfaction of those requirements.

---

You will recall that Barnard stated the importance of nonlogical behavior in administering organizations. The two following selections show you some of the ways in which nonlogical behavior exists side by side with logical behavior in the human relations of administration.

In the article below, Harbison, an institutional economist, presents the view that an organization can be considered a resource. He suggests that an investment in capital equipment usually necessitates a comparable investment in managerial resources to make the equipment effective. In the same light he also suggests that the efficiency of labor can be increased by a more intensive investment in managers. Finally, he observes that decisions made in organizations called businesses are influenced by many nonlogical and noneconomic factors.

The last article in this chapter is devoted to a look at some environmental features of an organization that affect behavior in it. The emphasis here is upon the ways in which the behavior of managers and executives is influenced by the environment an organization creates for itself. In Part VI the external environment of a business, which can be readily distinguished from the internal one, is examined.

---

## ORGANIZATION AS A RESOURCE

*Frederick Harbison*[*]

The functions of the modern entrepreneurial organization, whether it be privately or publicly owned and oper-

[*]Reprinted by permission of the publishers from Frederick Harbison, "Entrepreneurial Organization as a Factor in Economic Development," *The Quarterly Journal of Economics*, 70:365–378 (August 1956), (Cambridge, Mass.: Harvard University Press, Copyright 1956), by the President and Fellows of Harvard College.

ated, may be categorized as follows: (1) the undertaking or managing of risk and the handling of economic uncertainty; (2) planning and innovation; (3) coordination, administration and control; and (4) routine supervision. In the very small enterprise, of course, these functions may all be performed by a single person—the proprietor. In larger establishments, there may be a division of functions among a complex hierarchy of individuals. Ownership may be separated from management, and management itself may be subdivided into top, middle, and first-line supervisory management, and into line and staff management. Obviously, the large organization requires more managerial functionaries —and perhaps different types and combinations of people—than the small or medium-sized firm. Organizations can be quite simple or very complex, depending upon the nature of the business activity, the size of the firm, and the technology employed. . . .

Organization may be treated as any other resource such as capital, labor or natural resources. For example, one can conceive of "investment in organization" in the same terms as investment in machinery or equipment, and he may think of "accumulation of managerial resources" as a concept parallel to capital formation and accumulation. Industries requiring large investments in machinery and processes—capital intensive industries— may also be industries requiring great "depth" in organization, and thus might be called "organization intensive industries."

This concept of organization is perhaps most useful in analyzing the prerequisites for economic growth in underdeveloped countries[1] and the reasons for accelerated or retarded growth in more advanced countries. It provides a framework for tangible comparative studies of the role of entrepreneurship in industrial development. In this connection, let us now consider a few tentative propositions. . . .

[1]In using the term "underdeveloped countries," I refer exclusively to underdevelopment in the economic sense.

These propositions are based upon some acquaintanceship over the past two years with approximately seventy-five business enterprises in the following countries: England, France, Germany, Italy, Belgium, Holland, Egypt, Saudi Arabia, Peru, and the United States. This acquaintanceship consists of a visit of a day or two in about three-fifths of the cases and more intensive studies of the managerial organization and labor policies, averaging about two weeks per enterprise, in the other two-fifths.[2] Admittedly, the evidence at this stage of the research is more impressionistic than definitive. For this reason, the observations which follow are set forth as tentative propositions worthy of more exhaustive study rather than as final conclusions resulting from systematic research.

### A. ORGANIZATION AND CAPITAL

Industries requiring large capital investment appear to require a correspondingly heavy investment in organization. Or, put in a different way, machinery are likely to be quite unlarge expenditures for equipment and productive unless there is a corresponding investment in organization.

This proposition can be argued on logical grounds. Large investments in machinery and processes are usually associated with relatively large enter-

[2]The contact with these business enterprises was made by the author in collaboration with other associates who have been engaged in studies of management and organization in connection with the "Inter-University Study on the Labor Problem in Economic Development." The associates on the management studies have been Eugene W. Burgess, Franco Ferrarrotti, Heinz Hartmann, Ibrahim A. Ibrahim, William Scott, Ernst Köchling, and René Montjoie.

prises. A large enterprise, being more complex than a small one, naturally requires more and better trained managerial resources. Also, if the machinery and processes themselves are complicated, engineers, chemists, or other technical staff specialists are required. To the extent that machinery may displace unskilled or skilled labor, it usually requires greater investment in personnel who specialize in planning, production scheduling, engineering, and "control" of all kinds. Thus an additional cost involved in investment in modern processes or labor-saving machinery is that of procuring and developing the managerial resources necessary to utilize and to control it. If a business organization must employ a battery of technicians to supervise and control more complicated processes, there is also need for more experienced and expensive top management to co-ordinate their activities and to plan for future development.

On empirical grounds, this relationship can be illustrated by a rough comparison which we have made of steel mills in Germany, the United Kingdom, and the United States. The first comparison was made between a German and an American company, each producing a roughly comparable range of products and employing approximately the same total personnel (between 17,000 and 18,000 men). In comparison with the American company, the German enterprise had quite old machinery and processes which were in most respects inferior to those in the American company. Largely for this reason, the total annual production of the German company was only half that of its American counterpart.

The contrast in investment in managerial resources between the two companies was quite evident. In com-

parable steel-making and rolling departments, the American company used three foremen to every one in the German mill, and the educational level of the American foremen was in practically all cases much superior to that of the German foremen. In the German plant a greater burden of supervision was placed upon the group leader, an experienced skilled workman, whereas in the American company the supervisory functions were performed by full-time salaried foremen who were members of management. Some of the American foremen had Master's degrees and 15 per cent had college degrees, but none of the German foremen had any equivalent higher education. In the States, moreover, foremen quite frequently advance into the upper ranks of management; in Germany, the position of foreman is generally the highest step in the ladder of promotion for workers; only on rare occasions do the German foremen become members of middle or upper management. An even more striking contrast existed with respect to the senior technical staff, which comprises persons such as process engineers, chemists, specialists in industrial engineering, personnel, production control, and quality control. Here the American company employed 430 persons, as compared with only 43 in the German enterprise. It was obvious that the top managers and the superintendents in the States had a great many highly trained assistants actually to perform technical work. In Germany, the members of top and middle management did most of the technical work themselves. For this reason, a much higher proportion of the managers and superintendents in the German company were themselves highly trained engineers, whereas many of their counterparts in the American company had either no formal technical training or perhaps merely a liberal arts college education. . . .[3]

This American-German comparative study recently induced a British steel concern to send a team of experts to the States to make a similar comparison of its organization and manpower utilization with those of the same American company. In this case, the equipment and processes of the British company were fully as modern as those in the American; indeed, much of its machinery had been supplied by the same American manufacturer. In comparable departments, the labor force of the British concern averaged about 25 per cent in excess of that in the American company, the number of foremen was roughly equal, and the number of senior technical staff about half the number in the U.S. counterpart. The principal conclusion of the British company team was summarized in its report to the Board of Directors as follows:

"The most important single fact about managerial organization in America seemed to us to be the willingness of American companies to pay heavily for large management staff, while at the same time being minutely strict about the number of operatives; the argument being that if a plant was managed well everything else would follow."

The top management of this company concluded that it must attain more "depth in management" necessitating much greater attention to recruitment and development of managerial personnel at many critical levels.

[3]F. H. Harbison, Frank Cassell, Ernest Köchling and H. C. Ruebmann, "Steel Management on Two Continents" *Management Science,* II (Oct., 1955), 31–39.

This steel mill comparison, though it is admittedly suggestive rather than conclusive, indicates that there may be a direct and positive relationship between investment in technology and investment in organization. It also shows that where technology is comparable, labor productivity may be related positively to investment in managerial resources. We have noticed the same general relationships in the other companies with which we are acquainted. A thin managerial organization is usually associated with relatively extensive utilization of non-managerial labor forces and relatively primitive production methods, whereas a relatively deep managerial organization is almost always found in enterprises which have the largest investment in technology, particularly in labor-saving machinery. . . .

## B. ORGANIZATION AND LABOR RESOURCES

A second proposition is that organization is probably the principal factor determining the productivity of labor, assuming that capital and natural resources are constant. A labor force is recruited, trained, developed and managed by the organization, and the skills and qualities of manpower probably depend more on what the organization does than on any natural or innate characteristics of labor itself. This proposition, like the previous one, seems to be plausible on both logical and empirical grounds. . . .

In some respects, of course, the efficiency of labor resources may be independent of organization. The more important factors here may be levels of education, conditions of health, nutrition, and general experience with and attitudes toward work. The organization, however, is able to influence these factors at least in part. Attitudes toward work can be molded by management; companies can provide medical services and adequate diets for employees; and some firms in underdeveloped countries even provide facilities for general education of members of the labor force. In the industrially advanced countries, of course, the laboring population may be generally more efficient because of long tradition and previous experience with industrial enterprises, and the development of high labor productivity in a primitive society may thus require a much higher investment than in countries with a long industrial tradition. In short, I do not deny that some innate factors have influence on the quality of labor resources; my contention is simply that *the organization which employs labor* is probably the principal factor—the dominant force—in determining labor productivity with constant technology.

This contention has been fortified by observations of the utilization of labor resources in different enterprises. For example, in Egypt the productivity of labor is very low, even in factories which technologically may be among the most modern in the world. In the best Egyptian factories four to six workers are usually employed for every one in comparable establishments in the United States. But managerial resources are scarce and managerial methods are quite primitive. Although there is an impressive awakening to the need for improvement of management on the part of progressive Egyptian enterprises, systematic procedures of selection and training operatives are not yet used. Programs for training and development of supervisors or middle management in the skills of handling peo-

ple are almost nonexistent. Time and motion study, job evaluation, and other techniques for the systematic combination of labor with processes are still quite rare. The explanation for this "thinness of management" is obvious. First, labor is plentiful and cheap, so that there is no pressure to make a large investment in organization in order to economize in the utilization of labor; second, specialists in techniques of scientific management are scarce if they exist at all; and finally, the general level of existing managerial resources is not yet sufficiently high to utilize effectively modern techniques of manpower utilization.

Another convincing bit of evidence showing the relationship of labor productivity to organization is the "spotty" work performance which is evident in most factories, and particularly in those in the less developed countries. . . . In this connection . . . in Egypt, I visited two petroleum refineries located less than one-half mile apart. The labor productivity in one had been nearly double that in the other for many years. But recently, under completely new management, the inefficient refinery was beginning to make quite spectacular improvements in efficiency with the same labor force. All of this evidence, of course, is suggestive rather than conclusive. Nevertheless, it leads to a strong presumption that the productivity of labor may be primarily a function of organization.

## C. ORGANIZATIONAL "INEFFICIENCY"

Unlike land and capital, organization is a human resource. Business organizations are composed of animate human beings who are motivated by drives, hopes, desires, fears and frustrations. The actions of human beings and hence also the actions of organizations are not determined exclusively by economic forces. From the standpoint of economic analysis, organizational behavior as all other human behavior is not always "rational." Indeed, the economist who studies any form of management soon finds out that business organizations are surprisingly "inefficient." The decision-making processes in the modern enterprise are not so precise or so rational as the economic theorist might presume, and a great deal of energy within the organization is absorbed in clearly noneconomic activities. Thus the economist may have good grounds for assuming that all business organizations are inefficient in terms of economic theory, the distinction between them being only that some are more inefficient than others. . . .

First of all, there is no reason to believe that the heads of typical or representative business organizations are always or even primarily striving to maximize profits. As Reder has pointed out, an entrepreneur may at times strive to retain control over the organization rather than to maximize profits.[4] He may be interested in prestige and power rather than sheer financial reward. Many French businessmen, for example, are as much interested in using the firm as a means of maintaining or building the family name as in amassing a large fortune. Landes has said that to the French entrepreneur, "the business is not an end in itself, nor is its purpose to be found in any such independent ideal as production or service. It exists by

and for the family, and the honor, reputation and wealth of the one are the honor, wealth and reputation of the other."[5] Thus, the risk-taker, the innovator or the administrator may be as much concerned with getting his friends or his relatives into a business as he is with maximizing profits. In managing the enterprise, he may seek to maximize his social position or even his political power. He may be much more concerned with preserving his security than in seeking new opportunity. To the extent that he is concerned with such "extraneous" or non-economic goals, the firm may be "inefficient" from an economic standpoint.

Another factor explaining the inherent inefficiency of the firm is that of the imperfect knowledge upon which decisions must be made. The risk-takers, planners or administrators in any organization have at best imperfect facts concerning such things as the demand for their product, the marginal revenue productivities of capital or labor, the effects upon consumer demand of changes in either the price or the quality of articles produced, the future trend of costs of raw materials, and so forth. The business must operate on best guesses, hunches, and artificially constructed assumptions. Thus, the fact that business judgments must frequently be based upon imperfect knowledge makes completely logical and rational decision-making quite difficult.

An even more important factor explaining the economic inefficiency of business enterprise is organizational friction. This matter has received some

---

[4]M. W. Reder, "A Reconsideration of the Marginal Productivity Theory," *Journal of Political Economy*, LV (1947), 452.

[5]David Landes, "Business and the Businessman in France," in E. M. Earle (ed.), *Modern France* (Princeton: Princeton University Press, 1951).

recognition by economists.[6] In most business organizations there are perhaps three different types of frictions —(1) those resulting from "political" relations between persons, (2) those resulting from difficulties in communication, and (3) those resulting from imperfections in organizational structure. These are related to the behavior of human beings as functionaries in an organization.

Within most organizations there are personal jealousies and rivalries, conflicts of personalities, cliques and factions, prejudices and idiosyncrasies, and favoritism and nepotism. The successful member of an organization must know its internal politics as well as its formally stated purpose if he hopes to be successful. Persons who have actually lived with business organizations and studied them carefully will agree that "jockeying for position" and playing politics consume a substantial portion of the energies of a good many members of the managerial hierarchy. In short, in making almost any decision, individuals in the

------

[6]R. H. Coase, for example, points out that as a firm gets larger there may be decreasing returns to the entrepreneurial factor because of the increased costs of organization. (R. H. Coase, "The Nature of the Firm," *Economica*, IV [1937], 392.) And Austin Robinson states that the costs of greater division of labor are at some point offset by the greater cost of co-ordination, and then goes on to show that the scalar line of authority necessary for a business organization can be extended infinitely only if the necessary knowledge for decisions is very small, if the maximum amount of co-ordination is achieved at each level in the scale, and if the knowledge required for co-ordination at the next higher level need not descend into the lower levels of the scale. (Austin Robinson, "The Problem of Management and the Size of Firms," *Economic Journal*, XLIV [June, 1934], 250.) However, a more extensive and factual description of some of these frictions is necessary to clarify this point.

hierarchy are likely to ask themselves "how it will affect me and my position in the organization" rather than how it will contribute to profit maximization or to the formally stated goals of the enterprise.

Another cause of organizational friction is defective communication. The fact that people work side by side in the same organization does not mean that they understand each other. But understanding is necessary for agreement on goals, and agreement is a prerequisite of good teamwork. Communication is the cement which is supposed to hold the organization together.

Communication takes place through the written word, through speech, and also through behavior. It involves both giving and getting information, but information is always subject to varying interpretations. Authoritarian or "top-down" communication often breeds misunderstanding and determined resistance to authority in the lower levels of an organization, whereas lack of proper direction may lead to chaos. Another dilemma relates to the willingness of persons to communicate accurately. There is a very natural human reluctance to state facts which are known to be particularly unpleasant to the listener, especially when he is a superior. And the listener, when faced with bad news, is often reluctant to accept it objectively. Then, the same information may be construed quite differently by people in different strata of the organizational hierarchy. In all organizations, there are the official lines of communication and there is also the "grapevine." Even the most skilled administrators are unable to use either or both systems with complete precision. . . .

The third major source of organizational friction lies in the structure of the business organization itself. Specialization and division of labor increase the problems of integration, co-ordination, and control. This raises the very knotty question of the "span of control"—i.e., the number of persons who can be properly directed and supervised by each boss. The appropriate span of control varies, of course, with the nature of the business operations, but it is also dependent upon more intangible factors such as individual personalities, the communication process, authoritarian or democratic executive leadership, and the motivational patterns of working groups. . . .

Another related problem is the proper integration of the functions of the specialist-expert and the general administrator—in administrative jargon the relationships between staff and line. Modern business organizations require the services of specialists such as engineers, lawyers, industrial relations experts, and designers. Yet ideas coming from such advisors, particularly if they call for substantial innovation, are quite often resented and resisted by those in charge of operations. Consequently, a tremendous amount of energy must be devoted to "selling" the line management on new ideas and getting acceptance of necessary changes throughout the organization. . . .

If the above analysis is correct, one cannot conceive of organization in purely quantitative terms. Thus it would be misleading to say that greater financial investment in managerial resources will automatically increase the efficiency of the firm. There is as yet no exact science or technology of organization-building. But in a rough way it may be possible to distinguish between a relatively good organization and a bad one, a complex one or a simple one, and an expensive one or a cheap one. The typical business organization in the United States is probably relatively more efficient and much more expensive than that, for example, in France, Italy, or Belgium.[7] And within the United States it is possible for informed observers to detect the difference between a reasonably progressive and efficient organization and one which is very poorly designed and obviously using organizational energy in an excessively wasteful manner.

---

[7]For an analysis of management in these countries as compared with the United States, see F. H. Harbison and Eugene W. Burgess, "Modern Management in Western Europe," *American Journal of Sociology*, LX (July 1955).

---

## THE ORGANIZATION ENVIRONMENT

### *Robert Dubin**

Bakke[1] has pointed to the "organization charter" as the embodiment of the purpose and meaning of organizational activities. In his study of the telephone company he found that the

[1]E. W. Bakke, *Bonds of Organization* (New York: Harper & Bros., 1950).

organization charter was symbolized by asking the members of management and employees to describe what

*Reprinted with modifications by permission from Chris Argyris *et al.*, *Social Science Approaches to Business Behavior* (Homewood, Ill.: Dorsey-Irwin, 1962), pp. 25–30.

the name of the organization stood for in their minds. The charter appeared to have these meanings for the members (in the order of frequency of mention): expressing the purpose and function of the company, its general significance, its reputation, its major policies, and as an organization identified with a larger system. Two consequences were seen to flow from the members' recognition of the organization charter and its symbolization: (A) the charter provided important incentive values for the members by identifying uniquely and concretely the organizational image to which loyalties were attached; and (B) the charter, when internalized, tended to support the authoritativeness of the member and hence to support the stability of the authority structure.

The organizational charter is a very diffuse environmental feature of the organization. The charter of a business can be made very specific by describing the special products it manufactures, and the structure of the organization within which the production takes place. When this very specific sense of a "charter" of the organization is taken into account, it proves critical in establishing styles of leadership, as demonstrated in the study by Dill[2] of two Norwegian companies—one a clothing company, the other a light metal manufacturing company. The clothing company had a highly integrated technology, and the entire work flow was initiated by clothing orders received and their subsequent production for specified delivery dates. All operations were very interdependent. In this situation Dill found a high degree of centralization of manage-

ment with very limited autonomy distributed to subordinate levels of executives. By contrast, the second company had thirteen distinctive product divisions, each of which was autonomous in securing, handling, producing, and delivering its products. In this second company there was significantly more autonomy distributed among the ranks of management than in the first. This finding was established by recording the decision-making conferences of the respective managerial groups. Dill concluded that the organizational environment characterized in terms of division of labor and operating autonomy would affect leadership such that "the amount of autonomy of leaders' behavior was a function of four factors: (1) the ease of formulating independent task assignments for different work groups in the firm; (2) leaders' estimates of the probability that action on tasks would lead to unpleasant personal consequences by producing unwanted results for the organization or by producing conflict with other work groups; (3) the exclusiveness of each leader's control over information about tasks or activities that he was formally responsible for; and (4) leaders' estimates of the costs or gains associated with attempts to seek or to give advice."

McMurry,[3] in reporting the results of psychologically oriented interviews with 600 bank employees, concluded that the static nature of banking operations was mirrored in the undynamic and static nature of the banking employees' outlook and reactions to their environment. Thus, either one can argue that the "atmosphere" of banking tended to select out

[2] W. R. Dill, "Environment as an Influence on Managerial Autonomy," *Administrative Science Quarterly*, 2:409–443, (March, 1958).

[3] R. N. McMurry, "Recruitment Dependency, and Morale in the Banking Industry," *Administrative Science Quarterly*, 3:87–106, (June, 1958).

appropriate personality types to fill the operating positions of banking organizations (as McMurry does), or one can contend that the behavior systems of work were readily learned and were appropriate to the "atmosphere" of the organization, irrespective of the personality structure of employees, as I have suggested elsewhere in emphasizing the central importance of behavior systems as part of the organization environment.

Turning to still another feature of organizational environment as a determinant of managerial behavior, Fleishman and associates[4] found that foremen given human relations training were still impervious to its application in their supervisory behavior unless their own supervisors also practiced it. This carefully controlled study made clear that the leadership climate of the foreman was more determined by the climate created by the foremen's supervisors than by the training that the foremen received. Thus, other people as environment, especially direct bosses, materially determine the behaviors to be displayed toward subordinates.

It is interesting that in the folklore of managerial literature much is made of the need for total immersion of the individual in his organization and his complete dedication to it. One of the implications of this belief is that the individual member should have high interest in all aspects of the organization. Jaques[5] concluded from the long-term observational study of an English factory that man-

agers and executives *insulated* themselves by being inattentive to and indifferent toward many aspects of the organization that were not central to their own performance in it. Jaques concluded that this was functional for the expert performance of the executive and his concentration on his specific responsibilities and should not be interpreted as an index of apathy or lack of interest. Argyris[6] found this same phenomenon among production workers when management attempted to stir up an interest in the company as a whole, to which the production workers in effect replied "Nuts, leave us alone. We're doing our job; go do yours and leave us out of it."

Thus insulation or "adaptive segregation" (to use Jaques' happy phrase) may be one of the really necessary conditions for truly effective specialized performance in an organization. Pelz[7] found, for example, that govᵣᵤ.ᴊ₁-ment scientists tended to insulate themselves from central and departmental services staffs by such simple devices as using a telephone or written communication as a major means for avoiding face-to-face contacts in asking for services.

Still another aspect of the social environment of any organization is its past history as carried in the experiences and perceptions of those present members who experienced it. Jaques pointed out how the past behavior of older members of management colored their contemporary be-

[4]E. A. Fleishman, E. F. Harris, and H. E. Burtt, *Leadership and Supervision in Industry* (Columbus: Ohio State University Press, 1955).

[5]Elliott Jaques, *The Changing Culture of a Factory* (New York: Dryden Press, 1952).

[6]Chris Argyris, "Understanding Human Behavior in Organizations: One Viewpoint," in M. Haire (ed.), *Modern Organization Theory* (New York: John Wiley & Sons, Inc., 1959), Chapter 5.

[7]D. C. Pelz, "Interaction and Attitudes between Scientists and Auxiliary Staff," *Administrative Science Quarterly*, 4:321–336, (December, 1959).

havior, especially where there were status distinctions honored in the past that had to be defended against attack. It is not unreasonable to conclude that, where revolutionary changes in procedures, technologies, purposes, or other major features of organization are contemplated, the operations of "sweeping the rascals out" or "starting with a clean slate" may make sense, in order to sever links with the past carried in the behavior and outlook of those organization members who experienced it. This may sound drastic, but it seems realistic as one method of insuring reasonable "togetherness" about the new organization charter.

Moving into areas of perceptions that affect behavior, Weiss,[8] in studying research administrators in a government organization, found that those who described their own functions as a combination of policy-making and implementing policy also reported that they believed that colleagues in the organization were highly supportive of them; that the organization made full use of their abilities; and that relatively little opportunity was available on the job to learn more (or perhaps this response was their covert way of saying that they had nothing more to learn). Perhaps those who described themselves as running the organization by making its policy and carrying it out had a high sense of "self-realization," not necessarily because this was objectively true, but because the nature of their directing position made such a belief protection against the stresses of opposition and "problems."

Compare this with the report of Coates and Pellegrin,[9] who asked a sample of executives to describe their own characteristics they thought most important to their own success. These executives spoke of themselves as energetic, alert, aggressive, able to get along with and manipulate people, responsible, decisive, determined, adaptable, able to sell ideas, and get things done through groups—all of which gives the impression of high "self-realization." But when the same researchers asked career supervisors to describe the successful executives they knew, the same picture emerged from the responses with one addition— these supervisors were almost unanimous in denying any aspiration to be successful executives because they did not want the stress or "industrial suicide" that accompanied executive positions. Were these supervisors being extremely realistic in supporting the suggestion made above that an executive's sense of "self-realization" was one of his defenses against the stresses of his position? It may very well be that that outlook, attaching to a position as part of its environment, serves to protect the position incumbent from the stresses of his job.

Still another interesting facet of perceptions as environment for behavior was Jaques' observation, arrived at through content analysis of discourse, that, in the factory he studied, executives often used bromides and cliches as a defense against the reality of conflict and discord among themselves. For example, he pointed out that the belief that "if

[8]R. S. Weiss, *Processes of Organization* (Ann Arbor: Survey Research Center, University of Michigan, 1956).

[9]C. H. Coates and R. J. Pellegrin, "Executives and Supervisors: Contrasting Self-Conceptions and Conceptions of Each Other," *American Sociological Review*, 22:217–220 (April, 1957).

people were treated responsibly, they would behave responsibly," became a buttress for the idea that all opposition was responsible and well-intentioned. This is one illustration of "organization fictions" (See Chapter 21) and shows how beliefs may facilitate behavior in organizations, even though the beliefs are mythical and/or illogical.

One final and simple point about environment. It is a generally held precept in sociology that "like attracts like." In an organization this generalization means people of the same rank have each other as a social circle with little cross-over between ranks. This certainly seems to be borne out when examining the voluntary interactions of executives and members of management. Koontz and O'Donnell,[10] in quoting from an American Institute of Management study published in 1951, reported that, for 100 executives in ten leading operations, "out of a total of 817 activities of these executives . . . 72 per cent were in clubs, societies

and fraternities; . . . 17 per cent were in business associations. . . ." This means that 89 per cent of voluntary choices of social interaction for executives were either with other businessmen or with people who were similarly situated socially. As if to give the microcosmic picture of this, Ulrich, Booz, and Lawrence[11] reported: "At company parties and dinners the [management] team members made an attempt to circulate early in the evening and ended talking to their 'equals.'"

These are a few individual generalizations about organizational environment, all grounded in some systematic observation of executive behavior. Each of these generalizations tells us something about the impact of selective features of the organizational environment on managerial behavior. It is also clear that there is no pat or simple master conclusion that can be derived from these generalizations.

[10]H. Koontz and C. O'Donnell, *Principles of Management,* 2nd ed. (New York: McGraw-Hill Book Company, 1959).

[11]D. N. Ulrich, D. R. Booz, and P. R. Lawrence, *Management Behavior and Foreman Attitude: A Case Study* (Cambridge: Harvard Graduate School of Business Administration, 1950).

# 3

# Motivation in

# Organizations

By motivation we usually mean mechanisms inside the person that sustain his continued activity as a human being. This definition immediately raises three crucial problems. These analytical problems are: (1) *where* are these mechanisms located inside the individual? (2) *what* is it inside the individual that gives specific direction to his choices of particular activities? and (3) *how* does the specific content of particular motives get inside the individual?

One of the oldest traditions in psychology identifies motivation with inherited drives or instincts. This model of motivation solves the three analytical problems as follows: *where?*—motivation mechanisms are located throughout the body tissue; *what?*—the mechanisms are automatic physiological responses to tension states of the organism, designed to reduce these tension states regardless of whether the tension is generated inside or outside of the body; and *how?*—these mechanisms are inherited by each individual as the result of the evolutionary history of his species. For example, the hunger or sex drive is triggered by cell mechanisms when the cells are in a state of deprivation in which the response to the deprivation or tension has genetically established ways of reducing or eliminating the tension. Or, to take other examples, applying sudden heat to the finger tips, will result in a reflexive withdrawal of the hand from the heat source; increasing the volume of light striking the eye will automatically make the iris aperture smaller.

There are two important limitations in using the

**INTRODUCTION**

49

instinct model of motivation. We observe first that specific drives, like sex and hunger, result in wide variations of behavior for their satisfaction. Peoples around the world eat quite different foods, prepared in a bewildering variety of ways, using eating utensils in many forms. Even when hungry, some peoples will not eat certain foods tabooed by their customs. We observe, second, that the same people can be trained, educated, conditioned, or coerced into changing the form in which they satisfy their hunger, for example.

These two observations, of the variability in the satisfaction of identical drives, and the ability to change sources of satisfaction for the same individuals, call attention to an important consideration. We must view motivation as some form of exchange between the individual and his social environment. The social environment gives to the individual sets of preferences or values which constitute the goals towards which the instinctual drives are expressed. Furthermore, the social environment is the source of norms of behavior which draw the line between good and bad, right and wrong, legitimate and illegitimate. The values and norms come from the social environment and both are important guides for channeling the inborn drives of the individual.

The other half of the exchange in this motivational model is the degree to which the individual either conforms to social expectations in his behavior, or departs from these expectations. Conforming behavior tends to support the continued existence of the social system from which the norms and values are secured; departures from conformity may threaten the system. Thus, in exchange for the received values and norms, the individual gives back to the social system his loyalty and adherence in the form of meeting the system's behavioral expectations.

We then come to a modified model of motivation in which we can formulate the three analytical problems as follows: *where?*—in addition to physiological drives located throughout the body tissue, there are centered in the mind, emotional and rational mechanisms which act to sense and to choose among available behavioral alternatives; *what?*—in addition to automatic mechanisms for responding to bodily tension states, there are rational and emotional mechanisms that respond to the conditions of the social environment confronting the individual and which serve to minimize disparity in the exchange of values and norms received from the social environment to induce behavioral conformity; and *how?*—in addition to the inherited mechanisms, there are socially learned preferences among goals and norms of behavior and the means for their attainment.

When we see motivation as involving an exchange between the individual and his social environment, we have the key idea in understanding the meaning of motivation in organizations. It can now make sense to talk about "motivating soldiers to fight," or "motivating junior executives" or "motivating workers." In each instance we are talking about someone imbedded in a social system, an organization. These statements imply that we can reach these organization members from the outside in order to get them to perform to our highest level of expectation. Indeed, it is only because we can picture motivation as a form of exchange that it is even meaningful to talk about "motivating organization members." Without this notion of exchange between the person and the social system in which he operates, motivation would lie beyond social control and the managers of organizations would be helpless to channel motivations or to modify the level at which they operate.

Motivation then comes down to this. We all possess the basic instinctual drives. These drives do not by themselves result in determining behaviors, or the level of effort and performance put into the behaviors. The social environment provides the guide lines by which choices among alternative behaviors are made, and in exchange receives from the individual his conformity to the appropriate expectations placed upon him.

We have so far not introduced the notion of rewards and punishments as the payoff for motivated behavior. We can now fit rewards and punishments into the model of motivation. Something happens at the end of a motivated act. The actor gets "something" out of what he has just done. This "something" is his reward for doing what is expected of him, or for doing it with distinction. This "something" may also be punishment for not doing the expected, or for performing as planned, but poorly.

At the same time, the social system in which the actor participates also experiences "something" at the end of a motivated act. This "something" is either success or failure in the accomplishment of an expected organizational result. In this sense the organization is also rewarded or punished from the outcome of motivated acts by its members.

We can now see that the concept of exchange also applies to the *outcome* as well as the *initiation* of motivated behavior. At the end of an action sequence, the organization may mete out rewards or punishments, in accordance with the quality of the performance exhibited. Simultaneously, at the end of the action sequence, and because of it the organization may have achieved or failed to achieve a desirable goal. In both instances, the end of a motivated act is the signal for evaluating and reacting to its consequences.

In the accompanying chart we are able to visualize the exchange features of organizational motivation. This exchange between person and organization occurs at the beginning and end of an organizationally relevant act. At

MOTIVATION OF ORGANIZATION BEHAVIOR
AS AN EXCHANGE PHENOMENON

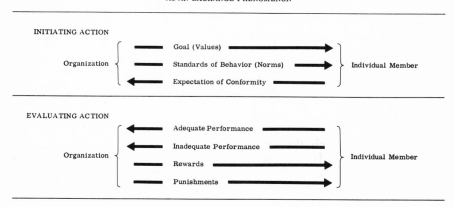

the start of the act, the individual "receives" from the organization some definition of the goals (values) towards which his behavior must be directed, and standards (norms) by which he can distinguish particular behaviors as being right or wrong, moral or immoral, for the accomplishment of these goals. At this point in the act, the person "gives" to the organization some reasonable expectation that he will conform to the defined goals, and to the norms governing their achievement.

When the action is completed, there is evident either some failure or achievement of expected outcomes. From an evaluation of these outcomes the organization is in a position to give its members rewards (more pay, recognition, promotion, etc.) for performance in achieving organization goals, or punishments (discharge, reprimand, demotion, etc.) because action failed to produce desired results.

It will be noted that the last stage in this double exchange between organization and individual member is the payoff in rewards and punishments to the individual. Indeed, an examination of the literature on motivation makes clear that most analytical attention has been centered on this payoff feature of motivation. We call these payoffs *incentives*. It is usually asserted that in the control of incentives, the amount and kind of rewards or punishments, management gains control of motivation. However, we should not overlook the fact that incentives are the end point of a chain of relationships between organization and individual. The control of motivation of organization members is also, and perhaps more importantly, achieved by inculcating organization values and norms as the basis for individual performance.

Let me illustrate. During World War II millions of civilian males (and females too) entered the fighting forces and succeeded in defeating a militarily competent opponent. The incentives for joining the fighting forces were minimal, as were those for retaining membership. Pay was low, working conditions (especially in combat) were poor to miserable, and the working day was twenty four hours. Furthermore, the military life departed in significant ways from the values and social norms of civilian existence, for example, "Kill or be killed" replaced "Thou Shall Not Kill," and "If it moves salute it" took the place of "Liberty, Equality, Fraternity." Now, if incentives (rewards and punishments) were, on the face of it, insufficient to turn civilians willingly into soldiers, how was this miracle accomplished? The explanation is to be found in the initial training of soldiers, during which time military values and norms were ceaselessly drummed into the recruits. It was possible in a very short training period to turn civilians into capable soldiers who were strongly motivated to perform successfully. This included even dying, if necessary, to achieve a military goal. Such strength of motivation could only be achieved by internalizing the values and norms of military existence as a basis for individual action. Indeed, we can highlight this conclusion by remembering that a mercenary army is one primarily motivated by incentives or payoffs, while a patriotic army is composed of soldiers who have adopted as their own the values and norms of military action. Ordinarily, given relative weapons equality, we would bet on the patriotic army's victory in any combat against a mercenary army.

That aspect of motivation that imbues each organization member with the values and norms of his organization is developed through participation, training, imitation, and learning. There is little that is spectacular about this side of motivation. Indeed, it is probably least amenable to conscious manipulation by management. On the other hand, the incentive side of motivation is readily manipulated and can be given spectacular forms if necessary (for example, stock options and liberal expense accounts for executives).

In the following selection will be found a general analysis of motivation as it relates to the behavior of organization members. Emphasis is placed on the exchange processes between the individual and his social environment that build and sustain personal motivation. Some attention is also directed at the functions of incentives in relation to motivation. This introduction together with the first selection, should establish for you a model of human motivation in organizations.

---

## MOTIVATION OF ORGANIZATION ACTIVITIES

### *Robert Dubin**

Motivation may be seen as a combination of forces maintaining human activity. Morale is the amount of zeal and zest people have for their activities. . . . Incentives are the inducements placed along the course of ongoing activities, keeping the activities directed toward one goal rather than another. Motivation, morale, and incentives are distinctive aspects of a person's connections with his work organization.

#### MOTIVATION DEFINED

Motivation may be defined as the complex of forces starting and keeping a person at work in an organization. To put it generally, motivation starts and maintains an activity along a prescribed line. Motivation is something that moves the person to action, and continues him in the course of

action already initiated. Furthermore —and this is important—motivation is part of an activity. . . .

Clearly there are forces inside the person starting and maintaining activity. Whether we call them drives, instincts, wishes, or tension states, they can be described as mechanisms of the organism. Psychologists and physiologists analyze these mechanisms.[1]

It is also clear that behavior is highly organized. Impulses to act have to find appropriate channels of expression. The social setting of behavior defines these channels of expression. Analysis of the channels of systematic behavior—or behavior sys-

---

*From *The World of Work* (Englewood Cliffs, N. J.; Prentice-Hall, Inc., 1958), modification of pp. 213–217.

[1]See, for example: M. R. Jones, ed., *Nebraska Symposium on Motivation* (Lincoln: University of Nebraska Press, 1954); Wayne Dennis *et al., Current Trends in Psychological Theory* (Pittsburgh: University of Pittsburgh Press, 1951), especially David Krech, "Cognition and Motivation in Psychological Theory," pp. 111–139; D. O. Hebb, *The Organization of Behavior* (New York: John Wiley and Sons, 1949); and B. F. Skinner, *The Behavior of Organisms* (New York: Appleton-Century-Crofts, 1938).

tems as we have called them—as part
of the motivational field surrounding
behavior is the task of the sociologist.
This is the viewpoint of our study of
work.[2]

## BIOLOGICAL MOTIVATION IS DIFFUSE

A wide variety of schemes have
been proposed by different kinds of
behavioral scientists for describing
and analyzing motivation. We can
take our choice. There is the relatively
simple formulation of W. I. Thomas,
who saw people motivated towards
new experience, response, recognition,
and security.[3] There was the very
complex formulation, now discarded,
of psychologists of the instinctivist
school who assume an instinct as the
basis for each separate and distinct
kind of human activity.

In recent years behavioral scientists
are more or less agreed that there is
not a general cause and effect connection between specific psychological
motivation mechanisms and specific
behaviors. The reasons for this are
simple. It has been found repeatedly
that the same activities can apparently be the consequence of quite different motivating forces. It has also
been found that the same motivating
force can give rise to widely different
activities. As a consequence it is difficult if not impossible, to see a one-to-
one relationship between something
called a motivating force inside the

person, and a resulting activity. The
current view suggests that internal
motivating forces start the human being in action, and keep his activity
going, but that we have to look outside the person for the determinants
of particular action patterns.[4]

The situation clarifies from an analytical standpoint if we turn our attention to the social practices that
organize human activities. It is here,
in the analysis of social structure, that
we find the pathways along which
human activity is directed. The society
comes to define each activity as to the
point of its origin, the nature of its
initiating behavior, the manner in
which it is continued, and the point
of its termination. The society defines,
for example, what earning a living
means; what being a father means;
and the activities that are related to
being an entertainer.

It is, in a sense, immaterial from
the standpoint of society what drives
underlie the activity of men who are
fathers, for example. Some might become fathers as a consequence of an
incidental sex act; others because they
like children; and still others because
of the authority the position would
give them in directing the lives of
their offspring. In the social system
these internal motivations, however
diverse, are of relatively little import
in defining what a father is and how
he shall behave.

---

[2]See: John Dewey, *Human Nature and
Conduct* (New York: Modern Library,
1930); and Kurt Lewin, *Resolving Social
Conflicts* (New York: Harper & Brothers,
1948), and *Field Theory in Social Science*
(New York: Harper & Brothers, 1951).

[3]First set forth in W. I. Thomas, *The Un-
adjusted Girl* (Boston: Little Brown and
Company, 1923).

[4]See, for example: A. H. Maslow, *Moti-
vation and Personality* (New York: Harper
& Brothers, 1954), especially Chapter 5, "A
Theory of Human Motivation," pp. 80–106;
Talcott Parsons *et al.*, *Towards a General
Theory of Action* (Cambridge: Harvard
University Press, 1951); John Gillin, ed.,
*For a Science of Social Man* (New York:
The Macmillan Company, 1954); and one of
the classics of the field, George Herbert
Mead, *Mind, Self, and Society* (Chicago:
University of Chicago Press, 1936).

Similarly, it makes relatively little difference to a business firm whether its junior executives are motivated toward advancement by vanity, by keeping up with the Joneses, by lust for authority, by a miserly desire to accumulate wealth, or by a dedication to the interests of the business firm. Any and all of these personal motivations in any combination might be found in a typical cross section of junior executives. To the business firm the main thing is that all of this cross section of its future principal officers are strongly motivated towards achieving the terminal positions of leadership in the firm.[5] Granting these diverse drives toward promotion and success, the business firm can use various forms of incentives to encourage the junior executives to keep striving toward their success goals.

It should be clear, then, that if we view motivation from the standpoint of driving forces within the person, it must be considered a general, rather than a specific attribute of the individual. The sum total of human drives can be seen as the forces that keep the human being in a state of sustained activity. These forces are, in most instances, difficult to detect in or infer from a given line of activity.

From the standpoint of the society, or any given organization with the society, the minimum test that is made of each individual is his capacity for activity. Only those individuals incapable of purposeful activity are rejected. Thus, society and its formal organizations tend to set aside those individuals who are so dissociated from reality that their activity bears no relationship to their immediate environment.[6] Also rejected are those individuals who are so overpowered by their environment that they are in a state of literal paralysis for meaningful activity.

Granting the capacity for meaningful activity on the part of most human beings, their behavior can be directed in specific and concrete ways. The systems for achieving direction of activity are the systems of motivation with which we are primarily concerned here. We will see below that motivation is sustained by social structure. We will examine specific ways in which this is done.

## MOTIVATION AND SOCIAL STRUCTURE

Social structure channels and sustains motivation. We can examine this proposition from two standpoints: (A) from the standpoint of the basic socialization of the person as a citizen of society; and (B) from the standpoint of learning to behave in specific organizations in which the individual carries out much of his daily activity.

The social structure sustains motivation in a specific way. When a person internalizes a value, norm, goal, or behavior pattern, these become guides for future activity.[7] Internalization means acceptance into the personal behavior systems, and ways of thinking. It means, literally, putting modes of activities and thoughtways inside the social personality so they become, in the future, the bases for be-

[5]As a general reference on this point see Clyde Kluckholn *et al.*, *Personality in Nature, Society and Culture* (New York: Alfred A. Knopf, Inc., 1953), which has a number of papers dealing with various facets of the problem of relating motivation to action.

[6]In our society they are usually labeled psychotics and institutionalized.

[7]See Mead, *op. cit.*, and also James Olds, *The Growth and Structure of Motives* (Glencoe: The Free Press, 1956), especially Chapters 2 and 3.

havior and thought. These activities and thoughtways, in turn, have their origins, for any given person, in social experience.[8]

We can now recognize the circular course of social motivation. Social experience provides the substance internalized by the person. Once internalized, the behavior systems and thoughtways become the motivational bases for future behavior.[9] After they are learned the social behavior patterns become the person's chosen channels for initiating, sustaining, and completing activities.

Of particular consequence as a motivation is the "payoff" resulting from chosen behaviors. Society defines the "payoff" for acceptable individual behavior in the rewards they bring. These rewards are general rather than specific. For example, a youngster is constantly reminded to be a good child. The adults fostering childhood "goodness" reward the right responses with affection, approval, and acceptance. This kind of reward can be summarized as payment in "status coin." Adults, and particularly parents, pay good children in the currency of higher ascribed status than bad children.

From this same example we can also learn the difference between motivation and incentive. Offering a child a piece of candy if he eats his spinach is an incentive to complete a specific activity. According the same child high status for being a good youngster in all his activities builds a motivational system. When the notions of goodness are internalized by the child,

he has standards for choosing channels of behavior in all areas of social interaction.[10]

Social motivational systems define their rewards for acceptable individual behavior in terms of basic human relationships. The "payoff" is in "power pay," or "authority pay," or "status pay." Correct behavior may be rewarded by the opportunity to perform more important functions, or to assume exclusive control of some functions; the reward is power. Such behavior may lead to the assumption of a decision-making position in relation to others; the reward is authority. Finally, socially appropriate behavior may be accorded higher ranking, being rewarded in "status pay." It is in this sense of broad types of rewards that the "payoff" of motivational systems is general rather than specific.

We are constantly learning to value and exhibit the behaviors that are defined by our society as important and desirable. From early childhood we learn correct and proper behavior and their appropriate rewards as well as the punishments that go with incorrect and improper activity. By the time we reach adulthood we have already learned a great deal about the specific channels of behavior that are acceptable in our society. In subtle areas we learn that there are kinds of rewards that are not so obvious and yet extremely important. The esteem of one's peers, the ceremonial recognition from one's parents or superiors, or the applause of an audience are all kinds of rewards to which we are early conditioned to respond as systems of motivation. The family, school, church, play group, and athletic team are all institutional settings in which

---

[8]This is the general point made by Talcott Parsons, "Motivation of Economic Activities," *Canadian Journal of Economics and Political Science*, 6:187–200. (May, 1940).

[9]Compare Olds, *op. cit.*

[10]See, for example: J. M. Whiting and I. L. Child, *Child Training and Personality* (New Haven: Yale University Press, 1951).

the growing child learns channels of proper activity and systems of reward and punishment. In this sense, then, the individual has already learned the basic motivational patterns of his society before he is thrown as an adult into active participation in work organizations.

In the work organization the adult learns the motivation system that is specific to that institutional setting. There is real continuity between childhood experiences in the society and adult experiences in the work organization. The work organization builds its motivation systems on societal foundations. What happens at work, however, is that these social motivation patterns are made more specific. They are also made appropriate to the work performed.

Motivational rewards in the form of "power pay" become, at work, the conferring of increased responsibility for job functions. For example, a man may be rewarded by being given sole responsibility for turning a valve at a critical moment in a liquid distilling process, a responsibility that he alone has, and that is highly essential in producing the proper distillates. The reward of "authority pay" may be promotion to the ranks of management, directing others in doing their work. High "status pay" may come as a result of exceptional skill in doing a task.

The motivation systems are not the same for all kinds of work organizations. The motivational patterns for a clergyman in a church organization will differ markedly from those of an accountant in a business firm. Furthermore, the motivational patterns of the United States Steel Corporation will differ, in some respects, from those in the General Motors Corporation. Particular systems of motivation have some characteristics that are unique for each work organization.

There is a very real learning process through which every individual goes in becoming a member of any organization. One of the most important things learned is the nature of the specific motivation systems of the organization.

Once a person becomes acclimated to his work organization, his church, his fraternal clubs, his recreational associations, and the like, he finds that his particular motivation is largely automatic in each organizational setting. That is to say, once accepted by, and accepting membership in, an organization, the person acknowledges his internalization of the motivational patterns established by that organization. It is in this sense that the systems of motivation are sustained by the organization, or the social structure.

## CONTINUITY AND STABILITY OF MOTIVATION

Motivation in the organization is continuous. The persons composing the organization, once they become a part of it, automatically fall into a pattern of motivation initiating and sustaining their organization activities.

In the context of motivation, three features of the work assignment—tasks, duties, and rights—are seen as impersonal environmental forces molding behavior in each work assignment. They channel technical activities and the activities concerned with general behavior in the work organization. The rights associated with a job are some of the specific rewards for adequate work performance.

Responsibility, obligation, and privilege are also components of each position. These three components represent, respectively, the personal internalization of the work values, the emotional commitment to these values through the sense of obligation about work, and the rewards coming out of interpersonal relations, in the form of privileges. Each member of the work organization discovers that some rewards of his work come in the form of rights and privileges. These rewards, in turn, require that he carry out the tasks and duties of his work and that he do so with at least minimum responsibility and sense of obligation.

We may conclude, then, that in the very components defining work assignments are to be found the channels of behavior appropriate to work, and the rewards that re-enforce compliance with these selected channels of behavior. The molding character of the work environment results in built-in, continuous, systematic motivation.

There is a permanence to the systems of motivation in organizations that tends to be little affected by personnel turnover and many other kinds of changes. There are several sources for this stability. The first and most obvious lies in the general purpose and philosophy governing the existence of the organization. In a business organization where the financial balance sheet is one of the primary indicators of economic health, it is scarcely surprising that emphasis is put on channeling motivational patterns in financial terms. However, in an educational institution the academic staff can scarcely be said to be motivated by strictly financial gain. In many instances professors could do far better financially in other pursuits. We can understand professors' motivational patterns if we know that the purpose of a college or university is not to earn money, but to produce educated persons. The way in which the goals of

the organization affect the motivational systems is even more evident in a religious organization. Here the creed of self-sacrifice and devotion to an idealistic goal becomes the center around which the motivational system is built. One tends to hold suspect the preacher who drives a Cadillac, but considers saintly the one whose clothes are threadbare.[11]

A second source of the stability of a motivational system lies in the fact that it affects a primary bond of organization.[12] The motivational system deals directly and immediately with the attachment of the person to the organization. Changes in the motivational system may entail vital and often disastrous changes in the bond between member and organization. Consequently, when members become acclimated to a particular motivational system in the organization in which they operate, they are often very reluctant to accept any significant changes that would tend to redefine their individual relation to the organization. We can see here the roots of the kind of resistance that workers are likely to display toward changes in the financial systems of rewards that are introduced as forms of incentives. The

----

[11]It sometimes happens, however, that the management's philosophy does not, in fact, determine the organization's motivation system. For example, paternalism in industry was supposed to generate a grateful response by workers to management's *noblesse oblige*. It seldom did. For a general discussion of paternalism, see Herbert Blumer, "Paternalism in Industry," *Social Process in Hawaii*, 15:26–31 (1951). For a specific case example, see Robert Dubin and D. E. Wray, in *Labor-Management Relations in Illini City*, Vol I (Champaign: Institute of Labor and Industrial Relations, 1953), "The Metal Products Company."

[12]E. Wight Bakke, *Bonds of Organization* (New York: Harper & Brothers, 1950), makes this general point.

very changes in the pay system are likely to be viewed as a fundamental change in the worker-manager relationship, and to be opposed as a consequence.

We can then conclude that a system of motivation is an essential ingredient in any organization.[13] Furthermore, it is a permanent feature of an organization and tends to reflect the nature of the organization, its goals, objectives, and underlying philosophy.[14] The motivational system is usually well-understood by all the participants in the organization. It is, furthermore, stable and permanent, known to the managers of the organization as well as its members. Indeed, a motivational system could hardly be effective unless it is understood, and its operations evident to all those affected by it.[15]

---

[13]See Rensis Likert, "Motivational Dimensions of Administration," in *America's Manpower Crisis* (Chicago: Public Administration Service, 1952). See also Daniel Katz and Robert Kahn, "Human Organization and Worker Motivation" in Solomon Barkin *et al.*, eds., *Industrial Productivity* (Champaign: Industrial Relations Research Association, 1951).

[14]This is the central point made by Rensis Likert, *et al.*, "Motivation: The Core of Management," *Personnel Series*, A 155 (New York: American Management Association, 1953), pp. 3–21.

[15]A general treatment of motivation together with an analysis of studies dealing with it is Morris Viteles, *Motivation and Morale in Industry* (New York: W. W. Norton & Company, 1953).

---

Whiting Williams coined the picturesque phrase, "Social handles of the pay-cup" over a quarter of a century ago. That was in the early infancy of the interest in human relations. Williams was then a journalist, intensely interested in the world of work. He used the journalist's technique of going and living with the people about whom he wrote. Traveling over the entire world he experienced the work of modern society by living and working with those who did it. Combining this intensive experience with genuine analytical skills, Mr. Williams wrote a number of books, from one of which the following selection is taken.

An important part of the motivation for work is the feeling that the job to be done is important, and preferably that others also feel the same way about it. This sense of importance of one's own job is first of all the product of the ways in which that job is valued in the society. But even with a low value placed on one's work, or some uncertainty in the way in which it is valued, the individual himself sees the work as important when his motivation is high. This internalization of the sense of worth of one's job permits the individual to give back to his employing organization a good performance in it, sometimes but not always earning the reward of a "Well done!"

What Williams points to as the sense of importance of the job has been labelled "power pay" in the previous selection. We will encounter the concept of "power pay" as an incentive again in Chapter 13 where it is contrasted with "authority pay" and "status pay."

## SOCIAL HANDLES OF THE PAY-CUP

*Whiting Williams**

Numberless other instances could be cited of this outstanding fact: *everywhere among the workers a man determines the social standing of himself and his family, not so much by the earning power as by the NATURE of his job.*

This universal connection between a man's work status and his community standing—this it is that constitutes by far the most important as well as the most elusive of all the "conditions" of work. This is what enlarges enormously the boundaries of a man's job. This is what provides those "social handles" of the pay-cup—that "social fringe" which makes a man's work infinitely more than that combination of mud, shovel, and arms which so fills the eye of the observer. Away out beyond these extends the thought of the doer of the task. Constantly he pictures the reward which is to follow. Of that reward only a part is put into the pay envelope. The rest of it spills over into satisfactions astonishingly intricate and imponderable—and indispensable. Among these, however, the assignment of a gratifying social status is only the final capstone set upon a whole series of lesser but ascending rewards.

What is this series?

Surely it starts with the simple gratification of mere physical activity. From the time of our mother's first urgent appeal to "Please sit still!" not one of us but has learned the genuineness of this first reward of action. Not one of us but knows, however, that in addition to this minimum delight of muscle exercise, we wish to see something worthy transpire through our effort.

"Deeg here, deeg dere! All-time for not'ing—like dam-fool! We quit!" A group of angry laborers threw down their shovels—to take them up again only after the boss had explained that he was looking for a lost water-pipe, and felt as helpless about it as they did.

Quite rightly, hospitals and insane asylums now try to utilize the huge curative value of such purposed and "resultful" effort rather than mere physical exercise. Almost inexplicable is the vast satisfaction which we get from even so slight a result as when, for instance, order and cleanliness displace disorder and dirt. All that is needed, apparently, is that *we* be the displacer!

"Yes, m'sieu'," a Belgian scrubwoman explained as she looked up from wringing out her cloth, "when my floor smiles at me like that over there—then it is easy to smile back at it. Then both of us are well content, is it not so?"

Similarly, after a day in a railroad warehouse, my companion and I took home scratched hands, bleeding knees, and exhausted backs. For nine solid hours we had piled 212-pound kegs of nails into neat tiers, one above the other. But, somehow, our injuries gave us an acute and pulsing joy. Both of us knew that we were also taking

*From *Mainsprings of Men* (New York, 1925), pp. 58–63. Copyright by Charles Scribner's Sons. Used by permission.

home something of the same pleasure which the Creator Himself must have enjoyed on the world's first Saturday night. We had positively thrilled when, after the whistle and the eveing "wash-up," we stood for a moment and "looked upon our labor and saw that it was good!"

"If it were desired," says Dostoievsky in *The House of the Dead*, "to reduce a man to nothing—to punish him atrociously, to crush him in such a manner that the most hardened murderer would tremble before such punishment—it would be necessary only to give his work a character of complete uselessness. . . . Let him be constrained to pour water from one vessel into another, or to carry earth from one place to another and back again, then I am persuaded that at the end of a few days the prisoner would strangle himself or commit a thousand crimes punishable with death, rather than live in such an abject condition and endure such torments."

The denial of exactly this simplest satisfaction probably explains that first great strike or "walk-out" of recorded history: the laborers there by the Nile doubtless felt that bricks—*good* bricks, mind you—simply could not be made without straw!

This reward of creation naturally grows greater just as rapidly as the creator finds it easier to picture the usefulness of his effort to others.

"The boys gotta stop work unless I keep after them pumps," the landlord in the mine town repeated proudly. In the same way "Old Evan" would call back after we had finished our job of bracing the roof and removing the "fall" of rock, which had completely stopped the work of all the colliers in that quarter of the pit:

"Wull, it been plain to see, now beunt it; they cawnt roon the bloody mine without *oos!*"

"Of course, we had to have the navy in them days," a half-drunken fisherman explained in a Swansea public house. "But 'twas us fishermen that won the war!—us with our trawlers always a-sweepin' of the seas and amakin' of it safe for the navy to do its work!"

"You remember," boasts the casual laborer, "that million-dollar dam they built up at Grand Forks fer savin' I don't know how many million acres o' good land—it was in all the papers everywhere? Well, *I* was on that job!"

"I'll show her I'm better'n her if she on'y knew it," the Hairy Ape in the stoke-hole sneers at the elaborately dressed woman visitor. "I belong and she don't! I move and she's dead! Twenty-five knots a hour, dat's me! Dat carry her, but *I* make dat. *She's* on'y baggage."

It is exactly this increasing measurement of the usefulness of the job—*and so of its doer*—which carries the thought of the measurer out beyond the factory walls and into the service he renders, in the highways and byways of the town and the nation. And by the same token, it is this measurement which makes the doer so sensitive to the weighing of his contribution by even his most distant fellow citizens. If these do not recognize his merit, perhaps his own weighing of the matter is wrong—*perhaps!* It is this uncertainty, accordingly, which helps to keep him "talking shop"—everlastingly weighing this job with that—until, finally, he discovers, in one way or another, that the question has been settled and his function has been given everywhere among his fellows something like a proper rating. Only then does he feel that he genuinely knows what his job really is, and what it truly pays him.

*It is impossible, therefore, to judge the effect of either wage or other*

conditions of *work apart from the
relationships the work permits with
other persons. What every worker
knows is this: that sooner or later the
final job of his work is settled, not by
him nor by his employer, but by the
social standing awarded him by his
fellow citizens.*

Thus with the brass-workers of Connecticut. During the war they knew
that their big brass cartridges were
helping to protect their country. After
the Armistice these men were hard to
get along with. In order to keep going,
the big plants had had to turn to making *lipstick-holders!* Yet the observer
would probably have assumed that
the more intricate manipulations required for the vanity-boxes gave the
worker something like delight, while
the cruder fabrication of the patriotic
cartridges furnished nothing but monotony and boredom!

Even the munitions worker wants,
of course, like every other worker, to
be sure that his high function is well
performed—that it represents a convincing proportion between effort expended and results achieved. The
laborer outside the Woolwich arsenal
had this fundamental in mind, as well
as its counterpart in the public's rating, when he urged me *not* to join him
and his fellows inside the gates. "It's

day after day of movin' things from
here to there, and then back from
there to here to-morrow! W'y, even
the tramway men call out at this stop
here: 'All out fer Convalescents'
Home!' or mebbe, 'Saints' Rest!' You'll
get your money, all right, but you'll
be disrespected by yourself and everybody else!"

No, nothing is more certain than
that it is impossible to squeeze a man's
work as its doer sees it into the puny
limits of a few mechanical operations,
or even of a whole factory. "What's
your job?" simply can't be answered
except by asking "What's it for?"

To better the conditions of a man's
task? By all means, improve the machine and the working place, if this
can be done—and it usually can. That
of itself will hardly fail, as we have
seen, to improve the type of worker
whom these selectors attract and retain. But if these cannot be improved
as much as could be hoped, large opportunity may still remain to change
the work's most important part—the
spiritual fringe which passes around
it, the worker, and us outsiders, and
ties all of us together. The best way to
improve the job may often be, in fact,
to *change what the outside public
thinks about it and its doers.*

---

In the introduction to this chapter
we pointed out that rewards and
punishments were essential ingredients in the exchange between the person and the organization. Now we will
examine the rewards that the organization has at its disposal. To do this
we will want to establish some of the
general features of incentive systems.

Incentives for work are analyzed in
a variety of ways at a number of
points in this volume. In Chapter 4,

dealing with the linkages between the
individual and the organization, we
consider some of the incentives that
make people want to be productive.
In a later section, Part 4, *Administrative Relationships,* we give detailed
attention to the three most powerful
non-financial incentives for work:
power pay, authority pay, and status
pay. This extensive treatment of incentives is reasonable. In the last analysis people want payoffs for what they

do as organization members. And these payoffs come increasingly from outside us, not from our self-satisfactions at doing a good job. It is very important to understand incentives, for they are the other side of the coin of motivations.

---

## INCENTIVES FOR WORK

### *Robert Dubin**

Incentives are what the working person gets from his employing organization for being a productive member. These incentives are pay for working. The pay comes in some form that is tangible. It is recognized as pay for work by both its recipient and those who make the payoff. Incentives must, therefore, be part of the working environment. Various kinds of incentives are built into the work organization, paying off in systematic ways as work is performed.

People work because they expect something out of it. They are likely to work for the Widget Company instead of the Gadget Company or the Trinket Company because they think Widget has a better payoff. Whatever incentives are important to the person may become the basis for his preference for his employer rather than another. Incentives are therefore important in keeping members in a work organization, as well as keeping them productive while working.

### TYPES OF INCENTIVES

We can look at incentives from two different but related standpoints. If

interested in designing incentive systems, we concentrate on the form they take. If we are concerned with how people react to the incentives offered for working, then attention is focused on their subjective reaction to them. We will first examine the general forms of work incentive systems. Then we will consider subjective reactions to incentives. . . .

### *Forms of Incentive Systems*

A common distinction is that made between financial and non-financial incentives. Any incentive that pays off either directly or indirectly in money is a financial incentive. Wages and salaries are the major financial incentives. However, bonuses, profit-sharing, retirement pay, vacation pay, health insurance, and free, company-sponsored medical service are obvious extensions of financial incentives that either pay out directly in money, or provide services that might otherwise require personal expenditures.

Non-financial incentives are forms of payment for working where the inducement is not a monetary one. Non-financial incentives may take the form of earning higher status, being given greater responsibility and participation in work decisions, receiving pub-

*Abridged and modified from *The World of Work* (Englewood Cliffs, N. J.: Prentice-Hall, Inc., 1958), Chapter 13.

lic praise from superiors, or receiving token rewards like service pins. Non-financial incentives are based on the clear recognition that people respond to a wide variety of inducements that are not expressed in monetary terms.

Many incentives have both a financial and non-financial aspect. A promotion, for example, can be viewed as a non-financial incentive in which the reward is greater authority and status. Promotions typically, however, also carry increased pay, so that they reward doubly. People seek promotions because they pay off in both financial and non-financial ways. Other examples of incentives that combine financial and non-financial inducements are recognition for merit (pay increases within the job rate range *plus* public recognition); seniority standing (retention on the job during layoffs, or preference for advancement *plus* rights and privileges); and designation as a permanent employee (often signalized by an increase in pay *plus* protection from firing except for cause).

The distinction between financial and non-financial incentives rests on the difference in the form of the payoff. It is important to recognize the different forms of inducements in order to design incentive systems of work organizations. We will analyze in detail below these two basic forms of incentives for work.

## Subjective Responses To Incentives

Incentives can also be viewed from the standpoint of their impact on the working person. Here we are concerned with the subjective response to inducements in whatever form they might be presented. From this subjective standpoint we can distinguish three types of incentives: (a) those based on present satisfactions; (b) those based on present dissatisfactions; and (c) those based on providing functional equivalents.

Incentives based on a person's present *satisfactions* are those features of his work that he likes, and wants to see continued. These kinds of incentives cut across the whole spectrum of job features toward which a liking may develop. Once a person likes aspects of his work, he develops an interest in seeing them preserved. Furthermore, these interesting features of work give the person reasons for wanting to continue work, or for wanting to continue employment in his present place of work. Examples of incentives based on present satisfactions are pride of craftsmanship, sense of creativity, feeling of meaningfulness of the task, enjoyment of the task, enjoyment of the company of co-workers; finding a "home" at work, habituation to pleasant routines; attachment to physical objects like a particular machine tool (truck drivers often have violent preferences for "their" truck and may even give it a name, usually feminine); a comfortable relationship with superiors, and the pleasure of being powerful (e.g., the only file clerk who can really find things in the files).

Incentives based on a person's present *dissatisfactions* are focused on those features of his work that he likes, but wants more of. Here again, almost all aspects of work can arouse dissatisfactions whose dissipation depends on getting more of what you now have. Indeed, the most common view of incentives is based on the dissatisfaction principle. We tend to think that a man works hard because he wants more pay, more authority, more power, or more status. Businessmen not uncommonly assert, for instance, that when their employees get hungry then they will work harder. We can surely recognize that incentives based on present dissatisfactions are important in making people want more of what they now have. We must also be prepared to acknowledge that people work because of the incentive value of preserving present satisfactions. As we will see immediately below, they also work to secure from the work organization things that are equivalent to what they might otherwise have to provide for themselves.

The third subjective response to incentives is based on the ability of the work organization to provide its members with *functional equivalents* of services or rewards that also can be secured on a private basis. The most general functional equivalent is the replacement of personal actions by organization programs for enhancing security. These company security programs take a number of forms. Included under the security heading are health and welfare services, hospital and life insurance, disability and retirement pay, job tenure, and security of employment through annual employment, or annual wage schemes. All of these aspects of personal living can be taken care of on an individual basis. It is significant that the work organization takes over the maintenance of features of personal security. This has important incentive value for members of the organization who typically lose benefits of security plans if they leave their employment.

The second kind of functional equivalent incentive is provision of substitutes for private activities. These substitutes may or may not be used by organization members. For those who use them, participation in the activity may have important incentive value. Examples of substitute activities include company sponsored recreation and cultural programs; company lunchroom and coffee service facilities; company medical, counseling or psychiatric services; and credit unions or other financial aid services.

We can now summarize types of work incentives. They take the form of either financial or non-financial systems of payoff. From the personal subjective standpoint, incentives either play on present satisfactions, present dissatisfactions, or substitute company services and rewards for those usually secured on a private basis. Generally, these three subjective aspects are intermingled for any single form of incentive. We can best organize our view of incentives by visualizing an example of the relations between their forms and the subjective response to them. This is done in the accompanying table, where illustrations are presented. The table shows only single illustrations. It should not be interpreted as representing an exhaustive list of possible examples.

In this chapter we are concerned with understanding how incentives are made systematic. We want to know how incentive systems are developed and why they take particular forms. Consequently, we will continue our analysis by focusing on the *forms* of incentive systems, dealing with financial and non-financial incentives, in that order.

### FINANCIAL INCENTIVES

"It is literally true that most workers in the United States do not make a living. They make money and buy a living." This conclusion by Noland and Bakke views the financial rewards

THERE ARE CHARACTERISTIC SUBJECTIVE RESPONSES TO EACH FORM OF INCENTIVE
(Some illustrations)

| Subjective Response to Incentives | Form of Incentive | | |
|---|---|---|---|
| | *Financial* | *Non-Financial* | *Financial and Non-Financial* |
| Present Satisfaction | "My wages are tops." | "My boss treats me like a human being." | "My seniority standing protects me." |
| Present Dissatisfactions | "Hope that raise comes through." | "Watch my smoke when I learn the ropes around here." | "I'm 'bucking' for a promotion." |
| Functional Equivalent:<br><br>(1)   Security | "I'd rather let 'them' worry about paying me than work for myself." | "My wife may not understand me but my boss sure does." | "When you work for this company for a long time you know they'll take care of you." |
| (2)   Substitutes | "It's cheaper to eat in the company lunchroom than outside." | "Our department bowling team will win tonight." | "I had a rough time until the counsellor in Personnel set me straight." |

of work as providing the worker with income to live in his community. It is a way of viewing money as a medium of exchange in which work is traded for income, and the income is then spent for personal consumption.

For our purposes we want to emphasize another aspect of income from work. The dollar is also a medium of evaluation. The financial payoff for working becomes an important way of stating the value of a man's work. If one man earns more than another, his productive efforts may be presumed to be more valuable. This concern with money as a measure of a man's value to a productive enterprise is the keystone of all financial incentive schemes.

The views that money provides a yardstick for measuring work performance, and that money is also a medium of exchange, supplement each other. The first statement tells us that money is a common measure of work performance. The second tells us that

money income is useful only when it is spent for personal consumption.

Ideally, all financial incentive schemes are planned to pay for work in accordance with the importance of the worker's contribution. Again ideally, it should be possible to take the jobs, positions, and offices of a work organization and range them on a dollar scale, so that the importance of the work assignment corresponds to the amount of pay received.

. . .

### Company Pay Scales

Let us turn our attention to what happens inside a work organization. What incentive values do pay scales provide for employees, or what purposes do the pay scales serve as incentives? How are pay and salary systems established and administered? What are some of the unanticipated consequences for working behavior of company pay scales and the methods by which they are designed? These questions will be answered in order.

## Incentives For Mobility and Stability

Differences in pay received by different persons have two incentive objectives. These objectives are: (a) to make employees want to move from lower to higher jobs, increasing their payoff as they move; and (b) to make employees want to stay in their present work, increasing their payoff for staying. Pay differentials are used to make people want to be upwardly mobile. They are also used to make people satisfied with their present jobs. These two objectives are achieved simultaneously by a method called job evaluation.

The mobility incentive is built into the job evaluation scheme by paying higher level jobs more than lower level jobs. The company president gets more pay than the general manager, and both get more than machine operators. In achieving the mobility incentive the company pay scale is graduated from low to high to correspond to the evaluation of jobs in terms of their productive contribution. It is assumed that many people will want to get ahead. Part of their reward for striving for advancement is the increased pay with each job promotion.

Not everybody, however, will make the promotion grade. In addition, not everybody will want to strive for promotion. Yet it will be desirable to provide an incentive for staying put on present work assignments. The incentive for keeping people stable in their present work is built into the job evaluation scheme by providing a pay range for increases within the same work category.

The two incentives are pictured in the accompanying chart, where the mobility and stability incentives can be visualized. All job evaluation schemes contain these two financial incentives. Individual job evaluation plans will vary in the amount of incentive pay attached to mobility as over against stability.

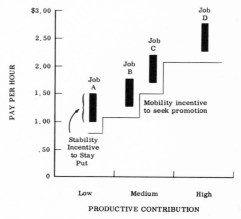

Both mobility and stability are necessary for the organization. Mobility provides a ready reserve of promotable people available to fill higher work assignments as they open up (people do die, leave, and retire from the organization, and new work assignments are established). Stability is necessary to maintain a trained and permanent work force capable of carrying on the organization tasks year after year. The bulk of employees reach promotion ceilings relatively early and have many years of future work at the same task. These are the "Thank God for" people who are a blessing because they do stay put. For them, merit increases on their present work assignment constitute financial incentives for continued effective performance. They, of course, also benefit from any upward movement in general pay levels.

## Balancing Stability and Mobility Incentives

Every financial incentive scheme attempts to provide stability and mobility incentives at the same time. It is necessary to organize the relationships among jobs so that it becomes attractive to move from a lower to a higher job. It is also necessary to provide some range of pay for each job so that over a period of years the worker can feel he is making some financial progress without changing his job.

A compromise is always required in achieving these two objectives. In order to achieve the incentive value of taking job promotions, the differences in pay between present and higher work assignments have to be relatively great. In order to maximize the incentive value of staying on the present job, the pay range for the job has to be increased. As the second is accomplished, there is a greater likelihood of overlap in pay between jobs, thereby diminishing the attractiveness of moving to the next higher job. Therefore the pay scales of a company reflect a compromise between these two incompatible objectives. This dilemma is visualized in the accompanying chart, where the two objectives are separately pictured.

The compromise between mobility and stability incentives is usually achieved in the light of the requirements of the particular company or industry. If the organization is a fast growing company, there are likely to be relatively narrow job and salary pay ranges accompanied by sharp differences between jobs in order to encourage people to move upward to fill the rapidly opening higher positions. If, on the other hand, the company is a stable one, not requiring rapid expansion of personnel, there are likely to be relatively wide pay ranges for each job in order to hire people for those jobs and keep them there for long periods of time until needed for promotions. At the same time, such companies will have narrower differences between jobs and a great deal more overlap between the pay scales of adjacent work assignments.

## Other Financial Payoffs

There is a wide variety of financial incentives other than wages or salaries. Profit-sharing, bonuses, free medical and other services, suggestion systems that pay in dollars, and at the executive ranks the generous expense accounts, company limousines, and

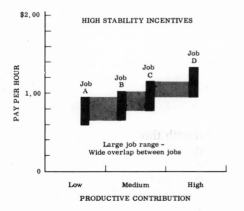

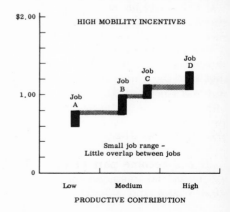

"working" vacations, are all examples of added financial incentives for working.

Periodically, interest turns to additional financial incentives in a search for new ways to stimulate employee effort. Perhaps the central reason for such interest lies in the fact that companies are less and less different from each other in their straight financial payoffs. The averaging of wages and salaries with those of the community or industry means that the distinctive company has to have added financial incentives.

The literature is full of special pleading for particular ways of making the additional financial payoffs. It is probably true that all added incentives work more or less successfully. That is, they work in the sense that employees will gladly accept any methods for "sweetening the take-home."

One of the pitfalls involved in using added financial incentives is the effort sometimes made to substitute uncertain special incentives for certain wages or salaries. In the most extreme case, where a salesman works on a straight commission for each sale made, with a bonus for exceeding a quota, the incentive value of the added earnings may be overwhelmed by the insecurity of no earnings in a bad week or month. In short, special financial incentives can only be effective when added to the basic financial incentives. The added incentives cannot take the place of a regular payoff for work performed.

## Money Makes The World Go Round

It has become part of the folklore of industrial management to assert that wages and salaries are not the most important incentive for work. Studies are cited to show that workers rank earnings below the top when asked what they like most about their work. Does this really prove that other incentives really take precedence over income from work? The answer is a clear negative.

In our society money does make the world go around. A worker wants economic advancement and economic security for himself and his family. Taking a job is a means to this end. In our society, as Veblen long ago suggested, we have measured most forms of human activity in money terms. Money is the universal medium of exchange that can buy anything from man's brainpower to, it is alleged, woman's virtue. Income remains the all-important means for satisfying human wants and needs. Income from wages and salaries is the major incentive to work.

### NON-FINANCIAL INCENTIVES

We have already suggested that non-financial incentives are forms of payment for working where the inducement is not a monetary one. The affirmative definition of non-financial incentives is the psychic rewards, or the rewards of enhanced position, that can be secured in the work organization.

There are two general forms of psychic rewards with which we will deal. The first is satisfaction with the work assignment, sometimes called job satisfaction. The second is "privilege pay," which is the free access to interaction with those in a superior organization rank.

There are three major forms of position rewards that can be won at work. The first is "power pay," which is an

*higher skill more satisfaction*

increase in the essentiality or exclusiveness of a work assignment. The second is "authority pay," an advancement into a position of greater authority. The last is "status pay," an increase in value attaching to a person on some comparative standard of judgment. These are all discussed in Chapter 13, "Status."

### Job Satisfaction

One of the rewards for some people at work is the satisfaction they get from their tasks. The work assignment itself is a source of job satisfaction. The big question is this: what is there about work assignments that provides personal satisfaction? Studies do not give us conclusive answers to this question. However, the partial answers are suggestive.

In general, there is strong evidence that job satisfaction increases with the skill required to do work. Harrell summarizes a number of studies reaching this general conclusion. A series of studies by Hoppock shows that more than 90 per cent of a group of 500 teachers like their work, while among a cross section of over 300 people in a Pennsylvania town an index of job satisfaction increased as one moved up the skill ladder. In a study of working youth, Bell found that 98 per cent of those working in canning factories and textile mills as unskilled laborers hated their jobs. In a study of an automobile assembly line, Walker and Guest found that most of the workers did not get satisfaction out of their work and wished that they did.

In a cross section of thousands of industrial workers who were asked about their satisfaction with work, Hull and Kolstad concluded that people in highly skilled trades responded with greater satisfaction about their work than did unskilled labor. Studies by Thorndike, Uhrbrock, and Super confirm the increase in amount of job satisfaction that comes with higher skill and more complex work.

What is there about a work assignment that makes it satisfying? Some partial answers are suggested by several studies. In the Morse study those who had higher job satisfaction scores tended to describe their jobs as being more varied and giving them some chance for decisions about their work. This conclusion is also reached by Walker and Guest in their study of the automobile assembly line. Another study by the Michigan Survey Research Center of 5,700 production workers in heavy industry revealed that 51 per cent would like to have more to say about the way their work is done, although 40 per cent were not interested in having more decision-making responsibility about their jobs. In this same study 65 per cent of the people felt that their work could be done better if they had more chance to make suggestions about such things as design, layout, and set-up of their own work.

We may conclude, then, that people doing more difficult and more skilled tasks get more rewards from their work in the form of job satisfaction. In particular, they seem to enjoy the variety of their work and the sense of personal responsibility they have for doing it.

These general conclusions suggest that at the lower reaches of most work organizations the non-financial reward of job satisfaction probably does not operate generally as a significant incentive. It is also true that most industrial workers start their working life at the lowest skill levels. This poses an interesting administrative problem. As some of these workers gradually move up into higher skill work assignments, they probably have to change from an indifferent or even hostile attitude toward job satisfaction to an outlook in which they value the satisfaction rewards they get from doing their tasks. This is another way of suggesting that different incentives operate at successive stages in working life histories. Industrial managers might well ponder this conclusion, and not expect job satisfaction comparable to their own from unskilled and semi-skilled subordinates.

We now come to an interesting consideration of motivation in the whole life of the individual. We start by recognizing that in our daily round of life we participate in a variety of institutions and organizations. Must it be true that in order to participate effectively our behavior must be highly motivated in each and every institutional setting in which we act?

This issue is fascinating. Modern man moves readily between work, recreation, worship, politics, intimate social relations, family life, and his special group activities like lodges and clubs. If we believe that he must be highly motivated to participate in all of these institutions surrounding his daily life, then there must be a terrific daily drain on his motivational energies. Perhaps this is a ready explanation for the alleged tensions under which we are supposed to live and the widespread use of tranquilizing drugs, energy pills, and other aids to "pick-up" our flagging energies and interests.

The next selection addresses itself to this issue and suggests that by modifying our model of motivation we can comprehend the possibility of being effective in activities without being strongly motivated. By drawing a distinction between necessary and voluntary action, it is proposed that motivation can be lower when acts are of a necessary type, and still be effective. If this analytical conclusion is correct, then we can conclude that organization members can contribute effectively without being motivated at maximum levels. This runs counter to much managerial thinking today which seems preoccupied with multifarious "morale programs" designed to raise individual motivation. Perhaps this is a misdirected effort and not really necessary to keep the organizations of our society efficient and effective. It is worthwhile to contemplate this possibility for it may actually make the functions of the executive easier. At a minimum, it may relieve administrators from a misplaced overconcern with the motivations of their associates and subordinates.

This selection also introduces the discussion of some linkages between the individual and his employing organization in terms of conformity and originality in individual behavior. This same subject is treated in more detail, and from other points of view, in the next chapter.

# NECESSARY vs. VOLUNTARY BEHAVIOR

## *Robert Dubin**

The historic trend of productive organizations is the specialization of functions within them and the development of unique technologies for their effective performance. The central fact of working life, as industrialization has proceeded, is that the worker behaves as he does while performing work because of the technologies with which he works. In industry we have developed machine technology to solve the problems of output, and fitted men to the jobs thus created. The same is true in the office and on the sales floor. In each instance the priority of technology over the human needs or requirements is evident.

The earliest use of social science knowledge was to take the insights about individual differences revealed through psychological studies and use them as a means for fitting people to tasks. The whole selection movement, grounded in psychological measurement and testing for individual faculties and capacities, was a direct and rational outgrowth of the recognition that the problem of people in industry was to fit men to machines and technical work tasks. If there is one enduring lesson in Taylor's work and the subsequent development of motion study it is this: that a man can be fitted to work tasks whose skill requirements are determined solely by

*From "Industrial Research and the Discipline of Sociology," *Proceedings of the 11th Annual Meeting* (Industrial Relations Research Association, Madison: The Association, 1959), pp. 152–160. Used by permission.

technological considerations. Man as employee was viewed as an animal whose capacity to perform useful work was limited only by his physiology and not his psyche.

More subtle forms of fitting man to work have been developed out of the original interest in his physiological capacities. Thus, we may counsel people into one occupation or another depending on their responses to a Strong Vocational Interest test. Complex personality profiles may be used to select administrative and executive personnel to fit the requirements of the jobs for which they are candidates. While we have succeeded in taking more subtle aspects of the human animal into account in employee selection and placement, we still work with the fundamental assumption: that the broad technology determining work tasks provides the criteria for selection of personnel.

The technologies of work in turn are determined by criteria other than the social characteristics of man. The blast furnace is designed to convert ore into pig iron. The consideration for designing the particular means of conversion are wholly independent of the characteristics of man as worker. At final stages in the design of the ore conversion process some decisions are usually made as to whether it is cheaper to use man as an integral part of the productive process, or to substitute mechanical, electronic, or other handling and control devices. This kind of decision usually rests solely on cost considerations. If man as worker is designed into the process, it is on the assumption that whatever the operating requirements are, there now exist workers with the requisite skills, or those who can be readily trained to perform the skills required.

Thus, the human actor is caught up in necessary behaviors that are organizationally relevant, and imperative, but normatively neutral in their consequences for the individual. This means that from the standpoint of the human actor his behaviors become imperative or necessary and are no longer within the range of voluntary social action. Once employed as a blast furnace charger, for example, the specific behaviors involved in carrying out this task are beyond the individual choice of the charger. These behaviors are built into his task as part of the larger process of converting ore to pig iron.

It is perhaps in industrial and business life that the sociologist is confronted with overwhelming evidence that much of the daily round of human life is caught up in necessary rather than voluntary social action. This is not a new datum for sociologists, but it is explicitly set forth with startling clarity in the facts of working life. Man is caught up in necessary behaviors, wholly legitimate in his society, but over which he exercises no control or choice other than the simple choice that he will or will not perform them. Even the choice not to perform them is often severely penalized, and therefore not a significant available choice.

What are some of the kinds of problems that flow from the necessary characteristic of working behavior? Let me briefly discuss three: (1) motivation for work; (2) control of necessary behaviors; and (3) the complimentariness of necessary and voluntary behaviors.

The literature on motivation seems to make clear that we have adopted simple theoretical models. Simpleness is first of all related to the assumption that motivation operates the same way whether the action ensuing is necessary or voluntary. The motivation models are also simple because they are grounded in the assumption that people's reactions to a course of behavior are polarized into liking or disliking the action. I think both of these assumptions require important modification.[1]

I do not think the motivation for necessary behavior involves the same kind of mechanisms as for voluntary behavior. Voluntary behavior implies some choice among alternatives on either rational or affective grounds. Necessary behavior, on the other hand, implies no such choice since by definition the choice is not available. Voluntary social behavior also implies that the choice of behavior selected can be expressed in some preferential terms over the courses of behavior not chosen. Since a choice is required in voluntary behavior, the condition of indifference automatically does not apply. The indifferent response would be to reject the need for any behavior among the alternatives available for choice. That is to say, the indifferent response for the person can only mean that he refuses to behave at all in the area in which a voluntary choice is possible.

If we now examine necessary behavior the indifferent category may become a crucial one. The necessary

---

[1] The application of motivation models to industrial work is summarized in Morris Viteles, *Motivation and Morale in Industry* (New York: W. W. Norton and Company, 1953); and William F. Whyte, *Money and Motivation* (New York: Harper & Brothers, 1955).

behavior may be carried on by the person because he likes it, or he may carry on the behavior even in the face of active dislike for it. It may also be true that he carries on this behavior with indifference toward it. Thus a subjective reaction of indifference becomes an important probability in necessary behavior.

Industrial studies have already revealed the prevalence of the indifferent orientation of workers toward their work. This is a result that students of industrial life have discovered with refined measuring instruments but which had already been well known to industrialists from their personal experiences in managing business organizations. The remarkable conclusion is that a good deal of working behavior is carried on by people who are indifferent to the things they are doing.[2]

This has obvious and important implications for the philosophy and practice of management. There has been a strong contemporary emphasis on finding means for making people like their work in employing organizations. The assumption is that they will be better workers as a result, better in the sense of more productive and less irascible, more loyal, or what not. When we understand that "indifference" is a coordinate response with "like" and "dislike" to the necessary behaviors caught up in working, we

---

[2]Representative studies include: Charles R. Walker and Robert H. Guest, *The Man on the Assembly Line* (Cambridge: Harvard University Press, 1952); Ely Chinoy, *Automobile Workers and the American Dream* (New York: Doubleday and Co., 1955); Joseph Shister and Lloyd G. Reynolds, *Job Horizons: A Study of Job Satisfaction and Labor Mobility* (New York: Harper & Brothers, 1949); and Robert Dubin, "Industrial Workers' Worlds: A Study of the Central Life Interests of Industrial Workers," *Social Problems*, III (Jan., 1956), 131–142.

may well be constrained to question whether management practices, designed to move a large segment of workers to a posture of liking work, are well advised.

This immediately raises the question as to what motivates people to work. It seems to me that the answer here is clear cut. Motivation is built into the social system. It is the general expectation that males of working ages will, in fact, be employed to earn a living. It is further general expectation that earning a living shall only be through legitimate channels defined in our society as gainful employment in legitimate occupations. Thus the social system provides the motive power to move major segments of the population into labor force. Once in the labor force, however, the performance of work may be responded to indifferently.

This poses the dilemma of how indifferent people are able to work effectively. How is our economic productivity increased from year to year and the fabulous production of goods and services of our society maintained?

There is nothing esoteric about the answer. The answer lies in the fact that necessary behavior is always surrounded by controls policing its performance. These controls operate to insure every work station is, in fact, occupied when it should be; that the quantity and quality of output is at acceptable levels; and that voluntary behavior does not interfere with the necessary behavior.

There are two basic requirements of necessary behavior: (1) that the behavior required be specifically set forth; and (2) that its performance be surrounded with controls that insure the desired outcome.

You are all familiar with the nature of these controls. Presence at a work station is controlled by time clock recording and physical nose counts. Quality of output is the province of inspection control in process and for the final product. Quantity of output is controlled by measured day-work standards or the built-in operating cycles of equipment. Voluntary social behavior that is inimical to necessary behavior is controlled by shop rules and personnel regulations. Furthermore, the controls just broadly outlined are supplemented by systems of rewards and punishments. Acceptable necessary behavior is rewarded in the pay envelope, through promotions and other forms of approval. Failure to perform the necessary behavior is punished with dismissal, fines, temporary lay offs, reprimands, and similar sanctions.

The point of the matter is that the logic of industrial and commercial output has always been implicitly grounded in the assumption of indifference on the part of workers employed in it. The multifarious control devices used in all productive organizations are the substitutes for voluntary work performance.

I think we will move forward very rapidly at the present time because we are now in a position to recognize the necessary or imperative character of working behaviors, and the generality of the indifferent response of workers to them. We can now see that the structuring of behavior as a consequence of the logics of production, together with the many control devices used to police this necessary behavior, present a whole facet of human action for which simple-minded voluntarism no longer is a meaningful theoretical concept.

Sociologists have long perceived the various kinds of necessary behavior caught up in such notions as folkways, mores, laws, and institutions. We have furthermore been quite aware of areas

we call social control where we have analyzed some mechanisms for policing necessary behavior. The data about industrial life now makes clear that we need more refined concepts to understand the detailed features of necessary behavior, and the tremendous range and variety of controls surrounding it.

Before you conclude that I have a picture in my head of man, the worker, as an automaton, let us consider the third topic under the general heading of necessary *vs.* voluntary actions. This is the topic of the complementariness of these two realms of behavior.

If a great deal of behavior is necessary to the functions of the social systems, and this is particularly true of productive systems, then where does modern industrial man have voluntary choices for his behavior? The working person has been caught up in imperative behavior surrounding his work performance. Does this mean that he still has available to him areas of life for voluntary actions? I think the answer is clearly "yes but" (and this is an important but) the realm in which voluntary social action is still open is different from the area of work.

Earning a living has become a highly segmentalized area of life, however imperative the behaviors demanded while working. Out of 168 available hours in a week, approximately one-fourth are spent at work. Approximately another quarter are spent at sleep or in activities associated with going to bed and awakening. This leaves approximately half the hours in each week available for activities other than working or sleeping.[3]

---

[3] A recent volume of readings deals with the many facets of the nonwork life of Americans at mid-century. See: Eric Larrabee and Rolf Meyersohn, eds., *Mass Leisure* (Glencoe: The Free Press, 1958). A

The great significance of this span of available time, not devoted to working or sleeping, is that the working citizen of our society has almost half of his total time available for voluntary activities. Caught up in this large block of time are activities associated with recreation, eating, participation in voluntary associations, sheer idleness (including spectatorism in entertainment) and the like. In short, the time freed from working provides the opportunity for use of this time on a voluntary basis.

We are inclined to view with alarm the conformity of modern industrial man. The principle of the squeezed balloon seems to operate to release him from conformity. The squeezed portion of the balloon is the area of necessary behavior while working. But the process of squeezing the balloon here expands the nonrestricted area of the balloon elsewhere. This is the analogy of the increased time available for voluntary activities.

There is ample evidence in the larger society that modern industrial man is making considerable use of this large block of free time for voluntary activities. The increase in the divorce rate can be interpreted as a form of voluntarism in the family institution. The persistent geographic mobility which sees approximately 1 in 5 citizens changing residence in the course of a year is another evidence of freedom in the area of voluntary choices. So is the tremendous growth of recreation in all its phases. The number of voluntary associations and the

amount of time devoted to participation in them is an unmeasured index of still additional free use of time. In recent years there has been a vast expansion in consumer activities, exhibited by the rate at which consumer goods are purchased, as well as the increasing range of consumer goods entering into the daily life of the average citizen. Here again is evidence of a form of voluntarism with respect to the consuming institution.

I personally do not view with alarm the destiny of modern industrial man, because of conformity in his working life. Like the squeezed balloon he finds release for voluntary action in many other realms of waking behavior. Indeed, one can go a step further by suggesting that even at work industrial man intrudes voluntary behavior within the restrictive confines of the work place. At this point I simply want to point out that the voluntary behavior during work does not have work as its subject matter. This is both evidence of the fact that industrial man's voluntary life lies outside the productive institution, and of the fact that the conformity in behavior demanded by the productive institution is not complete.

Our data about industrial life have served to clarify the nature of necessary human action by showing the priority that technological considerations have over other considerations in determining working behavior. At the same time, the data about work reveal that the impress of necessary behavior is neither complete at work, nor does it carry over into the larger segment of time available for the working citizen where he has a considerable measure of voluntarism in choosing his behaviors.

---

companion volume, Bernard Rosenberg and D. M. White, eds., *Mass Culture* (Glencoe: The Free Press, 1957) delineates the tremendous growth of popular arts as a source of activities or entertainment for a populace with leisure on its hands.

# 4

# Organization and the Person

Individualism has been a central feature of Western thought at least since the 18th Century. The individual has come to be viewed as endowed with certain rights and privileges, to be protected from invasion by the State or any lesser organized group. Our own Declaration of Independence and the United States Constitution contain classic statements of the individual's rights and freedoms.

In the modern world the concern with individual freedom has taken a new twist. It is no longer the oppressive, coercive force of the State against which the individual must be protected. Now it is the more insidious influence of the "organization" that must be combatted to protect individualism, according to some current beliefs. The organization is insidious in its influence because it appears to succeed in securing membership conformity without using force and overt coercion. People conform and become mediocre thereby, because of subtle and open demands made on them to be good "team men." The organization also seems to ally to itself the informal groups of its members to help enforce the leveling toward mediocrity that is the alleged result of conforming behavior. The end product is the "Organization Man," so sharply etched and clearly despised in the writings of Whyte and

**INTRODUCTION**      others.

Before we conclude that we are all destined for Hell, clothed in our snug little organization-men grey flannel suits, it is worthwhile to attempt a balanced consideration of the problem.

The emergence of individualism as a social value must be understood in its historical context. It was against the tyranny of an all-embracing State or State-Church that the doctrines of individual liberty were directed. It was held that the power of the State and/or the Church needed to be limited because they claimed supremacy in all areas of the individual's life. The nature of the limitation was essentially to provide some areas of privacy within which the individual would be relatively free to choose personal courses of action with more or less impunity. It should be noted that the State was still accorded the position of supreme power holder, and retained coercive powers absolutely in some areas, and under emergency circumstances in other areas. The Church was accorded supremacy in the area of the sacred.

What emerged was a pluralistic society exhibiting three kinds of individual freedom. The first individual freedom was the guarantee of areas of privacy, expressed in the notions of freedom of thought, freedom of religious beliefs, freedom and privacy of the home and property from arbitrary seizure and search. This freedom was generally institutionalized in the constitutions and sacred documents of the State, and sustained in the common law.

The second freedom of the pluralistic society was the freedom of choice of membership among the vast array of organized areas of daily life. Increasingly the individual became freer to choose his occupation and the employing organization in which he practiced it; his place and mode of residence; his voluntary associations like clubs, fraternal organizations, political parties, church organizations, and the like; his kinds and types of recreation and the groups with which he pursued them; his mate, friends, and close associates with whom he chose to ally himself intimately; and finally, even to choose a course of nonparticipation and seclusion from organized life. Part and parcel of this freedom of association was the freedom to give up particular associations for others. This freedom of association and choice of area of participation in social life is evidenced in the various forms of mobility in our society. People move up and down the social class ladder, in and out of occupations, between geographical areas. The apparent restlessness of a modern urban-industrial civilization exhibited in the constant mobilities of its citizens is a direct expression of the freedom of association which is a central feature of the pluralistic society.

The third freedom that came with the passing of the all-enveloping society, was the freedom to explore areas of social behavior not caught up in going institutions. The increased specialization of institutions and the organizations that embodied their practices led to their segregation; one from the other. In between these institutions exist areas of human behavior that none covers. In these interstices grow up natural experiments in human behavior made possible only by the notion of limited responsibility and limited coverage of the pluralistic institutions of our society. For example, the "Beatniks" of today can come close to rejecting all normal behavior patterns; they can invent, propagate, and protect their own behavior norms by *organizing* independent little societies for this purpose. Most social innovation takes place in the interstices between existing organizations and institutions. Health and welfare benefits in collective bargaining comprise a wholly new institution filling up the void between individual responsibility for personal welfare, state responsibility, and employer responsibility. Executive training for employed, successful executives is an example of another institution that has developed because our colleges and universities do not sufficiently educate their students before they graduate into business, and because the students do not learn enough when they work at their employment. Neither the educational institution in the formal training of the young, nor the business institution in the experience it affords, succeeds in "educating" fully the present day executive. He has to be sent back to special college-level courses for intensive supplementation of his knowledge to make him a more effective executive. Such social inventions are a continuous and common feature of our pluralistic society. They are a product of the constant experiments that take place between the organized sectors of life in efforts to organize these unstructured areas of daily living.

The pluralistic society, then, is characterized by three fundamental freedoms for the individual: freedom for privacy, freedom of association, and freedom for innovation in social behavior. All of these freedoms are close to maximum today. By contrast with our ancestors of the Middle Ages, or even the Classic Ages of Rome and Greece, modern man is exceptionally favored with individual freedom.

Wherein then comes the concern with the individual as a conformist, "Organization Man," who has sold his soul and individuality for a mess of comfort? This concern of students of modern life is grounded in two facts. *First,* there is evidence that we tend to be almost driven to be like our contemporaries. "Keeping up with the Jones'" seems to be the national pastime in work, home life, recreation, and morals. *Second,* this conformity seems to be all the more grotesque because it is voluntary. We are not literally coerced into being like our fellows —we seem to fear being different and accordingly bend every effort to copy their image. The result, then, is an alleged uniformity in our lives, made all the more unpalatable because we seem to strive for the sameness voluntarily. So runs the current indictment of the pluralistic society as the creator of "Organization Men."

Obviously this conclusion is controversial. It can be argued that we have sold our hard-won individualism for the security of the organization society and the creature comforts it affords. But the same set of facts also supports the conclusion that we have not given up the three freedoms of a pluralistic society in spite of the surface appearance of conformity to popular (and presumably low) standards of behavior.

This chapter is designed to examine the pros and cons of this issue. The purpose is to pose the problem as one means of understanding the linkages between individual and organization. The nature of these linkages, or "bonds of organization" as Bakke called them, helps in understanding the limits within which human relations policies of administrators operate and are effective.

A secondary purpose of this chapter is to examine still another aspect of motivation that centers on the connection between individual and organization. Within the framework of motivation viewed as an exchange between organization and individual, we will examine the organization level at which this exchange takes place.

In the following selection an excellent statement is made of the conflict between individual goals and organizational goals. This argument pictures the individual overpowered by organizational demands, and responding to organizational rewards, that lead to conformity with the lowest common denominator of behavior. Two fundamental consequences are drawn. *First,* the individual is alleged to have lost the spark of his uniqueness and individuality by being submerged in the conforming mass of his fellows. *Second,* the organization is also held to lose the benefits of individual initiative, inventiveness, and drive, that would otherwise result if less conformity were demanded of its members. These are serious charges deserving careful attention.

---

## PERSONAL vs. ORGANIZATIONAL GOALS

### *Chris Argyris**

A discussion of some of the basic properties of personality will be followed by a similar discussion regarding formal organization, from which an attempt will be made to derive some of the basic characteristics of the relationship that will tend to arise when these two initial components are "married" to form the beginning of a social organization.

The self, in this culture, tends to develop along specific developmental trends or dimensions which are operationally definable and empirically observable. The basic developmental trends may be described as follows. Human beings, in our culture:

1. Tend to develop from a state of being passive as an infant to a state of increasing activity as an adult.

2. Tend to develop from a state of dependence on others as an infant to a state of relative independence as an adult. Relative independence is the ability to "stand on one's own two feet" and simultaneously to acknowledge healthy dependencies.[1] It is characterized by the individual's freeing himself from his childhood determiners of behavior (e.g. family) and developing his own set of behavioral determiners. This individual does not tend to react to others (e.g., the boss) in terms of patterns learned during childhood.[2]

3. Tend to develop from being capable of behaving in only a few ways as an infant to being capable of behaving in many different ways as an adult.

4. Tend to develop from having erratic, casual, shallow, quickly dropped interests as an infant to a deepening of interests as an adult. The mature state is characterized by an endless series of challenges in which the

*From *Yale Scientific* (February, 1960), pp. 40–50. Used by permission.

[1]This is similar to Erikson's sense of autonomy and Bronfenbrenner's state of creative interdependence.
[2]R. W. White, *Lives in Progress* (New York, 1952), pp. 39 ff.

reward comes from doing something for its own sake. The tendency is to analyze and study phenomena in their full-blown wholeness, complexity, and depth.[3]

5. Tend to develop from having a short time perspective (i.e., the present largely determines behavior) as an infant, to a much longer time perspective as an adult (i.e., behavior is more affected by the past and the future).[4]

6. Tend to develop from being in a subordinate position in the family and society as an infant to aspiring to occupy a more equal and/or super-ordinate position relative to one's peers as an adult.

7. Tend to develop from a lack of awareness of the self as an infant to an awareness of and control over one's self as an adult. The adult who tends to experience adequate and successful control over his own behavior tends to develop a sense of integrity (Erikson) and feelings of self-worth.[5]

These dimensions are postulated as being descriptive as a basic multidimensional developmental process along which the growth of individuals in our culture may be measured. Presumably, every individual, at any given moment in time, could have his degree of development plotted along these dimensions. The exact location on each dimension will probably vary with each individual and even with the same individual at different times. Self-actualization may now be defined

more precisely as the individual's plotted score (or profile) along the above dimensions.

A few words of explanation concerning these dimensions of personality development:

1. The dimensions are continual in which the growth to be measured is assumed to be continuously changing in degree. An individual is presumed to develop continuously in degree from the infant end to the adult end of each continuum.

2. It is postulated that as long as one develops in a particular culture, one will never obtain maximum expression of these developmental trends. Clearly, all individuals cannot be maximally independent, active, and so forth, all the time and still maintain an organized society. It is the function of culture (e.g., norms, mores, etc.) to inhibit *maximum* expressions and to help an individual adjust and adapt by finding his *optimum* expression.

A second factor that prevents maximum expression and fosters optimum expression is the individual's own finite limits set by his personality. For example, some people fear the same amount of independence and activity that others desire. Also, it is commonplace to find some people who do not have the necessary abilities to perform specific tasks. No individual is known to have developed all known qualities to their full maturity.

Finally, defense mechanisms also are important factors operating to help an individual to deviate from the basic developmental trends.

3. The dimensions described above are constructed in terms of latent or genotypical characteristics. If one states that an individual needs to be

---

[3]*Ibid.*, pp. 347 ff.

[4]E. W. Bakke, *Citizens Without Work* (New Haven, 1940); and K. Lewin, "Time Perspective and Morale," in G. W. Lewin ed., *Resolving Social Conflicts* (New York, 1948), p. 105.

[5]C. R. Rogers, *Client-Centered Therapy* (New York, 1951).

dependent, this need will probably be ascertained by clinical inference because it is one that individuals are not usually aware of. Thus, if one observes an employee acting as if he were independent, it is possible that if one goes below the behavorial surface, the individual may be quite dependent. The obvious example is the employee who seems to behave always in a manner contrary to that desired by management. Although this behavior may look as if he is independent, his contrariness may be due to his great need to be dependent on management, which he dislikes to admit to himself and to others.

One might say that an independent person is one whose behavior is not caused by the influence others have over him. Of course, no individual is completely independent. All of us have our healthy dependencies, i.e., those which help us to maintain our discreteness, to be creative, and to develop.

One operational criterion to ascertain whether an individual's desire to be, let us say, independent and active is a true manifestation, is to ascertain the extent to which he permits others to express the same needs. Thus, an autocratic leader may say that he needs to be active and independent; he may also say that he wants subordinates who are the same; however, there is ample research to suggest that his leadership pattern only makes him and his subordinates more dependence-ridden.

### SOME BASIC PROPERTIES OF FORMAL ORGANIZATION

The next step is to focus the analytic spotlight on the formal organization. What are its properties? What are its basic "givens"? What probable impact will they have on the human personality? How will the human personality tend to react to this impact? What sorts of "chain reactions" are probable when these two basic components are brought together?

### FORMAL ORGANIZATIONS ARE RATIONAL ORGANIZATIONS

Probably the most basic property of formal organization is its logical foundation or, as it has been called by students of administration, its essential rationality. It is the "mirror image" of the planners' conception of how the intended consequences of the organization may be best achieved. The underlying assumption made by the creators of formal organization is that man within respectable tolerance will behave rationally, i.e., as the formal plan requires him to behave. Organizations are formed with particular objectives in mind, and their structure mirrors these objectives. Although man may not follow the prescribed paths, and consequently the objectives might never be achieved, Simon[6] suggests that, by and large, man does follow these prescribed paths. He points out:

Organizations are formed with the intention and design of accomplishing goals; and the people who work in organizations believe, at least part of the time, that they are stiriving toward these same goals. We must not lose sight of the fact that, however far organizations may depart from the traditional description . . . nevertheless most behavior in

---

[6]H. A. Simon, *Research Frontiers in Politics and Government* (Washington, D. C., 1955), p. 30.

organizations is intendedly rational behavior. By "intended rationality" I mean the kind of adjustment of behavior to goals of which humans are capable—a very incomplete and imperfect adjustment, to be sure, but one which nevertheless does accomplish purposes and does carry out programs.

Most of these experts emphasize that although no organizational structure will exemplify the maximum expression of the principles, a satisfactory aspiration is for optimum expression, which means modifying the ideal structure to take into account the individual (and any environmental) conditions. Moreover, they urge that the people must be loyal to the formal structure if it is to work effectively. Thus Taylor emphasizes that scientific management would never succeed without a "mental revolution." Fayol has the same problem in mind when he emphasizes the importance of *esprit de corps.*

However, it is also true that these experts have provided little insight into *why* they believe that people should undergo a "mental revolution," or why an *esprit de corps* is necessary if the principles are to succeed. The only hints usually found are that resistance to scientific management occurs because human beings "are what they are," or "because it's human nature." But, *why* does "human nature" resist formal organizational principles? Perhaps there is something inherent in the principles which causes human resistance. Unfortunately, there exists too little research that specifically assesses the impact of the formal organizational principles on human beings.

The formal organizational experts believe that logical, rational design, in the long run, is more human than creating an organization haphazardly. They argue that it is illogical, cruel, wasteful, and inefficient not to have a logical design. It is illogical because design must come first. It does not make sense to pay a large salary to an individual without clearly defining his position and its relationship to the whole. It is cruel because, eventually, the participants suffer when no clear organizational structure exists. It is wasteful because, unless jobs are clearly predefined, it is impossible to plan logical training, promotion, resignation, and retirement policies. It is inefficient because the organization becomes dependent on personalities. The "personal touch" leads to "playing politics," which Mary Follett has described as a "deplorable form of coercion."

Unfortunately, the validity of these arguments tends to be obscured in the eyes of the behavioral scientist because it implies that the only choice left, if the formal, rational, predesigned structure is not accepted, is to have no organizational structure at all, with the organizational structure left to the whims, pushes and pulls of human beings. Some human-relations researchers, on the other hand, have unfortunately given the impression that formal structures are "bad" and that the needs of the individual participants should be paramount in creating and administering an organization. However, a recent analysis of the existing research points up quite clearly that the importance of the organization as an organism worthy of self-actualization is now being recognized by those who, in the past, have focused largely on the individual.[7]

---

[7] C. Argyris, *The Present State of Research in Human Relations* (New Haven, 1954), Chap. 1.

In the past, and for the most part in the present, the traditional organizational experts based their "human architectural creation" on certain basic principles (more accurately, assumptions) about the nature of organization.

Although these principles have been attacked by behavioral scientists, the assumption is made in this paper that to date no one has defined a more useful set of formal organization principles. Therefore, the principles are accepted as "givens." This frees us to inquire about their probable impact on people, *if they are used as defined.*

In introducing these principles, it is important to note that, as Gillespie suggests, the roots of these principles may be traced back to certain "principles of industrial economics," the most important of which is the basic economic assumption held by builders of the industrial revolution that "the concentration of effort on a limited field of endeavor increases quality and quantity of output."[8] It follows from the above that the necessity for specialization should increase as the quantity of similar things to be done increases.

## Task (Work) Specialization

If concentrating effort on a limited field of endeavor increases the quality and quantity of output, it follows that organizational and administrative efficiency is increased by the specialization of tasks assigned to the participants in the organization.[9] Inherent in this assumption are three others. *First,*

that the human personality will behave more efficiently as the task becomes specialized. *Second,* that there can be found a one best way to define the job so that it is performed at greater speed.[10] *Third,* that any individual differences in the human personality may be ignored by transferring more skill and thought to machines.

A number of difficulties arise with these assumptions when the properties of the human personality are recalled. *First,* the human personality, as we have seen, is always attempting to actualize its unique organization of parts resulting from a continuous, emotionally laden, ego-involving process of growth. It is difficult, if not impossible, to assume that this process can be choked off and the resultant unique differences of individuals ignored. This is tantamount to saying that self-actualization can be ignored. *Second,* task specialization requires the individual to use only a few of his abilities. Moreover, as specialization increases, it tends to require the use of the less complex doing or motor abilities which, research suggests, tend to be of lesser psychological importance to the individual. Thus the principle violates two basic "givens" of the healthy adult human personality. It inhibits self-actualization and provides expression for few, shallow, skin-surface abilities that do not provide the "endless challenge" desired by the healthy personality.

## Chain of Command

The principle of task specialization creates an aggregate of parts, each

---

[8]J. J. Gillespie, *Free Expression in Industry* (London, 1948), pp. 34–37.

[9]H. A. Simon, *Administrative Behavior* (New York, 1947), pp. 80–81.

[10]G. Friedmann, *Industrial Society* (Glencoe, Ill., 1955), pp. 54 ff.

performing a highly specialized task. However, an aggregate of parts busily performing their particular objective does not form an organization. A pattern of parts must be formed so that the interrelationships among the parts create the organization. Following the logic of specialization, the planners create a new function (leadership) whose primary responsibility is to control, direct, and coordinate the interrelationships of the parts, and to make certain that each part performs its objective adequately. Thus the assumption is made that administrative and organizational efficiency is increased by arranging the parts in a determinate hierachy of authority in which the part on top can direct and control the part on the bottom.

If the parts being considered are individuals, then they must be motivated to accept control, direction, and coordination of their behavior. The leader, therefore, is assigned formal power to hire, discharge, reward, and penalize the individuals in order that their behavior is molded toward the organization's objectives.

The impact of such a state of affairs is to make the individuals dependent on, passive, and subordinate to the leader. As a result, the individuals have little control over their working environment. At the same time, their time perspective is shortened because they do not control the information necessary to predict their future. These requirements of formal organization act to inhibit four of the growth trends of personality because to be passive and subordinate and to have little control and short time perspective exemplify dimensions, in adults, of immaturity, not adulthood.

The planners of formal organization suggest three basic ways to minimize this admittedly difficult position. *First,*

ample rewards should be given to those who perform well and who do not permit their dependence, subordination, passivity, etc. to influence them in a negative manner. The rewards should be material and psychological. Because of the specialized nature of the job, however, few psychological rewards are possible. It becomes important, therefore, that adequate material rewards are made available to the productive employee. This practice can lead to new difficulties, since the solution is, by its nature, not to do anything about the on-the-job situation (which is what is causing the difficulties) but to pay the individual for the dissatisfactions he experiences. The end result is that the employee is paid for his dissatisfaction while at work and his wages are given to him to gain satisfactions outside his immediate work environment.

Thus the management helps to create a psychological set which leads the employees to feel that basic causes of dissatisfaction are built into industrial life, that the rewards they receive are wages for dissatisfaction, and that if satisfaction is to be gained, the employee must seek it outside the organization.

To make matters more difficult, there are three assumptions inherent in the above solution that also violate the basic "givens" of human personality. *First,* the solution assumes that a whole human being can split his personality so that he will feel satisfied in knowing that the wages for his dissatisfaction will buy him satisfaction outside the plant. *Second,* it assumes that the employee is primarily interested in maximizing his economic gains. *Third,* it assumes that the employee is best rewarded as an individual producer. The work group in which he belongs is not viewed as a relevant factor. If he produces well, he should be rewarded. If he does not, he should be penalized even though he may be restricting production because of informal group sanctions.

The *second* solution suggested by the planners of formal organization is to have technically competent, objective, rational, loyal leaders. The assumption is made that if the leaders are technically competent, presumably they cannot have "the wool pulled over their eyes"; which should lead the employees to have a high respect for them. The leaders should be objective and rational and personify the rationality inherent in the formal structure. Being rational means that they must avoid becoming emotionally involved. As one executive states, "We must try to keep our personality out of the job." The leader must also be impartial. He does not permit his feelings to operate when he is evaluating others. Finally, the leader must be loyal to the organization so that he can inculcate the loyalty in the employees that Taylor, Fayol, and others believe is so important.

Admirable as this solution may be, again it violates several of the basic properties of personality. If the employees are to respect an individual for what he does rather than for who he is, the sense of self-integrity, based on evaluation of the total self which is developed in people, is lost. Moreover, to ask the leader to keep his personality out of his job is to ask him to stop actualizing himself. This is not possible as long as he is alive. Of course, the executive may want to *feel* that he is not involved, but it is a basic "given" that the human personality is an organism always actualizing itself. The same problem arises with impartiality. No one can be com-

pletely impartial. As has been shown, the self concept always operates when we are making judgments. In fact, as May has pointed out, the best way to be impartial is to be as partial as one's needs predispose one to be but to be aware of this partiality in order to "correct" for it at the moment of decision.[11] Finally, if a leader can be loyal to an organization under these conditions, there may be adequate grounds for questioning the health of his personality make-up.

The *third* solution suggested by many adherents to the formal organizational principles is to motivate the subordinates to have more initiative and to be more creative by placing them in competition with one another for the positions of power that lie above them in the organizational ladder. This solution is traditionally called "the rabble hypothesis." Acting under the assumption that employees will be motivated to advance upward, the formal organizational adherents add another assumption; that competition for the increasingly (as one goes up the ladder) scarcer positions will increase the effectiveness of the participants. Williams, conducting some controlled experiments, shows that the latter assumption is not necessarily valid for people placed in competitive situations. Deutsch, as a result of extensive controlled experimental research, supports Williams' results and goes much further to suggest that competitive situations tend to lead to an increase in tension and conflict and to a decrease in human effectiveness. Levy and Freedman confirm Deutsch's observations and go further

---

[11]R. May, "Historical and Philosophical Presuppositions for Understanding Therapy," in *Psychotherapy Theory and Research*, O. H. Mowrer, ed. (New York, 1953), pp. 38–39.

to relate competition to psychoneurosis.[12]

## Unity of Direction

If the tasks of everyone in a unit are specialized, then it follows that the objective or purpose of the unit must be specialized. The principle of unity of direction states that administrative and organizational efficiency increases if each unit has a single (or homogeneous set of) activity (activities) that is (are) planned and directed by the leader.

This means that the work goal toward which the employees are working, the path toward the goal, and the strength of the barriers they must overcome to achieve the goal are defined and controlled by the leader. Assuming that the work goals do not ego-involve the employee (i.e., they are related to peripheral skin-surface needs), then ideal conditions for psychological failure have been created. The reader may recall that a basic "given" of a healthy personality is the aspiration for psychological success. Psychological success is achieved when each individual is able to define his own goals, in relation to his inner needs and the strength of the barriers to be overcome in order to reach these goals. Repetitive as it may sound, it is nevertheless true that the principle of unity of direction also violates a basic "given" of personality.

---

[12]L. C. S. Williams, "Effects of Competition Between Groups in a Training Situation," *Occupational Psychology*, 30:85–93 (April 1956); M. Deutsch, "The Effects of Cooperation and Competition Upon Group Process," *Human Relations*, 2:129–152 (1949); and S. Levy and L. Freedman, "Psychoneurosis and Economic Life," *Social Problems*, 4:55–67 (July 1956).

## A BASIC INCONGRUENCY BETWEEN THE NEEDS OF A MATURE PERSONALITY AND THE REQUIREMENTS OF FORMAL ORGANIZATION

Bringing together the evidence regarding the impact of the formal organization principles on the individual, it is concluded that there are some basic incongruencies between the growth trends of a healthy personality and the requirements of the formal organization. If the principles of formal organization are used as ideally defined, then the employees will tend to work in an environment where (1) they are provided control over their workaday world; (2) they are expected to be passive, dependent, subordinate; (3) they are expected to have a short time perspective; (4) they are induced to perfect and value the frequent use of few skin-surface, shallow abilities; and (5) they are expected to produce under conditions leading to psychological failure.

All of these characteristics are incongruent to the ones healthy human beings are postulated to desire. They are much more congruent with the needs of infants in our culture. In effect, therefore, formal organizations are willing to pay high wages and provide adequate seniority if mature adults will, for 8 hours a day, behave in a less mature manner! *If the analysis is correct, this inevitable incongruency increases as (1) the employees are of increasing maturity; (2) as the formal structure, based on the above principles, is made more clear-cut and logically tight for maximum formal organizational effectiveness; (3) as one goes down the line of command; and (4) as jobs become more and more mechanized, i.e., take on assembly-line characteristics.*

The resultants of this lack of congruency are frustration, failure, short-time perspective, and conflict. If the agents are predisposed to a healthy, more mature self-actualization:

1. They will tend to experience frustration because their self-actualization will be blocked.[13]

2. They will tend to experience failure because they will not be permitted to define their own goals in relation to central needs, the paths of these goals, etc.[14]

3. They will tend to experience short-time perspective because they have no control over the clarity and stability of their future.[15]

4. They will tend to experience conflict because, as healthy agents, they will dislike frustration, failure, and short-time perspective which are characteristic of the present job. However, if they leave, they may not find a new job easily; and/or even if a new job is found, it may not be much different.[16]

It can be shown that under conflict, frustration, failure, and short-time perspective, the employees will tend to maintain self-integration by creating specific adaptive (informal) behavior such as:

1. Leaving the organization.
2. Climbing the organizational ladder.
3. Manifesting defense reactions

such as daydreaming, aggression, ambivalence, regression, projection, etc.

4. Becoming apathetic and disinterested toward the organization, its make-up, and goals. This leads to such phenomena as:

   a. Employees reduce the number and potency of the needs they expect to fulfill while at work.

   b. Employees "goldbrick," set rates, restrict quotas, make errors, cheat, slow down, etc.

5. Creating informal groups to sanction the defense reactions and apathy, disinterest and lack of self-involvement.

6. Formalizing the informal groups.

7. Evolving group norms that perpetuate the behavior outlined in items 3, 4, 5, and 6 above.

8. Evolving a psychological set that human or nonmaterial factors are becoming increasingly unimportant while material factors become increasingly important.

9. Acculturating the youth to accept the norms discussed in items 7 and 8.

The basic problem is to decrease the degree of dependency, subordination, submissiveness, etc. It can be shown that job enlargement, employee-centered (or democratic or participative) leadership are a few factors which, if used correctly, can go a long way toward ameliorating the situation. However, these are limited because their success depends on having employees who are ego-involved: highly interested in the organization. The adaptive behavior listed above predisposes the employee to disinterest, non-ego-involvement, and apathy. The existence of such states of affairs, in turn, acts to require the more directive leadership

[13] R. B. Barker *et al., Frustration and Regression* (Iowa City, 1941); and J. Dollard *et al., Frustration and Aggression* (New Haven, 1939).

[14] K. Lewin *et al.,* "Level of Aspiration," in J. McV. Hunt (ed.) *Personality and Behavior Disorders* (New York, 1944); and R. Lippitt and L. Bradford, "Employee Success in Work Groups," *Personnel Administration,* 8:6–10 (December 1945).

[15] K. Lewin, "Time Perspective and Morale," *op. cit.,* pp. 103–124.

[16] T. M. Newcomb, *Social Psychology* (New York, 1950), pp. 361–373.

pattern to "motivate" and control the disinterested employee. The directive leadership pattern, in turn, requires strong management controls if it is to succeed. But, as we have seen, directive leadership and management controls actually create the human problems that one is trying to solve.

This dilemma between the needs of the individuals and the demands of the organization is a basic, continual dilemma, posing an eternal challenge to the leader. How is it possible to create an organization in which it is possible for the individuals to obtain optimum expression and, simultaneously, for the organization to obtain optimum satisfaction of its demands?

Although a few suggestions may be found in the literature, they are, by and large, untested and wanting in systematic rigor. Here lies a fertile field for future research in organizational behavior.

---

One possible way out of the dilemma of conflict between individual goals and organizational goals, so ably presented by Argyris, is suggested in the next selection. It is held that this basic dilemma is, in fact, solved by the citizens of an urban-industrial society on their own terms. The solution neither destroys individual self-realization, nor makes productive organizations less efficient.

The basic mechanism by which the dilemma is resolved is that of partial involvement of individuals in particular institutional settings. Given the wide range of areas of daily life, each person selects only a few as central life interests. In those realms of action that are central to the individual, strong attachments and involvements are developed. It is in such areas that "self-realization" and "mature, healthy" personality expressions are achieved. But, and this is of critical importance, in the remaining areas of required behavior, not central to the person's interests, there may be no need for "self-realization," and hence behavior ensues that does not appear as the product of a healthy, mature personality.

This implies, of course, that we dissemble in our relations with others. We act out roles and expectations of others, whether or not the actions fit our own unique personalities. But, it is argued in the following, we do this easily in areas *not* central to our life interest, and with no loss of our own sense of personality integrity and feelings of self-worth. Thus, it is concluded, we can meet organization goals readily, irrespective of their conflict with personal goals, in situations where the behaviors are not central to our life interests. In short, if you really do not care about something, then your actions in relation to it are not really important to you.

This conclusion may, at first blush, seem shocking for it suggests that productive organizations of our society are efficient and effective precisely because their participants *are not* heavily involved in them as central life interests. Remembering the selection from Chapter 3 distinguishing between necessary and voluntary action, it begins to make sense to view working behavior as a form of necessary action with the accompanying indifferent orientation towards it. As is pointed out in the following: "This is the magic of social organization—the ability to sustain required behaviors even when the institution is not central to the actors' interests."

## PERSON AND ORGANIZATION

### Robert Dubin*

Why the current hue and cry about the individual oppressed by the work organizations or unions of which he is a member? The answer seems to be that as students of human behavior, and as educated laymen, we can observe everywhere about us the extent to which behavior as members of organizations is imperative rather than voluntary.

What is the underlying assumption involved in the view that industrial man is the captive of his employing organizations and unions? It is this: Man participates in all institutions of his life with equal intensity. This assumption sees man as moving in his daily round of life from one institutional setting to another, participating with equal enthusiasm and affective attachment to each. Thus, he moves from the productive institution or work to the family institution, to the recreational institutions, etc., making each institutional setting an intensive focus of interest while in it.

I submit that this is an inaccurate way of characterizing man's attachment to the institutions of his society. A more accurate model would be this: Most men have certain central life interests at any given time focused in one, or at most, several institutional settings. They have to participate in other institutions, but do so in terms

of the behaviors required in them, and without reference to the voluntary choices that may be available in them. Thus the areas for voluntary social action are precisely the institutions that are central to a man's life interests and that are therefore at the focus of his attention.

With this formulation we can perhaps begin to understand the perfunctory character of much of social life and the apathy the citizen of modern society displays for many of its institutional facets. A man may go to church only on Sunday, or even less frequently on high holidays, carrying out the perfunctory obligations to the religious institution. He is part of the institution, but it is not part of him, since he only fulfills the minimum required behaviors to publicly acknowledge his participation in it. It is curious that sociologists have not really focused on the problem of differential institutional participation in the life history of the person. It seems clear that with the kind of formulation of this relationship just presented we are able to grasp and comprehend the apathy of industrial workers for their companies, their unions, and their work. It is a startling fact of our studies of industrial workers that they uniformly reveal this apathy in a number of ways.

The fact of the matter is this. Work, for probably a majority of workers, and even extending into the ranks of management, may represent an institutional setting that is not a central life interest for its participants. The

*From "Industrial Research and the Discipline of Sociology," *Proceedings of the 11th Annual Meeting* (Industrial Relations Research Association, Madison: The Association, 1959), pp. 160–163. Used by permission.

consequence of this is that while participating in work a general attitude of apathy and indifference prevails. The response to the demands of the institution is to satisfy the minimum expectations of required behavior without reacting affectively to these demands. Thus, the industrial worker does not feel imposed upon by the tyranny of organizations, company, or union. He is indifferent to this area of his life, considering it only a necessary part of his round of life, but not central in his interests. It is only the analysts, making value judgments about the dehydrated character of work, and fearing its consequences for the meaningfulness of life to industrial workers, who are alarmed by this problem. Bakke and Argyris, for example, write about "self-realization" at work.[1] Self-realization may, however, be a matter of indifference to people for whom work is not a central life interest. Their self-realization comes in other institutional settings outside the productive institution.

What about those people in industry and commerce for whom work is a central life interest? These are the people who find the fulfillment of their life goals in work itself. They make the work institution central to their lives. The interesting fact is that for such people the work environment is challenging and rewarding. This is another way of saying that an institution, when it is a central life inter-est for the person, is perceived as full of choices of behaviors, and opportunities for rewards to which the person is fully sensitive. The consequence is that he becomes a real striver in the institutional setting, securing many rewards and often encountering deprivations and frustrations. But this is no different from the man who experiences his family life as the institutional center of his interests. The point is that there is nothing about the organization of productive work, or the supervision of people while doing it, that is so antithetical to human personality needs as to result only in frustration and disappointment.

Elton Mayo began his pioneering studies of human relations in industry by examining the reveries of industrial workers. He conceptualized this as a means of escaping the "dehydrated" or depersonalized atmosphere of the workplace.[2] I would argue that a more inclusive conceptualization would be to conclude that the workers *never entered into* the work situation by making it central to their life interests. Their reveries were the continual, albeit imaginative, living out of their lives in institutional settings central to them while performing the necessary labor of industrial work.

The big point is this. Before we can use concepts of individual freedom, self-realization, satisfactions, and gratifications for the person, we have to ask what is his relationship to the specific social setting from which they are derived. If the social setting is one

[1]Cf. E. Wright Bakke, "The Function of Management," in E. M. Hughes-Jones, ed., *Human Relations and Modern Management* (Amsterdam: North-Holland Publishing Company, 1958) Chap. 8; and Chris Argyris, *Personality and Organization* (New York: Harper & Brothers, 1957). Their general point about self-realization in work is well taken for those to whom work is a central life interest.

[2]See: Elton Mayo, "Revery and Industrial Fatigue," *Journal of Personnel Research*, Vol. 3 (December 1924), 273–281; and his "Day Dreaming and Output in a Spinning Mill," *Journal of the National Institute of Industrial Psychology*, II (January, 1925), 203–209.

not central to his life interests, then he will participate in it as required (as is true in work) without expecting or needing these rewards to continue his effective performance. It is sufficient that the required behaviors be clearly specified, and that the payoffs (wages, fringe benefits) be readily apparent. He finds the rewards that sustain his personality integrity in other institutional settings central to his life. If this makes sense, then the argument is simple. We can now understand the data of indifference and apathy toward work and the organizations embodying it if we first understand the way in which persons are attached to the institutions in which they behave.

Work in our society does not appear to be a central life interest for a substantial proportion, if not a majority of our citizens. Their apathy and indifference result from this. But this does not mitigate against their effective performance as workers so long

as their required behaviors are adequately set forth for them and the incentives in the form of payoffs are calculable. This is the magic of social organization—the ability to sustain required behaviors even when the institution is not central to the actors' interests.

That this has implications for managing decisions is obvious. The broad struggle against apathy and indifference has been waged with a variety of personnel techniques designed to elicit loyalty and enthusiastic participation. The success of these techniques rests on the assumption that work *ought* to be a central life interest for workers. It becomes obvious that where work is not such a central life interest, then the techniques may be futile in making it so. Is this why personnel gimmicks proliferate at almost the same rate as styles in women's clothing?

---

You will have noted that Argyris started with the person and described his growth toward maturity. He then described organization as requiring individuals to behave in ways that prevented "self-actualization." For Argyris, the culprit is the organization.

In the preceding selection it was pointed out that the problem lies in neither the personality nor the organization, but rather in their mutual adaptation. The features of work organizations against which Agyris cried out are important for their technical operations. These organizational features may produce indifference in men without depriving them of their ability to be productive. This can happen because persons are able to achieve "self-actualization" in some areas of their life without requiring it in all

areas. For example, a professor may be a brilliant historian, an indifferent tennis player, an absent-minded husband and father, and an atrocious administrator as department head. This may leave him very contented in spite of the unequal quality of his performance in these various roles.

In the following selection George Strauss directly challenges the conclusions so ably presented by Argyris. When Argyris attacks the organizational disabilities, Strauss centers his criticism on the model of man used by Argyris and his colleagues. In addition, Strauss goes one step further and indicates that the costs of changing the organization may be very great and exceed the alleged profit to be gained by so doing.

Strauss uses the general term

"power-equalization" for what appears to be the organizational solution proposed by Argyris, namely, that all organization participants be made more equal by minimizing or eliminating hierarchy.

The most lively controversy in the whole field of human relations in administration is the battle between personality advocates and organizational proponents. Every student of the subject and every operating administrator and executive needs to be aware of the nature of this controversy and to have a personal position that resolves the conflict in his own mind. The three selections in this chapter provide you a very adequate basis for understanding the issues and reaching your own conclusions.

## PERSONALITY-VERSUS-ORGANIZATION HYPOTHESIS

### George Strauss*

Over the years, out of the contributions of individuals such as Argyris (1957), Hertzberg (1960), Maier (1955), Maslow (1954), and McGregor (1960) has come a consistent view of human motivation in industry.[1] With due credit to Chris Argyris, I would like to call it the "personality-versus-organization" hypothesis. I will state this hypothesis briefly first and then criticize it.

1. Human behavior in regard to work is motivated by a hierarchy of needs, in ascending order: physical, safety, social, egoistic, and self-actualization. By "hierarchy" is meant that a higher, less basic need does not provide motivation unless all lower, more basic needs are satisfied, and that, once a basic need is satisfied, it no longer motivates.

Physical needs are the most fundamental, but once a reasonable (satisficing, as Simon would put it) level of physical-need satisfaction is obtained (largely through pay), individuals become relatively more concerned with other needs. First they seek to satisfy their security needs (through seniority, fringe benefits, and so forth). When these, too, are reasonably satisfied, social needs (friendship, group support, and so forth) take first priority. And so forth. Thus, for example, hungry men have little interest in whether or not they belong to strong social groups; relatively well-off individuals are more anxious for good human relations.

Only when most of the less pressing needs are satisfied will individuals turn to the ultimate form of satisfaction, self-actualization, which is described by Maslow (1943) as "the de-

---

*Reprinted by permission from George Strauss, "Some Notes on Power Equalization," in Harold J. Leavitt (ed.), *The Social Science of Organizations* (Englewood Cliffs, N. J.: Prentice-Hall, Inc., 1963), pp. 41–84.

[1]For an excellent summary of this hypothesis and its application, see Clark (1960–61). Somewhat the same position is taken by Merton (1957) and Selznick (1949); both suggest that organizational attempts to obtain conformity lead to unanticipated consequences, such as lack of innovation and even rebellion.

sire to become more and more what one is, to become everything that one is capable of becoming. . . . A musician must make music, an artist must paint, a poet must write, if he is to be ultimately happy. What a man *can* be, he *must* be." (p. 372.)

2. Healthy individuals desire to mature, to satisfy increasingly higher levels of needs. This, in practice, means that they want more and more opportunity to form strong social groups, to be independent, creative, to exercise autonomy and discretion, and to develop and express their unique personality with freedom.

3. The organization, on the other hand, seeks to program individual behavior and reduce discretion. It demands conformity, obedience, dependence, and immature behavior. The assembly-line worker, the engineer, and the executive are all subject to strong pressures to behave in a programmed, conformist fashion.[2] As a consequence, many individuals feel alienated from their work.

4. Subordinates react to these pressures in a number of ways, most of which are dysfunctional to the organization. Individuals may fight back through union activity, sabotage, output restriction, and other forms of rational or irrational (aggressive) behavior. Or they may withdraw and engage in regression, sublimation, childish behavior, or failure to contribute creative ideas or to produce more than a minimum amount of work. In any case, employees struggle not to conform (at least at first). To keep these employees in line, management must impose still more re-

strictions and force still more immature behavior. Thus, a vicious cycle begins.

5. Management pressures often lead to excessive competition and splintering of work groups and the consequent loss of cooperation and social satisfaction. Or work groups may become even stronger, but their norms may now be anti-management, those of protecting individuals against pressures from above.

6. A subtle management, which provides high wages, liberal employee benefits, "hygienic," "decent" supervision, and not too much pressure to work, may well induce employees to *think* they are happy and not *dissatisfied*.[3] But they are not (or should not be) truly *satisfied;* they are apathetic and have settled for a low level of aspiration. They do as little work as they can get away with and still hold their jobs. This is an unhealthy situation which is wasteful both to the individual and to the organization.

7. There seem to be some differences in emphasis among authorities as to whether the behavior of the typical subordinate under these circumstances will be rational (reality-oriented) or irrational (frustration-oriented). In any case, organizational pressures, particularly being subjected to programmed work, may lead to

---

[2]These three groups are discussed in Walker and Guest (1952), Shepard (1960), and Whyte (1956).

[3]Hertzberg, Mausner, and Snyderman (1960) distinguish between dissatisfiers (basically, the absence of "hygienic" factors such as good "supervision, interpersonal relations, physical working conditions, salary, company policies, and administrative practices, benefits and job security") (p. 113) and motivators (basically challenge, autonomy, and interesting work). Similar conclusions are reached by Guerin, Vernoff, and Feld (1960). The Herzberg, Mausner, and Snyderman analysis is criticized by Vroom and Maier (1960).

serious personality disturbances and mental illness.[4] Thus, traditional organizational techniques not only prevent the organization from operating at maximum efficiency, but, in terms of their impact on individual adjustment, they are also very expensive to society as a whole.

8. The only healthy solution is for management to adopt policies which promote intrinsic job satisfaction, individual development, and creativity, according to which people will willingly and voluntarily work toward organizational objectives because they enjoy their work and feel that it is important to do a good job.[5] More specifically, management should promote job enlargement, general supervision, strong cohesive work groups, and decentralization. In a nutshell, management should adopt "power-equalization techniques."

### CRITICISM

The above is, in a sense, a hypothesis as to human behavior in organizations. But it is more than a coldly objective hypothesis: it is a prescription for management behavior, and implicit in it are strong value judgments.[6] With its strong emphasis on individual dignity, creative freedom, and self-development, this hypothesis bears all the earmarks of its academic origin.

Professors place high value on autonomy, inner direction, and the quest for maximum self-development. As much as any other group in society, their existence is work-oriented; for them, creative achievement is an end in itself and requires no further justification. Most professors are strongly convinced of the righteousness of their Protestant ethic of hard work and see little incongruity in imposing it upon the less fortunate.

And yet there are many misguided individuals (perhaps the bulk of the population) who do not share the professor's values and would not be happy in the professor's job. Further, the technical requirements of many lines of work are very different from those of academia. Academic work is best accomplished by those with academic values, but it is questionable whether these values are equally functional in other lines of work—where creativity is not required to get the job done, but only the ability to follow orders.

In the pages which follow, I shall seek to re-evaluate the personality-versus-organization hypothesis. I shall suggest, first, that it contains many debatable value judgements and, second, that it ignores what Harold Leavitt has called "organizational eco-

---

[4]Recent evidence suggests that unskilled workers are significantly more likely to suffer from personality disturbances and psychosomatic illnesses than are skilled workers, and that these differences become manifest only after the individuals take up their work. (In other words, once individuals land in unskilled jobs, they tend to become more maladjusted.) (Kornhauser, 1962; French, Kahn, and Mann, 1962.)

[5]Perhaps the most general statement of this position is McGregor's Theory Y. See McGregor (1960).

[6]There seems to be a certain amount of confusion as to whether prescriptions for power-equalization are written from the point of view of organizational efficiency or that of mental health (and possibly the degree of confusion has increased since the primary source of research funds in this area has shifted from the military to the National Institute of Mental Health). There are those who claim that what is good for the individual will, in the long run, be good for the organization, and vice versa. Regardless, it is useful to keep one's criteria explicit.

nomics." I shall conclude that a broad range of people do not seek self-actualization on the job—and that this may be a fortunate thing because it might be prohibitively expensive to redesign some jobs to permit self-actualization.

## VALUE JUDGMENTS

It seems to me that the hypothesis, as often stated, over-emphasizes (1) the uniqueness of the personality-organization conflict to large-scale industry, (2) the universality of the desire to achieve self-actualization, and (3) the importance of the job (as opposed to the community or the home) as a source of need satisfaction. Thus, too little attention is given to economic motivation.[7]

*The uniqueness of the problem*

At least some authors seem to over-dramatize the personality-organization conflict as something unique to large-scale organization (particularly to mass-production industry). But this conflict is merely one aspect of what has been variously characterized as the conflict between individual and society, individual and environment, desire and reality, id and superego. "Thus the formal organization . . . is not truly the real villain; rather any kind of organized activity, from the most democratic to the most authoritarian, contains within itself the necessary conditions for conflict."[8]

Similarly, the impact of the industrial revolution on work satisfaction

can be overemphasized. Much is made of "alienation" (dictionary meaning: turning away) from work. Comparisons are constantly made between the old-time craftsman who did the entire job and the mass-production worker of today. But I doubt whether the medieval serf or the Egyptian slave enjoyed much sense of autonomy or creativity (although one might perhaps argue that he had more of a sense of identification and less of a feeling of anomie than does his better-fed modern counterpart). Perhaps there is less job satisfaction today than there was 100 years ago. Obviously, there are no objective ways of measuring this, but my surmise is that the "turning away" has been less dramatic than some have suggested. There have been boring, programmed jobs throughout history.

Others are as skeptical as I am regarding the theory of increased alienation. In his conclusion to a survey of job-satisfaction studies, Robert Blauner (1960) questions "the prevailing thesis that most workers in modern society are alienated and estranged. There is a remarkable consistency in the findings that the vast majority of workers, in virtually all occupations and industries, are moderately or highly satisfied, rather than dissatisfied with their jobs. . . . The real character of the [pre-mass production] craftsman's work has been romanticized by the prevalent tendency to idealize the past. . . ." (pp. 352–353). And J. A. C. Brown (1954) asserts "that in modern society there is far greater scope of skill and craftsmanship than in any previous society, and that far more people are in a position to use such skills" (p. 207).

---

[7]I must confess that many of these criticisms apply to my own writing. See Strauss and Sayles (1960), especially Chapters 4-8 and 12, chapters for which I was responsible. See the review by Brayfield (1962).

[8]Bennis (1959, p. 281). Ironically, some

of those most concerned with the tyranny of the organization would substitute for it the tyranny of the participative group.

*The universality of the desire
for self-actualization*

The basic hypothesis implies a strong moral judgment that people should want freedom and self-actualization,[9] that it is somehow morally wrong for people to be lazy, unproductive, and uncreative. It seems to me that the hypothesis overemphasizes individuals' desire for freedom and underemphasizes their desire for security. It can even be argued that some of the personality-versus-organization writing has a fairly antisocial, even nihilistic flavor; it seems to emphasize individual freedom and self-development as the all-important values. Yet "mature" behavior does not mean freedom from all restrictions; it means successful adjustment to them.

As Eric Fromm has suggested, most people do not want complete freedom. They want to know the limits within which they can act (and this is true both on and off the job). To put it another way: most people are willing to tolerate and may even be anxious for a few areas of their life which are unpredictable and exciting, but they insist that, in a majority of areas, events occur as expected. The research scientist, for example, may relish the novelty and uncertainty of laboratory work, but he insists that his secretary be always on call, that his technician give predictable responses, and that his car start with complete regularity.

True, some people seek much broader limits than do others, and some are not too upset if the limits are fuzzy. However, there are many who feel most comfortable if they work in a highly defined situation. For them, freedom is a burden; they want firm, secure leadership. And there are many more who, if not fully happy with programmed work, find it rather easy to accommodate themselves to it.

Argyris, for example, might reply that such individuals are immature personalities who have adjusted to organizational restrictions by becoming apathetic and dependent. Were the organizational environment healthy, these individuals would react differently. But in many cases, the restrictions which made these people this way occurred in childhood or are present in the culture. Such individuals may be "too far gone" to react well to power equalization, and their attitude is not likely to be changed short of intensive psychotherapy. Indeed, many people may have internalized and made part of their self-concept a low level of aspiration regarding their on-the-job responsibilities and their ability to handle these. What psychologists call the *theory of dissonance* suggests that sudden attempts to increase their sense of autonomy and self-determination might be quite disturbing.

Impressive evidence of the need for self-actualization is provided by the preliminary results of the mental health studies, which suggest that poor mental health is correlated with holding low-skilled jobs. And yet the evidence is still not complete. Apparently, not everyone suffers equally from unskilled work, and some adjust more easily than others. (Perhaps these studies will help us to improve the prediction process, so that we can do a better job of selecting and even training people for this kind of work.)

Further, it is far from clear whether this lower mental health is caused primarily by the intrinsic nature of

---

[9] Though the concept of self-actualization is insightful, I tend to agree with Bennis (1959) that it "is, at best, an ill-defined concept . . . [and that] self-actualized man seems to be more myth than reality" (p. 279).

unskilled work or by the fact that such work pays poorly and has low status both off and on the job.[10] Insofar as mental disturbances are caused by economic and social pressures at home, higher wages may be a better solution than improved human relations on the job or a rearrangement of work assignments.

A hasty glance at the research in this field, as summarized in two reviews (Kasl and French, 1962; Vroom and Maier, 1960; see also Guerin *et al.*, 1960), makes it abundantly clear that unskilled workers are not the only ones to suffer from poor mental health. Depending on which study one looks at or what mental health index is used, one can conclude that executives, clerical personnel, salespeople, and lower-level supervisors *all* suffer from below-average mental health. The evidence makes one sympathize with the old Quaker, "All the world is queer save me and thee; and sometimes I think thee a little queer."

### The job as the primary source of satisfaction

There is an additional value judgment in the basic hypothesis that the *job* should be a primary form of need satisfaction for everyone (as it is for professors). But the central focus of

many peoples' lives is not the job (which is merely a "way of getting a living"), but the home or the community. Many people find a full measure of challenge, creativity, and autonomy in raising a family, pursuing a hobby, or taking part in community affairs. As Robert Dubin (1959) puts it:

Work, for probably a majority of workers, and even extending into the ranks of management, may represent an institutional setting that is not the central life interest of the participants. The consequence of this is that while participating in work a general attitude of apathy and indifference prevails. . . . Thus, the industrial worker does not feel imposed upon by the tyranny of Organizations, company, or union (p. 161).[11]

In my own interviewing experience in factories, I often ran across women who repeated variants of, "I like this job because it gets me away from all the kids and pressures at home." One girl even told me, "The job is good because it gives me a chance to think about God." Such individuals may feel little need for power equalization.

In any case, as Kerr, Dunlap, Harbison, and Myers (1960) predict, work, in the future, will doubtless be increasingly programmed and will provide fewer and fewer opportunities for creativity and discretion on the job. On the other hand, the hours will grow shorter and there will be a "new bohemianism" off the job. All this

---

[10]Both the Wayne State and the Michigan studies emphasize that no single factor explains the relationship. Kornhauser (1962) concludes: "Both on rational grounds and from empirical evidence, I see no reason to think that it is useful to single out one or a few of the job-related characteristics as distinctly important. . . . If we are to understand why mental health is poorer in less skilled, more routine factory jobs, we must look at the entire pattern of work and life conditions of people in these occupations— not just at single variables." (p. 46).

[11]Maslow (1954) himself suggests that self-actualization can be obtained off the job, as "an ideal mother [or] . . . athletically" (p. 373). Dubin's point may also be exaggerated. I would guess that *for the most part* those who participate actively (seek self-actualization) off the job also seek to participate actively on the job.

suggests the irreverent notion that *perhaps* the best use of our resources is to accelerate automation, shorten the work week just as fast as possible, forget about on-the-job satisfactions, and concentrate our energies on making leisure more meaningful.

## Underemphasis on economic rewards

Since the hypothesis over-emphasizes the job as a source of need satisfaction, it also underemphasizes the role of money as means of motivation. The hypothesis says that, once employees obtain a satisficing level of economic reward, they go on to other needs and, presumably, are less concerned with money. However, the level or reward which is *satisficing* can rise rapidly over time. Further, money is a means of satisfying higher needs, too—ego, safety, and, for some, even self-actualization needs, for example, the individual who (perhaps misguidedly) seeks to live his life off the job engaging in "creative" consumption. True, employees expect much better physical, psychological, and social conditions on the job today than they did fifty years ago. But they also expect more money. There is little evidence that money has ceased to be a prime motivator.

### "ORGANIZATIONAL ECONOMICS"

Perhaps the most fundamental criticisms of the personality-organization hypothesis is that it ignores (or at least misapplies) "organizational economics;" that is, it fails to balance carefully the costs and gains of power equalization. To be sure, most power-equalization advocates point out the hidden costs of autocracy: apathetic and resentful employees, turnover, absenteeism, sabotage, resistance to change, and all the rest. Traditional forms of supervision may be expensive in terms of the lost motivation and energy which might have been turned to organizational ends; they are even more expensive in terms of mental health. Yet some writers, in their moments of wilder enthusiasm, tend to overestimate the gain to be derived from eliminating autocracy and to underestimate the costs of power equalization.

## The gains from eliminating autocracy

Carried to excess, anxiety and aggression are undoubtedly harmful to both the organization and the individual. But many psychological studies suggest that dissatisfaction and anxiety (and even aggression, depending on how it is defined) spur individuals to work harder—particularly in simple, highly programmed tasks. Autocratic, work-oriented bosses very often get out high production; on occasion, their subordinates even develop high morale and cohesive work groups.[12]

Still, beyond certain limits, dissatisfaction, anxiety, and aggression are not in the organization's interests. There is much more doubt about apathy and conformity. It is often argued that an apathetic worker who is subject to "hygienic" supervision will only work enough so as not to get

---

[12]For a list of the conditions under which "authoritarian leadership might be as effective as its alternatives," see Wilensky (1957). Interestingly, the personality-organization hypothesis is strongly influenced by Freud. Yet Freud postulated that "productive work is partially a function of the expression of hostility to the leader" (Bennis, 1959, p. 292).

fired, that he will never exercise creativity or imagination or put out an outstanding performance.

On many jobs, however, management has no use for outstanding performance. What is outstanding performance on the part of an assembly-line worker? That he works faster than the line? That he shows creativity and imagination on the job? Management wants none of these. *Adequate* performance is all that can be used on the assembly line and probably on a growing number (I know no figures) of other jobs in our society. Here the conformist, dependent worker may well be the best.[13] As Leavitt and Whisler (1958) put it, "The issue of morale versus productivity that now worries us may pale as programming moves in. The morale of programmed personnel may be of less central concern because less (or at least a different sort of) productivity will be demanded of them" (p. 46).

Even at the management level, there may be an increasing need for conforming, unimaginative types of "organization men" if Leavitt and Whisler's prediction comes true that "jobs at today's middle-management levels will become highly structured. Much more of the work will be programmed, i.e., covered by sets of operating rules governing the day-to-day decisions that are made" (p. 41). Despite the *organization man,* it might be argued that nonconformity will be useful to the organization only in increasingly limited doses.

### The costs of power-equalization

On the other hand, power-equalization can be quite costly to the organi-

zation. To make general supervision or participative management work many of the old-line autocratic supervisors must be retrained or replaced this is an expensive process which may result in the demoralization or elimination of the organization's most technically competent individuals Since it is extremely difficult to de velop internalized motivation on many routine jobs, once the traditional, ex ternal sanctions (monetary rewards fear of discharge, and so forth) are removed, *net* motivation may fall on balance. And it is fairly meaningless to talk of permitting exercise of dis cretion to assembly-line workers or girls on a punch-card operation; the very nature of the technology requires that all essential decisions be cen trally programmed.

"But if the nature of the job makes power-equalization techniques im practical," some may argue, "change the nature of the job." Rensis Likert (1961) put this well:

To be highly motivated, each member of the organization must feel that the organization's objectives are of signifi cance and that his own particular task contributes in an indispensable manner to the organization's achievement of its objectives. He should see his role as diffi cult, important, and meaningful. This is necessary if the individual is to achieve and maintain a sense of personal worth and importance. *When jobs do not meet this specification they should be reorganized so that they do* [p. 103, my emphasis].

True, there are many opportunities to redesign jobs and workflows[14] so as to increase various forms of job satis-

------

[13]For an outstanding example, see Goode and Fowler (1949).

[14]See, for example, Davis and Werling (1960); Friedmann (1955); Chapple and Sayles (1961); Strauss and Sayles (1960) Chapters 2 and 16.

faction such as autonomy and achievement. But whether such changes should be made is a matter for organizational economics.

In many instances these changes, when accompanied by appropriate forms of supervision and proper selection of personnel, may result in substantial increases of productivity. (Purely technological losses in efficiency may be more than offset by increased motivation, less work-flow friction, and so forth.) Obviously, in such instances organizational economics would dictate that the changes should be introduced.

But there are other areas where technological changes can be made only at a substantial cost in terms of productivity—and the impact of automation and information technology seems to be increasing the number of jobs where this may be true. Should we scrap the advances of technology in these areas in order to foster good human relations? Or should we say, "Thank God for the number of people who have made an apparent adjustment to routine jobs; would that there were more"? Perhaps—as has been suggested earlier—it would be best to devote our resources to ever shortening the work week and helping people to enjoy their leisure more fully.

There seems to be considerable evidence (Argyris, 1960, Chapter 5) that a relatively stable situation can exist in which workers perform relatively routine, programmed jobs under hygienic supervision. Although these workers may not be satisfied (in the Hertzberg sense) and may be immature, apathetic, and dependent (in the Argyris sense), they are not actively dissatisfied, they do not feel a need for additional responsibility, and they seek meaning in life from their home and community rather than from their jobs. To be sure, these individuals are maximizing neither their productive efforts nor their possible job satisfaction. But both management and employees find the situation satisficing (in the Simon sense). Barring sudden change, it is stable. It may well be the best we are likely to get in many situations without costly changes in technology, child upbringing, and so forth.

## THE PERSONALITY-ORGANIZATION HYPOTHESIS SUMMARIZED

My concern . . . has been with the personality-versus-organization hypothesis. I have tried to demonstrate:

1. Although many individuals find relatively little satisfaction in their work, this may not be as much of a deprivation as the hypothesis would suggest, since many of these same individuals center their lives off the job and find most of their satisfactions in the community and the home. With these individuals, power-equalization may not liberate much energy.

2. Individuals are not motivated solely to obtain autonomy, self-actualization, and so forth. With various degrees of emphasis, individuals also want security and to know what is expected of them. Power-equalization may certainly stir up a good deal of anxiety among those who are not prepared for it, and at least some individuals may be reluctant to assume the responsibility that it throws upon them.

3. Power-equalization techniques are not too meaningful when management needs no more than an "adequate" level of production, as is often the case when work is highly programmed. Under such circumstances, the costs entailed by modification in job design and supervisory techniques may be greater than the gains ob-

tained from increased motivation to work.

All of the above does not mean either that the personality-organization hypothesis is meaningless or that power-equalization techniques are not useful. Quite the contrary. What it does mean is that many individuals can accommodate themselves to the demands of the organization without too much psychological loss, and for them the personality-organization conflict is not particularly frustrating. Similarly, in many circumstances the gains to the organization from power equalization may be moderate and more than offset by its costs.

For other individuals (for example, scientists working in large companies), the personality-organization conflict may be felt quite acutely. For the most part, these are the very individuals whose work cannot be pro-

grammed and from whom management wants more than merely "adequate" production.

All this re-emphasizes the often-made point that no single style of leadership can be universally appropriate. The techniques which work on the assembly line will almost certainly fail with research scientists. Indeed, it is fair to predict that, over time, the differences among supervisory styles may increase. Perhaps, in the future, we shall have at one extreme research scientists and others doing creative work who will be putting in a 40-hour or longer work week under conditions of relative power-equalization. At the other extreme may be those who submit to close supervision on highly programmed jobs, but for only 20 hours or so. Shades of *Brave New World*: the alphas and the gammas!

---

## BIBLIOGRAPHY

Argyris, Chris, *Personality and Organization*. New York: Harper & Row, Publishers, 1957.
————, *Understanding Organizational Behavior*. Homewood, Ill.: Dorsey-Irwin Press, 1960.
Bennis, Warren G., "Leadership Theory and Administrative Behavior," *Administrative Science Quarterly*, December 1959, 4.
Blauner, Robert, "Work Satisfaction and Industrial Trends in Modern Society." In Walter Galenson and Seymour Martin Lipset, *Labor and Trade Unionism*. New York: John Wiley & Sons, Inc., 1960.
Brayfield, Arthur H., "Treating Faint Workers," *Contemporary Psychology*, March 1962, 2, 92–93.

Brown, J. A. C., *The Social Psychology of Industry*. Baltimore: English Pelican edition, 1954.
Chapple, Elliot R., and Leonard Sayles, *The Measure of Management*. New York: The Macmillan Company, 1961.
Clark, James V., "Motivation and Work Groups: A Tentative View," *Human Organization*, Winter 1960–61, 19, 199–208.
Davis, Louis E., and Richard Werling, "Job Design Factors," *Occupational Psychology*, April 1960, 34, 109–132.
Dubin, Robert, "Industrial Research and the Discipline of Sociology." In *Proceedings of the 11th Annual Meeting*, Madison, Wisconsin: Industrial Relations Research Association, 1959.

French, John R. P., Robert L. Kahn, and Floyd C. Mann, eds., "Work Health and Satisfaction," *The Journal of Social Issues,* July 1962, 18.

Friedmann, George, *Industrial Society.* Glencoe, Ill.: The Free Press, 1955.

Goode, William J., and Irving Fowler, "Incentive Factors in a Low-Morale Plant," *American Sociological Review,* October 1949, 14, 619–624.

Guerin, Gerald, Joseph Vernoff, and Sheila Feld, *Americans View Their Mental Health.* New York: Basic Books, Inc., Publishers, 1960.

Hertzberg, Frederick, Bernard Mausner, and Barbara Snyderman, *The Motivation to Work.* New York: John Wiley & Sons, Inc., 1960.

Kasl, Stanislov V., and John R. P. French, Jr., "The Effects of Occupational Status on Physical and Mental Health," *Journal of Social Issues,* July 1962, 18, 67–89.

Kerr, Clark, John T. Dunlap, Frederick H. Harbison, and Charles A. Myers, *Industrialism and Industrial Man: The Problems of Labor and Management.* Cambridge: Harvard University Press, 1960.

Kornhauser, Arthur, "Mental Health of Factory Workers: A Detroit Study," *Human Organization,* Spring 1962, 21, 43–46.

Leavitt, Harold J., and Thomas Whisler, "Management in the 1980's" *Harvard Business Review,* November, 1958, 36.

Likert, R., *New Patterns of Management.* New York: McGraw-Hill Book Company, 1961.

McGregor, Douglas, *The Human Side of Enterprise.* New York: McGraw-Hill Book Company, 1960.

Maier, Norman R. F., *Psychology in Industry.* Boston: Houghton Mifflin Company, 1955, 2nd ed.

Maslow, A. H., "A Theory of Human Motivation," *Psychological Review,* July 1943, 50, 372.

———, *Motivation and Personality.* New York: Harper & Row, Publishers, 1954.

Merton, Robert K., *Social Theory and Social Structure.* Glencoe: The Free Press, 1957, rev. enlarged ed.

Selznick, Philip, *TVA and the Grass Roots.* Berkeley: University of California Press, 1949.

Shepard, Herbert, "Nine Dilemmas in Industrial Research," *Administrative Science Quarterly,* Fall 1960, 1, 245–259.

Strauss, George, and Leonard R. Sayles, *Personnel: The Human Problems of Management.* Englewood Cliffs, N. J.: Prentice-Hall, Inc., 1960.

Vroom, Victor, and Norman R. R. Maier, "Industrial Social Psychology," *Annual Review of Psychology,* Paul Farnsworth, ed., Palo Alto: Annual Reviews, 1960, 12.

Walker, Charles R., and Robert H. Guest, *The Man on the Assembly Line.* Cambridge: Harvard University Press, 1952.

Whyte, William H., Jr., *The Organization Man.* New York: Simon and Schuster, Inc., 1956.

Wilensky, Harold L., "Human Relations in the Workplace." In *Research in Industrial Human Relations,* Arensberg and others, eds. New York: Harper & Row, Publishers, 1957, 25–50.

# 5

# Informal Groups:

# Structure and Processes

From the standpoint of personal experience, most of us have spent more time in small, informal groups than we have in any other kind of human association. In early childhood we found in our play groups the informal association that Cooley, the sociologist, has called the primary group. Throughout our schooling, much time was spent in group associations on teams, in gangs, and as members of cliques. Even when we went to work, we found ourselves living in a series of social circles made up of our bowling team, bridge group, coffee club, gossip center, lunch associates, drinking companions, and the like. In short, a large part of our life is spent in informal activity.

We start the analysis of informal organization by drawing a distinction. The weekly bridge group is one kind of informal group. The work group acting together to restrict output is another type of informal association. The major difference between the two lies in the fact that the first is independent of any formal organization, while the second is an integral part of one. Most of us have an intuitive grasp of what an informal group within a formal organization is like. We tend, however, to be less well oriented regarding the connections between the formal and informal organizations.

**INTRODUCTION**

The most commonly held view is that informal groups are subversive of the purposes of the formal organization. Such informal groups oppose demands coming from higher authority and work counter to the purposes set by management. By now it is common knowledge that restriction of output is a product of the informal group that sets output standards below management's expectations and then polices the observance of the lower standards. It should be recognized that this is just one way informal and formal organizations are linked.

Where antagonism dominates the outlook of work group members, the informal group can be exceedingly strong. Formal control from the top down depends on a system for catching a culprit in violation of a rule or regulation, and then punishing him in an appropriate way defined by the rules of the organization. Such controls tend to be remote, and unless constantly policed, are unable to apprehend all rule violations. The informal group is in almost constant contact with all its members and maintains an all-seeing surveillance of their activities. Very little is missed in the behavior of a group member and the possibility of "getting away with something" is small. What the informal group may lack in ability to confront the formal organization head-on, it makes up in the intense and constantly policed surveillance of its members that makes for near unanimity in their behavior. As Gardner quotes a worker: "You gotta decide whether to go along with the group or to stand in with the boss. And if you don't go along, the gang can make it mighty unpleasant."[1]

The informal group can also cooperate directly and indirectly with management of the formal organization. When direct cooperation occurs, the informal group works to meet or even exceed management expectations. The research literature is beginning to produce examples of this kind of cooperation that has long been known to operating executives. Indirect cooperation has already been noted in the preceding chapter where we discovered how the informal group was the social unit within which motivation to get work done is sustained. Recent management attention has turned to the Group Dynamics movement for techniques by which cooperation of informal groups is secured and sustained. The mechanism by which member compliance with informal group goals is attained obviously also works when the group is interested in cooperating with management expectations. Thus, the informal group is self-policing, and can relieve management of much of the burden of supervision when the group is cooperatively oriented.

We also have to consider a third orientation of informal groups to the formal organization—neutrality. A neutral stance by the informal group may result because its private interests have no relationship to the work of the organization. Thus, the informal group may focus on pure sociability as the reason for existence. The activities of informal group members with each other can be independent of their working relations. Under these circumstances the group can well be neutral toward the organization. However, a management dedicated to keeping its people "looking like they are working all the time" may turn the neutrality of informal groups into antagonism by demanding that all unnecessary interaction and "horseplay" be eliminated. What then had been thought of as independent activity by informal group members seems to them infringed upon by management. Antagonism toward management can result.

[1] W. F. Whyte, ed., *Industry and Society* (New York: McGraw-Hill Book Company, Inc., 1946), p. 7.

_Informal Groups:_

We can better understand the antagonism, cooperation, and neutrality of informal groups towards the formal organization by examining the functions such groups have for their members. These functions have been set forth in detail elsewhere and will be summarized here.[2]

One of the important functions of an informal group is to carry out its assigned tasks efficiently. This is accomplished through cooperation among group members, group decisions, and sharing of job knowledge.

Most work tasks require some judgment and even decision, however minor, for their execution. In the vast majority of instances, judgment and decision are shared among several people whose work is interdependent. The most primitive level of such interdependence is found in the informal group, so that it is among close working associates that shared judgments and decisions are made about getting work done.

Informal groups also set the patterns of inter-personal behavior among their members. This establishes who is most competent and least competent at work, who is most entertaining, who is the greatest lover (by his own claims), the biggest braggart, and the like. In short, the daily interaction among informal group members establishes the status of each (see Chapter 13) in relation to all other members. There also grows up agreement about who will have the last word about group decisions, or the acknowledged authority in the group (see Chapter 12).

We can then summarize by suggesting that informal groups contribute to effective work performance by providing: (1) the social unit within which agreement on working judgments and decisions are reached, and (2) the patterns of inter-personal relations defining the many subtle nuances of person-to-person interaction that, in the nature of the case, cannot be defined in job descriptions and job analyses. On both of these counts the informal group of working associates contributes to effective work performance.

A second broad function of informal groups is to provide the environment for encouraging individual innovation and originality in getting tasks done. The society of close associates is the realm in which detailed knowledge about work tasks is shared, and it is here that alternative ways of accomplishing things are known and discussed. The approval of fellow-workers becomes important in supporting innovation and original ideas, while their disapproval may be sufficient to squelch new ideas. The informal group is the breeding ground in which the individual can experiment with unique ideas without having to "sell the boss" before trying them.

A third function of informal groups for their individual members is to establish and maintain standards of conduct. Standards of conduct are the dividing lines between good and bad behavior, between moral and immoral acts, between legitimate and illegitimate activities. Broad standards of conduct require some reality context to be meaningful for an individual. Abstract notions like honesty, faithfulness, cooperation, and self-sacrifice have no immediate meaning except as they are put to use. The operating situations in which these ideas of moral conduct are constantly applied are those involving informal groups.

---

[2]_Cf._ Robert Dubin, _The World of Work_ (Englewood Cliffs, N. J.: Prentice-Hall, Inc., 1958), Chap. 16.

It is largely in the peer group situation that there is immediate response by fellow human beings to an individual's behavior. This response is direct and personal. There is no need to be self-policing of moral standards. The policing is by one's close associates who react immediately to your conduct, either to confirm and approve, or condemn and censure it.

The fourth general function of informal groups is to sustain the individual's image of himself, and therefore his personality integrity. A minimum amount of pure sociability is required by every person. Each individual at work has to find some opportunity to carry out free and unstructured social relations with fellow men. The obvious unit within which such social relations can be established is the fellow worker group. The informal group fills the voids of social life at work. It is in such groups that each person is treated as an individual, accepted for all his unique personality characteristics. The informal group constantly emphasizes and reinforces each member's individual personality. It is here that at the end of a work day the individual finds himself still a man, a whole personality, and not just a tired "operative" of a machine.

We may summarize the functions of informal groups for their members as follows: (1) they are the natural unit in which are determined the actual operations for getting work done; (2) providing at the same time the environment for supporting experiments with new ways of working; (3) establishing and maintaining standards of conduct for members; and (4) giving to each member the sympathetic kind of human consideration that serves to buttress his self-image and his personality integrity.

In the light of this analysis of the three orientations of informal groups to the formal organization, and the four functions such groups perform for their members, we can now consider the structure and types of such groups. In the following selection Mayo and Lombard suggest an empirical classification of groups based on two general criteria: the function of the group in establishing standards of conduct, and the internal structure of the group. The test of regularity of attendance at work was used to determine if group members did behave alike in this respect, and if they did, to use this as the criterion of their sharing a common standard of conduct. In all three types of groups delineated was found this shared standard of conduct.

The "natural," "family," and "organized" groups are distinguished from each other by the fact that the first exhibits little or no internal structure, the second has a core of "regulars" who are influential in affecting the behavior of all members, and the "organized" group has an acknowledged leader. This classification of types of informal groups can be contrasted with the one presented by Sayles in the second selection of this chapter, or with still another classification presented elsewhere.[3] Any such classification highlights particular features of informal groups, and therefore, helps to improve understanding of their linkage with formal organizations.

---

[3]See Dubin, *op. cit.,* Chap. 6.

## TYPES OF WORK TEAMS

*Elton Mayo* and *George F. F. Lombard**

What number of people can naturally associate themselves together in work? Many arbitrary or empirical answers have been given to this question. The Army, for instance, places it at from 8 to 14 according to function; certain industrial psychologists say 5 without any convincing reason for doing so. We found that we had in our hands some evidence of definite interest in this connection. There seemed to be three types of groups in our studies: the "natural" group, the "family," and the "organized." These distinctions are empirical and tentative, but they indicate something in fact that demands further inquiry.

*a. The "natural" group.* In the records of 69 work centers given earlier in this report, there are 12 with a regular attendance record of over 80 per cent. Since one of these consists of only 1 worker (we do not know the "company" reason for this), we shall ignore it. The other 11 groups are all small, several of 2 or 3 workers, the highest numbers are 6 and 7. The regularity of attendance does not occur independently of supervision, for Department I has definitely more good working teams than the other two, and this accords with the reputation in the plant of the department's foreman. But regular attendance may occur in the most unlikely places. Actually it is evidence in support of the claim that human beings like regular

association with others at work; such association will happen in the natural order of events without explicit attention from management to the organization of human needs, unless some interference prevents. *In the absence of an internal plant organization deliberately designed to foster the habit of daily association, almost anything may operate as interference. . . .* This point should be borne in mind by every executive and supervisor. It should also be remembered that in the fall of 1943 the aircraft companies had existed at their peak size for only a short time. Particularly under such conditions it is not surprising that the "natural" group remains small in size.

*b. The "family" group.* The "natural" group, if not too much discouraged, may develop in size, by way of a move toward organization almost as equally automatic and unguided by supervision as the formation of a "natural" group. Work Center 3, Department I, second shift, to which we have previously referred, is an example. It consisted of 30 workers of whom 80 per cent had a regular attendance record. Of the 30, 8 were veterans [in service with company], 5 with almost perfect attendance records, only 1 at all doubtful. Twenty-two were relative newcomers; of these 17 had almost perfect attendance records, and only 3 could be classified as irregulars.

Our term "family" is purely arbitrary as a description; it is intended to denote a situation in which a core of regulars may, if they have prestige, determine, almost by inadvertence,

---

*From *Teamwork and Labor Turnover in the Aircraft Industry of Southern California* (Harvard Business School, Division of Research, Business Research Studies No. 32, 1944), pp. 22–23. Used by permission.

the group attendance. Wise parenthood, we are told, builds on the principle that "example is better than precept." This is all that the word "family" is here intended to denote; a situation in which the behavior of newer members is determined by the example set them by those who have been there longer. This situation is, of course, more common in the industrial centers of the East than in California; yet it occurred there in Work Center 3 of Department I. Its significance for management is limited to situations where a "natural" group can be held together long enough to act as a core for a larger group. Our researches have given us little insight on how long such a period must be. Our estimate is that, except under conditions of emergency or unusual stress when even larger teams may be achieved overnight, the minimal period necessary for the formation of teams the size of which we are speaking, and without explicit attention from management to the organization of human needs, may be between six months and a year of continuous working together.

*c. The "organized" group.* "Natural" and "family" groups achieve their integration, not by direct action of management, but spontaneously and because management establishes around the workers a "climate" of technical and operating aspects of organization such that groups can grow. The relationship of management to such growth is thus indirect; whereas in an "organized" group it is direct. This type of group we have already discussed in the description of the B work center of Department IV. It differs from both other types in that someone—leadman Z—with the respect and confidence of the workers and with the support of management as indicated by his selection as leadman, *has set himself deliberately, with intelligence and skill, to achieve a group integrity of association* and to order the relations of his own integral group with other departments in the plant.

Given sufficient experience, intelligence, and skill in management, the problem of number therefore does not arise. For the first type of group, the number limit seems to be in the neighborhood of 6 or 7; we have given an instance of the second type numbering 30; but there is no reason why the third type should not extend over an entire plant and include persons of widely different backgrounds. The desiderata are the group integrity of small groups, and, beyond this, an integral relationship among all groups. But this is the proper task of administration and management.

---

In order to study the behavior of people in work groups, Leonard Sayles examined 300 such groups in 30 industrial plants. By contrast with the above classification of informal groups, Sayles in the following selection presents a typology of groups based essentially on their orientation toward the formal organization. It will be recalled that in the Introduction to this chapter, it was suggested that informal groups can be cooperative, antagonistic, or neutral towards the formal organization of which they are a part. It is the particular orientation among these three that constitutes the basis for Sayles' classification of the types of informal groups. Thus, his "Apathetic" group is one consistently indifferent to the formal organization;

the "Erratic" groups cycle between antagonism and cooperation; the "Strategic" group maintains a relatively consistent antagonism; while the "Conservative" group is cooperatively oriented most of the time except when highly specific goals are sought by group members acting in concert, at which time the group displays antagonism towards management.

These two views of informal group structure and orientation provide the basis for understanding the reality of informal groups and their linkages with the formal organization. The last two selections of this chapter present empirical materials on the operations of such groups so that the processes by which they connect with the formal organization are also laid bare.

---

## INFORMAL WORK GROUPS AND THE FORMAL ORGANIZATION

*Leonard R. Sayles**

It will be observed that most of the qualities of the work groups described relate to their participation in the grievance process, as very broadly defined. That is, our observers in the plants, when referring to "hot spots" or "cooperative groups," placed most of their emphasis on the level of acceptance of and cooperation with management decisions, or, contrariwise, on the frequency and nature of challenge issued by the group to management. . . .

As the data were accumulated and reviewed it appeared that what was being described to us was not one but a variety of work groups. These groups differed from one another very substantially, particularly in the way they dealt with any problems they faced. For the sake of convenience we have attached names to the four types most

*Reprinted with permission from Leonard R. Sayles, *Behavior of Industrial Work Groups: Prediction and Control* (New York: John Wiley & Sons, Inc., 1958), excerpts from pp. 7–9, 11–14, 18–19, 32–35, and 38–39.

clearly distinguishable: The *Apathetic,* the *Erratic,* the *Strategic,* and the *Conservative.* It will be well to remember that the name is only a convenience, a shorthand method of referring to a set of distinguishing characteristics. . . .

### TYPE I: THE APATHETIC GROUPS

By almost any measure these departments were the least likely to develop grievances or engage in concerted action as a means of pressuring management or the union. Although incidents did occur on occasion, compared with other groups these workers were disinclined to challenge decisions or attempt to gain something "extra" for themselves. Surprisingly, however, these departments were not ranked highest by management for their consistent productivity and "cooperativeness." Apparently the Apathetics were not trouble-free, but only superficially so. Put in another way, there was evidence of worker discontent, but often it was not focused in terms of specific demands or grievances.

These same groups were also less prone to engage in union politics and to participate in the internal life of their unions. Within these departments petty jealousies and inter-personal problems were somewhat more common than in the other groups. Although management and union representatives could identify certain influential members of the group, real leadership seemed to be dispersed among a relatively large number of individuals. Group cohesion, as such, did not seem to be a primary characteristic of these Apathetic groups. . . .

These groups are not likely to challenge management or union decisions. . . . Certain common characteristics of the groups we have described are readily apparent. A number of the jobs included are relatively low skilled and low paid, particularly in terms of the general wage pattern of the plants in which they are located. The Apathetic groups that do not fit this description are primarily performing operations that involve a degree of interworker cooperation. These include crew operations, such as the hammershop, where each member of the crew performs a different operation having a separate job classification. . . .

We use the term "crew" to refer to a group of employees dependent on one another to accomplish a common work task. The crew differs from the assembly operation . . . in that the members all interact with one another in the work process. The assembly line, on the other hand, involves a chain of interaction: *A* with *B*, *B* with *A* and *C*, *C* with *B* and *D*, etc., as its flow of work. We found *long* assembly lines, typical in many industries,

also behaving like Apathetic groups. . . .

The behavior characteristics of the Apathetic group are:

1. Relatively few grievances or use of pressure tactics.

2. Lack of clearly identified or accepted leadership.

3. Internal disunity and frictions.

4. Evidence of suppressed discontent.

*Leadership!*

## TYPE II: THE ERRATIC GROUPS

The most distinctive characteristic of some work groups was their tendency toward "erratic" behavior. By this statement it is meant that there seems to be no relation between the seriousness of their grievances (from the point of view of the employees themselves) and the intensity of their protests. Issues that both management and union observers consider minor . . . might erupt without warning into a major conflagration—a mass demonstration of some kind, such as a wildcat strike. At the same time, deep-seated grievances may exist within these groups over long periods with no apparent reaction in terms of group behavior. . . .

This explosiveness is matched by a management evaluation that places such groups at the top of the plant's "very dangerous" list. In fact, a great deal of time and energy of both management and union officials that is devoted to the grievance procedure is concentrated on these tension areas. Even so, the managers and union leaders often admitted frankly that they were at a loss to understand what was "really going on" in such departments. . . .

There was some scattered evidence that these kinds of groups are subject to rather sudden "conversions"—a department that has been a source of endless grief to all concerned became, literally overnight, one of the showplaces of the plant, where unanimity and harmony prevailed, and then perhaps at some later time, reverted to its earlier condition. . . .

Internally these groups followed highly autocratic leadership that would "keep them in line," either in support of management objectives or in direct defiance of the rules. Unlike some of the more complex groups we shall deal with, the leadership in these departments was usually clear-cut and centralized—the same "strong" individual often served as the internal social leader and the external representative to union and to management. . . .

The members of Erratic groups had jobs in which everyone has an identical or nearly identical task. Most significantly, in this category there was a high preponderance of groups in which workers are required to interact with one another by the work process. These crews and assembly lines, however, differed from those we often found exhibiting behavior that would cause them to be included in our Apathetic classification. Rather, these were homogeneous crews and short assembly lines in which job descriptions and rates matched nearly perfectly. Many of the jobs involved operations which were primarily worker controlled as distinct from machine controlled.

The behavior characteristics of the Erratic groups are:

1. Easily inflamed.

2. Poorly controlled pressure tactics, behavior inconsistent.

3. Quick conversions to good relations with management.

4. Often highly centralized leadership.

5. Active in organizational phase of union.

### TYPE III: THE STRATEGIC GROUPS

In many plants, one or two groups seem to be at the very center of most of the really important grievances, important in the sense of involving major economic considerations. Often these groups were also a part of the core of union "regulars," who kept close track of how well their specific economic interests were being advanced by the officers. . . . These were not the departments characterized by sudden flashes of activity. Rather, they seemed to be shrewdly calculating pressure groups which never tired of objecting to unfavorable management decisions, seeking loopholes in existing policies and clauses that would redound to their benefit, and comparing their benefits with those of other departments in the plant. They demanded constant attention for their problems and had the ability to reinforce their demands by group action.

Unlike the Erratic work groups, however, the amount and kind of pressure the Strategic groups exert are carefully measured, both against the objectives they seek and the immediate strategy of the total situation. . . . To that degree their behavior is predictable, and this consistency is seen as a virtue, both by management and the union. In fact, these work areas ranked substantially above the Apathetic and Erratic groups in general plant performance and cooperation.

We have selected the term *strategic* for these groups, to emphasize their ability to adapt their pressure tactics to the situation and to engage in sustained and carefully thought out wars of attrition with both management and the union. The appellation does not refer to the location of the group in the plant or in the production flow. It is a behavioral description to which we have reference here, and not an attribute.

The departments so classified seemed highly cohesive. The leadership consisted of a small core of highly active and influential group members, each of whom specialized in such functions as dealing with management, dealing with the union, maintaining internal unity, or taking the lead in voicing dissatisfaction. . . .

The most consistent concentration of high self-interest activity was found in a number of related groups we have called Strategic. . . . In the process they come to set new standards for the plant as a whole for such matters as appropriate work loads, idle time, incentive earnings, and countless noneconomic working conditions. As pace setters in the struggle to better themselves, they attract and require an unbelievably high proportion of management and union energies. Thus, identifying them and answering the question, "Why these groups rather than others?" becomes an important task for the administrator.

The groups we have called Strategic had a number of identifying characteristics in common:

1. Most of the jobs, with the exception of some of those in automobile manufacture, were individual operations; the jobs were not technologically interdependent as were most of those of the Erratic groups. . . .

2. These jobs were better jobs than the majority of those in either of our two previous categories. In fact, they were close to the top in terms of worker preference among production jobs. However, it is important to note that they were not the best jobs in the plant. They were in a sense in the middle, between the relatively poor and the most desired position.

3. The skills required by the jobs were often identified with personal-worker-judgment factors that made exact time standards difficult to apply. Even when tolerances were controlled by the settings of the machine, the operator sensed an important skill element because the finished product had been held to such close tolerances. Grieving over time and motion study standards was relatively easy.

4. The job was often one that was relatively important in the plant to management and employees. There was a significant concentration of employees working at them, often senior employees who expected to make them "good" jobs, by pressure if necessary. Over the years they had looked forward to moving into such jobs and where the "goodness" of the job didn't meet their expectations, they sought to change the job, not their expectations. These positions were also in fact, if not in theory, the top of the promotional ladder for most of the men holding them. Promotions upward were few because the better jobs were limited in number and nearly always required apprenticeships or very good luck to obtain. Thus being committed to their present positions indefinitely, it was natural to expect concerted effort to make these positions the best ones.

The behavior characteristics of the Strategic groups are:

1. Continuous pressure.

2. Well planned and consistent grievance activity.

3. High degree of internal unity.

4. Sustained union participation.

5. Relatively good production records over the long run, for many of the groups, but not all.

### TYPE IV: THE CONSERVATIVE GROUPS

Of all the groups we observed, the Conservative groups were the most stable, in the sense of being least likely to use concerted action without warning. Also, they were less likely to participate in union affairs. Management tended to be impressed with their overall record, while recognizing and accepting the fact that occasional well founded formal grievances do arise in such departments.

Their strength is assured by their economic position—a monopoly of critical, scarce skills. In those instances when they have sought and obtained top union leadership positions, they were known for their selfish approach to the leadership job. . . .

When they are not concerned with union politics, which is more typical than not of their group, they are also above the strains of the less skilled production worker. For example, in one company, the only group that had a paid lunch period was the automatic screw machine operators, the most skilled machining group in the plant. This exception to the general rule had been in existence for some years. The Conservatives often insisted on doing their own negotiating, so as not to be bound by the settlements of the majority. Some, in effect, have their own union; they are that self-sufficient.

The niche they have carved for themselves is often so satisfactory, in terms of their compensation and working conditions, that it is more common for management to have grievances against them, than for the men to have grievances against the management. It was not unusual to find the company attempting to negotiate a higher level of output with the group. . . .

Summarizing, these kinds of groups are much more conservative in their grievance activities. On the surface, at least, we saw little evidence of turmoil, trouble, or concerted activity. At some time or times in the past such a group had to exercise its strength; but once "proved," like the strength of any great power, it was accepted at face value by those whom it affected, until such time that they can match this power with greater force. . . .

For most of the men in the Conservative groups there is the probability that if the company does not provide satisfactory employment opportunities, there are an adequate number of jobs available requiring their specialization in the local labor market. . . .

For the most part these were groups at the top rungs of both the promotional and status ladders of the plant. They were self-assured and successful, and they only went into action when some existing benefit was threatened or when they found themselves "behind the parade"—due to the ceaseless pressures of some less well endowed (and therefore less "worthy") work area.

Most of their work involved individual operations, but on occasion several employees will work together in a repair or maintenance crew. Common also is a wide distribution of their members throughout the plant—what we have called scattered groups.

Behavior characteristics of Conservative groups are:

1. Restrained pressure for highly specific objectives.

2. Moderate internal unity and self-assurance.

3. Activity — inactivity cycles in terms of union activities and the plant grievance procedure.

---

*The American Soldier,*[1] discussed below, is a four-volume report on a monumental study of the United States Army during World War II. In re-analyzing certain facts contained in this study, Shils developed the idea that the informal, face-to-face groups in the army are important in supporting the command structure. Soldiers in combat, when the chips are really down for them to do their job, identify with their battle mission by giving their loyalty to and finding their inspiration among their combat comrades. Soldiers feel attached to their army and its missions *through* their informal groups of fellow soldiers.

It should also be noted that the informal organization is effective in sustaining the formal organization by strengthening motivation only where there exists ". . . a set of generalized moral predispositions or sense of obligation," to use Shils' words. Translated into a business situation, this means that members have to believe that their employing organization has legitimate goals and means for achieving them. The strengthening of individual motivation that comes through the informal group is grounded in a set of prior beliefs that the organization as a whole is worthy. This explains why public relations programs are designed to present a worthy corporate image to the public, and especially to members of the organization. When this image is accepted, then organization members have a basis for developing moral predispositions and a sense of obligation to their employing organization.

[1]Samuel A. Stouffer and others, Vol. 1, *The American Soldier: Adjustment During Army Life*; Vol. 2, *The American Soldier: Combat and Its Aftermath*; Vol. 4, *Measurement and Prediction;* and Carl I. Hovland and others, Vol. 3, *Experiments in Mass Communication.* (Princeton, N. J.: Princeton University Press, 1949–1950).

---

## ORGANIZATION GOALS AND PRIMARY GROUPS

*Edward A. Shils**

The first problem of primary group analysis in relation to corporate bodies is: how does the influence of membership in the group affect the operation

of the corporate body; and particularly, the attainment of the goals of the corporate body. This problem is forthrightly faced in *The American Soldier.*

*From "Primary Groups in the American Army," *Continuities in Social Research: Studies in the Scope and Method of "The American Soldier,"* eds., Robert K. Merton

and Paul F. Lazarsfeld, pp. 19–22. Copyright 1950 by The Free Press. Used by permission.

The re-discovery of the primary group (or the informal group as it is usually called in *The American Soldier*) has not blinded them [the authors of *The American Soldier*]—as it has blinded some of its other re-discoverers—to the fundamental fact that a large corporate body like an Army is more than an assembly of primary groups accidentally coordinated with one another by primary group relationships. They are well aware that the army is an organization in which formally constituted agencies exercise authority over persons with whom they have no primary group relations whatsoever. The fundamental significance of command and sanction never disappears from their field of vision. . . .

The crucial data bearing directly on the limited power of expectations of coercive sanctions are relatively scanty and not entirely free from self-contradiction at certain points. The appearance of contradiction is however diminished by the relative infrequency with which soldiers mention coercion and the fear of sanctions in explaining their *own* behavior in battle. It is also diminished by the insight . . . that moral considerations (i.e., conceptions of duty and legitimacy), primary group sanctions and formal military sanctions in most cases move in the same direction, reinforcing one another in ways which present research techniques and conceptual schemes do not allow us easily to disentangle from one another. "One important general function of the existence of formal sanctions was . . . that when imposed they called into automatic operation informal sanctions both social and internalized. The existence of these informal sanctions gave the formal sanction much of its force."[1]

The formal coercive powers of the Army must moreover lose some of their directive force in the very situation toward which the entire military organization is directed: namely, the situation of battle. Here, as a result of the high probability of the unforeseen, the need for discretion is at a maximum and the dangers can be faced and contended with only if there is a positive self-impelled effort coming from within the general disposition of the individual soldier. . . .

One of the most significant contributions to . . . our knowledge of the importance of primary groups in the execution of the goals of large corporate organizations comes from certain inquiries made by the Research Branch into the soldier's own assessment of the factors which caused him "to keep going." Two major inquiries conducted on different occasions and somewhat differently phrased both indicate that the desire to avoid "letting the other fellow down" was one of the most important of all factors and was surpassed only by prayer when the "going was tough,"[2] or by the "desire to get the job over with" in the second inquiry.

In reply to the query: "Generally in your combat experience, what was most important to you in making you want to keep going and to do as well as you could?" addressed to infantry combat veterans in Europe, 39 per cent mentioned "ending the task;" 14 per cent, solidarity with group, "cannot let the other fellows or the outfit down;" "sticking together;" "buddies depending on me;" "my friends around me;" 9 per cent, "sense of duty and self-respect;" 10 per cent, "thoughts of home and loved ones." Five per cent mentioned "idealistic reasons;" 2 per cent vindictiveness; only 3 per cent

[1]Vol. II, p. 114, *The American Soldier.*

[2]Vol. II, p. 174, *The American Soldier.*

indicated absence of alternatives, leadership, discipline.[3] In another inquiry into the factors which helped when the "going was tough," Pacific and Mediterranean veterans; answered as follows: "prayer helped a lot," was indicated by 70 per cent of the Pacific veterans and 83 per cent of the Mediterranean veterans, "couldn't let the other men down," by 61 per cent and 56 per cent, respectively; "had to finish the job in order to get home again," 42 per cent and 28 per cent; "thoughts of hatred for the enemy," 38 per cent and 28 per cent; "what we are fighting for," 34 per cent and 29 per cent.[4]

It will be noted that in both inquiries and in both theaters, motives connected with primary group solidarity were estimated as very important and that none of the preponderant "motives" refers to the acceptance of a formal command from a formally appointed authority although obviously a good share of their importance consists in the extent to which they furthered the execution of commands or the exercise of initiative within the general framework of commands.

These data support the more complex hypothesis that primary group solidarity functions in the corporate body to strengthen the motivation for the fulfillment of substantive prescrip-

[3]Vol. II, *The American Soldier,* pp. 108–109.
[4]*Ibid.,* p. 174.

tions and commands issued by the official agents of the corporate body, within the context of *a set of generalized moral predispositions* or *sense of obligation.*

The latter need not be strongly present in consciousness but some measure of identification with the collectivity and some sense of generalized obligation and readiness to acknowledge the legitimacy of its demands in numerous particular situations must exist. Thus, for example, the soldiers who first thought of getting the job done, must, in some way, have accepted the legitimacy of the "job" and felt some degree of obligation to carry it out. The general setting of their goal was given by their identification with the United States and this made for an acceptance of specific commands from their officers. But even the 39 per cent who mentioned "ending the task" as a motivating consideration might have been lax and reluctant if they had not been subject to the pressure of their comrades who, more or less hiding the same belief, added the autonomous weight of their approval and affection for those who conformed and disapproval for those who were deviant. In other words then, it cannot be said that goals are set by membership in the primary group but only that efforts to achieve the legitimate formally prescribed goals may be strengthened by such membership.

---

We now turn attention to the complex problem of *personal relations* among the members of organizations. So far in this chapter we have considered the difference between the formal and informal *structure* of an organization and have drawn out some of the behavior characteristics of in-

formal groups. But this is only part of the story of informal organization.

The second major aspect of informal organization deals with the personal relations among individuals. Here we are concerned with the failure of prescribed routines of action to secure the expected productive outcome.

Even when the "book" way of getting work done is inadequate (because of conflicting expectations, incomplete specification of action, failure to cover the situation) the people involved still have to produce. They do so by resorting to their own inventiveness and initiative in solving the problems of getting their work done.

We can draw a distinction between two types of personal relations in getting work done.[1] *Informal relations* are personal interactions based on knowing each other as individual personalities and displaying spontaneity toward each other. They serve to satisfy personal goals as well as organizational goals. . . .

We distinguish *non-formal relations* by the fact that they are always work oriented and designed to get the job done at a minimum cost to the individuals involved. . . . In the concluding selection of this chapter, Whyte gives several illustrations of non-formal relations, such as the bar-keep who mixes drinks by type rather than in the order received (claiming "efficiency" as the grounds for such action but really solving the problem of maintaining his status in relation to lower status waitresses). Non-formal relations take into account some of the unanticipated social problems of people relating to each other in the flow of work. These non-formal relations solve such problems so that the individual gains some peace in doing his work. A recent study[2] has demon-

strated, for example, how the social status of fellow workers can play a key role in determining the degree of their cooperation with each other, and their work effectiveness. The assignment of people to work teams in terms of the compatability of their respective social statuses involves taking into account non-formal relations of the work place.

The concluding selection of this chapter deals with a structurally simple kind of organization, the restaurant. Because of this fact it is possible to study the processes of human interaction among those who work in a restaurant. Professor Whyte here provides us with an excellent summary of his larger study.[3]

Whyte presents the hypothesis that origination of interaction should be more frequent from high to lower status persons than the reverse. He predicts that this will reduce personal frictions among people who have to interact because of the organization of work, and will also reduce the wear and tear on their emotions. Many of his illustrations show how means are invented to achieve the "proper" frequency and direction of originations of action. The bulk of the data presented in this summary of the study deals with non-formal relations in the work place. It should be noted that these non-formal relations are not particularly spontaneous, free-flowing and "friendly." Indeed, it is data precisely of this sort that has made it necessary to distinguish between *informal* and *non-formal* relations in order to catch up the full range of behaviors of people at work.

[1] See in this connection: Robert Dubin, *The World of Work, op. cit.,* pp. 67–73, "Non-formal Behavior Systems" and "Informal Behavior Systems."

[2] Abraham Zaleznik *et al., The Motivation, Productivity, and Satisfaction of Workers* (Cambridge: Harvard Graduate School of Business Administration, 1958).

[3] William Foote Whyte, *Human Relations in the Restaurant Industry* (New York: McGraw-Hill Book Company, Inc., 1948).

## SOCIAL STRUCTURE OF THE WHOLE ORGANIZATION: THE RESTAURANT

### William Foote Whyte*

. . . Sociologists who are concerned with working out the comparative structures of economic organizations must . . . look beyond as well as into the factory. This paper represents one effort in that direction. It grows out of a fourteen-month study of restaurants.[1] We do not claim to have studied a representative sample of restaurants. In an industry having so many types of operations and sizes of units, such a task would have taken years. We did aim to find out, at least in a general way, what sort of structure a restaurant is and what human problems are found within it.

Here I shall present a schematic picture of the findings as they bear upon problems of social structure. . . .

### CHARACTERISTICS OF THE RESTAURANT

The restaurant is a combination production and service unit. It differs from the factory, which is solely a production unit, and also from the

*From "The Social Structure of the Restaurant," *American Journal of Sociology,* 54: 302–308 (Jan. 1949). Used by permission of The University of Chicago Press.
[1]The research was financed by the National Restaurant Association. The field work was done by Margaret Chandler, Edith Lentz, John Schaefer, and William Whyte. We made interview or participant-observation studies of twelve restaurants in Chicago and did some brief interviewing outside Chicago. From one to four months was spent upon each Chicago restaurant. In *Human Relations in the Restaurant Industry* (New York: McGraw-Hill Book Co., 1948), I report the study in detail. Since the book is primarily addressed to restaurant operators

retail store, which is solely a service unit.

The restaurant operator produces a perishable product for immediate sale. Success requires a delicate adjustment of supply to demand and skillful coordination of production with service. The production and service tie-up not only makes for difficult human problems of coordinating action but adds a new dimension to the structure of the organization: the customer-employee relationship.

The contrast between factory and restaurant can be illustrated by this simple diagram, representing the di-

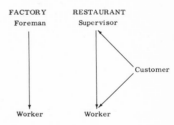

rection of orders in the two structures.[2]

The problems of coordination and customer relations are relatively simple in the small restaurant, but they become much more difficult as the organization grows. This may be illus-

and supervisors, the sociological frame of reference given here does not duplicate the more detailed publication.
[2]This is, of course, an oversimplified picture, for many factory workers interact also with inspectors, engineers, time-study men, etc., but the frequency of such interaction does not compare with that which we observe between customers and waiters or waitresses in a restaurant.

trated structurally in terms of five stages of growth.[3]

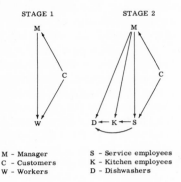

STAGE 1   STAGE 2

M - Manager
C - Customers
W - Workers

S - Service employees
K - Kitchen employees
D - Dishwashers

In the first stage, we have a small restaurant where the owner and several other employees dispense short orders over the counter. There is little division of labor. The owner and employees serve together as cooks, countermen, and dishwashers.

In the second stage, the business is still characterized by the informality and flexibility of its relationships. The boss knows most customers and all his employees on a personal basis. There is no need for formal controls and elaborate paper work. Still, the organization has grown in complexity as it has grown in size. The volume of business is such that it becomes necessary to divide the work, and we have dishwashers and kitchen employees, as well as those who wait on the customers. Now the problems of coordination begin to grow also, but the organization is still small enough so that the owner-manager can observe directly a large part of its activities and step in to straighten out friction or inefficiency.

As the business continues to expand, it requires a still more complex or-

[3] I am indebted to Donald Wray for the particular structural approach presented here.

ganization as well as larger quarters. No longer able to supervise all activities directly, the owner-manager hires a service supervisor, a food production supervisor, and places one of his employees in charge of the dishroom as a working supervisor. He also employs a checker to total checks for his waitresses and see that the food is served in correct portions and style.

STAGE 3

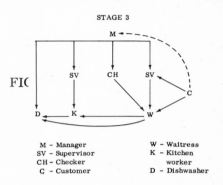

FIC

M - Manager
SV - Supervisor
CH - Checker
C - Customer

W - Waitress
K - Kitchen
     worker
D - Dishwasher

In time, the owner-manager finds that he can accommodate a larger number of customers if he takes one more step in the division of labor. Up to now the cooks have been serving the food to the waitresses. When these functions are divided, both cooking and serving can proceed more efficiently. Therefore, he sets up a service pantry apart from the kitchen. The cooks now concentrate on cooking, the runners carry food from kitchen to pantry and carry orders from pantry to kitchen, and the pantry girls serve the waitresses over the counter. This adds two more groups (pantry girls and runners) to be supervised, and, to cope with this and the larger scale of operation, the owner adds another level of supervision, so that there are two supervisors between himself and the workers. Somewhere along the line of development, perhaps he begins serving drinks and adds bartenders to his organization.

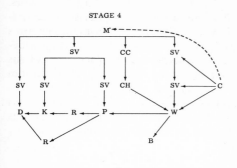

STAGE 4

M - Manager
SV - Supervisor
CH - Checker
CC - Cost control
    supervisor
C - Customer

W - Waitress
B - Bartender
P - Pantry worker
K - Kitchen worker
R - Runner
D - Dishwasher

stance, this involves the customer relationship, for here is where the flow of work begins. The handling of the customer relationship is crucial for the adjustment of the restaurant personnel, and a large part of that problem can be stated in strictly quantitative interaction terms: Who originates action for whom and how often? In a large and busy restaurant a waitress may take orders from fifty to one hundred customers a day (and perhaps several times for each meal) in addition to the orders (much less frequent) she receives from her supervisor. When we add to this the problem of adjusting to service pantry workers, bartenders, and perhaps checkers, we can readily see the possibilities of emotional tension—and, in our study, we did see a number of girls break down and cry under the strain.

Stage 5 need not be diagrammed here, for it does not necessarily involve any structural changes in the individual unit. Here several units are tied together into a chain, and one or more levels of authority are set up in a main office above the individual unit structures.[4]

This expansion process magnifies old problems and gives rise to new ones. They may be considered under three headings: administration, the customer relationship, and the flow of work. Whenever we lengthen the hierarchy, adding new levels of authority to separate top executive from workers, the problem of administration becomes more complex. However, this is true for any organization, and therefore these problems of hierarchy need not be given special attention in an article on restaurants.

The particular problem of the large restaurant is to tie together its line of authority with the relations that arise along the flow of work. In the first in-

Our findings suggested that emotional tension could be related directly to this quantitative interaction picture. The skillful waitress, who maintained her emotional equilibrium, did not simply respond to the initiative of customers. In various obvious and subtle ways she took the play away from customers, got them responding to her, and fitted them into the pattern of her work. She was also more aggressive than the emotionally insecure in originating action for other waitresses, service pantry people, and supervisor.

While in the rush hour the waitress works under a good deal of tension at best, the supervisor can either add to or relieve it. Here again we can speak in quantitative terms. In one restaurant we observed a change in dining-room management when a supervisor who was skillful in originating action for customers (thus taking pressure off waitresses) and who responded

---

[4]The structural changes arising with union organization are beyond the scope of this article. They are discussed in the book, *op. cit.*, in the chapter, "The Role of Union Organization."

frequently to the initiation of waitresses was replaced by a supervisor
who had less skill in controlling customers and who originated for the
girls much more frequently and seldom responded to them. (Of the new
supervisor, the waitresses would say,
"She's always finding something to
criticize'; "She's never around when
we need her"; "She's always telling
you; she doesn't care what you have
to say"; etc.) This change was followed by evidences of increased nervous tension, especially among the less
experienced waitresses, and finally by
a series of waitress resignations.

Here we see that the customer-
waitress, waitress-supervisor, waitress-
service-pantry-worker relationships are
interdependent parts of a social system. Changes in one part of the system will necessarily lead to changes
in other parts. Furthermore, if the
people involved in the system are to
maintain their emotional balance,
there must be some sort of compensa-
tory activity to meet large interactional changes. For example, when
waitresses are subject to a large increase in the originations of customers (at the peak of rush hours), the
supervisor allows them to originate
action for her with increasing frequency and diminishes the frequency
with which she gives them orders.
This is, in fact, the sort of behavior
we have observed among supervisors
who enjoy the closest cooperation
with waitresses, as reported by the
waitresses.

The customer relationship is, of
course, only one point along the flow
of work which brings orders from
dining-room to kitchen and food from
kitchen to dining-room. In a large
restaurant operating on several floors,
this is a long chain which may break
down at any point, thus leading to

emotional explosions in all quarters.
The orders may go from waitress to
pantry girl and then, as the pantry
girl runs low in supplies, from pantry
girl to pantry supplyman, from pantry
supplyman to kitchen supplyman,
and from kitchen supplyman to cook.
And the food comes back along the
same route in the opposite direction.
Where drinks are served, the bar must
be tied in with this flow of work, but
there the chain is short and the problem less complex.

We have here a social system whose
parts are interdependent in a highly
sensitive manner. Thus the emotional
tension experienced by waitresses is
readily transmitted, link by link, all
the way to the kitchen.

I have already noted how a skillful
dining-room supervisor may help to
relieve the tension on the entire system at its point of origin. Here we
may consider other factors which
affect the relations among employees
along the flow of work: status, sex relations, and layout and equipment.

I would propose the hypothesis that
relations among individuals along the
flow of work will run more smoothly
when those of higher status are in a
position to originate for those of lower
status in the organization and, conversely, that frictions will be observed
more often when lower-status individuals seek to originate for those of
higher status. (This is, of course, by
no means a complete explanation of
the friction or adjustment we observe.)

While more data are needed on this
point, we made certain observations
which tend to bear out the hypothesis.
For example, in one kitchen we observed supplymen seeking to originate
action (in getting food supplies) for
cooks who were older, of greater
seniority, more highly skilled, and

much higher paid. This relationship was one of the sore points of the organization. Still, we discovered that there had been one supplyman who got along well with the cooks. When we got his story, we found that he had related himself to the cooks quite differently from the other supplymen. He sought to avoid calling orders to the cooks and instead just asked them to call him when a certain item was ready. In this way, he allowed them to increase the frequency of their origination for him, and, according to all accounts, he got better cooperation and service from the cooks than any other supplyman.

Much the same point is involved in the relations between the sexes. In our society most men grow up to be comfortable in a relationship in which they originate for women and to be uneasy, if not more seriously disturbed, when the originations go in the other direction. It is therefore a matter of some consequence how the sexes are distributed along the flow of work. On this question we gave particular attention to the dining-room-service pantry and dining-room-bar relationships.

In the dining-room-pantry situation there are four possible types of relationship by sex: waiter-counterman, waiter - pantry girl, waitress - pantry girl, and waitress-counterman. We were not able to give much attention to the first two types, but we did make intensive studies of two restaurants illustrating the third and fourth types. Ideally, for scientific purposes, we would want to hold everything else constant except for these sex differences. We had no such laboratory, but the two restaurants were nevertheless closely comparable. They were both large, busy establishments, operating on several floors, and serving the same

price range of food in the same section of the city.

Perhaps the chief differences were found in the dining-room-pantry relationship itself. In restaurant A, waitresses gave their orders orally to the pantry girls. On the main serving floor of restaurant B, waitresses wrote out slips which they placed on spindles on top of a warming compartment separating them from the countermen. The men picked off the order slips, filled them, and put the plates in the compartment where the waitresses picked them up. In most cases there was no direct face to face interaction between waitresses and countermen, and, indeed, the warming compartment was so high that only the taller waitresses could see over its top.

These differences were not unrelated to the problems of sex in the flow of work. One of the countermen in restaurant B told us that, in all his years' experience, he had never before worked in such a wonderful place. Most workers who express such sentiments talk about their relations with their superiors or with fellow-employees on the same job or perhaps about wages, but this man had nothing to say about any of those subjects. He would discuss only the barrier that protected him from the waitresses. He described earlier experiences in other restaurants where there had been no such barrier and let us know that to be left out in the open where all the girls could call their orders in was an ordeal to which no man should be subjected. In such places, he said, there was constant wrangling.

This seems to check with experience in the industry. While we observed frictions arising between waitresses and pantry girls, such a relationship can at least be maintained with relative stability. On the other hand, it is difficult to prevent blowups between countermen and waitresses when the girls call their orders in. Most restaurants consciously or unconsciously interpose certain barriers to cut down waitress origination of action for countermen. It may be a warming compartment as in this case, or, as we observed in another restaurant, there was a man pantry supervisor who collected the order slips from the waitresses as they came in and passed them out to the countermen. There are a variety of ways of meeting the problem, but they all seem to involve this principle of social insulation.

The rule that all orders must be written also serves to cut down on interaction between waitresses and countermen, but this in itself is not always enough to eliminate friction. Where there is no physical barrier, there can be trouble unless the men who are on the receiving end of the orders work out their own system of getting out from under. Such systems we observed at one bar and at one of the serving counters in restaurant B. The counter in this case was only waist high. While the girls wrote out their orders, they were also able to try to spur the men on orally, and there was much pulling and hauling on this point both at the bar and at the pantry counter.

The men who did not get along in this relationship played a waiting game. That is, when the girls seemed to be putting on special pressure for speed, they would very obviously slow down or else even turn away from the bar or counter and not go back to work until the offending waitresses just left their order slips and stepped away themselves. Thus they originated action for the waitresses. While this defensive maneuver pro-

vided the men with some emotional satisfaction, it slowed down the service, increased the frustrations of the waitresses, and thus built up tensions, to be released in larger explosions later.

One bartender and one counterman not only enjoyed their work but were considered by waitresses to be highly efficient and pleasant to deal with. Both of them had independently worked out the same system of handling the job when the rush hour got under way. Instead of handling each order slip in turn as it was handed to them (thus responding to each individual waitress), they would collect several slips that came in at about the same time, lay them out on the counter before them, and fill the orders in whatever order seemed most efficient. For example, the bartender would go through the slips to see how many "Martinis," "Old Fashions," and so on were required. Then he would make up all the "Martinis" at once before he went on to the next drink.

When the work was done this way, the girl first in was not necessarily first out with her tray, but the system was so efficient that it speeded up the work on the average, and the girls were content to profit this way in the long run. The men described the system to us simply in terms of efficiency; but note that, in organizing their jobs, they had changed quantitatively the relations they had with the waitresses. Instead of responding to each waitress, they were originating action for the girls (filling their orders as the men saw fit and sending them out when the men were ready).

Along with our consideration of layout and equipment in the flow of work, we should give attention to the communication system. Where the restaurant operates on one floor, the relations at each step in the flow can be worked out on a face to face basis. There may be friction, but there is also the possibility of working out many problems on a friendly, informal basis.

When a restaurant operates on two or more floors, as many large ones do, face to face interaction must be supplemented by mechanical means of communication. We saw three such mechanical means substituted for direct interaction, and each one had its difficulties.

People can try to coordinate their activities through the house telephone. Without facial expressions and gestures, there is a real loss of understanding, for we do not generally respond solely to people's voices. Still, this might serve reasonably well, if the connection between kitchen and pantry could be kept constantly open. At least in the one restaurant where we gave this subject special attention, that solution was out of the question, as one call from kitchen to pantry tied up the whole house phone system and nobody could call the manager, the cashier, or anybody else on this system as long as another call was being made. Consequently, the telephone could be used only to supplement other mechanical aids (in this case, the teleautograph).

The public address system has the advantage over the telephone that it can be used all the time, but it has the great disadvantage of being a very noisy instrument. Busy kitchens and service pantries are noisy places at best, so that the addition of a public address system might be most unwelcome. We do not yet know enough of the effect of noise upon the human nervous system to evaluate the instrument from this point of view, but we should recognize the obvious fact that surrounding noise affects the ability of people to communicate with each other and becomes therefore a problem in human relations.

The teleautograph makes no noise and can be used at all times, yet it has its own disadvantages. Here we have an instrument in the service pantry and one in the kitchen. As the pantry supplyman writes his order, it appears simultaneously on the kitchen teleautograph. The kitchen's replies are transmitted upstairs in the same way. The machine records faithfully, but it does not solve the problem of meaning in interaction. We may pass over the problem of illegibility of handwriting, although we have seen that cause serious difficulties. The more interesting problem is this: How urgent is an order?

When the rush hour comes along, with customers pushing waitresses, waitresses pushing pantry girls, and pantry girls pushing supplymen, the supplyman is on the end of the line so far as face to face interaction is concerned, and he is likely to get nervous and excited. He may then put in a larger order than he will actually use or write "Rush" above many of his orders. If he overorders, the leftovers come back to the kitchen at the end of the meal, and the kitchen supplymen and cooks learn thus that the pantry supplyman did not really know how much he needed. They take this into account in interpreting his future orders. And, when everything is marked "Rush," the kitchen supplymen cannot tell the difference between the urgent and not so urgent ones. Thus the word becomes meaningless, and communication deteriorates. Stuck in this impasse, the pantry supplyman may abandon his machine and dash down to the kitchen to try to snatch the order himself. The kitchen people will block this move whenever they can, so, more often, the pantry supplyman appeals to his supervisor. In the heat of the rush hour, we have seen pantry supervisors running up and down stairs, trying to get orders, trying to find out what is holding up things in the kitchen. Since they have supervisor status, the kitchen workers do not resist them openly, but the invasion of an upstairs supervisor tends to disrupt relations in the kitchen. It adds to the pressures there, for it comes as an emergency that lets everybody know that the organization is not functioning smoothly.

It is not the function of this article to work out possible solutions to this problem of communication. I am concerned here with pointing out a significant new area for sociological investigation: the effects on human relations of various mechanical systems of communication. It is difficult enough to coordinate an organization in which the key people in the supervisory hierarchy are in direct face to face relations. It is a much more difficult problem (and one as yet little understood) when the coordination must be achieved in large measure through mechanical communication systems.

# part 3

# ADMINISTRATIVE

# PERSONNEL

**OVERVIEW**

We now have enough substantive knowledge about organizations in general and their operating features, so that we can place the managers of organizations within them. This section on Administrative Personnel is concerned with the executives, staff specialists, and supervisors who make up the ranks of management.

It takes people to run organizations. These are not, however, *just* people. The managers of organizations have selective and unique characteristics that are a product of the responsibilities they hold. These special characteristics of managers are a compound of personality traits and the role expectations of the organization offices they fill. It is meaningful to describe executives as possessing self-confidence, aggressiveness, assurance, and equanimity in waiting for and confronting results of past decisions. These are personality characteristics of successful executives.

We also have to look at the other side of the coin. We have to ask: "What is there about the organization office of executive that demands these personality characteristics for successful performance?" When we examine what it is that executives do, how they do it, and the consequences of their performance for the future of the organization they direct, we can see that the demands of the positions they hold select certain personality characteristics. Thus, self-confidence may be important in supporting the exercise of authority by an executive; aggressiveness may be necessary in ferreting out incipient problems and anticipating their solutions; assurance may be essential in making de-

*127*

cisions about an imperfectly understood future; and equanimity may be a requisite for taking chances about such decisions, anticipating exceptionally high pay-offs, but not overlooking potential failure.

Throughout the rank of managerial positions the issue of matching personality characteristics with role expectations is a major one. We can best understand this issue by focusing attention on role expectations since this gives us the organizational framework against which to measure personality features.

In the following five chapters we examine the three major types of managers: executives, staff specialists, and supervisors. These three types can be distinguished from each other on simple grounds. *Executives* typically exercise top direction of the organization, making its major decisions and holding responsibility for over-all levels of performance. Staff *specialists* are the internal consultants to operating management at the executive and supervisory levels. These specialists bring to the organization unique knowledge of their specialty and seek to apply it to the problems of the organization. In "pure" form (which is seldom realized in actual practice), the specialists are presumed to have no directing functions over the activities of the line. *Supervisors* are the managers who direct the activities of the work force, the first line of management responsible for work performance by the rank-and-file.

As a prelude to analysis of administrative personnel we will examine two analytical features of the positions they hold. Chapter 6 discusses organization office and the features of role expectations that determine the limits within which managers operate. Chapter 7 examines the structure of managerial organizations under the general title of bureaucracy—used in its technical and not derogatory sense. All five chapters should contribute to your understanding of the offices that make up modern management, and the administrative personnel who fill these offices. Material on the interrelationships among the three broad classes of managers is also included to provide insights into the human relations problems that exist among managers.

When we think of human relations we are considering an interaction phenomenon. Part of the process of understanding human relations of administration is to understand the managers who administer—their characteristics, their problems, and the limits imposed on their behavior by the offices they occupy. From this we gain insights into the orientation that managers bring to their interactions with each other, and with the workers whose productive destiny they govern. Thus we can better understand the interactions involved in human relations of administration by gaining detailed knowledge of those interacting with each other. In this section we seek to do this for the managers of organization.

# 6

# Organization Office

On being hired into an organization, an individual generally is selected to fit a job description. Each position in an organization is described in its formal operating characteristics. Furthermore, those who will occupy the position, and all others who will interact with them, come to understand the rights and obligations involved in fulfilling the position.

The most general label we give to the established positions of an organization is that of *organization office*. People fill the established offices of an organization whose functional performance is necessary to get the work of the organization accomplished.

This chapter on organization office provides the analytical concepts for the subsequent consideration of the three general levels of managerial positions. In Chapter 8 we deal with the top level—executives. Chapter 9 examines the offices of staff specialists, so characteristic of modern organizations. In Chapter 10, the first line of management, supervisors, are discussed in detail.

**INTRODUCTION**We start Part III with the analysis of organization office. This is followed by an appraisal of the widely used administrative system called "bureaucracy." We will then move to the discussion of executives, specialists, and supervisors, the three important types of offices found in typical business firms, and paralleled in most organizations.

What do we mean by organization office? We want to make this definition specific: *An office is a standardized group of duties and privileges that are part of a job and its performance in an organization.*

A person fills an office. The office is prior in time to the individual in the usual organization situation. It is in terms of this time priority that we can see the manner in which the organization molds the individual. When we take a job in an organization, the job is more than merely the physical or mental tasks that we perform. Each job includes a set of duties and privileges that set that job, or class of jobs, off from the rest in the organization. If we fulfill our job adequately, we are accepting and carrying out the duties surrounding it. At the same time we accept and use the privileges accorded to us because of the job we do. Thus, when we have a clearly defined set of physical and mental tasks, *accompanied by* duties and privileges that are not an immediate part of task performance, we have an office. We can, for example, consider the executive rank as constituting a modern organization office. In fact, we call executives *officials*—holders of offices.

When an individual distinguishes himself in some special way, he is acting in a role that is unique to him. The status that attaches to him as a member of a class of men in part determines his role behavior, and in part determines the reception of it by those around him. Should his role behavior be highly valued, others will attempt to succeed him in that role with his passing. This is the point at which the role created by the individual becomes institutionalized into an office.

Ritual solidifies an office. It makes its performance and the rights and duties surrounding it fixed and unchanging. This, among other things, makes it possible to transfer the office to a successor with a minimum of disturbance in the organization. When

sufficient stability surrounds an office, we react more and more to the office, and less to the individual occupying it. The Queen of England occupies an almost completely ritualistic office. Her subjects react very little in terms of her personal qualities, and almost completely in terms of the office.

We should not overlook the importance of offices in giving stability to an organization. An army could not operate without rigidly defined offices. If a commander is killed in battle, he can be replaced immediately, and with a high probability that his successor will be successful in taking over the reins at once. In politics, "sweeping the rascals out" does not create anarchy before the new politicians can take over their jobs. Government efficiency is little disturbed by turnover in personnel. It is also true in business organizations that turnover in top offices need not be disturbing to the organization. Thus, *part* of the cement holding an organization together is the development of fixed offices in a standard relationship to one another.

The less ritualistic an office, the greater is the possibility that the individual can change it or even create a new one. In the relationship between personal role and official role, the more "rational" the office, the greater the personal freedom in fulfilling it. We can see, then, that while the offices of an organization are part of the cement that holds it together, changes in the offices are evidence that the organization is responding to its environment.

In his pioneering and excellent study of business leadership, Gordon devoted a great deal of attention to the professionalization of such leadership. His conclusions in this field are presented in the following selection.

You may ask: What is the relationship between organization office and professionalization? The answer is clear. As an occupation or a class of jobs becomes stabilized and is surrounded with the characteristics of office it is possible to set forth objectively the prerequisites for selection to the job. When reliance on individual idiosyncrasies for defining a job is supplanted by reliance on the job characteristics themselves, we have the foundation for professionalizing the job. Thus, professionalization of an occupation, or at least its designation by a distinctive name, is one result of transforming the occupation into an office.

In Gordon's analysis, one of the principal features of the professionalization of business leadership is that the owner-entrepreneur plays a less prominent role in modern business organizations. His place is being filled, especially in our large corporations, by professional executives. Gordon points out that professional executives do not necessarily react to business situations in the same way as owner-managers. The differences are set forth in detail, and with real insight, based upon his research.

---

## PROFESSIONALIZATION OF BUSINESS LEADERSHIP

*Robert A. Gordon**

We stressed the importance of the function of business leadership in our complex, dynamic, and closely articulated economic system. We emphasized the fact that, particularly in the large firm, the business leader's decisions are not necessarily predetermined by underlying economic forces. What he does and the decisions he makes depend in part upon the kind of person he is, the leadership organization within which he operates, the institutional pressures which bear upon him, and the incentives to which he reacts. The wider the range of alternatives which underlying economic forces leave open to the business leader, the more important are the institutional, organizational, and personal factors mentioned to an understanding of why our business leaders act as they do. We therefore asked the question: Who does exercise the function of business leadership in the large corporation, with its hierarchy of delegated responsibility and with a variety of groups competing for power and influence in the firm's affairs? . . .

Our chief findings in this connection have already been stated. In the very large corporation of today, the main elements of business leadership are exercised by the executive group. This general conclusion is subject to some, but essentially only minor, modifications as a result of our study of the power, influence, and activities of directors, minority stockholders, bankers, and the other groups. . . .

When we speak of the "executive group," the second of these two words needs to be stressed. The chief execu-

*From *Business Leadership in the Large Corporation* (Washington, D. C.: 1945), pp. 317–326. Copyright by the Brookings Institution. Used by permission.

tive is the most important single figure in the large corporation, but he is only one of a sizable body of professional managers who individually and collectively make the decisions and provide the coordination that give unity and direction to the firm's activities.

The primary responsibility for business leadership in the large corporation has devolved upon a group of men who are professional managers. Their position is not achieved through ownership. They are salaried experts, trained by education and experience in the field of management. Though only salaried managers, they find themselves responsible for making the decisions which affect not merely the dividends their stockholders receive but also the prices consumers pay, the wages their workers earn, and the level of output and employment in their own firms and in the economy as a whole.

As far as the facts are concerned, there is nothing startlingly new about these conclusions. They have been sensed by the man in the street, and they are part of the everyday experience of those closely associated with big business. The detailed picture, however, has not been presented before in systematic form, and it has been obscured by loose generalizations about the "control" exercised by influential banking and stockholding groups. It is probably safe to say that the full extent to which professional executives have assumed the mantle of business leadership has not been adequately appreciated, either by economists or by the public generally. . . .

## FACTORS AFFECTING DECISION-MAKING BY PROFESSIONAL EXECUTIVES

Our reasoning about the working of a private enterprise system has long

been predicated on the assumption that the business decisions entering into the leadership function are made by owner-entrepreneurs seeking to maximize profits for their firms and thus for themselves—or at least, if concerns are not managed by their owners, that business leaders will make exactly the same decisions as profits - maximizing owner - entrepreneurs would have made in similar circumstances. . . .

Professional executives do not necessarily react to business situations in the same way as owner-managers. The personal attributes, background, and training of the salaried manager are likely to differ from those of the owner-entrepreneur of an earlier day or of most owner-managers operating in the modern industrial scene. The incentive systems to which the two types of business leaders react differ in significant respects. Institutional pressures are by no means the same in the two cases. Finally, the transition from personal to professional management tends to invite more formal and ultimately more bureaucratic patterns of organization. These tend to grow in complexity with the size of the firm. It is in the giant corporation with which we are dealing that professional management is likely to depart to the greatest degree from the pattern of owner-leadership in the small business concern that has been the basis of much of our economic reasoning.[1] In the pages that follow

---

[1] Of course, the larger the concern the less likely are we to encounter cases of owner-management. Indeed, bigness requires that some entrepreneurial decision-making be delegated to salaried managers. Large size inevitably professionalizes business leadership for two reasons. First, ownership tends to become diffused with increase in size of the firm, requiring a transfer of leadership from stockholders to salaried managers. Secondly, even if ownership is con-

we shall be concerned with this contrast—in which size, as well as professionalization . . . plays a part.

. . . Decision-making has been specialized and diffused through the various layers of management in the large corporation. In particular, a great deal of the initiation of decisions must come from the lower levels. Are lower-ranking executives as willing and able to pioneer and break from the beaten path as the individual owner-entrepreneur?[2] What are the effects of internal financial controls and other checks and balances, especially those inherent in large-scale organization, as plans are initiated at one level and thread their way upward for approval? Can functional and other departmental executives be expected always to give full consideration to the consequences of particular decisions on the enterprise as a whole? It would be surprising if organizational conditions such as these did not frequently result in decisions significantly different from those which an owner-entrepreneur would make in response to a given set of underlying forces.

There are also important differences between the responses and leadership activities of the chief executive and those of the owner-entrepreneur. We have noted the fact that the chief executive must stress the coordinating aspects of this job. This coordinating function, however, is of minor importance to the ordinary owner-enterpriser who, just in proportion as his business is small and personal, can make the important decisions himself, thus reducing the coordinating function to a minimum. As a matter of fact, part of the coordinating job imposed upon the chief executive of the large concern is for the small business performed by the external forces of the market.

The professional chief executive in the large corporation must attempt to coordinate the decisions of many lesser executives. The larger the firm, the more must original decision-making be delegated. What the chief executive approves depends in good part on what filters up to him for approval. And in exercising his approval function he is likely to apply very broad, particularly financial, criteria. Standards of solvency and liquidity not infrequently take precedence over those of profitability and efficiency. In the very large corporation, the size of the stakes often impels the professional manager to emphasize financial caution at the expense of imaginative and creative leadership.[3] The owner-enterpriser may be more willing to gamble his own money than the chief executive of a great corporation may be to jeopardize the financial empire of which he is trustee. The daring of the owner-entrepreneur may be checked by the investment or commercial banker, but the chief executive of the large corporation is more likely to feel the responsibilities of the financier upon his own shoulders.

In general, the bureaucratic tendencies inherent in large-scale organization lessen the ability of professional executives to perform their functions effectively, even if they conscientiously seek to serve the best interests of the firm. Big business, like

---

centrated in one or a few persons, such owners of a very large concern would find it a sheer impossibility to make all the entrepreneurial decisions necessary—hence the need for some delegation to professional managers.

[2] Assuming that the owner of the business himself were able to make the decisions at these lower levels.

[3] These considerations are likely to hold even more for the board of directors, insofar as it is active, than for the chief executive.

large-scale government, tends to suffer from a bureaucratic stiffening of the joints.[4] The result is to impair management efficiency, to create inflexibility of operation and some resistance to change, and to increase the strain placed on the personal and leadership qualities of the chief executive.

On the other hand, the professional manager's emphasis on organization and the organizational techniques permitted by the size of the large corporation have contributed to management's efficiency and have permitted constructive programs to be carried through that would have been impossible otherwise. The management structure within the large corporation has its positive as well as its negative side, so far as its effects upon business leadership are concerned.

In addition to problems of internal organization, top management in the large corporation must also deal with directors and with important outside interest groups. The "institutional environment" of the salaried executive, therefore, differs from that of the owner-entrepreneur, particularly of the small concern. In many companies, of course, the role of the non-officer director is a nominal one. But where the influence of leadership of directors is important, the resulting business decisions may well reflect an undue degree of financial caution. On occasion, they may reflect interests, outside the business, which particular directors wish to further.

From his stockholders and perhaps from powerful banking interests associated with the firm, the chief executive of the large corporation is subject to pressures which the owner-entre-

preneur avoids, although on occasion the latter may also have his problems with (chiefly commercial) banks.[5] The large firm with outstanding securities is subject to more government regulation than the small owner-managed concern; its legal problems are more varied, hence the influence of the legal profession is greater; and its management must ordinarily be more sensitive to public opinion. The results on decision-making are twofold. These influences create additional data which management must take into account in making its decisions.

Equally important, the character of the chief executive's job is affected. He must spend a substantial part of his time handling these and other external relations of the firm. For this reason, as well as because of the complexities of internal management organization, he must stress the coordinating aspects of his job and leave largely to subordinates the initiation and to some extent even the approval of important operating decisions.[6]

No two business executives are exactly alike. Nonetheless there are certain characteristics which we can attribute to professional managers as a group, and these attributes condition the business thinking and decision-making of the professional business leader.

The modern corporation executive is better educated and in many respects better trained than the owner-

---

[4]See: TNEC Monograph No. 11, *Bureaucracy and Trusteeship in Large Corporations,* Pts. 2 and 3.

[5]The owner-entrepreneur may also have occasional difficulties with partners or minority stockholders—as, for example, did Henry Ford.

[6]These considerations regarding the importance of external pressures hold not only for the giant concerns we have studied but also for many corporations in the smaller size brackets.

entrepreneur of an earlier or even the present day.[7] With this education and training has gone a marked development of a scientific approach to business problems, as evident in the increasing emphasis on careful planning, the use of advisory and research staffs, the development of accounting techniques and budget procedures, the attention being paid to problems of internal organization and executive personnel, and so on.[8]

Among some professional executives, scientific caution may degenerate into a tendency to play safe. They do not receive the profits which may result from taking a chance, while their position in the firm may be jeopardized in the event of serious loss.[9] This is an aspect of the bureaucratic tendencies mentioned previously making for inflexibility and some resistance to change.

In spite of the better education and training of the professional executive,

his general business background may not be as wide as that of the man running his own business. In the lower executive ranks, it is particularly likely to be narrow, while the chief executive himself is apt to have come up through the ranks and to have devoted most of his career to one or a few functions. Even at the top, the latter may continue to be primarily a specialist in his decision-making; hence the dependence on influential directors and bankers for advice, the development of advisory staffs, and the great reliance on management committees and group decision-making.[10]

Of course, the greatest contrast between the professional manager and the owner-entrepreneur lies in the character of their respective stakes in the business. A considerable literature has developed concerning the implications, especially from the point of view of the stockholder, of the separation of management and "control" from ownership.

. . . Management's small stockholdings have significantly diminished the strength of the profits incentive among professional business leaders, and this has been accompanied by a strengthening of the various non-financial attractions which the large corporation has to offer. For example, satisfaction of the creative urge and professional interest in the job compete with profit-making as a guide to action, although profits for the firm remain the primary criterion. Power and prestige for the individual executive are not dependent on the personal receipts of

---

[7]The educational backgrounds of the presidents of 100 large corporations are summarized in *Fortune,* February, 1940, p. 61. See also F. W. Taussig and C. J. Joslyn, *American Business Leaders* (1932), Chap. 17, for further data on the backgrounds of corporation executives.

[8]Many large and small concerns, including those managed by their owners, acquire a good deal of specialized managerial services from accounting, management, sales promotion, and similar service companies, and also through trade association channels. Thus many untrained businessmen can benefit in some degree from the knowledge of trained experts without needing to hire them full time. Nonetheless, it is generally true that the scientific approach to management problems is most marked among the larger firms well staffed with trained professional executives.

[9]For further discussion of the tendency among salaried managers to play safe, see P. S. Florence, *The Logic of Industrial Organization,* pp. 197, 219, 224–25. For an overdrawn statement of the same sort of tendency, see Miriam Beard, *A History of*

*the Business Man,* p. 727. The tendency to play safe is, as has been noted, also found among directors.

[10]For further discussion of the limited backgrounds and experience of professional executives, see TNEC Monograph No. 11, pp. 46, 49–50.

profits, and they are only loosely correlated with profits for the firm.

These considerations regarding incentives raise important questions. Do professional managements seek always to maximize profits for their firms, and is their distribution of earnings always equitable to stockholders and such as to facilitate the smooth functioning of the economic system?[11] Equally important is the broader question as to what role profits may play in a private enterprise system if they are not the reward for active business leadership.

---

[11]See, for example, N. S. Buchanan, *The Economics of Corporate Enterprise* (1940), pp. 448–49. Buchanan concludes that, on the whole, the economic effects of the separation of ownership and management are not particularly significant.

---

There is no better way to grasp the significance of organization offices than to examine across several cultures the different ways in which functionally similar offices have been defined. In a pioneering study, Harbison and Myers have brought together just such a body of data. The following is a general summary of their extensive and detailed volume as it illuminates the variety of ways in which duties and obligations of managerial offices are defined in different cultures.

It will be noted the authors repeatedly emphasize that the larger culture is crucial in determining the character of the business organization offices. For example, the British system seems to place emphasis on "aristocratic" values, the German on "authoritarian" values, the Japanese on "feudal" values, and the Russian on "materialistic" values, all of which has affected differentially the recruitment of managerial personnel, the authority structure of industry, and the class characteristics and outlook of managerial officials.

This is an important insight for it tells us that the offices of an organization may be defined uniquely in any given culture even though the organization serves the same function in each. Furthermore, even in a single culture there may be differences in the organization offices of similar types of organizations, as the case of Italy illustrates with its small, family-owned companies and its large corporate industrial firms, each having its special definition of managerial offices.

It is only because we have the general concept of "organization office" that we can comprehend these differences as varieties of the same phenomenon. This is a good illustration of how general concepts help to make sense out of complex reality without oversimplifying the complexity. Throughout this volume we aim to use general concepts in a similar fashion.

## CROSS-CULTURAL COMPARISONS OF MANAGERIAL OFFICES

*Frederick Harbison* and *Charles A. Myers**

In each of the countries whose managerial development has been summarized in Part II [of the source volume], industrialization has been an important objective of national policy. In each case, moreover, the conditions generated by the process of industrialization have required increasing attention to managerial organization, attitudes, policies, and development. There are, however, significant differences among the countries both in the problems faced and in the types of reactions; these differences reflect various cultural patterns as well as variation in the stage and pace of economic development.

Four of the essays are on countries less developed industrially which are seeking to industrialize rapidly: India, Egypt, Chile, and Israel. Two discuss France and Italy, Western nations in which industrialization (at least until fairly recently) seems to have been retarded, relative to the pace in other comparable European countries. Other essays deal with the advanced industrial nations (which differ among themselves): Japan, Germany, Sweden, Great Britain, the Soviet Union, and the United States. We have considered, finally, foreign management as it operates in the underdeveloped countries.

Cultural differences obviously have affected the growth and development of managerial resources and the na-

ture of management as a system of authority and as an elite. In Chile, for example, the landed and traditional commercial aristocracy tended in the past to regard new entrepreneurs as social upstarts, whereas in Egypt the resurgent wave of Arab nationalism has placed high social value on efficient administrators and entrepreneurs. In Israel, the desire for higher productivity in order to achieve economic goals has brought about a recognition of the critical role of management in economic development, which is in sharp contrast to the earlier disregard for the managerial function and the glorification of manual labor. After the departure of the British, India was left with a well-established and well-trained civil service, but the bulk of the private entrepreneurs came from restricted social classes which were looked down upon by other elites in the society. These attitudes, too, have been changing under the pressure of industrialization, as government finds that public enterprises, no less than private ones, require competent professional managers.

In general, France and Italy have been characterized by a large number of small enterprises, looked on by the family as a source of personal security and conducted in an atmosphere of widespread absence of trust. In both countries there are indications that new industries, pacing the recent increase in the rate of economic development, have been directed by managements selected on the basis of qualifications and performance, rather

*From *Management in the Industrial World: An International Analysis* (New York: McGraw-Hill Book Company, Inc., 1959), pp. 122–130. Used by permission.

than on the basis of family connections. In Italy, these large companies dominate the industrial scene.

The British social system, although much more flexible than it was fifty years ago, still carries over a strong feeling of the virtue of "aristocratic" values and gives a high mark to the "right" background in a man. In this respect, it may be less egalitarian than that of the Swedes, although in Sweden the business elite is still drawn predominantly from a small group. Japan, among the advanced industrial countries, appears to have retained many of the precapitalistic features of an earlier period and has managed to harness many supposedly "feudal" values to the service of its economic development. The German social system has also had a strong authoritarian element, but this has been modified to some extent by the early development of organizations outside of the dominant classes and the need, in a political democracy, for the elite groups to make concessions of various sorts in order to maintain their power. For these reasons, along with the pressure of an efficient educational system, the Germans have had a larger supply of technically competent personnel upon which to draw for intermediate and junior managerial positions. The Bolshevist Revolution in Russia destroyed the pre-existing social structure, but to meet the requirements of rapid industrialization, the Soviet government has consciously and forcefully set about the task of creating an administrative and managerial elite. Finally, in the United States, the social status of entrepreneurial and business groups has always been relatively high, and this has been an important factor in attracting the high-level human resources needed for our own economic development.

## MANAGEMENT AS A RESOURCE

The depth and quality of managerial resources are clearly greater in the advanced industrial countries than in the less developed ones discussed in the essays. The experience of firms in the United States over the past several decades shows the increasing proportion of technical and managerial personnel relative to wage earners. This has resulted from the growing complexity of technology as well as from the wider responsibilities which management is called upon to fulfill in an advanced industrial society.

The same tendency is found in Great Britain, where technology and size of firms are important factors in the postwar emphasis on more professional management. Market forces through the export trade have had an important influence on the need for better managerial resources both in Great Britain and in Sweden. The postwar resurgence of German and Japanese management, with the re-entry of these two nations into world markets, has had a similar impact on the need for improved managerial resources in these countries.

In France, modern managerial resources are growing in those private enterprises which are responding to the impact of rapid technological advances in equipment and methods, as in the automobile, chemical, rubber, oil, plastic, and electronic industries. The same is true of some of the larger public enterprises. Closer integration between all phases of production and distribution is necessary with more complex technology and wider markets, as these French firms have found. Market competition from German firms, furthermore, has put pressure on French employers to pay greater attention to strengthening managerial resources, and this pressure may be expected to increase under the European Common Market.

In the less developed industrial countries, on the other hand, thin managerial resources continue to function with limited technology and limited markets. Perhaps the small-scale industry, family-owned and -operated, will survive for many years in such countries as India, Egypt, and Chile. But even here, the impact of modern large-scale technology and wider markets, in such industries as steel, chemicals, oil refining, and fertilizer manufacture, have compelled management to add engineers, technicians, staff men of various types, and several layers of supervision. Managerial resources that were adequate for a retarded industrial society are supplanted by new skills and levels of management. The Israel essay is instructive here, as is the Soviet experience.

### MANAGEMENT AS A SYSTEM OF AUTHORITY

Many of the differences which can be discerned in the varying patterns of managerial authority are due to the different stages of industrialization of the countries studied. The economic power of labor and management both in terms of relative "scarcity" and organizational power may be affected. The stage of industrialization may also condition the way in which "the public" looks at management, and the degree to which social and economic needs can be met by alternative institutions. In short, management is likely to be most powerful and successfully authoritarian when, other things being equal, it is drawn from narrowly restricted groups which have a high degree of social prestige, when the jobs to be supervised are fairly simple, and when management is the unilateral supplier of "welfare" benefits which are urgently required by their recipients.

The process of industrialization tends, other things being equal, to limit managerial authority, both as a consequence of its direct effects on the industrial system and of its indirect effects on society as a whole. Directly, the increasing complexity and interdependence of many tasks make it necessary to elicit the cooperation of subordinates; the much larger size of establishment makes it necessary to increase the number of people in key managerial posts and makes it much more difficult to recruit them entirely from a narrow group, such as the family. Indirectly, the broadening of educational opportunities, the assumption of welfare responsibilities by governments or independent institutions, and the growth of rival organizations (such as labor unions), place checks on the power of management and prompt it to seek accommodation rather than arbitrary power. These pressures also force the managerial group to base its claim for leadership on rational acceptance rather than on appeal to its status as a social elite.

Authoritarian and paternalistic managerial attitudes and practices, both within the managerial group and toward workers, are found more frequently in India and Egypt, where the pressures on management for change are still relatively weak, than in Sweden or Great Britain, where strong labor movements have forced constitutional management on an increasing number of firms. Similarly, the relative weakness of the Chilean labor movement at the plant level, as well as the absence until recently of other similar pressures, has left much of Chilean management still comparatively authoritarian and paternalistic. Of course, the absence of community facilities, such as housing, schools, medical care, etc., in the less industrialized countries makes new industrial workers dependent upon the paternalistic policies of even enlightened employers, and this is seen in our studies of India, Chile, and Egypt.

Authoritarian management is still prevalent in Egypt, where there has been little effort to enlist employee cooperation and more concern for establishing management's rule-making power, which demands first obedience and then loyalty. Governmental labor legislation in Egypt, as in India and in Chile, has limited somewhat the unilateral authority of managers, although in each country enforcement measures vary in their effectiveness. In none of the less developed industrial countries except Israel did we find "constitutional" management of the type prevalent in Sweden, England, or the United States, but labor codes (in Chile) and labor legislation and tribunals (in India) have moved managerial attitudes and practices in the direction of constitutionalism. Labor shortages, which have put pressure on management in advanced industrial countries, are inoperative in the less industrially developed countries. This has resulted in a managerial mentality of "cheap labor," as against high capital costs, and a feeling that unsatisfactory employees can be replaced—though with increasing difficulty in countries (such as India and Egypt) where discharges are subject to government approval.

Authoritarian and paternalistic practices are also common in France and Italy, despite the presence of labor movements. These, however, are politically oriented. For the most part, French and Italian unions are weak at the plant level and have been unable to force many marginal concessions. Moreover there have been few other pressures to narrow the wide social gap that separates French and Italian owners or top managers from their employees. Centralization of control is characteristic in the French firm, as it is in the Italian or the Indian firm, for example. Despite the advanced stage of industrialization, the same pattern of authoritarian and paternalistic management seems to prevail in Japan—largely because of the social structure which, in prewar Japan at least, emphasized the unquestioning loyalty of subordinates to their superiors, as in the Japanese family.

In each of these countries, of course, there are exceptions. Some managements, both domestic and foreign, have attempted to move toward a constitutional or even democratic-participative type of management. Foreign firms in India, for example, are generally regarded as having more enlightened managerial policies toward Indian subordinates in the management hierarchy than do most Indian firms, and their personnel policies with respect to workers are more generous. Even these firms, however, find it difficult to avoid being paternalistic in a society which places a high premium on that type of personal dependency.

Although constitutional management has developed in most advanced industrial countries, the British case points to a further development which seems likely to occur in others. British employers share their power at the industry level with trade unions through industry-wide bargaining, but have as a consequence won increasing control at the plant level, where a new form of paternalism in employee relations seems to have developed. Personnel policies, including welfare programs, sports, and recreational activities, are initiated by management unilaterally or in consultation with plant or works committees which are usually separate from the union. Somewhat the same tendencies have occurred in Sweden, although the unions appear to be more active in the plant committees, which are a form of "joint consultation." The popularity of "human relations" programs among employers in all advanced industrial countries, including the United States, however, indicates that management is trying to regain some of the original control over the work force (albeit with kid gloves) which it had before the labor-union challenge to its authority. The popularity of the "organization man" in the managerial ranks is no less an indication of the control mentality of top management.

The recent assertion of managerial authority is also illustrated strikingly in the case of Israel but for different reasons. At first the ideology of the new state was, on the whole, hostile to the exercise of managerial authority, particularly as against the strong trade-union federation (Histadrut). But as industrialization has underlined the need for competent managers, especially in the public and Histadrut-owned enterprises, managerial authority has been established. Managers have been able to retrench surplus labor, despite the protests of trade-union leaders. However, as the essay on Israel points out, the environment within which Israel's economic growth is occurring has favored more demo-cratic-participative management than that of many other comparable industrializing countries.

In contrast, despite the development of "codetermination" in some German industries by law, the authority position of German management seems now to be greater than in most other Western industrial countries. The *Unternehmer* (top executive) claims total authority over subordinates as a trustee of private property, a person with a "calling," a member of a social elite, and an individual with extraordinary powers. Although these values are not always accepted by subordinates, the peculiar circumstances of postwar Germany have minimized the conflicts which might otherwise occur in favor of a nationally oriented drive for economic rehabilitation and recognition. As a consequence, top management's authority tends to be direct and concentrated; there is delegation of only routine operations. German management is also paternalistic, making heavier investments in voluntary social services for employees than most other European countries.

Factory managerial authority in the Soviet Union seems to have increased with the era of "one-man management" which supplanted the earlier period of divided authority between the manager and the political commissar. Soviet trade unions recently appear to constitute more of a check on managerial actions than formerly, but their power is far less than that of trade unions in the advanced industrial countries of the West. Further, it would be a mistake to suppose that the objectives of communist trade unions are similar to those of noncommunist unions, and the Communists would, in their more honest moments, be the last to deny this divergence.

## MANAGEMENT AS A CLASS

The managerial elite in the industrializing countries is a mixture of patrimonial management in family-owned enterprises and somewhat more professional management in the public enterprises. But the variations are as striking as the similarities. In Egypt, where stronger government control has been directed toward economic development since the Revolution of 1952, managers have high prestige; in some of the public enterprises, they have been drawn from the army. There is relatively little patrimonial management. In India, on the other hand, patrimonial management is entrenched in many parts of the private sector through the managing-agency system, and professional management is found largely in the more progressive Indian firms, the foreign companies, and in the growing number of public enterprises. Some political management is found in the latter, however, as it was in several of the public enterprises in Israel and, in an earlier period, in Soviet industrialization.

Patrimonial management, as we have stressed earlier, can absorb professionals and is not necessarily backward. But generally it has been a drag on dynamic industrial development, as illustrated in the essays on management in France and Italy. The French study points out that "the nature of the family-based enterprise is not only to limit the number of persons in management, but it also tends to expand this aridness by an excessive centralization of control and the assumption of full direction of the enterprise by the head of the family without an adequate organization." In France and Italy, as in Chile and India, a newer professionally oriented mana-

gerial elite is rising to challenge the old order. The Chilean management association known as ICARE is in the forefront of this effort there, and the newer Indian Management Association is a parallel.

Although patrimonial management is still strong in Japan, access to subordinate managerial positions is almost exclusively on the basis of university affiliation and record. Similar importance is placed on the graduates of the *grandes écoles* in France, and Oxford-Cambridge graduates in Great Britain. Despite the apparent exclusiveness, these managerial appointments are based as much on competence as on connection, and this is one test of professionalization of management. When the opportunities for professional training are broader, as they are in both the United States and in the Soviet Union, then access to managerial positions can increasingly be based on competence, even though "whom you know" still plays a part in both countries, as well as in the less industrialized societies.

German managers apparently tend to think of themselves not as professional managers but as engineers, lawyers, accountants, etc. The high status role of the German *Unternehmer*, many of whom are owner-executives, means that there is a gulf between the man at the top and lower managerial ranks. The top managers resist professionalization in the belief that it may threaten their formal authority position. Moreover, German top managers are organized in various associations and federations which tend to strengthen the cohesion of the German managerial class. Although works councils are imposed by law in Germany, their influence on management tends to be slight, and the basic determinant of labor-management relations is the relative power of the parties rather than specific governmental labor legislation.

With the growing professionalization of management in all industrial countries, is the managerial elite gaining so much power that it is the dominant economic and political force in each country? Our studies show clearly that the power of management is counterbalanced by strong trade unions and government in the advanced industrial countries. Management in Sweden and Britain, for example, is checked by the power of the labor movement in negotiating industry-wide agreements as well as by labor's political power. Furthermore, in each country the state regulates and controls the authority of employers and of management both in economic matters and more specifically, in aspects of the labor-management relationship. Although the latter is still *relatively* free for negotiation between management and labor in the advanced industrial countries of Britain, Sweden, and the United States, labor codes and labor legislation are more restrictive on employers and attempt to be more protective of employees in such countries as India, Chile, Egypt, and even Japan. The role of the state in regulating the authority of management is also great in countries like France and Italy, where the power of employees through their industry and national associations is stronger than in the less developed countries.

Soviet management has clearly moved from the political to the professional type, and the Soviet manager today enjoys high status and remuneration. But speculation that this might mean superior political power for industrial managers, engineers, and technical administrators at the expense of the Communist party seems to have little foundation in recent Soviet developments. The chances for a "managerial revolution" displacing the party's monolithic control are dubious in the foreseeable future.

In summary, employer and managerial authority is not unchecked by rival organizations or by government in any of the countries we have studied. Although the importance and influence of management as an economic resource is rising with advancing industrialization, there is no evidence of the development of a "managerial state" or a power elite in which management is the dominant element. The German case is the nearest to the latter; but the German government has limited cartels by legislation over employer opposition, and the German trade-union movement still possesses considerable political power.

# 7

# Administrative Systems—
# Bureaucracy

Our first reaction to the word *bureaucracy* is negative. In the common view of this term, a bureaucracy is an organized system for *not* getting things done efficiently. A bureaucrat, from this same every-day standpoint, is an expert in wasting time, money, and energy. In fact, the bureaucrat institutionalizes his inefficiency and raises it to the level of a fine art. This is the common man's view of bureaucracy and bureaucrats.

We have no quarrel with this viewpoint. There are people occupying positions and offices in organizations who behave in precisely this manner. It is highly desirable to have some nasty-sounding word or term to label such people and such ways of behaving. One way we can help to get rid of the cancer of wasteful administration is to call attention to it.

Now let us see if we can learn to use the term *bureaucracy* in an analytical and constructive sense. The only purpose in saving the term is that it has come to have a technical meaning (which we will use) in the literature of organization theory. There is no point in inventing another term just for the sake of invention.

**INTRODUCTION** Stop for a moment and think of some possible alternatives for organizing a large body of people. Suppose we start with 1,000 people. One way to organize them into a cooperating group is to have each one in direct relationship with a leader. But, you will say, that is manifestly impossible. What about span of control? Can one man be in constant interaction with a thousand and direct their activities effectively? Obviously, the answer is No. What you will propose immediately is some kind of structure of delegated authority and responsibility. We must have a group of subleaders standing in an intermediate position between the leader and the followers or members of the group. This in-between group of administrators we can label the bureaucracy of an organization.

Let us start on our problem of organizing our thousand people from the opposite extreme. Suppose we say that the group will be able to work out its cooperative activity without any direction or leadership. Pure democracy will reign. Yes, you will say on slight reflection, but in order to give continuity to the group's activities, some body of men, smaller in number than the total, must carry on certain delegated activities. Furthermore, you might contend, if for no other reason than to stand as a symbol of the group as a whole, there will be one or several people designated in the office of leader. Starting from quite a different standpoint, we still come out with an in-between group, which is neither membership alone nor leadership alone, to which we can apply the label, bureaucracy.

Does this give us our point of departure for understanding the technical concept of bureaucracy? We need some way of talking about the group of organization functionaries who are more than members but less than over-all leaders. To this in-between group of an organization we apply the term bureaucracy. The individual we call the bureaucrat.

Every organization that is big enough will develop a bureaucracy. We find bureaucracies in government (the classic instance), in religious organizations, in fraternal groups, in educational institutions, in business firms, and even in organized sports.

With what would we contrast a bureaucratic form of administration? In primitive groups, the central social unit is often the family. The social, religious, political, economic, educational, and recreational life of the members of some primitive groups is oriented around the family. One man heads the family unit. He is the leader of the entire family group and the one who deals directly with all family members. There is no delegation of authority to an administrative staff. The family head occupies his position by virtue of tradition and has a separate status that marks him off from the subordinate members of the family group. Here, certainly, is one kind of social group that does not have a bureaucratic form of administration.

If we go back to our discussion of informal organization, you will recall that there are modern kinds of groups that likewise do not have a bureaucratic structure. The boys' gang is one such group; so is the sewing circle, the clique, the bowling team, and countless other kinds of small, face-to-face groups. In other words, there are many kinds of social groupings that do not exhibit the bureaucratic administrative form.

Bureaucratic administration was invented when large formal organizations were developed, bringing together mixed groups of people with dissimilar backgrounds to perform a complex, coordinated task.

Max Weber has distinguished three basic types of administration.[1] The leader-oriented organization is one in which all members serve as loyal subjects of a leader. In such an organization every member holds his position by virtue of decisions of the leader.

[1]Max Weber, *The Theory of Social and Economic Organization* (New York: Oxford University Press, Inc., 1947), especially Part III.

Dependence on the leader makes followers exceptionally sensitive to the leader's whims and desires. No delegations of management functions are made that cannot be recalled by the leader. A leader-oriented organization has a clear-cut break between the leader as *the* management (*charismatic* leader), and all followers, regardless of their position.

A second type of administrative structure suggested by Weber is one in which positions are assigned on the basis of tradition. Managerial positions may be handed down from generation to generation. The leader accepts the traditional or hereditary basis of position assignment in the organization. Schooling for positions is built into the education of each individual whose productive destiny is determined by traditional criteria. Certain classes of people, for example, may be designated by tradition as the officer group of armies, as among the German Junkers. Who you are rather than what you can do, becomes the primary criterion for work assignment in tradition-oriented organizations. We saw in the last chapter, as Harbison and Myers pointed out, that in some countries of the world tradition still plays a leading part in determining the administrative form and personnel policies of business organization.

The third major type of administration suggested by Weber is the bureaucratic. Here the delegation of management responsibilities is based on reasonable judgments as to how best to design the organizational structure. Members of management are then recruited to fill established positions. Recruitment is based on the ability, either already demonstrated or promised by virtue of schooling and training, to fill the established positions. In bureaucratic administration no one can claim a particular position because of exceptional and unwavering loyalty to the leader. Nor can anyone claim a position because that position has been traditionally held by members of his family or class. People earn positions because they are presumed to be the best capable of filling them.

These three basic types of administrative organization show, in the contrast among them, the importance of bureaucratic administration. Bureaucratic administration breaks the absolute power of the leader to determine the fate of the organization and its members. Bureaucratic administration also breaks the hold that tradition and social custom have on assignment to positions of authority. In short, bureaucratic administration frees the organization from absolute rule by a single individual, and from the dead hand of the past.

Bureaucracy can be viewed as the logical extension of management, when it becomes impossible for one person to fulfill all management functions. The management organization becomes specialized, with specific responsibilities and functions delegated to positions created within the ranks of management. Once the management positions are established, recruitment is concerned with finding and securing the persons best able to carry out the requirements of each position.

Let us summarize now what we are going to do in this chapter. We want first to understand what the bureaucratic form of administration is, and what are its advantages. This is accomplished in the first two selections. Second, we want to examine the pathologies of bureaucratic administration, for every form of social invention has its disadvantages too. This is done in the last two selections of the chapter.

## TECHNICAL CHARACTERISTICS OF A BUREAUCRACY

*Robert Dubin*

The organization and structure, the direction and coordination of a formal organization[1] depend upon some kind of administrative form. Most modern, large-scale organizations have an administrative form that we call a *bureaucracy.*

A formal organization has, in general, three levels of direct participants. First, there is the top level of leadership, which may be centered in one person, but is usually in the hands of some kind of governing board of the organization. There is, as a second important group, the rank and file of members, who carry on the actual work of the organization. The third major group is composed of functionaries who carry out the directions of leadership and who supervise and control the activities of the rank and file. The members of this third group we call the bureaucrats of the organiza-

tion, and the group as a whole is the organization's bureaucracy. It is upon the bureaucracy that we want to focus our attention.

### GENERAL CONDITIONS FOR BUREAUCRATIC ADMINISTRATION

The conditions that give rise to the bureaucratic form of administration can be examined briefly. Three basic factors appear most important in the development of this form: (1) the size of the organization; (2) the limited purpose of the organization; and (3) the heterogenous background of those who are members of the organization. Let us examine each of these factors in turn.

When the size of an organization increases, the problem of leadership contact with the members becomes crucial. The number of people who can have direct access to the leader is limited by the time the leader has to devote to his function and the knowledge the leader has of the various functions of the organization. In the literature on organization, this problem is discussed under the concept of *span of control.* For our purposes, it is only necessary to point out that the span of control is limited. When more people are subject to the direction of the leader than can fall within his personal span of control, a delegation to a sub-leader or intermediary is necessary. Thus, as an organization grows in size, it becomes

---

[1]We use the terms "formal organization" and "corporate group" interchangeably. Barnard favors the first term; the second was used by Max Weber. Weber was an outstanding German social scientist. He made important contributions in sociology, economics, political science, and history. He was one of the first to give emphasis to the analysis of the forms of administration in formal organizations and to use the term "bureaucracy" to designate a widespread form of administration. Our discussion is based, in part, upon his analysis, which will be found in English translation in: *The Theory of Social and Economic Organization* (New York: Oxford University Press, Inc., 1947), pp. 329–341; and *From Max Weber: Essays in Sociology* (New York: Oxford University Press, Inc., 1946), pp. 196–244.

an organizational imperative that some of the tasks of direction be delegated below the level of the top leader. This is the first condition for the rise of a bureaucracy.

As a society becomes more complex, the business of carrying out and sustaining its daily activities becomes the special task of individual organizations. That is one of the basic meanings we attach to the concept of division of labor in society. This division of labor among special organizations means that each individual participates in such an organization as a segmental activity of his daily round of life. These two points are important enough to deserve illustration.

We know that our society has special organizations to carry out the economic, governmental, political, religious, and other basic functions. But it goes further than that. There are thousands of businesses, each performing some economic function in the society. Government is not one organization; it is subdivided both territorially and functionally. We have local and Federal governments. We have Departments of Commerce, Labor, State, and so on. We have bureaus in the departments, divisions and sections in the bureaus. Each of these units is a separate organization. The smaller the organization gets, the more limited and specialized become its purpose and function as a general rule. Thus, we have as one of the conditions for the development of the bureaucratic form of administration the fact that the organizations of society have limited purposes that are sometimes very hard to relate to the general goals of the society. This fact gives us a basis for seeing how the bureaucrat can operate oblivious of the goals of the society, and some-

times even against them. It suggests, for example, one basis for understanding why the specialist can be indifferent to the consequences of his work, as Merton points out in Chapter 9.

Let us look at the division of labor from the standpoint of the individual. We work at a job eight hours a day, five days a week. We are members of a church one or two hours a week in terms of active participation. We may go to lodge meetings twice a month. The parent-teachers group meets only once a month. We may vote only once a year but still consider ourselves members of a political party. In short, the individual participates in the whole round of life in a variety of organizations, but only part-time, and with varying intensity in each. Thus, there is created another kind of imperative in an organization demanding a particular kind of administrative form. How can individuals who give only partial attention to their participation in an organization learn how to behave appropriately, to produce at the proper level of output with a minimum of friction? This requires an extensive development of training and control functions in the organization. Thus, the groundwork is laid for functional specialization, which means the extension of the administrative staff of the organization—the development of a bureaucracy.

The third general factor we want to consider is the heterogeneity in background of participants in organizations. In a primitive society, there is a uniformity in social experience, which means that the training of each individual makes him suited for carrying out the tasks of daily living in a way very close to that of all similar individuals in the society. In a modern urban-industrial society, there is wide variation in social experience and background. When a business organization recruits personnel, it finds uniformity relatively rare in those it hires. People differ in education and in class and ethnic background. They have different values of right and wrong, good and bad. This creates problems in fitting people of widely different backgrounds into a cooperative structure we call an organization. These problems center around the selection of proper personnel and the provision of proper incentives for acceptable work in the organization. These, too, are problems that find a particular solution (which we will discuss below) in the bureaucratic form of administration.

To summarize, then, large organizations require an administrative staff between leaders and followers. This is the basic factor in the development of the bureaucratic form of administration. Secondly, the limited purposes of the thousands of individual organizations of modern society necessitate the development of functionally specialized staffs to train and control the members of the organization. This is a second kind of imperative that leads to the development of the bureaucratic form of administration. Third, the heterogeneous backgrounds of those who enter into the service of the formal organizations of society create administrative problems in the recruitment and motivation of organization members. This is another kind of imperative that leads to the bureaucratic form of administration.

## Organization Office and Bureaucracy

It will be recalled from Chapter 6 that an organization office was defined as "a standardized group of duties and privileges that are part of a job and its performance in an organization." It was pointed out that a job becomes an office when the physical and mental tasks are accompanied by additional duties and privileges that the job-holder fulfills and enjoys. In terms of this definition, any job in an organization has the potentiality of being transformed into an office in the organization. It is necessary, then, to examine the distinctive features of the offices of a bureaucracy. There are six important features of bureaucratic office.[2]

1. The office is considered to be the primary or the only occupation of the office-holder. This suggests that the bureaucratic office-holder is highly specialized in occupation and that a bureaucratic form of administration is both the product of and a contribution to the division of labor in society.

2. The official of a bureaucracy is subject to organizational authority only with respect to his impersonal official obligations. In other respects he is personally free. Thus, his after-work behavior is not subject to control by his organization superiors.

3. Closely allied to Point 2 is the fact that each office has a clearly defined area of competence within the organization. Each official knows the area in which he operates and the areas in which he abstains from action. Typically in an organization, the defined area of competence will be set forth in job descriptions, procedures manuals, and work-flow diagrams. In Chapter 10, we see some consequences of ill-defined positions in the office of foreman, which is pres-

---

[2]After Max Weber, *The Theory of Social and Economic Organization* (New York: Oxford University Press, Inc., 1947), pp. 333–336.

ently undergoing a major redefinition in our industrial establishments.

4. The office-holder is subject to clearcut and systematic control and discipline in the conduct of his office. We have only to remember the statistical and administrative controls of modern organizations to understand this point. This feature of organization is analyzed separately in Chapter 18. For our present purposes, we want to emphasize that it is the office that is controlled, irrespective of the personal idiosyncrasies of the office-holder. The bureaucratic system controls the individual as office-holder, not as an individual personality.

5. The official operates without owning the organization and he has no means, ordinarily, for gaining personal possession of his office. In every respect, the bureaucratic official is a hired hand.

6. Membership in the administrative bureaucracy ordinarily constitutes a career. There is usually an organized system of promotion or salary advancement based upon achievement, seniority, or both. Advancement or promotion is always based upon the judgment of organizational superiors.

These six features of office in the bureaucratic form of administration are all clearly recognizable to anyone who has had experience with modern organizations of whatever kind. As a matter of fact, a large part of scientific management, in the area of organization administration, involves the elaboration of techniques for clarifying and making objective these six conditions of bureaucratic office.

## HIERARCHY AND BUREAUCRACY

The offices of a bureaucracy are arranged in a pyramid of authority and responsibility. This is fundamental to the whole concept of bureaucracy. It will be recalled that the bureaucracy is the administrative segment of the organization between leader and rank and file. The top level bureaucrats have larger amounts of authority and responsibility than do those at the bottom levels. The top levels are closest to the leader, the ultimate level of organizational authority.

Furthermore, the hierarchy is not unitary. There are sub-pyramids of offices within the larger structure corresponding to the functional subdivisions of the organization. At all levels there are offices with the same *amount* of authority but with different *kinds* and operating in different areas of competence. You will see this in Dalton's study of staff-line relationships in Chapter 9, and the problems arising from the distinction between amount and kinds of authority.

## FUNCTIONAL SPECIALIZATION AND BUREAUCRACY

We have already examined in this selection, and will in Chapter 8, some conditions of modern organizations that lead to internal division of labor and specialization. We have paid particular attention to the development of staff functions in Chapter 9. These staff functions are largely service functions within the organization. In the functioning of these staffs, there are either advisors to administrators or operating departments handling auxiliary service operations. Thus, the advisory staff operates at the level of authority of the administrator being advised, and is an integral part of the administrative bureaucracy. The operating staff, like a personnel department, possesses all the features of a functionally specialized portion of the administrative bureaucracy. We can see, then, that functional specialization in the organization, when it appears as a staff operation, makes the staff offices clearly a part of the administrative bureaucracy.

### RECRUITMENT, MOTIVATION, AND BUREAUCRACY

There are two features of the recruitment of members of the bureaucracy that are important to recognize.

First, the offices are filled by a free contractual relationship. Whether in government or in any other kind of organization, both the organization and the applicant for office are equally free to enter into the hiring agreement. There is no compulsion that particular individuals must be hired or that special classes of individuals will be favored. Furthermore, the office-holder, once hired, is always free to resign his job and terminate the employment agreement. Only in military and some secret organizations is this freedom limited. The authorities of the organization are also free to terminate the employment of an official in accordance with the rules of the organization.

Second, candidates for office are usually selected on the basis of technical qualifications. The government selects its bureaucrats by examination. Many private organizations do likewise. In other instances, graduation from a prescribed course of study or other certifications of technical competence are used for selection. The college interviewers from large corporations and government bureaus who annually visit colleges to recruit young officials give particular emphasis to the marks of technical qual-

ification that the applicants for jobs have on their records.

The problem of motivation and incentive in relation to bureaucracy is complex. Viewed from the standpoint of the organization, it is a problem of (1) providing incentives to make the official consider his attachment to the organization as a career, and (2) to secure the necessary compliance with the requirements of office-holding.

The first problem is usually met by providing security in the form of advancement opportunities and pension privileges. Furthermore, the offices are remunerated with fixed salaries that are usually graded in accordance with rank in the hierarchy of offices. This security is further extended in a subtle fashion by careful initial selection and equally careful definition of the sphere of competence of each office. This tends to maximize the "fit" between individual and office and thereby reduce the fear of not adequately fulfilling the office. When there is some reasonable assurance that, for seniority reasons, if no other, certain progress can be made up the hierarchy of offices, the security for the office-holder is further enhanced. This emphasis on security will be found in both public and private organizations.

In relation to compliance with the requirements of being an official of the organization, there is the obvious problem of over-compliance and the consequent pathology of bureaucratic behavior. This problem is dealt with in the last two selections of this chapter. The primary technique for securing compliance is a system of organization controls that operate to insure that deviant behavior is apprehended and penalized. This is, of course, largely a negative approach. The more positive approach is the regular, in-service training program, which orients the official to his present office and those to which he aspires. The emphasis on in-service training as an incentive for compliance with organizationally correct behavior will probably be greatly increased in the future when it is more generally recognized as a form of incentive as well as a means for technical training.

### SUMMARY

The bureaucratic form of administration in formal organizations has the following central features:

1. It is the administrative official-dom of the organization that composes the bureaucracy.

2. These officials occupy objectively defined offices for which they are recruited according to objective, technical standards.

3. These offices are arranged in a hierarchy and sub-hierarchies that correspond to the levels of administrative authority and the specialization of technical functions.

4. The officialdom comes to be professionalized by virtue of technical training and specialization and comes to occupy a position distinguished by the fact that it is a salaried professional group rather than owners or leaders of the organization.

## THE EFFICIENCY OF BUREAUCRATIC ADMINISTRATION

*Robert Dubin*

The case for the efficiency of the bureaucratic form of administration is the same as that for modern scientific management. Scientific management has been concerned with perfecting bureaucracy at the administrative level and developing techniques at the rank and file level that will make bureaucratic administration more efficient.

There are two basic features characterizing the efficiency of this form of administration: (1) it is highly rational; and (2) it allows the greatest possible prediction of future events in the organization. Let us examine each point separately.

Bureaucracy is rational by virtue of the fact that it involves control of the organization on the basis of knowledge. Bureaucrats operate in terms of the technical knowledge required in performing their specialized offices. Furthermore, their performance is judged by superiors, not in terms of who they are, but in terms of what they do.

The rationality of bureaucratic administration is ultimately exhibited in the objective standards employed in controlling the behavior of office-holders. This control of bureaucratic behavior is based upon a double use of knowledge. In the first place, the standards of judgment are made objective and based on rational considerations. In the second place, the official is judged against these standards (known both to himself and to his superiors) on the basis of knowledge about his actual job performance. Thus, knowledge as a basis for control means establishing factual standards of judgment and factual records of performance.

The second rational aspect of bureaucracy is its impersonality, which is revealed in the objective methods for selecting and promoting officials, the objective standards of discipline, and the objective systems of control. In the previous selection, we have already examined the impersonal methods of selection and promotion of officials. Much effort in the personnel field has recently been directed toward making more reliable these selection and promotion methods. Industrial psychology has become an important contributor to this effort.

Discipline, and particularly the systems of sanctions used in controlling the behavior of officials, has likewise been developed to a high level of impersonality. It has reached the point where numerical values can be attached to the degrees of penalty. Thus, a bonus system for officials rewards and punishes in direct ratio to productivity with no room left for extenuating personal circumstances. Furthermore (and this is still another aspect of the impersonality of discipline), the penalties are universal. They apply to everyone equally. No one is exempted and no one is shown special favor.

The second great aspect of bureaucracy as an administrative system is the high degree of predictability it provides in anticipating the future of organizational behavior. This results from the reliability of the offices and the fixed and formal relations that exist between them. In a bureaucracy, every organization function is specifi-

cally assigned to an office. That office is responsible for carrying out the function. No other office is presumed to share the responsibility, or if it is shared, it is done so under specifically designated circumstances. This is essentially what we mean by the delegation of authority and responsibility. With complete and nonconflicting delegation, we have the basis for reliability in bureaucracy.

A necessary part of this reliability is fixed and formal relations among organization offices. We not only have to know how each official will behave with respect to his individual responsibility, but also, how the offices are interrelated with one another. In bureaucratic organization of administration, there is a great deal of attention paid to the interrelation of offices. In particular, emphasis is placed on making relations between offices impersonal in order to avoid the disturbances resulting from changes in officials. When the interaction between offices is defined in fixed and formal ways, the impact of the individuality of a given official is minimized.

It is particularly in modern industrial systems that predictability in administration is crucial. A business organization has to maintain stability in the face of widely fluctuating conditions affecting business operations. Price and product demands change; supply of materials varies; personnel turns over; and in many industries there are periodic seasonal changes in styles and volume of output. These and similar kinds of changes have to be met by the organization with a minimum of disturbance to the business. Hence, any factors in the system of administration that maximize predictability help to sustain the business organization in the face of highly variable conditions of operation. Small wonder it is, therefore, that the rise of the bureaucratic form of administration and its universal application to all kinds of formal organizations parallel the rise of modern industrial and commercial enterprise. This has led Weber to conclude that "though by no means alone, the capitalistic system has undeniably played a major role in the development of bureaucracy. Indeed, without it capitalistic production could not continue. . . ."[1]

---

[1]Max Weber, *The Theory of Social and Economic Organization* (New York: Oxford University Press, Inc., 1947), p. 338.

---

We are now ready to consider the pathologies of the bureaucratic form of administration.

Merton's famous paper on "Bureaucratic Structure and Personality" treats this problem. He points out that the "trained incapacity" of the expert or specialist provides the bridge to a consideration of the negative aspects of bureaucracy. You will have this restated when we meet the notion of trained incapacity in considering specialists in Chapter 9.

The pathological bureaucrat is, among other things, involved in making ends out of means. The purposes served by rules and procedures are lost—the rules and their literal enforcement become the end toward which the bureaucrat is striving. Merton examines, in detail, the "built-in" features of bureaucratic administration that contribute to this pathology.

Another general kind of pathology dealt with is the formalized relationship often developed between the bureaucrat and the clients he serves. Although this discussion is cast in terms of government organization, we should not lose sight of the fact that most businesses serve a public clientele and the same kind of pathology can develop within the business bureaucracy. If you have ever tried to pursue a complaint in a retail establishment, you will know what I mean. Again, Merton emphasizes the "built-in" characteristics of this form of administration as the causes of this particular kind of malfunctioning.

Finally, Merton shows how relations between bureaucrats tend to be impersonal. When carried to an extreme, this leads to shunting aside the informal interaction that we examined in Chapter 5. This conflict which exists between the official demand for formal relations and the human need for informal interaction is still another kind of pathology of bureaucratic administration.

## THE NATURE AND SOURCES OF PATHOLOGICAL BUREAUCRATIC BEHAVIOR

### Robert K. Merton*

The transition to a study of the negative aspects of bureaucracy is afforded by the application of Veblen's concept of "trained incapacity," Dewey's notion of "occupational psychosis," or Warnotte's view of "professional deformation." Trained incapacity refers to that state of affairs in which one's abilities function as inadequacies or blind spots. Actions based upon training and skills which have been successfully applied in the past may result in inappropriate responses *under changed conditions*. An inadequate flexibility in the application of skills will, in a changing milieu, result in more or less serious maladjustments. Thus, to adopt a barnyard illustration used in this connection by Burke, chickens may be readily conditioned to interpret the sound of a bell as a signal for food. The same bell may now be used to summon the "trained chickens" to their doom as they are assembled to suffer decapitation. In general, one adopts measures in keeping with his past training and, under new conditions which are not recognized as *significantly* different, the very soundness of this training may lead to the adoption of the wrong procedures. . . .

The concepts of both Veblen and Dewey refer to a fundamental ambivalence. Any action can be considered in terms of what it attains or fails to attain. "A way of seeing is also a way

of not seeing—a focus upon object A involves a neglect of object B." In his discussion, Weber is almost exclusively concerned with what the bureaucratic structure attains: precision, reliability, efficiency. This same structure may be examined from another perspective provided by the ambivalence. What are the limitations of the organizations designed to attain these goals?

For reasons which we have already noted, the bureaucratic structure exerts a constant pressure upon the official to be "methodical, prudent, disciplined." If the bureaucracy is to operate successfully, it must attain a high degree of reliability of behavior, an unusual degree of conformity with prescribed patterns of action. Hence, the fundamental importance of discipline which may be as highly developed in a religious or economic bureaucracy as in the army. Discipline can be effective only if the ideal patterns are buttressed by strong sentiments which entail devotion to one's duties, a keen sense of the limitations of one's authority and competence, and methodical performance of routine activities. . . .

At the moment, it is sufficient to observe that in order to ensure discipline (the necessary reliability of response), these sentiments are often more intense than is technically necessary. There is a margin of safety, so to speak, in the pressure exerted by these sentiments upon the bureaucrat to conform in his patterned obligations, in much the same sense that added allowances (precautionary overesti-

---

*From "Bureaucratic Structure and Personality," *Social Forces*, 18:560–568 (May, 1940). Used by permission. (The lengthy technical footnotes have been omitted.)

mations) are made by the engineer in designing the supports for a bridge. But this very emphasis leads to a transference of the sentiments from the *aims* of the organization onto the particular details of behavior required by the rules. . . . This may be exaggerated to the point where primary concern with conformity to the rules interferes with the accomplishment of the purposes of the organization, in which case we have the familiar phenomenon of the technicism or red tape of the official. An extreme product of this process of displacement of goals is the bureaucratic virtuoso, who never forgets a single rule binding his action and hence is unable to assist many of his clients. A case in point, where strict recognition of the limits of authority and literal adherence to rules produced this result, is the pathetic plight of Bernt Balchen, Admiral Byrd's pilot in the flight over the South Pole.

According to a ruling of the department of labor Bernt Balchen . . . cannot receive his citizenship papers. Balchen, a native of Norway, declared his intention in 1927. It is held that he had failed to meet the condition of five years' continuous residence in the United States. The Byrd antarctic voyage took him out of the country, although he was on a ship carrying the American flag, was an invaluable member of the American expedition, and in a region to which there is an American claim because of the exploration and occupation of it by Americans, this region being Little America.

The bureau of naturalization explains that it cannot proceed on the assumption that Little America is American soil. That would be *trespass on international questions* where it has no sanction. So far as the bureau is concerned, Balchen was out of the country and *technically* had not complied with the law of naturalization.

## STRUCTURAL COURSES OF OVERCONFORMITY

Such inadequacies in orientation which involve trained incapacity clearly derive from structural sources. The process may be briefly recapitulated. (1) An effective bureaucracy demands reliability of response and strict devotion to regulations. (2) Such devotion to the rules leads to their transformation into absolutes; they are no longer conceived as relative to a given set of purposes. (3) This interferes with ready adaptation under special conditions not clearly envisioned by those who drew up the general rules. (4) Thus, the very elements which conduce towards efficiency in general produce inefficiency in specific instances. . . .

. . . The bureaucrat's official life is planned for him in terms of a graded career, through the organizational devices of promotion by seniority, pensions, incremental salaries, et cetera, all of which are designed to provide incentives for disciplined action and conformity to the official regulations. The official is tacitly expected to and largely does adapt his thoughts, feelings and actions to the prospect of his career. But *these very devices* which increase the probability of conformance also lead to an over-concern with strict adherence to regulations which induces timidity, conservatism, and technicism. Displacement of sentiments from goals onto means is fostered by the tremendous symbolic significance of the means (rules).

Another feature of the bureaucratic structure tends to produce much the same result. Functionaries have the sense of a common destiny for all those who work together. They share the same interests, especially since there is relatively little competition insofar as promotion is in terms of seniority. In-group aggression is thus minimized and this arrangement is therefore conceived to be positively functional for the bureaucracy. However, the *esprit de corps* and informal social organization which typically develop in such situations often lead the personnel to defend their entrenched interests rather than to assist their clientele and elected higher officials. As President Lowell reports, if the bureaucrats believe that their status is not adequately recognized by an incoming elected official, detailed information will be withheld from him, leading him to errors for which he is held responsible. Or, if he seeks to dominate fully, and thus violates the sentiment of self-integrity of the bureaucrats, he may have documents brought to him in such numbers that he cannot manage to sign them all, let alone read them. This illustrates the defensive informal organization which tends to arise whenever there is an apparent threat to the integrity of the group. . . .

### PRIMARY vs. SECONDARY RELATIONS

Another feature of the bureaucratic structure, the stress on depersonalization of relationships, also plays its part in the bureaucrat's trained incapacity. The personality pattern of the bureaucrat is nucleated about this norm of impersonality. Both this and the categorizing tendency, which develops from the dominant role of general, abstract rules, tend to produce conflict in the bureaucrat's contacts with the public or clientele. Since functionaries minimize personal relations and resort to categorization, the peculiarities of individual cases are often ignored. But the client, who, quite understandably, is convinced of the "special features" of *his* own problem often objects to such categorical treatment. Stereotyped behavior is not adapted to the exigencies of individual problems. The impersonal treatment of affairs which are at times of great personal significance to the client gives rise to the charge of "arrogance" and "haughtiness" of the bureaucrat. Thus, at the Greenwich Employment Exchange, the unemployed worker who is securing his insurance payment resents what he deems to be "the impersonality and, at times, the apparent abruptness and even harshness of his treatment by the clerks. . . . Some men complain of the superior attitude which the clerks have."

Still another source of conflict with the public derives from the bureaucratic structure. The bureaucrat, in part irrespective of his position with*in* the hierarchy, acts as a representative of the power and prestige of the entire structure. In his official role he is vested with definite authority. This often leads to an actually or apparently domineering attitude, which may only be exaggerated by a discrepancy between his position within the hierarchy and his position with reference to the public. Protest and recourse to other officials on the part of the client are often ineffective or largely precluded by the previously mentioned *esprit de corps* which joins the officials into a more or less solidary in-group. This source of conflict *may* be minimized in private enterprise since the client can register an effective protest by transferring his trade to another organization within the competitive system. But with the monopolistic nature of the public organization, no such alternative is possible. . . .

Thus, with respect to the relations

between officials and clientele, one structural source of conflict is the pressure for formal and impersonal treatment when individual, personalized consideration is desired by the client. The conflict may be viewed then, as deriving from the introduction of inappropriate attitudes and relationships. Conflict with*in* the bureaucratic structure arises from the converse situation, namely, when personalized relationships are substituted for the structurally required impersonal relationships. This type of conflict may be characterized as follows.

The bureaucracy, as we have seen, is organized as a secondary, formal group. The normal responses involved in this organized network of social expectations are supported by affective attitudes of members of the group. Since the group is oriented toward

secondary norms of impersonality, any failure to conform to these norms will arouse antagonism from those who have identified themselves with the legitimacy of these rules. Hence, the substitution of personal for impersonal treatment within the structure is met with widespread disapproval and is characterized by such epithets as graft, favoritism, nepotism, apple-polishing, etc. These epithets are clearly manifestations of injured sentiments. . . .

Bureaucracy is a secondary group structure designed to carry on certain activities which cannot be satisfactorily performed on the basis of primary group criteria. Hence, behavior which runs counter to these formalized norms becomes the object of emotionalized disapproval. . . .

---

In the next selection, Dimock and Hyde discuss some of the common pathologies of bureaucratic administration as they are found in business organizations. These problems are characteristic of bureaucracy in general. This selection aptly illustrates how the malfunctioning of bureaucracy exhibits itself typically in business organizations.

It should be recognized that when we examine the faults of an aspect of

organization or administration, we are doing so in order to develop a sophistication about administration. Because the bureaucratic form of administration has its faults, we cannot condemn it in its entirety. Indeed, the approach that administrators take is to develop techniques and measures that will overcome the faults. There is no great administration invention in sight to replace the bureaucratic form of administration.

## BUREAUCRATIC PROBLEMS IN BUSINESS ORGANIZATIONS

*Marshall E. Dimock* and *Howard K. Hyde**

Whenever a large number of persons are brought together for the purpose of accomplishing an objective, it is essential that some direction be given to their efforts and that individual objectives be either subordinated to or harmonized with those of the group. For these purposes a hierarchy is established.

A system of hierarchy is as characteristic of business as it is of government, and in some respects the corresponding powers of the superior officers are more absolute in business. It is true that for crimes such as high treason, the state may deprive a person of his life. But for the great bulk of disciplinary action within a governmental hierarchy, the sanctions are no stricter than those of business and their application is surrounded by limitations. The private administrator, on the other hand, may deprive a subordinate of his means of livelihood almost at will and with few, if any, procedural requirements. In fact, the system of hierarchy and relatively unfettered authority is widely defended as an essential part of successful business administration.

Similarly the distribution of functions and activities among departments and their subdivisions is an accepted administrative method in business as in government. In business the means whereby these activities are allocated vary somewhat. The scope of a particular department may be determined by superior authority or

it may be left, within limits, to be decided by the department heads according to their individual capacities, interests, and aggressiveness. As an ideal, the first method, supported by staff study, is frequently held by corporation executives to be the more desirable. In actuality, however, the second method enjoys wide vogue, particularly at the top levels of the administrative hierarchy. In either case a means is provided whereby the scope of a department's jurisdiction is defined, even though its borders may be somewhat indistinct and transitory.

In the establishment of determinate qualifications for executive personnel, which Friedrich and Cole mention as a third characteristic of well-developed bureaucracies, there is a considerable diversity of practice. But among the large corporations there are distinct elements of such a tendency. Among the railroads, for example, executives are recruited almost entirely from within a given company or from other railroads. This practice is less strong but still present in the utilities, and is least prevalent among the industrials. Where ownership and management are separate—which is characteristic of the largest corporations—it is the boast of the executives that they are professional administrators. Nevertheless, there is a felt need for a better classification and record of executive requirements and capacities.[1] Though professionalization of management in private business var-

*From TNEC Monograph No. 11, *Bureaucracy and Trusteeship in Large Corporations* (Washington, D. C.: U.S. Government Printing Office, 1940), pp. 31–35.

[1]See, for example: Edward R. Stettinius, Jr., "The Selection of Executives," *Management Review* XXV (November 1936), 332–333.

ies, it is present and welcomed by those in control of the larger corporations.

To the extent, then, that these elements—distribution of functions, hierarchy, and professionalization—constitute the essential characteristics of bureaucracy, this term describes large-scale private business as accurately as it does public administration. There are, however, other characteristics of administration which are included in the concept of bureaucracy when used as an invidious term. These appear to stem from the more fundamental aspects which we have mentioned and are perversions, improper functionings, or undersirable accompaniments of them. The more important merit examination.

The most general criticism of bureaucracy is its unresponsiveness to the demands of the public and to hierarchical superiors. . . .

To the extent that unresponsiveness within the hierarchy exists, the purpose of the organizational structure itself is not being wholly fulfilled. The executives of the large corporations almost universally admit in interviews that they find varying degrees of organizational resistance among their subordinates, and that drastic means are sometimes necessary in order to overcome this tendency.

Unresponsiveness, it should be noted, is a broad term which includes four other more specific aspects of bureaucracy. These are an excess of rules or legalism, maladjustment, a low level of morale, and the tendency of persons and organizational units to enhance their own importance.

The extensive use of more or less rigid and precise rules and working procedures is well-nigh universal among the giant corporations. In no other way can such large administra-

tive units be made to operate consistently. However, what may be necessary from an administrative viewpoint is often irksome to the public, which does not understand the administrative implications of a given order. "Sorry, it's a company rule," doesn't help to make an exasperated customer feel that his particular case is being treated with much consideration. Within a corporation, furthermore, subordinate officials often complain that they are not permitted sufficient discretion, that transactions of any size must be referred through too elaborate channels. When questioned on this, however, the superior officials are quick to point out that there are aspects of such transactions which subordinates cannot understand. For consistency and safety, therefore, the top executives claim that limitations are necessary. Indeed, a whole philosophy of management—that of scientific management—is largely predicated on the idea of elaborate rules established for the most simple and routine actions. An unwieldy body of regulations is thus inevitably built up, and it becomes easy to forget the objectives of the system in a blind obedience to rules.

Maladjustment of the working parts of an organization is also frequently cited, both in business and in government, as evidence of the evils of bureaucracy. Instances are adduced where one part of a hierarchy worked at cross purposes with, or wasted its efforts by duplicating the efforts of, another. Illustrative is a case brought out in an interview. The company concerned is subdivided on the basis of products, though there is great similarity among them. Nevertheless, the officials of one division frequently consult with outside competitors on research, production, and other probems rather than attempt to discover what colleagues in their own concern had done along those particular lines.

It is anomalous that this malcoordination should be called a characteristic of bureaucracy. It exists because an essential purpose of bureaucracy, the coordination of effort, is not being fulfilled. Such, however, is the common conception. No official either of a large corporation or of government would claim that complete coordination exists in his organization. This lack, therefore, is attributable to the failure of bureaucracy rather than to its active effect.

A low level of morale is also considered part of the typical picture of bureaucracy. The bureaucrat is viewed as weighed down with rules, procedures, and red tape, mired in his own particular rut, uninterested in getting out of it and unable to do so if he would. Likewise he is loath to exert any great effort to advance the work of the enterprise.

The level of morale at a given time is difficult to measure because it is comparative and its elements are largely subjective.[2] Many executives, however, will admit that the morale of their employees is not especially high or that it was very low before a particular personnel policy was adopted. Among the corporate giants the company with a high level of morale is indeed rare. On the basis of interviews and observation, there appears to be a medium level around which most of the employees cluster.

Extra time and effort in cases of emergency are grudgingly given. Some officials complain that potential executive material is destroyed by the dulling environment at the lower levels of the hierarchy, causing irreparable loss to the company and employees concerned. Others say their men are in a rut and do not have a broad view.

Finally, a generally criticized characteristic of bureaucracy is the tendency of persons and organizational units to increase their own importance. "The inherent tendency of bureaucracy to expand" is one of the most common complaints directed at government.[3] This, of course, is an almost universal human tendency. Individuals cherish an increase in status; chambers of commerce seek to make "the biggest little town in America" a little bigger; a corporate management is looked upon with suspicion of inefficiency if it is unable to report that this year the company is larger or did more business than last, particularly if there has not been a general decline in the level of trade.

This tendency is recognized by corporation officials as operative within their enterprises. They complain that executives are too anxious to appear to have an individually outstanding record even though it may be at the expense of the corporation as a whole. Illustrative are these comments:

"The executive personnel has the short view. Their own achievement is all that counts, not the long-time corporation record. For example, one executive set up a hundred new deal-

---

[2] A rather extensive literature has been erected upon the base of some limited experimentation along this line at Western Electric's Hawthorne plant. For a summary, see Luther Gulick and L. Urwick, eds., *Papers on the Science of Administration* (New York: Columbia University Press, 1937), Chap. VII.

[3] Carl J. Friedrich and Taylor Cole, *Responsible Bureaucracy* (Cambridge, Mass.: Harvard University Press, 1932), point out that "under certain conditions, a bureaucracy shows no such tendency at all (postwar France, on the whole, for example)," p. 18.

ers in order to show an 8 percent increase in sales even though it was ruinous to the established agencies."

"A manager knows he will move on in 2 to 5 years. Therefore, he wants to squeeze everything out in profits instead of planning a long-term program."

It is apparent that the evils of bureaucracy, as evidenced by unresponsiveness, excessive internal legalism, maladjustment of working parts, low morale, and the tendency of persons and organizations to enhance their importance, are not confined to any particular class of human endeavor. Bureaucracy seems rather to inhere in large organizations. Business as well as government must use essentially the same human raw material to operate, and it is, therefore, subject to the same bureaucratic forces which take their administrative tolls. It is apparent, however, that some business concerns are more unfortunately bureaucratic than others, just as are some departments of government.

# 8

# Executives

One of the fascinating and distinguishing features of an organization is the fact that people are employed to fill *particular* positions in it. The consequence of this is clear. When we come to examine a general type of organization office we encounter a task of matching.

It is necessary to *match* the personality characteristics of people who hold the office, or aspire to it, with the requirements of the job. This has been neatly stated in the first selection: "the performance of an individual depends on what the *man* is, what the *job* is, and what the *situation* is."

We will approach this matching task in the instance of executives by first examining the executive as a man. We want to know what are the personality and character traits that seem to discriminate between successful and unsuccessful executives. This is accomplished through a broad survey of the literature and additional field research reported in the first selection.

You will re-encounter the personality problem again in Chapter 10 where we examine a study of the differences between the personality structures of executives and supervisors. At that point it will become strikingly clear that there are real differences that distinguish the man called "executive" from his permanent subordinates called "supervisors."

**INTRODUCTION**  The second general feature of the matching problem is to determine the characteristics of the positions occupied and the situations surrounding them. This we examine for business executives in the second selection of this chapter. By looking at the careers available to executives we gain a picture of the features characterizing the positions they hold.

A remarkable amount of folklore surrounds the actual behavior of executives. Much is written about what executives *ought* to do, but very little is known about what they actually do.

To remedy this situation and to provide the necessary realism for your view of executives, the concluding two selections deal with actual executive behavior. The first is a recent summary of studies of executive behavior. The second emphasizes the kinds of conflicts that arise among executives —an all too real feature of executive behavior.

In a very real sense, the executive and administrator is the central figure in all the succeeding chapters of this book. When we talk about staff specialists, one of the principal problems is the executive's relations to them. The same is true in examining the position of supervisor. Our whole discussion of bureaucracy, power, authority, status, decision-making, leadership, subordination, and relations with the larger society has the executive as the center of attention. This is equally true of the chapters on com-

munication, control, technology, and organization fictions.

We will re-encounter the executive countless times throughout the remainder of this volume. It is the purpose of this chapter to suggest the dominant features of the executive as a man, and the features of the office he occupies.

One word of caution: Remember we are dealing with studies of the *American* executive. Two chapters ago you learned that the position and situation of executives were different in cultures other than our own. We would confidently predict that the personality characteristics of successful executives in non-American cultures will differ from those in our own culture. This has practical significance for American companies, government bureaus, educational institutions, and religious organizations doing business abroad. It affects the type of executives they employ and will encounter in foreign lands. This also has theoretical significance for all students of administration in clarifying the meaning of the matching task involved in fitting man, office, and operating situation together.

## CURRENT OPINIONS ABOUT QUALIFICATIONS FOR SUCCESS IN BUSINESS

*Robert A. Gordon* and *James E. Howell**

Let us consider first the more systematic studies that have been made of the qualifications successful execu-

tives should presumably possess.[1] One type of study attempts to identify the personal traits which universally seem

*From *Higher Education for Business* (New York: Columbia University Press, 1959), pp. 76–81. Used with the gracious consent of the authors.

[1]The next several pages are based on a memorandum prepared for this study by Professor L. W. Porter and Mr. Irving Krauss of the University of California.

o identify successful executives and other types of leaders. Studies of this type suffer from a number of limitations: vagueness as to what constitutes an executive, failure to differentiate among businessmen according to the nature of the position held, lack of adequate criteria as to what constitutes successful performance, and so on. These studies emphasize personality traits. In utilizing various sorts of tests to uncover such traits, they run the risk of merely uncovering the stereotype-image of a successful executive which the persons tested happen to hold. In addition, they suffer from the fact that personality depends not merely on the possession of certain traits, but also on the way in which those traits are combined in an individual.[2]

In recent years, there has been some reaction against this kind of search for universal traits. More recent studies emphasize the importance of interaction between an individual's personal attributes and the nature of the situation in which he is expected to perform. According to this "situational" approach, leadership is not a passive phenemenon which automatically emerges out of a given bundle of personal traits, but is the result of the interaction between the nature of the organizational position to be filled and the particular characteristics of the person asked to fill it. As one student has put it, "the performance of an individual depends on what the *man* is, what the *job* is, and what the *situation* is."[3]

Somewhat related to these "situational" studies are several which at-tempt to discover whether managers at different administrative levels reveal significant differences in personality traits or other qualities. There is some indication that such differences do exist, although again serious difficulties in interpretation arise.[4] There is the danger, as before, that the findings merely show the stereotype-images of what the respondents think a person in their group should be like. We do not know whether the qualities revealed by these studies are those which an individual must possess to attain a given position or whether they are or can be developed as a result of holding a given position.

Further discussion of these methodological problems would carry us too far afield. In general, the literature we have examined suggests the following general conclusions.[5] No single set of personal traits essential to the performance of managerial jobs has yet been established to the general satisfaction of psychologists and personnel experts. Different combinations of qualities may carry different men equally far. The qualities needed depend to some extent on the nature of the job and of the organizational environment in which the job is placed. Even more important, we are handicapped in not having clearcut criteria

---

[2]For one useful critique of studies of this sort, see A. W. Gouldner, ed., *Studies in Leadership* (1950), pp. 21ff.

[3]Renato Tagiuri, "Research in Executive Selection," paper presented at Symposium on Management Selection Research, Sixty-sixth Annual Convention of American Psychological Association (1958, mimeographed).

[4]Cf. L. W. Porter and E. E. Ghiselli, "The Self Perceptions of Top and Middle Management Personnel," *Personnel Psychology*, X (Winter, 1957), 397–406; also, H. D. Meyer and G. L. Pressel, "Personality Test Scores in the Management Hierarchy," *Journal of Applied Psychology*, XXXVIII (April, 1954), 73–80; and C. G. Browne and R. P. Shore, "Leadership and Predictive Abstracting," *Journal of Applied Psychology*, XL (April, 1956), 112–16.

[5]See, for example: Mace, *The Growth and Development of Executives*, Chap. 2.

of successful performance to which to relate personal attributes.[6]

So much for the negative evidence. It does seem possible to say something on the positive side, provided this is done with appropriate qualifications and with full recognition of the fact that no list of managerial qualities can be expected to hold universally, for all successful businessmen or for all types of positions.

One reviewer of the literature in this field has concluded that, despite the contradictory evidence, the studies available do suggest that certain qualities are important for executive or managerial success. Thus, something better than average intelligence is required of persons in leadership positions. They tend to be well rounded in terms of interests and aptitudes; they have better than average facility in communication; they display mental and emotional maturity; they appreciate the value of cooperative effort and seem to know how to deal effectively with people and, more generally, to make effective use of the so-called executive skills. Perhaps most clearly of all, they possess a strong inner drive that impels them to strive for accomplishment and recognition.[7]

These qualities supposedly characterize leaders in general and therefore cover a broader area than administrative and staff positions in business. Nonetheless, this list of qualities provides a suggestive starting point.

If we turn now to some of the

studies concerned exclusively with th qualities presumably required for suc cess in business, we find that certai personal qualities tend to be men tioned more often than others, an that the list usually includes the lead ership traits mentioned above. E amination of a number of such studie indicates that the following traits ten to be emphasized most often: ment ability, skill in human relations, th ability to assume responsibility an make decisions, judgment, general ad ministrative skills, character, imagina tion, breadth and flexibility of min and loyalty to the organization. Tw others mentioned earlier, person motivation and ability to communicat were listed less often but probab should also be included as condition which all managers should meet.[8]

To this we can add some firsthan evidence of our own. In the course o the present study, intensive interview

<hr />

[6]The measurement of what constitutes effective performance in various types of jobs is a major objective of a study now being conducted by the Educational Testing Service in cooperation with a group of companies.

[7]C. E. Goode, "Significant Research on Leadership," *Personnel,* XXVII (March, 1951), 342–350.

<hr />

[8]The literature summarized in this para graph is described in Appendix A. It shoul be said here that the too brief discussio in the text, just because it is brief, suffe from a certain ambiguity. Some of the pe sonal qualities listed need to be describe more fully if the meaning we attach to th words used is to be perfectly clear. Th same semantic problem arises elsewhere i this section. As an illustration, "motivation can be directed toward different ends, an some kinds of motivation, which tend to b of a self-destructive character, can mak for failure rather than success as an execu tive. This has been brought out in studie by Gardner and Henry (see Appendix A Perrin Stryker has emphasized this semanti problem in a recent article in *Fortune,* goin so far as to say that the terms used to denot executive qualities "have no generally ac cepted meanings." ("On the Meaning of Ex ecutive Qualities," *Fortune,* June, 1958, 116). While we recognize these difficultie of definition and interpretation, we thin that the problem of communication is no insuperable, given the problem to which w are addressing ourselves. Sufficient agree ment on the meaning of the qualities liste

vere held with the officials of a sample f some ninety companies, chiefly arge concerns but with a sprinkling f smaller ones. While the sample was either random nor strictly representa-ve of all American business, we did ttempt to secure a broad representa-on by industry and by geographical rea. Within each company, questions 1 an eight-page interview form were ut to a group of executives ranging rom the president to the personnel irector and members of his staff. The itles and duties of those interviewed aried from company to company but sually included at least the top of-cials concerned with personnel and nanagement development.[9]

In each company, we asked the re-pondents to specify, on the basis of heir firm's experience, the personal ualities (including technical train-ng) that were most important for suc-ess in business management. The ualities that were given the greatest veight were motivation and personal lrive, skill in interpersonal relations, noral character, and superior (al-hough not necessarily extremely high) nental ability. Other qualities that ended to be stressed were breadth nd imagination, judgment, willing-ess to accept responsibility and to ake risks, ability to communicate, and ommand of general administrative kills.[10] Except for certain types of

jobs, possession of specialized knowl-edge and technical skills was consid-ered of only moderate or minor im-portance. This lack of emphasis on the need for specialized knowledge and technical skills, at least above the lower levels of supervision and except for some specialized staff positions, is in general confirmed by the other literature we have considered.[11]

We have examined the evaluation criteria actually used by a number of companies for selecting and promot-ing management personnel. The list of qualities used vary from company to company, and not infrequently a par-ticular company will have different sets of criteria for different types of positions. While it would be easy to add to the qualities we have already chosen to emphasize, there would be no great advantage in doing so. The more detailed the list, the easier it is to challenge any particular trait that is included.

We might, however, take a brief look at the qualities companies seem to stress when they recruit on the col-lege campus. In one study by the National Industrial Conference Board, the personal characteristics most em-phasized by a sample of 195 companies in their college recruiting were, in order: character, growth potential, personality, attitude toward work and company, intelligence, and appear-

---

s possible so that we can proceed to con-ider what they imply for the kind of edu-ation likely to be most useful to the usinessman. The problem would be more lifficult if, in a particular organizational con-ext, we were asking a group of executives o use this (or any other) list of traits in rder to identify the particular individuals nost likely to succeed in their companies.

[9]The sample and questionnaire are de-cribed further in Appendix B.

[10]Despite our interviews and the exami-

nation of evaluation forms and the like, we cannot say how much reliance these com-panies actually placed on such lists of per-sonal traits in selecting men for promotion —or how effective the use of such lists turned out to be.

[11]J. H. S. Bossard and J. F. Dewhurst reported that this same lack of emphasis on specialized knowledge prevailed among em-ployers at the end of the 1920's. Cf. *Uni-versity Education for Business* (1931), p. 108.

ance and health.[12] This study did not indicate the kinds of knowledge and training that were emphasized.

Another survey asked each of a group of companies to select from the college graduates recruited five years earlier the one who now seemed to show the greatest promise for advancement to the higher levels of management. Of the ninety-seven men selected, forty-eight had majored in engineering, twenty-eight in business administration, and twenty-one in liberal arts. The qualities most often cited as making these men outstanding were, in order of frequency of response: ability to work with people, ability to get things done, intelligence, initiative, leadership and administrative ability, capacity for hard work, judgment, adaptability, dependability, loyalty, and vision and imagination.[13] Again, the qualities are not greatly different from those we have derived from other sources.

In their college recruiting, the companies we interviewed seem to place the greatest emphasis on the evidence provided by student activities, personal impression, scholarship record, and psychological tests—in roughly that order. Specific courses were emphasized only for technical positions. As was to be expected, in recruiting for sales positions, these companies put the emphasis on personality and extracurricular activities more, and on grades and specific courses less, than for other types of positions.

One final piece of evidence may be cited. C. W. Randle recently reported on a study of executive qualities based on an intensive appraisal of some 1,400 executives.[14] This study, while subject to the limitations characteristic of all work of this sort, has a number of advantages, including differentiation among the executives studied by level of authority and type of functions performed. For all executives combined Randle found that the following characteristics, in addition to performance on the job, tended to differentiate the best from the poorest executives: motivation and personal drive, intelligence, leadership, administrative skills, initiative, creativeness, human relations skills, judgment, and flexibility.[15] Certain other qualities, though possibly important, did not discriminate between good and poor executives.

Again, the same qualities we have found mentioned in other studies tend to be repeated. Let us repeat what was said earlier. No list of traits has universal validity in identifying managerial talent, and different combinations of qualities may carry men equally far, depending on a variety of circumstances. It is highly probable that, to some extent, the qualities needed for success in particular positions, may emerge out of the demands of the job rather than represent traits which the individual previously possessed.[16] As one study has put it

---

[12]*Employment of the College Graduate* (Studies in Personnel Policy No. 152, 1956), p. 24. The evidence that was most emphasized in judging these characteristics was, in order of importance: impression made during the interview, personal history and background, grades, extracurricular activities, work experience, opinion of college authorities, and psychological test scores (p. 21).

[13]F. S. Endicott, "Employment Trends in 1955," *Journal of College Placement*, March, 1955, p. 48.

[14]"How to Identify Promotable Executives," *Harvard Business Review*, XXXIV (May-June, 1956), 122–134.

[15]We have combined a few of Randle' categories.

[16]For some discussion of the ways in which different managerial jobs may require

success as an executive depends not merely on the possession of a list of qualities, but on *"the proper organization* of abilities, knowledge, and personality traits."[17] Nonetheless, there seem to be certain basic abilities and skills which are generally required in business. The most important of these seem to be above average intelligence, including analytical ability and judgment; skill in inter-personal relations; the ability to accept responsibility and to make decisions in the face of uncertainty; general administrative skills, including the capacity to lead others, to plan, to organize and delegate, to develop subordinates, etc.; breadth and flexibility of mind as well as imagination; some facility in verbal communication; and strong personal motivation. Clearly, also, companies want loyalty and the ability to think in terms of the organization as a whole, even though this may make for the

different combinations of qualities, see the discussion by M. M. Mandell in M. J. Dooher and Elizabeth Marting, *Selection of Management Personnel*, vol. I (1957), 207–224.

[17]G. U. Cleeton and C. W. Mason, *Executive Ability* (1946), p. 26. Italics added.

conformity of the Organization Man and may to some extent conflict with the more dynamic aspects of some of the other qualities mentioned.

No doubt, other observers could prepare lists of personal qualities that would differ in some respects from the list we have presented. Any list, as a set of criteria for predicting success in business, would suffer from all of the limitations of the "personality" approach we have discussed. Nonetheless, it is difficult to believe that other types of evidence would change radically the general picture of the kind of person business needs for responsible administrative and staff positions. The evidence available is reasonably convincing that, in a rough and general way, the characteristics we have emphasized are those which the business schools should be seeking to develop. But we should like to point out again that potentially successful businessmen may possess these traits in varying combinations, and that the quality of performance depends not merely on a particular bundle of traits but on their interaction with the particular environment in which the performance takes place.

---

The next report deals with the influence of different kinds of business careers on the selection of new recruits to business management. This selection tells us a good deal about the characteristics of managerial positions in general. In so doing it reveals some of the interconnections between executive positions and staff and supervisory positions.

When an organization hires new members for the ranks of management it usually turns a critical eye on the characteristics of the positions to be filled. Gordon and Howell show how

the results vary according to the functions performed within the organization, the level of authority held, the kind of industry involved, and the size of the organization. There does not seem to be such a creature as a generalized "management man." It appears to be much more characteristic that the offices of business organizations have distinctive features that are a product of what you do, how much authority you carry in doing it, the size of the firm and the industry to which it belongs.

It is of particular interest to college

students preparing for management careers to follow the details of the Gordon and Howell data. This will lessen the possibility of falling prey to a personality cult viewpoint in which it is held that only personality counts in being hired by college recruiters from business organizations. A care-

ful reading of the section on "level of authority" will make clear that in executive ranks, demands of the positions go far beyond straight personality factors and include significant components of knowledge and skills characteristic of such positions.

## EXECUTIVE CAREERS IN BUSINESS

### Robert A. Gordon and James E. Howell*

Business is not one but a wide variety of occupations. What difference does this diversity make with respect to the kinds of knowledge and skills required for different kinds of business positions?

In considering this question, we have to take account of four kinds of diversity in careers. Businessmen may differ as to the nature of the function they perform within a company, the kind of industry in which they operate, the degree of authority they possess, and the size of firm with which they are associated.

#### DIVERSITY IN KINDS OF JOBS

Let us consider functional specialization first.[1] Most college graduates begin as either salesmen, staff special-

ists, or possibly first-line supervisors. In the latter two cases, and sometimes in selling jobs also, some specialized skill and knowledge are required. The amount of technical competence required tends to diminish as the degree of administrative responsibility increases. In general, also, it seems to be true that the kind of mental ability measured by intelligence tests is highest among staff specialists and lowest among salesmen.

Randle, in the study previously cited, divided his executives into four groups: sales, manufacturing, engineering and research, and finance and accounting. In only the latter two did technical knowledge seem to be a critical factor. Planning, flexibility, and analytical ability and judgment were "discriminating" factors in manufacturing but not in the other functional areas (except that planning was important in engineering and re-

---

*From *Higher Education for Business* (New York: Columbia University Press, 1959), pp. 84–96. Used with the gracious consent of the authors.

[1]Research now being conducted at the Educational Testing Service by J. K. Hemphill aims at providing a more useful classification of management positions (in terms

---

of the kinds of work, responsibilities, etc. involved) than is now available. The results thus far obtained suggest that positions in different functional areas may be quite similar in terms of the basic job elements involved.

search).[2] Ability to gain the confidence of others was important in all categories except accounting and finance. Accuracy and thoroughness were most important in accounting and finance, but creativeness was not a discriminating factor in this area. Personal leadership was more important in sales management and manufacturing than in the other two areas. Administrative skill was most important in manufacturing and in accounting and finance. Initiative was most important in manufacturing.[3]

None of these differences is very surprising. They must be interpreted in light of the fact that, as we noted earlier, the same study found a list of general abilities and skills that were common to all the functional areas.

Our own survey of companies yielded somewhat similar results. The majority of companies responding to this question thought that there were differences in the qualities needed for line and staff jobs. Thus, line and staff positions call for somewhat different sorts of human relations skills. The former require the ability to inspire others to do what is needed; the latter require the capacity to "sell one's ideas" to those with the authority to put them into effect.[4] Line positions, naturally, call for administrative skills much more than do staff positions, but imagination, breadth, and ability to handle abstract ideas were considered to be more important for staff than for line positions.

The great majority of those who re-

sponded did not think that staff and line positions called for materially different kinds of college training, although exceptions were made for accounting and sometimes for other specialties. This may be due in part to the very considerable amount of horizontal movement between line and staff positions that we discovered, in addition to the availability of company training programs. Only about 25 per cent of our companies reported little or no movement between administrative and nonadministrative positions. There was more movement from staff to line jobs than in the opposite direction, although half the companies reported moderate to considerable movement in both directions.

With some exceptions, our companies had no strong preferences for any particular kind of college training for line supervisors. When specialized training was mentioned, it was usually in connection with various types of staff positions, and the preference was somewhat greater for engineering students than for those with specialized business training. But the prevailing view was that it was not necessary to specify different kinds of college training for most line and staff positions, that much specialization within business administration was not necessary, that even in non-technical jobs, engineering and science provide a desirable training for a business career, and that specialized knowledge makes the least difference in sales positions, for which a liberal arts education may be as valuable as a major in business administration. . . .

There has been an increasing tendency for business firms, particularly the larger ones, to recruit for general training programs. In recruiting for such programs, much the strongest

---

[2] A characteristic was discriminating if it tended to differentiate between more and less successful executives.

[3] Randle, "How to Identify Promotable Executives."

[4] A similar distinction is made by Perrin Stryker in "Which Route Is Up?" *Fortune*, June, 1955, p. 158.

preference seems to be for business majors without regard to the field of concentration within business administration. According to the placement officers who responded to our questionnaire, companies are frequently willing to take liberal arts students into these training programs.

The reports of college placement offices partly confirm and partly contradict the information we secured directly from company officials. The nature of the contradiction has been the subject of many wry comments by college officials, who contrast the public statements of the company president praising the value of a liberal education and the practice of his recruiters who seek specialized training for particular jobs.

We frequently encountered this conflict within a business organization in our company interviews. The antagonists are top management and the central personnel department, on the one side, and the lower-level operating supervisors, on the other. It is the latter primarily who look to the colleges for specialized training.[5] When, with particular job specifications in hand, company recruiters visit a campus with a business school, they show a preference, *all other things*

*being equal,* for a student with special training in the functional area for which he is being considered.

Business schools are giving in much too easily to pressure from company recruiters; to some extent they are using this pressure as a rationalization for too much proliferation of special courses and fields of concentration within their institutions. It is important that they resist this pressure for a number of reasons. American business is beginning to put more emphasis on its long-range needs in the field of management development and less on the requirements of the first job. The shift involves a growing emphasis on the more general types of knowledge, abilities, and skills required for advancement to positions of administrative responsibility.[6] Both our company interviews and the replies of the college placement officers indicate that for many, if not most types of jobs, a general business education is considered entirely satisfactory. At the same time, our company

---

[5]In a sample of 240 companies, the Conference Board found that in one-third of the cases the final selection decision was made by a department head, in 18 per cent of the cases by a committee, in 17 per cent by a personnel department specialist, in 8 per cent by the head of the personnel department, and in 8 per cent by a plant or branch manager. A vice president or the president made the decision in 9 per cent of the cases. Thus, in 41 per cent of the companies the hiring was made by operating supervisors below the vice president level, and these officials presumably had an important if not the dominating voice in the 18 per cent of the cases representing selection by a committee. Cf. National Industrial Conference

Board, *Employment of the College Graduate,* p. 25. For some further discussion of this conflict between top management and first-line supervisors on the issue of specialized versus general training, see Herrymon Maurer, "The Worst Shortage in Business," *Fortune,* April, 1956, p. 204.

[6]In our company interviews, we asked if the firm emphasized primarily the first job or its long-term management needs in recruiting college students. Something less than a third did put the emphasis on the first job; about three-fifths said they emphasized long-term needs; and the remainder said they emphasized both. Among those emphasizing the first job, only a few thought this involved any serious conflict with their long-term needs; a slightly larger number thought there might be some but not a serious conflict between short-run and long-run recruiting objectives. For the sample as a whole, about one-third thought there was some conflict between their short-run and long-term recruiting objectives.

interviews suggest that, even for non-engineering jobs, there is a widespread belief in business that an engineering education equips a student for a business career as well as or better than a major in business administration. While recruiters may state a preference for particular types of business training, they will also take students with other kinds of training if the latter meet the companies' standards with respect to personal qualities, academic record, and other criteria.[7] It is worth noting that while the placement offices on campuses having a business school reported some difficulty in placing liberal arts students in other than selling jobs, the liberal arts colleges without business schools generally reported that ample opportunities in business were available to their graduates, and that it was possible to place their students in a number of functional areas other than sales, including production, personnel, and finance, as well as with companies having general training programs.

Bossard and Dewhurst pointed out nearly thirty years ago that business school graduates do not necessarily settle down in the particular fields in which they concentrate in college. Thus they found that only 38 per cent of the Wharton School alumni they surveyed had specialized in the field in which they were then working.[8]

Comparable data for all business school alumni are not available. It is well known, however, that a significant fraction of business school graduates take their first job in a field other than that in which they concentrated, and that a significant fraction also experience one or more changes in the type of work they do during their business careers.[9] Excluding the accountants, perhaps half of the business school graduates in recent years have taken their first jobs in a field other than that in which they majored.[10] Further changes occur as the years go by. In particular, the more successful move out of special areas into positions involving general administrative responsibility. . . .

### THE SPECIAL NEEDS OF PARTICULAR INDUSTRIES

So much for specialization by function or kind of position. Businessmen

---

[7] The placement officer in the business school of a large state university offered the following estimate of the situation on his campus. About 25 per cent of the company recruiters come with fixed specifications as to the training desired; 25 per cent have few or no specifications; the remaining 50 per cent announce specifications but frequently hire men without the training originally specified.

[8] *University Education for Business,* p. 171.

[9] A survey of Stanford Business School alumni in 1953 asked for the first and present jobs of respondents. For graduates of 1927–41, a comparison of present jobs and first jobs showed a significant movement out of the fields of public accounting, industrial accounting, financial research, production management and industrial engineering, sales, and retail merchandising, among others. The fields into which there was the greatest movement were general management (by far the most important), financial administration, sales management, industrial relations and personnel management, management consulting, and teaching. Stanford Business School *Alumni Bulletin* (July, 1953).

[10] This statement is based on conversations with college placement officers and some actual data supplied by a number of schools. The more a school and its students emphasize preparation for the first job, the more likely are the latter to take their first job in the field in which they concentrated in college.

also vary as to the industry with which they are associated. Does this make any difference? Many business schools allege that it does, and specialized training in preparation for careers in particular areas of industry—for example, real estate, insurance, retailing, banking, transportation, or construction—is fairly common.

Although there is very little evidence to support the need for this sort of specialized training, there is a good deal of evidence that points in the opposite direction. As we have already indicated, the personnel departments and top executives of the companies we interviewed did not place heavy emphasis on specialized business training except for some of the more technical jobs. We examined particularly the replies of the companies in fields for which the business schools tend to offer specialized training. With a few exceptions, these companies did not emphasize the need for specialization in the problems of their industry, although most wanted special training in particular functional areas such as accounting.

The four railroads in our sample were interested in getting engineers but evidenced no special desire for railroad or transportation majors. The airline displayed no great interest in specialized training in its field; this was also true of the four public utilities. The latter, like the railroads, had a strong preference for engineers. Three of the four banks wanted broadly trained recruits; the fourth wanted graduates who had taken "practical courses," although not necessarily in the details of bank operations. None of the four insurance companies emphasized college training in insurance, although one admitted that its branch offices took a different attitude. (In all these cases, we are reporting the views of personnel and other officers in the "home office.") In a number of cases, campus recruiters from these companies may have asked for special training in their particular fields.

Two of the three real estate firms we interviewed expressed an interest in recruiting graduates with a major in the field of real estate. Our two large construction companies wanted chiefly engineers, or those with an adequate background in science and mathematics; one hired practically no business school graduates.

The field of retailing calls for special comment. Most business schools offer one or more specialized courses in retailing; a large number permit it as a field of specialization; and a few universities have special schools of retailing. Yet there is considerable evidence, in addition to that supplied by our own company survey, that a specialized major in retailing is of limited value for students planning a career in the retail field.

Among the companies we interviewed, three of five retail firms did not want specialization in retailing, one wanted a moderate amount, and one wanted a good deal. Our survey of college placement offices suggested that recruiters in this field did not express a strong preference for retailing majors. Something of a paradox is involved. Retailing firms seek out retailing majors but, for the most part, do not seem to value very highly the training the latter have received. The answer to this paradox is not hard to find. In recent years, retailing has not been a popular field with college graduates; the department stores and merchandising chains have had difficulty in securing an adequate supply of qualified recruits. Retailers want the colleges to offer retailing programs in order to interest students in retailing as a career. A student with a major in retailing is presumably motivated toward a career in retailing. He is eagerly sought by retailers because of that motivation and not because of the virtues of his training. . . .

Our survey of college placement offices suggests that even company recruiters do not strongly emphasize the desirability of specialization in particular industry fields. We asked the placement offices at universities that had business schools to indicate, for a given list of fields, whether recruiters showed a "strong preference," "some preference," or "little or no preference" for students having a major in the field in question. In *no* field did the majority of replies indicate a "strong preference. . . ." These replies are summarized in Table 1. . . .

peculiarities of particular industries and are learned more thoroughly and with greater economy through experience and training programs in the industry than through formal courses in college. . . .

## DIFFERENTIATION BY LEVEL OF AUTHORITY

In addition to operating in different functional areas and industries, businessmen vary in the degree of authority they possess and the magnitude of the administrative problems they confront. There is fairly wide agreement as to how this sort of diversity is related to the qualities businessmen should have.

Table 1

REPORTS BY COLLEGE PLACEMENT OFFICES REGARDING PREFERENCES EXPRESSED BY COMPANY RECRUITERS FOR SPECIAL TRAINING IN PARTICULAR INDUSTRY FIELDS

| *Industry Field* | Number of Placement Offices Reporting | | |
| --- | --- | --- | --- |
| | *"Strong Preference"* | *"Some Preference"* | *"Little or No Preference"* |
| Transportation | 12 | 15 | 4 |
| Utilities, excluding transportation | 0 | 17 | 11 |
| Insurance | 2 | 12 | 21 |
| Banking | 9 | 15 | 11 |
| Real estate | 3 | 15 | 14 |
| Retail trade | 0 | 13 | 22 |
| Advertising | 16 | 15 | 2 |

Source: Tabulated from 37 replies to a questionnaire sent to a sample of college placement offices, but not all respondents completely answered this question. See Appendix C. This question was asked only of placement offices in universities having business schools. A few scattered replies referring to some industry area other than those included in this table have been omitted.

So far as we can determine, the basic abilities and skills emphasized earlier in this chapter are needed in much the same degree in all industries, and the similarities among industries in the qualifications needed are a great deal more important than the differences. The differences have to do with the technical and institutional

It is at the lower levels that specialized knowledge and technical skill may be important. Ability to fit into an organization and to get along well with associates, willingness to take orders and follow instructions, and qualities of thoroughness and dependability are particularly needed at the lower levels. At the higher levels, qualities of personal leadership, the general administrative skills, the ability to accept responsibility and to make decisions in the face of uncertainty, and strong personal motivation become particularly important. It is at the higher levels, also, that the businessman finds it necessary to give considerable thought to . . . the firm's nonmarket environment.[11]

This sort of distinction between the qualities required at the lower and upper levels of management must, at best, be very crude and obviously subject to a variety of exceptions. Some of the qualities required of top level managers are frequently needed at the lower levels also. Of course, the promise of these qualities must be present if a person is to advance to the higher ranks. One question we asked in our company interviews was: "For the higher levels of management, which of the qualities considered important are in shortest supply?" The qualities mentioned most often were human relations and general management skills, followed by "organization-mindedness" and willingness to accept responsibility and to take risks.

Randle, in his study of some 1,400 executives, attempted to distinguish the qualities that are particularly im-

portant at the top, middle, and lower levels of management. All of his general management qualities (see first selection of chapter) showed up more strongly in successful top executives than at the lower levels. The quality that showed up most strongly was motivation. At the middle level, flexibility and analysis and judgment were discriminating characteristics between more and less successful executives.[12] Mental capacity was a particularly discriminating factor in the lower level of management (where we should expect the range of mental ability to be fairly wide).

The larger business firms are today becoming increasingly concerned with the problem of "management development," i.e., of developing a supply of men with the qualities needed for the higher levels of management. These programs vary among themselves, and not all companies look for the same things in sending their executives to them. But it is fair to say that, taking these programs as a whole, American corporations are seeking ways of developing in their executives some or all of the following qualities: breadth of outlook (ability to view the company as a whole, to assess its place in the industry, and to appreciate the significance of changes in the nonmarket environment), flexibility of mind, a more rational approach to problem-solving and decision-making, improved human relations and com-

---

[11]For a forceful statement of the difference in qualities required by top and middle management, see R. N. McMurry, "Man-Hunt for Top Executives," *Harvard Business Review,* January-February, 1954, especially pp. 49–50. He emphasizes particularly "the magnitude of the risks which the two classes of executives are called upon to take." R. L. Katz emphasizes three kinds of skills needed by administrators: technical, human, and conceptual. The first is most important in the lower levels, and the last is most important at the top levels of management. "Skills of an Effective Administrator," *Harvard Business Review,* January-February, 1955, pp. 33–42.

[12]The fact that these qualities were "discriminating" at the middle but not the top level suggests that executives must have these qualities to rise to the top at all. Dependability was a discriminating characteristic at the top level but not at the middle or lower levels, suggesting that this was a fairly general quality below the top level. On all of this, see Randle, "How to Identify Promotable Executives," pp. 129–130.

munication skills, greater administrative proficiency, and greater capacity for self-analysis and self-development.

### DIVERSITY IN SIZE OF FIRM

The ingredients of business competence stressed in the early pages of this chapter hold for business firms of any size. The same qualifications can make a man successful in both a large and a small business. Such is the testimony provided by the careers of many businessmen.

There are, however, some differences in the problems posed by large and small business that should be noted. It is well to remember that a substantial fraction of business school graduates eventually settle down in firms of small or moderate size, and that a significant number take their first job with relatively small concerns.[13] Against this background, the business schools (particularly the graduate ones) have sometimes been criticized for teaching their students as if all of them would spend their entire business lives in large firms. While a minimum set of qualities are essential for success in large or small business, does small business have special needs of which the business schools should take account? To a limited extent, the answer is "yes." Some schools have been recognizing this by setting up courses with titles such as Problems of Small Business.[14]

Subject to some qualifications, we suggest that small firms present the following special problems. Their organizational problems are less difficult than in the larger firms. On the other hand, there is less specialization of function and considerably less use of specialized experts within the organization. As a corollary, there is less opportunity for staff research and greater difficulty in keeping up with the latest developments that affect the company's operations. Small firms cannot afford the kinds of internal training programs utilized by the larger companies, and only with some difficulty can they spare men to attend programs of any length conducted by other institutions. To the extent that small firms are also new and rapidly expanding, they raise special problems such as the need to secure adequate capital funds, the difficulty of maintaining working capital, and the need to develop a satisfactory distribution system for their products.[15]

Small firms cannot afford to rely on college recruitment as a source for

---

[13]According to a survey of Harvard Business School alumni published in 1956, more than one-third of those graduating during 1922–25 had become owner-managers, and more than one-half of all reporting alumni were associated with firms having fewer than 1,000 employees. Harvard Business School *Alumni Bulletin,* Summer, 1956. In 1958, about 44 per cent of Stanford Business School alumni were with firms having fewer than 1,000 employees. About a quarter were associated with firms having 100 or fewer employees. Stanford Business School *Alumni Bulletin,* January, 1959.

[14]There is no single dividing line between small and large business. A firm with less than 100 employees is today small by nearly any standard; for some purposes, a firm with two or three thousand employees may be small. Not long ago, *Fortune* considered the special management problems of "middle-sized" companies, defined as having from 500 to 2,500 employees. See Daniel Seligman, " 'Middle-Sized' Management." *Fortune,* May, 1955.

[15]"There is wide agreement, amounting to doctrine, that taxation, management, and finance together form an interrelated triumvirate of small-business problems." ("Does 'Small Business' Get a Fair Shake?" *Fortune,* October, 1953, p. 164.)

management personnel. It is not merely that such recruiting involves more immediate expense than these firms can afford. More important, they cannot afford the training (including the ripening through experience) that is necessary. The chief means of entry of college graduates into small firms seem to be the following: entry into a family business immediately after graduation, going into business for themselves (usually after some work experience), or moving into the management of a small firm after some years with a larger company. In addition, small firms hire some inexperienced college graduates "over the counter."

In our company survey, we found that the smaller companies tended to place somewhat greater weight on the importance of mental ability and human relations skills than did the larger companies. It was the largest companies that placed the greatest weight on skill in communication. General management skills were stressed more by the moderately large companies than by either the very large or by the smaller firms. We are not sure how significant these differences are. Such other differences as showed up in our respondents' replies when classified by size of company were not important enough to warrant reporting them.

Our survey of college placement offices yields some additional information. Smaller companies, when they use the college placement office, tend to hire for specific jobs rather than for long-run management needs. The small companies show a somewhat greater interest in business administration majors than the larger firms, and are more likely to be interested in a field of specialization within business administration. On the other hand, interest in holders of master's degrees comes almost exclusively from the large companies. All of this reflects the small firm's inability or unwillingness to provide as much training as the large firm. It also indicates that small firms tend to hire on an *ad hoc* basis as particular openings arise and to neglect their longer-run needs for upper-level management personnel (which they may satisfy by eventually bringing in experienced men from other firms). To the extent that small firms do emphasize college training for particular jobs, they also neglect the fact that, being small and without elaborate staff departments, they particularly need men with broad business training. However, the smaller firms frequently act as if such broad training, to be really valuable to them, can be acquired only by experience with some other (and usually larger) company.

---

Much of the knowledge about executive behavior is derived from personal accounts of individual executives. They describe what an executive does by describing their own daily work.

There is remarkably little systematic observation and controlled research on executive behavior. This is very surprising since executives are

so important to business operations.

The following is a recent summary of what is known about the behaviors of executives. If you read this summary carefully, you will discover that the systematic research on actual executive behavior reaches conclusions at odds with general beliefs about what executives do.

## MANAGERIAL BEHAVIORS

### Robert Dubin*

It is one of the curiosities of the literature on managerial behavior that we know almost nothing about it in any detail. Even such simple facts as the kinds of activities that managers engage in and the time distributions among them are not a matter of general knowledge in the literature. We can quote the plant manager cited by Guest, who says: "You know, I'd like to know what a foreman does, what he *really* does. . . ."[1]

The simplest and most obvious fact about executives is revealed by an account of their activities and interactions. Burns, in studying four departmental executives in an English factory, showed that, in 80 per cent of all the time spent by these executives at work, they were *talking*.[2] Carlson reported a 1949 study of twelve German industrial "directors" (top operating executives) who averaged 70 per cent of their time talking.[3] Stogdill and Shartle found that a sample of 470 Navy officers estimated that they spent 59.6 per cent of their time in contact with persons.[4] Ulrich, Booz, and Lawrence, in their study of an

American factory by observational methods, concluded that " . . . a rough estimate might be made that 50 to 60 per cent of a department head's time was spent in talking to men from outside the immediate ranks of his own subordinates."[5] That, of course, did not include the additional time he spent in discourse with his own people. Fox cited Kriesberg and Guetzkow as reporting for a large sample of executives that the businessmen estimated that they spent between one fourth and one half of their time in conferences.[6]

Perhaps the sheer investment in talking time accounts for one of Carlson's minor findings that there were chief executives who signed not more than one or two letters a week, with the maximum two or three letters a day. Written communication simply does not have a chance when oral communication demands so much of the executive's time.

Is it any wonder, then, that in any catalogue of executive abilities it seems clear why "ability to express himself" is a leading one? In the sheer volume of all activities demanded of him, verbal interaction is the No. 1 form of contact, consuming upward of 80 per cent of all the executive's

*Reprinted by permission from Chris Argyris *et al*, *Social Science Approaches to Business Behavior* (Homewood, Ill.: Dorsey-Irwin, 1962), pp. 12–20.

[1] R. H. Guest, "Of Time and the Foreman," *Personnel*, May, 1956.

[2] T. Burns, "The Direction of Activity and Communication in a Departmental Executive Group," *Human Relations*, 7:73–97, 1954.

[3] S. Carlson, *Executive Behaviour* (Stockholm: Stromborgs, 1951).

[4] R. M. Stogdill and C. L. Shartle, *Methods in the Study of Administrative Leadership*

(Columbus: Bureau of Business Research, Ohio State University, 1955).

[5] D. N. Ulrich, D. R. Booz, and P. R. Lawrence, *Management Behavior and Foreman Attitude: A Case Study* (Cambridge: Harvard Graduate School of Business Administration, 1950).

[6] W. M. Fox, "Group Reaction to Two Types of Conference Leadership," *Human Relations*, 10:279–289, 1957.

time. Bendix has argued that the so-called human relations movement was a response to the need for a new managerial justification for the exercise of authority with the passing of the owner-entrepreneur and his replacement by the professional, salaried executive.[7] He cited Dale Carnegie as the principal evangelist of this movement. But perhaps a simpler, less elegant, more realistic interpretation of the movement to "win friends and influence people" through verbal skills is to consider it a simple response to the behavioral demands of the executive role—the executive simply spends so much of his time talking that he has to be skillful at it in order to succeed.

As if to emphasize the other side of the coin of "togetherness," Carlson has some fascinating data on "aloneness" for a single top Swedish executive. The observational data showed that the average length of time that the executive was alone was only fourteen minutes for a given period. If uninterrupted time alone (undisturbed by visitors and telephone calls) was considered, then this averaged only eight minutes per alone period. Indeed, only twelve times in thirty-five days of observation was this chief executive able to work undisturbed alone in his office during intervals of twenty-three minutes or longer. Dale reported in a general way a recurrent complaint by American executives that they lacked the opportunity for time to be alone and uninterrupted.[8]

We start, then, with a picture of the executive scarcely able to close his mouth, with an extremely high proportion of his time spent in discourse with others in his environment. Assuming that he wanted to have time alone to think, read, relax, or even dream big for the company's future, the one study we have of a single executive in action reveals that there is pitifully little time to do this.[9]

With whom is this vast expenditure of time spent by executives in interacting with other people in the organization? Our data shift to middle managers, for, unfortunately, there are no data known to me dealing with top management. Rearranging Burns' facts about his four departmental managers, we secure the picture presented in Table 1. This table shows the distribution of time spent in contact with others and, of course, does not include time spent alone. Two notable features of the data call for comment.

First, as we go downward in rank, the proportion of time spent with superiors markedly increases, and, correspondingly, the proportion of time spent with subordinates decreases. That is to say, in the lower reaches of management more time is spent looking upward than downward in the rank system. This again accords with general observations (Roethlisberger,[10] Dubin[11]), but it is especially

---

[7]R. Bendix, "Bureaucratization in Industry," in A. Kornhauser *et al.* (eds.), *Industrial Conflict* (New York: McGraw-Hill Book Company, 1954), Chapter 12.

[8]E. R. Dale, *Planning and Developing the Company Organization Structure* (New York: American Management Association, 1952).

[9]I am willing to bet that there will even be executives who will have the content of this book "briefed," so that they may benefit without burdening themselves with reading the entire contents in the scraps of reading time available to them!

[10]F. J. Roethlisberger "The Foreman: Master and Victim of Double Talk," *Harvard Business Review*, 23:285–294, Spring, 1945.

[11]R. Dubin, *The World of Work* (Englewood Cliffs, N. J.: Prentice-Hall, Inc., 1958).

**Table 1**

PER CENT OF EXECUTIVES' TOTAL INTERACTION TIME SPENT
WITH PEOPLE OF VARIOUS RANKS

| Ranking of Person with Whom Interacting | Department Manager | His Senior Staff* | His Junior Staff† |
|---|---|---|---|
| Superiors | 6 | 23 | 34 |
| Peers | 29 | 50 | 46 |
| Subordinates | 65 | 27 | 20 |

Source: Burns (p. 90) observational data.
*Comparable to assistant departmental manager (actually one person).
†Comparable to section manager with foremen under him.

comforting to have actual data that substantially support the impression-istic observational conclusion. This conclusion, incidentally, helps to orient the data on foremen which we shall examine shortly.

Second, we observe that there is a very substantial increase in the pro-portion of time spent in interaction that is devoted to peers as we move downward in the rank system. This reaches half the total interacting time for the senior and junior staff men under the departmental manager. Now there is almost no notice taken in the literature (good *exceptions* being Richardson and Walker[12] and the anecdotal accounts of Dalton[13]) of the *horizontal* dimension of organiza-tion and the volume of business that is transacted among *peers* to keep the organization going. Indeed, it is prob-ably among organizational equals that much of the real co-ordination of work-flow and operations takes place in what we have called the "non-formal behavior system." The non-formal behavior system is the arena in which the organization is made to

work by supplementing the formal procedures, rules, etc., with realistic applications of them to operating situations. Jaques pointed to non-formal behavior systems when he con-cluded from his long-term observa-tional study of the English factory that " . . . it is an impossible task to make policy completely explicit. There remains always a residue of unrecog-nized and unidentified aspects of the culture of the concern. . . . The identi-fication and labeling of these is a never-ending process."[14] Weiss gives some brief descriptions of nonformal behavior among government research administrators, although not labeling it by this term.[15]

It cannot be too strongly empha-sized that horizontal relations among peers in management and the non-formal behavior systems through which such interactions are carried out constitute a dimension of organi-zational behavior long neglected and probably as important as authority re-lations. We shall see this same char-acteristic peer-to-peer interaction as an important form of contact among foremen in doing their work.

---

[12]F. L. W. Richardson and C. R. Walker, *Human Relations in an Expanding Com-pany* (New Haven: Labor and Management Center, Yale University, 1948).

[13]M. Dalton, *Men Who Manage* (New York: John Wiley & Sons, Inc., 1959).

[14]Elliott Jaques, *The Changing Culture of a Factory* (New York: Dryden Press, 1952).

[15]R. S. Weiss, *Processes of Organization* (Ann Arbor: Survey Research Center, Uni-versity of Michigan, 1956).

The mode of interaction up and down the ranks of management is revealed by examining the initiation of contacts. Again our hard data are meager, and we return to Burns' study. (Illustrative data are abundant in the work of Whyte [16] and Argyris,[17] but it is impossible to do more than accept their conclusions as plausible, since no distributions of data are presented by these investigations.) In Table 2 we have the distribution of

Our next concern is to ask, "What are principal areas of functional responsibility of executives?" The data from two studies are presented in Table 3. The Stogdill-Shartle study reports self-estimate data, while Carlson's data are based on observational records.[18] There may be other data of this sort, but we were not able to uncover it readily.[19]

The most outstanding (if not startling) fact presented by the table is

**Table 2**

INITIATION OF INTERACTION BY A DEPARTMENTAL MANAGER

| Interactions with— | Total Interactions Recorded | Per Cent Initiated by Manager |
|---|---|---|
| Superiors | 41 | 36 |
| Peers | 183 | 51 |
| Subordinates | | |
| Senior staff | 402 | 58 |
| Design-planning staff, foremen | 154 | 62 |
| Working supervisors, senior clerical, etc. | 27 | 74 |
| Apprentices, typists, etc. | 63 | 62 |

Source: Burns (p. 90).

870 recorded interactions of the departmental manager showing the proportion of each class of interaction which he initiated. It is notable that this one man initiated exactly half the interactions with his peers, much more than half and up to three quarters for his subordinates, and only about a third to his superiors. We seem to have confirmed here an inverse law of initiation of interaction in which the proportion of initiation increases from high to low rank, the greater the difference in rank between initiator and recipient.

the small proportion of time spent on making decisions.[20] If these studies are at all representative of what ex-

[18]In considering these data, it should be kept in mind that there may be real differences between observation of action and self-estimates of it. Burns, who did actual observational studies of executives and who also asked them to estimate their own time spent in activities, showed that there were significant discrepancies between the two methods of collecting the data.

[19]For example, Sayles and Chapple reported the distribution of time spent by two superintendents without any reference to comparable studies. Their data are not included here because it is used by them illustratively rather than as body of fact and is difficult to interpret for that reason. See L. R. Sayles and E. D. Chapple, *The Measure of Management* (New York: The Macmillan Company, 1961).

[20]Here the observational data reported a

[16]W. F. Whyte, *Human Relations in the Restaurant Industry* (New York: McGraw-Hill Book Company, 1948).

[17]C. Argyris, *Personality and Organization* (New York: Harper & Bros., 1957).

**Table 3**

PER CENT OF EXECUTIVES' TIME SPENT IN AREAS OF FUNCTIONAL BEHAVIOR

| Area of Functional Behavior | 470 Navy Officers* | 66 Wholesale Co-operative Executives* | Swedish Managing Directors, Centralized Organizations | Swedish Managing Directors, Decentralized Organizations |
|---|---|---|---|---|
| Getting information | 18 | 18 | 37.9 | 39.6 |
| Advising and explaining | 13 | 12 | 15.9 | 14.6 |
| Making decisions | 28 | 26 | 14.6 | 6.3 |
| Giving orders | 15 | 15 | 13.8 | 6.8 |
| Others | 26 | 29 | 17.8 | 32.7 |
| Data-gathering method | Self-estimate | Self-estimate | Observation | Observation |
| Source | Stogdill-Shartle (p. 49) | Stogdill-Shartle (p. 49) | Carlson | Carlson |

*Combination of reported categories.

ecutives do, it would seem that making decisions, which is often considered their cardinal function, occupies a remarkably small share of their total working time. Perhaps these samples of executives have learned what Barnard called the fine art of decision-making—"not deciding questions that are not now pertinent . . . not deciding prematurely . . . not making decisions that cannot be made effective, and . . . not making decisions that others should make."[21]

As if to support Barnard's conclusion by indicating how much preparation goes into decision-making, the observational studies of the Swedish top executives showed that they spend between a third and two fifths of their time getting information about their organizations, while the self-estimat-

relatively small proportion of time spent in making decisions, while the self-estimated figures reached an average of more than a quarter of the time. Does this mean that there may be some self-inflation of importance when executives evaluate their own work?

[21]Chester I. Barnard, *The Functions of the Executive* (Cambridge: Harvard University Press, 1938).

ing naval officers and American wholesale co-operative executives had to invest a major share of their time in simply getting information, suggesting, (a) that they may be genuinely isolated from their organization (an often-made observation—see Drucker's study of General Motors,[22] for example), this heavy investment in getting information being necessary in order to help overcome this isolation; and (b) that executives may be particular victims of dependency on flows of information within their organizations such that their decisions may be readily affected by what is fed to them, or withheld, by subordinates. Still another feature of Table 3 is the combined proportion of time spent in "giving orders" and "advising or explaining." For centralized organizations, including one group of Swedish companies, the Navy, and the wholesale co-operatives, explaining or ordering consumed about 28 per cent of an executive's time, while in the one example of decentralized organization (again Swedish data) these activities

[22]P. F. Drucker, *The Concept of the Corporation* (New York: John Day, 1946).

commanded only 20 per cent of the executive's time, the difference being entirely accounted for by the lesser amount of time devoted to giving orders under decentralization.

One of the curiosities of job descriptions is that they give the impression that the described components of the job are all brought into use at the same time or at least in closely connected bundles. This simple fact alone may have been important in leading academic investigators to assume that variety is a scarce commodity in business behavior and that, being the spice of life, its scarcity must thereby lead to characterizing the business world as tasteless and monotonous. Burns showed that over a five-week period there was significant variety in the business life of executives due to different "mixes" of the same content of their work through time.[23] As if to give added support to this idea from quite a tangential field of administration, Weiss showed that the self-described bundles of activities of research administrators in a governmental research agency varied considerably among men holding identical job classifications and organizational positions. Furthermore, he showed that these bundles tended to change through time when he compared the bundles of functions claimed by men of different lengths of tenure in the same kinds of administrative positions. Both these findings strongly suggest that there may be a rhythm of "content mix" comparable to that of business executives.

One final feature of the behavior of executives deserves notice because of its linkage with a popular claim that decentralization of management not only relieves top management of operating decision-making responsibility but also, by implication, makes the total job of top managers easier. It is easy to assume that there will be less work for top executives to handle if they shift some of their work to lower levels of management (incidentally also improving the morale and involvement of managers, according to the claims). Melman, in his penetrating study of the English automobile factory, demonstrated, first, that there was very considerable delegation of genuine authority down to and including the work level.[24] The major consequence of this was that top management turned its attention in greater and greater proportion to sales and the external problems of the firm. Management's total burden of work did not, in fact, become lessened by delegation—it simply shifted to focus on the external problems of the organization. Janowitz and Delaney pointed out this same phenomenon in a public bureaucracy where top management spent a significantly larger proportion of total time in public relations activities and maintaining contacts with external agencies, in contrast to lower-level officials, who really "ran" the organization day by day.[25]

This secular trend in the shifting functions of the top executive group that comes with modification of internal decision-making and authority is really another facet of the rhythm of

---

[23]A fact that I think equally characterized the work of foremen and rank-and-file workers. It takes real talent and determined effort at work simplification and job standardization to *remove* variation in "content mix" from a job.

[24]S. Melman, *Decision-Making and Productivity* (Oxford: Basil Blackwell, 1958).

[25]M. R. Janowitz and W. Delaney, "The Bureaucrat and the Public: A Study of Informational Perspectives," *Administrative Science Quarterly*, 2:141–162, September, 1957.

"content mix" in executive positions that takes place over long time spans. Haire, in his studies of the temporal, structural shifts in four firms in the balance between administrative and other employees, pointed to a changing condition of the organization that can also have its direct impact on the "content mix" of executive positions.[26]

[26]M. Haire, "Biological Models and Empirical Histories of the Growth of Organizations," in M. Haire (ed.), *Modern Organization Theory* (New York: John Wiley & Sons, Inc., 1959), Chapter 10.

---

It is desirable early in the game to recognize that conflict occurs, even among top executives. Furthermore, this conflict may be the consequence of non-rational considerations. The solutions to such conflicts may occupy a substantial proportion of the time involving executives.

One might very well ask: "Why doesn't the principal executive simply make the decision and tell the quarreling executives to shut up?" As Professor Stagner has indicated, this is indeed the most important basis on which executive conflicts are resolved. But he also points out that there are other means by which conflicts among executives are settled.

It is important to know that among the very top executives at the vice-presidential level will be found human beings. Even executives are subject to all the foibles and passions that characterize other people. The high offices they fill do not erase the very human qualities of the top executives.

---

## CONFLICT IN THE EXECUTIVE SUITE

*Ross Stagner**

How do major industrial corporations settle high-level conflicts on vital policy decisions? Is money the most important determining factor? Is there usually an internal power struggle, with one faction emerging on top? Are agreements reached through the force of winning personality and superior persuasive powers exerted in tête-à-tête conversations? Or, finally, if nothing else works, does the chief

officer simply move in and crack heads until he gets agreement?

All corporations establish policies about decision-making which are supposed to apply across the board to all departments and divisions; they are designated to minimize differences and help settle disputes. However, major disagreements between the heads of divisions can develop over the interpretation of corporate policy.

How do such disagreements, involving executives at the vice-presidential level and higher, get settled? . . .

In order to determine what execu-

*Reprinted by permission from Ross Stagner, "Conflict in the Executive Suite," *Transaction,* 3:39–41, January/February, 1966.

tives themselves believe to be the most important factors, I interviewed about fifty vice-presidents (or equivalents) in ten major corporations (employing from 2000 to 50,000 persons each) in the eastern United States.

The elements they considered most vital in such choices fell into three major categories which I call *dynamic, cognitive,* and *structural.*

■ *Dynamic* embraces motives and goals that the executives felt were best satisfied by choosing one solution over all others.

■ *Cognitive* refers to the way each executive saw or interpreted the situation.

■ *Structural* means the kind of corporation each belonged to, and its systems of communication and chains of command.

Let us examine each category more fully.

*Dynamic.* The dynamic factor most often cited by executives is, of course, *economics.* In practice, this factor is far more complicated than a simple computation of costs versus profits. One executive, who was just then in the process of spending a million dollars for a new warehouse, said quite frankly that he did not expect it to reduce materials handling costs significantly. "But," he added, "you don't want to live in a quonset hut *all* your life." Another, in a different industry, said of a particular decision, "Profitability had nothing to do with it."

On the other hand, in many companies cost figures were determined with considerable care before decisions were made. Amortization of new machinery, for example, might have to be accomplished within four years to be acceptable. This amounts to a 25 percent return on investment, which, to a layman like myself, seems pretty steep. However, the companies

setting this high figure apparently had a serious problem of rapid technological change. More stable industries showed figures as low as 6 percent for recouping costs, and this might give them more economic leeway in making decisions. . . .

It should be remembered that even under the best circumstances, costs—and profits—are often difficult to compute, and especially to project, accurately. They depend on such fluid concepts as estimated depreciation, allocation of overhead, anticipated volume (and sales), and the hope that no sudden or hidden fluctuations in labor or material costs will occur. Further, there is the old argument between short-term and long-term profit: for instance, the man who planned the new warehouse may well have felt that although no *immediate* return could be expected, it would save costs *in the long run.* In short, the economic yardstick contains so much rubber that it might well be stretched to cover many personal and power considerations, all claiming to be economic.

*Power* is a major dynamic factor. Certain high-level executives tried to maintain their own power or the power of their divisions with some open disregard for profit. For example, in one company it was proposed that three new installations be built, two in the USA and one in western Europe, each costing $5,000,-000. The heads of the English and the French subsidiaries got into a feud over which would get the European unit. After considerable negotiating, the executives in the American parent company decided to put *one each* in France and England. This kind of solution is, of course, simple if you have enough money.

In another case, two executives differed vigorously over who should get control of a new computer installation. Finally, two sections were set up, one to be involved in routine computer use, and one to concentrate on planning for future applications of automatic data processing. To no one's surprise, one section was put under Vice-President Smith and the second under Vice-President Jones.

Generally, executives would not talk about jealousy and personal feelings. However, one man did tell me that he protested the promotion of a colleague to executive vice-president; while he did not succeed in blocking the promotion, he did arrange to continue reporting directly to the president, not through the new executive vice-president. I was not surprised when informed later by others that he had expected to get the promotion himself.

Divisional heads will resent and often resist any change in central office policy which makes their units look less profitable. They become personally involved with the welfare of their divisions. One man told me: "Take Division A. They have increased their billings by 500 percent in four years, but have shown very little increase in profit. Naturally, they're critical of our pricing policy because they think it makes them look bad." Central office control over divisions may bring an intense struggle for power: "Conflicts are particularly acute with Division X, which was until recently an independent company and a competitor of what is now the larger portion of the merged corporation."

For the most part, however, overt "factionalism" in top management is muted. It is perhaps significant that in the only company in my survey where two vice-presidents were known leaders of competing factions, one was fired before the year was out.

This suggests that covert power struggles are permissible but open conflict is settled by eliminating the weaker. . . .

*Cognitive.* Decisions are also greatly affected by the fact that different people see and interpret the same things differently. These are the *cognitive factors.*

Depending on their jobs, and their personalities, executives will emphasize different elements in the same collection of information. Particularly, staff officials and operating executives have contrasting approaches. The most frequent example is the statement by production men that market researchers always overestimate demand for a proposed new product. Arguments may get to be so intense that some chief executives will even hire outside consultants in order to get an objective view of what is happening in their own companies.

Many executives I interviewed recognized the importance of learning to see things in a common frame of reference. Communication is especially easy if executives share a common background. One man commented, "When our chief executive was an engineer, I could communicate fairly easily. But our new chief is an economist, and I can't get through to him as well. I think a man will unconsciously listen more closely to someone with a background and experience like his own. Even though I've known this man for thirty years, he listens more to the officers who are economists."

Almost all respondents agreed that socializing with other executives outside of office hours improved communication and mutual understanding. As it happened, however, there was considerable friction in some firms where socializing was especially frequent. It may well be—as some people have said about husbands and wives —the real understanding may just make things worse.

In one company the opinion was expressed that "it takes a man about five years to become a member of the management team." In a way this corresponds with the statement by E. J. Cordiner, president of General Electric, who wrote not long ago that "The board of directors made me president of the company in 1950, but it took four years before the organization gave me the same honor." Decision making—and acceptance—do not occur automatically. There must be a process of learning, and of breaking old biases and ties, before new habits of perception and action are established.

*Structural.* Chief executives differ markedly in the style with which they participate in the communication process and dispute settlements.

Some will call in all of the executives affected and try to get an open expression of divergent points of view. Generally, the man using this technique is cautious to conceal his own preference until he has gotten all opinions. Otherwise there will be a rush to get on his bandwagon and the problem may suddenly be "solved unanimously."

Another pattern involves calling in the principals in a dispute separately, exploring the problem, and later announcing a decision. This seems to have the advantage of avoiding open controversy and facilitating face-saving devices. Nevertheless, it often upsets the "losing" executive, who implies that he has not gotten a fair deal.

Many firms use the technique of having the executive vice-president rule, leaving the president uninvolved so that appeals to him are still possible. If no one screams, the decision is allowed to stand.

My comments about the effectiveness of these techniques must be impressionistic. Nonetheless, it seemed clear that satisfaction was more widespread when more executives participated in a discussion of a problem. When the chief executive talked privately first with one, then with another vice-president, then laid down the decision, minimum satisfaction resulted. This impression may be in part caused by the vocal discontent of those whose solution was rejected. But it would, nonetheless, seem compatible with the findings of research on small groups—the man who has his preference argued down in open discussion before an "impartial" president will at least feel that he has taken part in the decision making process.

The most potent, and most often mentioned, influence toward accepting a non-preferred solution was the power of the chief executive. Regardless of widespread talk about decentralization and democratization, the boss is still the boss. "When we could not agree, we took it to the president and he settled it," was a typical report. Thus, the mode of conflict resolution by appeal to a higher authority is widely accepted in industry.

Centralized power also exerts influence indirectly. Controversies between divisions were occasionally played down because of concern for front office reaction. "It would not be good policy to embarrass another division," said one respondent. "It might have a bad effect on a man's chance for promotion."

The chief executive sometimes elects to function as a *mediator* rather than as an arbitrator. One vice-president described the chairman of the board as "a man who would bring two division managers into his office and ask them questions until they arrived at an acceptable conclusion." It is possible that some of the questions revealed the preference of the chairman and involved an implied coercion, but it was clear that no direct pressure was utilized.

Muzafer Sherif has laid great stress, in his recent writings, on the importance of a *superordinate* goal as the most important element to bring about cooperative behavior. Certainly the sharing of common goals—the profitability and viability of the corporation, for instance—favors compromise rather than last-ditch defense of preferred solutions. *Viability* means continued position, power, and prestige to the executive; *profitability* means more personal economic advantage. Most vice-presidents own stock in their corporation. They thus have an interest in corporate profits as well as in divisional power.

Another common type of pressure is similar to what we find in small-group discussion situations. One company reported a practice of having each vice-president bring in his budget for the following year, present it to the policy committee, and defend new expenditures. After all had done this, the requested sums were totaled and compared with estimated income. Since these never balanced, the executive vice-president would then ask everyone to go back and shave down his requests. Men who did not accept significant reductions were subjected to pressure from the group to conform. This did not always work; indeed, in some cases the group agreed that certain expansions were justified and necessary. However, the technique militated against "empire building."

Are vigorous, aggressive, persuasive individuals more likely to "win" controversies than less colorful persons? The consensus was negative. Two executives estimated that such personalities might be effective 20 per cent of the time, but in 80 per cent of the cases power of the division or status in the company would decide the issue. All respondents agreed that it would be rare for a persuasive man in a lower echelon to win out over a less fluent but higher placed objector.

Personalities do affect decision-making to some extent—but in a negative way. The individual who is unpleasant and irritating to his colleagues is cut out of the communications networks, becomes uninformed, and so loses effectiveness. An example: "One divisional manager is technically very competent, but he is blunt and often actually obnoxious. People try to schedule meetings *when they know he cannot attend.*" It is hardly surprising that this individual complained about poor communications in his company.

Over-all, what conclusions can we reach about decision-making among executives?

I cannot be sure without more evidence, but my strong impression is that the effectiveness of pressures to bring about an agreement in decision-making rank in the following order: first, the *power of the chief executive;* second, *shared goals* such as *profitability* of the company; third, *pressure from fellow executives* as a kind of group conformity process; and fourth, *persuasive pressure* by one individual upon another (not reinforced by status differences).

Although a few decisions were based on purely economic considerations, I found that the vast majority were determined in whole or part by these other factors. This would seem to give support to the picture of the corporation as a collection of pressure groups trying to arrive at compromise solutions.

# 9

# Specialists

We now turn our attention to another important group of organization officials who usually do highly technical things—the specialists.

Gordon, in his section on the professionalization of business leadership, Chapter 6, has shown how the dynamic, complex characteristics of modern, large-scale business lead to professional specialization. We want to examine that aspect of organization in detail in this chapter.

From the standpoint of their functional role in the organization, the problem of specialists is a critical one. We want to know first of all how far we can go in depending upon the expert. Second, we want to know how to fit the specialist into an organization. These are the basic questions the administrator asks about experts and specialists.

How reliable is the expert? That seems a stupid question on its face. If he is an expert, he knows his field better than a layman. The expert must of necessity be highly reliable in his own field. But it does not follow that he must be reliable in the total organization of which he is a functionary in one specialized field.

**INTRODUCTION**

Let us use Roethlisberger's question, asked in the first selection of this section: "What is that part of the situation which may be ignored or inaccurately stated by the limitations of a specialist logic, which must be understood and taken into account by the administrator if the control exercised is to be adequate?" Note that he mentions the limitations of a specialist logic.

*190*

That should give us a clew as to the nature of our problem. Is there something about specialization that makes difficult problems arise for the administrator?

The purpose of this chapter is *not* to prove that the specialist or expert in the organization creates problems for the organization, and hence, let us get rid of the specialists and organizations will be better off. That is manifestly impossible and undesirable.

The division of labor and functional specialization that pervade our society breed the specialist and expert. He is truly a product of the structure of our society, in the organizations that carry out the activities of our social life. We could not get rid of experts if we wanted to. They are built into the specialized niches and jobs that make up the fabric of society.

Thorstein Veblen suggested that the specialist was characterized by "trained incapacity." He not only is expert in one field, but by virtue of this very expertness, is inexpert or ignorant in other fields. The intensity of his training in one area means training in other areas is usually neglected. The intensity of concentration upon the problems of one area means that consideration of surrounding areas is often limited to the "all other things being equal" approach. To the administrator or executive who coordinates the work of different kinds of specialists, all other things are not equal. They must be considered as important variables in a total situation.

Suppose we agree that the specialist is likely to be characterized by "trained incapacity." Is there anything beyond that which is characterized of specialization? Yes, two important points: (1) regularizing, or, as the sociologists say, institutionalizing the distinctions between expert and nonexpert. The

selection by Moore and Tumin deals with this phenomenon; (2) the development of an ingrown view of things and the sense of limited responsibility, which is described by Merton in his selection.

These two typical facets of the behavior of experts constitute important additions to our knowledge of the function, position, and operating characteristics of experts.

Following the Merton selection, there is a summary of the limitations of the expert. These limitations all derive from the very intensity of training and concentration on limited problems that make the expert. These limitations are particularly significant for the executive and administrator to understand. They place the executive-expert relationship in proper perspective.

Let us now consider where the specialist fits into the organization. In the classical development of organization theory, the expert is viewed as occupying a staff position. We see this in pure form in certain kinds of military staffs. The expert is supposed to be a continuous consultant to the organizational doer-of-things, the line executive. Well and good—in theory. Unfortunately, this theoretical pure staff function is difficult to find in fact. Part of the reason for this is the expanded conception of *staff* that has grown up in the usage of this term. The concept of staff has been formulated in two broad senses.

First, a staff is composed of the personal, expert advisors of the executive or administrator. Staff in this sense means the specialized talents and brains that supplement, but do not supplant, the administrator or executive. This kind of staff is at the beck and call of the administrator. The only reason for such a staff existing is that the problems confronting the administrator are so technical, specialized, or complex, that one unaided man is incapable of making adequate decisions about them. In every respect, the administrator's or executive's office retains the full responsibility for action and decision. Neither action nor decision has its locus in the staff. Nothing is delegated to such a staff as an operating function. This kind of staff literally sits and waits to be consulted, or follows a long-range program of gathering and maintaining information that may conceivably be useful at some future time.

The second way in which we use the staff concept is in talking about certain activities of an organization that have become functionally distinct. Furthermore, these distinct functions are viewed as auxiliary to accomplishing the main purposes of the organization. The functionally distinct groups that carry out these specialized activities are usually designated as *staff groups.* Thus, the personnel department is often viewed as a staff department. The personnel operations are necessary to the functioning of the organization, but they are not the reason for the organization's existence. An automobile company is for making autos, not perfecting personnel practices.

It will be noted that a staff, in this second sense, will ordinarily do things in the organization. Action and decision that affect the organization are activities of such a staff. Administra-

tively, the structural problem relating to such a staff is to determine the area of staff activity and competence and to draw the boundaries between the staff's activities and the actions of other units of the organization. To return to our personnel example, where does the boundary fall between the personnel actions of the foreman (a line official) and the actions of the personnel department (a staff agency)?

These two structurally and functionally different conceptions of staff are clearly set forth in the sections dealing with the consultant, on the one hand, and Dalton's outstanding study of staff-line conflicts, on the other hand. In the short paper on the industrial consultant, we see the pure advisory role of the specialist. Dalton's study sets forth the problems of relationship between a staff that carries on functionally distinct activities and other units in the organization.

An even more detailed examination of staff-line relations is contained in the two studies concluding this chapter. The purchasing agent is an expert whose work is part of on-line operations but whose position is marginal to the departments using what he buys and the vendors selling the goods. Along with this kind of expert we will examine the way in which the industrial scientist is fitted into the organization as an expert.

In summary, this chapter on specialists deals with their limitations as contributors to the organization, and with the structural and functional relations of experts to an organization.

## THE ADMINISTRATOR'S OBJECTIVES AND STAFF SPECIALISTS

*Fritz J. Roethlisberger**

The problem [of directing an organization] is not a choice between two opposing alternatives—between "efficiency" on the one hand, and "morale" on the other; it is a problem of maintaining, under given conditions, a type and kind of equilibrium which will allow for maximum efficiency and collaboration. Now this is the problem with which any administrator is confronted every day. He is trying to use every method which will cut costs, increase output, improve quality, cut down waste and accidents, and make his department or division technically efficient. At the same time, he is trying to secure the cooperation of individuals in attaining these technical ends. Not only does he have to secure their willingness to contribute their services to these purposes, but also he must see to it that by giving their services to these ends they will obtain social satisfactions which make them continuously desirous of cooperating. Now this is not a static problem of black and white. It is a dynamic problem of equilibrium; it is a problem of knowing the technological limitations, the limitations of the human organization, and the particular objectives that can be accomplished under these limiting conditions. In part, it is a problem of sizing up a situation and knowing what needs to be done and know it should be done here and now in order

*Reprinted by permission of the publishers from Fritz J. Roethlisberger, *Management and Morale* (Cambridge, Mass.: Harvard University Press, 1941), pp. 156–159.

to attain the cooperative purpose. In part, it is the problem of a constant exercise of judgment in a situation of equilibrium, of assessing its nature, and of spotting possible sources of interference which may unduly disrupt the condition of balance.

To assist him in doing his job, the administrator has staff specialists or control agencies. Each of these specialists has specific functions. He selects from the total situation those aspects for which he is functionally responsible. Each is therefore evaluating the total situation in terms of the partial abstractions dictated by his specialty. Among these specialists in modern business must be included the personnel man. He too is responsible for certain functions: hiring, firing, placement, training, and welfare of employees. For each of these functions he too has specialized techniques: selection tests, job evaluation, employee-rating plans, conference techniques, pension plans, welfare plans.

Each of these specialists, control agencies, or functional staff groups can be arranged on a scale expressing the degree to which the application of its specialty involves cooperative phenomena. On one end would be the physicist, the chemist, the engineer. At the other end would be the rate setter, specialists engaged in job evaluation, measuring employee performance, and wage incentive systems. The latter groups are keenly aware of their relation to cooperative phenomena. They realize that their standards can be set only in cooperation with the different people and groups involved. At every turn the cooperation of employees, supervisors, and even top management must be sought. Only in this way can the desired results be achieved.

However, when the administrator has to conceive of his organization as a functioning whole and has to assess the contributions of each specialist group to it and make decisions in accordance with his size-up of the total situation, he is up against a concrete situation involving the interactions of people. And for this purpose what skills does he use? In terms of what data does he act? In what frame of reference is his thought set? If all the specialist skills are not the skill of the administrator, if all these partial controls of different specialist groups do not add up to the final control exercised by the administrator, then what is the administrative skill? What is that part of the situation which may be ignored or inaccurately stated by the limitations of a specialist logic, which must be understood and taken into account by the administrator if the control exercised is to be adequate? What, in short, does the administrator control?

It is the thesis of this book that "good judgment," "long experience," "common sense," "discretion," "a grain of salt," "being realistic," are not sufficient answers to these questions. Granted that some people exercise these skills successfully, how do they

do it? What is their point of view? How do they secure the cooperation of people? How does one conceive of a business organization as a functioning whole? What is the matrix from which can be made certain useful abstractions which ignore cooperative phenomena but which, when applied, have to be taken into account?

It would be absurd to imagine that the answers to these questions are simple; nor is there any claim that they have been completely, finally, or definitively answered in the preceding chapters. Rather, in each chapter an attempt has been made to suggest more fruitful ways of stating certain problems involving cooperative phenomena and more profitable avenues of inquiry. It has been the intention to provoke research, and not more talk, on problems relating to cooperative phenomena.

Therefore, in no chapter have there been given, let us say, ten specific rules for securing collaboration, or ten things which a rate setter needs to take into account in order to get the cooperation of employees. These omissions were not unconsciously made in order to avoid being specific and practical. Such rules and principles were deliberately omitted because in terms of the orientation which was suggested they are the height of impracticability. They substitute a verbal, ritualistic orientation for a diagnostic orientation to concrete situations. They try to solve a problem before they state it.

---

Roethlisberger has pointed out that the staff specialist is selected primarily to do a given task, not a general job. Each specialist is "evaluating the total situation in terms of the partial abstractions dictated by his specialty." The abstractions or points of view of the specialists can be arranged, says Roethlisberger, according to the degree to which they involve the human factor. A chemist can work with little or no reference to the human factor in the application of his results to the organization. The personnel specialist can work only in terms of the human factor in doing his job. In short, the "specialist logic" is characteristic of each specialty. But what about the administrator? Is the "administrator's logic" merely the sum of all the specialists' logic? The answer seems to be no.

I have purposely left the last two paragraphs of Roethlisberger's statement in this selection. He asserts here a general theme that runs through this book. It is worth repeating often.

The specialist is usually an intelligent and highly trained man. He is a *man,* not just a brain. His behavior in relation to other people is very human, often perverse, and sometimes irritating. Moore and Tumin point out for us how the specialist turns his special knowledge into an instrument for preserving his social status. He tries to keep the consumer of his special talents ignorant of his methods. In this way, his status is tied to his exclusive knowledge. Let us not forget that the consumer of the specialist's talents *in an organization* is the executive and the administrator!

Ignorance on the part of nonspecialists also provides a basis for limiting the competition for the specialist's job. This is a common phenomenon that we are likely to think of in terms of trade union activity. It is well to be reminded that this characteristic kind of behavior is much more widespread. By maximizing ignorance on the part of the nonspecialists, the specialist improves his job opportunities.

---

## SPECIALISTS AND THE IGNORANCE OF NONSPECIALISTS

*Wilbert E. Moore* and *Melvin M. Tumin**

The function of ignorance that is most obvious, particularly to the cynical, is its role in preserving social differentials. However, a purely cynical view is likely to overlook the extent to which the continuity of any social structure depends on differential access to knowledge in general, and, *a fortiori,* to specialized knowledge of various kinds. In many instances, of course, the counterpart of ignorance

*From "Some Social Functions of Ignorance," *American Sociological Review,* 14: 788–789 (Dec., 1949). Copyright by the American Sociological Society. Used by permission.

on the part of the outsider is *secrecy* on the part of the possessor of knowledge. Some of the outstanding examples of this general function of ignorance are summarized in the following paragraphs.

*The Specialist and the Consumer.* Ignorance on the part of a consumer of specialized services (for example, medical or legal advice) helps to preserve the privileged position of a specialized dispenser of these services. This is in some measure a by-product of the division of labor, and theoretically the same persons may occupy superordinate or subordinate positions as one or another service or skill is demanded. However, there are both theoretical and empirical bases for concluding that some persons whose skills are both scarce and functionally important will occupy a generalized superior position.[1] Although that status is not solely the product of the ignorance of others, in concrete instances it is partially maintained by such ignorance.

One evidence of the function of ignorance as a preservative of privileged position lies in the situation where the consumer acquires, through continuous exposure to the services of the specialist, a sense of his own ability to deal with his problems, and thus to dispense with the services of the specialist (for example, when we learn how to treat common colds, simple fevers, and bruises, and where we learn how to send stern notes concerning contractual obligations). Thus the range of situations in which the special services are believed to be required is altered from the original position.

On the other hand, the specialist commonly develops devices to protect himself against this sort of attrition. A common device is that of specialized and possibly esoteric vocabulary, or the use of instruments and techniques not intrinsically required for the solution but seemingly so.

However, the central point remains that real or presumed differential

knowledge and skills are inherently necessary to maintain mutually satisfactory relationships between specialist and consumer.

*The Specialist and the Potential Competitor.* Another facet to the preservation of the privileged position of the specialist is perhaps worthy of special mention. It was noted in the preceding paragraphs that the specialist's position may be endangered by "the patient becoming his own physician." A related danger is that the privileged position of the specialist will be so attractive that too many competitors will appear in the market. This is simply another, and more common, way of saying that ignorance operates to protect the specialist from potential competitors. Perhaps the commonest devices for guarding against this danger are "trade secrets" and their protection through the control by the specialists themselves of training and thus of access to the privileged positions. Examples in contemporary society are to be found in the limited access to certain professions and in the restriction of apprenticeship on the part of various craft unions. Although often justified as a means for protecting technical standards, these restrictions appear also to preserve a sharp distinction between the knowledge of specialists and the ignorance of aspirants. For the society as a whole the result may be a restriction in essential services, either directly through limitation of the number of specialists or indirectly through increasing costs so that other goods must be sacrificed by the consumer.

---

[1] Kingsley Davis and Wilbert E. Moore, "Some Principles of Stratification," *American Sociological Review,* 10: 242–249 (April, 1945).

## LIMITED PERSPECTIVE OF STAFF SPECIALISTS

*Robert K. Merton**

New applications of science to production by the engineer . . . do not merely affect the methods of production. They are inescapably social decisions affecting the routines and satisfactions of men at work on the machine and, in their larger reaches, shaping the very organization of the economy and society.

The central role of engineers as the General Staff of our productive systems only underscores the great importance of their social and political orientations; the social strata with which they identify themselves; the texture of group loyalties woven by their economic position and their occupational careers; the groups to whom they look for direction; the types of social effects of their work which they take into account—in short, only by exploring the entire range of their allegiances, perspectives, and concerns can engineers achieve that self-clarification of their social role which makes for fully responsible participation in society.

But to say that this poses sociological problems for "the" engineer is to make a reference so inclusive and vague as to mean little at all. The large and multifarious family of men called engineers have a far-flung kinship, but they also have much that marks sub-groups off, each from the others. There are military, civil, mechanical, chemical, electrical, and metallurgical engineers, and so on down through the hundreds of titles found among the members of national engineering societies. But whatever their specialty, so long as they are concerned with the design, construction, or operation of the equipments and processes of production, they are confronted with social and political implications of their position in society. . . .

### SPECIALIZATION

The intensified division of labor has become a splendid device for escaping social responsibilities. As professions subdivide, each group of specialists finds it increasingly possible to "pass the buck" for the social consequences of their work, on the assumption, it would seem, that in this complex transfer of responsibility there will be no hindmost for the devil to take. When appalled by resulting social dislocations, each specialist, secure in the knowledge that he has performed his task to the best of his ability, can readily disclaim responsibility for them. And, of course, no one group of specialists, the engineer any more than the others, alone initiates these consequences. Rather, within our economic and social structure each technological contribution meshes into a cumulative pattern of effects, some of which none has desired and all have brought about.

### THE PROFESSIONAL ETHIC

Deriving in part from the specialization of functions, engineers, not unlike scientists, come to be indoctrinated

*From "The Machine, The Worker, and The Engineer," *Science*, 105:79–81 (Jan. 24, 1947). Reprinted by permission.

with an ethical sense of limited responsibilities. The scientist, busy on his distinctive task of carving out new knowledge from the realm of ignorance, has long disclaimed responsibility for attending to the ways in which this knowledge was applied. (History creates its own symbols. It required an atomic bomb to shake many scientists loose from this tenaciously held doctrine.)

So, in many quarters, it has been held absurd that the engineer should be thought accountable for the social and psychological effects of technology, since it is perfectly clear that these do not come within his special province. After all, it is the engineer's "job"—note how effectively this defines the limits of one's role and, thereby, one's social responsibility—to improve processes of production, and it is "not his concern" to consider their ramified social effects. The occupational code focuses the attention of engineers upon the first links in the chain of consequences of technological innovation and diverts their attention, both as specialists and as citizens, from succeeding links in the chain as, for example, the consequences for wage levels and employment opportunities. "But we have to include consequences impartially"—this is John Dewey putting the issue in more general form. "It is willful folly to fasten upon some single end or consequence which is liked, and permit the view of that to blot from perception all other undesired and undesirable consequences."

## BUREAUCRATIC STATUS

The employment of large numbers of engineers and technologists in industrial bureaucracies further shapes their social perspectives. Knit into a bureaucratic apparatus, many engineers take their place as experts in a subaltern role with fixed spheres of competence and authority and with a severely delimited orientation toward the larger social system. In this status, they are rewarded for viewing themselves as technical auxiliaries. As such, it is not their function to consider the human and social consequences of introducing their efficient equipments and processes or to decide when and how they are to be introduced. These are matters for administrative and managerial concern. . . .

Max Weber and Thorstein Veblen, among others, have pointed to the danger that this occupational perspective, involving the rationalized abdication of social responsibility in favor of the administrator, may be transferred by engineers beyond the immediate economic enterprise. From this transference of outlook and the resulting trained incapacity for dealing with human affairs there develops a passive and dependent role for engineers and technologists in the realm of political organization, economic institutions, and social policy. The citizen-self threatens to become submerged in the occupational-self.

As technical specialists thus attend to "their own" limited tasks, the overall impact of technology upon the social structure becomes nobody's business through default.

---

Professor Merton has suggested some of the specialist's particular limitations and how they develop. The analysis is in terms of the engineer, but the generalizations apply to the entire class of people who are specialists or experts in any field. Merton shows how specialization, a professional ethics of limited responsibility, and a bureaucratic status combine to develop the specialist's indifference to the consequences of his work. Moore and Tumin tell us how and why the specialist posts the "keep out" sign around his specialty.

To the points already made by Roethlisberger, Moore and Tumin, and Merton about the expert and his limitations as a contributor to the organization, we can add several more that are developed by the late Harold Laski.[1]

Laski emphasizes the trained incapacity of the expert. This is expressed in four characteristic ways.

1. The expert sacrifices common-sense insights to the intensity of his experience in his special field. He fails to trust common sense in himself or others, because common sense is based on broad experience that goes beyond a field of special training. An example will illustrate the point. A large number of men in an army battalion are suddenly afflicted with diarrhea. The medics are in frantic search of a cause. The veterinary officer painstakingly investigates the meat served and also draws a blank in his searches. The battalion officers are baffled. Finally, a wise sergeant gives the common sense explanation: during a rainy period, the men of the battalion are permitted to enter the mess hall at the exit so that the waiting line can be placed around the outside aisle of the hall and more men can be put under cover from the rain while waiting. At the exit are the G.I. cans for washing mess tools. Ordinarily, a man leaving the mess hall stirs his mess tools in a

soapy solution, a chemical solution, and a clear-water rinse to clean them. The habit of cleaning the tools is so ingrained that the men do it automatically as they go past the can on their way into the mess hall on rainy days. They end up with GI soap, a highly laxative compound, on their mess tools. The medical men are so accustomed to looking for pathological causes that the common sense of the situation has completely escaped their consideration.

2. A second typical feature of the expert's trained incapacity is a marked aversion to new ideas. Experts in a field are usually the first to take up arms against innovation. Pasteur had a bitter struggle convincing some of his colleagues of the importance of his discoveries. Jenner fought a long and bitter battle with his medical contemporaries to gain the acceptance of vaccination. These examples could be multiplied. They seem to indicate clearly that broad innovations requiring modification of the systematic ideas of a field of specialization are likely to be met by active resistance from the specialists in that field.

3. Experts seldom see things in their entirety. This is the third feature of their trained incapacity. They take the subject of their specialty necessarily as the center of importance and relate everything to that. Roethlisberger touched this point when he called attention to the special logic of the expert, which includes a necessary emphasis on his field of specialization to the exclusion of other fields or objects of attention closely allied to it.

4. The fourth aspect of the expert's trained incapacity is the feeling of superiority that is likely to be associated with his position. This lack of humility often makes experts fail to see the obvious when it is in front of their noses. It is in this connection that the execu-

---

[1]Harold J. Laski, "The Limitations of the Expert," *Harper's Magazine*, 162:102–106 (Dec., 1930).

tive or administrator, if he keeps himself from being "taken in" by the expert's air of superiority, can often save
himself from bad advice.

Two more points should be made
about the expert's limitations. Experts
tend to have strong identification with
fellow specialists, so that the evidence
and arguments marshaled by nonexperts are viewed with suspicion. This
is the other side of the coin of the specialist's keeping the layman in the
dark. Experts not only try to keep the
layman ignorant, but also assume that
he is ignorant because he is a layman!

The final point about experts is that
they are likely to confuse the importance of their knowledge and facts
with the significance of what they
recommend be done with them. The
government bureau expert is likely to
view the legislator as standing in the
way of accomplishment. The president
of a company may be considered stub-
born because he fails to follow the

advice of his industrial relations spe
cialist. There are many examples o
this same point. The expert tends t
confuse knowledge with wisdom. Wis
dom is by no means the sole property
of specialists. The layman, the non
specialist, has his share of wisdom too

The importance of recognizing the
limitations of the expert lies in having
a proper perspective on the contribu
tions and difficulties of fitting the
specialist into an organization. I
should be emphasized again that thi
analysis is not meant to lead to the
conclusion that experts are "bad" o
should be avoided. They are necessary
and inherent in the complex division
of labor that characterizes our urban
industrial society. But society and the
organizations of society need both
expertness and wisdom, and cannot
be governed by expertness alone. We
can now turn to a consideration of the
place of experts in organizations.

---

You will recall that in the introduction to this chapter, we drew the distinction between the functionally distinct group performing auxiliary tasks
in the organization, as one kind of
staff, and the advisor, as another kind
of staff position. Let us look at this
advisory staff role.

In industry today, the advisory staff
role is found increasingly in the hands
of paid consultants. In almost every
area of business activity, it is possible
to hire a professional advisor. This is

an interesting commentary on the extent to which division of labor and
specialization have been carried out
in industry. It has reached the point
where some staff work is carried out
by people who are not even employees
of the firm!

The short statement from *Modern
Industry* lists what a staff consultant
can do, and sets forth four points
showing why the outside specialist is
able to accomplish what he does.

---

## THE MANAGEMENT CONSULTANT

*Modern Industry**

Management consultants have, in recent years, moved into respectability and general industrial acceptance.

For many years previously there were a number of incompetents—even some charlatans—in the field. Many able and conscientious consultants had rough going. Very few incompetents and charlatans are left. They were found out.

Hundreds of companies, big and small, have been discovering what consultants can do for them—and what they cannot tackle.

Here's what an expert consultant can offer the management man:

1. Time to study the client's problem, unhampered by routine.

2. Objectivity, unhampered by set habits of operational thinking, uninfluenced by personalities—the "outside point of view."

3. Experience gained from servicing many other clients—knowing, therefore, what is likely to work and what isn't.

4. Freedom from the suspicion of favoritism or prejudice; the ability to say what can't always be said from within.

If a consultant can deliver on all four of these points, he is likely to be worth his fee. (He doesn't work for peanuts.)

When is a consultant needed? First, when a tortuous, irritating company problem remains unsolved for years; second, when a specific project is to be undertaken, but permanent additions to the staff are unnecessary; and third, when the company needs physical or psychological face-lifting.

Most consulting firms supply specialized studies of individual problems as well as appraisals of the whole company. Some, generally smaller firms, deal in specialized studies only.

A consultant is occasionally hired only to analyze a problem and report what should be done about it. In other instances, management expects him to help carry out his recommendations.

Whatever use the consultant is put to, he should be carefully selected. Make sure his philosophy of business is at least similar to your own; that he won't antagonize or unnecessarily distract your staff; that his ability to produce has been proved in other companies. You'd be wise to query clients of two or three years ago. (Current clients are generally enthusiastic—before they have time to weigh long-range results.)

*Before* selecting the consultant: Make sure the job can't be done internally. *After* choosing the consultant: Tell your staff he's on his way, and why he's necessary.

When the consultant gets to work, he should receive sincere—not lip-service—cooperation. He should feel free to examine every record, every machine, every skeleton in the closet. He should be allowed to use any members of the organization—including the men who "can't" be spared.

In other words, avoid the "show me" attitude. Help him to succeed. After all the company has more to gain than he does.

*From *Modern Industry,* 20:6 (Dec. 15, 1950), p. 54. Used by permission.

Let us now turn our attention to the relationships between the functionally specialized staff, composed of experts, and the line organization. In an excellent study by Dalton, reported in the following paper, we see this relationship laid bare in its various dimensions.

Much of our academic thinking about staff-line relations is wholly unrealistic. It flows from a formal analysis rather than from the actual structure of relationships. Dalton decided actually to take a look at how staff and line got together or failed to do so. He studied the situation in three industrial plants. This is his report and analysis of the situations he encountered.

Note how the theoretical points made in the preceding sections of this chapter are illuminated in this empirical study. Note also, the additional general points made. These are summarized at the end of the study.

## STAFF AND LINE RELATIONSHIPS—A STUDY OF CONFLICTS

*Melville Dalton**

Industrial staff organizations are relatively new. Their appearance is a response to many complex interrelated forces, such as economic competition, scientific advance, industrial expansion, growth of the labor movement, and so on. During the last four or five decades these rapid changes and resulting unstable conditions have caused top industrial officials more and more to call in "specialists" to aid them toward the goal of greater production and efficiency. These specialists are of many kinds including chemists, statisticians, public and industrial relations officers, personnel officers, accountants, and a great variety of engineers, such as mechanical, draughting, electrical, chemical, fuel, lubricating, and industrial engineers. In industry these individuals are usually known as "staff people." Their functions, again, for the most part are to increase and apply their specialized knowledge in problem areas, and to advise those officers who make up the "line" organization and have authority[1] over production processes.

This theoretically satisfying industrial structure of specialized experts advising busy administrators has in a number of significant cases failed to function as expected. The assumptions that (a) the staff specialists would be reasonably content to function with-

---

[1]*Inside* their particular staff organization, staff officers also may have authority over their subordinates, but not over production personnel.

out a measure of formal authority[2] over production, and that (b) their suggestions regarding improvement of processes and techniques for control over personnel and production would be welcomed by line officers and be applied, require closer examination. In practice there is often much conflict between industrial staff and line organizations and in varying degrees the members of these organizations oppose each other.[3]

The aim of this paper is, therefore, to present and analyze data dealing with staff-line tensions.

Data were drawn from three industrial plants[4] in which the writer had been either a participating member of one or both of the groups or was inti-

mate with reliable informants among the officers who were.

Approached sociologically, relations among members of management in the plants could be viewed as a general conflict system caused and perpetuated chiefly by (1) power struggles in the organization stemming in the main from competition among departments to maintain low operating costs; (2) drives by numerous members to increase their status in the hierarchy; (3) conflict between union and management; and (4) the staff-line friction which is the subject of this paper.[5] This milieu of tensions was not only unaccounted for by the blue-print organizations of the plants, but was often contradictory to, and even destructive of, the organizations' formal aims. All members of management, especially in the middle and lower ranks,[6] were caught up in this

---

[2]To the extent that staff officers influence line policy they do, of course, have a certain *informal* authority.

[3]Some social scientists have noted the possibility of staff-line friction, and industrial executives themselves have expressed strong feelings on the matter. See Burleigh B. Gardner, *Human Relations in Industry* (Homewood, Ill.: Richard D. Irwin, Inc., 1945); and M. E. Dimock, *The Executive in Action* (New York: Harper & Row, Publishers, 1945). Dimock believes that we are too "staff-minded" and that we should become more "executive-minded" (p. 241). A high line officer in a large corporation denounced staff organizations to the writer on the ground of their "costing more than they're worth," and that "they stir up too much trouble and are too theoretical." He felt that their function (excepting that of accountants, chemists, and "a few mechanical engineers") could be better carried out by replacing them with "highly-select front-line foremen [the lowest placed line officers] who are really the backbone of management and pay them ten or twelve thousand dollars a year."

[4]These plants were in related industries and ranged in size from 4,500 to 20,000 employees, with the managerial groups numbering from 200 to nearly 1,000. Details concerning the plants and their location are confidential. Methodological details concern-

ing an intensive study embracing staff-line relations and several other areas of behavior in one of the plants are given in the writer's unpublished doctoral thesis, "A Study of Informal Organization Among the Managers of an Industrial Plant" (Department of Sociology, University of Chicago, 1949).

[5]Because these conflict areas were interrelated and continually shifting and reorganizing, discussion of any one of them separately—as in the case of staff-line relations—will, of course, be unrealistic to some extent.

[6]From bottom to top, the line hierarchy consisted of the following strata of officers: (1) first-line foremen, who were directly in charge of production workmen; (2) general foremen; (3) departmental superintendents; (4) divisional superintendents; (5) assistant plant manager; (6) plant manager. In the preceding strata there were often "assistants," such as "assistant general foreman," "assistant superintendent," etc., in which case the total strata of the line hierarchy could be almost double that indicated here.

In the staff organizations the order from bottom to top was: (1) supervisor

conflict system. Even though they might wish to escape, the obligation of at least appearing to carry out formal functions compelled individuals to take sides in order to protect themselves against the aggressions of others. And the intensity of the conflict was aggravated by the fact that it was formally unacceptable and had to be hidden.

For analytical convenience, staff-line friction may be examined apart from the reciprocal effects of the general conflict system. Regarded in this way, the data indicated that three conditions were basic to staff-line struggles: (1) the conspicuous ambition and "individualistic" behavior among staff officers; (2) the complication arising from staff efforts to justify its existence and get acceptance of its contributions; and, related to point two, (3) the fact that incumbency of the higher staff offices was dependent on line approval. The significance of these conditions will be discussed in order.

## MOBILE BEHAVIOR OF STAFF PERSONNEL

As a group, staff personnel in the three plants were markedly ambitious, restless, and individualistic. There was much concern to win rapid promotion, to make the "right impressions," and to receive individual recognition.

---

(equivalent to the first-line foreman); (2) general supervisor (equivalent to the general foreman); (3) staff head—sometimes "superintendent" (equivalent to departmental superintendent in the line organization). Occasionally there were strata of assistant supervisors and assistant staff heads.

The term "upper line" will refer to all strata above the departmental superintendent. "Middle line" will include the depart-

Data showed that the desire among staff members for personal distinctions often over-rode their sentiments of group consciousness and caused intra-staff tensions.[7]

The relatively high turnover of staff personnel[8] quite possibly reflected the dissatisfactions and frustrations of members over inability to achieve the distinction and status they hoped for. Several factors appeared to be of importance in this restlessness of staff personnel. Among these were age and social differences between line and

---

mental superintendent and assistants. "Lower line" will refer to general and first-line foremen and their assistants.

"Lower," "middle," and "upper" staff will refer respectively to the supervisor, general supervisor, and staff head.

"Top management" will refer to the upper line and the few staff heads with whom upper line officers were especially intimate on matters of policy.

[7] In a typical case in one of the plants, a young staff officer developed a plan for increasing the life of certain equipment in the plant. He carried the plan directly to the superintendent of the department in which he hoped to introduce it, but was rebuffed by the superintendent who privately acknowledged the merit of the scheme but resented the staff officer's "trying to lord it over" him. The staff organization condemned the behavior of its member and felt that he should have allowed the plan to appear as a contribution of the staff group rather than as one of its members. The officer himself declared that "By G— it's my idea and I want credit. There's not a damn one of you guys [the staff group] that wouldn't make the same squawk if you were in my place!"

[8] During the period between 1944 and 1950, turnover of staff personnel in these plants was between two and four times as great as that of line personnel. This grouping included all the nonmanagerial members of staff and line and all the hourly-paid (nonsalaried) members of management (about 60 assistant first-line foremen). Turnover was determined by dividing the average number of employees for a given year (in line or staff) into the accessions or separations, whichever was the smaller.

staff officers, structural differences in the hierarchy of the two groups, and the staff group's lack of authority over production.

With respect to age, the staff officers were significantly younger than line officers.[9] This would account to some extent for their restlessness. Being presumably less well-established in life in terms of material accumulations, occupational status, and security, while having greater expectations (see below), and more energy, as well as more life ahead in which to make new starts elsewhere if necessary, the staff groups were understandably more dynamic and driving.[10]

---

[9]Complete age data were available in one of the larger plants. Here the 36 staff heads, staff specialists, and assistants had a mean age of 42.9 years. This value would have been less than 40 years, except for the inclusion of several older former line officers, but even a mean of 42.9 years was significantly less (C.R. 2.8) than that of the 35 line superintendents in the plant who had a mean age of 48.7 years. The age difference was even more significant when the staff heads were compared with the 61 general foremen who had a mean age of 50.0 years. And between the 93 salaried first-line foremen (mean age of 48.5 years) and the 270 salaried nonsupervisory staff personnel (mean age of 31.0 years) the difference was still greater.

[10]One might also hypothesize that the drive of staff officers was reflected in the fact that the staff heads and specialists gained their positions (those held when the data were collected) in less time than did members of the line groups. For example, the 36 staff officers discussed above had spent a median of 10 years attaining their positions, as against a median of 11 years for the first-line foremen, 17 years for the general foremen, and 19 years for the superintendents. But one must consider that some of the staff groups were relatively new (13–15 years old) and had grown rapidly, which probably accelerated their rate of promotions as compared with that of the older line organization.

Age-conflict[11] was also significant in staff-line antagonisms. The incident just noted of the young staff officer seeking to get direct acceptance by the line of his contribution failed in part—judging from the strong sentiments later expressed of an age antipathy. The older line officers disliked receiving what they regarded as instruction from men so much younger than themselves, and staff personnel clearly were conscious of this attitude among line officers.[12] In staff-line meetings staff officers frequently had their ideas slighted or even treated with amusement by line incumbents. Whether such treatment was warranted or not, the effects were disillusioning to the younger, less experienced staff officers. Often selected by the organization because of their outstanding academic records, they had entered industry with the belief that they had much to contribute, and that their efforts would win early recognition and rapid advancement. Certainly they had no thought that their contributions would be in any degree un-

---

[11]E. A. Ross in *Principles of Sociology* (New York: D. Appleton-Century-Crofts, Inc., 1938), pp. 238–48, has pertinent comments on this.

[12]Explaining the relatively few cases in which his staff had succeeded in "selling ideas" to the line, an assistant staff head remarked: "We're always in hot water with these old guys on the line. You can't tell them a damn thing. They're bull-headed as hell! Most of the time we offer a suggestion it's either laughed at or not considered at all. The same idea in the mouth of some old codger on the line'd get a round of applause. They treat us like kids."

Line officers in these plants often referred to staff personnel (especially members of the auditing, production planning, industrial engineering, and industrial relation staffs) as "college punks," "slide-rules," "crackpots," "pretty boys," and "chair-warmers."

welcome. This naiveté[13] was apparently due to lack of earlier first-hand experience in industry (or acquaintance with those who had such experience), and to omission of realistic instruction in the social sciences from their academic training. The unsophisticated staff officer's initial contacts with the shifting, covert, expedient arrangements between members of staff and line usually gave him a severe shock. He had entered industry prepared to engage in logical, well-formulated relations with members of the managerial hierarchy, and to carry out precise, methodical functions for which his training had equipped him. Now he learned that (1) his freedom to function was snared in a web of informal commitments; (2) his academic specialty (on which he leaned for support in his new position) was often not relevant[14] for carrying out his formal assignments; and that (3) the important thing to do was to learn who the informally powerful line offi-

---

[13]John Mills, a research engineer retired from the telephone industry, has noted the worldly naiveté of research engineers in that field in his *The Engineer in Society* (Princeton, N. J.: D. Van Nostrand Co., Inc., 1946).

[14]Among the staff heads and assistants referred to earlier, only 50 per cent of those with college training (32 of the 36 officers) were occupied with duties related to their specialized training. For example, the head of the industrial relation staff had a B.S. degree in aeronautical engineering; his assistant had a similar degree in chemical engineering. Considering that staff officers are assumed to be specialists trained to aid and advise management in a particular function, the condition presented here raises a question as to what the criteria of selection were. (As will be shown in a separate paper, the answer appeared to be that personal—as well as impersonal—criteria were used.) Among the college-trained of 190 line officers in the same plant, the gap between training and function was still greater, with 61 per cent in positions not related to the specialized part of their college work.

cers were and what ideas they would welcome which at the same time would be acceptable to his superiors.

Usually the staff officer's reaction to these conditions is to look elsewhere for a job or make an accommodation in the direction of protecting himself and finding a niche where he can make his existence in the plant tolerable and safe. If he chooses the latter course, he is likely to be less concerned with creative effort for his employer than with attempts to develop reliable social relations that will aid his personal advancement. The staff officer's recourse to this behavior and his use of other status-increasing devices will be discussed below in another connection.

The formal structure, or hierarchy of statuses, of the two larger plants from which data were drawn, offered a frustration to the ambitious staff officer. That is, in these plants the strata, or levels of authority, in the staff organizations ranged from three to five as against from five to ten in the line organization. Consequently there were fewer possible positions for exercise of authority into which staff personnel could move. This condition may have been an irritant to expansion among the staff groups. Unable to move vertically to the degree possible in the line organization, the ambitious staff officer could enlarge his area of authority in a given position only by lateral expansion—by increasing his personnel. Whether or not aspiring staff incumbents revolted against the relatively low hierarchy through which they could move, the fact remains that (1) they appeared eager to increase the number of personnel under their authority,[15] (2) the personnel of staff groups *did* increase

---

[15]This was suggested by unnecessary references among some staff officers to "the

disproportionately to those of the line,[16] and (3) there was a trend of personnel movement from staff to line,[17] rather than the reverse, presumably (reflecting the drive and ambition of staff members) because there were more positions of authority, as well as more authority to be exercised, more prestige, and usually more income in the line.

Behavior in the plants indicated that line and staff personnel belonged to different social status groups and that line and staff antipathies were at least in part related to these social distinctions. For example, with respect to the item of formal education, the staff group stood on a higher level than members of the line. In the plant from which the age data were taken, the 36 staff officers had a mean of 14.6 years of schooling as compared with 13.1 years for 35 line superintendents, 11.2 years for 60 general foremen, and 10.5 years for 93 first-line foremen. The difference between the mean education of the staff group and that of the highest line group (14.6-13.1) was statistically significant at better than the one per cent level. The 270 non-supervisory staff personnel had a mean of 13.1 years—the same as that of the line superintendents. Consciousness of this difference

---

number of men under me," and by their somewhat fanciful excuses for increase of personnel. These excuses included statements of needing more personnel to (1) carry on research, (2) control new processes, (3) keep records and reports up-to-date. These statements often did not square with (1) the excessive concern among staff people about their "privileges" (such as arriving on the job late, leaving early, leaving the plant for long periods during working hours, having a radio in the office during the World Series, etc.), (2) the great amount of time (relative to that of line officers) spent by lower staff personnel in social activities on the job, and (3) the constantly recurring (but not always provoked) claims among staff personnel of their functional importance for production. The duties of middle and lower staff personnel allowed them sufficient time to argue a great deal over their respective functions (as well as many irrelevant topics) and to challenge the relative merit of one another's contributions or "ideas." In some of the staffs these discussions could go on intermittently for hours and develop into highly theoretical jousts and wit battles. Where staff people regarded such behavior as a privilege of their status, line officers considered it as a threat to themselves. This lax control (in terms of line discipline) was in part a tacit reward from staff heads to their subordinates. The reward was expected because staff superiors (especially in the industrial relations, industrial engineering, and planning staffs) often overlooked and/or perverted the work of subordinates (which was resented) in response to pressures from the line. This behavior will be noted later.

[16]In one of the larger plants, where exact data were available, the total staff personnel had by 1945 exceeded that of the line. At that time the staff included 400 members as against 317 line personnel composed of managerial officers and their clerical workers, but not production workers. By 1948, the staff had increased to 517 as compared with 387 for the line (during this period *total* plant personnel, declined over 400). The staff had grown from 20.8 per cent larger than the line in 1945, to 33.6 per cent larger in 1948, and had itself increased by 29.3 per cent during the three years as against a growth in the line of 22.1 per cent. Assuming the conditions essential for use of probability theory, the increase in staff personnel could have resulted from chance about 1.5 times in a hundred. Possibly post-war and other factors of social change were also at work but, if so, their force was not readily assessable.

[17]This movement from staff to line can disorganize the formal managerial structure, especially when (1) the transferring staff personnel have had little or no supervisory experience in the staff but have an academic background which causes them to regard human beings as mechanisms that will respond as expected; (2) older, experienced line officers have hoped—for years in some cases—to occupy the newly vacated (or created) positions.

probably contributed to a feeling of superiority among staff members, while the sentiment of line officers toward staff personnel was reflected in the name-calling noted earlier.

Staff members were also much concerned about their dress, a daily shave, and a weekly hair-cut. On the other hand, line officers, especially below the level of departmental superintendent, were relatively indifferent to such matters. Usually they were in such intimate contact with production processes that dirt and grime prevented the concern with meticulous dress shown by staff members. The latter also used better English in speaking and in writing reports, and were more suave and poised in social intercourse. These factors, and the recreational preferences of staff officers for night clubs and "hot parties," assisted in raising a barrier between them and most line officers.

The social antipathies of the two groups and the status concern of staff officers were indicated by the behavior of each toward the established practice of dining together in the cafeterias reserved for management in the two larger plants. Theoretically, all managerial officers upward from the level of general foremen in the line, and general supervisors in the staff, were eligible to eat in these cafeterias. However, in practice the mere taking of one of these offices did not automatically assure the incumbent the privilege of eating in the cafeteria. One had first to be invited to "join the association." Staff officers were very eager to "get in" and did considerable fantasying on the impressions, with respect to dress and behavior, that were believed essential for an invitation. One such staff officer, a cost supervisor, dropped the following remarks:

There seems to be a committee that passes on you. I've had my application in for three years, but no soap. Harry [his superior] had his in for over three years before he made it. You have to have something, because if a man who's in moves up to another position the man who replaces him doesn't get it because of the position—and he might not get it at all. I think I'm about due.

Many line officers who were officially members of the association avoided the cafeteria, however, and had to be *ordered* by the assistant plant manager to attend. One of these officers made the following statement, which expressed more pointedly the many similar spontaneous utterances of resentment and dislike made by other line officers:

There's a lot of good discussion in the cafeteria. I'd like to get in on more of it but I don't like to go there—sometimes I have to go. Most of the white collar people [staff officers] that eat there are stuck-up. I've been introduced three times to Svendsen [engineer], yet when I meet him he pretends to not even know me. When he meets me on the street he always manages to be looking someplace else. G— d— such people as that! They don't go in the cafeteria to eat and relax while they talk over their problems. They go in there to look around and see how somebody is dressed or to talk over the hot party they had last night. Well, that kind of damn stuff don't go with me. I haven't any time to put on airs and make out I'm something that I'm not.

## COMPLICATIONS OF STAFF NEED TO PROVE ITS WORTH

To the thinking of many line officers, the staff functioned as an agent on trial rather than as a managerial division that might be of equal importance with the line organization in achieving production goals. Staff members were very conscious of this sentiment toward them and of their need to prove themselves. They strained to develop new techniques and to get them accepted by the line. But in doing this they frequently became impatient, and gave already suspicious line officers the impression of reaching for authority over production.

Since the line officer regards his authority over production as something sacred, and resents the implication that after many years in the line he needs the guidance of a newcomer who lacks such experience, an obstacle to staff-line cooperation develops the moment this sore spot is touched. On the other hand, the staff officer's ideology of his function leads him to precipitate a power struggle with the line organization. By and large he considers himself as an agent of top management. He feels bound to contribute something significant in the form of research or ideas helpful to management. By virtue of his greater education and intimacy with the latest theories of production, he regards himself as a managerial consultant and an expert, and feels that he must be, or appear to be, almost infallible once he has committed himself to top management on some point. With this orientation, he is usually disposed to approach middle and lower line with an attitude of condescension that often reveals itself in the heat of discussion. Consequently, many staff officers involve themselves in trouble and report their failures as due to "ignorance" and "bull-headedness" among these line officers.

On this point, relations between staff and line in all three of the plants

were further irritated by a rift inside the line organization. First-line foremen were inclined to feel that top management had brought in the production planning, industrial relations, and industrial engineering staffs as clubs with which to control the lower line. Hence they frequently regarded the projects of staff personnel as manipulative devices, and reacted by cooperating with production workers and/or general foremen (whichever course was the more expedient) in order to defeat insistent and uncompromising members of the staff. Also, on occasion (see below), the lower line could cooperate evasively with lower staff personnel who were in trouble with staff superiors.

## EFFECT OF LINE AUTHORITY OVER STAFF PROMOTION

The fact that entry to the higher staff offices in the three plants was dependent on approval of top line officers had a profound effect on the behavior of staff personnel. Every member of the staff knew that if he aspired to higher office he must make a record for himself, a good part of which would be a reputation among upper line officers of ability to "understand" their informal problems without being told. This knowledge worked in varying degrees to pervert the theory of staff-line relations. Ideally the two organizations cooperate to improve existing methods of output, to introduce new methods, to plan the work, and to solve problems of production and the scheduling of orders that might arise. But when the line offers resistance to the findings and recommendations of the staff, the latter is reduced to evasive practices of getting some degree of acceptance of its programs, and at the same time of convincing top management that "good relations" exist with officers down the line. This necessity becomes even more acute when the staff officer aspires (for some of the reasons given above) to move over to the line organization, for then he must convince powerful line officers that he is worthy. In building a convincing record, however, he may compromise with line demands and bring charges from his staff colleagues that he is "selling out," so that after moving into the line organization he will then have to live with enemies he made in the staff. In any case, the need among staff incumbents of pleasing line officers in order to perfect their careers called for accommodation in three major areas:[18] (1) the observance of staff rules, (2) the introduction of new techniques, and (3) the use of appropriations for staff research and experiment.

With respect to point one, staff personnel, particularly in the middle and lower levels, carried on expedient relations with the line that daily evaded formal rules. Even those officers most devoted to rules found that, in order not to arouse enmity in the line on a scale sufficient to be communicated *up* the line, compromising devices were frequently helpful and sometimes almost unavoidable both for organizational and career aims. The usual practice was to tolerate minor breaking of staff rules by line personnel, or even to cooperate with the line in evading rules,[19] and in ex-

change lay a claim on the line for co-operation on critical issues. In some cases line aid was enlisted to conceal lower staff blunders from the upper staff and the upper line.[20]

Concerning point two, while the staff organizations gave much time to developing new techniques, they were simultaneously thinking about how

the chemical staff) twice daily checked these properties of the solution and submitted reports showing that all points met the laboratory ideal. Actually, the solution was usually nearly triple the standard strength, the temperature was about 10 degrees Centigrade higher than standard, and the rate of flow was in excess of double the standard. There are, of course, varying discrepancies between laboratory theory and plant practice, but the condition described here resulted from production pressures that forced line foremen into behavior upsetting the conditions expected by chemical theory. The chemists were sympathetic with the hard-pressed foremen, who compensated by (1) notifying the chemists (rather than their superior, the chief chemist) if anything "went wrong" for which the laboratory was responsible and thus sparing them criticism; and by (2) cooperating with the chemists to reduce the number of analyses which the chemists would ordinarily have to make.

[20]Failure of middle and lower staff personnel to "cooperate" with line officers might cause the latter to "stand pat" in observance of line rules at a time when the pressures of a dynamic situation would make the former eager to welcome line cooperation in rulebreaking. For example, a staff officer was confronted with the combined effect of (1) a delay in production on the line that was due to an indefensible staff error; (2) pressure on the line superintendent—with whom he was working—to hurry a special order; and (3) the presence in his force of new inexperienced staff personnel who were (a) irritating to line officers, and (b) by their inexperience constituted an invitation to line aggression. Without aid from the line superintendent (which could have been withheld by observance of formal rules) in covering up the staff error and in controlling line personnel, the staff officer might have put himself in permanent disfavor with all his superiors.

---

[18]The relative importance of one or more of these areas would vary with the function of a given staff.

[19]In a processing department in one of the plants the chemical solution in a series of vats was supposed to have a specific strength and temperature, and a fixed rate of inflow and outflow. Chemists (members of

their plans would be received by the line. They knew from experience that middle and lower line officers could always give a "black eye" to staff contributions by deliberate malpractices. Repeatedly top management had approved, and incorporated, staff proposals that had been verbally accepted down the line. Often the latter officers had privately opposed the changes, but had feared that saying so would incur the resentment of powerful superiors who could informally hurt them. Later they would seek to discredit the change by deliberate malpractice and hope to bring a return to the former arrangement. For this reason there was a tendency for staff members to withhold improved production schemes or other plans when they knew that an attempt to introduce them might fail or even bring personal disrepute.

Line officers fear staff innovations for a number of reasons. In view of their longer experience, presumably intimate knowledge of the work, and their greater remuneration they fear[21] being "shown up" before their line superiors for not having thought of the processual refinements themselves. They fear that changes in methods may bring personnel changes which will threaten the break-up of cliques and existing informal arrangements and quite possibly reduce their area of authority. Finally, changes in techniques may expose forbidden practices and departmental inefficiency. In some cases these fears have stimulated

line officers to compromise staff men to the point where the latter will agree to postpone the initiation of new practices for specific periods.

In one such case an assistant staff head agreed with a line superintendent to delay the application of a bonus plan for nearly three months so that the superintendent could live up to the expedient agreement he had made earlier with his grievance committeeman to avoid a "wildcat" strike by a group of production workmen.[22] The lower engineers who had devised the plan were suspicious of the formal reasons given to them for withholding it, so the assistant staff head prevented them (by means of "busy work") from attending staff-line meetings lest they inadvertently reveal to top management that the plan was ready.

The third area of staff-line accommodations growing out of authority relations revolved around staff use of funds granted it by top management. Middle and lower line charged that staff research and experimentation were little more than "money wasted on blunders," and that various departments of the line could have "accomplished much more with less money." According to staff officers, those of their plans that failed usually did so because line personnel "sabotaged" them and refused to "cooperate." Specific costs of "crack-pot experimentation" in certain staff groups were pointed to by line officers. Whatever the truth of the charges and counter-charges, evidence indicated (confidants in both groups supported this) that pressures from the line or-

---

[21]Though there was little evidence that top management expected line officers to refine production techniques, the fear of such an expectation existed nevertheless. As noted earlier, however, some of the top executives *were* thinking that development of a "higher type" of first-line foreman might enable most of the staff groups to be eliminated.

[22]This case indicates the overlapping of conflict areas referred to earlier. A later paper will deal with the area of informal union-management relations.

ganization (below the top level) forced some of the staff groups to "kick over" parts of the funds appropriated for staff use[23] by top management. These compromises were of course hidden from top management, but the relations described were carried on to such an extent that by means of them—and line pressures for manipulation of accounts in the presumably impersonal auditing departments—certain line officers were able to show impressively low operating costs and thus win favor[24] with top management that would relieve pressures and be useful in personal advancement. In their turn, the staff officers involved would receive more "cooperation" from the line and/or recommendation for transfer to the line. The data indicated that in a few such cases men from accounting and auditing staffs were given general foremanships (without previous line experience) as a reward for their understanding behavior.

### SUMMARY

Research in three industrial plants showed conflict between the managerial staff and line groups that hindered the attainment of organizational goals. Privately expressed attitudes among some of the higher line executives revealed their hope that greater control of staff groups could be achieved, or that the groups might

be eliminated and their functions taken over in great part by carefully selected and highly remunerated lower-line officers. On their side, staff members wanted more recognition and a greater voice in control of the plants.

All of the various functioning groups of the plants were caught up in a general conflict system; but apart from the effects of involvement in this complex, the struggles between line and staff organizations were attributable mainly to (1) functional differences between the two groups; (2) differentials in the ages, formal education, potential occupational ceilings, and status group affiliations of members of the two groups (the staff officers being younger, having more education but lower occupational potential, and forming a prestige-oriented group with distinctive dress and recreational tastes); (3) need of the staff groups to justify their existence; (4) fear in the line that staff bodies by their expansion, and well-financed research activities, would undermine line authority; and (5) the fact that aspirants to higher staff offices could gain promotion only through approval of influential line executives.

*If* further research should prove that staff-line behavior of the character presented here is widespread in industry, and *if* top management should realize how such behavior affects its cost and production goals—and be concerned to improve the condition—then remedial measures could be considered. For example, a corrective approach might move in the direction of (1) creating a separate body[25] whose sole function would be

---

[23]In two of the plants a somewhat similar relation, rising from different causes, existed *inside* the line organization with the *operating* branch of the line successfully applying pressures for a share in funds assigned to the *maintenance* division of the line.

[24]The reader must appreciate the fact that constant demands are made by top management to maintain low operating costs.

[25]This body, or "Board of Coordination," would be empowered to enforce its decisions. Membership would consist of staff and

the coordination of staff and line efforts; (2) increasing the gradations of awards and promotions in staff organizations (without increase of staff personnel); (3) granting of more nearly equal pay to staff officers, but with increased responsibility (without authority over line processes or personnel) for the practical working of

line men who had had wide experience in the plant over a period of years. The Board would (a) serve as an arbiter between staff and line; (b) review, screen, and approve individual recommendations submitted; and (c) evaluate contributions after a trial period. Such a body would incidentally be another high status goal for seasoned, capable, and ambitious officers who too often are trapped by the converging walls of the pyramidal hierarchy.

their projects; (4) requiring that staff personnel have a minimum supervisory experience and have shared repeatedly in successful collaborative staff-line projects before transferring to the line; (5) steps by top management to remove the fear of veiled personal reprisal felt by officers in most levels of both staff and line hierarchies (this fear—rising from a disbelief in the possibility of bureaucratic impersonality—is probably the greatest obstacle to communicate inside the ranks of management); (6) more emphasis in colleges and universities on realistic instruction in the social sciences for students preparing for industrial careers.

---

There are at least two classes of organizational specialists whose human relations problems differ significantly from each other. The first group is composed of those specialists whose work is essential in the daily operations of the business firm. This essentiality makes specialists of this kind an integral part of the work-flow. But the characteristics of the specialization make it marginal to the activities that it links. An important example of this kind of specialization is that of the purchasing agent.

The second type of specialist may perform an essential function but it is usually one not part of the daily work-flow. Members of the company legal department, the comptrollers division, and the research division are specialists in this category. We will examine the scientists in industry as a representative of this kind of specialist.

The essential human-relations problem of the first type of specialist is to

overcome the sense of marginality associated with this position. Typically, the people whose activities are linked by someone like a purchasing agent view the purchasing agent as a necessary evil at best and as an organizational barrier at worst. The operating department that needs to complete a purchase of equipment, materials, or supplies would often prefer to deal directly with vendors who sell these things. The vendors, in turn, often view the purchasing agent as a gatekeeper keeping them from direct contact with the ultimate user of their goods. Thus, from the standpoint of both the user and the supplier the purchasing agent is viewed as an intruder who prevents their direct negotiations.

In the next selection Strauss gives an excellent picture of the difficult position occupied by purchasing agents. These agents naturally want to eliminate their marginal status by being recognized as important to the purchasing operation. The users whom they serve are disinclined to grant this kind of recognition. Vendors openly court purchasing agents in order to win their favors but in so doing make clear that they would prefer to deal directly with the users.

The dilemma, therefore, of specialists like the purchasing agent is that they are essential in the work-flow activities but considered marginal by those whose activities they link. Their marginality therefore is a product of human relations and not technical position in the organization.

We will follow this discussion of the purchasing agent with an analysis of the industrial scientists to illustrate the contrasting kind of specialist.

---

## SPECIALISTS AND WORK-FLOW FRICTIONS: A CASE STUDY OF PURCHASING AGENTS

### George Strauss*

The causes of the Purchasing Agents' present discontent and [of] his desire for a more [prestigious] position in the corporate hierarchy are rooted deep in technology and work flow. The PA originally had but two functions: (1) to negotiate prices and place orders on the best possible terms, but only in accordance with requisitions placed by others, and (2) to expedite orders, that is, to check with suppliers to make sure that deliveries are made on time. This kind of arrangement seemingly gives the PA broad powers in dealing with salesmen, yet within the company his power and status are often limited. As one PA put it:

I spend half the day getting my ego blown up by salesmen and the other half getting it torn down by the rest of management.[1]

Many PAs feel that placing orders and expediting deliveries are but the bare bones of their responsibilities. In most circumstances they have become far more than just "order clerks."

1. They seek greater discretion in determining what the company will buy.

The difference between a successful and an unsuccessful PA [one commented] is the difference between the man who is authorized to procure an adequate amount of protective coating and the man who is told to buy ten gallons of Sherwin-Williams paint.

2. They seek to be consulted by other departments in regard to any

power of 'business or no business' with 90% of the company's suppliers, has yet to earn the confidence and respect of management. In pay and prestige he's a cut above the foremen in the shop. But rarely does he belong to the same country club as the heads of manufacturing, sales, and finance." Dean Ammer, "The Push toward Materials Management," *Purchasing*, January 5, 1959, 65. Whether this is true or not is perhaps not as important as the fact that many PAs think it is true.

*Reprinted by permission from George Strauss, "Work-Flow Frictions, Interfunctional Rivalry, and Professionalism: A Case Study of Purchasing Agents," *Human Organization,* 23:137–149, Summer, 1964.

[1]"The PA, although he usually has the

question dealing with components (this is called "value analysis").[2]

3. They seek, in many instances, to win control over allied functions such as receiving, inventory control, stores, and production control (this is called "materials management").

These objectives naturally involve sensitive inter-departmental relations. In fact, most PAs reported that such relations were at least as important to them as relations with salesmen. In larger companies, where there is a PA in charge of the office, with a number of buyers and expeditors reporting to him, the PA himself does little or no buying and spends only a small portion of the day with salesmen. Instead he devotes most of his time to internal problems—primarily with lateral relations. Many of these internal problems arise out of the PA's attempts to change the terms in which requisitions are drawn.

### REQUISITIONS

One of purchasing's primary functions is to place orders in response to *requisitions*. The normal requisition is concerned with three questions: quality, quantity, and time. It includes a *specification* as to the characteristics of the goods to be purchased (quality), the *lot size* (quantity), and the *delivery date* (time). Setting of specifications is normally the responsibility of engineers; lot size and delivery dates are usually determined by production scheduling.[3] The ambitious PA is anx-

ious to expand his discretion in regard to all three areas. He feels that he should be allowed to do more than merely buy a specified component at the lowest price, and that his technical knowledge should be accorded recognition equal to the technical knowledge of the engineer and the accountant. He looks upon his most important function as that of keeping management posted about new developments in the market: new materials, new sources of supply, price trends, and so forth. To make this information more useful, he seeks to be consulted before the requisition is drawn up, while the product is still in the planning stage. The Vice President of Purchasing at Westinghouse stated the PA's aspirations and problems as follows:[4]

Under ideal conditions, the purchasing officer participates in a project from its inception. He sits with engineering, manufacturing, and marketing on the first decisions, beginning with design, choice of materials, and level of quality. He contributes his own experience, knowledge and imagination; and he brings to the problem the rich technical experience of the company's suppliers. As a professional, he knows where the talent lies, and which supplier is equipped to make the greatest contribution. He brings this

---

[2] Understandably PAs object when Engineering Departments establish departments of "Value Engineering" and point out that PAs are far better qualified to perform this function. See Stuart F. Heinritz "The Claim Jumpers," *Purchasing*, August 18, 1958, 57.

[3] Although other departments are often involved, throughout this discussion we shall

use the term "engineering" to refer to the department which sets specifications and "production scheduling" to refer to the department which sets lot sizes and delivery dates. Actually, for example, the office manager may set specifications for clerical supplies and the maintenance foreman may set them for maintenance supplies. And many companies have a separate inventory control department.

[4] Andrew M. Kennedy, Jr., "Does Management Get Its Best from Purchasing?" *New York State Purchaser*, August 1959, 49–50.

supplier talent to bear early enough to really do some good, to conserve his own engineers' time, to get specialized knowledge working to supplement his company's efforts, to cost-reduce the product before it ever goes into production.

The situation is far less than ideal when the purchasing officer receives only a piece of paper containing specifications, scheduling and amount. The higher decisions have already been made; only the price and the supplier remain undetermined.

One way of looking at purchasing's expansionist desires is in interaction terms. Normally, orders flow in one direction, from engineering, through scheduling, to purchasing. But purchasing is dissatisfied with being at the tail end of the process and seeks to reverse the flow and to initiate for others. Such man-bite-dog behavior naturally results in ill feeling—primarily with engineering and production scheduling. Of my questionnaire sample of manufacturing PAs, 39 per cent said their biggest problem was with engineering, and 37 per cent with production scheduling (while the remaining 24 per cent scattered their votes among other departments such as stores, manufacturing, quality control, and even accounting and sales. Our attention here will be concentrated on conflicts with engineering and production scheduling.

### CONFLICTS WITH ENGINEERING

In many plants PAs are engaged in a running battle with engineers. Most of these disputes revolve around purchasing's never-ending effort to gain greater control over deciding what to buy, particularly in relation to specifications. One PA said:

The situation is so bad in our company that I could buy XXXX for $60,000 less if we could get Engineering to revise their specifications. But it is all tied up in power politics. Engineering won't admit they are wrong.

Purchasing's power and, in a sense, purchasing's status depends on how tightly specifications are worded. . . .

Control over salesmen has been an effective tool in the hands of a resourceful PA. By choosing which salesman he permits to see engineers, he can indirectly influence the specification process. In fact, once a PA decides that a product should be introduced, he and the salesman will often coordinate their strategies closely in order to get this product accepted by higher management.[5]

### CONFLICTS WITH PRODUCTION SCHEDULING

The size of the order and the date on which it is to be delivered are typically determined by production scheduling. Purchasing must seek to place the order on these terms and expedite suppliers to make sure that delivery is made on time.

PAs often feel more friendly towards production schedulers than they do towards engineers. In the first place there is less of a status barrier. Schedulers are less likely to be college men and they have little claim to being

---

[5] Significantly, PAs expressed quite friendly feelings towards salesmen as a group (even though they were antagonistic to individual salesmen whom they felt were incompetent or over-insistent). Typical comments were: "The vendor helps me, management doesn't," "They are our allies in dealing with engineering," "All I know, I've learned from salesmen," "They are the PA's biggest support."

professionals. Secondly, PAs are in a stronger position to turn down scheduling's requests than they are those of engineers. As we shall see, the purchasing-production scheduling relation involves certain elements of bargaining between equals.

*Conflict over lead time.* Still there are some points of conflict. Purchasing's chief complaint against scheduling is that delivery is often requested on much too short notice. There may be a number of reasons for the short lead time. Production schedulers sometimes cry wolf; they claim to need deliveries earlier than they really do, on the assumption that it is better to play it safe. Sometimes scheduling engages in sloppy planning and delays placing requisitions until the last minute. On occasion engineering completes blueprints too late. Or the sales department may underestimate sales and so cause inventory to be exhausted. Or, where the product is custom-made the salesmen may make a commitment on a delivery date without consulting other departments. In addition, there are genuinely unexpected events such as equipment break-down and the like.

Regardless of the cause, scheduling puts pressure on purchasing and purchasing must make the commitment good by scurrying around to find the components in a hurry. Since purchasing is at the end of the line, it must make up for all the accumulated delays. . . .

### INADEQUATE RECOGNITION FROM HIGHER MANAGEMENT

The PA tends to look to higher management for support in his interdepartmental disputes. But management tends to give purchasing less attention than purchasing feels it deserves. At times management treats purchasing almost as a routine, clerical operation —and when this happens purchasing men are naturally resentful. . . .

### THE VALUE OF INTERFUNCTIONAL CONFLICT

Further research is needed to see if the PA's experience is duplicated by other functional departments. However, the picture of the company we get from the PA's frame of reference is very different from that presented by many organizational theorists. It is not that of a highly coordinated organization, tightly controlled by top management. Rather it is one of a number of semi-autonomous departments which keep each other in line through a series of checks and balances.

On the surface, at least, this seems to be a highly inefficient way of doing things. Even routine decisions regarding inventory level, make-or-buy, the acceptance of new products, or quality standards seem to involve a number of departments, each with its special point of view. Decisions seem to be made as much on the basis of pressure politics and implicit bargaining as of rational analysis, and there is no one department to bear the final responsibility. Certainly a case can be made for a unified systems approach which would take all variables into account.

Inefficient as it may seem, perhaps the system of checks and balances has its virtues in the industrial scene just as it does in the national state. Special interests do require lobbyists if a balanced point of view is to prevail. The restricted "professional" viewpoint tends to counter-balance the excessive

conformity and rigidity of "organization man."[6]

Interdepartmental conflicts encourage the free competition of new ideas
(as well as giving top management a
chance to evaluate subordinates' behavior). Since each department has
only a partial picture of the entire or-

ganization, competition improves the
quality of each department's thinking
and forces it to take the other department's point of view into consideration. In large organizations such internal competition tends to substitute
for the external competition of the
market place. And

jurisdictional disputes are an important
means of bringing to the top administrator significant issues of policy, and of
preventing these from being decided at
lower levels without his knowledge.[7]

[6]This point is elaborated in George
Strauss, "Organization Man: Prospect for
the Future," *California Management Review,*
VI, No. 3, Spring 1964, 5–16. In addition,
it can be argued that the functional professional in industry has what Andrew G.
Frank calls an "under-defined administrative role" which permits him opportunity for
innovation; [see] "Administrative Role Definition and Social Change," *Human Organization,* XXII, No. 4, Winter 1963–64, 238–
242.

[7]Herbert Simon, *Administrative Behavior,*
Macmillan, New York, 1947, p. 145. The
same point is made by Wilfred Brown, *Ex-
plorations in Management,* Tavistock Publications, London, 1960.

---

Industrial scientists are a class of
specialists distinguished by two characteristics: (1) they have a highly
technical and usually very specialized
education like that of a science discipline, law, or accountancy; and (2)
their activities in the organization are
not part of the daily flow of work.

This type of specialist views his
position as requiring a high degree of
autonomy in relation to the work organization. He expects autonomy because he feels that ordinary nonspecialists are incapable of understanding the work he does. Such specialists, of course, do not go out of
their way to improve this understanding since they are likely to use language and behave in ways that are
designed to keep the layman in the
dark about their specialities, as we
saw in the selection by Moore and
Tumin. This type of specialist may
also expect a high degree of autonomy
because the practice of the specialization is judged by standards that are

different from those of the employing organization. Thus the lawyer
wants his legal advice to the business
firm to be judged by standards of the
legal profession and not those of commerce or industry. In the same way,
the scientist working in an industrial
laboratory wants his work judged by
the standard of his scientific discipline.

Where the human relations problem of the first type of specialist was
that of overcoming marginality and
being integrated into the organization, the second type of specialist
wants to maintain a human relations
position of independence from the organization. These are obviously different expectations that the two groups
of specialists have. It is, therefore, important to understand this difference.

In the next selection Marcson summarizes the basic features of his own
research on scientists in industry. This
selection makes clear the importance
of autonomy for the scientists. It
should be obvious that the manage-

ment of specialists, like scientists, is made difficult precisely because they want to be independent of supervision and management. We can now perhaps better understand why the services of a specialist may be purchased on a consulting basis from an independent organization. The consultant can provide the special knowledge required without having at the same time to be supervised and directed.

---

## SCIENTISTS AS EMPLOYEES IN INDUSTRY

*Simon Marcson**

Ever since the scientist became an industrial laboratory employee in large numbers, he has become an object of interest and scrutiny. He has been written about by novelists, psychologists, and journalists. Many generalizations are based on the assumption that he is peculiar and different. The results have provided interesting and even amusing reading but have thrown little light on him as an employee. I would suggest that it is as an employee that he is of interest, and it is as an employee that I wish to examine him.

The peculiar thing about the scientist as an employee is that his training does not prepare him to be an industrial laboratory employee. He is trained to be a member of a profession who engages in research. That is, he has internalized the values of his profession as to the importance of scientific achievement and the necessary methods of work for such an end. These commit him to a scientific and professional ethos regardless of the

goals of his industrial employer. In other words, he is not prepared to be an industrial employee.

My thesis is that since he is not prepared to be an employee, the industrial laboratory must undertake to make one out of him. How it accomplishes this is reflected in the particular managerial and personnel problems one finds in industrial laboratories. I want to look at this a little more closely by examining the problem-producing characteristics of the industrial laboratory which affect the molding of the scientist into an employee.

### RECRUITMENT

The university recruit is selected by the industrial laboratory both for the judgments about his competence and his future promise. He entertains visions of himself exploring the unknown and startling the world with his breakthroughs into the secrets of nature. The laboratory's recruitment process does not substitute more realistic expectations. Typically, the recruit enters the laboratory with the self-conception of himself as a profes-

*Reprinted by permission from Simon Marcson, "The Professional Commitments of Scientists in Industry," *Research Management*, 4:271–275, 1961.

sional scientist whose future will be largely dedicated to basic research. The industrial laboratory has the objective of adapting him to industrial research employment while at the same time not entirely destroying his self-conception. If this were begun in the recruitment process, the problems of adaptation would be lessened. If, however, the laboratory does this with too much vigor the man may be lost. The laboratory, therefore, postpones the day of realistic induction and thereby contributes to its future problems. The only other alternative the industrial laboratory has is that of selecting scientists who, with a high degree of certainty, will fit into industrial employment. This, too, has its problems, since competence may not always be correlated with this adaptability.

### CAREER ADAPTATION

The industrial research laboratory has fairly immediate tasks and goals which are vital to it as an ongoing economic enterprise. To meet its goals, the laboratory has developed an elaborate and expensive organization providing its research employees with all the necessary facilities.

The goals of the corporation are omnipresent. Once in the laboratory the recruit quickly discovers that his expectations need reorganization. As he sees it, initially he is engaged in changing the laboratory. In actuality, he adapts to the requirements of the work situation. In adjusting to his new role he goes through a process of change that permits him to internalize selected aspects of his new environment.

In the process of adaptation four types of career pathways emerge in the laboratory:

1. He may remain devoted to research and scientific professional career and shape his career goals in this direction.

2. He may become interested in administration and try to steer his career up the administrative ladder.

3. He may be interested in research but turn to administration because he sees a limited financial and status future for himself in research.

4. He may turn to administration because he cannot compete in research with his colleagues.

Career adaptation is productive of strain. It evokes resentment towards oneself and others. The individual scientist may feel resentful towards himself or towards the laboratory for having given up his goals for a high salary, or because he has accepted modification of his self-conception. Awareness of these strain-producing mechanisms and the adequate provision on the part of the laboratory in aiding the scientist's career adaptation would modify the ensuing problems.

### RECOGNITION

While the laboratory is engaged in making an employee out of a scientist, what it fundamentally wants to do is to release the dynamo of energy and creativity it has bet its recruit has. What it is really concerned with is motivating him as a scientist toward optimum goal attainment. The key to this objective, I would suggest, is recognition.

Recognition establishes the basis for the much sought after autonomy for the professional person. Recognition provides the scientist with increasing independence in his work. Since, in the final analysis, the scientist's achievement is subject only to the judgment of his peers, recognition is crucial. One might go as far as to say that in science there is a right to recognition. Recognition, then, is not only a basic need of the professional person, it is also a dynamic incentive of paramount importance to him.

The industrial laboratory has introduced a variety of formal systems of recognition, ranging from merit awards to titles. While the introduction of such systems in themselves are productive of strain, the failure to introduce them would provoke greater difficulties. There is no doubt in my mind that the industrial laboratory is valiantly trying to solve its problems of recognition. There is an aspect of the general problem of recognition, however, that is still missing. I refer to the understanding of the scientist's problem of self-esteem as a professional person. This respect of recognition depends upon the type of authority system within which the scientist must function.

## AUTHORITY

I have described the type of authority system which prevails in traditional business organizations as *executive authority*. Here ultimate control over policy and over the limits within which subordinates can make decisions rests with top executives and, in the final analysis, with the chief executive. On the other hand, the professions, and especially the academic profession, can be said to be characterized by *colleague authority*. In this system, authority rests in a group of professional colleagues.

The scientist, whether in industry or the university, has need of an authority system which recognizes the characteristics of his professional role. He has need of an authority system which permits him autonomy and protects his self-esteem. He has need of participation in decisions concerning his work.

To meet these needs, the industrial laboratory does grant varying degrees of autonomy. It has instituted varying forms of scientific recognition. It cannot, however, be said to have moved toward a colleague authority system. Its fluidity, however, bespeaks the latent possibility of a new organizational form containing some of the elements of both executive authority and colleague authority.

I want to emphasize that the introduction of a colleague authority system is not a simple matter of enlarging the freedom of the laboratory scientist. It requires extensive skill and expertness in the adequate development of indirect techniques of control. When it is carried out inadequately it arouses resentment on the part of scientists and contributes to conflict. When it is carried out adequately it molds the working environment into what Dean J. Douglas Brown has called a "climate for discovery."

The molding of authority in the industrial laboratory in the direction of colleague authority will permit the scientist to work out new self-conceptions of his role as scientist and employee. It will permit research management to develop new organizational models. This, in turn, will stimulate it to new insights about its managerial inadequacies and assist in undertaking its own change.

# 10

# Supervisors

Continuing our analysis of the major types of organization offices, we turn our attention next to supervisors. The position of supervisor is a central one in a business organization. This is true for two principal reasons. First, workers experience management as a whole primarily through the supervisor, who is their immediate boss. The supervisor is the ever-present daily and even hourly reminder of management. Second, management experiences its workers primarily through the supervisors. The office of supervisor is a central and critical link in a chain of command that connects management with the work force. In this office there is then a "built-in" and institutionalized need to be "Janus-faced"—to be able to look in two directions at the same time.

We will consider in this chapter the dilemmas and changes that are generated by the squeeze on the position of the supervisor between management and the work force. This is done by Roethlisberger in the first selection. Attention is then turned to the "working supervisor" who is one step below the foreman level and just one step above the actual working level. Here too, as Strauss makes clear in the second portion of the chapter, there are important changes taking place in the industrial institution that make this position a difficult one to fulfill.

**INTRODUCTION**

As we did with executives, we have included in this chapter a summary of studies of the actual behaviors of supervisors and foremen. This analysis helps to provide a realistic base from which to evaluate the office of

*222*

supervisor in industrial establishments.

The final portion of the chapter is an analysis by Coates and Pellegrin of (1) the differing self-images held by executives and supervisors; and (2) the rather considerable agreements between the ways in which executives see themselves and the ways they are perceived by supervisors. We conclude this chapter then, by coming the full circle back to a consideration of executives as they are shown to be different from supervisors.

For consistency in exposition we have limited the discussion in this chapter largely to supervisors of industrial work. The generalizations reached, however, apply to most supervisory offices wherever found. Supervisors in the office, on the sales floor, in government bureaus, schools, and hospitals undoubtedly face comparable problems and have to resolve similar dilemmas as their counterparts in the factory.

In the following paper by Roethlisberger, some of the distinctive features of staff offices and executive offices are described as they result in

demands and pressures on the managerial group called supervisors. Roethlisberger particularly emphasizes the alternative responses available to supervisors, and the high possibility that they will become "masters of double talk" in relating themselves to staff people and executives. This whole business of "double-talk"—or "translating *what is* into a semblance of *the way it ought to be*" to quote the author—is a good illustration of organization fictions, which we will consider separately in Chapter 21.

This selection also focuses on other key ideas dealt with in this volume. In the order in which they appear in this reading there is a discussion of status (which we deal with in detail in Chapter 13); subordination (analyzed in Chapter 17); communication (discussed in Chapter 14); and finally informal organization and informal relations (which we have already examined in Chapter 5). This selection puts to work and shows some of the interconnections among the important ideas that characterize the analytical framework of this volume.

---

## THE FOREMAN: "MAN IN THE MIDDLE"

### Fritz J. Roethlisberger*

Let us explore further this feeling of the modern foreman. Not only does he have to know more than his old-time counterpart about the "logics"

*From "The Foreman: Master and Victim of Double Talk," *Harvard Business Review*, 23:285–294 (Spring 1945). Used by permission.

of management, but also he has to relate himself to a wider range of people. In any mass production industry, the foreman each day is likely to be interacting (1) with his boss, the man to whom he formally reports in the line organization; (2) with certain staff specialists, varying from one to a dozen people depending on the size and kind of organization—production control men, inspectors, standards men, efficiency engineers, safety engineers, maintenance and repair men, methods men, personnel men, counselors; (3) with the heads of other departments to which his department relates; (4) with his subordinates—subforemen, straw bosses, leadmen, group leaders, section chiefs; (5) with the workers directly, numbering anywhere from 10 to 300 people; and (6) in a union-organized plant, with the shop steward. Exploring the interdependence of each of these relationships, as they impinge *in toto* upon the foreman, makes it easier to understand how the modern foreman may feel in his everyday life.

*Foreman-Supervisor*—In the modern business structure there is probably no relation more important than that of the subordinate to his immediate superior.[1] This statement applies straight up the line from worker to president. It is in the relation between a subordinate and his immediate superior that most breakdowns of coordination and communication between various parts of the industrial structure finally show up. It is here that distortions of personal attitude and emotional disturbances become more pronounced. Why this relation is so important could be indicated in any number of ways. But it is clear that any adequate analysis would go far beyond the confines of this article since it would involve a critique of modern business organization and the individual's relation to authority and, in part, an examination of the ideologies held by the leaders and execu-

tives of business.[2] It is enough that the importance of this relation and its consequences in terms of behavior, particularly at the foreman level, are matters of common observation; and it will be at this level of behavior and its associated *feelings* that we shall remain.

Personal dependence upon the judgments and decisions of his superiors, so characteristic of the subordinate-superior relation in modern industry makes the foreman's situation basically insecure. He feels a constant need to adjust himself to the demands of his superior and to seek the approval of his superior. Everything that he does he tries to evaluate in terms of his superior's reaction. Everything that his superior does he tries to evaluate in terms of what it means or implies about his superior's relation to him. Everything that his subordinates and workers do he immediately tries to evaluate in terms of the criticism it may call forth from his superior. In some cases this preoccupation with what the boss thinks becomes so acute that it accounts for virtually everything the foreman says or does and all his thinking about what goes on around him. He will refrain from doing anything even to the point of dodging responsibility, for fear of bringing disapproval from the boss. Hours at work and at home are spent in figuring and anticipating what explanations or reasons he will need to give the boss. And the boss's most innocent and unintentional acts —failure to say "good morning" for instance—are taken perhaps to imply disapproval.

It is hard to realize how much those

---

[1] See B. B. Gardner, *Human Relations in Industry* (Chicago: Richard D. Irwin, Inc., 1945).

[2] See Chester I. Barnard, *The Functions of the Executive* (Cambridge: Harvard University Press, 1938), pp. 161–184.

who are interested in improving the efficiency of industry have neglected this area. If the man-hours spent by subordinates both on and off the job in preoccupation about what the boss thinks were added up, the total hours would be staggering—not to mention the results this phenomenon has produced in nervous breakdowns and other forms of mental anguish. Stranger still, it almost appears as if modern industrial organization, which prides itself so much on its efficiency, has aggravated rather than reduced the amount of this preoccupation, with disastrous consequences for health and thus for efficiency. All this applies to the foreman in particular.

The crux of the foreman's problem is that he is constantly faced with the dilemma of (1) having to keep his superior informed of what is happening at the work level (in many cases so that his superior may prepare in turn for the unfavorable reaction of his superior and so on up the line) and (2) needing to communicate this information in such a way that it does not bring unfavorable criticism on himself for not doing his job correctly or adequately. Discrepancies between the way things are at the work level and the way they are represented to be by management cannot be overlooked, and yet the foreman feels obligated to overlook them when talking to his boss. This makes the foreman's job particularly "tough" and encourages him to talk out of both sides of his mouth at the same time—to become a master of double talk.

Each foreman, of course, resolves the conflict in terms of his own personal history, personality, and temperament. Some foremen become voluble in the face of this situation; others are reduced to stony silence, feeling that anything they say will be held against them. Some keep out of the boss's way, while others devise all sorts of ways for approaching him and trying to direct attention to certain things they have accomplished. And extraordinary are the skills which some more verbally articulate foremen develop in translating *what is* into a semblance of *the way it ought to be* in order to appease their superiors and keep them happy.

But, for the most part, the foreman, being loyal and above all wanting to be secure, resolves the conflict and maintains good relations with his superiors by acting strictly in accordance with his functional relations and the logics of management. In spite of what this may lead to in his relations to workers and other groups, his relations with his superiors at least are not jeopardized.

Thus the foreman, like each individual in the modern industrial structure, is in effect painfully tutored to focus his attention upward to his immediate superiors and the logics of evaluation they represent, rather than downward to his subordinates and the feelings they have. So rigid does the conditioning of supervisors and executives in the industrial structure become in this respect that it is almost impossible for them to pay attention to the concrete human situations below them, rich in sentiments and feelings. For them, this world of feeling does not exist; the territory is merely populated with the abstractions which they have been taught to see and the terms in which they communicate—"base rates," "man-hours," "budgets," "cost curves," "production schedules," etc.

*Foreman-Specialist*—Also of extreme importance are the foreman's relations to the technical specialists who *originate* the standards of performance which he must *uphold* and to which his subordinates and workers must *conform*. This experimentally minded group of engineers, accountants, and technologists can become one of the chief sources of change, and rapid change, at the work level; through them changes can be introduced at the work level at a more rapid rate than they can be assimilated by customary shop codes and practices. Through them, also, "controls" can be exercised far more precisely than heretofore. It is one thing for a foreman to know what his cost performance has been; it is another matter to know what his actual costs should be in relation to a standard. What was heretofore a matter of projective experimental judgment after the fact becomes now a matter of projective evaluation and of constantly shooting at a target—a target whose outlines become increasingly more clear-cut and demanding, at least in one area of his job.

It is little wonder that this group can become . . . a constant source of threat to the foreman's feelings of security. These men of course affect and often make more difficult his relations to workers. They also provide reports to management which can make his relations to his boss exceedingly uncomfortable. The result: more double talk.

It is well to note that these control groups can (as can the union) short-circuit foremen and levels of supervision lower in the line by providing information direct to higher levels of supervision.[3] Whatever the value of this information in evaluating the foreman's performance, it results in certain pressures upon him. Each su-

perior can request explanations from, or give orders to, his foreman based on such information; yet the foreman cannot control it and indeed may be unaware of it until his superior initiates action. Information flowing through the line the foreman can censor before it reaches the boss; but this way the boss can get information at the same time he does, or even before, and the foreman is no longer able to foresee or to gauge the boss' reaction. The results of this in mental anguish, in preoccupations, in worries about what the boss may think or do in preparation of explanations, "good reasons," and alibis, are tremendous. Because of the subjective nature of the data, the technologists of industry have not as yet decided to study this area or even to give it much attention. But the modern foreman, from the point of view of both his effectiveness and his satisfaction at work, finds the actual phenomena only too real.

*Foreman-Foreman*—By the very nature of the closely knit technological processes of a manufacturing organization, the foreman of one department often has to work very closely with a foreman of another department. These lateral relations are not formally defined, and their functioning depends largely upon the informal understandings which exist between foremen. Thus, the kind and amount of cooperation which one foreman is likely to obtain from another foreman is in good part determined by their inter-personal relations. Here again, the boss comes in, because the preoccupation with what the boss thinks may also affect the foreman's relation to his colleagues at the same level.

Although all foremen have equal formal status, they do not, as everyone in a shop knows, enjoy equal informal status. The individual fore-

---

[3]Discussed more fully by B. B. Gardner, *op. cit.*

man's relative status is determined by such factors as age, sex, service, earnings, and social symbols of one sort or another. But the chief determining factor is his direct relation to the boss, i.e., how close he is to the boss. Not only the foreman's need for security but also the closely allied strivings for status and recognition are therefore directed to his superior. He needs to feel "close" to him. Thus he may constantly be comparing his relation to the boss with that of his colleagues. If this comparison indicates his position to be weak, he may enter into competition with his colleagues for recognition from the boss. As can be imagined, such emotional disturbances in the work situation may impede rather than facilitate cooperation among foremen, and they constitute a peculiar kind of "headache" for the superior.

*Foreman-Worker*—It is in his relation to the workers, however, with the rise of "scientific" management and with the growth of industrial unions, that the modern foreman's position becomes especially difficult. Here "the straw that breaks the camel's back" is finally reached. Here the problem of getting smooth operation becomes acute because, as we have seen, the foreman according to the logic of industrial organization must (1) *uphold* at the work level the standards, policies, rules, and regulations which have been *originated* by other groups and see to it that the workers *conform* to them and, at the same time, (2) obtain if possible the workers' spontaneous *cooperation* to this way of doing business. As anyone who has been in such a position knows, this is not a very easy task. As a rule, people do not like to conform to matters when they have no say in them, when they do not participate or feel that their point of view is taken into account. This is not a popular way of evoking spontaneity of cooperation; it is not consistent with our basic social values. Yet over and over again both foremen and workers are told, merely told, to conform to conditions over which they have very little or no say—conditions, moreover, which shockingly fail at times to take into account what is of vital importance to them in their work situations.

This state of affairs affects the foreman's personal situation: his strivings to satisfy his needs for security, personal integrity, and recognition in the work situation. Further, it makes his job in relation to his workers very difficult. Again and again, he is put in a position either of getting the workers' cooperation and being "disloyal" to management or of being "loyal" to management and incurring the resentment and overt opposition of his subordinates.

For those who do not fully appreciate the conflicting position in which the foreman is placed, it may be desirable to show the nature of the two contrasting worlds in the middle of which the foreman stands and spends his workaday life. In business, as in any organized human activity, there are two sets of social processes going on:

(1) There are those social processes which are directly related to the achievement of purpose and which result in "formal organization." In business, for example, formal organization leads to such things as practices established by legal enactment or policy, specifications, standard methods, standard procedures, standards of time, output, quality, cost, and so on. They are concerned with those means most appropriate to achieve certain ends. And as such they can be changed rapidly.

It should be noted that these manifestations of formal organization are essentially logical in character. Through formal organization man expresses his logical capacities; in fact, it is one of the chief outlets for the expression of man's logical capacities. It should also be noted that in the past 25 years there has been a tremendous amount of attention given to this aspect of business organization. It is in part because of this that, as we tried to show, the modern foreman's environment is so radically different from the good old days. And yet the foreman, unlike some higher executives, cannot stay only in this logically sheltered atmosphere.

(2) There are those spontaneous social processes going on in any organized human activity which have no specific, conscious common purpose and which result in "informal organization." Informal organization leads to such things as custom, mores, folkway, tradition, social norms, and ideals. In business, for example, it expresses itself at the work level in such things as what constitute fair wages, decent conditions of work, fair treatment, a fair day's work, and traditions of the craft. It takes the form of different status systems: e.g., oldtimers should get preferential treatment; supervisors should get more money than their subordinates; and office workers are superior to shop workers. These are attitudes and understandings based on feeling and sentiment. They are manifestations of "belonging," and they do not change rapidly.

It should be especially noted that these manifestations of informal organizations are not logical in character. They are concerned with values, ways of life, and ends in themselves —those aspects of social life which people strive to protect and preserve and for which at times they are will-

ing to fight and even die. It should also be noted that a cursory examination of the periodicals, books, formal statements, and speeches of business executives and business experts shows that little systematic attention has been given to this aspect of business organization. This is indeed a curious state of affairs since, as every foreman intuitively knows, it is only through informal organization and its manifestations that he can secure spontaneity of cooperation at the work level.

Informal organization in any organized human activity serves a very healthy function. It binds people together in routine activity. It gives people a social place and feeling of belonging. It provides the framework for the fulfillment of human satisfaction. It gives people a feeling of self-respect, of independent choice, of not being just cogs in a machine. Far from being a hindrance to greater effectiveness, informal organization provides the setting which makes men willing to contribute their services.

Yet what is management's attitude toward these informal groups which form at the work level? Curiously enough, their appearance makes management uneasy. And sometimes management willfully tries to break them up. Such ill-conceived attempts inevitably produce open hostility to the aims of management. For informal organization cannot be prevented; it is a spontaneous phenomenon necessary wherever coordinated human activities exist.

More important still—for it is more often the case—these informal groups are ignored and not even recognized. Having no representation in the formal organization, which to many an executive is by definition the "reality," they just do not exist. As a result—not from malicious design but from sheer oversight born of over-logicized trainıg—these informal groups at the work ˀvel become inadvertently the victims f change, disruption, and dislocation. 'echnical changes are introduced ʋithout any attention to what is happening to the members of these ɾoups in terms of their group associaɔns. New methods of work and new tandards are initiated, newcomers are dded, someone is transferred, upɾaded, or promoted, and all as if this ɾoup life did not exist. What happens? There develops a feeling of beɪg "pushed around"—a very uncomɔrtable feeling which most people islike and which often provokes the ɛaction of trying to push the pusher ʋith equal intensity in the opposite ɹirection.

Because their way of life is conantly in jeopardy from technological hanges, new methods, raised stanards, and constant manipulation of ne kind or another by logically ninded individuals, these groups in ɪdustry take on a highly defensive nd protective character. Their major ɯnction becomes, unfortunately, the ɛsistance to change and innovation, nd their codes and practices develop t variance with the economic purpose ˀf the enterprise. Much pegging of ˀutput at a certain level by employees ɟ an expression of this need to proɛct their ways of life, as well as their ivelihood, from too rapid change.

As might be expected, these defenive and protective characteristics of ɲany informal groups at the work ˀvel—and they exist full blown in ɲany factories even before any formal ɯnion appears—have serious conseɟuences for foremen (not to mention ɪew workers and other individuals). \nny supervisor or foreman in charge ˀf such groups has two, if not three, trikes against him to begin with. Anyhing he does in relation to them is ikely to be "wrong." To ignore them

completely would be to fail in fulfilling his responsibilities to management. Yet the foreman is the key man of management in administering technical changes. He often has the impossible task of taking plans made by the specialists without thought of the realities of human situations and relating them to just such situations.

*Foreman-Union*—Once these patterns of behavior become formalized in a union, the foreman's debacle becomes complete. Into this situation, now, is introduced a new set of logics, verbal definitions, rules, and regulations, by means of which he is supposed to set his conduct toward the worker. The last vestiges of initiative, of judgment, and, what is perhaps more important, of personal relations with his subordinates are taken away from him. Literally the foreman is left "holding the bag"—a bag containing (1) the maximum of exquisitely logical rules, definitions, procedures, policies, standards that the human mind can devise, by means of which he is now supposed to do his job, and (2) the minimum of those relationships and their associated feelings through which he can obtain the wholehearted cooperation of people. Standing in the middle of a now formally bifurcated situation, where onehalf is trying to introduce changes and improvements into the factory situation and the other half by habit and conditioning is trying to prevent or resist them, the modern foreman is expected to "cooperate."

### THE FOREMAN'S SITUATION SUMMARIZED

The salient features of the foreman's situation should now be clear. In very broad outline—tentatively and approximately formulated—the failure on the part of top management, in mass production industries in particular, to understand the social implications of its way of doing "business" has resulted in the development of certain rigidities which do not make for co-operation in the industrial structure.

(1) At the bottom of the organization there are people called *employees* who are in general merely supposed to *conform* to changes which they do not originate. Too often the attitude is that employees are merely supposed to do what they are told and get paid for it. Directing them there is—

(2) A group of *supervisors* who again are merely supposed to *uphold* —"administer" is the popular word— the standards of performance and policies determined by other groups, one of which is—

(3) A group of *technical specialists* who are supposed to *originate* better ways and better standards through which the economic purpose of the organization can be better secured and more effectively controlled by—

(4) A group of *top management* men who in their *evaluation* of the workers' behavior assume that the major inducement they can offer to people to cooperate is financial (i.e., that they are merely providing a livelihood, rather than a way of life); that informal organization is either "bad" or not "present"; and that authority comes from the top, so that no attention has to be given to that authority which is a matter of individual decision and comes from the bottom. This group's whole explicit theory of human cooperation—but not necessarily the practice of it—dates back to the eighteenth century:[4] (a) society is

composed of a rabble of unorganized individuals; (b) these individuals ar only interested in the pursuit of prof and pleasure; and (c) in the pursu of these ends the individual is esser tially logical.

These rigidities in operation mak people in one group feel that they ar excluded from the activities of othe groups and prevent the wholeheartec participation of all groups in a fu attainment of the organization's objec tives.

These rigidities in the industria structure also have serious conse quences for the satisfactions of ind viduals. Man's desire to belong, to b a part of a group, is constantly bein frustrated. Things that are importan to him seem to be disregarded. Oppo tunities for personal and social satis faction seem to be denied. Yet, con trary to the assumptions made b management, all the evidence of mod ern investigation shows: (a) society i composed of people related to eac other in terms of group association: (b) the desire to belong, to be a par the desire for continuous and intimat association at work with other huma beings, remains a strong, possibly th strongest, desire of man; and (c) i the pursuit of these ends man is essen tially nonlogical and at times irra tional, i.e., willing to die or, as man agement should know only too wel to "cut off his nose to spite his face.

As a result of being constantly de prived of real social (not logical) in terrelationship and of those basic hu man satisfactions which come from i the worker becomes restless and dis satisfied, if not openly resentful anc hostile. And like any human being h expresses his dissatisfaction in a num ber of ways: by being absent, by quit ting, by pegging output, and by join ing a union where he hopes to satisf

---

[4]These assumptions are taken from Elton Mayo, *The Social Problems of an Industrial Civilization* (Cambridge: Harvard Business School, 1945).

ıe needs for self-expression that his
ɔb no longer provides.

In this environment the foreman
tands—victim, not monarch, of all he
ɪrveys. And what does he survey? On
ıe one hand, a monument of techni-
al achievement such as no civiliza-
ɪon has seen before, and on the other
ɪand, what Elton Mayo likes to refer
ɔ as "the seamy side of progress," a
ıleak and arid human scene scorched
ɪry by the babel of words and logics
ᴠhich have long ceased to have any
ᴠower to motivate or fill with renewed
ope and vigor the hearts of men.
eparated from management and sep-
ɪrated from his men, dependent and
ɪnsecure in his relation to his superiors
ɪnd uncertain in his relations to his
ɪnen, asked to give cooperation but in
ɪurn receiving none, expected to be
riendly but provided with tools which

only allow him to be "fair"—in this
situation of social deprivation our
modern foreman is asked to deliver
the goods.

In this predicament, how does this
foreman feel and behave? In one of
three ways: (1) he "stews in his own
juice" and, like Sir Hudibras's rusty
sword, "he eats into himself for lack
of something else to hew and hack,"
i.e., becomes obsessive; or (2) as current newspapers and periodicals have
kept us informed, he joins a union,
i.e., becomes aggressive; or (3) he too
—who knows?—may go to Washington
to be delivered from his social isolation and logocentric predicament, i.e.,
may seek a political solution for his
social void. So at the foreman level do
the "mills of the gods" grind out the
three major ills of our industrial civilization.

---

The working supervisor both super-
ises people and works along with
hem. This alone is sufficient to make
ıis position ambiguous. In addition,
here have been material changes in
he managerial definition of the super-
ᴠisory office of foreman, the working
upervisor's boss. This change has re-
ulted in greater demand for "human
ᴠelations skills" and a conscious re-
:ruiting of college trained people who
ɪnter management as foremen with
ull expectation of future promotions
ɔ executive positions. These college
ᴠeople, with their eyes on better jobs,
ɪnd with their special background
ɪnd training, have subverted the work-
ng supervisor, who has usually se-
:ured his education and technical
:kills in the school of hard knocks.
Γhis is the central point of Strauss'
study.

We can see then that recruiting
future executives from among college
graduates, and placing them in the
organization as foremen for their first
on-the-job training experience has had
as one of its unanticipated consequences the undermining of the working supervisor. Management, in trying
to provide broad working experience
for its future executive officials has
inadvertently damaged the effectiveness of the lowest level of supervision.
This serves to emphasize the below-
the-surface interconnections among
the operating parts of a business organization, and shows why we find it
necessary to consider any organization
as a social system. The operating parts
do hang together, and are each affected by what happens in surrounding parts of the organization.

# THE CHANGING ROLE OF THE WORKING SUPERVISOR

## George Strauss*

The working supervisor in industry is a key man whose position has often been misunderstood. In many companies his job has been downgraded or eliminated. In doing so, management may defeat its own purpose of increasing supervisory efficiency.

Most people think of the foreman as the lowest level of supervision. In fact, many workers take their orders from their *working supervisor*—the setup man, straw boss, crew chief, or group leader. In contrast to the foreman, the working supervisor spends most of his time in actual "production." Although he does not have the right to hire and fire or even (in a formal sense) to discipline, he is the one through whom the foreman channels his orders to the rest of the work group. He is the technical coordinator who keeps the team pulling together. And his job is often considered a stepping stone to higher managerial positions.

In the situations observed, the status of the working supervisor has tended to fall in past years. In some cases the job has disappeared altogether. In others it remains, but with vastly decreased authority. College-trained foremen tend to bypass working supervisors in giving orders, and the stress on academic training limits their chances for advancement. Staff activity and explicit personnel policies tend to limit their discretion. Unions often demand the elimination of this half-worker-half-management position.

These changes in many cases have caused serious decline in the working supervisor's status and morale even where his job has not been abolished. In turn, this has resulted in a severe shakeup in the pattern of human relations in the shop—a shakeup which has often reduced production. And in many cases management does not know what has happened, because it never appreciated the role of the working supervisor in the first place.

We shall consider the following questions in turn. What was the traditional role of the supervisor? How did he lose his authority and his prestige? What has been the impact of these changes on human relations and production? And, finally, what is the working supervisor's proper place in industry, and how can we reconcile it with demands of modern personnel practice?

Our analysis is based on four case studies dealing with four different kinds of working supervisors: (1) "poly" (polymerization) operators in newly developed cracking still; (2) "gaffers" on a glass-blowing team; (3) maintenance mechanics in a plant producing metal containers; and (4) head nurses.[1] Less intensive studies were

*Reprinted from "The Changing Role of the Working Supervisor," *The Journal of Business of the University of Chicago*, 30:-202–211 (July 1957). Used by permission.

[1] The gaffer study was conducted by Professors William F. Whyte and Frank Miller of the New York State School of Industrial and Labor Relations, Cornell University. The "poly" operator study was by Professor Whyte; the head-nurse study by Professor Edith Lentz, School of Public Health, University of Michigan. The others, made by

also made of setup men in an auto-motive-parts factory, chief substation operators in a public utility, and work-ing foremen in the building trades. In all these situations the power of the working supervisor was observed to decline. Although the basic research is too limited to be representative, it is felt to be suggestive.

### THE TRADITIONAL WORKING SUPERVISOR

There are two kinds of working su-pervisors. The most obvious form is the straw boss, sometimes called "working foreman," "leadman," "pusher," or "group chief." He is the leader of a group of men who do roughly the *same* sort of work. He shares their work and has some addi-tional quasi-supervisory duties as well. The other type of working supervisor exercises his authority by virtue of his

---

the author, were supervised by Professor Whyte. For reports on the over-all studies see William F. Whyte, "Engineers and Workers: A Case Study," *Human Organiza-tion,* XIV, No. 4 (Winter, 1955), 3–12; George Strauss, "The Set-up Man: A Case Study of Organizational Change," *Human Organization,* XIII, No. 2 (Summer, 1954), 17–25; Temple Burling, Edith M. Lentz, and Robert N. Wilson, *The Give and Take in Hospitals* (New York: G. P. Putnam's Sons, 1956). The author's work and that of Profes-sor Miller were sponsored by the Grant Foundation, Inc.

Each of the major cases involved a mini-mum of six months' study during which time working supervisors, their superiors, and their subordinates were extensively in-terviewed and (with the exception of the poly operators) observed on the job. The poly operator, the setup man, and the auto-parts cases were studied over a period dur-ing which it was possible to observe at first-hand the impact on human relations while the working supervisor actually was being downgraded.

technical position on the work team, because his work is different from and more skilled than that of the others. For example:

One of the cases dealt with a depart-ment of twelve "shops" (actually teams) engaged in producing high-quality glass crystalware for the luxury market. Head-ing each shop is a "gaffer." Because of his skill and his position at the final step of a complicated production process, the gaffer is the shop leader and is account-able to the management for the quality and quantity of ware produced by his team. Until recently, he had a substantial voice in the promotion, pay scale, and tenure of his subordinates; in addition, he had almost complete authority over their work performance. This combina-tion of technical and administrative au-thority gave him great disciplinary powers.

In many cases this second type of working supervisor receives no formal recognition of authority from manage-ment. Rather it is inherent in the tech-nological process itself: technical co-ordination is required by the work process, and it is the top skilled men who provide this coordination. The very fact that inadequate recognition is given on the organization chart of this type of working supervisor means that the new college-trained foreman tends to ignore his special position. Yet the foreman who comes from outside the department rarely has the time or experience to provide the technical and detailed coordination required.

The supervisory duties of both sorts of supervisors vary from plant to plant. They normally assign men to duties, coordinate operations where two or more men are involved, make techni-cal decisions as to which machine should be run and how fast, keep records, and inspect the product. In addition, they often informally discipline members of their work group—and recommend formal discipline to the foreman. Unlike the foremen, they wear overalls, get hourly pay, and (in most instances) belong to the union if there is one. How the working supervisor exercises his authority is illustrated by the following quotation from an operator in one factory:

The setup man asked me to sweep the floors this afternoon, but I told him I was too busy. He could have gone to the foreman on it or gotten someone else to do it, but he is a good guy, and he swept them himself.

Note here that the setup man was expected to give orders which would normally be backed up by the foreman. Sweeping is below him, but he is a "good guy," so he does it himself.

The working supervisor owed much of his authority to a natural alliance with the foreman, for in the past foremen were normally promoted from the ranks of working supervisors. Foreman and working supervisor had the same background, spoke alike, and thought alike. It was second nature for the foreman to consult with his former associates, to delegate powers to them, and to channel orders through them. Naturally, too, when a question of discipline arose, the working supervisor would be backed up with little question. Thus he assumed powers which were in many cases larger than those envisioned by formal company organization charts.

## THE "NEW" FOREMAN AND THE WORKING SUPERVISOR

As long as the "old-line" foreman was supreme, the working supervisor was secure. However, recent years have brought about substantial changes in management's concepts of the foreman's role. In particular, there is an emphasis on college training and on human relations skills.[2] Increasingly, the foreman's job is now a training ground for those being groomed for higher posts rather than a reward for years of service, although this may be occurring more slowly than some of the writers in the field of management development might believe.

The changes which occurred in the container plant may be typical of much which is happening in industry generally. Until recently the setup job was considered a stepping stone to higher things. In the old days the line of promotion ran from operator to helper to setup man and then to chief mechanic. If a man was exceptionally good, he might become master mechanic of an entire plant. Indeed, as everyone in the plant knew, a large number of former setup men held top jobs in the company's general offices.

This plant now has a supervisory training program. Its purpose is to bring into the company people who can eventually be promoted into middle- and top-management positions. Young college graduates receive a few months' training in each department and at the end of two years qualify as assistant foremen. Although ordinary workers in theory still have a chance to get ahead, actually no one has been promoted to a management job since the training program was introduced.

Having little understanding or sympathy for the working supervisor's position, the "new" foreman tends to undermine it. Thus changes which in theory affect the foreman alone have

---

[2] See William H. Whyte, Jr., *Is Anybody Listening?* (New York: Simon & Schuster, 1950), Chap. viii.

widespread implications throughout the shop.

Before examining the impact of these changes in the foreman's role, let us examine why they were made.

1. As production processes become more complicated, shop skills must be supplemented by engineering theory. With some processes even the man who directs the face to face group must have a scientific background which can be obtained only through a college education. This is particularly true where technology is rapidly changing and the ability learned by years on the job is largely outmoded.

2. Processes are becoming increasingly interrelated. Experience with a single work team or even one department may not be enough to enable one to coordinate activities adequately with other groups. A broader plant-wide (and even company-wide) point of view is highly desirable. Committee work and cooperation with other departments are becoming increasingly important. Furthermore, the very working-class background which makes it easy for working supervisors to get along with their subordinates makes it harder for them to communicate with college-trained men on higher levels. The personnel director of one plant justified the new policy on the grounds that "there is a lot you will never learn if you spend your whole life in one department. Somehow if you never use a single thing you learned in college, college training gives you a broader base by which to handle the day-to-day problems in the shop."

3. Today great attention is given to human relations skills. Increasingly, emphasis is placed on the ability to handle men rather than to handle process. By top-management standards the gruff autocrat who worked his way up from the ranks is not as good in human relations as the more socially "polished" college graduate. (However, as far as relations with the men on the job are concerned, it is entirely possible that the working supervisor is the man with the greater skill.)

What happened to the head nurse in one hospital is perhaps typical of a widespread tendency in industry. The nursing school is an important part of this large hospital (as it is in most large hospitals), and a large part of nursing education consists of on-the-job training. Traditionally, this was the responsibility of the head nurses of the various floors and wards, most of them women well along in years. As educational theories changed and the new profession of nursing administration developed, the feeling grew that these older head nurses were not providing adequate training. To coordinate their efforts, college-trained "clinical instructors" were introduced. Soon these instructors were engaged in general supervision and eventually were given the title of "supervisor." Thus they were placed over women who had considerably more years of age and experience than their own.

Furthermore, in many cases the foreman's authority has been seriously weakened. The areas of control which he once exercised now either are spelled out in contractual provisions about wages, seniority, or disciplinary procedure or have gravitated upward to middle management and the personnel department. These frequently settle grievances, grant merit increases, and so forth, usually in accordance with fixed rules. Even if the foreman wishes to, he can no longer give the working supervisor the kind of support he received in the past.

Just as on higher levels of management, the working supervisor's freedom to make arbitrary decisions has been limited by union contracts and explicit personnel policies. The old working supervisor exercised a highly autocratic pattern of control. Yet the author's research findings suggest that workers will be considerably more tolerant of a tough supervisor if they have respect for his technical ability.[3] Men speak with affection for someone who is a "hard driving devil, but the best damn widget-maker in the industry."

Tradition and personalized relations, such as that between the working supervisor and his men, are giving way throughout industry. In their place are coming a more rigid, impersonal set of relationships symbolized by the union contract and the company policy book.

The autocrat finds it hard to operate in an atmosphere where subordinates can question his decisions. In the old days the working supervisor might discipline the lazy apprentice by kicking him around. Today similar problems are handled with the union or by the apprentice training committee.

Furthermore, unions seek to draw a sharp line between management and workers. According to the union ethic, supervisors should not work and workers should not supervise. In effect, the union asks the working supervisor, "Which side are you on?" As we shall see, in some cases working supervisors take an active part in the union. Yet in many instances the union takes a strong position against them. As one union leader said, "The sooner we get rid of them, the better. Either they put on a white shirt [stop working],

[3]See also Stephen A. Richardson, "Organizational Contrast on British and American Ships," *Administrative Science Quarterly*, I, No. 2 (September, 1956), 189.

or they stop giving orders and acting like a foreman."

## HOW CHANGES IN JOB RELATIONSHIPS HAVE AFFECTED THE WORKING SUPERVISOR

The most obvious impact of these changes was a loss of opportunity for promotion and the consequent lowering of morale. Take a typical example:

In view of the rapid technological development in the natural gas company, it was decided that only college graduates would be appointed as foremen. Until this time, men had been rising out of the ranks. The poly operators were particularly upset by this ruling, for they were especially ambitious and had hoped for rapid promotion. Now many of them said, "We're just bumping our heads against the ceiling here."

One man in particular refused to believe he had been blocked. Enrolling in an International Correspondence Course in chemical engineering, he built a laboratory in his cellar and spent many long hours at his studies. No one in local management could say whether completion of this stiff course would be accepted as a substitute for a college degree—although he was one of the most intelligent and most competent of the younger men. As the months went by and he received no encouragement from management, he became increasingly upset about his relationship to the college-trained engineers. One day, after a minor blowup, he strode off the job in a fit of rage, never to return again.

However, more serious changes were involved than mere loss of promotional opportunities. In the old days foremen naturally channeled their orders through their former associates, the working supervisors. Today, the new foremen bypass them and give their orders to workers directly. For instance, the foreman might move an operator from one work team to another without consulting the working supervisors involved.

The "old-line" foreman and his working supervisors thought in the same terms; when the working supervisor faced insubordination, the foreman backed him up. Today foremen are likely to look upon the working supervisor's assertion of authority as a threat to their own. Take, for example, the followng two quotes from the same situation:

*Foreman:* Some of these working supervisors have been here so long that they run the place—and no one is going to tell them anything. Well, I'm going to cut them down to size.

*Working Supervisor:* I had one guy who was really making a mess, and I complained to the foreman. He watched him for about a half-hour before he finally transferred him away. Doesn't he take my word for it that the man is no good?

As a result, working supervisors lost much of their authority to direct and coordinate work teams, and in many cases cooperation within the work crew has declined markedly. Both working supervisors and operators now take less initiative and responsibility. Foremen rarely can coordinate the internal operations of every team at once. Often they do not even have the technical knowledge to do so.

One foreman's failure to know the proper nomenclature made him the laughing stock of the department—as well as costing the company considerable production.

The new college-trained foreman in the cracking still issued detailed instructions as to how the equipment was to operate and would accept no criticism of these instructions. When the instructions turned out wrong, the foreman insisted it was because the men had not followed them properly. So the poly operators operated the plant in the way which experience taught them would be effective and "boiler-housed" figures on the Daily Operating Sheet to make the foreman happy.

With differences in background and differences in "language," foremen and working supervisors had difficulty in communication. As one setup man put it:

The trouble with me is I haven't got a college education, and I can't explain things. I tried to explain this idea of mine to the foreman in three different ways. He just didn't get it—or maybe he didn't try. Finally, he said, "I don't understand what you are driving at, but go ahead and give it a try."

Gaffers in the glass plant found it difficult to communicate with their new production manager not only because of his lack of work-level experience but also because of the status difference:

He [the production manager] is too smart for us; we can't understand him half the time. You could talk to Shultz [the old foreman], and he knew what you meant to say.

From time to time setup men in the container plant had suggestions on how to improve the functioning of their machines. Management was too busy to listen. A foreman said, "Today you get your new developments from the laboratory, not from the plant floor." A worker pointed out, "They don't want you to think around here. As far as they are concerned, you are just a pair of hands."

To some extent working supervisors lost even their discretion to make technical decisions.

One of the contributing causes of discontent in the cracking still was the action of engineers in directing the hydrostillmen in detail as to how to make adjustments. Formerly these were made by the hydrostillmen and the poly operators [working supervisors] working together.

In the past, setup men in the container plant had considerable freedom to determine which line would receive first attention. The new foreman insisted on making these decisions himself, particularly since the product of some lines had a higher priority than others. The men looked upon this as arbitrary throwing of weight around, particularly since the new foreman never kept them informed as to priority requirements.

The immediate result of such changes was confusion. The working supervisor no longer had the authority to give orders; the new foreman did not have the ability, yet he found himself burdened down with far more duties than his predecessor had. Thus production fell down while the foreman tried to be every place at once.

In two of the situations observed someone of higher authority stepped in when the foreman was unable to provide the necessary technical coordination. In the container plant this was the plant superintendent, himself a former setup man (who, incidentally, worked much closer with the setup men than did the foreman). In the glass shop the production manager performed the same function. Yet,

such men could not afford to spend all their time in one department—and their very expertness tended further to reduce the prestige of both foreman and working supervisor.

As more and more trouble spots developed in the container plant, supervisors were brought in (management in effect assuming that two bad supervisors could equal one good one).

Because production was turning out so poorly, the plant superintendent began spending a disproportionate number of hours in this one department, the assistant superintendent made it a full-time assignment, and an assistant foreman was added. No wonder setup men began complaining of "too many bosses" and conflicting orders. At one critical moment six supervisors were observed hovering over a single setup man who later remarked, "It's getting so close with bosses around here that I can't turn around. Someday I am going to drop a wrench on someone's toes just to clear the way."

This picture was fairly general. In spite of a large number of management people, the average worker felt that he had lost contact with supervision. He was no longer able to get help from his working supervisor, while the foreman seemed too distant and too busy.

No exact measure of the impact on production of these changes in technology was made, and the effect of neither could be isolated. However, in all four situations there was general agreement that efficiency was not being maintained. In the container plant, for instance, even in the operations where technology remained unchanged, production dropped alarmingly; scrap, in this case a more acceptable measure of efficiency than raw-production data, increased 145 per cent. Yet, after changes were made (to be discussed later) which restored a good deal of the working supervisor's power, scrap and efficiency returned to normal in spite of a greatly accelerated program of technological change.

## THE WORKING SUPERVISOR'S REACTION

Shorn of authority and prestige, subject to duplicating and often clearly incorrect orders, it is not surprising that working supervisors suffered serious loss of morale. In many cases they lost interest in their work and refused to accept responsibilities. A typical comment was:

In the old days a setup man would never [make minor repairs] or clean the machine. Operators did that. Today an operator puts in a wrong piece and laughs at you because it breaks. If you gripe at them, you get in even more trouble. It's all management's fault. They see things, and yet they don't do anything. They don't back you up. I do what I can now, and that is it. I've stopped being so anxious and trying to get a good run.

Often, too, there was quasi-sabotage:

During union negotiations the superintendent of oil refinery replied to requests by poly operators for higher pay with the comment, "Down there everything is automatic. There is no skill in the work. You just watch the charts. If anything goes wrong, you call an engineer." The next day the columns were not operating properly. One of the staff engineers dropped in to ask the poly operator what seemed to be wrong. The workers shrugged their shoulders and replied, "You're supposed to tell us."

When the chief engineer of the division came in and asked the same question, he got the same answer. This was most embarrassing to the engineers.

A newly appointed bakery superintendent told his mixers [working supervisors], "From now on we are not going to have any prima donnas—we're going to follow the recipes from New York." The mixers complained that experience had taught them from day to day slight variations had to be made depending on the heat and humidity—but to no avail. As soon as the superintendent left, the senior mixer said, "They don't care what kind of bread they make," and lit a cigar and threw it into the batter.

In the container plant, where the college-trained foreman bypasses the setup man, nine setup men were regularly assigned to the day shift (no changes were made in the night shift, which consistently had higher production records throughout the change). One had a nervous breakdown, and another had a heart attack generally attributed to overstrain and overwork. Of the remaining seven, another five had serious illnesses, and in most cases no organic cause could be determined. All this happened during a period of twelve months.

In the glass-blowing shop some gaffers were completely demoralized by the changed situation, and shop morale and production suffered. A few outstanding artisans commanded respect for their proficiency in a trade where excellence of workmanship still reflects prestige on leader and his work crew alike.

## ACTIVITY IN THE UNION

In the old days, working supervisors were rarely active in the union. Once their authority and promotional opportunities were taken away, the picture changed, and they began participating actively. This gave them a chance to express their aggressions against the company and to display the leadership denied them in the plant. As respected natural leaders they soon attained high positions in the union.

In the container plant, for instance, setup men took a relatively inactive part in the union prior to the introduction of college-trained foremen. During the period of crisis they elected six out of seven officers. Once the foremen began channeling orders through them again, their participation dropped off rapidly.

As changes were made, the poly operators' status was gradually "clarified"—downward. About the time a CIO drive started among the lesser skilled men, the poly operators heard that in a neighboring plant men holding a job similar to theirs were receiving higher wages. Selecting a spokesman, they presented their case for more money to local management. In building up the importance of their position, they stressed their supervisory responsibilities. Management turned down the request and countered by ending the weekly meetings and announcing that they were now eligible for membership in the company union.

As the CIO drive made progress, the poly operators made one last attempt. They requested they be given the title of "shift foremen" so they would not have to make a choice between the CIO and the company union. This, too, was turned down.

Later, in negotiations with the company union, the general superintendent made the remark previously mentioned about the poly operator job requiring no skill. To this the leading poly operator commented, "The superintendent changed me from a Republican to a Democrat, anti-union to pro-union—overnight."

## CONCLUSION

The old-time working supervisor made an important contribution as the "non-com" who partially bridged the gap between management and the rank and file worker. The secret of his success was his lifelong knowledge both of the processes with which he worked and of the people who worked them. Above all, he was the leader of the "face to face" work group. In addition, working supervisors were the first rung in the promotional ladder which in many companies might lead through foreman and general foreman, right up into top management. Thus the working supervisor's job served the dual function of providing management with a reservoir of possibly promotable material and of symbolizing to the average worker the continuance of the American Horatio Alger ideal that every man can rise to the top.

It might well be argued that the position of the working supervisor was "ambiguous," yet this very ambiguity was its strength. In introducing college-trained foremen and clarifying the working supervisors' "ambiguous" position, management sought to achieve better human relations on the job. In fact, human relations often got worse. Management also felt that the engineering-trained college graduate would provide more expert technical direction.

It is undoubtedly true that more than mechanical "knack" is required to get maximum efficiency from increasingly complicated work processes. In spite of the working supervisor's disbelief, the new foreman often comes up with ideas which actually *are* better. Although he would be the last to admit it, technological change has frequently outmoded the working supervisor's special skills. Thus it would seem that management has good reason for many of the changes it makes. The trouble is that those changes are often made too far and too fast—and, above all, their impact on human relations has been ignored. The working supervisor still has an important (if reduced) role to play.

This is particularly true when the work is done by a team of men who must coordinate their efforts. Someone must provide the coordination, or the team falls apart. Even if the foreman had the technical competence, he must divide his attention among a number of work teams. Traditionally, coordination within the team is provided by the man whose job calls for the highest degree of skill (among other reasons because he has had the longest experience on the job). When the foreman fails to give this man special status, coordination becomes more difficult.

In the changes observed the working supervisor's status has been ignored or deliberately reduced. As a result his power over his fellows has declined and his efficiency brought to rock bottom. Even workers in lesser jobs look upon the working supervisor's apparent demotion as a threat to the security of their present position and their chance for advancement.

What can be done? Must the baby be thrown out with the bath? Not at all, for there is a natural division of responsibilities between the two jobs. The college-trained man can handle relations upward and outward (with higher management, staff agencies, and the union), while the working supervisor deals with purely internal problems. The chief requirement is that the foreman channels his orders through the working supervisor and gives him sufficient discretion to carry them out. Of course, on serious matters like formal discipline the foreman must have primary responsibility. However, before making his decisions, he should consult with the working supervisor.

Such adjustments were made in the container plant. The foreman now consciously channels orders through the set-up men, keeps them informed as to which particular item is most essential at the moment, and consults with them prior to moving men around.

As a consequence, the setup men's morale has substantially improved. They now report the foreman "has found himself—he knows what he is doing." Production has substantially improved. Recently a company emergency required the department to operate on a three-shift, seven-day week, concentrating on a particularly difficult item. Efficiency remained high, and setup men bragged about how well they were doing.

College-trained people are generally better than noncollege-trained people in dealing with management, who now are mostly college trained themselves. However, the selection of a college man at the foreman level tends to create a social gap between foreman and worker which may best be bridged by someone like the working supervisor.

On the technical level the relationship can be extremely productive. The engineering-trained foreman is an expert in theory; the working supervisor is an expert in practice. The foreman knows what should be done; the working supervisor knows how it can be carried out. College training and on-the-job experience are complements, not substitutes, for each other. As one working supervisor explained the difference in approach as follows:

When there are a set of adjustments to be made, these college guys want to make them all at once. But if it doesn't work out right, you don't know what is wrong; these machines never work the way the slide rule says they should. I like to make the changes one at a time and *wait* to see what happens. That way you creep up on it.

One of the main obstacles to fruitful foreman-working-supervisor cooperation is the fact that they speak different "languages." When the foreman's orders are not carried out, he blames it on the working supervisor's stubbornness rather than on poor communication; perhaps he takes direct charge of the process, since the working supervisor will not cooperate. The working supervisor, in turn, is frustrated because he cannot "get across." He feels that his foreman is either incompetent or pigheadedly refusing to admit that anyone else can have a good idea.

Once the foreman recognizes that there is a communication problem, it can be licked in time. However, the foreman must realize that the working supervisor does have an important contribution to make—and that it is worth making an effort to understand his advice. With patience, foremen and working supervisors can learn the other's language.

A perhaps more difficult problem is the common union demand that the working supervisor should stay either on one side of the fence or the other. Yet in the situations observed, this point of view was emphasized only when union-management relations were bad as a whole. Where the parties got along reasonably well, there was little insistence on drawing the line so sharply. In the building and printing trades, unions even insist that foremen belong to unions. Certainly, such problems can be settled through collective bargaining.

Indeed, particularly where it is no longer practical for foremen to be drawn from the rank and file, it would seem especially important to build up the job of working supervisor as a reward for service and skill. Furthermore, management would do well not to slam the door completely on the uneducated man's chance for advancement to higher jobs. Even if only a few pass the ever more distinct line which separates labor from management, the impact on morale is significant.

Of course, one of the main reasons for eliminating the working supervisor was his alleged autocratic behavior. The new college-trained foremen were expected to handle men in a more democratic manner. However, just as in higher management, the younger generation of working supervisors are showing more human relations skills. They look upon their job as being that of team leader and teacher and seek to solve problems through group discussion and voluntary cooperation rather than by bluster and command. With training, they should improve still further. In the glass-blowing shop, for instance, some of the gaffers developed a democratic leadership style which made cooperation possible even without support from management.

Foreman-working-supervisors cooperation can bring rich rewards. In many processes the working supervisor's function as technical coordinator is absolutely essential and cannot be well performed by those who have not had his years of experience on the job. Even where this is not true, the working supervisor has much to contribute as a link between management and rank-and-file workers. Certainly, management should devote more attention to defining more carefully his role.

---

There are not many individual studies of the actual behavior of foremen. In the following selection a broad sample of such studies is analyzed to determine what foremen actually do on the job.

One of the most notable findings of these studies is the amount of time foremen spend in horizontal relations. These are interactions with other foremen. The horizontal or peer relations are to be contrasted with relations between the foremen and his workers on the one hand and the foremen and his bosses on the other hand. Roethlisberger has emphasized the "man-in-the-middle" position of the foremen in the vertical structure of the organization. The more recent studies of foremen behavior summarized below emphasizes the position of the foremen as a link in the chain of horizontal relationships. This is, of course, the manner in which a great deal of coordination is achieved between operations in the work-flow. The horizontal flow of work of related activities is largely coordinated through non-formal human relations. This idea of non-formal human relations was developed in Chapter 5.

---

## THE BEHAVIOR OF FOREMEN*

### Robert Dubin

We now turn to examine the behavior of foremen as it has been reported in the literature. Here we are no more fortunate in having data any better than that available on executives.

In contrast with the very high percentage of total time that executives spend in talking, it appears that foremen are much more likely to be doers than talkers. Ponder[1] reported observational studies of twelve "high effective" General Electric foremen, showing that they spent 56 per cent of their total time talking, while "low effective" GE foremen devoted 45 per cent of their time to conversation. Guest's study of fifty-six automobile assembly plant foremen, again an observational study, showed that the foremen aver-

*Reprinted by permission from C. Argyris, R. Dubin, M. Haire, R. D. Luce, W. L. Warner, and W. F. Whyte, *Social Science Approaches to Business Behavior* (Homewood, Ill.: Dorsey-Irwin, 1962).

[1] Z. D. Ponder, "The Effective Manufacturing Foreman," *Proceedings of the Tenth Annual Meeting of the Industrial Relations Research Association* (Madison, Wis.: The Association, 1958), pp. 41–54.

aged 46.6 per cent of their time in conversation.[2] The Ponder study apparently counted all interaction contacts as "talking" contacts, while in the Guest study only actual talking was so counted. Guest reported that all interpersonal contacts accounted for 57.3 per cent of all the time of his fifty-six foremen, apparently a measure more comparable with Ponder's results.

It will be recalled that the farther down the ranks of management we went, the higher was the proportion of time spent with superiors relative to time spent with subordinates. When we get to the foreman level, however, the facts seem to indicate that foremen are so busy getting their work done that they do not have time to spend with their bosses. By recalculating the Ponder and Guest data, we secure the picture of Table 1,

here are only suggestive, since the classifications were very loosely drawn by the original investigators. Nevertheless, it is clear that a significantly higher proportion of all interaction time was spent by foremen with their subordinates than was true for any but the department manager in the executive study. If we were able to add in the subordinates included among the "others" in the table, this result would be even more apparent.

Perhaps we can surmise from these comparative data that the direct supervisory responsibility forces downward orientation for a boss, whether he is a department manager or a first-line foreman. On the other hand, it may be that line supervisors without a direct rank-and-file command or who perform both staff and line functions must spend more time interacting with the boss to find out what is expected

**Table 1**

Per Cent of Foremen's Total Interaction Time
Spent with People of Various Ranks

| Ranking of Person with Whom Interacting | 12 "High Effective" General Electric Foremen | 12 "Low Effective" General Electric Foremen | 56 Automobile Assembly Plant Foremen | 16 Midwest Production Department Foremen |
|---|---|---|---|---|
| Superiors | Not given | Not given | 10 | 30 |
| Subordinates | 34 | 39 | 46 | 60 |
| Peers | Not given | Not given | 12 | 10 |
| Others* | 66 | 61 | 32 | 0 |
| Data-gathering method | Observation | Observation | Observation | Observation |
| Source | Ponder | Ponder | Guest | Piersol** |

*Includes some superiors from other departments and areas, all the superiors in the two GE samples, and some subordinates and peers in other departments.
**"Communication Practices of Supervisors in a Mid-Western Corporation," *Advanced Management,* 23:20-21, February, 1958.

which is somewhat comparable to the similar table for executives. The data

[2]R. H. Guest, "Of Time and the Foreman," *Personnel,* May, 1956.

and/or to be one of his informational sources and advisers. However we interpret these data, it seems clear that there are significant differences in the proportions of contact time spent with superiors, peers, and subordinates by various levels of managers.

Jasinski,[3] using a portion of the data from Guest's study of the fifty-six automobile assembly-line foremen, found that in one department of eleven foremen there were about 300 contacts among them in a single eight-hour day. He observed that an average of three quarters of all contacts for the average foreman were either with the foremen immediately preceding him on the line or with the one immediately succeeding him. Simpson,[4] using reported contacts data and only accepting those contacts mutually reported for a group of eight foremen (general foreman, two shift foremen, five crew foremen) on two shifts in the same department, showed that among the five crew supervisors there was a range of 43–76 per cent of all contacts among foremen that were peer contacts. These two reports tell us again the importance of the horizontal dimension of management and give some clue as to the volume of non-formal relations involved in getting work done at the foreman level. To give some idea of how much this peer-level interaction is work-oriented, as our model of "non-formal relations" predicts,[5] Table 2 summarizes Jasinski's data for the eleven foremen he observed. Only 9.7

[3]F. J. Jasinski, "Foreman Relations outside the Work Group," *Personnel,* 33:130–136, September, 1956.

[4]R. L. Simpson, "Vertical and Horizontal Communication in Formal Organization," *Administrative Science Quarterly,* 4:188–196, September, 1959.

[5]We observe that there is a very substantial increase in the proportion of time spent in interaction that is devoted to peers as we move downward in the rank system. This reaches half the total interacting time for the senior and junior staff men under the departmental manager. Now there is almost

**Table 2**

SUBJECTS OF FOREMAN-TO-FOREMAN INTERACTION

| Subject | Per Cent of Interaction Time |
|---|---|
| Production | 27.1 |
| Personnel administration | 13.7 |
| Equipment and methods | 3.1 |
| Quality | 35.8 |
| Personal, non-work | 9.7 |
| Other | 10.6 |

Adapted from Jasinski *op. cit.,* p. 135.

no notice taken in the literature (good *exceptions* being Richardson and Walker in *Human Relations in an Expanding Company* and the anecdotal accounts of Dalton in *Men Who Manage*) of the *horizontal* dimension of organization and the volume of business that is transacted among *peers* to keep the organization going. Indeed, it is probably among organizational equals that much of the real coordination of work flow and operations takes place in what we, in *The World of Work,* called the "non-formal behavior system." The non-formal behavior system is the arena in which the organization is made to work by supplementing the formal procedures, rules, etc., with realistic applications of them to operating situations. Jaques, in *The Changing Culture of a Factory,* pointed to nonformal behavior systems when he concluded from his long-term observational study of the English factory that " . . . it is an impossible task to make policy completely explicit. There remains always a residue of unrecognized and unidentified aspects of the culture of the concern. . . . The identification and labeling of these is a never-ending process." Weiss, in *Processes of Organization,* gives some brief descriptions of non-formal behavior among government research administrators, although not labeling it by this term.

It cannot be too strongly emphasized that horizontal relations among peers in management and the non-formal behavior systems through which such interactions are carried out constitute a dimension of organizational behavior long neglected and probably as important as authority relations. We shall see this same characteristic peer-to-peer interaction as an important form of contact among foremen in doing their work.

per cent of the total interactions among foremen could be classified as personal—non-work, as Table 2 shows. Almost 80 per cent of the total time spent together among foremen was devoted to the four clearly work-oriented subjects of production, personnel administration, equipment and materials, and quality of output.

For both the executive data and the foremen data we find substantial support for the plea that the horizontal interactional aspects of managerial behavior among peers be accorded significant attention in the research and theorizing about managerial behavior.

There do not appear to be data for foremen comparable with the facts about the functional behavior of executives presented in Chapter 8. Ponder reported that his twelve "high effective" foremen gave orders 8 per cent of the time they were in interaction with subordinates, while the "low effective" foremen gave orders 16 per cent of the time. The "high effective" received information 25 per cent of the time during contact with subordinates, while the "low effective" foremen were getting information 37 per cent of the time that they were with subordinates. These figures are not directly comparable with the similar ones for executives, since the foremen data were based only on interactions with subordinates, while the executive data covered all interactions. The most significant thing we can conclude from these foreman data is that getting information from rank-and-file workers is a relatively important behavior of foremen, just as getting information about the organization turned out to be important behavior of executives. For those organizational theorists who still believe that some members of an organization can be power*less*, these data on the

dependence of all ranks of management on the upward flow of information should be a proper corrective. As a minimum, the rank-and-file, by controlling the information going to the foreman and then on upward, has significant power in its own hands.

There is only a single report on the balance of initiating contacts and receiving contacts by foremen. Guest reported that 60.3 per cent of all foremen contacts were initiated by them. Burns' data on the department manager yield a comparable figure of managers' initiations of 57 per cent. The similarity of the proportions may be noted, but in the absence of any further comparisons it is difficult to draw any meaningful conclusions from this fact.

One final fact of substantial agreement should be noted about the foremen's position. Three different studies, two of them based on direct observation and one based on self-records, indicated that the overwhelming content of the interaction of foremen with all other people was devoted to the close details of work. The four areas of production, personnel administration, equipment and methods, and quality account for between 63 and 78 per cent of all interactions. The data are shown in Table 3.

We emerge, then, with the following summary picture of the content and ecology of managerial behavior. Decision-making and giving orders—the classical functions of managers—seem to occupy a relatively minor amount of their time. At all levels of management a major investment of time is made in getting information from lower levels of the organization as a basis for knowing what is happening and presumably also as a basis for follow-up decisions and action. The environment of the executive is verbal

**Table 3**

PER CENT OF TOTAL TIME OF FOREMEN SPENT
IN AREAS OF OPERATING RESPONSIBILITY

| Area of Operating Responsibility | 12 "High Effective" General Electric Foremen | 12 "Low Effective" General Electric Foremen | 56 Automobile Assembly Plant Foremen | Radio Corporation of America Foremen |
|---|---|---|---|---|
| Production | 20 | 40 | 34.5* | ⎫ |
| Personnel administration | 23 | 12 | 13.2* | ⎪ |
| Equipment and methods | 14 | 8 | 16.3* | ⎬ 78 |
| Quality | 6 | 6 | 18.2 | ⎭ |
| Other | 37 | 34 | 17.8 | 22 |
| Data-gathering method | Observation | Observation | Observation | Self-record |
| Source | Ponder | Ponder | Guest | Zinck** |

*Composite of reported categories.
**"The Foreman and Productivity," *Advanced Management*, 23:12-16, January, 1958.

to a high degree, with the volume of time spent in conversation diminishing as we go down the ranks of management. A remarkable amount of time is spent by all ranks of management with organizational peers, which, by infer-ence, leads to the conclusion that much of the active co-ordination of actual work of the organization that "makes things really run" is carried out through non-formal relations.

In the concluding selection of this chapter we examine the very marked differences between the personality attributes executives see themselves possessing, and those possessed by career supervisors. Those who hold executive offices are a separate and distinctive group of people whose very personality characteristics seem to fit the demands of their offices. Further-more, and this is of crucial importance, supervisors confirm the self-images held by executives, by describing them largely as the executives describe themselves. This provides strong evi-dence that the office of executive is clearly recognized at both ends of the managerial ranks, and that there is considerable agreement in describing the personal characteristics of those who fill the office.

This study also tells us a good deal about supervisors. For all the char-acteristics on which executives are held to have "more than," supervisors have "less than." In addition, super-visors, when asked if they would like to become executives given the chance to do it over, were strong and united in rejecting this goal. Their success goals are set lower and they are ad-justed to these lower goals. Part of their rationalization is that the wear and tear of success at higher levels is not worth it. It is important to be aware that the rags-to-riches ideology has faded fast in American industry. Those who start at the bottom (rather than from a college education) see relatively low ceilings for themselves, and can find reasons for not being dissatisfied with this lot in life.

---

## EXECUTIVES AND SUPERVISORS: SELF-VIEWS AND VIEWS OF EACH OTHER

### *Charles H. Coates* and *Roland J. Pellegrin**

Cooley's "looking-glass self" and Mead's "taking the role of the generalized other" rank among the foremost concepts in sociology.[1] In spite of their utility and significance, however, these concepts have rarely been exploited in the investigation of why some individuals achieve more vertical occupational mobility and career success than others in the same or similar occupational environments.

Successful executives in business and industry have often been and are continually being studied through self-appraisals obtained by personal interviews and questionnaires.[2] Their success stories are widely publicized, and the top-level business and industrial executive has been popularized as an ideal type of successful American. From such self-appraisals by outstanding executives, so many generalizations have been made about "how to become successful" that it is often erroneously assumed that the means of achieving executive success have universal applicability. What is usually overlooked is that executive success, like leadership and success in other occupational fields, is subject to situational and environmental variability. It would therefore seem logical to study differential executive success situationally by asking top-level executives to appraise their "looking-glass selves," and to take the roles of "generalized others" on the top and bottom rungs of the executive ladder by appraising retrospectively their own personal attributes in contrast with those of subordinates in their own or similar occupational environments. It would also seem logical to compare these top-level appraisals oriented downward with similar lower-level appraisals oriented upward.

Essentially, this was the approach employed in a comparative study made in 1954 and 1955 of 50 top-level executives in 30 large and bureaucratically structured business, industrial, governmental, and educational organizations, and 50 first line supervisors in the same or similar occupa-

---

*From "Executives and Supervisors: Contrasting Self-Conceptions and Conceptions of Each Other," *American Sociological Review*, 22:217–220 (April 1957). Used by permission.

[1] Charles H. Cooley, *Human Nature and the Social Order* (New York: Scribner's, 1902); and George H. Mead, *Mind, Self and Society* ed. Charles W. Morris, (Chicago: University of Chicago Press, 1934).

[2] A recent example of such research is found in W. Lloyd Warner and James C.

Abegglen, *Big Business Leaders in America* (New York: Harper & Brothers, 1955).

tional environments.[3] The setting of the study was a dynamic Southern community, fictitiously called "Bigtown," which had experienced within a span of 30 years a growth to a population of 200,000 as a result of industrial and business expansion. The confidential personal interview was used in studying the comparative samples of top- and low-level individuals in management, all of whom had long occupational histories. Because of the effective matching of the samples on the basis of age and long occupational histories, the retrospective appraisals had a unique quality of depth in time. The confidential nature of the study made possible considerable interviewer-interviewee rapport, which brought forth a wealth of subjective data. Since standardized interview schedules were utilized, comparative analysis of the data was facilitated.

The following analysis is limited to the executives' and the supervisors' self-conceptions and conceptions of each other. In eliciting these self- and other-conceptions, open-ended questions were utilized on the interview schedule, and no pre-conceived list of desirable or undesirable attributes was employed. The attributes presented below are derived from a content analysis of equivalent terms most frequently mentioned by interviewees. There was virtually no disagreement

concerning the attributes of executives and supervisors, although some respondents listed more attributes than others. Each attribute was mentioned independently by at least 15 of the 50 persons involved in each self- or other-rating.

### RESULTS

Most executives conceived of themselves as possessing several of the dynamic personal attributes revealed in Henry's well-known study of 100 executives in the Chicago business community.[4] Among these were: strong achievement desire, high mobility drive, sympathetic conception of authority, considerable ability to organize, firm decisiveness, strong self-structure, much aggressive activity, and direct orientation toward reality. Mention of these executive attributes was to be expected, but of more interest were the main distinctions that executives made between themselves, their associates, and first-line supervisors they had known through the years.

These comparative self- and other-appraisals usually began with a statement of qualities that executives possess and that supervisors either lack or possess to a lesser degree. Among the distinctions most frequently made by executives between themselves and supervisors were: more energy, alertness, and initiative; aggressive as opposed to submissive attitudes; more understanding of and ability to get along with and manipulate people; greater willingness to assume responsibilities and make decisions; greater

---

[3]Further information on the scope, method, and content of the study is presented in the following papers by the authors: "Absentee-Owned Corporations and Community Power Structure," *American Journal of Sociology*, 61 (March, 1956), pp. 413–419; "Executives and Supervisors: A Situational Theory of Differential Occupational Mobility," *Social Forces* 31 (December, 1956), pp. 121–126; and "Executives and Supervisors: Contrasting Definitions of Career Success." *Administrative Science Quarterly*, 1 (March, 1957), pp. 506–517.

[4]William E. Henry, "The Business Executive: The Psychodynamics of a Social Role," *The American Journal of Sociology*, 54 (January, 1949), 286–291.

ability to deal with and impress superiors; better judgment and foresight; more magnetic, well-rounded, projective personalities; more tact and poise; better problem-solving ability; more adaptability to changing situations; more determination and strength of personal character; different definitions of the meaning of success; greater ability to sell themselves and their ideas, and to get things done through group effort; more education and training; different occupational and social contacts and opportunities; different loyalties and job interests. Illustrative of the self- and other-conceptions of the executives are the following:

*Executive A:* Successful executives are not "born," or "made" in college, but are products of their social environments. Compared to low level supervisors they have much more ability, personality, human understanding, and motivation. They have different attitudes and values and different definitions of organizational and personal success. Low level men simply lack the inner determination to climb further up the executive ladder.

*Executive B:* The main distinctions are: "spark" or lack of it, willingness to accept responsibility and make decisions or the lack of it, ability to handle people or the lack of it. I can't define "spark," but you know it when you see it. Maybe it is a combination of personality and drive.

*Executive C:* The big difference in the two levels is in the ability to analyze the motives of others and to foresee their reactions. Low level men are unable to realize why people react as they do. Because of this they lack the ability to plant ideas in others and get them to do things.

Like the executives whom Henry

studied, these executives placed high values on achievement and self-directedness, but they may also pay a high price for holding these values.[5] The executives were asked to give their conceptions of the penalties and sacrifices associated with the achievement of top-level executive success. Among those most frequently mentioned were: adverse effect of a pressure environment on personal health; considerably more worry than the average professional person; lack of time for recreation and leisure; insufficient opportunity for normal family life; a certain amount of loneliness associated with an isolated position; feeling that hard work would lead to even harder work; recurring invasions of personal privacy; forced suppression of personal desires; continuous disruption of personal plans; constant fear of making wrong decisions. One executive stated:

*Executive D:* This corporation has been reorganized just so I could turn over the presidency to a younger man. I wanted to get rid of all of these responsibilities, worries, and pressures. The ups and downs in the competitive business world are terrific. You're always on the 'phone, days and nights and holidays. I've got to get more time with my family and more time for recreation before it is too late. I haven't had a vacation in four years, and the only way to get one is to just pack up and leave town.

In order to compare the self- and other-conceptions of the executives oriented downward, the supervisors were invited to give similar self- and other-conceptions oriented upward.[6]

---

[5] *Ibid.*, p. 291.

[6] See Robert Dubin, "Upward Orientation Toward Superiors" in his *Human Relations in Administration* (New York: Prentice-Hall, 1951), 2nd ed., Chap. 17.

When asked to make the main distinctions between themselves, their supervisory associates, and executives they had known through the years, the great majority rather surprisingly tended to concede to executives greater amounts of the same personal attributes in which executives had tended to claim superiority. What was of more interest, however, were their reasons for conceding to executives this superiority. Their concessions seemed to have resulted not only from their conceptions of their own personal limitations and those of their associates but also from their conceptions of the differential role expectations of executives and supervisors. Supervisors tended to be acutely aware of the handicaps of their socio-cultural backgrounds, education and training, and occupational opportunities.[7] As derivatives of these self-conceived personal limitations, they tended to concede to executives: better social and educational backgrounds, more ambition and motivation; higher level attitudes, values and life goals; more energy, alertness, and initiative; better understanding of human nature; better rounded, more magnetic personalities; more ability to handle large numbers of people; more ability to solve problems and make long-range plans; more willingness to delegate authority, accept responsibility, and make decisions. Illustrative self- and other-conceptions of the supervisors follow:

*Supervisor A:* Top men are totally different from supervisors. Top men have better social backgrounds and education and thus have different abilities and goals. Most supervisors want to get so high and no higher because they don't want big responsibilities. They just want to carry out instructions without having to make decisions.

*Supervisor B:* Top level men are like Army Generals. They sit down, make the plans, and issue the orders, though in doing so they are thoughtful, courteous, understanding, and helpful. Supervisors carry out the orders like Army Sergeants. Some are hard-boiled, and some are soft-boiled. Some are drivers, and some are leaders. It all depends on how they think the boss wants them to behave.

*Supervisor C:* The top level is better at getting jobs done through group effort because they have more flexible, more magnetic personalities. They are the better planners, organizers, coordinators, decision-makers, and administrators. That's what top men are for, anyway.

To throw further light upon their conceptions of the roles of top level executives, the supervisors were asked the question, "If you could start all over again, would you like to become a top level executive?" The great majority of the supervisors stated emphatically that they would *not*. Usually they gave as their reasons, "too many worries, headaches, and responsibilities." As one veteran supervisor expressed it:

*Supervisor D:* Who, me? Hell no! Not way up top. Look at our head man. He has a wonderful education, makes a lot of money, and has a big reputation. But that kind of job commands a man's whole being, day and night, and almost commands his soul. He's always contending with worries, responsibilities, and decisions. The directors hound him to death. With the power and the glory go the headaches and the ulcers. One of my

---

[7] The effects of these factors upon career patterns are analyzed in the authors' "Executives and Supervisors: A Situational Theory of Differential Occupational Mobility," *op. cit.*

top level friends died the other day of "industrial suicide." As for me, I'd rather have a happy, pleasant life. What's the use of killing yourself?

Thus, there appeared in the self- and other-conceptions of supervisors an acute awareness, not only of their own personal limitations, but also of the penalities and sacrifices associated with top level executive roles.

## IMPLICATIONS

1. Superiors tend to judge their subordinates in terms of their own self-images, and to appraise low-level role performance by comparing it with their own high-level role performance.

2. Subordinates tend to judge their superiors in terms of their own images of high-level role expectations, and to account for their own personal limitations in terms of socio-cultural back- grounds and conceptions of low-level role expectations.

3. Both superiors and subordinates tend to be aware of the rewards, penalties, and sacrifices associated with high-level roles. Such an awareness differentially influences achievement desires on the two levels.

4. Such self-conceived achievement desires positively or negatively affect role performance and therefore differentially influence life-span career success.[8]

Further study of comparative samples of individuals at different levels in various occupational hierarchies may be helpful in increasing understanding of such factors as differential motivation, role performance, and status striving.

---

[8]On this point, see the discussion in *ibid.* and in our "Executives and Supervisors: Contrasting Definitions of Career Success,' *op. cit.*

# part 4

# ADMINISTRATIVE
# RELATIONSHIPS

To administer an organization involves the use of special kinds of relationships *among* the administrators, and *between* them and the subordinates they direct. We call these administrative relationships. Of special significance as administrative relationships are power, authority, and status as they are used as tools of administration.

Human relationships are interactions among people. These interactions have systematic qualities, obeying rules by which they are guided. Within limits, each individual administrator has personal choices he can make regarding the style and manner of his own administrative relationships with fellow members of management and with subordinates. There are, however, clear limits that guide these choices. It is the purpose of this section of the volume to examine the nature of these limits on administrative relationships. From the knowledge gained through this analysis should come insights about the content and quality of administrative behavior.

**OVERVIEW**

The administrator's interactions with other members of the organization relate his official duties with theirs. He is linked to the rest of the organization through power relations and authority relations. These two fundamental types of human relations are evidenced every day in the behavior of organization members. They can be called the *operating* administrative relationships. By this is simply meant that in the process of carrying out assigned duties, each organization member is linked to others in systematic ways.

253

Where the linking is achieved by establishing who performs what function
we are dealing with a power relationship. Where the linking is in terms
who makes the decisions about the quality of performance of functions, we a
dealing with an authority relationship. This distinction between power an
authority is drawn out in the next two chapters, in which definitions, illustr
tions and analytical consequences are set forth.

Status relations are distinguished from power and authority relations by tl
fact that they are a product of judgments about where people stand in con
parison with each other on some scale of judgment. Once people can be place
in their relative position on such a scale, we can then interact with them
accordance with our respective standings on the judgment scale. It is immed
ately apparent that there are two basic types of status relationships: that b
tween a higher and a lower person on a scale of judgment, and that betwee
equals who have the same standing on the scale. Status relations confirm tl
*location* of people in comparison with each other. When these respective loc
tions are established consistently by those interacting, they then behave towar
each other as equals, or as superior-inferior. It will become apparent fro
the discussion in the next three chapters that status relations are *confirmin*
administrative relationships as distinct from the characterization of *operatir*
administrative relationships applied to power and authority.

We call power, authority, and status the fundamental administrative rel
tionships because they are the three basic ways by which people are linked wit
each other in an organization. Power and authority establish who does wh
in the organization, and who decides the distribution of functions and tl
quality of their performance. Status establishes the standing of people in respe
to each other on some common scale of judgment and thereby determin
whether they interact as friends (when they view each other as equals) or wit
some constraint (when they mutually accept the belief that one is better tha
the other). Thus, it is possible to derive from the three fundamental administr.
tive relationships the full spectrum of administrative interactions found in o
ganizations, ranging from impersonal decision-making to personal friendship

Analytically it turns out to be most useful and practical to be able to reduc
administrative relationships to the three fundamental ones of power, authorit
and status without any loss of understanding of the full range of administrativ
behavior. Once the operating executive, and the student who expects to becom
one, finds that it makes sense to organize his thinking about administrativ
relationships around the three fundamental concepts, he can see order an
achieve understanding of what might have the surface appearance of rich co
fusion. Put another way, grasping the fundamental analytical components of
situation provides the "big picture" into which the specific details of the situ
tion can be fitted in comprehensible ways.

# 11

## Power

*[handwritten annotation: administrative relationships ① power ② authority ③ status]*

The concept of *power* is universally used in describing human relations. Yet it is one of the least understood ideas, and is a concept about which there is relatively little agreement.

The first theoretical selection is helpful in cutting through some of the difficulty with terminology. In particular, there are sharp distinctions, through mutually exclusive definitions of power and other concepts with which it may be confused, or to which it may be related.

The second selection of the chapter is one of the good empirical studies of power in organizations. Thompson compares two identical units of the Air Force by asking the members of management in them (the officers) to identify and rank the fellow officers among them who "have most to do with getting things done around here." You will note that this is asking about the people in each organization who produce important effects, through their actions, on the business of the organization. Put another way, the power of the rated individuals is determined by their functional importance to their respective units "in getting things done." This idea of functional importance as the content of power has been elaborated elsewhere.[1] It is sufficient to repeat here that the functional importance of the official in getting things done, as distinct from his formal authority (or his legitimate right to get things done) is what constitutes the measure of power used by Thompson.

The fundamental characteristic of society is that

**INTRODUCTION**

---

[1]See: Robert Dubin, *The World of Work* (Englewood Cliffs, N. J.: Prentice-Hall, Inc., 1958), especially Chaps. 2 and 3.

it orders the relations among individuals, between individuals and groups, and among groups. Groups and individuals do not interact haphazardly; the interactions are structured and organized. The element that underlies these systems of organized interactions is power.

The latent quality of power may be troublesome to grasp. Let us think in terms of an analogy, for a moment. Gravity is something latent in a body. When gravity is exercised, we talk about gravitational force or the pull of gravity. The expression of the quality of gravity is something we designate by the terms "force" or "pull." In the same sense we can view power as latent. We can never touch, feel, smell, or contact power. But certain classes of human actions that we can observe and contact can be given meaning only by assuming that the actor possesses power.

In other words, what we are trying to do when we use the concept of power is to distinguish certain kinds of human action from other kinds. Two people in love are not ordinarily thought of as being in a power relationship. Several youngsters playing together are not in a power relationship. On the other hand, a foreman makes use of power in the exercise of authority over his workers.

We are trying to understand a frame of reference for analyzing and comprehending leadership and subordination. Such a frame of reference is grounded in the concept of power.

The next several chapters are difficult. The ideas are complex and intricate. But we are, after all, dealing with the most complex and intricate of all phenomena—human relations.

In the first selection of this chapter, we have a broad-gauge analysis of the types of social action that are based upon power. Let us not get lost in maze of terminology. The term *power holder* is used. What the power holder *does* is exercise force, domination, or manipulation. He does not use power directly in his relations with subordinates. This is a crucial point to keep in mind.

Perhaps we ought to discuss the power-holder more fully. Power, although latent, also has a focal point, location. Power does not just float around unattached to anything. We know where power resides only when we observe people in interaction. We know that certain people or groups have power when the consequences of their actions can be observed in the behavior of other people. We specifically limit the kinds of initiating acts that we call power acts to those that involve the exercise of force, domination, or manipulation.

It is within this framework that we can find the location of authority which we deal with specifically in the next chapter. Bierstedt says that authority is institutionalized power. That means that in an organization, the right to exercise command is built into the organization. Authority is one element of a social structure, a social organization. Domination and manipulation, as defined by Goldhammer and Shils, are the *ways* in which authority is expressed in an organization: the authority of the legitimate power holder rests upon his recognized right of domination.

One other point should be called to your attention. The analysis of acts based upon power inevitably brings up the question of what happens when disobedience occurs. Goldhammer and Shils discuss this. So does Simon, in the next chapter, with specific reference to disobedience to authority. In Chapter 18, we examine

ontrol of the organization and behavior in it as one of the important
organization devices for minimizing
disobedience.

The following selection focuses our
attention on acts based upon power.

We will make this more concrete in
the next chapter when we deal with
the principal expression of power
within a formal organization—authority.

## TYPES OF POWER

### Herbert Goldhammer and Edward A. Shils*

A person may be said to have *power*
to the extent that he influences the behavior[1] of others in accordance with
his own intentions. Three major forms
of power may be distinguished in
terms of the type of influence brought
to bear upon the subordinated individual. The power-holder exercises
*force* when he influences behavior by
a physical manipulation of the subordinated individual (assault, confinement, etc.); *domination* when he influences behavior by making explicit
to others what he wants them to do
(command, request, etc.);[2] and *ma-*

*nipulation* when he influences the behavior of others without making explicit the behavior which he thereby
wants them to perform.[3] Manipulation
may be exercised by utilizing symbols
or performing acts. Propaganda is a
major form of manipulation by symbols. The undermining of confidence
in an enterprise by sabotaging its activities may be taken as an example of
manipulation by acts.

Most power-holders claim legiti-

---

*From "Types of Power and Status,"
*American Journal of Sociology*, 45:171–178
(Sept. 1939). Used by permission of The
University of Chicago Press.

[1]Behavior is here to be understood as both
covert and overt behavior. Influence is to be
understood as both an alteration of behavior
and a maintenance of behavior as it was, but
other than what it would have been without
the intervention of the power-holder.

[2]"Shoulder arms!" and "Please close the
door" are both cases of domination, provided, of course, that these utterances succeed in realizing the intentions of the
speaker. It may be that everyday associations render "Please close the door" as an
example of domination somewhat surprising.
A polite request, however, is as much a way
of getting people to do what one wants them
to do as is the most brutally uttered command. Polite requests often enable a person
to exercise power over another where a command containing no elements of deference

may fail. The relation between the exercise
of power over, and the granting of deference
to, subordinated individuals is not treated
here.

[3]Since the distinction between domination and manipulation rests on the degree to
which the power-holder makes his intention
explicit to the person whose behavior he
wants to influence, the two frequently shade
off into each other. It often happens, of
course, that the context in which the power-
holder's behavior takes place is such as to
enable him to assume that his intention is
quite clear to the person whom he is attempting to influence. It is desirable to include such cases under domination.

It is clear that manipulation excludes
modifications of behavior following the communication of factual representations in discussion. In the case of discussion the intentions of the discussants are evident to each
other. This, of course, does not preclude the
possibility of manipulatory elements entering into a discussion. As in the cases discussed in the first paragraph, the line between discussion and manipulation may (in
certain concrete cases) be difficult to draw.

*Force*
*Domination*
*Manipulation*

macy for their acts, i.e., they claim the "right to rule" as they do. If the legitimacy of the exercise of power is acknowledged by the subordinated individuals we speak of *legitimate power;* if it is not recognized we call it *coercion* (provided, of course, that the intention of the power-holder is realized). There are three major forms of legitimate power. Legitimate power is regarded as *legal* when the recognition of legitimacy rests on a belief by the subordinated individuals in the legality of the laws, decrees, and directives promulgated by the power-holder; *traditional* when the recognition of legitimacy rests on a belief in the sanctity of traditions by virtue of which the power-holder exercises his power and in the traditional sanctity of the orders which he issues; and *charismatic* when the recognition of legitimacy rests on a devotion to personal qualities of the power-holder. Usually, of course, these personal qualities are, or appear to the followers to be, extraordinary qualities such as sanctity and heroism.[4]

A person whose general position as a power-holder is recognized as legitimate may exercise force, domination, or manipulation. But, as far as the recognition of the legitimacy of individual acts of power is concerned, it is clear that manipulation cannot be legitimate power, since in the case of manipulation there is no recognition by the subordinated individual that an act of power has been effected. Persons who are subject to force (especially as an initial form of influencing behavior and not as a sanction) frequently do not recognize the legitimacy of such acts of power. Gener-

ally, therefore, the recognition of a power-holder as a legitimate exerciser of power rests on the recognition of the legitimacy of his acts of domination. However, this need not mean that he may not also exercise force or manipulation.

Attempted domination may meet with obedience or disobedience. The motivation for obedience and disobedience is *instrumental* to the extent that it is based on an anticipation of losses and gains, and *noninstrumental* to the extent that it is based on ethical or affective imperatives of conduct dictating obedience or disobedience to the command. In the case of obedience these imperatives may derive either (a) from a belief that the recognition of power as legitimate, i.e., as legal, traditional, or charismatic, imposes obedience as a norm of conduct or (b) from norms of conduct (e.g., the mores) which dictate, not obedience to the power-holder but the performance of the particular acts commanded. In the case of disobedience, the imperatives will likewise derive either (a) from a belief that the recognition of power as nonlegitimate, i.e., coercive, imposes disobedience as a norm of conduct or (b) from norms of conduct which dictate not disobedience to the power-holder but the nonperformance of the particular acts commanded.[5] Although one may rec-

---

[4]The classification of types of legitimate power is that of Max Weber (cf. *Wirtschaft und Gesellschaft* [Tübingen, 1925], I, 124).

[5]Motivation for conformity with, or rejection of, the expressed wish or demand of the power-holder is here considered only in terms of perceptions by the subordinated person of certain selected characteristics of the power-holder and the commanded act. Clearly a number of other factors would be relevant in a complete analysis of why one individual obeys or disobeys another, e.g., the personality of the obeying person. Such factors are not considered here since the above classification is not being used as a basis for a complete casual explanation of obedience or disobedience.

ognize the legitimacy of power, yet one may also obey or disobey out of instrumental considerations. This signifies in the case of disobedience that the instrumental considerations outweigh the motivation toward conformity arising from the recognition of legitimacy.

If the attempt of a person to exercise power fails, the power act may be followed either by a substitute power act or by a sanction. A *substitute power act* is intended primarily to attain the original aim of the first act. Substitution may take place both within or between types of power. Thus a command may be substituted for a polite request (both forms of attempted domination), or unsuccessful propaganda may be succeeded by an outright command (manipulation and domination). A *sanction* is a power act initiated primarily as a reprisal for nonconformity with a prior act of power; its intent is punitive and not primarily directed toward achieving the goal of the prior unsuccessful power act. Since persons who are subjected to attempted exercise of force or manipulation do not—unlike persons subjected to commands—either obey or disobey, sanctions may most properly be spoken of as a reprisal for disobedience to a command (domination) rather than as nonconformity to other types of power. However, it may be true that an unsuccessful propagandist or unsuccessful exerciser of force may (irrationally) take actions with punitive intent against persons who fail to succumb to his propaganda or to his attempt to exercise force.

A sanction may be either a deprivation of values already possessed or an obstruction to the attainment of values which would have been realized were it not for the punitive intervention of the power-holder. A sanction may be either a physical loss (beating, confinement, etc.) or a nonphysical loss (fining, confiscation, removal from office, ridicule, etc.).

Disobedience to the command of a power-holder may result not only in consciously intended sanctions but also in unintended penalizations (such as guilt feelings, loss of prestige, etc.), the anticipation of which may motivate the individual to conform. Market operations afforded an important case of unintended penalizations. The demands of buyers and sellers upon each other produce a collective compromise expressed in the price level. Intransigent buyers and sellers are not necessarily subject to intended losses, but their intransigence is, in fact, likely to squeeze them out of the market. The conformity of the buyers or sellers to the imperatives of market conditions involves, in this case, conformity not only to the immediate demands of those with whom they have direct relations but through them, indirectly, with all other persons in the market. Unintended consequences may also be derivative penalizations, i.e., they may be unintended results from the infliction of an intended sanction. Thus imprisonment may (even after release) result in the loss of job, prestige, and associations.

Sanctions may be exercised either directly by the power-holder himself or indirectly through others in official or nonofficial positions. Most power-holders of any consequence possess a staff of officials to whom the exercise of sanctions is delegated. Although power-holders may instigate persons without official position (mobs, the public, "the consumer," etc.) to take reprisals against nonconformists, the exercise of sanctions by nonofficials is perhaps most important in the case of unintended and derivative penalizations and in the case of intended sanctions without instigation from official power-holders.

A power relation is *unilateral* if only one party to the relationship exercises power over the other and *bilateral* if both parties exercise power over each other. The power relationships between officers and privates in an army are typically unilateral. A major form of bilateral power relation is the case of bargaining power, to the extent that each party influences the behavior of the other in the intended direction. In bargaining each party attempts to influence the behavior of the other either by depriving him of values already possessed or by obstructing the attainment of values not yet possessed but desired. Bilateral power relations exist not only in the case of domination (as when each party is able to make demands on the other) but also in the case of manipulation. That is, each party may influence the behavior of the other party without making explicit what behavior is desired. Thus parties may mutually influence each other's behavior in a desired direction by propaganda or by acts. The outcome of attempted bilateral domination or manipulation may be complete fulfilment of the intentions of both parties (provided they are not incompatible) or a compromise, i.e., a partial success by both parties or the fulfilment (partially or fully) of the intention of only one party or, finally, modes of behavior completely different from the intention of either party.[6]

The exercise of power is *direct* when the power-holder alters the behavior of others without utilizing an intermediary and *indirect* when a chain of direct power acts is initiated by a power-holder who utilizes one or more subordinate power-holders. The control of an army by a general or of factory workers by a large-scale entrepreneur is largely by means of indirect power. The chain of direct power acts constituting the exercise of indirect power may be composed of different types of direct power acts. Thus the initial act may be a command (domination) to a subordinate power-holder who may alter the behavior of others by propaganda (manipulation) in order to instigate mob violence (force) against certain groups, thus attaining the intention of the initiating power-holder. The personnel utilized in the sequence of direct power acts composing indirect power may be both official and nonofficial.

The amount of power exercised by an individual may be measured either by the ratio of his successful power acts to all of his attempted power acts or by certain criteria specified below. These measures may be used as a basis of comparison between different power-holders. The two "amounts" represent not alternative techniques of measurement but differences in what is measured. Amount in these cases does not mean the same thing. Most investigations of power, in so far as they deal with the amount of power, utilize "amount" in the second sense.

Two principal criteria may be used to measure the amount of power exercised by a power-holder: the number of actions of any given person, in each of any number of selected types of be-

---

[6]The last case is only an *attempted* bilateral power relation since neither party accomplished his intention. The case in which only one party accomplishes his intention is marginal to the definition of bilateral power and may be characterized as being a case of attempted bilateral power with culmination in unilateral power.

navior, over which control is realized (or potential[7]); and the number[8] of persons so controlled. The definition of dictatorship as "a form of government where everything that is not forbidden is obligatory" indicates complete power in terms of the spheres of behavior over which control is exercised.

Concentration of power is not diminished if the power-holder acts through many subordinates, provided he is able to exercise control over them. In fact, however, the utilization of a large subordinate staff is very likely to diffuse power, since the chief power-holder is rarely able to control fully the actions of his subordinates who may therefore exercise a certain amount of independent or initiatory, rather than dependent, power. Further, the impossibility of maintaining complete control over the subordinate staff and the reliance which the power-holder must place on them tends to set up a bilateral power relation between the chief power-holder and his subordinates, giving the latter power over the chief power-holder in addi-

tion to any independent power they may exercise over the mass. Subordinate power-holders, to the extent that they exercise independent power in the sphere claimed by the chief power-holder, will limit the power of the latter, and to that extent lose their character of subordinates. On the other hand, a plurality of independent power-holders (whether partially or completely independent) may not only limit but also reinforce or not at all affect one another's exercise of power. This will be true only to the extent that the power-holders influence the behavior of others in a manner which does not obstruct the intentions of their co-power-holders. With the growing interdependence of all aspects of social life, however, and consequently the increased probabilities that any act will have more extensive repercussions throughout the society than formerly, it becomes more essential for a power-holder both to control many aspects of behavior that formerly might have seemed quite unnecessary for carrying out his intentions and to prevent others from exercising powers that formerly might not have interfered with his intention. Although one finds in contemporary society, both in public and in private spheres, an increasing concentration of power, the necessity, as enterprises increase in size, of exercising power through the utilization of many subordinate power-holders tends to limit the actual if not the formal concentration of power.

The amount and stability of power exercised will be limited by the means which the power-holder has available for influencing the behavior of others by making them want to do what he wants them to do or by the sanctions which they anticipate that he can bring to bear upon them.

---

[7]It would be extremely difficult to determine how much control is possible in a given situation unless the power-holder actually attempts to exercise power. Although for some purposes it would be highly desirable to attempt estimate of the potential amount of power that could be wielded, the amount of power actually exercised would in most cases be the primary interest, and of course would involve the sounder empirical procedure. However, the predictions of the power-holder and those subordinated to him as to how much power the power-holder might wield if so inclined may be an important determinant of the behavior of the power-holder and those subordinated to him.

[8]"Number" here may be absolute number or the proportion of controlled persons in the total population. It may also be desirable to represent this as the ratio between those who are controlled to the total number over whom control is attempted.

Large amounts of power cannot be exercised in a purely coercive fashion, for even though the mass of subordinated individuals do not recognize the power-holder as exercising legitimate power, the necessity of utilizing a large staff would introduce other than purely coercive power into the total power system; for the subordinate power-holders, who exercise dependent power and carry out sanctions for cases of nonconformity among the mass, cannot themselves be controlled by coercion alone. The greater the amount of coercive power exercised, the greater is the dependence of the chief power-holder on his staff. For this reason and because the possible supervision over, and sanctions against, the mass often fall short of the requirements for the exercise of coercive power, the latter frequently has to be augmented and supported by manipulation. This may serve the purpose not only of getting people to act in a desired manner without exercising coercion but also of developing a belief in the legitimacy of the power exercised and thereby also limiting the need for coercive action.

It is sometimes assumed that a person who uses force or is in a position to impose very drastic sanctions in the event of nonconformity with his commands is somehow more powerful than one who exercises power without the use of these means. But, the amount of power exercised by a legitimate power-holder may be as great as, or greater than, the amount exercised by a coercive power-holder. If, however, we restrict comparison only to coercive power-holders, then it is true, all other things being equal, that power varies directly with the severity of the sanctions that the power-holder can impose.

---

The following study of two actual military organizations is one of the few attempts to analyze power in real situations, using the general framework here presented. Thompson finds that two identical units of the Air Force do not have the same power structures. He shows that "on paper" both of these organizations appear to be wholly similar. When those who participated in each as members of management were asked to determine, from their own experience, who beside the top commander had most to say about how their own unit got its work done and met requirements, they revealed distinctly different pictures of the power structures of the two units. This result is attributed to differences in top management outlook and expectations as well as to the degree to which specialized functions were tightly organized in each unit.

An important conclusion emerges from Thompson's study. The power structure of an organization may be unique to the present individuals who compose it, and may change with turnover of personnel. This fact gives rise to one of the characteristic problems of an organization, namely, the change in power structure accompanying turnover of managerial personnel. Often some of the most bitter contests among managers occur in their jockeying for new power positions when an important power-holder leaves the organization.

## POWER IN IDENTICAL ORGANIZATIONS

*James D. Thompson**

This paper reports some results of a study of authorized and real power structures in two Air Force wings with the same regulations, directives, and charts, reporting to the same headquarters, and comparable in equipment, personnel, length of time in existence, and mission. They operated under like weather conditions. Attention is focused on "top" executives and on differences in communication channels which were associated with differences in power structures.

It was hypothesized (1) that the real power structures in both wings would deviate from the more limited authority structures and (2) that the two power structures would differ from each other.

Power was defined as the ability to determine the behavior of others, regardless of the bases of that ability. Authority, in contrast, was defined as that type of power which goes with a position and is legitimated by the official norms. Power consists of some combination of authority and influence, but for purposes of this study influence was treated as a residual category.

A power structure was defined as a relatively fixed, regular, and continuous power relationship between two or more individuals or groups, and an authority structure as a relatively fixed, regular, and continuous power relationship between offices as they are formally prescribed.

Communication was defined as a kind of interaction in which sentiments, ideas, or facts become shared, and a communication channel as a relatively fixed, regular, and continuous communication relationship between two or more individuals.

### COLLECTION AND ANALYSIS OF DATA

Data were collected by the author and other members of the research team[1] during six weeks spent in each of two wings. The principal techniques were direct observation, semi-structured interviews, work-contact questionnaires, self-recorded schedules of contacts made by executives, and power ratings made by judges in the wings. Regulations, directives, and charts in effect at the time of field work also were analyzed.

Attention during field work was focused on two major aspects of coordination: *allocation* and *communication*. The allocation category was divided into five areas: tasks (or responsibilities); manpower; facilities; authority; and sanctions (rewards and punishments).[2] Data on allocation were obtained primarily through interviewing and observation.

---

*Reprinted from "Authority and Power in 'Identical' Organizations," *American Journal of Sociology*, 62:290–298 (November, 1956) by permission of The University of Chicago Press.

[1]Fredrick L. Bates, Jack L. Dyer, Raymond W. Mack, Richard Stephens and George S. Tracy.

[2]The frame of reference was taken, with modifications from Talcott Parsons, particularly from *Toward a General Theory of Action*, ed. Parsons and Edward A. Shils (Cambridge, Mass.: Harvard University Press, 1951).

A series of interviews was conducted with each of a dozen executives in each wing and organized around three general questions: (1) What allocation decisions were made? (2) Who made them? (3) What were the consequences for the groups and activities under the respondent's jurisdiction? Weekly "staff meetings" and other sessions of executives were observed and recorded in detail, and the data were classified according to the same general questions. Critical incidents which related to these questions were also observed and recorded.

Channels of communication were determined from work-contact questionnaires completed by all available members of each wing and from records of actual contacts kept by major executives during a critical week in each wing.

Questionnaires asked the respondent to list the individuals with whom he had contact as frequently as several times a week. Contacts within his own work group were separated from other contacts. The plan was to administer the questionnaires to all executives and all their assistants, who together made up the "executive subsystem" of the wings. Similar questionnaires were administered throughout the "maintenance subsystem" and in one of the three squadrons which comprised the "operations subsystem."

Completed questionnaires were obtained from 71 per cent of members of the executive subsystem in Wing A and from 68 per cent in Wing B. Percentages obtained in the other subsystems ranged from 67 to 81. The distribution of those from whom questionnaires were not obtained resembled randomness, and it is believed that the data obtained approximate the channels of communication within the wings.

All questionnaire entries were coded and entered into a matrix. The completed matrix was then "folded over," so that data regarding interaction between any two individuals appeared in one cell, regardless of whether the facts were supplied by one or both of the individuals.[3] (Results reported here refer to interaction as reported by either party; if reported by both parties, it is tabulated as one interaction.)

## THE AUTHORITY STRUCTURES

Each wing was composed of six working squadrons and a headquarters. Flying activities were carried out by crews belonging to the three tactical or combat squadrons, which "owned" the aircraft and performed minor maintenance on them. Specialized and heavy maintenance activities were the responsibilities of three maintenance squadrons.

The chief executive of a wing was the wing commander, whose principal assistants were his deputy, his six squadron commanders, and the three members of his "wing coordinating staff," namely, a director of operations, a director of matériel, and a director of personnel. These eleven, plus an assistant to the director of matériel known as the "maintenance control officer," were the key executives on whom this study focused.

Each squadron commander was officially responsible *directly* to the wing

[3]Slightly more than 30 per cent of contacts reported by one person were also reported by the other. This was true in both wings. There is evidence that men tended to list their more important contacts (at least outside their own work groups) and to omit the less important. This would explain the absence of mutuality: contacts between A and B might be quite important to A but insignificant to B.

commander for the control over and the quality of the activities of his squadron. Each had one or more squadron staff officers responsible for certain matters and answerable *directly* to him. To assist him in coordinating the activities of the six squadrons, the wing commander could turn to his coordinating staff. Regulations did not limit these offices to advisory positions, however. The director of operations was officially responsible to the wing commander for the development of the wing's combat capability; the director of matériel for the direction and coordination of all phases of maintenance, supply, and logistics within the wing; and the director of personnel for personnel actions in all squadrons.

Although relationships between squadron commanders and wing staff officers were not prescribed, regulations did specify that appropriate squadron staff officers would be "supervised and directed" by wing staff officers. At the same time, however, the squadron staff officers were officially responsible to their squadron commander.

A status differential existed among the executive offices, since the authorized ranks of the coordinating staff were one notch higher than those of squadron commanders. Movement "upward" in the hierarchy was movement from squadron command to wing staff positions.

In summary, the authority structure appeared to be a blend of the "line" and "functional" concepts of administration which left some authority in both types of channels without fully integrating the channels.

## OVERVIEW OF THE POWER STRUCTURES

In both wings members of the co-ordinating staffs were found to exert power *over* squadron commanders, despite the absence of authority to do so. This was particularly true of the directors of operations and matériel and less so of the director of personnel. Repeatedly and systematically, directors made decisions about allocation which limited the freedom of squadron commanders to act. Directors enjoyed priority in manipulating variables and could freeze these into conditions for squadron commanders.

Allocation of operation tasks was dominated in both wings by the directors of operations, who drew up monthly training plans which were then divided among the tactical squadrons, fixed dates and deadlines for many requirements, and decided which of the squadrons would perform special activities assigned to the wing. Within the limits of restrictions by higher headquarters, the directors of operations decided who, what, and when, thereby forcing squadron commanders to take as fixed conditions which, to the directors of operations, were variables.

Similarly, the directors of matériel controlled the allocation of tasks among maintenance squadrons—and within maintenance sections of combat squadrons. They, too, set deadlines and priorities.

Despite the presence of a director of personnel in the authority structure, the allocation of manpower in both wings tended to be dominated by the directors of operations and matériel, depending upon the experience and training of the men subject to allocation. Routine matters were handled by squadron commanders and the directors of personnel, but, when key men or positions were involved, initiative was retained by the director of operations or matériel. This was true because of the crucial relationship between allocation of tasks and of men capable of carrying them out.

The allocation of facilities was handled through regular command or "line" channels—squadron commander to wing commander—for routine items, but, when the facilities were directly linked to operations or maintenance performance, the appropriate director took control, deciding which squadrons or sections within them would receive scarce tools or supplies.

Detailed policies and procedural guides by higher headquarters succeeded in minimizing "politics" with respect to sanctions—such as promotions in rank and discipline. Other less tangible rewards—more or less covered by the term "job satisfactions"—were controlled, perhaps inadvertently, by those wielding power over task and manpower allocation. This meant that many things regarded as rewarding or punishing were decided by the directors of operations and matériel and were beyond the power of squadron commanders.

Qualitative data, then, indicated that *in both wings* directors of operations and matériel exercised unauthorized power over squadron commanders and over the directors of personnel. Less clear was the position in the power structure of the deputy wing commanders and the maintenance control officers: their roles appeared to differ in the two wings.

## MAJOR DIFFERENCES BETWEEN WINGS

In Wing A the director of operations dominated maintenance executives, on the theory that maintenance existed to serve operations. On several occasions he planned major operations on the basis of his own inaccurate estimates of maintenance capabilities and later, to the general confusion, was forced to change his plans. The director of matériel was handicapped,

in staff meetings, by the fact that he had to transact business with operations executives without the help of his chief assistant, the maintenance control officer, whose position gave him detailed information about maintenance schedules and capacities. Furthermore, when maintenance executives complained about lack of cooperation on the part of operations, it was the director of operations (not the combat squadron commanders) who promised and took action.

In Wing B the directors of operations and matériel worked more closely together, checking on each other's needs and capacities at several stages of their planning. Furthermore, they united sometimes against what they felt were arbitrary dictates of the wing commander. The director of matériel was strengthened, in executive discussions, by the presence of the maintenance control officer, who, being recognized in Wing B as a staff officer, attended all staff meetings.[4] (Because of the absence during part of the field work of the deputy wing commander of Wing A, qualitative data on his role were inconclusive.)

Finally, there were sharp differences between the two wings in the relationships of other executives to the wing commanders. In both, of course, the wing commanders were at the top of the hierarchy. But the commander of Wing A preferred to let his subordinates—in particular the director of operations—take the initiative; he reviewed and approved acts of his subordinates and held veto power. In Wing B, however, the wing com-

---

[4]One example of the complexity of power phenomena involves a comparison of maintenance control officers. In Wing A this position was weak, when viewed at the executive level. Other members of the research team, concentrating on maintenance activities, found that this officer was quite powerful *within* the maintenance system. In Wing B the locus of his power was reversed.

mander more often exercised initiative, with the result that the hierarchical distance between him and his subordinates appeared to be greater.

### POWER HIERARCHIES OBTAINED FROM JUDGES' RATINGS

As an independent check upon the qualitative analysis, the directors and squadron commanders were asked to give power rankings, that is, to "name the top five or six officers in the wing in addition to the Wing Commander, who have the most to say about how the wing gets its work done and meets requirements." *After* the executive had named those he considered most powerful, he was asked to rank them. When judges felt unable to rank more than three or four, they were not pressed, with the result that there were several "ties" in the lower ranks.

The rankings were weighted using the simple device of five points for first place, four for second, and so on. In cases of tie votes, the average value was given to each. The weighted ratings obtained by each officer named were then totaled, to give each a score (see Tables 1 and 2).

**Table 1**

POWER HIERARCHY IN WING A, EXCLUDING WING COMMANDER, AS DETERMINED FROM AGGREGATE SCORES RECEIVED FROM NINE JUDGES

| Executive | Ranking in Hierarchy | Score | Per Cent of Total Score | Cumulative Percentage |
|---|---|---|---|---|
| Total | .... | 133.0 | 100.0 | ...... |
| Director of operations | 1 | 39.0 | 29.3 | 29.3 |
| Deputy wing commander | 2 | 29.0 | 21.8 | 51.1 |
| Director of matériel | 3 | 21.5 | 16.2 | 67.3 |
| Director of personnel | 4 | 17.0 | 12.8 | 80.1 |
| Commander, Bomb Squadron A | 5 | 7.5 | 5.6 | 85.7 |
| Commander, Bomb Squadron B | 6 and 7 | 6.5 | 4.9 | 90.6 |
| Commander, Bomb Squadron C | | 6.5 | 4.9 | 95.5 |
| Executive officer | 8 | 4.0 | 3.0 | 98.5 |
| Maintenance control officer | 9 | 1.0 | 0.7 | 99.2 |
| Wing intelligence officer | 10 | 1.0 | 0.7 | 100.0 |

**Table 2**

POWER HIERARCHY IN WING B, EXCLUDING WING COMMANDER, AS DETERMINED FROM AGGREGATE SCORES RECEIVED FROM EIGHT JUDGES*

| Executive | Ranking in Hierarchy | Score | Per Cent of Total Score | Cumulative Percentage |
|---|---|---|---|---|
| Total | .... | 113.9 | 100.0 | ...... |
| Director of operations | 1 | 35.5 | 31.2 | 31.2 |
| Director of matériel | 2 | 30.5 | 26.8 | 58.0 |
| Deputy wing commander | 3 | 18.0 | 15.8 | 73.8 |
| Maintenance control officer | 4 | 12.0 | 10.5 | 84.3 |
| Director of personnel | 5 | 11.0 | 9.7 | 94.0 |
| Commander, Bomb Squadron A | | 2.3 | 2.0 | 96.0 |
| Commander, Bomb Squadron B | 6, 7 and 8 | 2.3 | 2.0 | 98.0 |
| Commander, Bomb Squadron C | | 2.3 | 2.0 | 100.0 |

*One prospective judge was unavailable.

The order of the deputy wing commanders and directors of matériel is found to be reversed between wings, and the maintenance control officer is much higher in Wing B than in Wing A. The director of personnel is also higher in one case than in the other.

Perhaps of more significance, however, is the distribution of percentages. In Wing A the deputy received 21.8 per cent of the total score, while the director of matériel received 16.2 per cent; but in Wing B the deputy received 15.8 per cent and the director of matériel 26.8. Cumulative percentages show the two directors of matériel in very different situations. In Wing A more than half of the total score went to men above the director of matériel, while in Wing B it was less than one-third of the total score.

Another important question about the power hierarchies is the extent to which judges agreed on the locus of power. Tables 3 and 4, showing the number of times each executive was

**Table 3**

DISTRIBUTION OF RANKINGS OF WING EXECUTIVES EXCLUDING WING COMMANDER, AS REPORTED BY NINE JUDGES

| Executive | Number of Times Named in Each Rank* | | | | |
|---|---|---|---|---|---|
| | 1 | 2 | 3 | 4 | 5 |
| All executives | 9 | 10 | 8 | 5 | 4 |
| Director of operations | 4 | 5 | .. | .. | .. |
| Deputy wing commander | 5 | 1 | .. | .. | .. |
| Director of matériel | .. | 1 | 3 | 3 | 1 |
| Director of personnel | .. | 2 | 2 | 2 | .. |
| Commander, Bomb Squadron A | .. | 1 | .. | .. | .. |
| Commander, Bomb Squadron B | .. | .. | 1 | .. | .. |
| Commander, Bomb Squadron C | .. | .. | 1 | .. | .. |
| Executive officer | .. | .. | 1 | .. | .. |
| Maintenance control officer | .. | .. | .. | .. | 1 |
| Wing intelligence officer | .. | .. | .. | .. | 1 |

*Tie votes given maximum value in each case rather than average value.

**Table 4**

DISTRIBUTION OF RANKINGS OF WING EXECUTIVES, EXCLUDING WING COMMANDER, AS REPORTED BY EIGHT JUDGES*

| Executive | Number of Times Named in Each Rank† | | | | |
|---|---|---|---|---|---|
| | 1 | 2 | 3 | 4 | 5 |
| All executives | 9 | 7 | 10 | 6 | 5 |
| Director of operations | 4 | 4 | .. | .. | .. |
| Director of matériel | 2 | 3 | 3 | .. | .. |
| Deputy wing commander | 3 | .. | 1 | .. | .. |
| Maintenance control officer | .. | .. | 2 | 3 | .. |
| Director of personnel | .. | .. | 1 | 3 | 2 |
| Commander, Bomb Squadron A | .. | .. | 1 | .. | 1 |
| Commander, Bomb Squadron B | .. | .. | 1 | .. | 1 |
| Commander, Bomb Squadron C | .. | .. | 1 | .. | 1 |

*One prospective judge was unavailable.
†Tie votes given maximum value in each case rather than average value.

named in the various ranks, reveal general agreement on the higher rankings. (Tables here show maximum value, not average.) In both wings the rankings for the top men cluster. The directors of operations were rated either first or second by all judges. But, with descending rank, clusterings of frequencies gradually disappear. Moreover, there is a major incongruity in the case of the deputy wing commanders. When they were named, they were ranked high—but they were not always named.

It appeared that power is perceived differently by various executives, depending upon their positions. If this were so, it should be possible to group judges according to similarity of position and find a higher degree of consensus than in aggregate scores. To examine this possibility, an "index of consensus" was developed. In order to demonstrate the logic and mechanics involved in the index, procedures used in computing one for the aggregate

scores will be described, using data in Table 1. Since in essence the purpose is to find the "goodness of fit" of a given hierarchy—the extent to which it agrees with estimates of the judges —it is assumed for the aggregate index that the five executives with the largest total scores actually were the five most powerful executives and that their relative rankings as determined by the scores are correct.

Since each judge named only five and score points were based on five possible rankings, only the first five in the hierarchy are considered. If the nine judges in Wing A had been in perfect agreement, the director of operations would have received 45 points, the deputy 36, and so on as indicated in Table 5, under "Expected Score." In the adjoining column are entered "reported scores," from Table 1. The differences between expected and reported scores are then computed and entered in the third column of Table 5. In this case the differences

**Table 5**

COMPUTATION OF INDEX OF CONSENSUS ON POWER HIERARCHY OF
WING A, AS DETERMINED FROM AGGREGATE SCORES OF NINE JUDGES

| Executive | Rank in Hierarchy | Expected Score (1) | Reported Score (2) | Differences (1 − 2) (3) |
|---|---|---|---|---|
| Total | .... | 135 | 133.0 | 40.0 |
| Director of operations | 1 | 45 | 39.0 | 6.0 |
| Deputy wing commander | 2 | 36 | 29.0 | 7.0 |
| Director of matériel | 3 | 27 | 21.5 | 5.5 |
| Director of personnel | 4 | 18 | 17.0 | 1.0 |
| Commander, Bomb Squadron A .... | 5 | 9 | 7.5 | 1.5 |
| Commander, Bomb Squadron B ⎱ | ⎰ 6 | 0 | 6.5 | 6.5 |
| Commander, Bomb Squadron C ⎰ ......... ⎱ 7 | | 0 | 6.5 | 6.5 |
| Executive officer | 8 | 0 | 4.0 | 4.0 |
| Maintenance control officer | 9 | 0 | 1.0 | 1.0 |
| Wing intelligence officer | 10 | 0 | 1.0 | 1.0 |

$$C = 100 \left[ \frac{\text{Total Col. 1} - \text{Total Col. 3}}{\text{Total Col. 1}} \right] = 70.4$$

total 40. This means that 40 points were "misplaced" by the judges or that there were 40 points of disagreement, leaving 95 points of agreement. This was converted into an index by determining the percentage of agreement (95 divided by 135) between reported and expected scores, and multiplying by 100.

The general formula for computing the index of consensus is:

$$C = 100 \times \frac{\text{Sum of expected scores minus difference between sum of expected scores and sum of reported scores}}{\text{Sum of expected scores}}$$

The index can vary between 0 and 100, with 0 indicating equal amounts of agreement and disagreement or absence of a pattern, and 100 indicating that all judges named the same executives in the same order.[5]

The aggregate index of consensus for judges in Wing A, on the hierarchy shown in Table 1, is 70.4, while there was more consensus among judges in Wing B, where the index was 78.4 on the hierarchy shown in Table 2. . . .

### TEST OF HYPOTHESES

It was hypothesized that the real power structures in both wings would deviate from the more limited authority structures. This can be accepted without reservation. At both

---

[5]Zero is theoretically possible but not practically so, since we determine expected scores from the hierarchy established from the estimates of judges. There must be some consensus before we can determine expected scores.

bases the directors of operations and matériel held more power than did squadron commanders. This was supported by observation and in the reports of staff judges as well as those of squadron commanders. While the panel judgments do not show that the power of directors was power *over* squadron commanders, they support observations that the directors of operations and matériel were at or near the top of their power structures.

It is also clear that in both wings executives concerned primarily with operations activities had greater power than those concerned primarily with maintenance activities. This appeared in observations and in the judgments of panel members. In both wings, moreover, combat squadron commanders appeared on the fringe of the executive power structure, but maintenance squadron commanders were excluded.

Both directors of operations exercised power *over* the directors of matériel which again was outside authorized relationships. This conclusion is supported by observation and also by interview data.

It was also hypothesized that the real power structures of the two wings would differ from each other. This can also be accepted without reservation. Domination of maintenance by operations executives was more pronounced in Wing A than in Wing B, where the director of matériel was in second place on the judge's lists. The maintenance control officer in Wing A was all but overlooked; his counterpart in Wing B was placed in the hierarchy by judges, a distinction confirmed by observation and interview data.

From analysis of the estimates of judges, a power hierarchy appeared sharply defined for operations executives in Wing A but poorly delineated for maintenance executives. In Wing B, by contrast, a power hierarchy was well defined for maintenance executives but poorly defined for operations executives. This leads to the conclusion that the operations system was more tightly structured than the maintenance system in Wing A, while the maintenance system was more tightly structured in Wing B. In the former the power of the deputy wing commander was felt primarily in operations, while in Wing B the power of the deputy was felt primarily in maintenance.

Finally, command and staff channels were more important in Wing B than in Wing A, where the "functional" concept of organization was favored.

---

It is usual to think of power being wielded from the top down in an organization. The higher one goes in an organization, the greater is one's power. It is therefore important to understand that subordinates may also have power. It is easy to understand how an individual may have power over those in a lower rank of the organization. It is not so easy to understand that a person may have power over those above him.

In the next selection David Mechanic deals specifically with the power of subordinates. This power is based upon the dependence that superiors have on them for information, for performance, or for the control of resources.[1] These are the categories that Mechanic suggests when he points out that the control of information, persons, and instrumentalities is the basis for making others dependent upon you.

The major share of the discussion is concerned with the sources of power available to subordinates. It was Lord Acton who suggested the aphorism

"Power tends to corrupt, and absolute power corrupts absolutely." The assumption underlying this conclusion is that power begets power; the more power a person has, the greater the possibility that he can accumulate additional power. What is overlooked is the fact that subordinates, by virtue of their own power, can introduce what Galbraith called "countervailing power." The power of subordinates provides an effective brake on the accumulation of absolute power by the top executives of an organization. There are, therefore, forces of counterbalancing power in every organization.

The advantages of counterbalancing power lie in the fact that it makes it more difficult for any single individual to lead the organization into a decline or to destruction. There is usually enough countervailing power among subordinates to prevent any single top executive from doing this. Correspondingly, there is enough power at the top of an organization to prevent subordinates from causing it to decline or die.

The power of subordinates may have the distinct negative consequences of slowing the rate of change in the organization or even of sabotaging desirable change. Much of the effort of top executives and middle

---

[1]The linkage between power and dependence was originally elaborated in Robert Dubin, *The World of Work* (Englewood Cliffs, N. J.: Prentice-Hall, Inc., 1958), Chapter 3, and further elaborated in "Power, Function, and Organization," *Pacific Sociological Review*, 6:16–24, Spring, 1963.

managers is often directed toward getting subordinates to cease using their power to oppose changes in operations. This is usually analyzed as a problem of effective communications and the use of communication techniques to influence behavior. It should be recognized, however, that the need for influencing behavior of subordinates lies in the fact that they have the power to disagree with the conclusions of the bosses. Thus, an understanding of effective communications requires a prior understanding of why bosses need to be persuasive and to exercise influence over subordinates. This is achieved when we understand that subordinates in an organization have sources of power over their bosses.

## POWER OF SUBORDINATES IN COMPLEX ORGANIZATIONS

### David Mechanic*

It is not unusual for lower participants[1] in complex organizations to assume and wield considerable power and influence not associated with their formally defined positions within these organizations. In sociological terms they have considerable personal power but no authority. Such personal power is often attained, for example, by executive secretaries and accountants in business firms, by attendants in mental hospitals, and even by inmates in prisons. The personal power achieved by these lower participants does not necessarily result from unique personal characteristics, although these may be relevant, but results rather from particular aspects of their location within their organizations.

### INFORMAL VERSUS FORMAL POWER

Within organizations the distribution of authority (institutionalized power) is closely if not perfectly correlated with the prestige of positions. Those who have argued for the independence of these variables[2] have taken their examples from diverse organizations and do not deal with situations where power is clearly comparable.[3] Thus when Bierstedt argues that Einstein had prestige but no power, and the policeman power but no prestige, it is apparent that he is comparing categories that are not compar-

*Reprinted by permission from the author and the publisher from David Mechanic, "Sources of Power of Lower Participants in Complex Organizations," *Administrative Science Quarterly*, 7:349–362 (December 1962).

[1]The term "lower participants" comes from Amitai Etzioni, *A Comparative Analysis of Complex Organizations* (New York, 1961), and is used by him to designate persons in positions of lower rank: employees, rank and file, members, clients, customers, and inmates. We shall use the term in this paper in a relative sense denoting position vis-à-vis a higher-ranking participant.

[2]Robert Bierstedt, "An Analysis of Social Power," *American Sociological Review*, 15 (1950), 730–738.

[3]Robert A. Dahl, "The Concept of Power," *Behavioral Science*, 2 (1957), 201–215.

able. Generally persons occupying high-ranking positions within organizations have more authority than those holding low-ranking positions.

One might ask what characterizes high-ranking positions within organizations. What is most evident, perhaps, is that lower participants recognize the right of higher-ranking participants to exercise power and yield without difficulty to demands they regard as legitimate. Moreover, persons in high-ranking positions tend to have considerable access to and control over information and persons both within and outside the organization, and to instrumentalities or resources. Although higher supervisory personnel may be isolated from the task activities of lower participants, they maintain access to them through formally established intermediary positions and exercise control through intermediary participants. There appears, therefore, to be a clear correlation between the prestige of positions within organizations and the extent to which they offer access to information, persons, and instrumentalities.

Since formal organizations tend to structure lines of access and communication, access should be a clue to institutional prestige. Yet access depends on variables other than those controlled by the formal structure of an organization, and this often makes the informal power structure that develops within organizations somewhat incongruent with the formally intended plan. It is these variables that allow work groups to limit production through norms that contravene the goals of the larger organization, that allow hospital attendants to thwart changes in the structure of a hospital, and that allow prison inmates to exercise some control over prison guards. . . .

## Clarification of Definitions

The purpose of this paper is to present some hypotheses explaining why lower participants in organizations can often assume and wield considerable power which is not associated with their positions as formally defined within these organizations. For the purposes of this analysis the concepts "influence," "power," and "control" will be used synonymously. Moreover, we shall not be concerned with type of power, that is, whether the power is based on reward, punishment, identification, power to veto, or whatever.[4] Power will be defined as *any force that results in behavior that would not have occurred if the force had not been present.* We have defined power as a force rather than a relationship because it appears that much of what we mean by power is encompassed by the normative framework of an organization, and thus any analysis of power must take into consideration the power of norms as well as persons.

I shall also argue, following Thibaut and Kelley,[5] that power is closely related to dependence. To the extent that a person is dependent on another, he is potentially subject to the other person's power. Within organizations one makes others dependent upon him

---

[4]One might observe, for example, that the power of lower participants is based primarily on the ability to "veto" or punish. For a discussion of bases of power, see John R. P. French, Jr., and Bertram Raven, "The Bases of Social Power," in D. Cartwright and A. Zander, eds., *Group Dynamics* (Evanston, Ill., 1960), pp. 607-623.

[5]John Thibaut and Harold H. Kelley, *The Social Psychology of Groups* (New York, 1959). For a similar emphasis on dependence, see Richard M. Emerson, "Power-Dependence Relationships," *American Sociological Review,* 27 (1962), 31-41.

by controlling access to information, persons, and instrumentalities, which I shall define as follows:

a. *Information* includes knowledge of the organization, knowledge about persons, knowledge of the norms, procedures, techniques, and so forth.

b. *Persons* include anyone within the organization or anyone outside the organization upon whom the organization is in some way dependent.

c. *Instrumentalities* include any aspect of the physical plant of the organization or its resources (equipment, machines, money, and so on). Power is a function not only of the extent to which a person controls information, persons, and instrumentalities, but also of the importance of the various attributes he controls. . . .[6]

### A Classic Example

Like many other aspects of organizational theory, one can find a classic statement of our problem in Weber's discussion of the political bureaucracy. Weber indicated the extent to which bureaucrats may have considerable power over political incumbents, as a result, in part, of their permanence within the political bureaucracy, as contrasted to public officials, who are replaced rather frequently.[7] Weber noted how the low-ranking bureaucrat becomes familiar with the organization—its rules and operations, the work flow, and so on, which gives him considerable power over the new political

incumbent who might have higher rank but is not as familiar with the organization. While Weber does not directly state the point, his analysis suggests that bureaucratic permanence has some relationship to increased access to persons, information, and instrumentalities. To state the hypothesis suggested somewhat more formally:

$H_1$ Other factors remaining constant, organizational power is related to access to persons, information, and instrumentalities.

$H_2$ Other factors remaining constant, as a participant's length of time in an organization increases, he has increased access to persons, information, and instrumentalities.

### SOURCES OF POWER OF LOWER PARTICIPANTS

The most effective way for lower participants to achieve power is to obtain, maintain, and control access to persons, information, and instrumentalities. To the extent that this can be accomplished, lower participants make higher-ranking participants dependent upon them. Thus dependence together with the manipulation of the dependency relationship is the key to the power of lower participants.

A number of examples can be cited which illustrate the preceding point. Scheff, for example, reports on the failure of a state mental hospital to bring about intended reform because of the opposition of hospital attendants.[8] He noted that the power of hospital attendants was largely a re-

---

[6]Although this paper will not attempt to explain how access may be measured, the author feels confident that the hypotheses concerned with access are clearly testable.

[7]Max Weber, "The Essentials of Bureaucratic Organization: An Ideal-Type Construction," in Robert Merton *et al.*, *Reader in Bureaucracy* (Glencoe, Ill., 1952), pp. 18–27.

[8]Thomas J. Scheff, "Control over Policy by Attendants in a Mental Hospital," *Journal of Health and Human Behavior*, 2 (1961), 93–105.

sult of the dependence of ward physicians on attendants. . . .

Similarly, Sykes describes the dependence of prison guards on inmates and the power obtained by inmates over guards.[9] He suggests that although guards could report inmates for disobedience, frequent reports would give prison officials the impression that the guard was unable to command obedience. . . .

## FACTORS AFFECTING POWER

*Expertise*

Increasing specialization and organizational growth have made the expert or staff person important. The expert maintains power because high-ranking persons in the organization are dependent upon him for his special skills and access to certain kinds of information. . . .

We can state these ideas in hypotheses, as follows:

H$_3$ Other factors remaining constant, to the extent that a low-ranking participant has important expert knowledge not available to high-ranking participants, he is likely to have power over them.

Power stemming from expertise, however, is likely to be limited unless it is difficult to replace the expert. This leads to two further hypotheses:

H$_4$ Other factors remaining constant, a person difficult to replace will have greater power than a person easily replaceable.

---

[9]Gresham M. Sykes, "The Corruption of Authority and Rehabilitation," in A. Etzioni, ed., *Complex Organizations* (New York, 1961), pp. 191–197.

H$_5$ Other factors remaining constant, experts will be more difficult to replace than nonexperts.

*Effort and Interest*

The extent to which lower participants may exercise power depends in part on their willingness to exert effort in areas where higher-ranking participants are often reluctant to participate. Effort exerted is directly related to the degree of interest one has in an area.

H$_6$ Other factors remaining constant, there is a direct relationship between the amount of effort a person is willing to exert in an area and the power he can command.

When an organization gives discretion to lower participants, it is usually trading the power of discretion for needed flexibility. The cost of constant surveillance is too high, and the effort required too great; it is very often much easier for all concerned to allow the secretary discretion in return for cooperation and not too great an abuse of power.

H$_7$ Other factors remaining constant, the less effort and interest higher-ranking participants are willing to devote to a task, the more likely are lower participants to obtain power relevant to this task.

*Attractiveness*

Another personal attribute associated with the power of low-ranking persons in an organization is attractiveness, or what some call "personality." People who are viewed as attractive are more likely to succeed in promoting a cause. . . .

H₈ Other factors remaining constant, the more attractive a person, the more likely he is to obtain access to persons and control over these persons.

## Location and Position

In any organization the person's location in physical space and position in social space are important factors influencing access to persons, information, and instrumentalities.[10] Propinquity affects the opportunities for interaction, as well as one's position within a communication network. Although these are somewhat separate factors, we shall refer to their combined effect as centrality[11] within the organization.

H₉ Other factors remaining constant, the more central a person is in an organization, the greater is his access to persons, information, and instrumentalities.

## Coalitions

It should be clear that the variables we are considering are at different levels of analysis; some of them de-

fine attributes of persons, while others define attributes of communication and organization. Power processes within organizations are particularly interesting in that there are many channels of power and ways of achieving it.

In complex organizations different occupational groups attend to different functions, each group often maintaining its own power structure within the organization. Thus hospitals have administrators, medical personnel, nursing personnel, attendants, maintenance personnel, laboratory personnel, and so on. Universities, similarly, have teaching personnel, research personnel, administrative personnel, maintenance personnel, and so on. Each of these functional tasks within organizations often becomes the sphere of a particular group that controls activities relating to the task. While these tasks usually are coordinated at the highest levels of the organization, they often are not coordinated at intermediate and lower levels. It is not unusual, however, for coalitions to form among lower participants in these multiple structures. . . .

## Rules

In organizations with complex power structures lower participants can use their knowledge of the norms of the organization to thwart attempted change. In discussing the various functions of bureaucratic rules, Gouldner maintains that such rules serve as excellent substitutes for surveillance, since surveillance in addi-

---

[10]There is considerable data showing the powerful effect of propinquity on communication. For summary, see Thibaut and Kelley, *op. cit.*, pp. 39–42.

[11]The concept of centrality is generally used in a more technical sense in the work of Bavelas, Shaw, Gilchrist, and others. For example, Bavelas defines the central region of a structure as the class of all cells with the smallest distance between one cell and any other cell in the structure, with distance measured in link units. Thus the most central position in a pattern is the position closest to all others. Cf. Harold Leavitt, "Some

---

Effects of Certain Communication Patterns on Group Performance," in E. Maccoby, T. N. Newcomb, and E. L. Hartley, eds., *Readings in Social Psychology* (New York, 1958), p. 559.

tion to being expensive in time and effort arouses considerable hostility and antagonism.[12] Moreover, he argues, rules are a functional equivalent for direct, personally given orders, since they specify the obligations of workers to do things in specific ways. Standardized rules, in addition, allow simple screening of violations, facilitate remote control, and to some extent legitimize punishment when the rule is violated. The worker who violates a bureaucratic rule has little recourse to the excuse that he did not know what was expected, as he might claim for a direct order. Finally, Gouldner argues that rules are "the 'chips' to which the company staked the supervisors and which they could use to play the game;"[13] that is, rules established a punishment which could be withheld, and this facilitated the supervisors' bargaining power with lower participants.

---

[12]Alvin W. Gouldner, *Patterns of Industrial Bureaucracy* (Glencoe, Ill., 1954).

[13]*Ibid.*, p. 173.

While Gouldner emphasizes the functional characteristics of rules within an organization, it should be clear that full compliance to all the rules at all times will probably be dysfunctional for the organization. Complete and apathetic compliance may do everything but facilitate achievement of organizational goals. Lower participants who are familiar with an organization and its rules can often find rules to support their contention that they not do what they have been asked to do, and rules are also often a rationalization for inaction on their part. The following of rules becomes especially complex when associations and unions become involved, for there are then two sets of rules to which the participant can appeal.

What is suggested is that rules may be chips for everyone concerned in the game. Rules become the "chips" through which the bargaining process is maintained. . . .

# 12

# Authority

We have already seen that authority is institution-ized power. That means that it is to be found in formal organizations, in corporate groups. Thus, we may now look specifically for the manifestations of power *within* an organized group situation. *Authority* is the concept we use to summarize this.

Let us look back for a moment on the road we have so far traveled. We started with a concept of power as a foundation stone of society. We then examined the kinds of human acts that are based upon power. In that examination, we found that the actions most interesting to us and most meaningful from the standpoint of human behavior in organizations were those involving subordination. That brings us to this chapter, in which we shall analyze authority concretely in terms of subordination.

With this chapter we shall add one additional initial refinement. You will recall that Goldhammer and Shils talked about the power-holder influencing the behavior of others. We shall now make this more specific. Simon in the first selection, defines authority as the power to make decisions that guide the actions of others. We are not talking about influence in its wide variety of forms (which Simon deals with also), but we focus our atten-

**INTRODUCTION** tion specifically on that kind of influence that involves decision-making. This lays the groundwork for a later chapter, which deals specifically with decision-making.

You will note that Simon builds his analysis within the framework that we have already developed. He treats authority in terms of behavior, as something to be comprehended and analyzed in the actions of people, not as an abstract entity.

You will also see that he deals with both sides of the coin of authority. Most formal treatments of this subject view authority from the standpoint of the superior. Simon gives us a very illuminating picture of the meaning of authority to the subordinate. It is worth underscoring that when authority is exercised, the subordinate holds "in abeyance his own critical faculties for choosing between alternatives and uses the formal criterion of the receipt of a command or signal as his basis for choice."

We have now moved the concept of power into an organizational framework. In this analysis of authority we are rapidly building toward our comprehension of leadership and subordination.

## AUTHORITY

### Herbert A. Simon*

Even the very simple illustrations that have been presented of organized behavior exhibit, in embryo at least, the phenomenon of authority. *Authority* may be defined as the power to make decisions which guide the actions of another. It is a relationship between two individuals, one "superior," the other "subordinate." The superior frames and transmits decisions with the expectation that they will be accepted by the subordinate. The subordinate expects such decisions, and his conduct is determined by them.[1]

The relationship of authority can be defined, therefore, in purely objective and behavioristic terms. It involves behaviors on the part of both superior and subordinate. When, and only when, these behaviors occur does a relation of authority exist between the two persons involved. When the behaviors do not occur there is no authority, whatever may be the "paper" theory of organization.

The behavior pattern of the superior involves a command—an imperative statement concerning the choice of a behavior alternative by the other—and an expectation that the command will be accepted by the other as a criterion of choice.[2]

The behavior pattern of the subordinate is governed by a single indeterminate decision, or criterion for

---

*From Herbert A. Simon, *Administrative Behavior* (New York: The Macmillan Company, 1947), pp. 125–134. Copyright 1945 and 1947 by Herbert A. Simon and used with the permission of The Macmillan Company.

[1] For other descriptions of authority see L. D. White, *Introduction to the Study of Public Administration* (New York: The Macmillan Company, 1939), pp. 44–46, and C. I. Barnard, *The Functions of the Executive,* p. 163.

[2] This idea was central to the utilitarian concept of the state. See, for example, Jeremy Bentham, *A Fragment on Government* (Oxford: Clarendon Press).

decision, to "follow that behavior alternative which is selected for me by the superior." That is, he holds in abeyance his own critical faculties for choosing between alternatives and uses the formal criterion of the receipt of a command or signal as his basis for choice.[3]

Now since the relation of authority involves a particular criterion of choice as the basis for the subordinate's behavior, it is clear that the two persons may stand in a relation of authority at one moment and not at the next. For the subordinate's behavior may be governed at the first moment by a command, and not at the next. Nor does it follow that when two persons recognize each other as "superior" and "subordinate" respectively, all the verbalizations of the first which affect the behaviors of the second are "commands." The willingness of the subordinate to accept a command, *if given,* does not imply that all, or even most, of his behavior choices are governed by commands.

It is necessary to distinguish, therefore, between specific behaviors which are momentary instances of the exercise of authority and the roles played by two persons over a period of time which involve an *expectation of obedience* by the one and a *willingness to obey* by the other.

## DISTINCTION BETWEEN INFLUENCE AND AUTHORITY

The relation of authority by no means comprehends all situations

where the verbalizations of one person influence the behavior of another. The verbs "persuade," "suggest," etc., describe several kinds of influence which do not necessarily involve any relationship of authority. The characteristic which distinguishes authority from other kinds of influence is one already mentioned above, namely, that a subordinate holds in abeyance his own critical faculties for choosing between alternatives and uses the formal criterion of the receipt of a command or signal as his basis for choice. On the other hand, a person who receives a suggestion accepts it as only one of the evidential bases for making his choice—but the choice he will make depends upon conviction. Persuasion, too, centers around the reasons for or against a course of action. Persuasion and suggestion result in a change in the evidential environment of choice which may, but need not, lead to conviction. Obedience, on the other hand, is an abdication of choice.

Confusion among these terms results from the fact that all three phenomena—persuasion, suggestion, and command—are frequently present in a single situation. Even when a behavior can be secured by the exercise of authority, a superior often and perhaps usually prefers to employ suggestion or persuasion. Some reasons for this will be discussed presently. But confusion will be avoided if it is remembered—as has been pointed out already—that the mere fact that two persons accept the roles of superior and subordinate does not imply that all, or even most, of their behaviors will be instances of the exercise of authority.

The line of demarcation between suggestion and command is perhaps not so clear as would be suggested by this discussion, however. Certain sub-

[3] Cf. Ordway Tead, *Human Nature and Management* (New York: McGraw-Hill Book Co., Inc., 1929), p. 149; and E. O Stene, "An Approach to a Science of Administration," *American Political Science Review,* 34:1131 (Dec., 1940).

tleties are concealed in the term "conviction," which was used as the distinguishing criterion.

A conviction, as used in this connection, is a belief in a factual or value premise which is relevant to a particular decision. Belief in a factual proposition may be induced in a number of ways, one of which is *proof.*

But we are convinced of a great number of things which never have been proved to us logically or empirically. Most persons in this country would agree that the atom bomb has been invented, though they would be hard put to demonstrate this either by pure logic or by the evidence of the senses. Likewise, few persons before taking prescribed medicines ask their physicians for a demonstration of the curative properties of the prescription.

In other words, conviction often results from the social transmission of factual statements, even in the absence of proof. So, a secretary who has been instructed by her employer to investigate a particular question of office procedure may report: "I have looked into the problem, and suggest that you act in this manner." This suggestion may be accepted without any review of its evidential basis by the employer, merely on the strength of his confidence in the secretary. Here is evident the same relaxation of critical faculties that we have said was characteristic of the relation of authority.

Statements, then, may convince without proving by virtue of the status or position of the person making the statement. An individual who does not have a recognized status, or who is not recognized by his associates as expert with respect to a certain kind of knowledge will have a more difficult time convincing his listeners that a recommendation is sound than

one who possesses the credentials of "expertness." Recommendations are judged partly on the merits of the persons making the recommendations. This is true both because the individuals acting upon the recommendations often do not have the expertise needed to judge them, and because pressure of time requires them to accept the recommendations of those whom they trust. This is an important reason for the resistance that is usually experienced in any organization to suggestions that are made outside the line of duty, or that are volunteered through other than the usual lines of communications.

It should not be implied that this resistance to "irregular" suggestions is entirely a weakness of organization. The specialization of decision-making functions, and the fixing of responsibility for particular kinds of expertness upon particular individuals are an important source of organizational efficiency that must be balanced against the potential loss of independent ideas which results.

At the expense of a possible abuse of the term, we shall use "authority" broadly, and comprehend under it all situations where suggestions are accepted without any critical review or consideration. If this definition is accepted, it follows that when A is superior to B at one moment, B may act as superior to A at the next moment. What is meant, then, when A is described as *the* superior of B?

## AUTHORITY AND THE "LAST WORD"

In the situations that have been discussed, a subordinate accepts commands in the absence of a determinate choice of his own. But a subordinate may also accept commands in opposition to a determinate choice of his own. In such a case, the element of authority in the behavior pattern is unequivocal. When there is disagreement between two persons, and when the disagreement is not resolved by discussion, persuasion, or other means of conviction, then it must be decided by the authority of one or the other participant. It is this "right to the last word" which is usually meant in speaking of "lines of authority" in an administrative organization. Too often, however, the element of disagreement in obedience is overemphasized at the expense of the other elements of the situation. The term "authority" would be too narrowly employed if it were restricted to such instances of disagreement.

A final complication must be added to the notion of authority. If authority were evidenced entirely in the acceptance of explicit commands, or in the resolution of disagreements, its presence or absence in any relationship could be sought in the presence or absence of these tangible concomitants. But it is equally possible for obedience to anticipate commands. The subordinate may, and is expected to, ask himself "How would my superior wish me to behave under these circumstances?" Under such circumstances, authority is implemented by a subsequent review of completed actions, rather than a prior command. Further, the more obedient the subordinate, the less tangible will be the evidences of authority. For authority will need to be exercised only to reverse an incorrect decision.

This phenomenon has been pointed out by Friedrich,[4] who calls it a "rule

of anticipated reactions." It affords a striking example of the manner in which expectations and anticipations govern human behavior, and the difficulties which result from this for the analysis of human institutions. The difficulty in determining authority relations because of the operation of the rule of anticipated reactions is common to all "power" situations. Any study, for instance, of a governor's veto power must take into consideration what bills failed of passage in the legislature because of the anticipation of veto, and what bills were passed for the very same reason.[5]

Any study of power relations which confines itself to instances where the sanctions of power were invoked misses the essential fact of the situation. To avoid this fallacy, authority has been defined in this study not in terms of the sanctions of the superior but in terms of the behavior of the subordinate.

## THE SANCTIONS OF AUTHORITY

Having decided, tentatively at least, what authority is, we must examine the circumstances surrounding its exercise. Why and to what extent will a subordinate accept the decision of another as governing his own conduct?

---

[4]C. J. Friedrich, *Constitutional Government and Politics* (New York: Harper &

Bros., 1937), p. 16. Cf. Bentham's very interesting definition: "A tacit *expression of will* is that which is conveyed by any other signs than words whatsoever; among which none are so efficacious as acts of punishment annexed in times past, to the nonperformance of acts of the same sort with those that are the objects of the will that is in question." (*A Fragment on Government*, p. 138.)

[5]Leslie Lipson, *The American Governor: From Figurehead to Executive* (Chicago: University of Chicago Press, 1939), pp. 210–212.

The superior-subordinate relationship is one of many possible examples of the role-taking which characterizes broad areas of human conduct. Perhaps the most important basis for such role-taking is custom. That is, a great deal of conduct requires no further explanation than that, under the circumstances, it is the socially "expected" conduct. For the reasons why particular conduct is dictated by custom it would be necessary to study the social history of the society in question.

The "institutions" of society may be regarded as rules specifying the roles that particular persons will assume in relation to one another under certain circumstances. The range of possible roles and possible behaviors is as broad as the ingenuity of man for dramatic invention.

One of the socially determined roles in many societies is that of "employee." The particular content of the role—the degree of obedience expected —will vary with the social situation. The American workingman today, for example, probably has a somewhat narrower zone of acceptance, so far as the employer's instructions are concerned, than his father had. In part this may be due to his stronger bargaining position, or conversely, the weaker sanctions of the employer; but there is probably also present here a more fundamental change in social attitudes as to what it is "proper" for an employer to ask an employee to do. This changed attitude is reflected also in social legislation limiting the terms of the employment contract.

There are wide differences, too, among different types of employees in their expectations of the authority relations in their positions. Professional men and skilled workmen are apt to have relatively narrow zones of acceptance, particularly in the areas of their professional competences or skills.

No attempt will be made here to explain the genesis of these social attitudes that establish an expectation of obedience in certain situations, nor their dependence upon and relation to other attitude clusters in the society. There has been much speculation that the central attitudes of a society must be reflected in administrative organization, so that administration in a democracy will be in some sense "democratic" while administration in a totalitarian system will be "authoritarian." Thus far, the thesis has been expounded, but by no means demonstrated.

There are a number of other, more specific, factors which induce acceptance of authority in organization. In a broad sense they might be called "sanctions," although that word is usually confined to stimuli which act through punishment, while some of the factors listed below are more properly classified as rewards.

(1) The social sanctions are the first to be noted, and perhaps the most important. Not only does society set up in the individual expectations of obedience in certain social situations, but the individual who fails to accept his role will feel, in one way or another, the social disapprobation of his fellows. Insubordination can be as embarrassing, under these circumstances, as failure to wear a necktie to church.

On the other hand, in so far as fellow employees may receive vicarious satisfaction when an individual "tells off" the boss, social sanctions may operate to decrease the effectiveness of authority. The extent to which group attitudes of acceptance or resistance will condition the individual's reactions to authority has been much emphasized in the Hawthorne studies.[6]

(2) Psychological differences between individuals may play an important part in enforcing such relations. Though the study of leadership is in a very primitive stage, there are some indications that there may be certain personality types that lead, and others that follow.[7]

(3) Purpose has been stressed by students of administration as a sanction of prime importance. . . . In voluntary organizations efforts are contributed largely because the contributor is sympathethic to the purpose of the organization. He is willing to obey commands because he realizes that the coordination secured thereby is useful to the attainment of the joint purpose.[8]

Several conditions must be satisfied if purpose is to be an effective sanction of authority. The subordinate must have confidence that the command is issued in furtherance of a purpose with which he is in sympathy. Second, he must have confidence that the command will be effective in achieving this purpose. This confidence may be based less on his own knowledge of the correctness of the command (as a matter of fact, such acceptance would fall outside our definition of authority) than on

his faith in the ability of those who issue the command, his recognition that they have information he does not have, and his realization that his efforts and those of fellow workers will be ineffective in reaching the desired objective without some coordination from above. Within limits, he will even accept commands he knows to be incorrect because he does not wish to challenge or unsettle a system of authority that he believes to be beneficial to his aims in the long run.

(4) More formal sanctions in our society are based on the relation between the "job" and economic security and status. Thus, obedience may be the price of retaining the position, securing a higher salary, or other advantages. The facts that most organizations will tolerate large quantities of insubordination—particularly if it is not verbalized—without dismissal, and that many organization members are not desirous of promotion, diminish the importance of these sanctions as a means for securing acceptance of authority in the day-to-day work of an organization.

(5) Particularly in the case of individuals not much affected by influences in the third and fourth categories, simple unwillingness or disinclination to accept responsibility may be a major reason for the acceptance of decisions made by others. If the assigned task is not unduly unpleasant, many individuals would prefer being told what to do to being forced to make the decisions themselves. As a matter of fact, this is probably characteristic of most individuals when the decision in question lies outside the area of their experi-

[6]See, for example, F. J. Roethlisberger and W. J. Dickson, *Management and the Worker* (Cambridge: Harvard University Press, 1939).

[7]Charles E. Merriam, *Political Power* (New York: McGraw-Hill Book Co., Inc., 1934), pp. 24–26; and Harold D. Lasswell, *Psychopathology and Politics*, pp. 38–64, 78–152.

[8]C. I. Barnard, *op. cit.*, pp. 165–166, and Luther Gulick, "Notes on the Theory of Organization," in Luther Gulick and L. Ur-

wick, eds., *Papers on the Science of Administration* (New York: Institute of Public Administration, 1937), pp. 37–38.

ence and competence. The psychological roots of this lie deeper than a mere fear of the consequences which may be forthcoming in case of an incorrect decision, and there is great variability among individuals in this characteristic.

### THE LIMITS OF AUTHORITY

The most striking characteristic of the "subordinate" role is that it establishes an area of acceptance[9] in behavior within which the subordinate is willing to accept the decisions made for him by his superior. His choice is then determined, always within the area of acceptance, by his superior, and the relation of superior-subordinate holds only within this area. Acceptance may be due to any of the influences discussed in the previous section, and may take place when the subordinate does not care which alternative is selected, or when the sanctions are sufficiently strong to induce him to carry out an undesired alternative.

The magnitude of the area is influenced by a large number of circumstances. A voluntary organization with poorly defined objectives has

perhaps the narrowest range of acceptance. An army, where the sanctions as well as the customs are of extreme severity, has the broadest area of acceptance.[10]

Restraint of the superior is as important as obedience of the subordinate in maintaining the relationship. Modern writers on administration have emphasized the need for restraint by recommending the use when possible of other means of influence, leading to conviction, rather than authority, leading often to nothing more than acquiescence.

The corresponding limitations of political authority have been discussed by Professor Charles E. Merriam.[11] Theoreticians of history have often questioned the extent to which "leaders" really lead. How broad is the area of indifference within which a group will continue to follow its leadership? In a very real sense, the leader, or the superior, is merely a bus driver whose passengers will leave him unless he takes them in the direction they wish to go. They leave him only minor discretion as to the road to be followed.

---

[9]This concept is adopted from Barnard (*op. cit.*, pp. 168–169), who, however, does not develop to any great extent the positive significance of what he calls the "zone of indifference."

[10]Military literature shows a clear recognition of the importance of the area of acceptance as a fundamental element in tactics. Cf. Col. J. F. C. Fuller's graphic description of the psychology of battle (*The Foundations of the Science of War* [London: Hutchinson & Co., 1925], pp. 140–141).

[11]See the chapter "The Poverty of Power" in his *Political Power* (pp. 156–183).

---

Amitai Etzioni presents an analysis of the structure of authority in an organization as it relates to staff and line distinctions among organization members. He reaches a number of conclusions which are briefly summarized in his introductory paragraph.

This discussion adds to the preceding analysis by Simon. It is particularly important to have a clear knowledge of the relations between professional staffs and line executives because the growing complexity of modern organizations, and especially business firms, has seen the addition of substantial numbers of technical staff experts. These technical experts have backgrounds and outlooks that differ from those of managers and executives. These differences should now be rea-sonably obvious to you from your reading of the chapters dealing with executives and specialists. The following selection summarizes some of the major features of these differences.

## MANAGERS, STAFF EXPERTS AND AUTHORITY

*Amitai Etzioni**

The three major generalizations to be discussed are as follows: (a) In the ultimate analysis staff authority is subordinated to line authority. (b) Organizational units, especially the organization as a whole, are therefore headed by managers and not by experts. (c) Organizations have one and only one ultimate center of authority.

### STAFF AND LINE

There are two approaches to the relationship between staff and line. According to one approach the staff has no direct authority whatsoever. It advises the executive (line authority) on what action to take. The staff in itself does not issue orders and is not responsible for action. According to the second approach the staff, while advising the line on various issues, also takes responsibility for limited areas of activity.[1] In spite of important differences between the two approaches

both agree that staff authority is subordinate to line authority, and they tend to identify line with managers or administrators and staff with experts and specialists. While it is obvious that there are some experts among the line personnel, it is suggested that there is a high correlation between line and managers and between staff and experts.

What is the relationship between these two groups and the organizational goals? Managers are generally considered as those who have the major (line) authority because they direct the major goal activity. Experts deal only with means, with secondary activities. Therefore it is functional for them to have none, or only limited (staff), authority.

*Manager* and *expert* are the two major terms used in this paper. Therefore a few lines will be devoted here to some conceptual clarification. Managers and experts may be differentiated from four points of view: (a) role structure, (b) personality, (c) background, mainly in terms of educational

---

*Reprinted by permission from Amitai Etzioni, "Authority Structure and Organizational Effectiveness," in *Administrative Science Quarterly*, 4:44–51, June, 1959.

[1] On the two approaches see H. A. Simon, D. W. Smithburg, and V. A. Thompson, *Public Administration* (New York, 1956), pp. 280–295; also A. W. Gouldner, *Patterns of Industrial Bureaucracy* (Glencoe, 1954), pp. 224–228.

and occupational experience, and (d) normative orientations.

The *role* of the expert is to create and institutionalize knowledge. The role of the manager is to integrate (create or maintain) organizational systems or subsystems from the point of view of the institutional goals and needs.[2] The expert typically deals with symbols and materials (although there are many who disagree with this point of view).[3] The manager deals with people. The two role types require different *personality* types. The expert, who has intensive knowledge in a limited area, tends to have a restricted perspective. The manager has extensive, though limited, knowledge of many areas, and the resulting broad perspective is essential for his role. Experts are committed to abstract ideas and therefore tend to be unrealistic, whereas managers are more practical. Managers are skilled in human relations; experts are temperamental.

Managers and experts differ in *background.* Experts usually have higher educations than managers and tend to enter their first job at a later age and at higher initial salaries. They often start at relatively high positions in the hierarchy but are limited in the range of their mobility. Managers enter their first job at a younger age, with less

education, and at lower positions, but they move upward faster than the experts and some of them eventually get higher than any expert. Whereas many experts remain more or less restricted to the same organizational functions, the typical manager is assigned to a large variety of tasks in what is called the process of broadening.

Managers' *orientations* differ considerably from those of experts. Managers are more committed or loyal to their specific organization than are experts.[4] Experts are often primarily oriented toward their professional reference and membership groups, while managers are often committed to the scientific and professional ethos regardless of the particular needs and goals of their institution.[5]

Obviously, though there is a high correlation among these four variables, they are not inevitably associated. Two major mechanisms explain how the correlation is maintained. First of all there is *selective recruitment.* People with managerial personalities and background are recruited to managerial roles, and those with the personalities and education of experts tend to enter staff positions. The second mechanism is *role adaptation.* People who enter roles which are initially incompatible with their personalities often adjust to their new roles. Whether they had latent tendencies to act in accordance with the new role or whether the new role meant deep changes in their personality structure need not be discussed here. In both

---

[2]The roles of managers will be discussed here only with regard to the internal functions of the organization. Their roles with regard to environment will be disregarded because of space limitations.

[3]Experts can be arranged in a continuum from the less to the more skilled in human relations. Chemists, for instance, are on the average less skilled from this point of view than labor relations experts. See L. E. Danielson, "Management's Relations with Engineers and Scientists," *Proceedings of Industrial Relations Research Association,* Tenth Annual Meeting, 1957, pp. 314–321.

[4]For a case study which brings out this point, see A. H. Stanton and M. S. Schwartz, *The Mental Hospital* (New York, 1954).

[5]A. W. Gouldner, "Cosmopolitans and Locals: Toward an Analysis of Latent Social Roles," *Administrative Science Quarterly,* 2 (1957), 444–480.

cases the actors will adjust to their new roles. In such adjustment the process of broadening produces managers from initial specialists; a parallel process produces semi-experts from managers who entered managerial roles in professional organizations. These processes explain in part also why there is no perfect correlation among the four variables discussed above. For example, people with the background of experts may fulfill managerial roles.

### INSTITUTIONAL HEADS

It is one of the basic characteristics of bureaucratic organizational structures to have one and only one center of authority. This is often vested in the role of the head of the organization. He is seen as the top of the chain of command, as the ultimate authority in the internal structure and as ultimately responsible for the organizational activity relative to external structures such as the community and the government. Institutional heads are often symbols of identification for members and employees of the organization.[6] Customers and other outsiders, such as the personnel of other organizations, tend to identify an organization with the organizational head. Institutional heads are in a strategic position to influence the implementation of proclaimed organizational goals.[7]

All organizations need to integrate their various activities into one operating whole.[8] This function is partially fulfilled by the organizational head. Since integrating is a managerial role, it follows that managers and not experts will head organizations. We shall return to this point.

### ORGANIZATIONS ARE MONOCRATIC

As noted above, bureaucratic organizations have one center of authority.[9] This is one of the important characteristics which differentiate bureaucracies from feudal regimes.[10] This does not mean that all activities are directed from one center. Authority is often delegated. Organizations can be compared with respect to the degree to which authority is centralized. But even in decentralized organizations there is one center of authority where final decisions are made and conflicts among lower authorities can be resolved. The monocratic structure is one of the more important reasons why bureaucracies are considered as the most effective form of organization. Such a structure enables the top central authority, which is often strongly committed to the organizational goals, to retain control of much of the organizational activity.

On the basis of existing theory, then, one would hold three expectations: (a) Managers have the major (line) authority whereas experts deal with secondary activities, and therefore have only limited (staff) authority. (b) Institutional heads have to be

---

[6]The University of Liverpool, *The Dock Worker* (Liverpool, 1951), pp. 95–96.

[7]See Philip Selznick, *Leadership in Administration* (Evanston, 1957).

[8]See Talcott Parsons, "Some Ingredients of a General Theory of Formal Organization," in Andrew W. Halpin, ed., *Administrative Theory in Education* (Chicago, 1958).

[9]For a discussion of this point, see M. Weber, *The Theory of Social and Economic Organization* (Glencoe, 1947), p. 337; Herbert A. Simon, "Decision-Making and Administrative Organization," in R. K. Merton, A. P. Grey, B. Hockey, and H. C. Selvin, eds., *Reader in Bureaucracy* (Glencoe, 1952), pp. 185–194.

[10]See G. Mosca, *The Ruling Class* (New York, 1939).

manager oriented because their role is a role of system integration. If an expert-oriented person were to hold this role, the system would be alienated from its goals and might even eventually disintegrate because some functions would be overemphasized while others would be neglected. (c) Organizational goals can be maintained more effectively in organizations with one center of authority. . . .

## THE PRIVATE BUSINESS: AN AFFIRMATION

The organizational goal of private business is to make profits. The major means are production and exchange. While experts deal with various aspects of the production and exchange process, that is, with means such as engineering, labor relations, quality control, and marketing, the manager is the one who co-ordinates the various activities in such a way that the major organizational goal will be maximized. Profit making is his responsibility. That seems to be one of the reasons why modern corporations prefer to have people with administrative experience as top executives rather than former specialists such as engineers. . . .

In general the goals of private business are consistent with managerial orientations. The economic goals of the organization and the bureaucratic orientations of the managerial role have in common the orientation toward rational use of means and development of rational procedures to maximize goals which are considered as given.[11] The social and cultural conditions that support modern economic activities also support modern administration.

[11]See H. A. Simon, "A Comparison of Organizational Theories," *Review of Economic Studies*, 20 (1952–1953), 40–48.

When people with strong expert orientations take over the managerial role of the institutional head, a conflict between the organizational goals and the expert orientation can be predicted. The case described in *Executive Suite*, where the design engineer with strong craftsman commitments takes over the presidency of a private corporation, should be considered atypical.[12] Usually commitment to professional values runs counter to the economic values of the organization.[13]

Homans reports an interesting case in which the influence of the experts was greater than it is in most corporations.[14] He discusses an electrical equipment company which was owned, managed, and staffed by engineers. Management, which was in the hands of manager-oriented engineers, suffered from pressure toward professional values from the design engineers. The design engineers in the eyes of management were "prima donnas" and "temperamental," terms often used by management to describe experts. Furthermore, they were indifferent "to the general welfare of the company," that is, to profit making, as "shown by their lack of concern with finance, sales, and the practical needs of the consumer and by their habit of spending months on an aspect of design that had only theoretical importance." This caused considerable tension between the managerial and expert-oriented groups, tension to which this company was especially

[12]See E. Larrabee and D. Reisman, "The Role of Business in *Executive Suite*," in B. Rosenberg and D. M. White, eds., *Mass Culture* (Glencoe, 1957), pp. 325–340.
[13]See Thorstein Veblen, *The Engineers and the Price System* (New York, 1921), esp. pp. 70–81.
[14]George C. Homans, *The Human Group* (New York, 1950), pp. 369–414.

sensitive because of its high dependence on expert work and the special structure of ownership. A power struggle resulted, ending with a clearer subordination of the design engineers (staff) to the managerial engineers (line). This was mandatory "if the company was to survive and increase its sales," as Homans puts it. The treasurer (a nonexpert in this context) became the most influential member of the new management. In short, in a corporation where the experts had a strong power position, the existence of the organization was threatened, considerable internal tension was generated, and finally the organizational structure was changed toward a more usual structure with a clearer subordination of the experts. In other words, the organizational authority structure was made more compatible with the goals of the organization. Manager orientations and the institutional goals of private business seem to match. When an expert orientation dominates, this is dysfunctional to the organizational purposes.

To sum up, the study of private business as an organization can be seen as an affirmation of the three generalizations of organizational theory presented above. Managers direct the major goal activities and have the major authority; experts deal with means and are in minor and subordinated authority positions. The organizational heads are manager oriented, and there is only one internal center of authority. All business organizations studied, including such decentralized organizations as General Motors and Bata, seem to have one center of authority.[15]

---

[15]See George Friedmann, *Industrial Society* (Glencoe, 1955), pp. 325–329.

---

The following study makes clear the proportion of the interactions recorded by the heads of important business departments that were with their organizational equals. While the study does not present data on the content of these interactions, we may properly infer that an authoritative exchange took place many times during these interactions. Furthermore, the interactions originated and interactions received by the head of each department in each company are closely balanced. There appears to be some sort of reciprocity between department heads, so that one who initiates many interactions with heads of other departments will receive an approximately equal number of interactions from them.

It is between equals in a business firm that a substantial amount of authority is exercised. This is related to actually getting the work done and coordinating the operations of related departments. Perhaps the equality among the department heads in initiating and receiving interactions is evidence of the fact that equals keep the authority relations between them balanced so that no single individual can achieve more informal authority than any of his organizational peers.

## THE HORIZONTAL DIMENSION OF INTERACTION

*Henry A. Landsberger* and *Frank B. Miller**

Despite the fact that "conflict of interest" is our basic concept in examining the horizontal dimension of organization, we still believe that the various subsidiary concepts used in examining vertical, hierarchical phenomena have applicability also to horizontal relationships, i.e., that they have lateral content.

For example, in order to discharge their functions properly, officials are *dependent* on their equal and opposite numbers in other departments. They must and do *anticipate* their views and probable reactions on issues of joint concern. Opposite numbers possess and display *power* and exercise tacit *authority* toward one another in areas where they share responsibility for joint decisions or joint execution of tasks. They try to *legitimate* their lateral authority on the basis of specialized functional knowledge rather than organizational level. Moreover, the authority of one department over another is *institutionalized* through rules in the same way as is the authority of a superior over a subordinate. Likewise, *codification of rules* exists as much to limit and channel the areas where conflict between departments is acceptable or not, as to limit friction between organizational levels and to

define appropriate organization levels for executive action. Systems of *control* are not only a tool for evaluating subordinates' performance; they profoundly affect lateral line and line-staff relationships as demonstrated by the 1951 Argyris-Miller study on budgets.

We would like to re-emphasize that division of labor in an organization takes place along both main dimensions of decision-making. Under the hierarchical principal there is a *quantitative* division, with decisions made at appropriate levels according to their magnitude. Under functional specialization, there is a *qualitative* division, with decisions made according to type of *expertise*. The concepts of authority, power, control, etc. must be seen as having *both* kinds of connotations of division of labor—not just the hierarchical. . . .

### EMPIRICAL ILLUSTRATION

The conflict-of-interest approach may be illustrated with data gathered by one of the authors during a study of three factories. The three factories produced a similar product, and each employed a mixed labor force of 300 to 500 persons.

The focus of the study was the position of the Production Control, sometimes called the Production Planning, department relative to other departments. We studied the tasks and functions which this department is expected to perform; how successfully it performs these functions; its formal

*Reprinted by permission from Henry A. Landsberger and Frank B. Miller, from a paper presented at the 1957 annual meeting of the American Sociological Association. A revised version under the authorship of Professor Landsberger was published as "The Horizontal Dimension in Bureaucracy," *Administrative Science Quarterly*, 6:299–332, (December 1961).

and informal power; authority and prestige; and so on.

Production *Control* departments issue weekly or monthly production schedules to various subdepartments of the Production department proper. These schedules are based on incoming orders received from the Sales Liaison department, which in turn receives them from the Field Sales offices. One should therefore visualize a chain of departments along which orders flow, and along which the various planning functions must be performed. All of these departments are vitally interested in the schedules of the Planning department. The chain stretches from Field Sales through Sales Liaison, Planning, Production, to Purchasing, with "branches" to the

Thus we are *excluding* relationships between ego and his superiors, subordinates, or peers in the same department.

In order—among other reasons—to obtain such illustration we made detailed observations in two of our three factories of all the oral interactions of the four responsible officials in the three departments. These departments —Sales Liaison, Planning, and Production—are the *key* ones from the planning point of view. Using a modified Bales technique, we counted and scored all oral, interpersonal contacts for each of the four relevant executives for two mornings and two afternoons.

Table 1 contains the relevant summary data from these observations.

**Table 1**

THE INTERACTION OF THREE DEPARTMENT HEADS
WITH THEIR EQUALS IN TWO FACTORIES*

| | Proportion of All Interactions Which Were with Equals in Other Departments | | | |
| | *Interactions Originated* | | *Interactions Received* | |
| *By Head of—* | *In Co. A* | *In Co. B* | *In Co. A* | *In Co. B* |
| --- | --- | --- | --- | --- |
| Production, Planning & Control[a] | 31.5% | 40.1% | 30.7% | 48.9% |
| Production | 16.8 | 41.2 | 22.4 | 40.2 |
| Sales Liaison[b] | 61.7 | 61.5 | 56.9 | 63.7 |
| Total | 39.1 | 48.2 | 38.4 | 51.9 |

*Recorded for 2 mornings and 2 afternoons.
[a]In factory B, two persons, heading two separate departments, supervised the Production Planning and stock control functions respectively, which were supervised by a single person in factory A. In constructing this table, the interactions of these two persons were added to each other. Interactions between them were treated as "internal."
[b]In factory A, two persons in the same department performed the sales liaison function performed by one person in factory B. Their interactions were likewise added to each other.

Design and Industrial Engineering Departments.

The first point we wish to illustrate here is the sheer quantitative importance of horizontal inter-departmental relationships—i.e., those completely outside normal authority relationships.

We present here the per cent of interactions which were *external* by our definition, broken into originations (ego's statements) and responses (alter's statements).

Table 1 shows that the per cent of external interactions is quite high—

hence no theory seeking to explain organizational behavior is complete if it does not account for such interactions. The figures vary from a "low" of 16% to a "high" of 63%, with an average per factory—at least for these four key persons—of around 50% or just under. Moreover, for a variety of reasons into which we cannot go here, these figures are extremely conservative.

You may now notice from Table 1 that differences in external interaction rates are certainly a role phenomenon (contrast the two Sales Liaison departments with the two Production departments). They may also be an organizational phenomenon. This is especially noticeable for the Planning and Production superintendents who had different rates in the two factories. It is suggestive that economic data indicates that factory A is the less efficient of the two. The main points we want to illustrate here, then, are, first, the substantial quantity of horizontal interaction; and second, the important differences in the functioning of organizations with which differences in rates of external interaction may possibly be linked. . . .

---

The following selection examines the specific relationships between authority and bureaucracy. In understanding the role of leadership in organizations, it is necessary to understand the nature of the ties that bind the leader's staff to him. In a previous selection, Simon has discussed the "area of acceptance" of authority on the part of a subordinate. He examined the acceptance of authority and subordination to it in general terms without distinguishing among different patterns of acceptance that are organizationally determined.

One way of distinguishing different patterns of organizational authority is to consider the bases upon which that authority is established. In the following selection, three distinct kinds of authority are examined. In this respect the discussion follows Max Weber's development of his analysis of legitimate authority.

There are three central reasons for examining the different kinds of organizational authority. The very nature of the administrative staff of an organization varies with different kinds of leadership authority. Similarly, the modes for exercising authority within the organization vary in accordance with the nature of leadership authority. Finally, the object of obedience on the part of the administrative staff is different for different kinds of leadership authority. These points are examined in some detail in the next selection.

# AUTHORITY, BUREAUCRACY, AND LEADERSHIP

## Robert Dubin

One of the particular aspects of authority in formal organizations that deserves special attention is the authority relationship between the leader and his administrative staff, the bureaucracy. This aspect of authority is important because we have already seen how the staff specialist stands in a peculiar subordinate relationship to the leader. The leader does have the power to make decisions that guide the actions of his administrative staff. But at the same time, there enters into this very decision-making process the contribution of the staff specialist in his area of competence. Thus, the executive vice-president of a company may issue the orders establishing the company's production schedule. These orders are binding upon the operating departments. However, before the schedule was validated by the vice-president and issued as a directive, the staff specialists in production, purchasing, and marketing, at a minimum, have had their say regarding the schedule. In this example there is an initial presumption that the leader is not wholly independent of his administrative staff. There is the further assumption that the administrative staff and the individuals particularly concerned with a given decision have not held "in abeyance [their] own critical faculties for choosing between alternatives and used the formal criterion of the receipt of a command or signal as [their] basis for choice," as Simon suggests in a preceding selection.

This special kind of relationship between the leader and the bureaucracy of an organization leads us directly into the analysis of different kinds of organizational authority. Following Weber, we will distinguish among three kinds of authority: (1) that which is based upon rational grounds, (2) that which is based upon traditional grounds, and (3) that which is based upon charismatic grounds (derived from charisma—the "gift of grace").

The authority based upon rational grounds rests on the belief by subordinates in the legality and propriety of the rules governing the organization and the right of those elevated to leadership to issue commands under such rules. Thus, in the military organization the Articles of War are the legal governing rules, so accepted by members of the Army. A commanding officer is considered to have the right to exercise and enforce these rules irrespective of his personal attributes or his past accomplishments. He has this right of authority by virtue of the office he fulfills. Where organizational authority is rational in its basis, the rules of the organization are enacted by conscious decision and are subjected to tests of adequacy in performance.

Authority based upon traditional grounds rests on the belief by subordinates in the sanctity of time-honored traditions and the legitimate right or status of those exercising authority under them. In Japan, the authority of the emperor was based upon a long tradition of belief in his direct descent from heaven, "son of heaven," and the person of the emperor was considered the sole source of ultimate authority in the country.

Charismatic authority rests on the

devotion of subordinates to an individual who is believed to have exceptional personal characteristics that set him above and beyond mere mortals. These exceptional personal qualities may be unusual piety, exemplary character, or heroism. Such a leader reveals or ordains the rules or codes of behavior for his followers.

With this distinction among the three kinds of authority in mind, it is possible to indicate how the staff of a leader is related to him and to the organization. We will examine the typical organization of the administrative staff, the typical mode for exercising authority, and the object of staff obedience for each kind of authority. The following table summarizes the analysis.

Where authority is established on rational grounds, the typical administrative staff is a bureaucracy in which authority is rationally delegated both in terms of specialized function and in terms of level of command. The staff is obedient to the body of rules and regulations that we can call the *constitution* of the organization. The leader under these circumstances is the one with the greatest amount of authority derived from his position in the organization. The particular leader may change, and usually does, but the office of leader retains the authority that goes with it. Thus, the president of a company may be replaced, but his successor will have the same

amount of authority, unless—and this is important—the constitution of the organization is changed so as to modify the authority of the new president. The enacted rules of the organization determine the authority structure. Authority is derived from them. Staff obedience to the leader and to the organization is in terms of the impersonal body of rules that establish the governmental framework of the organization.

Many modern formal organizations have an authority structure based upon rational grounds. This is generally true of business organizations, for example. This fact is of considerable significance to us because it conforms to a pattern we have already encountered. In the general discussion of bureaucracy, great emphasis was placed upon the rationality of this form of administration. We now see that leadership in many modern organizations is likewise grounded in authority that has rational roots.

For purposes of better grasping the meaning of rational authority, it is worth while contrasting it with traditional and charismatic authority. Within an organizational context, these latter types of authority are found less frequently than rational authority.

In the case of traditional authority, the typical administrative staff of the leader is a group of retainers. To these retainers the leader makes limited and revocable delegations of authority at

| Type of Authority | Typical Organization of Staff | Typical Mode of Exercising Authority | Staff Is Obedient to— |
|---|---|---|---|
| Rational | Bureaucracy | Rational delegation | Legally established impersonal order |
| Traditional | Retainers | Ad hoc delegation | Person of leader |
| Charismatic | Personal staff—servants | Directly—no delegation | Idealized person of leader |

his convenience and whim. The leader can discharge a member from his staff of retainers at will. Under these circumstances, it is clear that the obedience of the staff is to the person of the leader and not to some impersonal order. The leader operates within a body of tradition that defines his office in broad terms and that, in particular, provides the traditional legitimate justification for the leader to exercise the authority he possesses. The classical monarchy is a good example of an organization grounded in traditional authority. A modern counterpart of this kind of authority is found in some business organizations that are considered one-man companies. The general pattern of our culture legitimizes the authority of the president as leader of such a firm. His relation to subordinates is precisely that of leader to retainer. Thus, Sewell Avery had operated in terms of traditional authority in Montgomery Ward and Company to the point where he dismissed the president and 10 top executives for differing with his policies.[1] This kind of one-man rule is fast losing ground in the management of modern organizations.

Authority based upon charismatic grounds is the opposite of rational authority. The leader is invested by his entire group of followers with supernatural powers that place him above ordinary mortals. There can be only one role for the administrative staff in relation to such a leader—that of per-

sonal staff or servants. There is little or no delegation of authority. All authority is exercised in the name of the leader as a direct extension of his personal authority. Obedience is owed only to the idealized person of the leader. This charismatic authority is well illustrated by modern examples. Hitler was a charismatic leader. So was Gandhi in India. Father Divine also exercised charismatic authority over his flock. It will be recalled that Hitler, for example, treated his generals as though they were his personal servants in spite of the fact that his own military knowledge was developed from the vantage point of a corporal's rank. The generals, who operated with rational authority within the army, were in turn subjected to charismatic authority at the hands of Hitler, the over-all leader. Gandhi played a less demanding leadership role in India, but regular visits were made to him by the party leaders and they approached him with reverence to secure his blessing and word of approval. Policies or actions that bore the stamp of his approval were automatically preferred. Father Divine spoke with the supernatural authority of God and exercised far-reaching control over his flock.

The three kinds of authority that we have examined represent the analytically distinct types of authority. In most organizational situations, there is likely to be more than one type of authority present at the same time. The different kinds of authority may be called into play under varying conditions in which the organization is operating. Franklin D. Roosevelt exercised all three kinds of authority in the office of President. Many New Dealers were completely devoted to

---

[1] The executives actually resigned, but there is a strong probability that they had no other course and would have been dismissed if they had failed to do so. For an interesting and sympathetic account of Mr. Avery's leadership role, see "The Stewardship of Sewell Avery," *Fortune*, 33:111–113, 179–186 (May 1946).

him as a charismatic leader, as were a significant part of the electorate. In some situations he was wont to use authority grounded in tradition, especially, for example, in the direction of the armed forces, where great emphasis was placed upon our traditional superiority of civilian over military leadership. Finally, the proliferation of bureaus to carry out specialized tasks under his administration represented a widespread use of rational authority in carrying out the business of government.

---

The increased valuing of the image of the modern corporate organization as a family of cooperating individuals with its accompanying "human relations" emphasis for administrators has led to the development of research on styles of leadership. In particular, the group dynamics movement, inspired by the theory and research of the late Kurt Lewin, has placed great emphasis on the virtues of democratic leadership.

This has led to a fundamental dilemma of discovering how the exercise of authority and the maintenance of democratic relations between authority holder and subordinate could be achieved simultaneously. In the next selection this problem is tackled with the suggestion that the subordinate gets a payoff of "privilege pay" when an authority holder follows a demo-cratic style of leadership. The implication of this for the behavior of administrators is two-fold. (1) It means that authority is not diminished or set aside when the administrator behaves democratically toward his subordinates. (2) It also means that the incentive value of "privilege pay" depends on the skill of the administrator in making the amount of payoff fit the particular circumstances of democratic interaction with, and contributions of subordinates. Inconsistent use of "privilege pay" may readily destroy its incentive value.

When "privilege pay" is used effectively, the desirable consequences of democratic administration in the form of high morale and cooperation may be forthcoming. At the same time, the exercise of industrial authority is not eroded.

---

## AUTHORITY AND PRIVILEGE PAY

*Robert Dubin**

Privilege pay, like job satisfaction, is essentially a psychic reward. Both result in a feeling or attitude of well-being and pleasure. We mean by privilege pay the freedom with which authority holders permit subordinates to interact with them. People in authority can accord to their subordinates opportunities for interaction, or

*From *The World of Work* (Englewood Cliffs, N. J.: Prentice-Hall, Inc., 1958), pp. 243–244. Used by permission.

these opportunities can be withheld. It is a genuine privilege to a subordinate to be able to talk with his boss as another human being.

Privilege pay is highly valued. Subordinates like to feel, in particular, (A) that they are free to talk to the boss about working problems, (B) that their boss values their professional and technical opinion, and really wants them to be free to express their opinions about operating problems troubling the boss (e.g., to be the opposite of "yes men"), and (C) that they can be man-to-man with each other. When the boss is able to create an atmosphere in which these goals of subordinates are achieved, then the subordinates have been paid off in privilege pay. They have earned the privilege of setting aside the boss-subordinate relationship, under some conditions, and at some times.[1]

There has been a very vigorous movement in personnel circles to encourage bosses to make more liberal use of privilege pay as a work incentive. This general movement goes under the name of "group dynamics." The formal rationalization for using a group dynamics approach as a boss is that it succeeds in unlocking hitherto unused human resources of the organization. By involving people in making decisions about their own work, more effective brain power is mobilized on behalf of the work organization. Many studies, of which the report by Kahn and Katz[2] is rep-

resentative, establish this conclusion.

The fact that people enjoy and value participation in determining their own working destiny appears undisputed. The "group dynamics" approach, initiated through the research of Kurt Lewin,[3] has been extremely valuable in providing an alternative to what Worthy has called the "machine theory of organization," or what Mayo had earlier called the "rabble hypothesis" of industrial administration. In the more mechanical view of industrial administration, it is assumed that the work organization operates most effectively only by using its formal structures and official channels and means of interaction.

In the group dynamics view, it is recognized that human beings respond to a wide range of incentives, of which privilege pay is an important one. It has not generally been recognized by the proponents of the group dynamics approach that what the subordinate gets out of the group dynamics situation is privilege pay. Most of the studies of employee reaction do not go beyond pointing out the greater satisfaction reported by subordinates.[4] It should be recognized, however, that the principal reason for such satisfaction is the opportunity to interact with the boss as a relative equal, under particular circumstances. It is the boss who is conferring this privilege on his subordinates. He is giving them privilege pay.

---

[1]For general insight into the nature of "privilege pay," see: Henri de Man, *Joy in Work* (New York: Holt, Rinehart & Winston, Inc., 1929); Russell Davenport, "Enterprise for Everyman," *Fortune*, 41:55–59 (January 1950); and T. H. Hargrave, "Working Conditions and Morale," *Human Factor*, 6:382–84 (October 1932).

[2]R. L. Kahn and Daniel Katz, "Leader-

ship Practices in Relation to Productivity and Morale," in D. Cartwright and A. Zander, eds., *Group Dynamics* (Evanston: Row, Peterson & Co., 1953), pp. 612–628.

[3]See especially his *Field Theory in Social Science* (New York: Harper & Brothers, 1951).

[4]See, for example: R. B. Wolf, "Nonfinancial Incentives," *Advanced Management*, 5:168–170 (October-December 1940).

Indeed, management literature makes this crystal clear. The great difficulty in making a group dynamics approach work is getting the boss to accept and use it. Only when the boss is willing to accord this privilege pay to his subordinates will the method work.

Privilege pay is an important non-financial incentive for work. In particular, it works because it modifies the authority structure of work organizations. It changes the boss from an "oracle" to a troubled administrator, seeking the best help he can get from his working associates and subordinates. Privilege pay substitutes for an unquestioning response to authority by subordinates, an attitude of cooperation. In order for privilege pay to be an effective incentive, the boss must be willing to admit that he "doesn't know," and be willing to pay off his subordinates with the privilege of expressing their best ideas to him, in helping him be a more effective boss.

# 13

# Status

We now have a picture of the organization as a social system in which there is specialization in terms of function, and differentiation in terms of authority. We know these distinctions exist because we can detect them in the different kinds of behavior that characterize various people in the organization. But we know that not all the behavior of each individual, while he is participating in the organization, is official behavior. Yet, in spite of this, we can usually tell where each person fits into the organization.

How can we do so? The answer is that we judge the position of an individual or a group in a system of positions by the marks of *status* that they possess. Status is the external markings and trappings that visibly distinguish and rank people in relation to one another.

To put it differently, status is an important kind of cement that binds an organization together. When authority becomes relatively stable, and when functional specialization is established, the development of status symbols for each position in the organization serves to institutionalize and regularize the structure. An established organization always has a status system.

There is another point about status to emphasize. Status is always evident in a system of rankings—there is no such thing as a solitary status. There always have to be two individuals or groups to compare. Furthermore, the comparison has to result in the conclusion that one is "better," "higher," "more important," than the other. Thus, we see that a status system is also a set of value judgments that rank individuals and groups in relation to one another.

There is still another point about status in organizations: the status system covers all members of the organization. Every individual finds his rank in the system. Where there is no ascribed status for an individual or a group, there is a strain to assign status created in the organization.

We can now define status as follows:

*It is a set of visible, external markings that systematically ranks individuals and groups in relation to each other, and that includes all the members of the organization some place in the scheme of rankings.*

This definition does not exactly accord with the definitions of either Hughes or Barnard in their selections of this chapter. Let us not quibble about definitions. What has been said in the previous paragraph summarizes, in the form of a definition, what Hughes and Barnard are talking about. We are concerned with *what* they are talking about, not with what they say they are talking about. The above definition seems to deal with the substance of what they are analyzing. If you think either one of their definitions, or even another, is better, by all means use it.

To summarize, then, the marks of status tell us *who* and *what* an individual is in an organization. If we know, in addition, the organizational office he occupies, we will also know *what he does* and the authority he possesses.

---

The following selection, from an article by Barnard, is a classic. You will be richly rewarded in reading it carefully.

Barnard distinguishes between functional status and scalar status. The first corresponds to specialization and division of labor along technical lines. The second corresponds to the structure of authority. This ties in closely with our framework of analysis.

There are three functions that Barnard notes for status systems in organizations. First, a status system facilitates communication. It does so in terms of establishing the legitimacy of the communication. You can readily see how this idea fits into our discussion of specialists in Chapter 9, and of authority in Chapter 12. The expert legitimizes his position to communicate as an expert by developing a specialized jargon and keeping nonexperts out of the field of specialty. In Dubin's treatment of authority in Chapter 12, he analyzes the bases upon which authority is made legitimate. Second, a status system provides an important form of incentive in an organization. This discussion can be related back to Chapter 3, where we deal with motivation. Third, a status system is a means for imposing and fixing responsibility among the members of an organization. In terms of our framework, status helps to define the office for the individual. We examined organization office in detail in Chapter 6.

This is another one of the key selections of this book. We have just indicated some of the interrelationships it has with other parts of the book.

## FUNCTIONS OF STATUS SYSTEMS IN FORMAL ORGANIZATIONS

*Chester I. Barnard**

The following is a report of a preliminary inquiry into the nature and functions of systems of status in formal organizations. So far as I am aware this subject has not been given extensive consideration by students of organization. This neglect appears not to be due to failure to recognize the importance of problems of status in organizations, but rather to failure to recognize that status is systematic, and that systems of status have a considerable degree of independence of other structural aspects of organization. Status systems are very closely related, for example, to systems of specialization, to systems of organization communication, and to systems of authority, so that differences of status have appeared to be incidental to these other structural aspects of organization and not to constitute a separate system. This view appears to be inadequate. . . .

### I. THE NATURE AND TECHNICAL APPARATUS OF SYSTEM OF STATUS IN FORMAL ORGANIZATIONS

By "status" of an individual in an organization we mean in the present text that condition of the individual that is defined by a statement of his rights, privileges, immunities, duties, and obligations in the organization and, obversely, by a statement of the

restrictions, limitations, and prohibitions governing his behavior, both determining the expectations of others in reference thereto. Status becomes systematic in an organization when appropriate recognition of assigned status becomes the duty and the practice of all participating, and when the conditions of the status of all individuals are published by means of differentiating designations, titles, appellations, insignia, or overt patterns of behavior.

Two kinds of systems of status may be discriminated, both being simultaneously observed in nearly all organizations and being partly overlapping and interdependent. The first kind, which we shall call *functional* systems of status, is that in which status does not depend upon authority and jurisdiction but upon function. The ranks are vertically divided into lateral groups of different callings, trades, crafts, metiers, divisions of labor, specializations, and professions. One common characteristic of them all is the authority of command of one over another is lacking, or is irrelevant at least to the functional status. But this does not mean that functional statuses are equally valued. On the contrary, the variation is wide, from the "low" of common, unskilled, and casual labor, intermittently attached to organizations, to the "high," *e.g.*, of the expert accountant, lawyer, architect, physician, and clergyman. Though lateral differentiation of status is not confined to formal organizations, it is a characteristic of such organizations generally and especially of the larger

*From W. F. Whyte, (ed.), *Industry and Society* (New York, 1946), pp. 46, 47–53, 55–67, 68–70. Copyright by The McGraw-Hill Book Company, Inc. Used by permission.

organizations conspicuous for their elaborate divisions of labor.

Functional status is a general attribute. For example, merely performing carpentering at a given place, which would determine specific status varying for each individual from time to time and from place to place, is not what we mean by functional status. The "carpenter" is presumed by all to have certain capacities regardless of who he is or what he is doing and conversely is presumed to have limitations, *e.g.*, he is not authorized to give medical advice. It is the presumption of capacities and limitations without necessary regard to the immediate concrete activities of the individual that is the essential feature of systematic status. The emphasis is upon the potentialities of behavior, not necessarily upon the immediately observable behavior.

In the second kind of status system, which we shall call the *scalar,* status is determined by (1) the relationship of superiority or subordination in a chain of command or formal authority and (2) by jurisdiction. In this kind of status system the primary relationships are customarily conceived as being along vertical lines, of above and below, of superior and subordinate. Status is distinguished by horizontal levels, and integration is by vertical groups, several such groups exemplifying a "pyramid of authority." It should be noted that status is a general attribute of an individual associated with the occupation of a usually rather narrowly restricted position. For example, a naval captain possesses certain prerogatives not enjoyed by those of inferior rank and is deemed qualified for positions for which those of inferior rank will not ordinarily be acceptable; but the position of command actually occupied at a given time will be confined to a particular ship or shore station or staff position, and the immediate authority and responsibility will be correspondingly restricted.

Although the status systems of general societies will not be treated in this paper, the close interrelation of general social status and status in organizations should be noted. Wherein a general society a low status is assigned based, *e.g.*, on race, nationality, sex, age, education, ownership of property, or family, it is difficult in general to acquire high status in formal organizations in that society; and where there is high social status it tends to facilitate attainment of high organization status, though less so in democratic than in aristocratic societies. Conversely, those having low status in a formal organization are not likely to have high social status, though there are many exceptions; and those having high status, especially in important organizations, tend thereby to acquire higher general social status. The bearing of this is that if status systems are necessary in formal organizations, it is probable that they will extend into general social relationships, in greater or less degree depending upon the society.[1]

Nearly all members of formal organizations may be observed to be much preoccupied with matters of status; and the leaders or managers of such organizations are almost constantly concerned with problems of

---

[1]During the last several generations, when scalar organizations were developing rapidly in Germany, organization status was carried over widely into generalized status in German society, formally, that is, by title. See Talcott Parsons, "Democracy and Social Structure in Pre-Nazi Germany," *Journal of Legal and Political Sociology,* November, 1942.

status for reasons that will be treated in some detail later. But to fix more clearly what we mean by status, it seems desirable to present briefly here the organization apparatus by which status is established and maintained. This apparatus may be described as of the following categories: (1) ceremonies of induction and appointment; (2) insignia and other public indicia of status; (3) titles and appellations of office and calling; (4) emoluments and perquisites of position and office; (5) limitations and restrictions of calling and office.

(1) The use of ceremonies of induction and appointment varies widely in different types of organizations. Ceremonial induction is common to all grades and ranks in military and religious organizations, is quite widely used in governmental and educational organizations, and is almost absent in business organizations (at least in the United States).

(2) Insignia and other indicia of status are nearly universal in military organization, especially in time of war, and in many religious organizations, especially to the clergy. They are also used in many education organizations on ceremonial occasions. They are little used in civil government organizations (except by the departments for police and fire protection) or in business organizations except for the wearing of union labor insignia in many trades and, in Europe, distinctive garb for those employed in some trades.

(3) Titles and appellations of address are universal in formal organizations both for scalar and for functional status. In the case of functional status, the title often begins as a mere designation of the function performed, as "clerk," "bookkeeper," "lineman," "typesetter," etc., and initially has no implication of systematic status; but very quickly, since classification by functions is attended by other distinguishing conditions such as differences in compensations, such titles become also the designations of status.

(4) Emoluments, perquisites, and privileges are highly important evidences of status and are often highly valued. Care should be taken, however, to distinguish between the valuation of them as material rewards and as evidences and elements of status. They are almost universally employed in organizations of all kinds. In business and in some other organizations they are even more important than titles in fixing status. The use or non-use of restricted quarters, automobiles, chauffeurs, private offices, private secretaries, and other perquisites in various combinations, time clocks, etc., provide a complex code that describes the system of status in effect, thoroughly understood by the initiated and fairly easily sensed by the outside observer.

(5) Both higher and lower statuses are also established and published by restrictions and limitations of behavior that relate almost exclusively to maintenance and protection of status and the status system. For example, those of higher status often cannot go to places where those of lower status are free to go, or do things that those of lower status may do, or say things, or use language, etc. Though this is well understood, these limitations are not often made explicit and they are among the most subtle elements of status systems.

This, it is hoped, is sufficient to make clear the nature and in general the technical features of systems of status in scalar organizations so far as necessary for present purposes. If so, we may proceed to the main business of studying the functions and the consequences of such systems.

## II. THE FUNCTIONS OF SYSTEMS OF STATUS WITH RESPECT TO INDIVIDUALS

Systems of status of different kinds and of various degrees of elaborateness and complexity are found in most if not all formal organizations. The establishing of a nucleus of such a system is one of the very first steps in creating an organization.[2] Are these facts merely reflections of habitual attitudes and needs transferred from general society and coming down from antiquity? The view to be developed here is that systems of status, though they may be affected in degrees and in details by habitual attitudes and needs projected from the customary beliefs of people, are fundamentally determined by the necessities associated with the needs and interests of individuals as biological and social units, and upon the requirements arising from the physical and social limitations inherent in systems of cooperation. In the present section we shall deal with the relation of status systems to the needs of individuals. I shall discuss these in five topical divisions, as follows:

I. The differences in the *abilities* of individuals.

II. The differences in the *difficulties* of doing various kinds of work.

III. The differences in the *importance* of various kinds of work.

IV. The desire for formal status as a social or organizational tool.

V. The need for protection of the integrity of the person.

I

Differences of ability with respect to any kind of effort in which there is social interest obviously lead to a recognition of difference of status of individuals in respect to that kind of effort. This does not necessarily imply superiority or inferiority in general, although, in fact, usually the lack of capacity of individuals for most kinds of effort, or even for any valued effort whatsoever, does inescapably establish for them a general position of at least technical or productive inferiority. . . .

II

Differences in the capacities of individuals undoubtedly lead to differences of informal status quite aside from the requirements of formal organization. For example, some groups tend to form on the basis of educational level, or physical strength, or endurance, etc. But the important significance of differences of ability stems from differences in the nature of various kinds of activities. Many kinds of work, unskilled labor, for example, usually require only sound health and normal physiological abilities. Other work, say that of a laboratory chemist, may require unusual delicacy of physiological reaction in the use of labora-

---

[2]In the case of corporations, corporation law provides at least often for both boards of directors and for two or more general officers. Bylaws almost always provide for additional general officers. In the case of individually owned businesses and partnerships, the nucleus of the status system rests initially directly upon property ownership.

Similarly with noncommercial organizations, the first steps in organizing are likely to be to create an initial governing board and a set of officers.

tory equipment, long arduous technical education, powers of imagination, thorough experience, and a willingness to work persistently without supervision or instruction. The work requires an exceptional combination of powers, some of which may need to be developed to an exceptional degree. Recognition of the status of being exceptional is forced upon such a man by his own experience. He is made aware of it by the difficulty of finding those competent to carry on his work to assist him. He is also elevated to exceptional status by those who wish his work to be done and who find that there are few competent to do it. Those whose interests are narrowly concentrated in one field for this reason often regard exceptional ability in that field as indicating not only special but general superiority. The banker finding few who can function effectively in his field, whatever their condition of education and experience, may be led to believe that those who can do so are of status generally superior to all others. A broader view, of course, recognizes that great superiority in one field does not imply general superiority.

Thus the second base for status is, as contrasted with personal ability, the relative difficulty of things to be done. The difficulties will usually be appraised on judgment based on general experience and observation, or, more objectively, on the basis of the numbers or proportions of individuals who can or cannot do well the various tasks.

III

The exceptional ability to do things that are exceptionally difficult, while it is a sufficient basis for establishing

differences of status in the general estimation, is not sufficient to establish a *system* of status involving authority or responsibility. Superiority in formal organizations depends upon exceptional ability for exceptionally difficult work of exceptional *importance*. "Importance" in this context includes more than economic importance. High status is not accorded to superior ability to do unusually difficult things of trivial character, except perhaps in very restricted circles. On the contrary, if an activity is regarded as exceptionally important, even though not very difficult, superior status is nevertheless likely to be accorded to superior ability with respect to it. This is probably most evident in the economic world, but it is readily seen in other spheres, for example, in military organization.

The importance of the work, then, establishes the importance of the position that "seeks" those of exceptional ability. Relative difficulty is a factor but is usually of minor importance except when importance is approximately equal. Status becomes systematic because activities regarded as important are systematized and organized.

IV

The next basis for status is pragmatic. Insignia and titles of status have the effect of credentials. They create a presumption with respect to the character, ability, and specific skills or functions of individuals. They are not conclusive, of course, but as preliminaries, as introductions, they save time and prevent awkwardness and embarrassment. The general's stars indicate at a glance the nature of his responsibilities and the probable relative reliability of his utterances in certain fields. The title "M.D." creates a presumption that the holder of that degree may usefully be approached without reticence about bodily ills. The degree of "Ph.D." may be granted to a fool, but very generally it is a sign of the possession of considerable intellectual experience, scholarly or scientific skill, and mental discipline. "Vice-president" of a corporation indicates one who probably understands business language and organization. "Foreman" indicates the man through whom the most effective approach may probably be had respecting the group under him and the work they are doing. "Bishop" is the title of one whom the communicant may accept as having certain ecclesiastical responsibilities and authority and as being able to perform certain spiritual functions, though the communicant may never before have seen him or been told about him.

Generally, the possession of title and of other indicia of rank certifies that those in the best position to have responsible judgment acknowledge and publish the status indicated, which all whom it may concern may accept at least tentatively. The convenience and efficiency of the status system is such that men seek status as a necessary tool in their work; and for the same reasons it is imposed upon them by those responsible for their work. It is to be noted that this applies as much to functional status as it does to scalar status.

V

Insofar as systems of status are imposed "from the top" they are expressions of the requirements of coordination rather than of the ambi-tions of the most able and powerful acting on the basis of personal motives. The personal motivation of most profound effect, applying equally to those of superior and to those of inferior status, is the need for protecting the integrity of the person in a social environment. This leads some to seek superior formal status, but it also leads others to refuse superior status and even to seek inferior status, depending upon the individual and the circumstances. This may be demonstrated sufficiently by presenting four modes in which the need for status is expressed: (1) the need of integrating personal history by the conferring of status; (2) the need of imputing superior status to those from whom commands are to be received; (3) the need of imputing superior status as a means of symbolizing possession of personal value in participating in an organization; and (4) the need of status as a protection against excessive claims against the individual.

(1) The need of integrating one's personal history into one's personality by the attainment of improved status and by the conferring of status publicly is exceptionally important to those who by deliberate effort or sacrifice condition themselves to the possession of superior knowledge, skill, or experience. The need is for an endorsement of the individual's past history as a creditable element in his existing personality. The granting and attainment of improved or different status here is not reward but anointment. It serves a ceremonial function of announcement, or proclamation, that an approved course has been followed by this person. Without such endorsement the effort often appears to the individual to have been in vain. A sense of frustration, sometimes devastating may follow. Even when the

individual is one of extraordinary self-sufficiency, the attainment of recognized distinction of status may be desired to maintain standing with relatives and supporting and cooperating friends. No one who watches the contemporary parade of diplomas, degrees, public honors, and the award of innumerable insignia of achievement and distinction, and who observes the reaction of individuals, of families, of organizations, and of the public to them can doubt the importance of these recognitions in nearly every field of individual and social activity. If such distinctions, often of ephemeral value, are an important element in individual behavior, it is evident that permanent possession of status is even more so. It may be thought that the need of status here discussed is merely a reflection of the effect of attitudes, inculcated by mores and institutions that no doubt do reinforce the need, but the response of small children to status and the use made of status in instruction and discipline of the very young suggest that the need is more primitive and is individual.

(2) The need of imputing higher status to those from whom commands come is rather certain though it is not often obvious. It is apparent to nearly everyone on the basis of even simple and limited experience that the co-ordination of effort necessary for effective cooperation can be practically secured only by specializing the function of command. It is obvious that everybody cannot give orders to everybody else at the same time and for the same activity. But except at times of great danger, to receive orders from a nondescript "someother" is felt to be an injury to the self-respect, to the integrity, of the person. This can be avoided or alleviated only if it is felt that command is exercised by "right" either conferred by supernatural authority, or, more generally in our present society, conferred by superior ability, or by the burden of superior responsibility. Men are eager to be "bossed" by superior ability, but they resent being bossed by men of no greater ability than they themselves have. So strong is this need of assigning superior status to those in positions of command that, unless the obvious facts preclude it, men will impute abilities they cannot recognize or judge. They want to believe that those of higher authority "know what they are doing" when they appoint someone over them. Since men in the ranks are not capable of judging or are not in a position in advance to judge the competence of men in posts of command remote from them by two or more grades or even of those in immediate command if special technical abilities are required (for example, the surgeon in the operating room or the navigator of a ship), this desire for the justification of subordination leads often to profuse rationalization about status and even to mythological and mystical explanations of it; but the ways in which a need is manifested ought not to be permitted to obscure its nature or the function of the means that satisfy it.

What has just been said as respects the need of imputing higher scalar status to those from whom commands are received applies somewhat less definitely and more subtly to differences in functional status where authoritative advice rather than formal authority is involved. Thus the advice or even the directions of one having the status of an expert in a particular field will be accepted against that of someone recognized as being equally expert but not having status. The subjective factor involved may be that of a diffuse feeling of public authorization to transfer responsibility to one having functional status. Though there is wide variation in the competence of those having the same status, and reliance upon mere formal status is subject to much error and abuse, nevertheless there can be little doubt that the system of functional status affords great relief to nearly everybody in practical everyday social behavior.

(3) The need felt by those of subordinate rank for imputing personal superiority to those in command, that is, the need of protecting the integrity of the person, is also expressed in sentiments of valuation of an organization as a whole. To be a member of a good organization is a personal asset. It is among the claims to distinction of most men. To be ejected from an organization is a serious, sometimes a catastrophic, injury to the integrity of the person. "Patriotism," "sense of communion," "loyalty," "*esprit de corps*" are common expressions of this attitude. Few, if any, with experience of command will doubt this, and those who observe behavior of men in military organizations in war know how powerful and indispensable this sentiment is, though perhaps not many would express the facts in terms of personal integrity.

One of the effects of this need is to sustain the system of status. For if it is not practicable for all to command, and command, that is, coordination, is essential to organization, then a system of status is indispensable. Office becomes symbolic of the organization. The commander in chief not only occupies the supreme position of command, but he speaks for the army and in his person symbolizes it.

(4) Individuals of superior ability and those of inferior ability can com-

fortably work together only on a basis of physical or social segregation. If no formal segregation is established, either friction and noncooperation occur or there is spontaneous informal segregation, "natural" leaders leading "natural" groups, without being adequately integrated into the system of formal command. The necessity for differentiation from the standpoint of those of inferior ability is that without it they are constantly in a position of disadvantage, under pressure to exceed their capacities, perpetually losing in a race in which no handicaps are recognized, never able to attain expected goals so long as they are treated as the equals of those who are in fact superior; therefore they are always in a position of never securing respect for what they do contribute, of always incurring disrespect for what they cannot do. Men cannot stand this kind of inferiority and its frustrations. The inferiors will group themselves and command respect by various means if they are not protected by being assigned a formal status, which, though inferior, recognizes their position as being more or less indispensable and participating, even though individually less important. The practice of labor unions of restraining the production of the more able workers of an undifferentiated craft to a level approximating that of the poorer workers, though in practice doubtless of complex motivation, seems clearly in accordance with the human needs of the situation.

Concordantly, the abler individuals press for segregation corresponding to the observed differences in abilities and in contributions. To be lumped in with inferiors in ability seems an unjust withholding of recognition, an injury to the integrity of the person. Their escape from this position will probably be more individualistic than that of those of inferior abilities who must more often resort to group solidarity. One escape, or attempt to escape, for the superior individual is to try to organize the group, to adopt a function of leadership, or to dominate without authority. Another is to leave the group for various alternative activities—found a new sect, start a new business, establish a party, and so on.

Much experience demonstrates that those who are unequal cannot work well for long as equals. But experience also demonstrates that where differences of status are recognized formally, men of very unequal abilities and importance can and do work together well for long periods.

This discussion of the relationship of integrity of the person to systems of status is not exhaustive or comprehensive, but it is enough to suggest that personal need of status system is one of their foundations.

### III. THE FUNCTIONS OF STATUS IN COOPERATIVE SYSTEMS

Up to this point the approach to systems of status has been in terms of the characteristics of human beings and their bearing on behavior and fundamental relationships in formal systems of cooperation. The differences in abilities arising from biological characteristics and from social conditioning and experience, the variation in the difficulties of work, the variations in importance of work, the systematic character of cooperation arising from valuation of effort, the common sense of the necessity of centralizing and specializing the function of command, the need of formalizing differences of status to protect

the integrity of the socialized individual, and the symbolic functions of systems of status—all of this may be taken as the basis of the evolution of systems of status. The patterns may be as unplanned or undevised, as "spontaneous" or "instinctive" as languages. But having been evolved, they have been subjected to observation and analysis and deliberate modification, development, and design in much the same way that old languages are to some degree modified by intention and new languages have been constructed. Executives have to have a practical understanding of systems of status and are persistently occupied with concrete operations of selection, appointment, changes of status, modification of hierarchical relationships, inculcation of doctrines of command or management, and ceremonial activities, all directed to maintaining and improving the system of status and assuring that it performs its function in coordinating behavior. Much of the theory stated above appears to be sensed by executives, though not necessarily comprehended intellectually and not made explicit. The observations of practical executives would not be in terms of social psychology but in the technical terms of specific organization practice and forces.

Proceeding, then, on this level of discourse it appears necessary to the executive to recognize by some formal means differences in the ability of individuals and differences in the importance of their work or of their contribution to cooperative effort. However, executives are probably much more conscious of the necessity of systems of status as (I) a function of the system of organization communication, the fundamental process in cooperation; (II) as an important part of the system of incentives; and (III) as an essential means of inculcating and developing a sense of responsibility and of imposing and fixing responsibility.

I

A system of organization communication, in order that it may operate with sufficient accuracy and rapidity, has to be so designed that it may easily and quickly be assured that particular communications are (1) authentic, (2) authoritative, and (3) intelligible.

(1) Under ordinary circumstances, and especially with respect to routine matters, explicit authentication of communications is not required. Personal acquaintance with or knowledge of the communicator together with the relevance of the communication to the general context and to previous communications are sufficient. The status system is not of great importance in this connection. But in times of emergency and great danger or in respect to important matters, explicit authentication of communications often becomes necessary. Witnessed written communications or letterheads indicating the name, position, and title of the communicator and personal introductions by mutually known third parties are among the means used. There is no doubt that here the status system greatly facilitates authentication—it is one of the practical uses of insignia of office.

(2) It is in respect to the authoritativeness of a communication, however, that we find the basic need for systems of status. The primary question of the recipient of a communication, assuming that it is authentic, that is, comes from whom it purports to come, is whether the contents of the communication may be relied upon as a basis for action. This is what we mean by authoritativeness. Authoritativeness in this context is of two kinds: functional authoritativeness; and scalar or command authoritativeness.

Whether a communication reflects the facts and needs of the situation depends upon whether the individual (or body) that emits it has the general qualifications for understanding what he (or it) communicates about and whether he is *in a position* to have the essential concrete knowledge.

A report from a carpenter about the condition of a generator in a power house is initially not credible; that of the electrician in charge is credible, though not conclusive; that of an electric power engineer is more credible and *may* be accepted as final. The authoritativeness of the report depends in part upon the qualifications of those reporting, and these are presumptively established by formal status. But a report by an electrician in Des Moines about a generator in New York is not credible. He has the qualifications in general, but he is not in a position to apply them to the situation in New York.

The purpose of the report may be to secure help in the correction of some fault. The help needed may be in the form of superior technical instruction; it may be in the form of the application of some maintenance skill or of a replacement part. The electrician is not in a position to know the status of those whose services are needed. His superior does—he knows less of the concrete situation, but he has more technical knowledge or more knowledge of the relevant status system.

The functional status system is so extraordinarily convenient in providing prima-facie evidence of the authoritativeness of communications that we depend upon it almost exclusively in the conduct of daily affairs generally as well as in all organizations. It does not imply any generalized superiority or inferiority of status in this aspect. It does not exclude discrimination as between individuals having the same status, nor does it assume errors may not occur in relying upon the prima-facie evidence granted by status. The plumber, or electrician, or lawyer, or doctor may be immature or poor or even bad, as determined by experience or surmised from observation, but even so may often be presumed to be superior to those of other statuses. A poor doctor, even though inadequate, will generally be a better advisor on medical matters than an expert plumber. Systematized functional status would seem to be absolutely indispensable for the effective operation of complex divisions of labor, and it may also be indispensable even for relatively simple divisions of labor although in the latter condition there may be some acceptable "jacks of all trades."

(3) The special system of status associated with chains of command or hierarchy of authority depends upon each position being a "communication center," the inferior command being associated with restricted areas or fields, the higher command being more comprehensive. Outside the technical competence special to each field of organization, the general functions common to all hierarchies of command are: to evaluate the meaning of communications received in the form of advices and reports, largely affected by the status of the transmitter; to know to whom communications should be relayed (that is, to know the relevant status system or "the organization"); to select that which needs to be re-layed; and to translate communications, before relaying, into language appropriate to the receiver.

The system of command communication cannot effectively work except on the basis of a status system. For very small organizations communication may effectively be addressed to persons, but for larger systems status becomes primary. Contrast saying to the new office boy, "Take this order to Bill Jones in building K" (in which there are two Bill Joneses) and "Take this order to the foreman of section 12 in the Y Department in building K." Contrast the following orders: "Capt. Jones of Station Y and Capt. Smith of Station X will advise each other by telephone each morning as to their respective situations and will advise Major Allen of any unusual circumstances." "The Commandants of Stations X and Y will advise each other and this office each morning of their respective situations and of any unusual circumstances." In the first case any change of personalities calls for a new order—otherwise the desired collaboration will fail.

Although both functional and scalar systems of status are essential to establishing in a practicable degree the authoritativeness of communications, authoritativeness is not sufficient. Unless communications are intelligible, they cannot be acted upon correctly or effectively. Now, it is apparent that the intelligibility of a communication depends not merely upon the capacity of the communicator but also upon that of the receiver. Thus communications of the same content will differ very greatly, depending upon the status of those to whom they are addressed. Whether a communication is intelligible depends upon the use of language having the same meaning to the originator and to the receiver of the communication. This requires a selection of language, depending upon from whom and to whom the communication is made. Systems of status are an indispensable guide to the selection of appropriate language. . . .

The executive, then, is much preoccupied with systems of status because they are important in the authentication of communications, indispensable in establishing a working presumption of the authoritativeness of their content, and essential to their intelligibility.

## II

Systems of status are also important because maintenance of status and improvement of status are among the essential incentives to cooperation. The scarcity of effective incentives calls for use of many kinds of incentives; and their wise use requires, especially in larger organizations, their systematic use.

Status as an incentive has two aspects suggested earlier. The first is that of prestige for its own sake, as a reinforcement of the ego, as security for the integrity of the person. This is an important need of many individuals. They will work hard to satisfy it and forego much to attain it. The second aspect is that of prestige as a valuable or indispensable means to other ends. Thus some men endure publicly or accept conspicuous positions of onerous character as a means of supporting organizations or of eliciting the support of others because they like philanthropic, or scientific, or cultural work, which is their fundamental incentive.

The importance of status as an incentive is shown by the immense amount of work and sacrifice made by innumerable volunteer heads of social, philanthropic, religious, political, and scientific organizations. For some the motive is directly personal. For others it is the "good of the cause" and the personal incentive is satisfaction in the promotion of that cause.

These are perhaps the most obvious instances of the importance of status as incentive. The executive is frequently concerned with the instances where material rewards are by themselves ineffective and status proves to be the controlling or a necessary supplementary incentive. He is also concerned with the still less conspicuous cases where prestige is a negative incentive, where preferred status is regarded as too burdensome, and where it is believed to be a limitation on personal liberties.

## III

The system of status is a strong and probably an indispensable developer of the sense of responsibility and therefore of stability and reliability. Loss of status is more than loss of its emoluments; it is more than loss of prestige. It is a serious injury to the personality. Thus while improvement of status is important, especially to the more able, and desirable to many, loss of status is much more generally resisted. It is difficult to accept, or to be accepted in, a reduced status. Indeed, the fear of losing status is what leads some to refuse advancement of status. The desire for improvement of status and especially the desire to protect status appear to be the basis of the sense of general responsibility. Responsibility is established and enforced by specific penalties for specific failures and by limitation of status or by loss of a particular status for failure in general. Although both methods in conjunction are most effective, of the two it would appear that the second is much more effective than the first, especially as to those above low levels of status. In view of the extreme importance of dependable behavior, the function of status in creating and maintaining dependable behavior is probably indispensable. The extent of criminal behavior suggests that specific sanctions are not sufficient in general to establish adequate responsibility.

We have now completed an abbreviated presentation of the rationale of status systems universally found in scalar organization. What has been set forth may well be summarized. . . .

Status systems have their origins in differences in the biological and socially acquired characteristics of individuals, in differences in the difficulties of the various kinds of activities, and in differences in the valuation of these activities. Systems of status are a means of protecting the integrity of the person, especially of those of inferior ability. Superior status is often necessary to the effectiveness of the

work of those of superior ability. All this on the level of biology and social psychology. Additional observations on the level of sociology and the technique of organization show that systems of status are necessary to specialization of function; that they are essential to the system of organization communications for purposes of coordination; that they are important and sometimes indispensable as affording incentives; and that they are important in promoting the sense of responsibility and, therefore, the dependability and stability essential to cooperation. These inductions from experience and observation and from history are not scientific proof of the theory outlined; but they are believed to present a fair basis, of considerable probability of correctness, for the assertion that systems of status are not the product of irrational mores, mythologies, and rationalizations, but are specific modes of adaptation of behavior to fundamental characteristics of individuals and to the fundamental physical, biological, and social properties of systems of scalar organization.

---

While Barnard pays little attention to what he calls "insignia and other indicia," it has long been observed that distinctive dress characterizes people of different statuses in business firms. The man in the gray flannel suit is very likely to be located somewhere among the managers or executives of a business firm.

Indeed, according to *The Wall Street Journal* the pressure to dress up to one's position has reached such proportions that some business firms now prescribe standard uniforms for nonmanual employees. This idea has

been received with considerable enthusiasm by the affected employees, since it relieves them of the bother and expense of constantly having to dress up to their positions. Even stenographers and clerks value the uniforms, since it has the effect of reducing clothing expenses and standardizing at least one element in their competition for male attention.

The following is a study of the attitude toward clothing for work among male manual and non-manual employees. It is notable that while manual workers value work clothing for its utility on the job, non-manual employees value clothing for the impression it makes. In other words, non-manual employees apparently want to be certain that those observing them will clearly understand that they are white-collar workers, a term which itself helps to describe clothing as an indicator of status.

---

## CLOTHING AND THE MAN AT WORK

### *William H. Form* and *Gregory P. Stone**

Although American men like to think that they are seldom preoccupied with clothing, about one-half of the men studied in this research ascribed relatively high importance to clothing in general. It was established that this finding was a function of both the type of occupation men were engaged in and the social standing of those occupations. White collar workers and workers employed in occupations accorded high social standing attached high importance to clothing in general, while manual workers and workers employed in occupations of relatively lower community prestige attached less importance to clothing. These differences were even more clearly shown in specific evaluations of work clothing.

The meaning that clothing had for the occupational groups studied was found to vary with occupational type. Although many other differences were disclosed, the most significant was that white collar workers appraised clothing in terms of its potential for favorably impressing the other people with whom they came in contact at work. As a consequence, white collar workers viewed dress as a symbol capable of manipulation in the work situation to influence others. Manual workers were more concerned with the durability of work clothing and its usefulness in facilitating work performance. Manual workers, on the other hand, felt that their use of work clothing was restricted by job demands.

It follows, then, that the white collar worker is extremely concerned about the attention others in his work environment give to his occupational dress, while the manual worker is often unaware that others may judge him on the basis of his clothing.

The recognition by white collar workers that clothing can influence others at work was present from the time they first entered the job market. Over a third "dressed up" to impress the hiring agent when they applied for their first employment. Over four-fifths of the manual workers, however, did not recall dressing up for their first job application. It is difficult to determine exactly how this early use of clothing influenced the occupational careers of the men. Yet one-half of

---

*Reprinted by permission from William H. Form and Gregory P. Stone, *The Social Significance of Clothing in Occupational Life* (East Lansing, Mich.: Agricultural Experiment Station, Technical Bulletin 247, Michigan State College, 1955).

those engaged in white collar occupations at the time of the study were first employed in the higher prestige positions, and only one-tenth of those who were manual workers when interviewed reported white collar positions as their first employment.

In response to a question asking what might happen to a foreman who, when promoted to an office position, failed to dress according to the demands of his new job, 61 per cent of the men in the study said that he would be fired, demoted, or transferred to another position. An additional 14 per cent foresaw no future advancement for the man; and 17 per cent thought that he would quit his new job or accept a voluntary demotion. In short, over nine-tenths of the sample believed that failure to dress as expected would adversely affect the occupational mobility and the future of the man in question. Other data confirmed this general recognition of clothing influence on occupational success.

In response to direct questions on the subject, more than one-half of the informants agreed that one's mode of dress affects his job opportunities, and two-thirds either knew someone who had advanced occupationally by using dress or thought it was possible to do so. In the face of this widespread recognition of the relationship between dress and success on the job, only one-sixth of the men interviewed took such information specifically into account in planning their choice of clothing at work. . . .

Nine-tenths of the respondents interviewed expressed satisfaction with their work clothing, but more white collar workers than manual workers felt they did not have enough money to purchase all the clothes they needed at work. . . .

The general satisfaction expressed by all workers with their occupational attire indicated that there was little desire for change in work dress, and this was confirmed in the study. Reluctance to change one's clothing behavior is reinforced by a number of mechanisms of social control. These mechanisms differed sharply between white collar workers and manual workers. Men in business occupations felt that deviation in dress would impair relationships with customers and elicit expressions of disapproval from others. The agents of control for this group were vaguely and diffusely defined. Specifically, white collar workers said that reactions to deviant dress would originate among the members of such broad and general groupings as "the public," "customers," or the entire work force.

Manual workers, on the other hand, felt that deviations in dress would draw ridicule from others, or that others would actively intervene to control the deviation. For them, the agents of control were the members of their immediate work group. These data demonstrate that social control is more direct and interpersonal among manual workers and more indirect and impersonal among white collar workers. Thus, self-evaluation for the latter group is difficult to achieve with adequate certainty, and this may engender considerable anxiety. On the other hand, the manual worker has more security in this respect, for he gains immediate approval or disapproval of his dress from work associates whom he knows and who show less interest in clothes generally.

The next selection concludes this chapter as well as this section of the volume. Here are summarized the general forms of nonfinancial payoffs characterized as "power pay," "authority pay," and "status pay." The selection clarifies the fundamental administrative relationships of an organization by showing how administrators use power, authority, and status as important features of the incentive systems they manage.

This selection, then, makes very practical application of the three theoretical concepts we have employed in this section of the book. In the process some of the common precepts of managerial behavior are shown to have sound grounding in existing theory.

---

## POWER PAY, AUTHORITY PAY, AND STATUS PAY

### Robert Dubin[*]

We may consider the applied aspects of power, authority, and status in the form of payoffs for adequate performance as a member of an organization.

#### POWER PAY

We have already indicated that power pay, authority pay, and status pay are rewards of enhanced position that can be secured at work. Each form of pay serves to improve the position of the person receiving it.

Power pay is the reward conferred on a person by making his tasks more important in the organization. It is one of the precepts of management that subordinates should be encouraged in many ways to feel that their work is important to the organization. This is the way in which power pay as a nonfinancial incentive is usually discussed. When we stop to ask what

is meant by importance, we discover it can be described in two ways. The work is important because its performance is essential; or the work is important because no one else does it or can do it.

The most direct forms of power pay are to make the work more important, or to give the worker more exclusive jurisdiction over it. This usually involves actual changes in tasks and the assignment of work responsibility. For example, a man operating a machine tool may be told that the accuracy of his work determines the functioning of a finished product. He may not only be told the tolerance dimensions within which he is expected to hold the items he produces, but may, in addition, be given instruction in using micrometers and gauges to measure his output. He may also be given the responsibility for checking his own work, and making adjustments in the machine to correct for inaccuracies. The worker now knows that his output is considered highly essential and is given the means for insuring that

---

[*]From *The World of Work* (Englewood Cliffs, N. J.: Prentice-Hall, Inc., 1958), pp. 244–46. Used by permission.

he will fulfill his critical responsibility. He has been paid off in power pay.

To take another example of power pay, a branch plant accountant may be given the sole responsibility for forwarding accurate accounting reports to the home offices of the firm. Here the person is impressed with his critical importance as the only link between the records of the branch plant and the home office. The power pay comes in the form of exclusive jurisdiction over a work assignment.

The subjective response to power pay is clear. A person feels his own importance when he is aware of the position of power he holds. Whiting Williams long ago reported this sense of power among the lowly workers with whom he worked as an observer.[1]

Power pay can be an exceedingly strong incentive. It applies at all levels of the organization. The satisfaction resulting from it does not depend on the absolute amount of power a person actually holds. The satisfaction with this kind of nonfinancial payoff results from a clear recognition that work is somehow important, and that superiors recognize its importance. In short, there is a real reward in knowing that one's work has an important function in the organization.

### AUTHORITY PAY

Authority pay is the promotion to a position of greater authority. It is the most generally used of the nonfinancial incentives. For all those employees who aspire to get ahead at work by moving into the ranks of

[1]Whiting Williams, *Mainsprings of Men* (New York: Scribners and Sons, 1925), especially Chapter 4 "What the Worker Wants in His Job."

management, authority pay is a potent incentive.

In relatively simple organizations the authority pay is reasonably clear-cut. For such organizations there tends to be a close correspondence between promotions in management and increased authority.

In more complex organizations promotions and authority may not have a simple relation to each other. If we examine the kind of authority involved, the reason will become clear. As persons are promoted to higher levels of management, they tend to move from directing authority to coordinating and controlling authority. They may also move from a staff to a line position, or move in the opposite direction. Under the circumstances of a change in kinds of authority, or kinds of management position, it is not always clear that a promotion is necessarily accompanied by more authority pay. Indeed, one of the ways to get rid of people without firing them is to "kick them upstairs." This involves a nominal promotion accompanied by actual lessening of authority—some of the authority pay is taken away from the person.

Authority pay is a not very subtle form of payoff for working. People tend to measure authority pay in very practical terms. "How many people do you supervise?" or "How many departments are under your jurisdiction?" are obvious questions designed to determine the level of authority pay. For those employees who are particularly attracted by authority pay, "empire building" may become a method for forcing more authority pay from management.

Of all the nonfinancial incentives for working, authority pay comes the closest to being a substitute for a financial payoff.[2] It is not uncommon in industry to encounter supervisors who make less money than some of their subordinates. What probably accounts most for the supervisor's tolerance of the situation is his greater authority pay, although he is fully aware of his income disadvantage and actively seeks to overcome it.

### STATUS PAY

Status pay is the increased value that management places upon you. This sense of value may be grounded in any scale of measurement that permits comparative judgments. Members of management may consider one employee the neatest, another the most loyal, and another the most skilled. If there is some public acknowledgment of these evaluations, each employee is being rewarded with status pay by management.

We recall, however, that status conferred by management is not to be confused with status accorded by the primary group at work. When management and worker goals differ, the former may backfire on the recipient, who has accepted some token of company approval; the latter seems thus to be more durable. Status pay accorded a person by peers is potentially a large element in the payoff of a given job, conceivably enough to keep a man from starting elsewhere.

The difference between status pay and power pay is real, although in an operating situation they may be confused at first glance. Status pay is the reward for some valued attribute of the person. Power pay is the reward for some valued attribute of the work

assignment. For example, all secretaries in a firm may be expected to produce neat letters. Some will, in fact, do neater work than others and will be accorded higher status for it. The president's secretary may or may not turn out the neatest letters of them all (she is probably near the top in neatness anyway), but she has a powerful job in the organization if only because she controls access to her boss.

Status pay is the "cheapest" form of payoff for the organization. It involves only some kind of public recognition by a member of management of a person's particular merits. The individual so singled out receives some acknowledgment that he is valued, usually in a way that other employees will be aware of the high regard of management.[3]

The incentive value of status pay depends on the good judgment of those according it. The attributes of a person that are valued should have some relevance to the work situation. To prefer an employee for the way he parts his hair, or because he is tall, is to accord status, but for reasons irrelevant to the work situation. This kind of preferential selection does not turn out to be status pay at work because it does not use a criterion of selection that could apply to all employees for their work performance.

Because status pay is so cheap to give, it is likely to be given lavishly, and thereby lose its incentive value. If everyone gets praised for something, then the value of the praise is diminished, and it becomes a debased form of payment. The very value of

[2]Cf. C. A. Drake, "When Wage Incentives Fail," *Advanced Management,* 7:42–44 (January-March, 1942).

[3]See a simple, yet effective treatment of this in Walter Brown, "Our Way of Putting Creative Interest into Humdrum Jobs," *Factory,* 33:39–137 (July, 1924).

being accorded high status lies in the fact that this is a position shared with few others. Differentials in status must be recognized and preserved if status pay is to have incentive value.

Status pay is a nonfinancial incentive found in all kinds of work organizations, and providing incentives for all kinds of personnel.

# part 5

# ADMINISTRATIVE ACTION

Administration action includes the whole range of actual behaviors of executives in directing the destinies of their organizations. Involved is communication with other members of the organization and decision-making about organization affairs. Also included is the exercise of leadership in the organization and the connections between leadership and subordination. Finally, the control of working behaviors to achieve organization goals is another important dimension of administrative action. These issues are dealt with, in order, in the next five chapters.

We can distinguish administrative relationships, as discussed in the preceding section of the book, from administrative action. Administrative relationships are the *fundamental modes of interaction* in terms of which any executive behavior can be characterized. Administrative actions are the *actual behaviors* employed in directing an organization, and are composed of combinations of the three basic kinds of administrative relationships. For example, when an executive exercises leadership in choosing the goal of product diversification for his company, his act of leadership (1) depends on his function to choose organization goals (power); (2) is supported by the belief that he has genuine wisdom underlying his choice (status); and (3) is carried into action within the organization because he has "the last word" about the choice (authority). Every administrative action displays combinations of the three fundamental components of administrative relationships, in varying amounts, depending on the particular action involved.

**OVERVIEW**

*321*

The connections between administrative relationships and administrative action can be seen from an analogy. Physical particles interact with each other in accordance with the electrical charge they carry, and are either attracted to or repelled from each other depending on the like or unlike charges they carry. This is the fundamental relationship of particles to each other. Given two substances or elements like hydrogen and oxygen, their interaction to produce water ($H_2O$) is grounded in their respective electrical charges, but occurs only when appropriate quantities of the elements under special circumstances are brought together. We can understand *why* the interaction takes place from a knowledge of the fundamental relationships among particles; we can predict *what* the interaction will be from the characteristics of the situation in which the particles are exposed to each other. In like manner, administrative relationships reveal the *why* of organization behavior, while administrative actions tell us *what* will happen under given circumstances when executives carry out their tasks.

In the next five chapters important areas of executive behavior are examined to determine what executives actually do in their daily round of activities. In each instance the discussion combines description with analysis. The description locates the particular kinds of behaviors under consideration. The analysis sets forth the characteristics of the situations in which the executive is acting, and the ways in which he combines the fundamental administrative relationships to achieve successful outcomes of his actions.

This section of the book builds on the ideas set forth in the preceding chapters. It constitutes a summary in the sense that the analytical ideas already discussed are put to work to make sense out of the complex realm of human behavior called administrative action.

# 14

# **Communication**

Barnard has called communication the foundation of cooperative group activity. There is no question that an organization depends upon a system or systems of communication. Indirectly, we have already dealt with important aspects of communication. We could hardly have avoided it.

It is therefore desirable at this point to select certain aspects of communication for emphasis. Those selected supplement what has already been said and what will be said in Chapter 21, which deals with organization fictions.

Communication involves the use of symbols. A word or a gesture stands for something—it is symbolic. Symbols not only point to something, but often indicate the meaning that that something has, as well.

Roethlisberger, in the first two selections of this chapter, calls our attention to two central points about communication. The first is that the status or authority position of a person in an organization is correlated with the kinds of symbols he uses. The language of the executive and that of the floorsweeper are different. Roethlisberger's second point is that the meanings of symbols can be determined only in the context in which they are used. The subtleties of meaning even of single words are familiar to all. Those with military experience can recall the yeoman service performed by certain Anglo-Saxon monosyllables in a vast array of different situations.

It is particularly necessary for the executive and administrator who is an initiator and recipient of vast

**INTRODUCTION**

quantities of communications to have a real appreciation of the status-associated feature in symbol selection, and of the varieties of meanings associated with different contexts. Indeed, nothing so obviously shows an individual to be out of place as a slip of language. The executive who tries to fraternize with the worker at the latter's level does so at the peril of vast embarrassment with the first slip in language that does not ring true.

There follows an important discussion by Simon of the role of communication in developing teamwork.

Three important studies of actual behavior among business executives describe respectively the relations between authority and communication, between decision-making and communication, and between remembering and communication. These studies have the special value of making clear that there are problems of communication unique to the world of the executive.

One of the little-realized features of communication is the variety of modes available for carrying it out. Meissner shows how speech, signs, symbols, and objects all serve as means of communication among industrial workers.

In the final selection Simon examines the grapevine as a significant feature of organization communication.

---

## COMMUNICATION AND SYMBOLS

*Fritz J. Roethlisberger**

The problem of communication is very important in the effective integration of any group or of a group of groups, of which industry is composed. Successful communication between individuals depends upon something more than a common language, a common set of words. People and groups with different experiences and social places, although having in common many of the same words, may vary widely in mental attitudes. These differences in modes of thought and ways of viewing things may make communication in some instances al-

most impossible. The trained expert with his precise and logical vocabulary has difficulty in communicating with the layman. The customary ways of thinking of the skilled toolmaker, for example, are quite different from those of the nonmachine-minded unskilled worker. They differ also from those of the engineer, the accountant, the marketing expert, the executive, or the administrator. As it is commonly expressed, people with different ways of thinking do not "get" each other.

If there is to be successful communication between the top and bottom of an industrial organization, these differences in modes of thought must be clearly recognized. The same symbols do not necessarily have the same

*Reprinted by permission of the publishers from Fritz J. Roethlisberger, *Management and Morale* (Cambridge, Mass.: Harvard University Press, 1941), pp. 62–63.

referent for different groups. Most symbols not only point out something, they also convey certain emotions. There is no better example than the case of the language of efficiency. The top of the organization is trying to communicate with the bottom in terms of the logical jargon and cold discriminations of the technical specialist, the engineer, the accountant, etc. The bottom of the organization, in turn, is trying to communicate with the top through its own peculiar language of social sentiments and feelings. Neither side understands the other very well. To the bottom the precise language of efficiency, instead of transmitting understanding, sometimes conveys feelings of dismay and insecurity. The bottom, in turn, instead of transmitting successfully its fears of social dislocation, conveys to the top emotional expressions of petty grievances and excessive demands.

---

## THE EXECUTIVE'S ENVIRONMENT IS VERBAL

*Fritz J. Roethlisberger**

That a good portion of the executive's environment is verbal seems hardly open to question. In discussions, meetings, and conferences the verbal atmosphere is thick. The executive is dealing largely with words, symbols, and abstractions. Of course, this applies to any of us. We are all responding to words and other stimuli involving meaning. It seems to me obvious, however, that the higher the executive goes in an organization the more important it becomes for him, if he is to handle effectively one aspect of his job, to deal competently with his verbal environment.

On the other hand, he has to become skillful in using words that will appeal to his listeners' sentiments. In trying to secure the cooperation of individuals in the common purposes of the enterprise the executive often has to practice the art of persuasion. He uses words that he hopes will produce the appropriate effects on his listeners. In statements to stockholders, employees, and customers, the executive has to resort to words, both oral and written. In handling complaints and grievances, the executive is using, as well as listening to, words.

On the other hand the executive has to be able to interpret skillfully what people say, for in so far as his work involves the interactions of human beings his data comes from what he hears as well as from what he sees and does.[1] Whether he likes it or not, he has to practice this difficult art; yet he has no explicit tools for doing it. He either picks up the skill intuitively or tries to organize his work so that the need for exercising it is at a minimum. This latter method is likely to

*Reprinted by permission of the publishers from Fritz J. Roethlisberger, *Management and Morale* (Cambridge, Mass.: Harvard University Press, 1941), pp. 88–92.

[1]The statements are similar to those made about the social scientist by Professor L. J. Henderson in *Three Lectures in Concrete Sociology* (privately distributed), p. 13.

be unsuccessful because it leads him to busy himself more and more with logical, statistical, and oversimplified abstractions or lofty principles about human motivation and conduct. In doing so he loses touch with the concrete situation before him.

In short, words play an important role in all the major functions of the executive. If this proposition is true, it seems sensible to ask what the executive needs to know about words and their functions and what skills he can explicitly develop in interpreting what people say.

Let us consider some of the different functions of language or words.[2] In the first place, words can be used to refer to events and happenings outside of our skin: this can be called the logico-experimental function of language. In this way words are used by scientists or by two or more people engaged in a discussion of matters with which they have firsthand, familiar, and intuitive acquaintance, as well as a common background of systematic knowledge. The words and symbols used by the speaker refer to events, and uniformities among events, which occur primarily outside of him or the listener, and to which they can go for observation and check in case of disagreement. Most of us spend only a very small portion of our day using words in this strict sense. We are much more likely to be engaged in less arduous and more pleasant verbal practices.

In a social conversation, for example, the situation is likely to be

quite different. When two or more people are talking together, what is primarily happening is an interaction of sentiments rather than anything strictly logical. One person is using words to express certain sentiments, to which the other responds with similar or opposite sentiments; or one person tries to influence the other by using symbols that will have a favorable reaction on the latter's sentiments. This can be called the "emotive"[3] function of language, as opposed to the logico-experimental. The skillful politician is a good example of a person using words in this way.

There is a third function of language which has received considerable attention during the past two or three decades. Through words man not only communicates but satisfies his desires. I refer to the day-dreaming, revery, and air-castle building in which we all indulge and from which we obtain considerable satisfaction. A good portion of our day is spent in using words to satisfy our desires in this way.

That "Language serves a man not only to express something but also to express himself,"[4] every executive should realize and explicitly take into account. The fact that language has different functions and that these functions, except under special circumstances, are rarely distinguished complicates our problem. Words refer not only to things happening outside our skins, but also to our attitudes, feelings, and sentiments toward these objects and events. This means that many statements are expressed which have little or no meaning apart from

---

[2] For the purposes of this paper it would be inappropriate to discuss the many different theories of language. Only three well-recognized functions of language will be mentioned to illustrate some of the problems involved in interpreting what people say.

[3] Taken from C. K. Ogden and I. A. Richards, *The Meaning of Meaning* (New York: Harcourt, Brace & Company, 1925), p. 257.

[4] *Ibid.*, p. 261 (statement by O. von der Gablentz, quoted by Ogden and Richards).

the personal situation of the person who makes them. This not only makes the interpretation of what people say difficult, it also makes it imperative to do a skillful job, because if we refer words to a wrong context we are likely to misunderstand what a person is telling us. The channels of communication in a business organization often become clogged because words are referred to wrong contexts.

The problem would be simple if when people spoke they labeled what it was they were telling us; if, for example, they would say: "Now I am talking about simple events and uniformities among them in our common experience." "Now I am expressing my sentiments and attitude toward something." "Now I am day-dreaming and satisfying my ego." "Now I am trying to disguise my sentiments as logic." "Now I am trying to influence your sentiments by using these particular words." "Now you may think I am talking about my supervisor but really I am talking about my unhappy experiences with my father." Unfortunately (or fortunately, depending upon our point of view), this is not often true. We very seldom express our sentiments *as sentiments*. One of the most time-consuming pastimes of the human mind is to rationalize sentiments and to disguise sentiments as logic.

All I have said so far shows clearly that the interpretation of what people say is a difficult business. There is nothing to be gained by pretending that the job is simple. It is something that some people learn from experience and at which some people—physicians, lawyers, and businessmen—become exceedingly skillful. (These skillful people, however, often cannot communicate their skill.) The technique cannot be learned without practice but, again, for some people practice is not enough. No matter how much experience they have in listening to or in using words, they never acquire any great ability in this field. They continue to deal with words as constants rather than as variables, as if they had universal meanings rather than different meanings for different people under different conditions and situations.

---

In the next selection, Simon points out the crucial role of communication in teamwork. For the members of the team to be effectively coordinated, in theory, each must have a knowledge of the behavior of all others as a basis for determining his own behavior. Thus, the more profound meaning of coordination is not a mechanical putting together of automatons called organization members. If individual initiative is to be retained in appropriate degree in the organization, then the individual must have enough knowledge to coordinate his actions with others effectively. This is the more significant sense of coordination and its basis in communication.

In some respects, the kind of control that establishes appropriate patterns for behavior in organizations is one of the necessary conditions for teamwork. However, organization controls serve to relate the individual to the organization in general. They do not orient him completely to the specific individuals with whom he will have to work in a team relationship. He needs more information. That information comes from intensive communication between the team members prior to embarking on a course of action. You will find in this the genesis of that ubiquitous characteristic of organization, the conference. The conference is one way of sharing information about what each is going to do as a member of a team before action is undertaken. Don't be bored when the other fellow is telling you what he will do. He is really establishing for you a basis for determining what you will do in coordinating your actions with his own.

---

## SHARED KNOWLEDGE AND TEAMWORK

*Herbert A. Simon**

At the opposite extreme from a purely competitive situation is one where two or more participants share a common goal, and where each has sufficient information as to what the others are going to do to enable him to make correct decisions. This is precisely what is meant by "teamwork." The purpose of signals in football, or bidding in bridge, is to enable each player in a team to form accurate expectations as to what his teammates are going to do, so that he can determine the proper means for cooperating with them to reach the common aim. A major purpose of the planning and organizing that precedes any administrative activity is not merely to put each participant in the job he can best fill, but to permit each to form accurate expectations as to what the others are going to do. Perhaps it would clarify discussion of administrative theory to use the term "cooperation" for activity in which the participants share a common goal, and

"coordination" for the process of informing each as to the planned behavior of the others. Hence, cooperation will usually be ineffective—will not reach its goal, whatever the intentions of the participants—in the absence of coordination.

If the activity is competitive, then, it may exhibit a certain instability, for each individual will readjust his behavior if he "finds out" the intentions of his opponent, or even as a defensive tactic to prevent the opponent from finding out his own. But this same instability may result even if the activity is cooperative, provided the participants are insufficiently informed. In an organization, for example, where responsibilities have not been allocated with sufficient definiteness, two executives may write conflicting letters to the same person on the same matter, while in another case a letter may remain unwritten because each expects the other to do it.

To state the matter formally, in a cooperative pattern both participants prefer the same set of consequences; hence, if each anticipates the other correctly, they will both act so as to secure these consequences. In a com-

*From Herbert A. Simon, *Administrative Behavior* (New York: The Macmillan Company, 1947), pp. 71–73. Copyright 1945 and 1947 by Herbert A. Simon and used with The Macmillan Company's permission.

petitive pattern, the optimum outcome for the first participant is not the optimum for the second. Hence the realization by the first participant of the consequences he prefers will frustrate the other participant—e.g., the rule of the market is to buy cheap and sell dear, but if the buyer buys cheap the seller will not have sold dear. Even a cooperative pattern may be unstable if each participant is unable to predict what the other is going to do. In these cases, coordination of the behaviors of the two participants is necessary in order that they may realize the possibility that they both prefer. Here conflict of aims is not in question, but imperfect knowledge.

Administrative organizations are systems of cooperative behavior. The members of the organization are expected to orient their behavior with respect to certain goals that are taken as "organization objectives." This leaves the problem of coordinating their behavior—of providing each one with knowledge of the behaviors of the others upon which he can base his own decisions. In cooperative systems, even though all participants are agreed on the objectives to be attained, they ordinarily cannot be left to themselves in selecting the strategies that will lead to these objectives; for the selection of a correct strategy involves a knowledge of each as to the strategies selected by the others.

---

In a pioneering study of an English factory, Burns studied the communication and interaction behavior of a group of four department executives, the manager of the department, the chief designer of products manufactured by the department, and the two production engineers who were each in charge of a production line in the department. The department manager was the immediate superior of the other three men, with the chief designer ranking somewhat above the engineers.

Each of the four men kept a standardized record of all communications with anyone else in the entire organization for every working day of the same five week period. These data were then analyzed to reveal a picture of the subjects about which managers interacted,[1] the amount of time spent on each subject, the people who entered into each interaction, and the perceptions these four men had about what they were doing when they interacted with each other.

We will focus attention only on a small section of Burns' study dealing with the differences in perceptions of what was happening when the boss talked with his immediate administrative subordinates. The outstanding finding is that half of the time the boss thought he was giving instructions or decisions to his subordinates, they perceived the same communications as being only information or advice.

This conclusion has an important bearing on the relationship between the exercise of authority and the communication content of authoritative acts. Burns emphasizes the fact that the subordinates "refused" to see the boss acting authoritatively when he

---

[1] Burns' study was inspired by the unique study of Sune Carlson, *Executive Behavior* (Stockholm: Stromborgs, 1951), which was one of the first attempts ever made actually to measure the amount of time top executives spend on various aspects of their responsibilities.

gave instructions and made decisions because it was necessary for them to protect their personality integrity and self-esteem by appearing to be independent of him, at least in their own minds. This Burns calls "status protection." There is no reason to believe that the three subordinates were not wholly honest in thinking that their boss was only informing and advising them, when the boss saw himself as instructing or deciding for them.

A second conclusion also needs to be drawn from Burns' data. Some of the curse of authoritarian leadership behavior is dispelled when subordinates make their own translations of authoritative communications from bosses to reinterpret the content of the communications as being non-coercive.

If we can properly talk about the "magic" of communication, it is this: initiator and recipient can differently interpret identical symbols of communication as to their role in relating the two persons; at the same time the intent of the initiator is carried out by the recipient. Applied to Burns' data this means that the boss could act authoritatively and expect his decisions to be carried out without his subordinates viewing him as authoritarian in his manner. This very malleability in communication processes materially improves the probability that authority in organizations can be exercised effectively.

---

## AUTHORITY AND COMMUNICATIONS TO SUBORDINATES

### *Tom Burns**

The same record forms were also examined for conflicting accounts of the exchange of information and advice as against decisions and instructions. Whenever the department manager noted that he had given an instruction or a decision, while the other had recorded merely advice or information, the lack of concurrence was noted by +. The reverse situation, of information or advice being received as instructions or decisions was noted as −.

Major discrepancies in such exchanges occurred in about two cases

out of every five. . . . The discrepancies had mostly the same bias: when the manager records giving instructions or decisions, the other records receiving information or advice; or, he records information only when the manager notes giving information, advice, and decisions or instructions. Only rarely did the deputy or the production engineers record receiving decisions or instructions when the manager noted giving information or advice.

Hunt [Dept. manager] noted giving instructions or decisions in 165 of the 237 episodes; the others recorded receiving instructions or decisions on only 84 of these occasions. Half the time, what the manager thought he

*From "The Direction of Activity and Communication in a Departmental Executive Group," *Human Relations*, 7:73–97 (selection from pp. 94–95). Used by permission.

was giving as instructions or decisions was being treated as information or advice.

This result may be regarded as an aspect of status protection. The tendency for the three senior staff to treat instructions from the head of the department as information or advice amounts to a rejection of the subordination implied in being instructed to take this or that action. Their status as executives—in an elastic status system, moreover, in which promotion is part of a normal career—appears to act as a force compelling them to treat their situation as one in which they could proceed for the most part not in response to instructions from a superior but as a result of their own judgments arrived at after consulting and obtaining information from the department's manager, as well as from other sources.

The element of status protection, in which the authority concomitant of communication downwards is tacitly rejected, may throw some light on the conception earlier advanced of the functioning of lateral communication as an integral feature of the organization. In its turn, the latter concept may indicate a means whereby the subordinate is enabled to protect his view of his own status. In dealing with individuals at a lower level in the system, a departmental manager will be conscious not merely of their subordinate position, but also of the fact that he provides their main link with the circuit in which he himself operates, and where "decisions are taken." They, on their side, while they may be conscious of their subordinate position, will also be aware of the "circuits" in which they too operate. These include people of their own status similar to those included in the circuit appropriate to their manager. As far as they are concerned, "decisions are taken" at their level, too, and in opposition with colleagues over a fairly wide range of positions from all of whom information relevant to action may be derived. It seems, therefore, reasonable that what appears "instruction" to the manager who delivers it, may well be looked on as "information" by the recipient. If this account of what happens in the organizational structure is true, the customary view—among top management —of the organization as a system of vertical communication is quite inadequate, apart from the individual case of the chief person in a concern or within a department, who has nobody to communicate with apart from subordinates.

---

There is a widespread belief among executives of all kinds of organizations that "group thinking" is a desirable alternative to individual analysis. This idea finally resulted in developing "brainstorming" as a technique by which creativity could be increased among a group of individuals. The basic idea was that several persons, each thinking out loud, would be mutually stimulated to produce better and more original ideas than any could develop individually.

The following study by Professor Dunnette is an especially important test of the brainstorming idea. Dunnette used the personnel from a major American corporation as his subjects. These men had worked together in the corporation and therefore did not have to overcome the fact of being strangers to each other in their brainstorming groups. The conclusion to this study is clear: brainstorming does not measure up to the claims made for it. Furthermore, individual thinking appears to be *more* productive than group thinking.

Underlying the idea of brainstorming is the notion that communication among individuals is stimulating to their thinking. As we shall see in the two selections following this one, communication is very inefficient in "getting the message across" as well as in even being remembered as a contact. Burns shows that what the boss intended was perceived differently by

his subordinates. Weinshall shows that when executives communicate with each other they do not remember the subject matter of many of their contacts and do not remember a high proportion of their contacts at all.

When we put all three of these experimental results together, it becomes very clear that a simple belief in the effectiveness of oral communication is unwarranted, at least in the business world. All three of these studies were made of executives, managers, and specialists in business organizations.

---

## COMMUNICATION AND DECISION-MAKING

### Marvin D. Dunnette*

A few years ago, the technique of brainstorming was developed and widely promoted by Osborn.[1] The cornerstone of the process was the rule that an absolute moratorium be placed on all criticism. By temporarily doing away with criticism, Osborn reasoned that a group could have its cake and eat it too—that problem solving meetings could take advantage of the diversity of talents and social stimulation of several people focusing on a difficult problem without suffer-

ing the deleterious effects of critical comments. For a time, it seemed that brainstorming was the answer to increased group effectiveness. Osborn even went so far as to claim that "the average person can think up twice as many ideas when working with a group as when working alone" (p. 228).

However, a widely cited study by Taylor, Berry, and Block[2] showed that group participation apparently retained inhibiting qualities even in brainstorming situations. Taylor and his colleagues presented 3 different

*Reprinted by permission from Marvin D. Dunnette, "Are Meetings Any Good for Solving Problems?" in the March-April 1964 issue of *Personnel Administration*, copyright 1964, Society for Personnel Administration, 1221 Connecticut Avenue, N.W., Washington, D. C. 20036.

[1]A. F. Osborn, *Applied Imagination*, rev. ed. (New York: Scribner's, 1957).

[2]D. W. Taylor, P. C. Berry, and C. H. Block, *Does group participation when using brainstorming facilitate or inhibit creative thinking?* (New Haven: Technical Report No. 1, Yale University, Department of Psychology, and Office of Naval Research, 1957).

problems to 96 Yale University juniors and seniors who had previously been together in group discussion sections. Forty-eight of the subjects were divided into 12 real 4-man groups who brainstormed the problems: the other 48 brainstormed the problems alone. The number of different ideas produced by the real groups was compared with the number produced by so-called "nominal" groups formed after the experiment by randomly dividing the 48 individual subjects into 12 groups of 4 each. For each of the 3 problems, the nominal groups produced an average of twice as many ideas as the real groups. This means that brainstorming was better by far when done *individually* than when done in a group—a rather startling conclusion in view of the strong support for group brainstorming expressed by Osborn. However, it can still be argued that the Taylor study does not entirely prove the case for individual thinking—particularly in a business setting. The study can be criticized on at least 2 rather crucial points:

1. The study was conducted on college students rather than on industrial employees. Thus, groups were necessarily *ad hoc* groups. It is possible that real functioning groups comprised of employees and their co-workers would more likely show an advantage for the group situation.

2. Taylor and his colleagues employed an experimental design which did not provide for each subject to participate in *both* group and individual brainstorming situations. Results did not, therefore, yield direct comparisons of the behavior of the same person in both situations. Conclusions from the study demanded the assumption that persons assigned to the 2 conditions were not different from one another in their brainstorming abilities.

Because of these criticisms, the Taylor study has not been widely interpreted as necessarily detrimental to the use of problem solving meetings in industry. In order to test the usefulness of such meetings, I and my colleagues (Dunnette, Campbell and Jaastad[3]) repeated the Taylor study with industrial employees as subjects, and with an improved experimental design. The subjects were 48 research scientists and 48 advertising personnel employed with 3M Co. of St. Paul, Minnesota. It was believed that group participation might show different effects in the 2 groups; we expected scientists to do better in the individual condition, advertisers to be superior in the group situation. The subjects had worked together for varying periods of time and were closer to being real functioning groups than were the *ad hoc* groups in the Taylor research. Each of the 2 sets of subjects was divided into 12 groups of 4 men who had worked together and who were well acquainted with one another. In no case were persons of different job levels placed in the same group and no persons with advanced degrees participated in the study. Thus, an effort was made to rule out the more obvious potentially inhibiting influences of differences in job and educational status. Our design also provided that each subject serve as his own control by participating in *both* the group and individual conditions. This required a counter-balanced experimental design; that is, half the subjects participated first in the individual condition followed by the group condition, the other half experienced the group situa-

[3]M. D. Dunnette, J. P. Campbell, and Kay Jaastad "The effect of group participation on brainstorming effectiveness for two industrial samples." *J. Appl. Psychol.*, 1963, 47, 30–37.

tion first followed by the individual condition. Equated problem sets were used in the 2 conditions; pre-tests conducted on University of Minnesota students (in engineering and business) showed that the following problems possessed nearly the same degree of idea-eliciting qualities, and they are the ones which were used in our experiment:

*Thumbs problem.* We do not think this is likely to happen, but imagine for a moment what would happen if everyone after 1960 had an extra thumb on each hand. This extra thumb will be built just as the present one is, but located on the other side of the hand. It faces inward, so that it can press against the fingers, just as the regular thumb does now. Here is the question: What practical benefits or difficulties will arise when people start having this extra thumb?

*Education problem.* Because of the rapidly increasing birth-rate beginning in the 1940s, it is now clear that by 1970 public school enrollment will be very much greater than it is today. In fact, it has been estimated that if the student-teacher ratio were to be maintained at what it is today, 50% of all individuals graduating from college would have to be induced to enter teaching. What different steps might be taken to insure that schools will continue to provide instruction at least equal in effectiveness to that now provided?

*People problem.* Suppose that discoveries in physiology and nutrition have so affected the diet of American children over a period of 20 years that the average height of Americans at age 20 has increased to 80 inches and the average weight has about doubled. Comparative studies of the growth of children during the last 5 years indicate that the phenomenal change in stature is stabilized so that further increase is not expected.

What would be the consequences? What adjustment would this situation require?

*Tourists problem.* Each year a great many American tourists go to visit Europe. But now suppose that our country wished to get many more European tourists to come to visit America during their vacations. What steps can you suggest that would get more European tourists to come to this country?

Each experimental session was begun by emphasizing the rules[4] of brainstorming which had been outlined in a lecture a week previously. Each problem was presented by reading it aloud and distributing typed copies to each of the subjects. Ideas and consequences were recorded on a dictating machine using a conference microphone. In every session, nearly all ideas for a given problem had been expressed at the end of 10–12 minutes, but the time limit was extended to 15 minutes to be certain that no flow of ideas would be cut off by the time limit. Each subject participated in both experimental conditions on the same afternoon. The individual brainstorming condition was conducted by placing subjects in 4 widely separated offices where each was free to brainstorm without interruption.

### RESULTS

The first step in analyzing the results was a comparison between the number of different ideas or solutions produced by group participation and the number of different ideas or solutions produced by the same group members during the individual brain-

---

[4]The *rules* of brainstorming are: the more ideas the better, the wilder the ideas the better, improve or combine ideas already suggested, and *do not be critical.*

storming condition. It should be emphasized that the score or number of ideas under the individual condition includes only *different* ideas. Thus, if 2 or more members of a group, during their individual sessions, suggested the same idea or solution to a problem, it was counted as only a single contribution to the total score of the nominal group.

Comparisons between individual and group brainstorming totals showed the effect due to the experimental condition to be highly significant statistically and practically. For the research personnel, the mean number of ideas produced by groups of 4 brainstorming as individuals was 141; the corresponding mean number of ideas produced by the groups brainstorming as groups was only 110. The corresponding means for the advertising personnel were 141 and 97 for the individual and group conditions respectively. We concluded, therefore, that the pooled sum of individual effort produces about 1/3 more different ideas than the output of the same individuals serving in a group situation.

Of the 24 groups, only one failed to produce more ideas under the individual condition than under the group condition, and the difference in this one instance was only 163 to 162 in favor of group participation. Our hypothesis that group interaction would facilitate the output of advertising personnel and inhibit the output of research personnel failed to be sustained. Apparently, the inhibiting influence of group participation cuts across the kinds of personal and occupational differences represented by the subjects participating in this study. Clearly, individual brainstorming achieves more different ideas than group brainstorming.

However, it could be argued that the advantage of individual effort over group effort in the volume of ideas produced might be accompanied by a decrease in the quality of ideas. Thus, we rated the quality of each of the hundreds of ideas on two 5-point scales. Ideas elicited by the Education and Tourists problems were rated on an *effectiveness* scale ranging from a score of *zero* for "no conceivable contribution to the solution of the problem" to *four* for "clearly a major contribution to the solution of the problem." Ideas elicited by the Thumbs and People problems were rated on a *probability* scale ranging from a score of *zero* for "very highly improbable or clearly impossible" to a score of *four* for "highly probable."

The mean quality ratings for research personnel were 2.12 and 2.04 for individual and group conditions respectively; this difference is not significant statistically. The corresponding means for advertising personnel were 2.18 and 2.02 for the individual and group conditions; this difference is statistically significant at the 5% level.

It is evident, therefore, that individuals produce responses of quality equal to or greater than that of the ideas produced in groups. The evidence seems clearcut: brainstorming is most effective when undertaken by individuals working alone in an atmosphere free from the apparently inhibiting influences of group interaction.

### DISCUSSION

These results confirm those of Taylor *et al.* and tend to refute Osborn's argument that individuals are stimulated by group interaction to produce more ideas than they would produce alone.

It seems particularly noteworthy that it has not been possible to demonstrate a group advantage either for the *ad hoc* groups of Yale students or for the real groups of industrial research scientists and advertising personnel.

Even so, these results seem to be in sharp disagreement with the widely held belief that group activity is somehow superior to individual effort. Earlier research studies (Shaw[5]; Lorge, Fox, Davitz, and Brenner[6]) gave apparent support to this belief by comparing the average group with the average individual. The average of groups was usually higher than the average of individuals, thereby leading to the widespread misconception of group superiority. However, such a comparison ignores the more crucial question of whether it is more or less efficient for a given number of persons to hold a meeting or simply to pool the products of their individual efforts. The Taylor study and our study were focused on this question, and the answer (at least for brainstorming) seems clearcut: the time of people for solving problems is *not* efficiently utilized in group situations.

Since our studies were, however, restricted to brainstorming, we might still hold out hope for the group for problems requiring a single best answer on which to base a definite decision or action. Recently, Tuckman and Lorge[7] studied such a situation,

using as subjects Air Force cadets who worked on a problem as individuals and in *ad hoc* groups of 5 men each. The problem required the formulation of a plan of action for getting a cadre of 5 men across a road mined with supersensitive enemy mines which could neither be neutralized nor dug up. The road was 12 feet wide, bordered with trees about 40 feet tall. Scattered about one side of the road were a variety of potentially usable materials and debris including beams, ropes, a discarded auto tire, pulley, etc. It is apparent that the problem is not of the brainstorming variety; indeed, it is of the general type usually encountered in business settings in the sense of requiring an immediate practical solution. Furthermore, the solutions could be reliably scored for quality by assigning various point values to significant elements of the solution, yielding a Quality Point Score (QPS).

Tuckman and Lorge asked 70 men to work on the problem alone and to write their solutions. The men were then divided into 14 5-man groups which met to discuss the problem and to prepare written group solutions. A simple comparison between group and individual averages showed the traditional apparent superiority for group problem solving (average QPS for the 14 groups was 53 compared to an average for the 70 individuals of only 25, a difference highly significant statistically). However, the crucial test of the presumed facilitating influence of group interaction came via the comparison between group solutions and the best individual solutions of the members. Presumably, if a group is a more effective problem-solving unit, the group solution should be better than the best ideas of its individual members. This was found *not* to be

[5]M. E. Shaw, "Comparison of individuals and small groups in the rational solution of complex problems." *Amer. J. Psychol.*, 1932, 44, 491–504.

[6]I. Lorge, D. Fox, J. Davitz, and M. Brenner, "A survey of studies contrasting the quality of group performance and individual performance, 1920–1957." *Psychol. Bull.*, 1958, 55, 337–372.

[7]J. Tuckman, and I. Lorge, "Individual-ability as a determinant of group superiority." *Human Relations*, 1962, 15, 45–51.

the case in the Tuckman and Lorge study. The average "concocted" Group Quality Score based on choosing the best individual solutions from the members of each group was 69, which is well above the average QPS of 53 obtained for the actual group solutions. The group performance rarely exceeded the performance of the best member individually. In fact, the performance of the most effective member was often inhibited and was not, therefore, reflected in the group solution. The quality of the group interaction is described by Tuckman and Lorge as follows:

"They tended to form cliques or subgroups working independently, with one clique attempting to convince any other of the soundness of its thinking. In most groups at least one individual did not even participate in the deliberations. In some groups a single member dominated the discussion to the extent of coercing the acceptance of his solution, and, in one group, so much antagonism was engendered among its members that communication ceased" (p. 49).

Tuckman and Lorge concluded that meetings do not constitute an efficient way of capitalizing on the intellectual resources of different individuals. Their study leads us to view with extreme pessimism the possibility that meetings can be so constituted and conducted as to be worth the time taken in group problem solving endeavors.

Furthermore, it appears highly significant that even the rules of brainstorming are insufficient to overcome the inhibiting influences of group interaction. Future research should devote more effort to identifying the exact nature of the factors inhibiting the quality of group outcomes. With

research, perhaps we will someday be able to define the properties of groups which can be expected to be better than the pooled sum of individual efforts. As of now, however, the burden of proof is on those who advocate group meetings as efficient means of solving problems. Identification and dissolution of inhibiting interactional patterns in groups, if they serve no other purpose, ought at least to assure that the contributions of the best members of groups will be allowed to emerge rather than being suppressed, as appears to be the case now in most group situations.

In the meantime, what clues do these studies provide for the typical manager who still must solve problems and who desires to use the intellectual resources of other persons in his firm? We believe the results present a compelling argument for no longer using meetings for problem solving. Instead, they should be used primarily as communications devices —the giving and receiving of information and for keeping people informed about decisions affecting them.

How then should the resources of other persons for solving problems be utilized? The answer is not clear, but we suggest that the following sequence of steps might be worth trying:

1. Select persons who presumably possess information relevant to the solution of a problem. Write a memo to each person broadly stating the nature of the problem and outlining specific areas of relevant knowledge which each should gather and be prepared to present.

2. Hold a brief meeting (not to exceed 30–40 minutes) designed to define more fully the exact nature of the problem. The meeting should be devoted almost exclusively to a sharing of the information gathered by each

of the participants. Ideas or suggested solutions to the problem should be scrupulously avoided. At the end of the meeting, each participant should be given a second written statement of the problem to be solved.

3. Have the participants return to their offices and spend at least one uninterrupted hour working out their individual solutions to the problem. Some may want to brainstorm by dictating ideas and solutions into a recording device. Others may simply jot down the broad outlines of their solutions. Regardless of their individual methods, each should summarize his solution in the form of a written protocol of his problem solving activity.

4. Review the written solutions, and derive from them a final answer utiliz-

ing what appears to be the best elements of each of the individual solutions.

5. Finally, hold a brief 10–15 minute meeting for the purpose of summarizing the results of the problem solving efforts and communicating the final decision to the participants.

These procedures allow a manager to take advantage of the diversity of intellectual resources available to him without exposing participants to the inhibiting and channeling influences of a group problem solving session. Thus, the time of each person is spent efficiently, and safeguards are established to allow the emergence rather than the inhibition of the best that may be available from individual problem solving efforts.

---

The next study takes us one step further in understanding the complexities of communication among members of a business firm. This is a study of communication contacts among thirty-four executives of an American business firm.

Only about one-quarter of the communications between each two members of this group of executives was identified by both members as having taken place. Part of this "loss" of memory about interaction may be the result of the method used to recall the interaction, which was to have each executive make a list of his contacts twice a day. But even this tells us something, for if an executive did not

remember having contacted a fellow executive in the previous four hours there is some reason to believe that the content of the contact might also have faded from his memory. As if to confirm this second conclusion, Weinshall shows that the proportion of communication content that was received as it was intended is even lower than the proportion of contacts recalled by both parties.

Apparently, the communication channels among executives may reach a condition of overload. The result seems to be that many messages "go through" but never "get through" to the receiver.

## THE RECIPROCAL PERCEPTION OF COMMUNICATION

*Theodore D. Weinshall**

Fifty persons were chosen from among the management of the Devon Corporation (pseudonym for an American company) for participation in the communications study. They were mostly higher-echelon managers (with annual salaries of $10,000 and upwards) interconnected in their daily work.

Each person was given a form of the "Daily Management Interactions," which he was asked to fill at least twice daily (before leaving for lunch and for home), over a period of two weeks. The forms were collected daily from the participants. This form included information pertaining to every interaction the respondent could recall, and it was to be expected that a certain proportion of the interactions to which he was a party would escape

*Reprinted with modifications by permission from Theodore D. Weinshall, "Communicogram: A Way to Describe the Pattern, Frequency, and Accuracy of Organization and Communication" (Haifa: Technion, Israel Institute of Technology, July, 1964), pp. 10–18 (an occasional paper, mimeographed).

his memory, having failed to produce an impression.

### MODE OF INTERACTION

Thirty-four out of 50 chosen as participants reported their daily interactions during the two weeks chosen for the experiment.

These 34 persons reported 5135 interactions, of which only one third (1708 out of 5135) were interactions with other members of the 34 group.

We thus see that the telephone was perceived as having been used only in 30% of the total interactions (1514 times out of 5135). The proportion of conference versus telephone interactions was higher within the group (78% as compared with 22%) than in out-of-group communications (only 67% in conference as compared with 33% over the phone). Naturally, members of the organization would prefer the phone as physical distances between them grew.

It should be emphasized that we are dealing with perceived interactions.

**Table 1**

PERCEIVED INTERACTIONS BY 34 GROUP MEMBERS
(OVER 2 WORKING WEEKS)

| | Total | Daily Average per Person | Within Group | | Outside Group | |
|---|---|---|---|---|---|---|
| | | | Interactions | % of Total | Interactions | % of Total |
| Telephone | 1514 | 4.5 | 380 | 22% | 1134 | 33% |
| Conference | 3621 | 10.5 | 1328 | 78% | 2293 | 67% |
| Total | 5135 | 15 | 1708 | 100% | 3427 | 100% |

The findings of this experiment strongly indicate that the actual numbers of interactions, both total and daily average per person, were much higher. The balance of the interactions, those not perceived by either party, "drifted into oblivion."

The data indicate, however, that the fact that about 15 interactions per day were perceived, on the average, in the group of 34, does not mean that these communications "went through" in every one of the perceived interactions.

We can assume that the actual proportion of such "lost" interactions was much larger. The reason is that undoubtedly some interactions remained unperceived by either party involved. This means that probably more than three-quarters of the interactions in this group were "wasted," not being recalled several hours later. This is a surprising result even to one who expected, like myself, that when you deal with perceived interactions certain proportions are bound to be "lost."

### CONSENSUS AS TO THE EXISTENCE OF THE INTERACTION

When the perceived interactions were checked against one another for a consensus as to their occurrence, it

### CONSENSUS AS TO THE MEANING OF THE COMMUNICATION

The fact that the participating parties in an interaction agree as to its existence does not necessarily mean

**Table 2**

MUTUALLY PERCEIVED INTERACTIONS AMONG GROUP MEMBERS
(CONSENSUS AS TO OCCURRENCE OF INTERACTIONS)

|  | Total Perceived Interactions in Group | Mutually Perceived (Consensus as to Occurrence) | |
|---|---|---|---|
|  |  | Interactions | % Out of Total |
| Telephone | 380 | 80 | 21% |
| Conference | 1328 | 356 | 27% |
| Total | 1708 | 436 | 25% |

turned out that only in 25% of the cases were the perceptions of one party reciprocated.

We thus see that 75% of the reported interactions registered in the mind of one party only, and therefore could to an extent be regarded as "lost" from the communications point of view.[1]

that the communication "gets through." Table 3 shows that only in less than one half of all the mutually perceived interactions did the "recipient" of the communication understand the spirit in which it was meant to be delivered by the "transmitter" of the communication.

Table 3 clearly shows that in only 47% of the mutually perceived interactions did there exist an understanding of the meaning of the interaction. This means that the communication

[1] A certain proportion of the perceived interactions were unreciprocated because of errors in registration of the time of occurrence. Even so, the proportion "lost" would remain amazingly high.

**Table 3**

CONSENSUS AS TO WHAT TOOK PLACE IN THE INTERACTIONS

| | Total Mutually Perceived Interactions | Consensus as to Meaning of Interaction | |
|---|---|---|---|
| | | Number of Interactions | % Out of Total |
| Telephone | 80 | 48 | 60% |
| Conference | 356 | 158 | 44% |
| Total | 436 | 206 | 47% |

did not "pass" ("go through") in the spirit in which it was intended—in 53% of the recorded mutually perceived interactions.

Contrary to the consensus as to the existence of the interaction, where the conference did better than the telephone, the consensus as to the meaning of interaction shows that the telephone did better than the conference.[2] Thus, if the phone conversation is recalled, it is more accurate. We find that only 44% of the communications "went through" in a conference, while 60% "went through" over the phone. One speculation why this is so refers to the relative brevity of telephone conversations (the expectation being that telephone conversations are usually shorter than face-to-face meetings

and cover fewer subjects than conferences usually do). Perhaps there is a stronger tendency, in face-to-face meetings, to go from one subject to another (even when the original reason for the meeting was a specific topic). When the meeting terminates every participant might "take away" a different impression of what seemed to him the core of the meeting. These dynamics are worthy of more detailed study.

Interestingly enough, the advantage of the conference over the phone in "registering" the occurrence of an interaction was found to be almost equal to the advantage of the phone over the conference in "transmitting" the meaning of the communication. This is shown by their respective ratios of:

[2]The differences in this case were found to be significant (between .02 and .01 levels).

$$\frac{27\%}{21\%} = 1.29 \qquad \frac{60\%}{44\%} = 1.36$$

**Table 4**

PROPORTION OF COMMUNICATIONS THAT "GOT THROUGH" OUT OF TOTAL INTERACTIONS PERCEIVED WITHIN GROUP

| | Reported Interactions Within Group | Total Mutually Perceived Interactions | Consensus as to Meaning of Communication | |
|---|---|---|---|---|
| | | | Number of Interactions | % out of Reported Interactions |
| Telephone | 380 | 80 | 48 | 13% |
| Conference | 1328 | 356 | 158 | 12% |
| Total | 1708 | 436 | 206 | 12% |

The same results hold when we consider the interactions in which the communication "went through" as percentages of the *total* reported interactions in the group.

As Table 4 shows, in only 206 (12%) out of the 1708 perceived interactions in the group did there exist a consensus as to their occurrence as well as to their character. The telephone did almost as "poorly" as the conference (13% versus 12%).

---

If you are still unconvinced that communication is a very complex process, perhaps the following unique and original study will convince you. Martin Meissner analyzed all communication acts among industrial workers. In this brief selection from his comprehensive report he sets forth three forms of non-verbal communication and compares their frequency with that of verbal communication between pairs of workers.

These four modes of communication are correlated with the distance between the people communicating, the noise level of the environment, and the existence of visual barriers.

As might be expected, the use of non-verbal communication increases as distance, noise in the environment, and visual barriers increase. We may therefore conclude that teamwork and person-to-person co-ordination in getting work done requires constant communication among work-group members. All forms of communication are employed to accomplish this. Especially interesting is the communication that results through objects, which are typically pieces of work in process. As a piece moves from one work station to another, the worker at the second station sees it and realizes he has to get to work on it.

A portion of the much larger study here reported deals with the manner in which industrial workers use sign language to communicate with each other about non-work subjects. It seems clear that the understanding of communication is basic to understanding human relations in administration. It seems equally clear that we have to continue to broaden our knowledge upon which this understanding is based. The four research reports included in this chapter have been selected purposely in order to help you appreciate how good research changes old ideas about human communication and adds new ideas to our store of knowledge.

---

## NON-VERBAL COMMUNICATION ON THE JOB

*Martin Meissner**

We classified our workers' conversations by four kinds of methods of transmitting messages or cues, and counted frequencies separately for each:

1. *Speech*—direct talking or shouting

---

*Reprinted by permission from Martin Meissner, "Workers' Communication and the Means of Production" (1964), pp. 11–14 (unpublished study).

from one person to another, unaided by technical means.

2. *Signs*—cues produced by the emitter's body (other than speech sounds) and directly perceived by sight or touch. This category includes such things as one man tapping his finger on another man's shoulder, a gesture like shrugging shoulders, or a symbol from a sign language. The facial expressions and gestures that ordinarily accompany speech in our culture were not separately counted, but deliberate signs and gestures in excess of this definition were. The imprecision obviously contained in this distinction is difficult to avoid in sustained observations in "natural," and particularly industrial, settings.

3. *Signals*—cues produced by means of a technical transmitter, and received by hearing or sight, such as pushing a button that turns on a red light elsewhere, pulling a rope to blow a whistle, a chalk mark on a work piece, and the use of telephone and public address system (the last two very rare in our cases).

4. *Objects*—cues produced by control over the movement or positioning of a material object, and received by visual, audial, or tactile perception. Pulling a lever and setting a machine in motion is a way of transmitting information to another man. Similarly, a work piece sent down the line may tell the next man to get working on this one. Throwing rotten avocados has the power to express your feelings exquisitely. We include this category as communication when the perception of the object in question is given meaning by the receiver, and thus effects his behavior. The bulk of our frequencies of communication by object consists of work-piece movement from one position to another.

Frequencies will be summarized by

arithmetic means. In our case this can only be taken as a crude indicator of differences. The distribution of these frequencies does not approach the bell-shaped normal curve which many phenomena take when put together in large numbers, and which makes the mean an effective summary of information.

## PERCEPTUAL LIMITS TO COMMUNICATION

We can begin by putting communication rates in relation to the brute facts of industrial life: noise, visual barriers, distance between work stations, and spatial confinement. In our observations we roughly coded both noise and visual restrictions as barriers to communication between the two positions of a pair of workers on a four-point scale. Distances between positions were estimated from layout sketches. A man was regarded as spatially confined when, in the course of his work, he could not move to other work stations.

Table 5 generally indicates that talking declines, and communication by objects and signals increases, as barriers to perception become more severe. In addition the use of signs obviously demands clear vision, and becomes prominent in very noisy places. One of the explanations for increased noise is that the hourly frequency of operation cycles is twice as high for the two more noisy categories than for the two quieter ones.

Increasing distance reduces verbal communication. The effect of distance can be overcome, however, when workers are free to move to other work stations in the course of their work. Table 6 demonstrates that there is no verbal communication at distances above fifty feet. Workers whose ordinary work stations are separated by these extended distances communicate only when both are free to move and thus reduce the distance temporarily.

**Table 5**

PERCEPTUAL BARRIERS AND COMMUNICATION IN WORKER PAIRS

| Noise | *Mean hourly frequency of communication by* | | | |
| | *Speech* | *Signs* | *Signals* | *Objects* |
|---|---|---|---|---|
| 1 Quiet | 10.3 | .4 | .0 | 12.0 |
| 2 | 8.2 | .1 | .0 | 34.7 |
| 3 | 7.9 | .8 | .1 | 87.0 |
| 4 Very noisy | 2.4 | 7.0 | 2.1 | 101.2 |
| Visual barriers | | | | |
| 1 No restrictions | 9.5 | 6.1 | .7 | 77.2 |
| 2 | 5.3 | 2.0 | .3 | 96.4 |
| 3 | 5.6 | .9 | .3 | 11.7 |
| 4 Positions not visible to each other | .4 | .0 | 2.5 | 122.1 |
| Distance | | | | |
| 25 feet and less | 9.0 | 4.4 | .3 | 69.7 |
| 26 – 50 feet | 3.3 | 1.2 | .7 | 87.0 |
| 51 feet and more | .6 | .7 | 2.8 | 60.2 |

**Table 6**

DISTANCE, SPATIAL CONFINEMENT, AND VERBAL COMMUNICATION
(MEAN HOURLY FREQUENCY OF COMMUNICATION BY SPEECH)

| Spatial Confinement | *Distance Between Two Workers in a Pair* | | |
| | *25 feet & less* | *26–50 feet* | *51 feet & more* |
|---|---|---|---|
| Both workers can move | 13.7 | 6.9 | 2.4 |
| One worker confined | 4.1 | 1.2 | .0 |
| Both workers confined | 7.4 | .4 | .0 |

In spite of all the planning to ensure that communication systems exist to carry on the necessary message exchanges among people, there still remains an area where informal communication dominates. This is often called the grapevine. In discussing the grapevine, Simon makes clear that the very human qualities of freely interacting with people with whom we are in daily contact provides the basis for informal communication. The grapevine cannot be eliminated; it may even have positive consequences for the organization, as Simon suggests.

## INFORMAL COMMUNICATION AND THE "GRAPEVINE"

*Herbert A. Simon**

No matter how elaborate a system of formal communications is set up in the organization, this system will always be supplemented by informal channels. Through these informal channels will flow information, advice, and even orders (the reader will recall that, in terms of our definitions, an authority relation can exist even though the superior is not vested with any sanctions). In time, the actual system of relationships may come to differ widely from those specified in the formal organization scheme.

The informal communications system is built around the social relationships of the members of the organization. Friendship between two individuals creates frequent occasions for contact and "shop talk." It may also create an authority relationship if one of the individuals comes to accept the leadership of the other. In this way "natural leaders" secure a role in the organization that is not always reflected in the organization chart.

The informal communication system takes on additional importance when it is remembered that the behavior of individuals in organizations is oriented not only towards the organization's goals but also to a certain extent toward their personal goals, and that these two sets of goals are not always mutually consistent. Hence, when organization members deal with one another, each must attempt to assess

the extent to which the other's attitudes and actions are conditioned by personal rather than organizational motives. When a primary relationship has been established between them, it becomes easier for each to make this assessment, and easier for them to be frank in regard to their motives. Requests for cooperation will less often meet with the reaction: "You run your department, and I will run mine."

Primary relationships can be unfriendly, of course, just as easily as they can be friendly, although there is what might be called a "presumption of friendliness" in most social relationships in our society. It becomes a major task of the executives, then, to maintain attitudes of friendliness and cooperation in these direct personal relationships so that the informal communication system will contribute to the efficient operation of the organization rather than hinder it.

The informal communications system is sometimes used by organization members to advance their personal aims. From this arises the phenomenon of cliques—groups that build up an informal network of communications and use this as a means of securing power in the organization. Rivalry among cliques, in turn, may lead to general unfriendliness in social relationships and defeat the purpose of the informal communications system.

There has been little systematic analysis of the way in which the formal organization structure encourages or hinders the formation of cliques, or of the techniques that can be used by executives to deal with cliques and

*From Herbert A. Simon, *Administrative Behavior* (New York: The Macmillan Company, 1947), pp. 160–162. Copyright 1945 and 1947 by Herbert A. Simon and used with The Macmillan Company's permission.

minimize their harmfulness. On the first score, it may be conjectured that the weakness of the formal system of communications and failure to secure an adequate measure of coordination through that system probably encourage the development of cliques. The coordinating function that cliques perform under such circumstances is closely analogous to the coordinating function performed by political machines in a highly decentralized governmental structure like the American system.

A great deal of the informal communication in any organization is far less deliberate than the activities of cliques or even the conversations of executives who lunch together. In addition to these there is the great mass of communication that goes under the head of "gossip." In most organizations the "grapevine" probably plays, on the whole, a constructive role. Its chief disadvantages are, first, that it discourages frankness, since confidential remarks may be spread about, and second, that the information transmitted by the grapevine is often inaccurate. On the other hand, in addition to transmitting information that no one has thought to transmit formally, the grapevine is valuable as a barometer of "public opinion" in the organization. If the administrator listens to it, it apprises him of the topics that are subjects of interest to organization members, and their attitudes towards these topics. Even for this latter purpose, of course, the grapevine needs to be supplemented by other channels of information.

# 15

# Decision-Making

In this chapter we consider four important aspects of
decision-making. First we examine the general processes of decision-making and their consequences in
organizations. Second the imperatives that limit and
modify decisions in business organizations are analyzed. Third the techniques of "muddling through" and
of the use of mathematical models are considered as
methods available for making decisions. Finally, attention is given to sharing decisions with subordinates.

In the past decade an extremely powerful mathematical technology has been applied to decision-
making within organizations under the titles of operations research and linear programming. Very material
benefits have resulted in the *quality* of decisions
reached because of the precision of the decisional
models made necessary by the mathematical logic and
language employed. Nevertheless, it is desirable to
emphasize that the processes by which decisions become necessary in an organization, and their consequences for the organization, are independent of the
technical means employed in coming to the decisions.
A "seat-of-the-pants" decision and one derived from
a mathematical model may be identical as to need
or consequences.

**INTRODUCTION**

It is, therefore, particularly important that we
distinguish the technologies for reaching decisions
from the broad processes of decision-making itself.
This chapter is focused on the latter problem.

Barnard, in the first selection, provides the central
framework for our analysis of decision-making. He

347

particularly emphasizes the differences between organizational decisions as a product of operating circumstances and encircling environment, on the one hand, and personal decisions as a product of psychological processes, on the other. An interesting side issue also raised by Barnard illuminates the art of decision-making when he emphasizes the circumstances and reasons for deciding *not* to make a decision. This selection by Barnard treats the organization as a social system and shows how decision-making for and on behalf of the organization is primarily a social process.

## DECISION-MAKING IN ORGANIZATIONS

### Chester I. Barnard*

This distinction between the two types of decision is frequently recognized in ordinary affairs. We very often say or hear sentences similar to this: "If this were my business, I think I would decide the question this way —but it is not my personal affair"; or, "I think the *situation* requires such and such an answer—but I am not in a position to determine what ought to be done"; or, "The decision should be made by someone else." This is in effect a restatement, with a different emphasis, of the suggestion . . . that a sort of dual personality is required of individuals contributing to organization action—the private personality, and the organization personality.

These two kinds of decisions—organization decisions and personal decisions—are chiefly to be distinguished as to process by this fact: that personal decisions cannot ordinarily be delegated to others, whereas organization decisions can often if not always

be delegated. For example, what may be called a major decision by an individual may require numerous subsidiary decisions (or judgments) which he also must make. A similar important decision by an organization may in its final form be enunciated by one person and the corresponding subsidiary decisions by several different persons, all acting organizationally, not personally. Similarly, the execution of a decision by one person may require subsequent detailed decision by him as to various steps, whereas the execution of a similar decision in an organization almost always requires subsequent detailed decision by several different persons. Indeed, it may be said that often the responsibility for an organization decision is not a personal responsibility until assigned. Responsibility for organization decision must be assigned positively and definitely in many cases because the aptness of decision depends upon knowledge of facts and of organization purpose, and is therefore bound up with organization communication. Thus central or general organization decisions are best

---

*Reprinted by permission of the publishers from Chester I. Barnard, *The Functions of the Executive* (Cambridge, Mass.: Harvard University Press, 1938), pp. 188–199.

made at centers of the communication system of the organization, so that such decisions must be assigned to those located at these central positions. Persons located at such positions are known as executives; so that the necessities of communication as an essential element in organization imposes the assignment of responsibility for some kinds of organization decision to executives. In short, a characteristic of the services of executives is that they represent a specialization of the process of making organization decisions—and this is the essence of their functions.

The circumstances surrounding the making of concrete decisions are of course of indefinitely large variety, but we will give attention here only to certain general conditions, which may be presented under three headings: the occasions of decision, the evidences of decision, and the environment of decision.

## I. THE OCCASIONS OF DECISION

The making of decisions, as everyone knows from personal experience, is a burdensome task. Offsetting the exhilaration that may result from correct and successful decision and the relief that follows the terminating of a struggle to determine issues is the depression that comes from failure or error of decision and the frustration which ensues from uncertainty. Accordingly, it will be observed that men generally try to avoid making decisions, beyond a limited degree when they are rather uncritical responses to conditions. The capacity of most men to make decisions is quite narrow, although it is a capacity that may be considerably developed by training and especially by experience.

The executive is under the obligation of making decisions usually within approximately defined limits related to the position he has accepted; and is under the necessity of keeping within the limits of his capacity if he is continuously to discharge this obligation. He must, therefore, to be successful, distinguish between the occasions of decision in order to avoid the acceptance of more than he can undertake without neglecting the fields to which his position relates. For the natural reluctance of other men to decide, their persistent disposition to avoid responsibility, and their fear of criticism, will lead them to overwhelm the executive who does not protect himself from excessive burdens of decision if he is not already protected by a well regulated and habitual distribution of responsibilities.

It is for this reason necessary in the making of decisions to maintain a balance between the fields from which the occasions of them arise. I suppose this is rarely a matter of conscious selection, and is probably subject to no general rules. It involves in itself important decisions. For our purposes, however, it may be helpful to note that the occasions for decision originate in three distinct fields: (a) from authoritative communications from superiors; (b) from cases referred for decision by subordinates; (c) from cases originating in the initiative of the executive concerned.

(a) Occasions for decision are frequently furnished by instructions or by general requirements of superior authority. Such decisions relate to the interpretation, application, and distribution of instructions. These occasions cannot be avoided, though the burden may be reduced by delegation of responsibility to subordinates. They involve serious decisions when the instructions seem morally wrong, harmful to the organization, or impossible of execution.

(b) The cases referred for decision may be called appellate cases. They arise from incapacity of subordinates, uncertainty of instructions, novelty of conditions, conflict of jurisdiction or conflicts of orders, or failure of subjective authority. The control of the number of appellate cases lies in adequacy of executive organization, of personnel, of previous decision; and the development of the processes of informal organization. The test of executive action is to make these decisions when they are important, or when they cannot be delegated reasonably, and to decline the others.

(c) The occasions of decision on the initiative of the executive are the most important test of his capacity. Out of his understanding of the situation, which depends upon his ability and initiative, and on the character of the communication system of his organization, it is to be determined whether something needs to be done or corrected. To decide the question involves not merely the ordinary elements but the executive's specific justification for deciding. For when the occasions for decision arise from above or below the position of the executive, others have in advance granted him authority; but when made on his own initiative, this always may be (and generally is) questioned, at least tacitly (in the form of whether decision was necessary, or related to scope of obligations, etc.). Moreover, failure to decide is usually not specifically subject to attack, except under extreme conditions. Hence there is much incentive to avoid decision. Pressure of other work is the usual self-justification. Yet it is clear that the most important obligation is to raise and decide those issues which no one else is in a position to raise effectively.

From the point of view of the *relative* importance of specific decisions, those of executives properly call for first attention. From the point of view of *aggregate* importance, it is not decisions of executives but of nonexecutive participants in organization which should enlist major interest. Indeed it is precisely for this reason that many executive decisions are necessary—they relate to the facilitation of correct action involving appropriate decisions among others. In large measure this is a process of providing for the clear presentment of the issues of choices. At any event, it is easily evident merely from the inspection of the action of the nonexecutive participants in organization that coordination of action requires repeated organization decisions "on the spot" where the effective action of organization takes place. It is here that the final and most concrete objectives of purposes are found, with the maximum of definiteness. There is no further stage of organization action. The final selection of means takes place at this point.

It should be noted, however, that the types of decisions as well as the conditions change in character as we descend from the major executive to the nonexecutive positions in organization. At the upper limit decisions relating to ends to be pursued generally require the major attention, those relating to means being secondary, rather general, and especially concerned with personnel, that is, the development and protection of organization itself. At intermediate levels the breaking of broad purposes into more specific ends and the technical and technological problems, including economic problems, of action become prominent. At the low levels decisions characteristically relate to technologically correct conduct, so far as the action is organization action. But it is at these low levels, where ultimate authority resides, that the *personal* decisions determining willingness to contribute become of relatively greatest aggregate importance.

## II. THE EVIDENCES OF DECISION

Not the least of the difficulties of appraising the executive functions or the relative merits of executives lies in the fact that there is little direct opportunity to observe the essential operations of decision. It is a perplexing fact that most executive decisions produce no direct evidence of themselves and that knowledge of them can only be derived from the cumulation of indirect evidence. They must largely be inferred from general results in which they are merely one factor, and from symptomatic indications of roundabout character.

Those decisions which are most directly known result in the emission of authoritative communications, that is, orders. Something is or is not to be done. Even in such cases the basic decision may not be evident; for the decision to attempt to achieve a certain result or condition may require several communications to different persons which appear to be complete in themselves but in which the controlling general decision may not be disclosed.

Again, a firm decision may be taken that does not result in any communication whatever for the time being. A decision properly timed must be made in advance of communicating it, either because the action involved must wait anticipated developments or because it cannot be authoritative without edu-

cational or persuasive preparation.

Finally, the decision may be not to decide. This is a most frequent decision, and from some points of view probably the most important. For every alert executive continually raises in his own mind questions for determination. As a result of his consideration he may determine that the question is not pertinent. He may determine that it is not now pertinent. He may determine that it is pertinent now, but that there are lacking adequate data upon which to base a final decision. He may determine that it is pertinent for decision now, but that it should or must be decided by someone else on the latter's initiative. He may determine that the question is pertinent, can be decided, will not be decided except by himself, and yet it would be better that it be not decided because his competence is insufficient.

*The fine art of executive decision consists in not deciding questions that are not now pertinent, in not deciding prematurely, in not making decisions that cannot be made effective, and in not making decisions that others should make.* Not to decide questions that are not pertinent at the time is uncommon good sense, though to raise them may be uncommon perspicacity. Not to decide questions prematurely is to refuse commitment of attitude or the development of prejudice. Not to make decisions that cannot be made effective is to refrain from destroying authority. Not to make decisions that others should make is to preserve morale, to develop competence, to fix responsibility, and to preserve authority.

From this it may be seen that decisions fall into two major classes, positive decisions—to do something, to direct action, to cease action, to prevent action; and negative decisions, which are decisions not to decide. Both are inescapable; but the negative decisions are often largely unconscious, relatively nonlogical, "instinctive," "good sense." It is because of the rejections that the selection is good. The best of moves may be offset by a false move. This is why time is usually necessary to appraise the executive. There is no current evidence of the all-important negative decisions. The absence of effective moves indicates failure of initiative in decision, but error of action probably often means absence of good negative decisions. The success of action through a period of time denotes excellence of selection and of rejection of possible actions.

### III. THE NATURE OF THE ENVIRONMENT

Whatever the occasions or the evidences of decision, it is clear that decisions are constantly being made. What is the nature of the environment of decisions, the materials with which they deal, the field to which they relate? It consists of two parts: (a) purpose; and (b) the physical world, the social world, the external things and forces and circumstances of the moment. All of these, including purpose, constitute the objective field of decision; but the two parts are of radically different nature and origin. The function of decision is to regulate the relations between these two parts. This regulation is accomplished either by changing the purpose or by changing the remainder of the environment.

(a) We may consider purpose first. It may seem strange perhaps that purpose should be included in the objective environment, since purpose of all things seems personal, subjective, internal, the expression of desire. This is true; but *at the moment of a new decision,* an existing purpose, the result of a previous decision under previous conditions, is an objective fact, and it is so treated at that moment in so far as it is a factor in a new decision.

This is especially true because organization decisions do not relate to personal purposes, but to organization purposes. The purpose which concerns an organization decision may have been given as a fact and accepted as such by the person who is responsible for making a new decision. But no matter how arrived at, when decision is in point, the purpose is fact already determined; its making is a matter of history; it may be as objective as another man's emotions may be to an observer.

We must note, however, that purpose is essential to give any meaning to the rest of the environment.[1] The environment must be looked at from *some* point of view to be intelligible. A mere mass of things, atoms, movements, forces, noises, lights, could produce some responses from a sensitive creature or certainly would have some effect on it, or on other things, but the reduction of this mass of everything to something significant requires a basis for discrimination, for picking out this and that as pertinent, relevant, interesting. This basis is that in *this* situation something is or is not to be done. The situation aids, obstructs, or is neutral from *this* point of view. The basis for this discrimination is a purpose, an end, an object to be accomplished.

Purpose itself has no meaning, however, except in an environment. It can only be defined in terms of an envi-

---

[1] I am under the impression that in a general way both the form of expression and the concepts stated in the next several paragraphs were derived from or influenced by A. N. Whitehead's *Process and Reality.*

ronment.[2] Even to want to go some-where, anywhere, supposes some kind of environment. A very general purpose supposes a very general undifferentiated environment; and if the purpose is stated or thought of it must be in terms of that general environment. But when formed, it immediately (if it is not in suspense or dormant, so to speak) serves for reducing that environment to more definite features; and the immediate result is to change purpose into a more specific purpose. Thus when I decide I want to go from A to B my idea of terrain is vague. But as soon as I have decided, the terrain becomes less vague; I immediately see paths, rocks, obstacles that are significant; and this finer discrimination results in detailed and smaller purposes. I not only want to go from A to B, but I want to go this way, that way, etc. This constant refinement of purpose is that effect of repeated decisions, in finer and finer detail, until eventually detailed purpose is contemporaneous accomplishment. But similarly with each new edition of purpose, a new discrimination of the environment is involved, until finally the last obstacle of progressive action represents a breaking up of a general purpose into many concrete purposes, each as it is made almost simultaneously associated with the action. The

thing is done as soon as decided; it becomes a matter of history; it constitutes a single step in the process of experience.

Thus back and forth purpose and environment react in successive steps through successive decisions in greater and greater detail. A series of final decisions, each apparently trivial, is largely accomplished unconsciously and sums up into an effected general purpose and a route of experience.

(b) We may now consider the environment of decision exclusive of purpose. It consists of atoms and molecules, agglomerations of things in motion, alive; of men and emotions; of physical laws and social laws; social ideas, norms of action, of forces and resistances. Their number is infinite and they are meaningless in their variety and changes except as discriminated in the light of purpose. They are viewed as static facts, if the change is not significant from the viewpoint of the purpose, or as both static and dynamic facts.

This discrimination divides the world into two parts; the facts that are immaterial, irrelevant, mere background; and the part that contains the facts that apparently aid or prevent the accomplishment of purpose. As soon as that discrimination takes place, decision is in bud. It is in the state of selecting among alternatives. These alternatives are either to utilize favorable factors, to eliminate or circumvent unfavorable ones, or to change the purpose. Note that if the decision is to deal with the environment, this automatically introduces new but more detailed purposes, the progeny, as it were, of the parent purpose; but if the decision is to change the purpose rather than deal with the environment, the parent is sterile. It is abandoned, and a new purpose is selected,

---

[2]Care should be taken to keep in mind that environment throughout does not mean merely physical aspects of the environment, but explicitly includes social aspects, although physical rather than other aspects are used for illustration as simpler. In many organizations, however, the physical aspects are constant and it is the social aspects which are pertinent. This is the case especially when the purpose is a concrete expression of social ideas or attitudes, as, for example, in ritualistic types of action whether religious or political.

thereby creating a *new* environment in the light of *that* purpose.

This looks like metaphysical speculation if one thinks of it as individual and personal—undemonstrable assumptions, speculative reasoning. But it can be observed in an organization, at least sufficiently to corroborate it roughly. Thus if the president of a telephone company for good reasons orders[3] two poles carrying a cable removed from the north side of First Street between A and B Streets to the opposite side of First Street, it can, I think, be approximately demonstrated that carrying out that order involves perhaps 10,000 decisions of 100 men located at 15 points, requiring successive analyses of several environments, including social, moral, legal, economic, and physical facts of the environment, and requiring 9000 redefinitions and refinements of purpose, and 1000 changes of purpose. If inquiry be made of those responsible, probably not more than a half-a-dozen decisions will be recalled or deemed worthy of mention—those that seemed at the moment difficult or momentous, or that were subject to question or proved erroneous. The others will be "taken for granted," all a part of the

business of knowing one's business. However, a large part of the decisions, purposes, and descriptions and analyses of the various environments will be a matter of record—short-cut, abbreviated, to be sure, but marking the routes of decisions with fair definiteness. Only in the case of individual workmen shall we be almost completely reduced to speculation as to the number and character of the decisions required, because many of them certainly will relate to physiological action.

The purpose of this chapter has been to suggest the climate of concrete decisions as they occur in organizations and to emphasize the radical difference between the process of decision in organizations, when decision is in its important aspects a social process, and the process of decision in individuals when it is a psychological process socially conditioned. Perhaps the most important inference to be drawn from this description is that within organizations, especially of complex types, there is a technique of decision, an organizational process of thinking, which may not be analogous to that of the individual. It would appear that such techniques differ widely among the various types of organization—for example, religious, political, industrial, commercial, etc. This is perhaps conveyed by the remark often made about the "differences in approach" to similar questions. It may be suspected that more than differences in technological character or even of the ends or purposes are involved.

---

[3]Partly to illustrate several statements in this essay I may say that it is necessary to imagine extreme conditions to suppose he would issue such an order. Ordinarily what he would do would be to inquire whether it would be feasible to take the action suggested, or what would be involved in doing so, or he would state the problem and ask for its solution, etc. The executive art is nine-tenths inducing those who have authority to use it in taking pertinent action.

In the following selection, Tannenbaum makes more concrete the organization decision-making processes by casting them in the framework of authority and subordination. By now we should be thoroughly familar with this framework.

He points out the manner in which the holder of authority limits and prescribes the actions of subordinates through various kinds of decisions. Thus, he spells out for us seven areas of decision in which authority is exercised, areas that serve to limit or specify the organization behavior of subordinates. In the last part of his selection, he introduces the second major topic of this chapter: some of the influences that are known to have a bearing upon the decision-maker.

## LIMITATIONS ON DECISION-MAKING

*Robert Tannenbaum**

### THE MANAGED AND DECISION-MAKING

It has previously been pointed out that managers make decisions to affect, both directly (through authority) and indirectly (through influence), the behavior of their subordinates. In this section consideration will be given to the implications of these managerial decisions to the behavior of the subordinates—the managed.

It has been seen that the relatively isolated individual is faced with insurmountable difficulties in his attempt to achieve rational behavior. But when individuals become members of organized groups, it is at least possible for their behavior to achieve a high degree of rationality when viewed in terms of group purposes. The decisions of managers, operating upon the managed through authority and influence, make this possible in ways which will be examined below.

*From "Managerial Decision-making," *The Journal of Business,* 23:33–37 (Jan. 1950). Used by permission of The University of Chicago Press.

In the discussion which follows, it will be important to remember that the term "managed" includes most managers and all nonmanagers. A manager is such only with respect to his subordinates; he is managed with respect to his superior. Of all the managers in an enterprise, only the head of the supreme complex is a manager who is not at the same time being managed. The concern in this section is with the managed as such, including individuals who are both managers and nonmanagers.

The decisions of managers (made to organize, direct, or control responsible subordinates) operate to increase the rationality of the behavior of subordinates—when viewed in terms of enterprise purposes—in the following ways.

1. Decisions are made by superiors which define enterprise purpose. This purpose is the end for the attainment of which the specialized services of the members of the group are being contributed. It is important that the decisions made by each member of

the group be made with reference to the group end and not a differing personal end. Through training it is possible to indoctrinate individuals in the enterprise purpose; through incentives, to induce individuals to accept it; and through supervision, to insure that the enterprise purpose will guide individual decisions.

2. Superiors establish the criterion of rationality to guide subordinates in making the choices which they are called upon to make. It will be remembered that this criterion requires that a choice be made between alternatives which will maximize results (the degree of attainment of the relevant end) at a given cost. For a business firm seeking to maximize profits, this cost is a money cost. As in the preceding case, training, incentives, and supervision are the relevant managerial devices to be used in establishing the criterion of rationality as the basis for individual choice.

3. In establishing the degree and type of specialization to be effectuated within an enterprise, superiors thereby define the general kind of activity to be expected of individuals filling particular positions. Such definition significantly reduces the number of spheres of discretion which are relevant to the particular activity to which an individual is assigned. This limitation is an aspect of the managerial function of organization.

4. Another relevant aspect of the function of organization is the determination of lines of formal authority. This determination establishes for the subordinate the individual (or individuals) to whom he is to look for decisions made to affect his behavior.

5. With respect to those spheres of discretion relating to the general kind of activity expected of a subordinate, superiors frequently impose additional constraints, thereby limiting the number of available behavior alternatives from among which the subordinate is expected to choose.

6. Superiors can provide subordinates with relevant information. This information may relate to behavior alternatives about which the subordinate is not aware. Or it may relate to the consequences attendant upon specific behavior alternatives. This information may be supplied through training, through the use of reports and memoranda, through conversation, and the like.

7. Superiors may request that particular decisions be made at or by a specified time. Such requests are stimuli which direct the attention of subordinates to designated problems and therefore initiate the decision-making processes at particular moments of time.

8. With respect to given problem areas, superiors may expect specific behavior responses of their subordinates which permit no discretion to them. Here the subordinate is not expected to make a decision to guide his own behavior but simply to act in the manner specified by his superior. The superior may specify the action of the subordinate through an on-the-spot order; or he may use such devices as rules, regulations, routines, standing orders, policies, standard methods and procedures, and the like to accomplish the same purpose. In this connection it should be noted that the same purpose can also be accomplished by selecting people with desired attributes or by training them. Through selection or training, particular individual modes of response can reasonably be insured so that the number of direct orders which must be given can be reduced. Thus, if a novice is hired to do clerical work, his superior must specifically tell him what to do, how to do it, etc. But if

a trained person is hired or the novice is trained, then such specific orders are no longer necessary.

By way of summary, the subordinate (the individual managed) is expected to focus his attention on a greatly restricted number of problems calling for decision. With respect to these problems, authoritative constraints are often imposed on the pertinent spheres of discretion which further limit his range of choice. Information is provided which calls the subordinate's attention to behavior alternatives relevant to particular decisions and which adds to his knowledge of the consequences attendant upon those behavior alternatives under consideration. The ends toward which his decisions must be directed are specified for him, as is the criterion of rationality to guide the choices which he must make. Lines of formal authority are specified for him which designate the individual (or individuals) to whom he is to look for decisions to affect his behavior. His superior often determines for him the particular problems calling for his decision to which he should direct his attention at specified moments of time. The superior often expects specific behavior responses of the subordinate which permit no discretion to him. And through incentives and supervision the superior reasonably insures that all the behavior responses of the subordinate are in conformance with those desired. As a result of these factors which originate with superiors, it is possible for the behavior of the subordinate to achieve a high degree of rationality when viewed in terms of enterprise purposes.

## THE MANAGERS AND DECISION-MAKING

The decisions of managers are made to affect the behavior of responsible subordinates in the ways considered in the preceding section. But these decisions are themselves not made in a vacuum. They are subject to all the restrictions which have previously been discussed and to influence. In this section, particular attention will be given to the sources from which stem the authority and influence which can directly and indirectly affect the managerial decision-making process.

In making decisions, managers can be subject to the authority of many individuals and groups. The determination as to whether they will be subject to such authority, of course, always rests with the managers. They, like others, can either accept or reject any exercise of authority. If they accept the exercise of authority (because of positive inducements or coercion), they thereby assume a role of subordination with respect to the individuals or group possessing the authority. The superior can directly affect the behavior of the subordinate in the ways previously discussed—by imposing constraints on spheres of discretion, by completely eliminating spheres of discretion from the province of the subordinate, and by imposing a decision on the subordinate to the effect that the subordinate act in a particular manner.

There are many individuals and groups who do, at varying times, exercise authority with respect to managers. While no attempt will be made in the discussion which follows to consider all those who might authoritatively impinge upon managers, the principal ones will be given attention.

First, nearly all managers, as managed, are subject to the authority of their managerial superiors. This relationship was probed in the preceding section. At this point it is simply necessary to point out that this exercise of authority directly affects, among other things, the decisions made by the subordinate manager to affect the behavior of his own subordinates.

Second, managers are subject to the authority of individuals who, from the formal point of view, are their own subordinates. At first glance, this may be difficult to visualize, but it is a fact the understanding of which is crucial to the effective performance of the functions of management.

It has previously been stated that the sphere of authority possessed by a superior is defined for him by the sphere of acceptance of his subordinates. It is likewise true that the sphere of nonacceptance of authority of formal subordinates defines the sphere of nonauthority of the formal superior. This limiting effect imposed upon the managerial decision-making process by formal subordinates is indeed real. Barnard has stated the case in these positive terms:

There is no principle of executive conduct better established in good organizations than that orders will not be issued that cannot or will not be obeyed. Executives and most persons of experience who have thought about it know that to do so destroys authority, discipline, and morale.[1]

---

[1]*The Functions of the Executive* (Cambridge, Mass.: Harvard University Press, 1938), p. 167. Donald C. Stone has commented upon this same point as follows: "The executive is often seen as the man sitting at the top of the organization possessed of a dangerous amount of authority, hiring and firing at will, whose every suggestion or order is responded to promptly and completely. This view reflects one of the greater misconceptions about the nature of executive work. The government executive may have a large grant of legal authority, but he will find that in actual fact it must be used in an economical fashion. If he lacks discrimination in the use of his power, he will debase its value and perhaps find himself

One of the arts of leadership is that of widening the sphere of acceptance of formal subordinates and, therefore, the sphere of authority of the leader.

Third, managers are subject to the authority of individuals and groups who are not members of the formal organization of the enterprise. Among these are the following:

1. *Governmental agencies: local, state, and federal.*—Government agencies impinge upon the decision-making processes of management through the adoption of constitutions or characters, the passage of legislation, the interpretation of legislation by the courts, and the action of administrative bodies. They establish the rules of the game (the institutional framework within which enterprises operate), impose restrictions, demand specific action, settle disputes, and approve certain managerial decisions before these can become effective.[2]

2. *Parties to contracts with management.*—When management enters into a contract with another party (an act involving the acceptance of the authority of another), it thereby agrees to meet certain obligations or to accept certain restrictions upon its activities.[3]

---

impotent at the moment of crucial importance" ("Notes on the Governmental Executive: His Role and His Methods," *New Horizons in Public Administration* [University, Ala.: University of Alabama Press, 1945], pp. 50ff.). See also Marshall E. Dimock, *The Executive in Action* (New York: Harper & Bros., 1945), pp. 236–240.

Charles E. Merriam has analyzed the authority relationship here under discussion primarily with reference to a government and the governed (see his *Political Power* [New York: Whittlesey House, 1934], chap. vi).

[2]See R. A. Gordon, *Business Leadership in the Large Corporation* (Washington, D. C.: Brookings Institution, 1945), chap. x.

[3]Roscoe Pound, the eminent legal scholar, implies this in the following statement: "A

3. *Monopolistic and monopsonistic economic groups.*—In those areas of economic activity where conditions of perfect competition do not exist, buyers of the enterprise's products and sellers to the enterprise of productive services are often able, through the use of monopsonistic and monopolistic power, respectively, directly to affect the behavior of managers. Among the monopsonists are consumer's organizations and large private buyers of the products of the enterprise. Among the monopolists are large suppliers of capital funds (banks, bondholders, etc.), raw materials, and labor services (unions).[4]

Because of the growing importance of unions in relation to managers, it is desirable to give additional attention to these monopolistic groups. The kinds of restrictions and the demands for particular actions which they impose upon managers are numerous.[5] And they often impose these restrictions and demands through the threat or use of coercive economic power.[6]

It has previously been stated that managers are subject to the authority of individuals who, from the formal point of view, are their own subordinates. In this case the limitations to the exercise of managerial authority are imposed by isolated individuals and informal groups. These same individuals, by joining together in unions, can impose the limitations much more effectively because of the coercive power available to strong, formal groups. Finally, in this connection, it should be pointed out that, although coercion is an important device of the union in obtaining managerial acceptance of its exercise of authority, positive inducements are also used. For example, a union may offer something of value to managers in return for an accepted limitation of managerial authority.

4. *Arbitrators.*—When managers accept arbitration as a means for the settlement of a dispute (labor or otherwise) to which the enterprise is a party, they thereby assume a role

---

contract . . . is a legal transaction in which the declared will takes the form of a promise or set of promises; in which the intent to which the law gives effect is that one of the parties shall be bound to some performance—either by way of action or abstaining from action—which the other may exact, or that each of the parties shall be bound toward the other" ("Contract," *Encyclopaedia of the Social Sciences*, Vol. IV [1930]).

[4] I recognize that these monopolists and monopsonists are often parties to contracts with management. However, managers also often become subject to their authority where contractual relationships are not involved.

[5] For examples see Neil W. Chamberlain, *The Union Challenge to Management Control* (New York: Harper & Bros., 1948), chap. iv and Appendices A–D; and Robert M. C. Littler, "Managers Must Manage," *Harvard Business Review*, XXIV (Spring, 1946), 367–370.

[6] The Labor Committee of the Twentieth Century Fund (including W. H. Davis [chairman], W. L. Chenery, H. Coonley,

C. S. Golden, S. H. Slichter, R. J. Watt, and E. E. Witte) has had this to say about the coercive elements underlying collective bargaining: "In genuine collective bargaining such an interruption [through strikes and lockouts] should be the last resort, and indeed it is, but the possibility of a strike or lockout is, nevertheless, an ever-present and controlling factor in the realistic processes of collective bargaining. Those processes lose all color of reality if the workers have not the right to reject management's offer and quit, or if management has not the right to refuse the workers' terms and close the plant. It is the overhanging pressure of this right to strike or to lockout that keeps the parties at the bargaining table and fixes the boundaries of stubbornness in the bargaining conferences" (*Strikes and Democratic Government* [New York: Twentieth Century Fund, 1947], pp. 13ff.); also see Raleigh W. Stone, "Trade Unionism in a Free Enterprise Economy," *University of Chicago Law Review*, XIV (April, 1947), 399ff.

of subordination with respect to the arbitrator.[7]

5. *Cartels, trade-associations, and other business associations.*—Enterprises often are members of one or more such business associations. Decisions are frequently made in these associations which are accepted as being authoritative by the managers of the member enterprises.

6. *The general social order.*—The decisions of managers are always subject to the general social order. Cus-

tom, tradition, convention, mores, and the like are the relevant authoritative principles; and sanctions (both positive and negative) are the factors which determine managerial acceptance or rejection of the authority.

Authority exercised by these individuals and groups, external to the enterprise, is always an extremely important factor in the direct determination of the behavior of the managers of the enterprise.[8]

---

[7]For a discussion of the degree of authority possible to an impartial umpire in labor disputes see Sumner H. Slichter, *The Challenge of Industrial Relations* (Ithaca: Cornell University Press, 1947), pp. 60ff.

[8]For an excellent discussion of the problem of managerial adaptation to these individuals and groups see Philip Selznick, "Foundations of the Theory of Organization," *American Sociological Review*, XIII (February, 1948), 25–35.

---

The next two selections are even more specific in setting forth the organizational imperatives affecting decisions.

Gordon, in an incisive analysis of the organization context of profit and price decisions, makes vividly clear the extent to which bureaucratic administration in large scale business has affected business operations. In

the second selection are set forth some of the organization imperatives affecting industrial relations decisions. The general theme of the two selections is the same. There are certain requirements of the business organization, as organization, that definitely tend to mold the decision-making patterns of executives.

---

## IMPERATIVES AFFECTING PROFIT AND PRICE DECISIONS

*Robert A. Gordon*[*]

Basically, the characteristics of large-scale professionalized business leadership . . . may affect entrepreneurial decision-making, and hence

the functioning of the economy, in either of two ways. . . . There may not be the same emphasis on maximizing profits for the firm and the stockholders, as we should expect from a proprietor running his own business.[1]

---

[*]From *Business Leadership in the Large Corporation* (Washington, D. C., 1945), pp. 326–335. Copyright by the Brookings Institution. Used by permission.

[1]Actually, two issues are involved here. Management may not seek to maximize

If this is the case, not only is the stockholder affected but, more important, the economic system does not behave entirely in accordance with the profit rules under which it is supposed to function. Secondly, even if we assume for the moment that professional managers do seek always to maximize profits, the leadership conditions under which they operate may still result in decisions significantly different from those which would have been reached under a different set of leadership conditions. For example, complexities of internal organization may prevent management from exploiting fully every profit opportunity; or the more scientific approach of professional managers may uncover investment opportunities that might have escaped the old-fashioned type of owner-entrepreneur using hit-and-miss methods.

We run into difficulties when we try to evaluate in greater detail the effects on decision-making of the leadership conditions in the large corporation. What can be said lies almost entirely in the field of conjecture; factual evidence is largely lacking; and the tendencies which seem to be at work do not all point in the same direction.

We have already stated our opinion that the goal of profit-making, while still paramount, has been weakened in the large corporation. In view of management's small ownership and the incentive system . . . it would be surprising if this were not the case. The delegation of much decision-making to specialists in the lower executive ranks, professional characteristics emphasizing security of tenure and interest in the job for its own sake, and possible pressures from nonman-

agement groups put further obstacles in the way of complete adherence to the goal of profits-maximization for the firm as a whole.

The profits criterion can never be disregarded by salaried executives. As a minimum, it is necessary to keep directors and stockholders passive.[2] Beyond this, however, the executive group may or may not seek, with every decision to be made, to enlarge profits still further. There is considerable opportunity to follow other goals. Today, executives are not likely to use extensively the criterion of maximum financial gain for themselves.[3] But they may very well adopt, at least in part, such criteria as personal position and power, the desire to see the firm larger, or even more socially desirable goals such as the welfare of workers, consumers, or other broad groups. Perhaps more important, they may seek to some extent to play safe and to avoid some of the change and uncertainty which result from assiduous pursuit of every possible opportunity to increase profits further.

To the extent that salaried executives do not take advantage of every change in profit opportunities, an additional element of inflexibility is introduced into the large corporation's responses to changing conditions—over and above the inertias normally inherent in large-scale organization. In

---

profits for the firm. Secondly, given total profits, it may divert some part of them away from stockholders. We are interested chiefly in the first of these problems.

[2]We saw . . . how impotent most stockholders are. But directors and large minority stockholders can and on occasion do intervene when profits results are particularly unsatisfactory.

[3]Today executives are prevented by law from trading in and out of their own stock on the basis of "inside" information. A minority, however, exploit their positions to secure the largest possible salary and bonus for themselves. Other opportunities for maximizing personal income also exist. In general, however, executives are much more restrained in this respect than they were before the thirties.

short, such managements are likely not to be as sensitive as they might to short-period changes, which are continually occurring in market conditions and profit expectations—price behavior and other economic variables being affected accordingly.[4] In this connection, large-scale business leadership has shown a marked tendency to concentrate upon long-term strategic considerations, particularly on maintaining the competitive and financial position of the firm. Prices may be maintained or changed, for example, not so much with the specific aim of maximizing profits over some period as to protect a competitive position over the very long run, or investment decisions may be based on a variety of financial and strategic considerations, not all of them concerned with a precise balancing of expected returns against cost.[5]

Even long-period profit calculations may be subordinated to such considerations as protecting the firm's position in the industry, plans for further growth, maintenance of a liquid position, and so on.[6]

---

[4]Insofar as directors are active, they are likely to add little if anything to making the large firm more sensitive to short-period changes in profit opportunities.

[5]Owner-managers also use such criteria where the size of their firms or other advantages give them the opportunity to do so. However, they are more likely than professional executives to link their strategy directly to some concept of maximum profits for the firm, and they are also likely to pay more attention to short-period market changes.

[6]Executives and many economists would argue that emphasis on these "strategic considerations" merely represents a far-sighted evaluation of profit opportunities over the long-term future. They would argue that maintaining or enlarging the firm's share of the market (say, through the formulation of certain price policies) was merely a way of maintaining or enlarging profits in the long

When we turn to particular types of business decisions—investment and price decisions, for example—it is not easy to assess the significance of the leadership conditions prevailing in the large corporation. If we are to have full employment, business leaders must maintain the volume of private investment, and, to make such investment possible, they must continue to pioneer —with new products, new production techniques, and so on. Is the professional business leader likely to do a better or worse job in this respect than the owner-entrepreneur? The evidence is contradictory.

Offhand, we should expect that the tendencies making toward a less dynamic type of leadership in the large corporation would have a depressing

---

run. This may be true in particular cases. But emphasis on these broad strategic considerations may also represent, consciously or subconsciously, a desire to manage a bigger firm and other motives related only indirectly to profits maximization over any period whatsoever. Further, certain non-profit criteria may come to be accepted as representing short-cut approximations to the criterion of maximum profits for the firm. Thus maintaining the firm's position in the industry may be the chief criterion used in determining price policy because this is considered the most effective way of maintaining or enlarging profits over the long run. However, these short-cut approximations tend to be accepted unthinkingly by executives and are frequently used without further consideration as to whether future profits are in fact always furthered thereby.

The need of negotiating with organized interest groups also requires the use of broad, strategic criteria which often cannot be readily translated into a quantitative effect on profits. Management's decision, for example, to accept or reject a proposal for a "closed shop" or to grant a particular wage increase may be made with a view to the "best interests of the firm," but it would be difficult indeed to translate the qualitative considerations which entered into the final decision into any clear-cut forecast of the probable effects on future profits.

effect upon the volume of private investment. Professional executives, emphasizing care and caution and reacting only imperfectly to the lure of profits, may be slow to exploit new and unfamiliar lines of activity, and even investment in familiar channels may be temporarily postponed if the risks involved seem to be substantial.[7] The desire to play safe is likely to be particularly important during depressions, but it may evidence itself during other phases of the business cycle.[8]

---

[7]It is possible, of course, that dealing with "other people's money" may lead an executive to place a lower valuation on investment risks than would an owner-entrepreneur hazarding his own capital. I have already indicated my opinion, however, that the reverse is more likely to be the case today in the large corporation. The factors making for caution and financial conservatism among salaried executives are likely to outweigh any propensity to take chances because they personally do not stand to incur the losses that may be involved.

Such lack of risk-taking leadership as may be evident in the large corporation is not confined to the executive group. Directors also show a tendency to play safe, to emphasize the state of the firm's treasury, and generally "to make decisions that will at least keep their own records clear." (*Fortune*, February 1940, p. 108.) Even more than executives, directors have personally little to gain and much to lose from approving decisions involving a high degree of risk. Among the outside interest groups discussed in earlier chapters, the considerable influence of bankers may also be exerted to restrain risk-taking investment, although the desire of some bankers for new business may on occasion lead them to press management to undertake unwise expenditures.

[8]However, the large firm does not hesitate in depressions to introduce technical improvements which lower costs but which do not involve substantial expenditures or much risk. While not necessarily involving much if any net new investment, these operating economies may put the firm in a good position to exploit new investment opportunities in the late stages of depression and to some

The bureaucratic nature of large-scale organization also tends to be a restraining factor in this respect. A substantial distance separates the chief executive from the lower ranks of the executive hierarchy, whence must come much initiation of investment decisions, and internal financial controls and the checks and balances inherent in such an organization militate against prompt exploitation of investment opportunities.

On the other hand, some characteristics of a professionalized business leadership should tend to stimulate investment.[9] The professional executive's emphasis upon industrial and commercial research has opened up investment opportunities that would have been missed by an earlier generation of business leaders. Modern management methods, emphasizing full knowledge of the facts and careful estimation of costs and prospective revenues, may uncover investment opportunities promising moderate returns that would have been overlooked by business leaders not employing such modern tools. On the other hand, more careful reckoning of probable costs and returns may lead the professional execu-

---

extent may offset the lack of risk-taking initiative mentioned in the text.

[9]Of course the mere size of big business, apart from the nature of its management, creates a situation favorable to investment. The size and financial resources of a large firm mean that risks can be spread; no single undertaking need involve a very large part of the concern's capital; and hence the "marginal value" of the funds tied up in a given investment is less than to a smaller concern. The large firm also will have more ready access to the capital markets, and at lower cost, than the smaller concern; its cash and credit resources permit it to undertake projects beyond the financial means of the smaller company; and it can utilize financial procedures and devices which the small firm cannot so readily employ.

tive to reject investment possibilities that the old-fashioned entrepreneur might have accepted because of the possibilities of large gain if the venture succeeded at all. The profit-receiving entrepreneur is likely to over-value small probabilities of large returns.

Long-range planning and the professional executive's ability to ignore to some extent short-run profits expectations may lead to the undertaking of some long-run projects that might not have been made if attention had been concentrated on short-run problems. Further . . . the urge for greater personal power and prestige and the tendency to identify himself with his enterprise may lead the professional executive to continue expansion even in the face of declining profits prospects.

This urge to expand may result in some maldistribution of investment in the economy as a whole. Frequently cited in this connection is the supposed tendency of large-scale corporate managements to retain an undue share of earnings in their enterprises. If retention of earnings goes so far as to bring the rate of profit on further increments of investment in a particular firm below what could be earned by stockholders through investment in other directions, capital is not being ideally allocated.[10] There is probably a tendency in this direction among the managements of American corporations.[11]

But the tendency may be no stronger than among many owner-entrepreneurs, whose devotion to their firms may lead them to continue to plow back earnings (or even to invest new capital) when larger returns could be secured elsewhere.

What is the net effect of these conflicting tendencies upon the volume of new investment—in particular firms and in the economy as a whole? It is impossible to say in the absence of more indication as to the relative weight to be attached to the various factors mentioned. It is clear, however, that professionalized business leaders in the large corporation do not necessarily make the same investment decisions as would an owner-entrepreneur confronted with the same set of underlying conditions.[12] It is also clear

---

[10]Obviously, retention of earnings in the business does not mean that real investment necessarily increases correspondingly. The "reinvested" earnings may go, in some part, into increases in cash or securities or into purchases of existing rather than new fixed assets and inventory.

[11]See N. S. Buchanan, "Theory and Practice of Dividend Distribution," *Quarterly Journal of Economics*, Vol. 53 (1938), pp. 64ff.; also by the same writer, *The Eco-*

*nomics of Corporate Enterprise*, Chap. 9. Various other writers have questioned the advisability and profitability of reinvestment of earnings on the scale practiced by many American corporations, and they have also called attention to the non-financial incentives which may lead corporate managements to reinvest earnings. As Buchanan points out ("Theory and Practice of Dividend Distribution," pp. 71ff.), it is practically impossible to test statistically the profit results which ensue from reinvestment of earnings.

[12]The owner-entrepreneur of a small concern, of course, would never be confronted with exactly the same set of underlying conditions as would the management of a large enterprise. The former would be much more restricted by his market environment, he would not have the same set of technical and financial resources, and so on. (See, for example, note 9, above.) From this point of view, the contrast in the text is unrealistic. Nonetheless, it is significant and needs to be made. . . . Nearly all economic reasoning about our private enterprise system proceeds by asking what action a profit-maximizing owner-entrepreneur would take if he were faced with a particular set of underlying conditions. The purpose of our analysis is to show that the answers thus obtained are not necessarily the correct ones if the decisions

that certain characteristics of large-scale professionalized leadership tend to restrain the free flow of investment and innovating decisions. Anything done to remove or offset them would tend to stimulate the volume of private investment.

Similar uncertainty surrounds the question as to whether these tendencies accentuate or mitigate the instability inherent in the economic system. The effects on economic stability of some of the factors mentioned in the preceding pages are not altogether clear; and where the effects are obvious, we do not know to what extent the conflicting tendencies offset each other.[13]

We may feel somewhat more confident about our knowledge of the probable effects on price-making of the leadership conditions characteristic of the large corporation. In making their price decisions, corporation executives (consciously or unconsciously) undoubtedly follow in part other goals in addition to that of profit maximization. And even to the extent

---

are in fact made by professional managers operating in a particular type of leadership organization and reacting to the array of incentives that we have described.

[13]For example, conservatism and careful planning should result in the professional business leader's avoiding some of the excesses of boom periods and should thus mitigate the effects of subsequent depressions. On the other hand, tendencies toward reinvestment of earnings and overexpansion and toward avoiding risk-taking in depression may have the opposite effect. Some inflexibility in the large firm's responses to changing conditions may accentuate maladjustments and tend to lengthen or deepen depressions. Further, the professional managers of our largest firms seem to be as susceptible as any owner-entrepreneur to waves of optimism, although we should expect the professional manager's scientific approach, his increasing familiarity with economic processes, and his tendency to take a long-run view of things to exercise a mitigating influence on the cycle. Schumpeter has called attention to the fact that in the large corporation economic progress and the entrepreneur's innovating function tend to become depersonalized and automatized. (See Schumpeter, *Capitalism, Socialism, and Democracy*, pp. 132–33; also his *Business Cycles*, Vol. I, pp. 96, 108–09.) We have given some indication of the extent to which this is true. Following Schumpeter's analysis, the "routinizing" of the innovating func-

tion and growth of large-scale enterprise (his "Trustified Capitalism") should significantly modify the factors giving rise to business cycles. (*Business Cycles*, Vol. I, pp. 96–97, 108–09, 144–45; also *The Theory of Economic Development*, pp. 230, 253.) Presumably, in an economy of very large concerns under professional managements, innovations would be introduced more continuously than in an economy of small concerns; the process of adaptation would go on in part within individual firms and to that extent would not necessarily involve the serious competitive readjustments he envisages; very large firms can and do react to a new situation in ways different from small concerns which have less power to manipulate their environments; there would generally be less resistance to new ways of doing things, and hence the innovations would presumably be carried through more quickly and with less serious repercussions on the economy. Actually, so far as I can see, cyclical disturbances are not less severe today than they were when the very large firm was not particularly important, and waves of innovating and adapting investment show up in the very large as well as in the smaller concern. Professor Schumpeter does not think the giant firm yet covers a large enough sector of the economy to make his theoretical structure inapplicable, but in light of our findings . . . we cannot agree with him in this. However, the fact that the large firm modifies his explanation of the way in which business cycles occur does not imply that wide cyclical fluctuations might not also occur in a world of large corporations, although in a different way. It is interesting to note that Schumpeter suggests that increasing familiarity of businessmen with the cycle, along with "trustification," is "the chief reason why the real crisis phenomena . . . are becoming weaker." *The Theory of Economic Development*, p. 253.

that the profits goal is adhered to, executives will not necessarily make the same price decisions as would an owner-entrepreneur in the same circumstances.

We have noted the leeway that executives have in adhering to the profits criterion. In view of this and the tendency of large-scale leadership to emphasize strategic considerations such as the firm's position in the industry, prices are certain not to be altered with every change in market conditions and profits expectations. These tendencies making for price inflexibility are strengthened by the probable disinclination of professionalized business leaders to pioneer in the field of price changes, particularly in view of the low level within management at which much initiation of price decisions takes place and the inertias and inflexibilities which result from the complexities of internal organization in large firms. In general, the leadership conditions created by the large corporation make for inflexible rather than flexible prices and for some dissociation of price-making from changes in costs and demand.

Important price decisions are likely to be group decisions, in the making of which various individuals and departments participate. In the large firm, data regarding costs and demand "are not ordinarily transmuted into an entrepreneurial decision through a single mind guided by a total view of the situation; rather they are interpreted by various interests and emerge as a group decision influenced in important ways by the internal organization of the firm in question." Rules-of-thumb and formal procedures determine at what levels and by whom different sorts of price decisions are made; this in turn affects significantly the range of considerations likely to

be taken into account in making these decisions.[14]

Of course the competitive conditions surrounding large-scale industry, entirely apart from the question of leadership organization and incentives, profoundly affect the executive's price decisions. In considering pricing in the large firm, however, we need to take into account the leadership factors mentioned as well as such matters as company size, degree of concentration in the industry, extent of product differentiation, and other factors not directly concerned with leadership organization and personnel which are ordinarily cited in this connection.

The reader may care to examine for himself the possible effects of these leadership conditions upon other fields of decision-making. In each case, account must be taken of considerations discussed in the preceding pages. How important these factors will be depends on a variety of circumstances.

---

[14]For discussion of some of the issues raised in this and the preceding paragraph, see *Cost Behavior and Price Policy,* prepared by the Committee on Price Determination for the Conference on Price Research (National Bureau of Economic Research, 1943), pp. 18–19, 43–47, 272–274. The quotation in the text is from p. 47 of this volume. Other factors not mentioned in the text and which cannot be fully examined here might also affect the price-making of professional executives. One of these is the professional business leader's increasing desire for knowledge concerning the nature of his costs and of the demand for his product.

The need for a more dynamic type of price-making in large-scale enterprise is examined in E. G. Nourse and H. B. Drury, *Industrial Price Policies and Economic Progress,* and by E. G. Nourse in *Price-Making in a Democracy.* Both of these volumes consider some of the problems of internal organization and external relations of the large firm with which the present study is concerned.

But given the latitude which the large corporation in any event enjoys in determining its course of action, its leadership setup—particularly its incentive system and its method of delegating and specializing decision-making—will in many cases significantly affect the kinds of decisions made and the consequent functioning of the affected parts of the economic system.

## IMPERATIVES AFFECTING INDUSTRIAL RELATIONS DECISIONS

### Robert Dubin*

There are important imperatives arising out of the organization of business itself which affect decisions concerning industrial relations. These organizational imperatives deserve serious study. They profoundly influence the kind and timing of decisions made in collective bargaining by business managers.

Immediate expediencies and the compromises of collective power relations determine much of what happens in union-management relations. Yet, within the context of this rapidly shifting relationship, it is possible to detect repeating uniformities, some of which are directly attributable to the requirements of business organizations.

#### GOVERNING BY RULES

In a large company with multiple plant operations the most obvious single consideration affecting labor relations decisions is the need for standardization and uniformity. Un-questionably, the administration of a work force of several hundred thousand, or fifty thousand, or even five thousand is a staggering job. It would be totally impracticable to attempt individualized treatment of so many workers. The almost nostalgic plea for the "clinical" approach,[1] that is, for the setting-forth of "all the facts" in every employee problem, is hardly possible in the large-scale enterprise.[2] This is not to say that it would not be desirable or humane to treat each worker as an individual. The emphasis is rather on the fact that administration in the big firm necessitates standardization through rules and uniform procedures as a basis for prediction of future events. Management must be in a position to predict what will be the outcome, granting a given personnel situation. Similarly, employees are provided with a basis for predicting the effect of their own action or that of management representatives in the light of the rules governing their relationship to each other.

*From "Decision-making by Management in Industrial Relations," *American Journal of Sociology*, 54:292–296 (Jan. 1949). Used by permission of The University of Chicago Press.

[1]Cf. B. M. Selekman, *Labor Relations and Human Relations* (New York: McGraw-Hill Book Co., 1947), chap. v.
[2]See, e.g., P. Pigors and C. A. Myers, *Personnel Administration* (New York: McGraw-Hill Book Co., 1947), chap. v.

The "reign of rules" is the administrative answer to the problems of governing in large-scale organizations. This rule-making habit is all-pervading. It takes its most obvious form in shop rules governing personal conduct and in the union agreement which sets forth the mutual rights and obligations of the contracting parties and their constituents. But job descriptions, production standards, standard procedures, wage-rate structures, and policy manuals are rule-making, too. Even a casual examination of the manuals of procedures, operating codes, standards, and specifications to be found in most any industrial or commercial firm should be convincing evidence that rule-making and enforcing for the class rather than decision-making in the individual case plays an increasing role in the functions of the executive.

There is an interesting paradox involved in the growth of governing by rule in large businesses. The goal of standardization and hence of predictability is certainly achieved. But making the rule for the class rather than the individual does two things to the individual worker. He becomes aware of his personal inability to make an individual "deal" for himself outside the company rules and procedures, except under the circumstances of a "lucky break." He tends also to view himself as part of a group of similarly situated fellow-employees who are defined by the rules as being like each other.

In addition, uniform rule-making and administration of the rules makes unionism easier and, in a sense, inevitable. It should be reasonably clear that collective bargaining is joint rule-making. It is no great step to the joint determination by union and management of rules governing employment from the determination of them by management alone. Both proceed from the basic assumption that generally applicable rules are necessary to govern the relations between men in the plant. . . .

The paradox stands out clearly. Governing men by general rules in a business makes for administrative efficiency. At the same time it is likely to assist the growth of unionism, if not make it inevitable. The question is then raised as to how much efficiency in decision-making is lost through collective bargaining as over against decision-making solely through the management structure.

This paradox is not the sole result of governing by rules. In a company which bargains with a single union for many plants, as General Motors does with the U.A.W.-C.I.O., company-wide bargaining reinforces the existing tendencies toward standardization. From the union standpoint a gain or loss made in the contract is shared by all members of the bargaining unit in all plants of the company. From the company standpoint a master-contract is necessary lest bargaining in the individual plant should result in local gains which would then be pressed by the union for application throughout the company. The company seeks to protect itself from such whipsaw tactics with a master-contract, standardized for all company bargaining units.

A second result of governing by rules is centralization in decision-making on industrial relations problems. It is clear that high-level decisions are required for broadly applicable rules. Personnel and collective bargaining policies tend to be applied generally throughout the organization. The decisions affecting them gravitate to a central point, less and less discretion being permitted to the local or department management. Thus, General Motors, with a highly developed theory of decentralized management, has perfected centralized control in the industrial relations field—even individual job rates negotiated locally must be reviewed and approved in Detroit before becoming effective.

What, then, are the organization imperatives affecting industrial relations decisions which can be related to size of firm? We can expect uncoordinated decisions dealing, case by case, with individual workers to be replaced by rules which apply impartially to classes of employees. The real decision-making power and skill are involved in establishing the rules. Their administration tends to be reduced to mechanical formula or may even be permitted to go completely outside the company structure by the settlement of disputes by umpires or arbitrators. In addition, centralized decision-making is generally associated with standardized rules. Unionism is both an effective means for worker intervention in company rule-making as well as a force amplifying the tendency for centralized management decision-making.

What the union regards as the "buck-passing" sometimes displayed by lower-level supervisors and executives is, in reality, logical behavior in a system of centralized decision-making. In addition, the slowness with which systems of rules are permitted to change through collective bargaining or administrative decision is a product of the cohesion of the rule systems and the internal logic which binds the rules into systems. . . .

## THE RULE-MAKING PROCESSES

A business is characterized by a high degree of organization. This is exemplified in the formal organization chart and the minute functional divisions of work. A consequence of the complicated structure of a firm is its sensitivity to changes in operations; indeed, the very existence of an individual business may depend upon its ability to adjust to changing conditions affecting operations.

It is typical for a business to operate on a crisis basis. There are always problems, either internal or external, whose solution requires constant choices among several courses of action. Conscious and explicit decisions are repeatedly being made throughout the company which solve immediate problems. Such problems arise constantly in all phases of the business. Generally minimized in a business are the areas in which common understandings and traditional solutions to problems are prevalent. The "new" and "novel," the "better" way of doing it, "bigger" and "better" products, are commonly used adjectives reflecting the premium placed upon change. But change resulting from meeting crises in the business is not given unlimited range.

Decisions affecting the firm are made in the light of a body of policy and practice already in existence. This provides a practical limit on the extent to which innovations can be incorporated into the operating creed of the business. Moreover, decision-making areas have different degrees of susceptibility to change. In the fields of production processes and methods engineering, changes which produce greater efficiency or lower costs are constantly being sought. The highest premium on change is probably in those areas. The same is true of the sales field and advertising. In the area of industrial relations or personnel management changes may be accepted much more reluctantly. In fact, the objective of management policy may be stability rather than change.

Within particular areas of decision there is a tendency toward consistency in policy. This consistency may be seen in two ways: (1) decisions making changes from established policy or practice are tested and generally brought into alignment with (or necessitate a change in) the existing body of procedure and policy; and (2) in putting the change into practice organizational realignments may be necessary. In any event, the very segregation of areas of decision from each other creates an imperative only for consistency within rather than between areas. Sometimes one of the most difficult functions of the key management decision-makers is to resolve conflicts in policy or practice between areas of business operations. For example, the sales department may insist on a particular design of the product because of its consumer appeal. The production people argue against the design on grounds of difficulty or expense of manufacture. Both groups are right and consistent within their respective areas of operation. When the choice is finally made, it will represent a tactical defeat and not a defeat in principle to the losing group. The loser would urge the same course under similar circumstances in the future.

This point has an important bearing on decision-making in industrial relations. Observers have often been struck by what appears to be an abandonment of strict business thinking in certain decisions about labor relations. For example, very severe financial risks may be accepted in pursuit of a labor policy—witness the year-long strike at the J. I. Case Company after the war which practically halted production and sales during most of the period of the strike. A decision to risk such a lengthy interruption in sales, if based upon considerations of production or raw materials or design, would certainly be viewed with skepticism. But a decision leading to the same result in labor relations was judged on quite other grounds than its influence on profit and loss. What such an instance illustrates is that policy formation on labor issues can readily proceed from premises unlike those behind other business decisions. Management decisions in the field of industrial relations are not always characterized by the logic of the market.

The characteristic of specialized areas of decision following the functional division of labor is common to all organization. It represents a feature of bureaucracy in which the job-holder succeeds in making his job self-contained and as independent as possible of all other jobs. The "let George do it" attitude, when found in a firm, is an excellent index that George operates in a separate compartment of business action and decision, recognized as discrete by both himself and his fellow-workers. Contrariwise, emphasis on "coordination" or "integration" or "rationalization" in the business firm is another evidence of concern with over-specialization of action and decision.

The officials responsible for accounting or production or personnel come to think in terms of their professional specialization within a framework peculiar to their own line of work. As the ideas unique to a specialty become more specialized, associates in other departments of the firm are more inclined to stay out of the area of the specialist, partly because they are no longer familiar with his frame of reference or comfortable with his jargon. The specialist follows the logic of his specialty and tends to bring his actions and decisions into conformity with it. The segregation of industrial relations as a separate field of business activity has resulted in the designation of distinct functionaries and the rise of outside paid consultants. The specialization, however, does not insure a broad consensus regarding a frame of reference for industrial relations men. What, then, is the basis for the logical system within which the individual industrial relations executive operates?

An industrial relations specialist typically does not have firsthand knowledge of production processes and plant operations. His knowledge is about people and the operations of hiring, placement, training, promotion, layoff, discharge, retirement, etc. All these processing operations are standardized and of general application. They are most easily controlled through general rules. Again we come

back to the question of rule-making, but this time in terms of specific policy problems rather than as previously considered in terms of the broad movement toward governing by rules. It is one of the important advisory functions of the industrial relations specialist to emphasize to line officials the need for hewing to the line of shop rules, company policy, and the union agreement.

The logic of the industrial relations specialists can then best be characterized as a preoccupation with the internal consistency of rules, procedures, and operations concerning the processing of groups of people within a company. Increasing separation from production and operations has tended to divorce many of the decisions of policy in industrial relations from production decisions, whether the labor decisions are made directly by the industrial relations specialist or by top executives on his advice.

---

When behavioral scientists encounter a widespread phenomenon, they are likely to ask: "If this behavior occurs so frequently, it must make some contribution to society. What contribution does it make?" In this vein the political scientist Lindblom has analyzed "muddling through" as an essential feature of organizational decision-making. He is probably right that many decisions are made on a muddling-through basis.

In the next selection Dror points out

some significant limitations of muddling through as a basis for decision. One of his important points is that there is a sharp discontinuity between the past and the future when genuine innovation is attempted. This is true whether the emphasis is on policy, technology, or procedure. "Muddling through" guarantees continuity with past policy or practice, and is therefore especially inappropriate for developing innovative decisions.

---

## "MUDDLING THROUGH"—SCIENCE OR INERTIA

### *Yehezkel Dror**

In a much-quoted article published in the *Public Administration Review* in 1959, Charles E. Lindblom put forth a brilliant justification of policy and decision making through "muddling through," that is, through incremental change aimed at arriving at agreed-upon policies which are closely based on past experience.[1] As developed and expanded in other articles,[2] he presents a well-considered theory fully geared to the actual experience of practicing administrators and well designed to reinforce their actual behavior patterns by giving them the blessings of scientific approval.

Indeed, there can be no doubt that in comparison with the "rational-comprehensive" models of decision making commonly accepted in management sciences and their related disciplines, Lindblom's approach constitutes a very valuable contribution. It is more closely tied to reality, a more sophisticated theory, and more adjusted to human nature. Nevertheless, the question must be asked whether the favorable evaluation of "incremental change" and "muddling through" (in the sense of policy making through successive limited comparisons) does not, in some respects, constitute a dangerous overreaction.

More specifically, it is necessary to reexamine the "Science of 'Muddling Through'" thesis both in respect to its inherent validity and its potential impact on actual policy making and decision making practices. The possibilities for constructing a mixed optimum model of policy making, superior to both the "muddling through" and "rational-comprehensive" ones, also requires attention, especially because of the neglect of such a possibility in the professional literature.

### CONDITIONS LIMITING THE VALIDITY OF THE "SCIENCE OF 'MUDDLING THROUGH'" THESIS

Conceding the many penetrating insights in Lindblom's paper, there may nevertheless be a critical examination of two main elements of the "Science of 'Muddling Through'" thesis, namely the incremental nature of desired changes in policy, and agreement on policy as the criterion of its quality.

The basic strategy of incremental change, as stated by Lindblom, is one

---

*Reprinted by permission from *Public Administration Review*, 24:153–157 (September, 1964).
[1] See Charles E. Lindblom, "The Science of 'Muddling Through,'" 19 *Public Administration Review*, 79–88 (Spring, 1959). Unless otherwise noted, quotations from Lindblom included in the present paper are taken from that article.
[2] See especially Charles E. Lindblom, "Policy Analysis," 48 *American Economic Review*, 298–312 (June, 1958), and Albert O. Hirschman and Charles E. Lindblom, "Economic Development, Research and Development, Policy Making: Some Converging Views," 7 *Behavioral Science*, 211–222 (April 1962). Both these papers are more careful in their conclusions than "The Science of 'Muddling Through,'" both recognizing some limitations inherent in the method of "change through incremental comparison" and its locality-bound assumptions. In a recent book Lindblom further develops his ideas, but without changing this basic rationale. See David Braybrooke and Charles E. Lindblom, *A Strategy of Decision* (The Free Press, 1963).

of maximizing security in making change. All reliable knowledge being based on the past, the only way to proceed without risk is by continuing in the same direction, limiting consideration of alternative policies "to those policies that differ in relatively small degrees from policies presently in effect."[3] This is sound advice, provided certain conditions obtain—a requirement not adequately faced by Lindblom.

Unless three closely interrelated conditions are concurrently met, incremental change by "successive limited comparison" is not an adequate method for policy making. *These three essential conditions are: (1) the results of present policies must be in the main satisfactory (to the policy makers and the social strata on which they depend), so that marginal changes are sufficient for achieving an acceptable rate of improvements in policy results; (2) there must be a high degree of continuity in the nature of the problems; (3) there must be a high degree of continuity in the available means for dealing with problems.*

When the results of past policies are undesirable, it is often preferable to take the risks involved in radical new departures. For instance, in newly developing states aspiring to accelerated socio-economic development, the policies followed by the former colonial policy makers clearly do not constitute an acceptable basis to be followed with only incremental change. Similarly, in modern countries when changes in values make formerly accepted policy-results unacceptable, radical departures in policy are required despite the risk, for instance in respect to the segregation problem in the United States.

When there are no past policies in respect to a discrete policy-issue, incremental change is in fact impossible. For instance, many of the problems faced during the New Deal had novel characteristics, making most policies (other than doing nothing) a radical departure from the past.

Changes in knowledge—technological and behavioral—put at the disposal of policy makers new means of action, which, unless ignored, lead to radically new policies. The best illustrations are provided in military technology, where "incremental change" results in the often noted tendency of a nation's armed forces to be excellently prepared for the last war. Similar illustrations can be cited in most spheres of social action where innovations in knowledge take place, such as medicine (policy making in regard to smoking) and education (utilization of programmed teaching machines).

The three conditions essential to the validity of the "muddling through" thesis are most likely to prevail where there is a high degree of social stability. Under conditions of stability, routine is often the best policy, and, change being at a slow rate, incremental policy-change is often optimal. But, even in the most stable societies, many of today's qualitatively most important problems are tied up with high speed changes in levels of aspirations, the nature of issues, and the available means of action, and requires therefore, a policy making method different from "muddling through."[4]

---

[3]Lindblom, "The Science of 'Muddling Through,'" p. 84.

[4]In his "Policy Analysis," *ibid.*, Lindblom explicitly recognizes that his analysis applies to the United States and other "stable, well-established, deeply rooted democracies" (p. 30). But he fails to pursue this limitation and does not realize that there is today no country, including the United States, "stable" enough to fit his analysis.

A similar conclusion may be reached from examination of the reliance on agreement on policy as the criterion of the policy's quality. Under conditions of stability, when all relevant parties have a more or less clear image of the expected results of a certain policy, with a high correlation of subjective and objective probability, a policy agreed upon will ordinarily involve little risk of catastrophe; also, under such conditions, it is in fact much easier to agree on a discrete policy than on abstract goals. In contrast, under conditions of high rate change, ignorance can produce agreement upon a catastrophic policy; under such conditions, moreover, it is often much easier to agree on abstract or operational goals (e.g., "raising the standard of living," "increase net per capita product by 2% annually") than on policies, there being no background of shared experience to serve as a basis for consensus on policy. Lest the reader reach the conclusion that these comments apply only to new developing countries, let him consider military policy, where decisions agreed upon by experienced military personnel were rejected following their dissection by McNamara's "whiz kids."

The formula that "agreement" equals "high quality" is the more dangerous because of its appeal to a value highly regarded in democratic ideology, as attested to by the abundance of "administration by consent" literature. It is, therefore, highly necessary to emphasize that agreement should follow examination of the consequences of policy and not be substituted for it, in all save the most familiar and stable policy areas.

The conclusion is inescapable, therefore, that the "Science of 'Muddling Through'" thesis has limited validity. It may be more valid for a larger number of policy areas in a relatively stable society, such as the United States, than in countries engaged in high rate directed social change. But even in the United States many of the most critical policy problems involve factors changing at a high rate of speed.

---

There is abroad in the land general knowledge about the new super-science employing mathematical models and computer technologies in decision-making. No modern executive or administrator can avoid being caught up in discussions of this newest era in scientific management. It is therefore necessary for you to have a sensible and detailed enough knowledge of the new science of decision-making so that you can employ it intelligently in your own executive and administrative practices.

The following selection is a brief but excellent summary of this field. It is especially noteworthy because of the constant emphasis upon the need for thinking through a model before any of the mathematical technologies can be applied to it. Indeed, if the new scientific methods are to be employed meaningfully, then work of the executive is increased, for it is upon his thinking through the objectives to be achieved and the variables influencing their achievement that adequate mathematical models can be constructed. This selection is designed for the use of the executive and because of that gets right down to the central issues involved in utilizing mathematics for decision-making. You will find this particularly useful because it establishes the proper relationship between the thought and effort necessary to define a problem and the mathematical technologies available for its solution.

## HOW USEFUL ARE "SCIENTIFIC" TOOLS OF MANAGEMENT?

*Edward F. R. Hearle**

During the past few years, considerable attention has been focused on "scientific" tools of management. The quotation marks usually placed around the word *scientific* in this context suggest some uncertainty as to whether the normal attributes of science apply to these tools. But the intimation of "science" suggests we suspect that these tools have qualities different from the traditional judgment or wisdom that administrators have always exercised in management decisions. These "scientific" qualities are explicitness, rigor, and quantification. None of these qualities is new to administration. There is, in fact, a historical and inevitable trend toward increasing the proportion of these three ingredients in the management process. Accounting, budgeting, work measurement have all been efforts—tools—to replace the hunch with more explicitness, rigor, and quantification. What are these newer tools which take us another step toward greater management precision?

The titles are dazzling: linear and dynamic programming, queuing theory, game theory, simulation, and monte carlo, to name a few. The dominant characteristic which is common to all of these tools is that they are efforts toward an accurate representation of some part of the world: a reflection, a *model*. *Model* is the single word most descriptive of the newer so-called scientific tools of management.

### CONSTRUCTING A MODEL

For this discussion, a model may be defined simply as a symbolic representation of a problem to be studied. The problem may be a process, an organization, or an operation. In each of these, the significant elements and the relationships between them are represented symbolically—in numbers and letters. This representation is generally in algebraic notation. Constructing a model usually involves the following steps, each of which describes a component of the real world problem being studied:

1. Identification of the variables that are significant to the problem under study. In a simple inventory control model such variables could include the items in the inventory, the demand for each, and the costs of purchasing and holding them.
2. Specification of the relationships among the variables. In an urban

---

*Reprinted by permission from *Public Administration Review*, 21:206–209 (Autumn, 1961).

analysis model one such relationship might be that there are 1.3 cars per single family residence.

3. Specification of the objectives and the criteria by which progress toward achievement of these objectives may be measured. Since several objectives are often present, relative weights may be assigned to each. . . .

4. Specification of restrictions or constraints that are present, including uncertainties. Such constraints could be capacity limitations, or prohibitions against utilizing over-time or exceeding a specified budget. They could also be "value" judgments about the limits within which policies can operate. Uncertainties are generally expressed as probabilities.

A moment's reflection suggests that these steps are not unique—managers follow them implicitly in making decisions every day. But in formulating them in the structure of a model, these steps must be expressed in *explicit* and *quantitative* terms. The "science" is not in the identification of these factors—it is in the manner of their *expression* and *manipulation*. This point cannot be too strongly stressed. Decisions about what variables are relevant require human judgment coupled with careful empiricism. Relationships, objectives, constraints, and the numerical parameters of each: none of these is inherent in the tools. The tools are used to manipulate the factors according to formal, rigorous rules.

### THE NEED FOR EXPLICIT STATEMENT OF OBJECTIVES

Consider two examples of what explication and quantification mean in real problems. Take the case of the ever-present uncertainty in many management decisions—some things are just not known or cannot be precisely predicted. So we may say "the chances of this happening are about even." In a model we must specify, on the other hand, that the probability is .5 or .6 or .4—still our "judgment" but explicitly expressed.

Of special importance in model construction is the explicit statement of objectives and criteria. . . . Using this objective, plus data as to demands for service, resources, and constraints, a model can be used to determine and test the cost of alternative policies to achieve the objective.

### THE PROBLEM DETERMINES THE TOOL EMPLOYED

Throughout the process of explicitly stating and assigning numerical values to relevant variables, their relationships, objectives, and constraints, the properties of the tools to be used in solving the problem thus described must be kept in mind. All of these tools are models; that is, they are designed to represent symbolically observable characteristics and relationships in the real world. Because different characteristics and relationships exist in the world, the tools are designed to solve different kinds of problems. Some of the tools are deterministic or exact for dealing with problems or parts of problems that exhibit this behavior. Others deal with problems where uncertainties are present and explicitly recognized. In the following listing the more exact tools are described first.

*Linear programming* is a technique for optimally allocating specified resources to meet certain objectives subject to specific restrictions. "Optimum" can be measured in terms of the minimization or maximization of a specified criterion such as dollars of cost or units of time. Linear means that the relationships between the variables are expressed in first degree equations. Linear programming has been used with considerable success in solving such management problems as minimizing transportation, improving personnel assignments, and locating retail stores.

*Dynamic programming* is designed to solve problems that have many stages, often measured in time intervals. It takes into account the effect changes made during prior stages have on the present stage, thus reflecting the dynamic character of many management processes. Dynamic programming can be useful in dealing with such problems as estimating changes in the traffic flow on a road system brought about by a progressive opening of additional highways.

*Queuing theory models* are concerned with the waiting line problem. Waiting lines "queue up" in banks, unemployment claim offices, court cases, even in correspondence awaiting reply. The problem is either too long a line—indicating insufficient facilities to handle demand—or excessive facilities standing idle. Time is the major dimension, and queuing models deal with the randomness with which the events occur which require the use of the facilities. They operate to find the optimum balance between the cost of facilities and the costs associated with delays caused by the "queue."

*Game theory* involves the choice of strategies in a competitive situation. Probability plays a large role, but the major characteristic of game theory is the presence in the model of a rational opponent. A primary strategy in game theory is based on the minimax princi-

ple. Minimax is designed to hold to a minimum the maximum loss one can suffer in a competitive situation. . . .

*Simulation* models are designed to deal with problems where the analytic tools described above cannot adequately or realistically handle the interrelationships and complexities which are in fact present. Simulation models take specified variables and specified rules about their relationships and calculate from these the numerical result of alternative ways of solving the problem. Simulation is not designed primarily to produce the optimum answer. It narrows the alternatives and identifies the consequences of particular policies. This characteristic has led to simulations in which persons participate by providing human choice of one of the alternatives specified at various points by the model. This technique is also being widely used in management training programs to illustrate the effects of specific decisions in particular business situations.

In simulation and gaming models, *monte carlo* methods are often used to approximate unpredictable real world situations under study. By numerous random draws from probability distributions, monte carlo models are able to reflect the inexact behavior of the operation involved by approximating actual experience in a compressed time period. Monte carlo methods might, for example, be part of models which represent such unpredictable situations as the occurrence of fires.

## WHAT GOOD ARE THE TOOLS?

This has been a very simplified description of some major characteristics of several newer tools of management. An important question still remains: what is achieved by the use of the formal mathematics which the analytic tools involve? First, the reliability of mathematical rigor is obtained in solving the problem described by the model. Human wisdom is remarkable but not perfect in solving problems. We do forget; we are inconsistent. To the extent of our forgetfulness or inconsistency, our decisions are deficient. The logical consistency of mathematical rigor is strong in these areas where human decision making often is weak.

Second, models and the tools associated with them provide a reliable means of testing out the consequences of alternative actions open to management. The need for costly trial and error in the real world can therefore be reduced. For example, if our police chief is satisfied with a twelve-minute response time, this number can be "plugged into" the model in place of ten. The model will then show the precise effect of a different policy on all other phases of the operation included in the model, and we can be certain of the cause-effect relationship. These tools therefore both provide solutions to specific problems and furnish a structure which enables the human decision maker to improve his performance because he is better able to see the ingredients and consequences of his actions.

This does not mean that these tools are suitable for solving all management problems. Far from it. Generally, the problems for which spectacular solutions have been found are relatively small problems where the relevant variables, objectives, and constraints could be clearly identified. And even in simple problems there is the ever-present danger that the abstraction and simplification which the

model usually involves will excessively dilute reality. If a model poorly represents the problem, the mathematically precise answer may be totally irrelevant and misleading. Accurate description is a prerequisite to correct solution. Futhermore, these tools do not deal with some of the more exciting parts of the total management process —such as building support for a program.

However, the value of these tools to management is considerable and lies in those qualities that we earlier said characterized them: explicitness, rigor, and quantification. The discipline of explication forces clear thinking. Rigor guarantees logical consistency. Quantification demands data we often fail to gather and reveals values we recognize but seldom specify. Many an inconsistent objective and many a fuzzy criterion has been revealed in the process of building a model.

Administrators should therefore set themselves two objectives with respect to these tools. First, to become familiar with formulating problems in the explicit symbolism of the model, striving to make goals and criteria fully explicit even if the explication is a little forced. Second, to become generally familiar with the mathematical properties of these tools so that real world problems suitable for solutions by their use can be recognized. Such problems do exist; resource allocations must be made, waiting line delays must be dealt with, competitive strategies must be selected. Both the form and the substance of the scientific tools of management can make a substantial contribution to the solution of these and other problems of public administration.

We should now have clearly established the first three purposes of this chapter: we have examined the decision-making processes in the context of organization; we have dealt, with some considerable elaboration, with the environment of decisions; we have also looked at several technologies for making decisions. There remains the final task of examining the possibility of sharing decision-making with subordinates.

By a broad extension of the decision-making processes, Tannenbaum and Massarik find the possibility of limited participation by subordinates. But note that subordinates never make the actual decision. The authors say that making the decision is the manager's task. Subordinates can suggest alternatives and point out the consequences of each. To that extent they participate in preparing for the decision.

If our analysis has been reliable up to now, this conclusion makes sense based upon our knowledge of authority and of subordination as it relates to authority. A level of authority is a level of the organization at which relevant decisions are made. If subordinates are included in the decision-making, or if they make the decision, and it is a legitimate one, the authority attached to making that decision automatically moves down to their organizational level. This is what we mean by delegation of authority. But delegation of authority and sharing in decision-making at a higher level of authority are two entirely different things. Inadvertently, the sharing of decision-making might turn out to be a covert form of delegation of authority. There is no meaningful sense of sharing decision-making with subordinates except in the special way suggested in the next selection:

---

## SHARING DECISION-MAKING WITH SUBORDINATES

### *Robert Tannenbaum* and *Fred Massarik**

Decisions are made by managers in order to organize, direct, or control responsible subordinates to the end that all service contributions be coordinated in the attainment of an enterprise purpose.[1] Since managers are those who accomplish results through subordinates, the latter are always directly and intimately affected by managerial decisions and therefore may have a considerable interest in them. Because of this possible interest, subordinates may have a strong desire, particularly in a nation with deeply-ingrained democratic traditions, to participate in the determination of matters affecting them. It is of importance, therefore, to consider the form which such participation might assume.

*From "Participation by Subordinates in the Managerial Decision-making Process," *Canadian Journal of Economics and Political Science,* 16:410–413, 416–418 (Aug. 1950). Used by permission of the *Journal* and of its publishers, the University of Toronto Press.
[1]See Tannenbaum, "The Manager Concept: A Rational Synthesis," *Journal of Business,* Oct., 1949.

Decision-making involves a conscious choice or selection of one behaviour alternative from among a group of two or more behaviour alternatives.[2] Three steps are involved in the decision-making process. First, an individual must become aware of as many as possible of those behaviour alternatives which are relevant to the decision to be made. Secondly, he must define each of these alternatives, a definition which involves a determination of as many as possible of the consequences related to each alternative under consideration. Thirdly, the individual must exercise a choice between the alternatives, that is, make a decision.

In enterprises, managerial subordinates, as subordinates, can participate in the first two steps of the managerial decision-making process. They cannot participate in the third step. The actual choice between relevant alternatives must be made or accepted by the manager who is responsible to his superior for the decision.[3] However, subordinates can provide and discuss with their manager information with respect both to relevant alternatives and to the consequences attendant upon specific alternatives. In so doing they are participating in the managerial decision-making process.[4]

The participation with which we are here concerned may take place in two different ways. First, it may involve interaction solely between a subordinate and his manager.[5] This would be the case where a worker

[2]This discussion of the decision-making process is based upon Robert Tannenbaum, "Managerial Decision-Making," *Journal of Business*, Jan., 1950.

[3]In a democratic group, the choice can be made through a vote participated in by the rank and file. But, in such a case, the leader is organizationally responsible to the rank and file, and the members of the rank and file are not properly, in so far as the decision is concerned, subordinates of the leader.

Members of a democratic group, making the final choice in matters directly affecting them, may be more highly motivated as a result thereof than managerial subordinates who are granted the right to participate only in the first two steps of the managerial decision-making process. For evidence of the motivational effects of group decision, see Kurt Lewin, "Group Decision and Social Change" in T. M. Newcomb and E. L. Hart-

ley, eds., *Readings in Social Psychology* (New York, 1947).

[4]It is this type of participation that most writers, who deal with human relations in enterprises, have in mind when they use the concept. The following examples illustrate this contention: "One of the most important conditions of the subordinate's growth and development centers around his opportunities to express his ideas and to contribute his suggestions before his superiors take action on matters which involve him. Through participation of this kind he becomes more and more aware of his superiors' problems, and he obtains genuine satisfaction in knowing that his opinions and ideas are given consideration in the search for solutions" (D. McGregor, "Conditions for Effective Leadership in the Industrial Situation," p. 60); "I am not suggesting that we take over intact the apparatus of the democratic state. Business cannot be run by the ballot box. . . . We must develop other inventions, adapted to the special circumstances of business, which will give employees at all levels of our organizations a greater sense of personal participation and 'belonging'" (J. Worthy, "Changing Concepts of the Personnel Function," p. 175); "Action initiated by the responsible head to bring his subordinates into the picture on matters of mutual concern is not a sharing of prerogatives of authority. Rather, it is an extension of the opportunity of participation in the development of points of view and the assembly of facts upon which decisions are made" (H. Carey, "Consultative Supervision and Management," p. 288).

[5]The concept of interaction as used here is not restricted to direct person-to-person, two-way communication (as in the process of superior-subordinate discussion), but encompasses more indirect forms (such as, for example, written communication) as well.

originates a suggestion which he transmits to his boss. Secondly, it may involve interaction between a group of subordinates and their manager. This would be the case where a manager calls his subordinates together to discuss a common problem or to formulate a recommendation.[6]

## POSSIBLE ADVANTAGES OF PARTICIPATION AS A MANAGERIAL DEVICE

It becomes useful to inquire why managers might find it advantageous to use this device. In other words, what are the possible benefits which might accrue to an enterprise whose managers made it possible for subordinates to participate in the decision-making process? In providing an answer to this question, it is first necessary to indicate the criterion which would guide the managerial choice relating to the use of participation. A manager of an enterprise (profit or nonprofit) who behaves rationally will attempt to make a selection from among alternatives related to any problem which will maximize results (the degree of attainment of a given end) at a given cost or which will attain given results at the lowest cost.[7] This is the criterion of rationality.

Guided by this criterion, rational managers will find it advantageous to use participation whenever such use will lead to increased results at a given cost or to the attainment of given results at a lower cost.

There are many advantages which *may* stem from the use of participation as a managerial device. The following are the principal ones:

(1) A higher rate of output and increased quality of product (including reduced spoilage and wastage) as a result of greater personal effort and attention on the part of subordinates.[8]

(2) A reduction in turnover, absenteeism, and tardiness.

(3) A reduction in the number of grievances and more peaceful manager-subordinate and manager-union relations.

(4) A greater readiness to accept change.[9] When changes are arbitrarily introduced from above without explanation, subordinates tend to feel insecure and to take countermeasures aimed at a sabotage of the innovations. But when they have partici-

---

[6]It may be observed that participation in the latter way, where there is communication between participators and where the act of participation is carried out through the medium of the group (as in cases of "group decision"), may often yield the more useful results. The level of derivable benefits may be higher than if participation had proceeded through channels in which there had been no interparticipator communication. Some factors important in this context are the following: (a) the feeling of "group belongingness" obtained by means of "action together" and (b) the role of norms, set as a result of group discussion, toward which behaviour will tend to gravitate.

[7]The term *cost* is here used in its highly

precise form to refer to whatever must be given or sacrificed to attain an end. See "Price," *Webster's Dictionary of Synonyms*. The term *end* is broadly conceived to embrace whatever factors (monetary or nonmonetary) the managers themselves define as the formal ends of the enterprise.

[8]For examples, see Lippitt, "A Program of Experimentation on Group Functioning and Productivity"; John R. P. French, Jr., Arthur Kornhauser, and Alfred Marrow, "Conflict and Cooperation in Industry," *Journal of Social Issues*, Feb., 1946; *Productivity, Supervision and Morale* (Survey Research Center Study No. 6, Ann Arbor, 1948).

[9]See, for example: Alex Bavelas, "Some Problems of Organizational Change," *Journal of Social Issues*, Summer, 1948; Elliott Jaques, "Interpretive Group Discussion as a Method of Facilitating Social Change," *Human Relations*, Aug., 1948; Lewin, "Group Decision and Social Change."

pated in the process leading to the decision, they have had an opportunity to be heard. They know what to expect and why, and they may desire the change. Blind resistance tends to become intelligent adaptation as insecurity is replaced by security.

(5) Greater ease in the management of subordinates.[10] Fewer managers may be necessary, the need for close supervision may be reduced, and less disciplinary action may be called for. Subordinates who have participated in the process leading toward a determination of matters directly affecting them may have a greater sense of responsibility with respect to the performance of their assigned tasks and may be more willing to accept the authority of their superiors. All managers possess a given amount of formal authority delegated to them by their superiors. But formal authority is not necessarily the equivalent of effective authority. The real source of the authority possessed by an individual lies in the acceptance of its exercise by those who are subject to it. It is the subordinates of an individual who determine the authority which he may wield. Formal authority is, in effect, nominal authority. It becomes real only when it is accepted. Thus, to be effective, formal authority must coincide with authority determined by its acceptance. The latter defines the useful limits of the former. The use of participation as a managerial device may result in a widening of these limits, reducing the amount of resistance to the exercise of formal author-

ity and increasing the positive responses of subordinates to managerial directives.

(6) The improved quality of managerial decisions. It is seldom if ever possible for managers to have knowledge of *all* alternatives and *all* consequences related to the decisions which they must make. Because of the existence of barriers to the upward flow of information in most enterprises, much valuable information possessed by subordinates never reaches their managers. Participation tends to break down the barriers, making the information available to managers. To the extent that such information alters the decisions which managers make, the quality of their decisions may thereby be improved.

These, then, are the principal advantages which *may* stem from the use of participation as a managerial device. The conditions under which it *will* accomplish them—under which participation will lead to motivation—is the concern of the section which follows.

### EXTRA-PARTICIPATIONAL CONDITIONS FOR EFFECTIVE PARTICIPATION

Beyond the factors governing the relationship between participation and possible resultant motivation, certain conditions "outside" the individual must be considered by the managers in deciding whether or not this particular device is applicable.[11] It would be possible to distinguish a great number of such outside conditions that

---

[10]See, for example: L. P. Bradford and R. Lippitt, "Building a Democratic Work Group," *Personnel*, Nov., 1945; O. H. Mowrer, "Authoritarianism vs. 'Self-Government' in the Management of Children's Aggressive (Anti-Social) Reactions as a Preparation for Citizenship in a Democracy," *Journal of Social Psychology*, Feb., 1939, pp. 121–6.

[11]For analytical purposes, this article differentiates between conditions regarding the dynamics of participation as a psychological process and all conditions outside this psychological participation-to-motivation link. The latter category of conditions is treated under the present heading.

may determine whether or not the use of participation is feasible in a given situation. Those here indicated are suggestive rather than fully definitive. All are viewed with this question in mind: "Granting that participation may have certain beneficial effects, is it useful in a given instance if the ends of the enterprise are to be achieved?"

To answer this question affirmatively, the following conditions must be met:

(1) *Time Availability.* The final decision must not be of a too urgent nature.[12] If it is necessary to arrive at some sort of emergency decision rapidly, it is obvious that even though participation in the decision-making process may have a beneficial effect in some areas, slowness of decision may result in thwarting other goals of the enterprise or even may threaten the existence of the enterprise. Military decisions frequently are of this type.

(2) *Rational Economics.* The cost of participation in the decision-making process must not be so high that it will outweigh any positive values directly brought about by it. If it should require outlays which could be used more fruitfully in alternative activities (for example, buying more productive though expensive equipment), then investment in it would be ill-advised.

(3) *Intra-Plant Strategy.*

(a) *Subordinate Security.* Giving the subordinates an opportunity to participate in the decision-making process must not bring with it any awareness on their part of unavoidable catastrophic events. For example, a subordinate who is made aware in the participation process that he will lose his job *regardless* of any decisions towards which he might contribute may experience a drop in motivation.

Furthermore, to make it possible for the subordinate to be willing to participate, he must be given the feeling that no matter what he says or thinks his status or role in the plant setting will not be affected adversely. This point has been made effectively in the available literature.[13]

(b) *Manager-Subordinate Stability.* Giving subordinates an opportunity to participate in the decision-making process must not threaten seriously to undermine the formal authority of the managers of the enterprise. For example, in some cases managers may have good reasons to assume that participation may lead nonmanagers to doubt the competence of the formal leadership, or that serious crises would result were it to develop that the subordinates were right while the final managerial decision turned out to be in disagreement with them and incorrect.

(4) *Inter-Plant Strategy.* Providing opportunities for participation must not open channels of communication to competing enterprises. "Leaks" of information to a competitor from subordinates who have participated in a given decision-making process must be avoided if participation is to be applicable.

(5) *Provision for Communication Channels.* For participation to be effective, channels must be provided through which the employee may take part in the decision-making process. These channels must be available continuously and their use must be convenient and practical.[14]

---

[12]See Chester I. Barnard, *Organization and Management* (Cambridge, 1948), p. 48.

[13]See McGregor, "Conditions for Effective Leadership in the Industrial Situation," *passim.*

[14]For a rigorous mathematical treatment of channels of communication within groups see Alex Bavelas, "A Mathematical Model for Group Structures," *Applied Anthropology,* Summer, 1948, pp. 16ff.

(6) *Education for Participation.* For participation to be effective, efforts must be made to educate subordinates regarding its function and purpose in the over-all functioning of the enterprise.[15]

It must be stressed that the conditions stipulated in this section are dynamic in their own right and may be affected by the very process of participation as well as by other factors.

---

[15]See French, Kornhauser, and Marrow,

"Conflict and Cooperation in Industry," p. 30.

# 16

# Leadership

Complexity and size of organization lead to the development of bureaucratic forms of administration. We have traced this development by considering organization office and the division of labor. In Chapter 7, we developed the theory of bureaucratic administration and pointed out its inherent strengths and weaknesses.

Throughout the first four sections of the book covered by Chapters 1 through 13 we have assumed one important thing. We have considered the organization as having a directing head, a leadership involved in over-all coordination. Now we are in a position to examine the nature of this leadership and the processes that characterize leadership behavior.

Leadership in organizations involves the exercise of authority (see Chapter 12). It also involves making decisions for the organization. In Chapter 15, we focused our attention on the nature of such decisions, the organizational and environmental conditions that influence them, and the difference between delegating authority and sharing decision-making with subordinates.

The substance of the preceding chapters dealing with power, authority, and decision-making is this:

**INTRODUCTION**

*Order in society is grounded in power. The organizations of society institutionalize power and are the means for carrying out the ordered and regular daily activities of society. Within organizations, the activities of the members and functionaries must be directed in systems of cooperation and coordination. These co-*

*ordinating functions are grounded in authority—the expectation that direction will be followed. Involved in coordination and the exercise of authority is organization decision-making by the authority-holder.*

It follows from this that there are some basic dilemmas in democratic leadership that *flow from the organizational context in which leadership is exercised.* This is the central thesis of the first two selections in this chapter. It is the nature of formal organizations that leaders possess authority and make decisions. How, then, can a formal organization be democratic in its administration?

This question has important practical implications for the management of all organizations of our society. In fact, it is one of the dilemmas of modern political democracy. It is not an insoluble dilemma.

If authority is based upon power, then the central area of contest in our society is the possession of power. If authority is to be modified, then it is done through the shifting of power from one group of individuals or class members to another. We have examples of this in our own experience. The growing intervention of government in the multifarious aspects of our life, including business activity, is an important example of the shift of social power from private to public hands. Take another large area of our modern life. The extensive development of collective bargaining represents the transfer of power from one private group to another—from management to organized labor. These two examples are enough to make the point. The change in the authority structure of an organization comes about only with a change in the possession of power.

How does this tie in with our firm belief in democracy? The democratic state and democratic organizations are democratic because the leaders do not have unrestricted authority since they possess only limited power. Our whole constitutional system of checks and balances is one expression of this. Government regulation of business and the power of trade unions is another system of checks and balances that modifies private power.

It has been necessary to say what has just been said: there has grown up around the notion of "human relations" the idea that it is either some magical way to build democracy into organizations, or that it makes people willing subjects of manipulation. These are shallow and worthless ways to view the meaning of a "human relations outlook." The significant orientation to a human relations approach is to seek an understanding of how people behave *in* organizations. Members of an organization understand authority and leadership and their functions. The problem is not to destroy authority or get rid of leadership. That would inevitably destroy the organization itself. The real problem is to make leadership and the exercise of authority operate according to the accepted values and beliefs of our society.

We can put the argument another way. We are not saying that the nature of formal organizations or corporate groups makes dictatorship inevitable. We *are* saying that order in society and the institutionalization of order in formal organizations involve both exercise of authority and development of the offices of leadership.

There are four major aspects of leadership upon which we are focusing in this chapter. First, we will examine the functions of leadership as they affect the character and destiny of the organization. Second, we will see why the essentially political character of the leadership functions produces dilemmas with respect to democracy in organizations. Third, attention will be turned to the recruitment of new cadres of leaders from the rank and file as this is affected by bringing in outside leaders and the sponsorship of successors. Finally, we will note a built-in feature of all leadership—the isolation of the leader from full and unstructured contacts with people from the internal and external environment of his organization.

Selznick, in the first selection, presents a broad view of the special functions performed by leaders for their organizations. In a passing reference ("When an organization lacks leadership, these tasks are inadequately fulfilled, however expert the flow of paper and however smooth the channels of communication and command.") Selznick distinguishes between leadership and command. This distinction deserves special mention.[1]

Command is exercised when administrators carry out established policies and orders by presenting them to the work force in ways to insure their execution. Command is a necessary condition of all "line" administrative positions, for without the command functions being performed, the operating divisions of the organization could not long get their work done. Indeed, we distinguish "staff" and "line" positions in management by the fact that commanding is a feature of the latter only.

Leadership, on the other hand, is a continually creative function involving

constant appraisal of the dynamic internal and external environments of the organization. From such appraisals flow broad policy decisions determining "what the organization can do and to some extent what it must do."

Ordinarily, leadership is exercised at the very top of an organization by its "top executives." This is largely because the legitimate right and obligation to make broad policy decisions rest at that level of the organization. We must not overlook the fact, however, that leadership can be exercised at any level of the organization. Its appearance at low administrative levels is usually signalled by the fact that the low level administrator takes action outside established policy limits which then commits the organization to legitimize that action by creating the necessary new policy justifications. In this special sense, then, leadership in the lower administrative reaches of an organization may be unsettling and even potentially dangerous to organizational viability.

This becomes one of the basic dilemmas always posed by the choice between centralization and decentralization of organizational structure. One of the positive payoffs of decentralization is the increased probability that the diffusion of leadership functions will produce constructive and imaginative innovations, improving the organization as a whole. One of the penalties of decentralization is that lower levels of administrators may commit the organization to undesirable courses of action through the exercise of their leadership. These rewards and penalties, of course, become prime entries in the balance sheet when a decision is made regarding decentralization and its conse-

---

[1]See, in this connection, Robert Dubin, *The World of Work* (Englewood Cliffs, N. J.: Prentice-Hall, Inc., 1958), chaps. 20 and 21, in which the distinctions between leadership and command are set forth.

quent diffusion of leadership on an organization.

Selznick's analysis of the functions of leadership was published almost two decades after the first appearance of the succeeding selection by Barnard. Selznick obviously draws on Barnard's insights in presenting his incisive description of the leadership functions. Barnard, in turn, examines in depth the fundamental dilemmas generated by the fact that "leadership" implies "led." The linkages and interdependencies between leaders and followers serve as limits on the wholly arbitrary determination of group policy by a leader. Barnard examines this as a series of dilemmas when viewing the relationship primarily from the standpoint of the leader.

It is well to pay particular attention to Selznick's opening discussion of the connections between leadership and a political orientation. This theme reappears in an important way in Barnard's subsequent analysis.

## FUNCTIONS OF ORGANIZATIONAL LEADERSHIP

*Philip Selznick**

We have argued that policy and administration are interdependent in the special sense that certain areas of organizational activity are peculiarly sensitive to policy matters. Because these areas exist, creative men are needed—more in some circumstances than in others—who know how to transform a neutral body of men into a committed polity. These men are called leaders; their profession is politics.

A political orientation is greatly needed if we are to reach a proper understanding of institutional leadership. But this orientation should not be too narrowly identified with the struggle for power. The link between "polity" and "politics" must constantly be kept in mind. To be sure, the political process always involves an actual or potential contest of wills, but it

also includes the continuous redefinition of public interest and the embodiment of those definitions in key institutions. The German term *Politik,* as distinguished from *Verwaltung,* nonpolitical administration, has some of these connotations. *Politik* is not so much concerned with technical efficiency as with decisions that are open and potentially controversial. While at any given moment there may be consensus, this does not signify indifference. *Verwaltung,* on the other hand, does deal with areas of indifference. Some matters (*Politik*) are part of critical experience because they affect the way the group's character is formed, whereas other matters (*Verwaltung*) are constant despite changes in character. The existence of a contest of wills is prima facie evidence (though not conclusive) that political issues in this sense have been raised. This holds for all organizations that have freedom of self-definition, not just for public agencies.

*From Philip Selznick, *Leadership in Administration* (Evanston, Ill.: Row, Peterson & Company, 1957). Used by permission.

Leadership sets goals, but in doing so takes account of the conditions that have already determined what the organization can do and to some extent what it must do. Leadership creates and molds an organization embodying —in thought and feeling and habit— the value premises of policy. Leadership reconciles internal strivings and environmental pressures, paying close attention to the way adaptive behavior brings about changes in organizational character. When an organization lacks leadership, these tasks are inadequately fulfilled, however expert the flow of paper and however smooth the channels of communication and command. And this fulfillment requires a continuous scrutiny of how the changing social structure affects the evolution of policy.

The relation of leadership to organizational character may be more closely explored if we examine some of the key tasks leaders are called on to perform:

1. *The definition of institutional mission and role.* The setting of goals is a creative task. It entails a self-assessment to discover the true commitments of the organization, as set by effective internal and external demands. The failure to set aims in the light of these commitments is a major source of irresponsibility in leadership.

2. *The institutional embodiment of purpose.* The task of leadership is not only to make policy but to build it into the organization's social structure. This, too, is a creative task. It means shaping the "character" of the organization, sensitizing it to ways of thinking and responding, so that increased reliability in the execution and elaboration of policy will be achieved according to its spirit as well as its letter.

3. *The defense of institutional integrity.* The leadership of any polity fails when it concentrates on sheer survival: institutional survival, properly understood, is a matter of maintaining values and distinctive identity. This is at once one of the most important and least understood functions of leadership. This area (like that of defining institutional mission) is a place where the intuitively knowledgeable leader and the administrative analyst often part company, because the latter has no tools to deal with it. The fallacy of combining agencies on the basis of "logical" association of functions is a characteristic result of the failure to take account of institutional integrity.

4. *The ordering of internal conflict.* Internal interest-groups form naturally in large-scale organizations, since the total enterprise is in one sense a polity composed of a number of sub-organizations. The struggle among competing interests always has a high claim on the attention of leadership. This is so because the direction of the enterprise as a whole may be seriously influenced by changes in the internal balance of power. In exercising control, leadership has a dual task. It must win the consent of constituent units, in order to maximize voluntary cooperation, and therefore must permit emergent interest blocs a wide degree of representation. At the same time, in order to hold the helm, it must see that a balance of power appropriate to the fulfillment of key commitments will be maintained.

---

Chester I. Barnard has often been called the father of modern organization theory. He certainly was one of its most able contributors. The following is a portion of an address delivered by him at Princeton University in 1939. At that time he was primarily interested in the problems and dilemmas of running government organizations and bureaus, though he was also perceptive of the nature of dilemmas of leadership in any organization which operated on a democratic basis.

In this particular expression of his thinking Barnard examines a facet of leadership which has been widely extolled, but whose dilemmas have been ignored. "Consultative management" and "democratic leadership" are concepts worthy of application to all kinds of organizations. We have already seen from the preceding chapter that the sharing of decisions with subordinates does not mean letting subordinates make the decisions. This is certainly a significant limitation on the full flowering of democratic leadership. Barnard expands these notions by suggesting three dilemmas faced by leaders in any circumstance of democratic governance. There are always solutions to dilemmas—but they are dilemmas precisely because their solution is difficult. Barnard makes his points in order to alert leaders of all kinds of organizations to some of the problems they will confront in fulfilling their offices.

## DILEMMAS OF LEADERSHIP IN THE DEMOCRATIC PROCESS

### Chester I. Barnard*

Leaders as functioning elements of organization are not formally nominated, selected, elected, or appointed, nor are they born to leadership; they are accepted and followed; and are sometimes pressed or (rarely) coerced into leading. Indeed, I have never observed any leader who was able to state adequately or intelligibly why he was able to be a leader, nor any statement of followers that acceptably expressed why they followed. Also leaders historically and logically precede all systems of formal organization decision. They have been primary factors in the selection or adoption of every system of governance; but once established, such a system becomes a conditioning element of the functions of leaders and also a means by which their functions are carried out. This arises from the facts that positions of control are essential to the coordination of effort—a common element in all systems of governance; and that leaders must operate chiefly through such formal positions.[1] . . .

### I. THE DILEMMA OF EFFECTIVE ACTION AND POLITICS

In an autocratic system of governance every leader or executive is constantly confronted with the dilemma

*Reprinted by permission of the publishers from Chester I. Barnard, *Organization and Management* (Cambridge, Mass.: Harvard University Press, 1948), pp. 39–47.

[1]See Chester I. Barnard, *The Functions of the Executive* (Cambridge, Mass.: Harvard University Press, 1938), chap. xv, pp. 217–223. This book is referred to hereinafter as *The Functions*.

involved in the fact that a specific aim most appropriate to the *purpose* of organization effort is in some degree out of accord with the means available for its accomplishment, that is, the human beings whose efforts are to be utilized. The choice to be made usually requires some modification of the ideal aim to one adapted to the capacities, emotions, and wills of the individuals whose efforts must accomplish it; and simultaneously some modification of the latter by training, precept, example, and inspiration. Thus there are involved initially nice questions of judgment of a technical character as to the range of acceptable aims on one side, and on the other, concerning the capacities and dispositions of the persons whose efforts are involved. . . .

Either of the horns of such dilemmas usually will be modified where the democratic process is employed. The aim may be determined by this process, or the means—for example, the number of persons and rates of pay. The initial dilemma of the leader should be usually conceived as not relieved by democratic decision in either respect.[2] The task still remains of coordinating numerous efforts with precision to obtain a concrete effect. Indeed, it can readily be observed that the dilemma is frequently made more severe. Decision as to one part of the problem is often made without attention to the other part, because the requisite intimate knowledge and concentration and sense of the situation are not available to the individual participants in the democratic process. That process therefore in general adds a second dilemma to the initial one. It

creates for the leader a trilemma. He must seek a concrete program of action which is at once adapted (a) to the technical (external) situation; (b) to the internal operative organization condition; and (c) to at least the majority abstract "democratic" opinion, and usually also to the minority opinions, both as to aim and means. The latter is the political factor. In principle it is ineradicable from the democratic process.[3]

The complication introduced by the political factor is so great that it has heretofore made impossible the direct use of the democratic method in determining most concrete activities. The exclusion of a wide field of activities from the application of the democratic process is so much a matter of course and so little consciously perceived that this statement of the nature of the political complications may seem theoretical and remote from observable events. However, it is well known that committees, boards, and legislatures frequently determine upon aims which cannot be accomplished under the conditions, or prescribe means which prevent their accomplishment, or establish conditions which destroy the power of effective leadership.

It is probable that unfavorable consequences of the political factor can rarely be avoided and that many situations theoretically available to the democratic process are for this sole reason not practicable of solution by it. The reasons are clear. The addition of the political to the more primitive factors of cooperative effort adds greatly to the complexities of leadership. These complexities may be regarded for illustration as increasing as the cube of the number of factors

---

[2]Usually, in general, not always. As later noted, sometimes the process of formal assent is an important and even necessary aid in securing willing subordination.

[3]It is in some degree usually present in any other process.

involved, so that they might be stated as of the order of three times as great under the democratic process as under an autocratic method. . . .

This means that the democratic process in general will be less effective and less efficient, at least for short time periods, than autocratic processes *unless the quantity of leaders is greater and their quality better than would be otherwise sufficient.* It would be a great disservice to the ideal of democracy to underestimate this.

## II. THE DILEMMA OF PERSONALITY AND POSITION

Effective leadership in organizations depends upon *leaders* of appropriate qualities on one hand and *a system of positions* to be filled by them on the other—upon communicators in communication positions.[4] Usually only a few alternative schemes of communication or of official organization may be regarded as practicable at a given time; and usually personnel available is limited. The most suitable combination of positions and personnel requires modification of the scheme of positions on one hand to meet the limitations of personnel, and on the other hand the selection of personnel with respect to the available schemes of communication. This is a fundamental problem of all cooperative effort under *any* method of governance. In the democratic process the dilemmas arise chiefly from three sources: (1) the scheme of positions must be relatively rigid; (2) the selection of leaders must be based in part upon political as distinguished from organizing abilities; (3) the subtleties in the precise combining of leader and offi-

cial position are generally beyond the capacities of any democratic system.

1. Regarding the scheme of positions, it is clear that under any plan of operations it must usually be stable, not only from the standpoint of the convenience of administration but also from the standpoint of the habituation of organization and especially of the stability of constituent unit organizations.[5] But under the democratic process the changing of the scheme of positions introduces not merely confusion of ideas but also the political elements. . . .

2. Since leaders under the democratic process must function with respect to the political factor in addition to others, it is obvious that political abilities become important qualifications. But the appraisal of the latter by the democratic process is necessarily confused by lack of unity and the division into groups and parties which it probably requires. The difficulties are apparent. It is a generally valid criticism of the democratic process that it is relatively ineffective in selecting men on their merits for organization positions. . . .
cribed solely to the party element in the democratic process. The extreme

3. This difficulty need not be ascribed—delicacy of the judgment of abilities required in complex situations and the destructive effect of open discussion of such matters on confidence itself—both of leaders and followers—are even more important, in my opinion, than the more obvious and tangible difficulties.

## III. THE DILEMMA OF DIFFUSED RESPONSIBILITY

The democratic process involves not

---

[4] *The Functions,* chap. xii, pp. 172–181.

[5] *Ibid.,* chap. viii, p. 104.

only a diffusion of responsibility within an electorate, but in addition it requires that leaders shall carry out policies of others. They are publicly blamed for faults not their own; and conversely, they are credited with false merits. Their influence with their followers is thereby weakened. Thus this process restricts the initiative, enthusiasm, and confidence of leaders and followers and greatly reduces the incentives to leaders and their personal responsibility. The quality of leadership is reduced, and the quantity of leaders narrowed, under the very conditions which require that both should be increased.

There is a general disposition of the public and also of many politicians and public officials to assume insufficiency of leadership capacity upon the part of public officials appointed by the democratic process or of those directly dependent upon those so appointed. In my opinion the deficiency is at least greatly exaggerated. I do not rely upon such sentiments here. A small *proportion* of leadership positions is today filled by the democratic process—chiefly major public officials, officers of labor organizations, social organizations; also principal officers of corporations and universities—but as to these classes the process is often nominal. This makes it quite possible that adequate leadership is available in this limited degree despite the depressive effect of the democratic process on the ambitions of persons otherwise competent to lead. The important measure of the effect of the irresponsibility of the democratic process would only be indicated by what we might expect if a large proportion of important organization positions were to be filled by this process. I believe that a much wider extension of the democratic process to the formally organ-

ized efforts of our society—so far as appointments are concerned—would quickly break down through the inability to secure the much higher quality and the quantity of leaders then necessary. It should be noted that the proportion of positions filled democratically has probably been decreasing in major degree in recent years due to the extension of civil service systems, the development of large-scale corporations, the exceedingly "practical" methods of continuity of tenure in some other organizations, the increasing extent of perfunctory legislative approvals of "career" men, and the rapid spread of "administrative law," not only in government but —under other conceptions or names— in corporations. . . .

It would be shamefully stupid to underrate the dilemmas of the democratic process as they affect the selection and development of leaders or as they discourage followers, thereby diminishing cohesion and coordination. They are by no means decisive when contrasted with the corresponding dilemmas of other processes, and for many situations the démocratic process seems clearly superior to others. But probably for many situations it is so inferior that it is in practice impossible, and this should be definitely recognized.

## THE ADOPTION OF
## SYSTEMS OF GOVERNANCE

Notwithstanding that in practice the democratic process is persistently subject to major dilemmas such as I have described, yet this process is widely used with success and satisfaction. However, a similar statement may be made respecting other methods of government. What determines fundamentally the choices in great and small organizations? How is it that the democratic process is adopted when no democracy is available to determine its adoption? How is it that it is abandoned despite the interests that become vested in it? In what way are determined the limits of fictions and of circumventions attendant upon the democratic process—and upon others as well—that seem to permit their nominal retention notwithstanding their *de facto* abandonment?

The answer to these questions refers to the informal processes of cooperation that underlie all formal processes. The answer is that the formal system is confirmed by the conformatory behavior of leaders and followers jointly. A silent "democracy of behavior" determines all systems of

government, public or private. Not what the King says but how he acts, not what his subjects say but what they do, determines this question. If he in fact leads, and they in fact follow, he is King, they are subjects. And if they call him King and themselves subjects, but decide their course by a Parliament and execute it through its leaders, they are using the democratic method. What men will and can do decides the issue. They can and will use the democratic process under some conditions; they cannot or will refuse to do so under others. In conditions of complexity, or great danger, or rapidity of action, they have rarely been willing or able to follow a committee or to elect a leader, as for example in battle.

---

There is an important segment of the field of personnel administration that deals with selection of executives and leaders. We are not here concerned with the admittedly great problems of finding round pegs to fit in round holes. In the following selection, by Selznick, we will examine a significant process of organization that leads to the selection of certain kinds of organization leaders.

Selznick calls our attention to the fact that an organization may be threatened when at least some of its members no longer consent to be governed by the existing leadership. Under such circumstances, the incumbent leadership may often act to bring into its ranks leaders of the dissident forces. By this technique the insurgent group may be brought back into allegiance to the organization. This process works itself out in a number of dif-

ferent ways in the organization, as Selznick suggests. An example that characterizes the process is the instance of a business merger where top executives of the newly acquired unit are taken into the leadership of the parent company. This may be dictated, at least in part, by the established leadership position of the executives in the newly acquired unit. With their transfer to the parent organization, the sentiments and loyalties of their employees are likely also to transfer more readily to the parent company.

We might look at the process analyzed by Selznick as the opposite of the old adage—"if you can't beat 'em, join 'em." To parallel that phrase, we might say, "if you can't beat 'em get 'em to join you." The first looks at it from the standpoint of the outsider; the second, from the standpoint of the insider.

## STRENGTHENING LEADERSHIP—COOPTATION

### Philip Selznick*

*Cooptation is the process of absorbing new elements into the leadership or policy-determining structure of an organization as a means of averting threats to its stability or existence.* This is a defensive mechanism, formulated as one of a number of possible predicates available for the interpretation of organization behavior. Cooptation tells us something about the process by which an institutional environment impinges itself upon an organization and effects changes in its leadership and policy. Formal authority may resort to cooptation under the following general conditions:

(1) When there exists a hiatus between consent and control, so that the legitimacy of the formal authority is called into question. The "indivisibility" of consent and control refers, of course, to an optimum situation. Where control lacks an adequate measure of consent, it may revert to coercive measures or attempt somehow to win the consent of the governed. One means of winning consent is to coopt elements into the leadership or organization, usually elements which in some way reflect the sentiment, or possess the confidence of the relevant public or mass. As a result, it is expected that the new elements will lend respectability or legitimacy to the organs of control and thus reestablish the stability of formal authority. This process is widely used, and in many different

*From "Foundations of the Theory of Organization," *American Sociological Review*, 13:34–35 (Feb. 1948). Copyright by the American Sociological Society. Used by permission.

contexts. It is met in colonial countries, where the organs of alien control reaffirm their legitimacy by coopting native leaders into the colonial administration. We find it in the phenomenon of "crisis-patriotism" wherein normally disfranchised groups are temporarily given representation in the councils of government in order to win their solidarity in a time of national stress. Cooptation is presently being considered by the United States Army in its study of proposals to give enlisted personnel representation in the court-martial machinery[1]—a clearly adaptive response to stresses made explicit during the war, the lack of confidence in the administration of army justice. The "unity" parties of totalitarian states are another form of cooptation; company unions or some employee representation plans in industry are still another. In each of these cases the response of formal authority (private or public, in a large organization or a small one) is an attempt to correct a state of imbalance by *formal* measures. It will be noted, moreover, that what is shared is the *responsibility* for power rather than power itself. These conditions define what we shall refer to as *formal cooptation.*

(2) Cooptation may be a response to the pressure of specific centers of power. This is not necessarily a matter of legitimacy or of a general and diffuse lack of confidence. These may be well established; and yet organized forces which are able to threaten the

[1]Since the writing of this article the change has been made by the Army. [Ed.]

formal authority may effectively shape its structure and policy. The organization in respect to its institutional environment—or the leadership in respect to its ranks—must take these forces into account. As a consequence, the outside elements may be brought into the leadership or policy-determining structure, may be given a place as a recognition of and concession to the resources they can independently command. The representation of interests through administrative constituencies is a typical example of this process. Or, within an organization, individuals upon whom the group is dependent for funds or other resources may insist upon and receive a share in the determination of policy. This form of cooptation is typically expressed in informal terms, for the problem is not one of responding to a state of imbalance with respect to the "people as a whole" but rather one of meeting the pressure of specific individuals or interest-groups which are in a position to enforce demands. The latter are interested in the substance of power and not its forms. Moreover, an open acknowledgment of capitulation to specific interests may itself undermine the sense of legitimacy of the formal authority within the community. Consequently, there is a positive pressure to refrain from explicit recognition of the relationship established. This form of the cooptative mechanism, having to do with the sharing of power as a response to specific pressures, may be termed *informal cooptation.*

Cooptation reflects a state of tension between formal authority and social power. The former is embodied in a particular structure and leadership, but the latter has to do with subjective and objective factors which control the loyalties and potential manipulability of the community. Where the

formal authority is an expression of social power, its stability is assured. On the other hand, when it becomes divorced from the sources of social power its continued existence is threatened. This threat may arise from the sheer alienation of sentiment or from the fact that other leaderships have control over the sources of social power. Where a formal authority has been accustomed to the assumption that its constituents respond to it as individuals, there may be a rude awakening when organization of those constituents on a nongovernmental basis creates nuclei of power which are able effectively to demand a sharing of power.[2]

The significance of cooptation for organizational analysis is not simply that there is a change in or a broadening of leadership, and that this is an adaptive response, but also that *this change is consequential for the character and role of the organization.* Co-

---

[2]It is perhaps useful to restrict the concept of cooptation to formal organizations, but in fact it probably reflects a process characteristic of all group leaderships. This has received some recognition in the analysis of class structure, wherein the ruling class is interpreted as protecting its own stability by absorbing new elements. Thus Michels made the point that "an aristocracy cannot maintain an enduring stability by sealing itself off hermetically." See Robert Michels, *Umschichtungen in den herrschenden Klassen nach dem Kriege* (Stuttgart: Kohlhammer, 1934), p. 39; also Gaetano Mosca, *The Ruling Class* (New York: McGraw-Hill, 1939), pp. 413ff. The alliance or amalgamation of classes in the face of a common threat may be reflected in formal and informal cooptative responses among formal organizations sensitive to class pressures. In *TVA and the Grass Roots: A Study in the Sociology of Formal Organization* (Berkeley and Los Angeles: University of California Press, 1949), the author has made extensive use of the concept of cooptation in analyzing some aspects of the organizational behavior of a government agency.

optation involves commitment, so that the groups to which adaptation has been made constrain the field of choice available to the organization or leadership in question. The character of the coopted elements will necessarily shape (inhibit or broaden) the modes of action available to the leadership which has won adaptation and security at the price of commitment. The concept of cooptation thus implicitly sets forth the major points of the frame of reference outlined above: it is an adaptive response of a cooperative system to a stable need, generating transformations which reflect contraints enforced by the recalcitrant tools of action.

---

One of the characteristics of leaders in an organization is the ability to choose their own successors. There is an important social process involved in the selection and grooming of future organization leadership. We call the process *sponsorship*.

In the next selection, sponsorship is examined in detail. Hughes examines sponsorship in developing industrial leadership. He shows what happens in newly industrialized countries to which industry has been brought by managers and capital from other countries. He finds parallel behavior in an examination of American industry today.

In addition to the central consideration of sponsorship, Hughes raises some interesting questions about ambition and mobility in industry. Every organization needs its "Thank God for" people, as he indicates. To what extent does sponsorship of a selected class of individuals to fill the management positions act as an effective block to the ambitious but unacceptable people? To what extent does management say it wants everyone to be ambitious when it means that it wants only certain acceptable kinds of people to display an ambition to "get ahead?" You will want to refer back to our discussion of motivation in Chapter 3, and to relate the sponsorship process to its impact on motivation.

---

## AMBITION, MOBILITY, AND SPONSORSHIP

*Everett C. Hughes**

. . . Industry in the Western world promoted an ideology of mobility, that is, of ambition. In the colonial world,

*From "Queries Concerning Industry and Society Growing Out of Study of Ethnic Relations in Industry," *American Sociological Review*, 14:218–220 (April 1949). Copyright by the American Sociological Society. Used by permission.

ambition is often regarded an unjustified and dangerous. Even in the Western world, managers speak with nostalgia of the unambitious first-generation of Poles, French-Canadians or peasant-workers of other ethnic groups; people who were content with their jobs, willing to work hard without hope of advancement. Of course, such people often had objectives outside industry to keep them at work and content; notably, the desire to save money for buying property. In spirit, they were not completely industrialized. A second or later generation which insists on advancement within industry is compared unfavorably with their fathers. The hostile reaction of many managers to ambitious Negroes is too well-known to require documenting.

Here is apparently a contradiction: industry encourages ambition, and complains a good deal about lack of it. On the other hand it praises some people for not having it, and complains of others who do. This raises another general question: just how much ambition does an industrial organization want, and in how many people and what kinds of people does it want it? In the colonial world, there is generally a limit on the possibilities of promotion for persons of each ethnic category, although this may change through time. For certain kinds of work, it may actually be to the advantage of industry to hire only people whose ambitions are directed to goals completely outside the industrial system. For others, they may want ambitious people. There may, however, be some balance between the proportion of ambitious and unambitious people which works best even in the oldest of the industrial regions. A clue appears in a phrase current in a large concern in this country. They have a breed known as the "Thank God for" people; the unambitious people who can be counted on to stay where they are, and who keep things running while others are busy climbing the mobility ladder from one job to another. . . .

Just what proportion of ambitious workers industrial organizations of various kinds can tolerate is a ques-

tion which merits comparative analysis, although it may be difficult to make the necessary observations in a society where people generally claim to believe in ambition and to be ashamed of lack of it. In colonial regions, the talk on the subject is often franker.

I have already noted that ethnic exclusiveness tends to develop at all levels of colonial industrial hierarchies. The dominent managerial and technical functions remain pretty much in the hands of the founding ethnic group. . . .

Even in American industry, such a tendency shows clearly. A number of forces apparently play upon hiring and selection to reinforce or to break up this tendency. If I were to venture an hypothesis it would be something like this: the tendency to exclusiveness is present in all organizations, and in the segments thereof, but the power to maintain it varies. In industry, the necessity of keeping a full labor force operates against exclusiveness in those categories where large numbers are required; generally, the lower levels of skill. The people at these levels have little or no formal power of hiring. They have, in varying degree, informal power of selection and rejection.

The people in the higher levels of the hierarchy have the power to keep their own ranks ethnically exclusive. . . . They may operate through the mechanism of sponsoring, by which promising young people are picked and encouraged in their mobility efforts by their superiors. In the course of their rise, they are not merely given a technical training, but also are initiated into the ways and sentiments of the managerial group and are judged by their internal acceptance of them. Ethnic, national, and class loyalty are undoubtedly factors in the original choice of people to be sponsored and in their later rise. In the Western world individuals ethnically different from those at the top of management may be drawn into the sponsorship circle, but in the course of it effectively lose all symbols of identification with the ethnic group from which they have come and take on those of the receiving group. Where skin-color and other racial features are involved, this is not so easy to do. Thus, while modern industry is opposed to nepotism, as contrary to the choice of the best people in an open market, as an operating organization it tends to hold power in the hands of a group whose new members are picked from among people thought to be loyal not merely to the particular organization but to the management class and its culture. . . .

The sponsoring power of lower ranks may be less, but is by no means lacking in many situations. Coal miners and railroad workers notoriously have great sponsoring power. And even in the colonial regions the members of an ethnic group or clan, or the inhabitants of a village, may have, in effect, the power to recruit new workers. In a sense, when industry brings in some new ethnic group it has to do it in opposition to the present workers.

The actual ethnic composition and changes therein seem then to be a resultant of the operation of demand for new help against the exclusive tendencies of the various segments of the existing working organization. The search of modern industry for new help that can be used with profit has certainly been active and persistent. On the other hand, for a given kind or level of job, the field in which the search is made may be limited by management's own state of knowledge and sentiments. . . .

The role of sentiments is, however, made somewhat stronger in the hiring and utilization of human labor than in the buying and selling of inanimate commodities by the fact that the human labor is, so to speak, consumed by industry. Industry is not a labor broker, for it uses the labor to build a continuing organization for work; it must live with its laboring people. And in the course of working together the social and political processes get under way as they do in any organization. Industry thus considers its people not merely as technical help, but as actual or potential participants in a struggle for power within industry and society, and as potential close colleagues (or as unfit to be such). . . .

In the next selection we deal with a characteristic of top leadership—isolation from contacts within the organization. It has been said that this executive isolation "not only breeds a parochialism of the imagination comparable to the 'military mind' but places a considerable premium on it."[1]

You will recall from Chapters 7 and 9 the development of the concept of "trained incapacity." In the isolation of the executives, we see one of the organizational processes leading to the top executive's trained incapacity to see the facts as others see them.

[1]Peter F. Drucker, *Concept of the Cor-*

*poration* (New York: John Day Company, 1946), p. 88.

## LEADERSHIP AND EXECUTIVE SUBORDINATION

### Tom Burns and G. M. Stalker*

The head of the concern stands for the concern and its relative successes —he symbolizes or personifies it. The management of the concern is also a career system, and the man standing on the topmost rung has to serve as a showcase for the characteristics which must be attributed to the person who is by definition the most successful, or their absence must be condoned by the presence of equally highly valued personal qualities.

So, while there is a regular succession of increments of authority and higher status positions as one moves up the management hierarchy, the topmost position differs from the others by more than a matter of degree. As the ultimate controller of direction, he sets the goals the whole concern is to achieve and so sets the parameters of the task and activities of groups and persons. As the 'patron' of the concern, he specifies—by example, by adjudication, by remonstrance, by permissive silence, by approval—the measure of privilege and rights attached to lower positions. The system and structure of management are both determined largely by him. Above all, he is the ultimate authority for appointment and promotion.

The head of a concern, therefore, exerts a powerful influence over its members in their conduct in many ways apart from the actual and overt authority he possesses. In addition, he

occupies a socially isolated position at the top of the management hierarchy.

'Social isolation' comprehends more than the 'loneliness of command', the familiar notion of the burden of responsibility which is carried by the person to whom is ascribed ultimate authority in any organization. It has to do rather with the social peculiarities of the position. People in working communities in our society normally have to deal with others who are subordinate, equal, or superior in social standing and power. In doing so, they are continually testing out the answers they have themselves arrived at to such all-important questions as 'Am I a likeable person?', 'Am I doing my job well?', 'Did I act on such and such an occasion intelligently, or unjustly, or dishonestly, or with enough warmth, or with enough detachment?' In the relatively crowded millieux of our occupational lives, we are presented with plenty of hints, clues, and even downright statements from equals and superiors which we can trust as evidence of fairly disinterested judgment on these matters. We do usually trust them, at least when they are favorable; it is the unfavorable judgments which we can often dismiss as unreliable, because of the element of competitiveness which enters into all our dealings with colleagues and superiors.

As soon as a man reaches the top position in the hierarchy of a working organization, this normal situation is reversed. He enters what is in many respects an unreal world, one in which all responses to his actions and to him-

*Reprinted by permission from Tom Burns and G. M. Stalker, *The Management of Innovation* (London: Tavistock Publications Limited, 1966), pp. 211–220.

self are filtered through the knowledge that he is in supreme command, and in a position to control the careers and occupational lives of all the members of the organization. People below him have to be—and have much experience and training to help them be —circumspect in their dealings with him. They have as a matter of unthinking habit to control not only their utterances but also the manner in which they are delivered, their non-verbal conduct. For they have first to present themselves in the best light and secondly to display to him the precise responses, hints, and clues which will give him the kind of reassurance about himself and his conduct which they think he needs at that moment. None of this should be identified with the cruder forms of displayed subservience, which, indeed, is characterized as such only when it is failing in its purpose. Disagreement and even, in certain circumstances, criticism is normally possible if the timing and style are correctly judged; indeed, they may convey a deeper reassurance to the head of the concern by appearing to discard some essential elements of his isolation.

The managing director [the top executive of an English business firm] may seek either to exploit his position or to escape from it. In doing either, he may act in accordance with ideas prevailing in the concern about what a man in his position can legitimately do, or he may not. This gives four kinds of relationship with the members of the concern, each of which promotes a specific array of responses, and so acts as a chief determinant of the management system. These four kinds of relationship, which are also four ways of dealing with the fact of isolation, are elucidated below.

(i) Exploitation of the managing director's position of isolation and supremacy which is accepted as legitimate can approximate very closely to 'natural' (charismatic) leadership. This was visible in one concern in many instances, but was particularly apparent in the manner in which changes in the management structure were carried out. They seemed to be decided and acted upon with formidable speed, and to emerge from the managing director's personal appraisal of situations.

The task of analyzing and changing the system was seen as implicit in the managing director's role. People in the organization sanctioned this because of his identification with the company's success and because he acted as a focus for the general orientation of the system towards swift, imaginative, and intelligent appreciation of user needs in relation to the firm's capacities. . . .

Charismatic leadership of this kind has served as an archetypal model for all leadership roles. It has often been regarded as the one essential quality demanded of the person at the head of any organization or group. Its existence has been regarded, too, as a substantial justification for organization according to hierarchic forms and the concentration of power in the person at the top. Yet any concern operating on such a system of beliefs, however successful and forceful the leader, is ill-equipped to survive the end of the careers of the pioneer group. When such beliefs become weakened or extinct, the commitments created have to be sanctioned first by explicit principles of loyalty to the boss, or to the firm, and then by routines of subordination. . . .

(ii) When the beliefs of the managing director in his capacities are not shared by his subordinates, attempts to sustain the role of charismatic or even of authoritarian leader may in fact result in over-playing or under-playing. Over-playing the role is the more familiar of these two illegitimate uses of the characteristics of the position. It leads to a more complete social isolation. A sudden change of policy, the upsetting of promotion prospects by importing a senior manager without consultation, wayward changes of intention during a meeting, outbursts of temper, dismissals or promotions on what appear to subordinates as insubstantial grounds may, when they intrude themselves into the traffic of conversations and meetings between the managing director and his subordinates, prompt the same, equable, non-committal responses and comments or even the same compliance or applause that other more acceptable or even successful strokes in the past have won. The perpetual encounter, universally within the concern, with responses which are either fabricated or blank sets an increasing distance between the man at the top and his subordinates. . . . So far as the organization itself is concerned, the positive aspect of the response is the building-up of a tacitly or explicitly collusive understanding among subordinates, which may develop into team-play against the managing director. This requires a substantial and comprehensive network of loyalties, from which any persons have to be excluded who are suspected of buying favor by acting as informants to the managing director.

Under-exploiting the role is perhaps less familiar, at least in this industry, and was observable in only one case. It consists in a partial abdication from the role. The head of the concern, in this instance, was said to be 'involved' in the big decisions about financial and commercial policy and to interest himself in people and things which had meant much to the company in the past; he was accorded very high prestige because of the 'personal achievement' which the history of the firm, founded by him, represented. But the center of gravity, so far as general matters of direction and organization were concerned, was among his immediate subordinates.

In this case, the collusive arrangements between subordinates, while necessary in order to stabilize the division of power between themselves and their superior, took on an additional function. The ties of loyalty derived not so much from mutual self-protection as from a kind of tacit non-aggressive understanding. In order to ensure that no single member of the ruling group extended his influence at the expense of the others, a peculiar formal structure was arrived at. A hierarchy of committees on which they all sat *ex officio* enabled them to make or influence executive decisions or recommendations at two or three levels below their own, *and* to review them subsequently. The degree of central control exercised over all aspects of the concern's activities was therefore abnormally high.

(iii) The managing director, however, may escape from most of the circumstances of his social isolation, although since such escape always requires deliberate acts of choice, it does not necessarily affect his ultimate seniority and responsibility. Legitimate escape from isolation was evident in one concern, in which there was a conscious and deliberate effort by the managing director to involve other directors and subordinates along with himself in every decision of a directional or organizational kind. He put it in these words: 'What has emerged in our way of trying to run this business is that although we have believed in the need for committee decisions, we have found that we have had to try and evolve a system of having committees to voice opinions, leaving no doubt that some joker has to go off and take action having heard what everybody else says. This is more sensible if he has said his piece. Even then, the decision may not be the one you'd made. . . . In our set-up we are feeling our way towards the new types of organizational structure which are going to be required—they are based much more on discussion than they were.' . . .

In describing a mode of playing the role of managing director as 'escaping from' its isolation, therefore, the phrase should be understood in terms of a perpetual intention and endeavor rather than final achievement. The difference between this and the first two modes is nevertheless material. It may be roughly indicated by the distinction in common usage between 'directing' and 'leading'. In terms of the top management organization, the difference lies in the location of indeterminacy in the situation of the individual subordinate. Under 'direction', indeterminacy is largely confined to the behavior of the man at the top. He may propose, or dispose, 'without consulting anybody'. One measure of his superlative qualities as head of the concern is, indeed, his unpredictability (although another may also be the subsequent success of his decisions) as showing his confidence in his capacity for thinking farther and faster than his subordinates. So, even though believing in his capacities and stimulated by the success of the enterprise under his control, subordinates are compelled to devote attention to reading his in-

tentions and analysing the factors affecting them, obscure though they are. Under 'leadership', indeterminacy attaches not to the person at the top, but to the situation the subordinate finds himself in, along with his superior and his colleagues and the firm; decisions do not arrive like 'thunderbolts' from above; the only way out of the difficulties of reaching decisions in the most indeterminate of situations is by consulting his superior and his colleagues.

What should be apparent is that both systems equally originate in a line of conduct pursued by the head of the concern, both are equally forms of organization, both equally dependent on his powers and the use he makes for them. For their success, also, both are equally dependent on the extent to which both superior and subordinate share a common system of beliefs about the way the managing director should perform in his role. Because only in so far as the system operates in a context of trust can the energies of subordinates and chief alike be directed to solving the problems presented by the situation of the concern, rather than the problems of their relationships with each other.

(iv) When a manager makes a confidant of someone who is not accorded the rank of deputy or next-in-line, or 'plays off' individuals and groups against each other in order to weaken potential competition for his position or pressure from below, he may be said to seek an illegitimate escape from isolation. If one took all comments made in interviews at their face value, this strategy would be regarded as the most frequent of all four. Some discounting of such statements is necessary for a number of reasons. Allegations of favouritism and of playing-off are useful as a means of saving one's self-esteem on occasions when a superior has shown a preference for others, more attention than one expects to others' affairs, or less to one's own, or has offered criticism or shown disfavour. Also, most managers react strongly and immediately to the slightest suspicion in their superior's conduct of such tendencies.

These sensitivities are aroused because such conduct by the managing director exploits the ambiguities of the positions occupied by members of a concern. They are at one and the same time co-operators in the common enterprise of the concern and rivals for the rewards of successful competition with each other, just as the management hierarchy is at the same time a single control system and a career ladder. So far as the working organization is concerned, managers are co-operators and the hierarchy is a control system. It is assumed that this is the aspect which the head of the concern wishes to be dominant. If, however, he becomes pre-occupied with the weaknesses in his own position, some of which may be unavoidable, such as being less technically expert than this juniors, he may feel driven to making use of the competitiveness of his subordinates and to exploiting the absolute control he has over the success ladder. But he may also do this in an attempt to buy relief from the rivalries themselves.

At all stages of the management hierarchy, some feelings of insecurity and self-doubt enter into individuals' occupancy of their several positions. Reassurance of some kind, even spurious, becomes an absolute necessity at times. For the most part, such reassurance is gained through gossip. In gossip, judgments are passed on to other people, mostly of a depreciatory kind. In this way one can gain a tem-

porary 'fix' of one's own standing or prestige; one can also detect what styles of conduct and directions of activity win approval from one's peers. Also, "Gossip offers the guarantee that because one is united with at least one other in judging A to be deficient in technical knowledge, B to have made a gaffe, C to be sycophantic, D to spend too much time chatting in the canteen, the speaker and his hearer—compared with these others—are at least free from such faults. In gossip, speaker's and audience's status claims are underwritten, relative to these being discussed."[1]

Clearly the greatest possible reassurance is obtained when gossip is exchanged with a managing director. One managing director remarked that he seemed to spend most of his time 'keeping his departmental and lab chiefs happy'. This appeared to involve long gossipy chats with one or other of them, in which a fairly cosy intimacy could develop. The fact that he had to do so with each in turn, and reject any special intimacy in meetings with more than one of them, kept the jealousies and suspicions he was contending with well stoked. Because, in such a group, it is not long before it is apparent to those who are privileged to enter such relationships that they may also well form the subjects of gossip on other occasions.

Whether he allows himself to be captured by one or other careerist subordinate or by one or other caucus seeking a political victory, or 'keeps the peace' (his own peace) by making diplomatic use of confidential gossip, the managing director is endeavouring to escape from the isolated position

---

[1]Burns, Tom. 'The Reference of Conduct in Small Groups; Cliques and Cabals in Occupational Milieux." *Human Relations*, 8 (1955), pp. 467–86.

which he must occupy before he can insist on the co-operative aspect of each managerial role and the operation of the management hierarchy as a control system. The difficulties of relationships among the top management of which so many managing directors complain are 'presenting problems' of symptomatic rather than fundamental nature. The essential problem is the unbearable isolation of his own position.

# 17

# Subordination

We could not have dealt with many of the aspects of organization already discussed without implicitly or explicitly considering subordination. The purpose of treating subordination separately is to orient meaningfully this aspect of organization to other characteristics of group life.

Certainly, the exercise of authority implies subordination. Leadership implies subordination—being led. Status ranking means that somebody or some group has to be low man on the totem pole, just as somebody has to be the crowning figure at the top.

Among a number of possible aspects of subordination that might be given special emphasis here, we have chosen four. First, how does being in a subordinate position affect relations with those above and below? You will recall Roethlisberger's discussion of the position of the foreman in this connection. You will also recall the discussion of the power of subordinates in the Chapter 11. Second, does subordination have positive social values to the individual? Put another way, does the person, in relating himself to an organized group, find this group association satisfying, even though he plays a subordinate role in it? Third, what are the preconditions for insubordination? When does subordination become irksome? Fourth, we **INTRODUCTION** will turn to an examination of the balance between doing what is ordered (and only that), and using initiative in fulfilling an organizational position. This is the general problem of the balance between initiative and compliance in administrative behavior.

406

Implicit in all four of these questions are the ideas of coercion and control. However, we can put aside until the next chapter a formal consideration of control within organizations. In Chapter 18, we will undertake a systematic analysis of control.

In the first selection of this chapter, the ranks of an organization are pictured as looking upward to take cues for behavior. This is obviously an oversimplification, but perhaps it is justifiable in order to make a point. It is an oversimplification for several reasons. In the discussions of informal organization and informal relations, we concluded that individuals behave in organizations with reference to their peers—the people on the same level with them. This certainly is leveling attention horizontally to find cues

for organization behavior. In the discussion of sponsorship, in the chapter on leadership, the point was made that even the ranks of workers have power to sponsor and reject groups of individuals. This is evident in the often-heard statement by management officials that "we would do it but our workers will not stand for it." This certainly is looking downward into the organization for cues to action.

The reason for the emphasis of the first selection is obvious. Being "boss-oriented" is encountered in all ranks of an organization. It is also one of the first things that usually happens to a new member of an organization. Let us remember, however, that it is not the only orientation to which the usual organization member responds.

## UPWARD ORIENTATION TOWARD SUPERIORS

*Robert Dubin*

It is one of the paradoxes of organization that delegation of authority is supposed to permit an individual to concentrate on getting his subordinates to carry out a task while at the same time directing his own attention toward the source of delegated authority. Thus, we are expected to be oriented toward subordinates and at the same time toward the boss. In occupying such a position, there is likely to be a strain characteristic of any subordinate rank.

What are the factors that contribute to making everyone in an organization look upward along the lines of authority? There are three important

factors: (1) the process of delegation itself; (2) the control and direction that delegation implies; and (3) the superior's evaluation of performance.

Delegation of authority and responsibility implies that the source of the delegation is in a superior organization position whose incumbent is theoretically capable of performing the task or function delegated. Thus, there is implicit in every delegation of authority the idea that responsibility still rests at the level from which the delegation has been made. This works itself out in two primary ways.

In the first place, the superior retains some control and direction of a delegated function. The subordinate usually feels impelled to inform his superior about what he is doing and to secure approval for it. Carried too far, this dependence upon a superior destroys the very effectiveness of the delegation. The superior might as well do it himself if the subordinate fails to assume some initiative in implementing the authority delegated to him.

In the second place, the superior is constantly evaluating the performance of his subordinates. Out of such evaluation comes advancement, salary increases, or censure. Inevitably, the rewards and punishments of the organization are controlled by those of superior rank. This obviously bends the efforts of subordinates toward pleasing the boss and being wary of his ire. Carried to an extreme, this sensitivity to the boss leads to over-concern with the superior's every whim, gesture, and expression of approval or displeasure.

Within this framework of upward orientation toward superiors arises an important problem of relations with one's own subordinates. The organizational success of a foreman is in part dependent upon the performance of his subordinates; that of the superintendent upon the performance of his foremen, and so on up the line. Accordingly, each supervisor is likely to feel that his success is at the mercy of those he supervises. In such a situa-

tion there is a tendency to shift blame for failure upon one's subordinates.

In a real sense, then, there is built into the very structure of authority in an organization the conditions making for critical and fault-finding relations with subordinates.

At the same time, there is built into an organization a subservience to superiors arising from the structure of authority.

These two conditions of organizations often give rise to considerable strain on personnel. The intermediate subordinate tends to be driving with respect to his own subordinates and fawning with respect to his superiors; the personnel in the middle levels of administration behave in mutually contradictory ways at the same time.

Around this contradictory role expectation often arises a rationale that takes the following general form: the driving supervisor is tolerated by his subordinates because it is recognized that he is acting under organizational imperatives over which he has no control. The corporal is demanding of the private, the sergeant of the corporal, the lieutenant of the sergeant, and so on up the line. Imperious command is tolerated in the organizational situation where it would be rejected in other kinds of social relations. The fact that both the superior and the subordinate are operating within the framework of an organization makes the difference.

---

Turning to the second aspect of subordination that we want to examine, we find in the following selection, from the writings of Georg Simmel, the great German sociologist, an elaboration of the positive functions of subordination for the individual.

Simmel starts by suggesting that whether or not it is historically accurate, it is useful to think of primitive subordination as bending to the personal superiority of another individual. With the growth in size of the organizations of society comes the development of authority in relation to office, or, in Simmel's phrase, positions. Subordination is no longer to individuals who possess outstanding qualities, but rather to offices arranged in a hierarchy of authority or superordination. This part of the analysis should already be one that is familiar to us.

Simmel then goes on to raise the question of what happens to the individual in this structure of impersonality. Is he satisfied to be under the coercion that inevitably accompanies subordination? Simmel concludes that the order and orderliness essential to participation in group life and activity are derived from subordination to authority. In other words, participation in organizations and subordination to group goals and values are essential to the individual.

---

## SUBORDINATION

### *Georg Simmel**

The fact of domination poses the following quite general sociological problem. Superordination and subordination constitute, on the one hand, a form of the objective organization of society. On the other hand, they are the expression of differences in personal qualities among men. How do these two characteristics compare with one another, and how is the form of sociation influenced by the differences in this relationship?

In the beginning of societal development, the superordination of one personality over others must have been the adequate expression and consequence of personal superiority. There is no reason why, at a social stage with no fixed organization that would *a priori* allocate his place to the individual, anybody should subordinate himself to another, unless force, piety, bodily or spiritual or volitional superiority, suggestion—in brief, the relation of his personal being to that of the other—determined him to do so. . . .

Thus, in primitive times, the prince is required or assumed to have perfections which are extraordinary in their extent or combination. The Greek king of the heroic period had to be, not only brave, wise, and eloquent, but also outstanding as an athlete and, if possible, an excellent carpenter, shipbuilder, and husbandman as well. It has been noted that the position of King David rested largely upon the fact that he was, at the same time, a singer and warrior, a layman and prophet, and that he had the capabilities needed for a fusion of secular state power with spiritual theocracy. This origin of superordination and subordination, of course, still operates constantly in society and continuously creates new situations. But out of it have developed, and are developing, fixed organizations of superordination and subordination. Individuals are

*From *The Sociology of Georg Simmel* (Glencoe, Ill., 1950), pp. 291–294, 298–300. Translated by Kurt H. Wolff. Copyright by The Free Press. Used by permission.

either born into them or attain given positions in them on the basis of qualities quite different from those which originally founded the super-subordination in question.

This transition from the subjectivistic relationship of domination to an objective formation and fixation, is effected by the purely quantitative expansion of the sphere of domination. Two actually contradictory motives are significant in it. The increase in number of people entails an increase in the qualitative characteristics existing among them. This greatly increases the improbability that any one person with a strong subjective individuality has identical or even generally satisfactory relations to all others. To the extent that there is an increase in the differences within the group over which domination extends, the ruler . . . must shed all individual character and adopt, instead, a general character, above subjective fluctuations.

On the other hand, this same expansion of the group leads to the division of labor. . . . Unlike the Greek king, the ruler of a large group can no longer be the standard and leader of all its essential interests. What is required, rather, are manifold specialization and specialized division of the regime. . . . The results of activity, now circumscribed in purely objective terms, form a unit along with those of other personalities. It is probable that the totality of such causal chains has transformed the relation of domination, which originated from case to case and from person to person, into an objective form in which not the person, but the position, so to speak, is the superordinate element. . . . The firmer and the more technically articulated the organization of the group, the more objectively and formally do the patterns of superordination and subordination present them-

selves. Individuals suited for the positions are sought only "afterwards," or else the positions are filled by the mere accidents of birth and other contingencies. . . .

There operates quite generally the conviction that coercion is necessary for social organization. The idea is that human nature simply needs coercion lest human actions become completely purposeless and formless. For the general character of this postulate, it is irrelevant whether subordination be under a person and his arbitrariness, or under a law. There are, admittedly, certain extreme cases where the formal value of subordination no longer makes up for the senselessness of its content; but, aside from these, it is of only secondary interest whether the content of the law be a little better or a little worse—exactly, it will be remembered, as was the case concerning the quality of the ruling personality. . . .

The advantages of subordination are similar to the prerogative of marriage over free love. Nobody can deny that the coercion of law and custom holds innumerable marriages together which, from the moral standpoint, ought to break apart. In these instances, the persons concerned subordinate themselves to a law which simply does not fit their case. But in other instances, this same coercion—however hard, momentarily and subjectively, it may be felt to be—is an irreplaceable value, because it keeps together those who, from the moral standpoint, ought to stay together but, for some momentary ill-temper, irritation, or vacillation of feeling, would separate if they only could, and thus would impoverish or destroy their lives irreparably. The content of marriage laws may be good or bad, may be or may not be applicable to a given case: the mere coercion of the law to stay together develops individual values of an . . . ethical nature (not to mention values of social expediency) which, according to the pessimistic, perhaps one-sided standpoint presupposed here, could never be realized in the absence of all coercion. The mere consciousness of everyone that he is bound to the other by coercion may, in some cases, make the common life utterly unbearable. But in other cases, this consciousness will bring about a tolerance, self-discipline, and thorough psychological training which nobody would feel inclined to undergo if separation were possible at all times. These traits are produced, rather, only by the desire to make the unavoidable life in common at least as bearable as possible.

Occasionally, the consciousness of being under coercion, of being subject to a superordinate authority, is revolting or oppressive—whether the authority be an ideal or social law, an arbitrarily decreeing personality or an executor of higher norms. But, for the majority of men, coercion probably is an irreplaceable support and cohesion of the inner and outer life. In the inevitably symbolic language of all psychology: our soul seems to live in two layers, one of which is deeper, hard or impossible to move, carrying the real sense or substance of our life, while the other is composed of momentary impulses and isolated irritabilities.

This second layer would be victorious over the first and even more often than it actually is; and, because of the onslaught and quick alternation of its elements, the second layer would give the first no opportunity to come to the surface if the feeling of a coercion interfering from somewhere did not dam its torrent, break its vacillations and caprices, and thus, again and again, give room and supremacy to the persistent undercurrent.

In comparison with this functional significance of coercion as such, its particular content is of only secondary importance. Senseless coercion may be replaced by sensible coercion, but even the latter has its significance, which is relevant here, only in that which it shares with the former. Moreover, not only the toleration of coercion, but also opposition to it—both to unjust and to justified coercion—has for the rhythm of our surface life this same function of inhibition and interruptions: to make conscious and effective the deeper currents of the most intimate and substantial life, which cannot be inhibited by any external means. Insofar as coercion is associated with some form of domination, the association reveals that element in domination which is, as it were, indifferent to the quality of the ruler and to any individual right to dominate, and which thus shows the deeper sense of the claim to authority as such.

---

The following selection deals with the preconditions for insubordination. In this selection, de Man sets forth the conditions under which subordinates react adversely to the exercise of authority. In the terminology we have already become familiar with, we can say that the subordinates are reacting by questioning the legitimacy of the authority or the authority-holder. This is an old but thoughtful analysis, more objectively viewed by us, perhaps, because it is based upon German, not American, data. The reports from which de Man draws his conclusions were autobiographical work histories that he collected.

---

## REACTION TO SUBORDINATION

### *Henri de Man**

Levenstein, in the previously quoted book, in which he reports on a mass study of working-class mentality, comes to the conclusion that: "Only to the extent of securing a minimal subsistence is the worker interested in the material things of life. . . . What he finds most intolerable is his dependent position." The reports I collected fifteen years later from the students of the Frankfort Labour College confirm this impression. To put the matter epigrammatically, we may say that the worker regards as his worst enemy, not the machine, but the boss. Among the causes of distaste for work, the social causes predominate over the technical; and among the social causes, the most important is disciplinary subordination of the worker.

In the seventy-eight reports, thirty of the writers expressly declare that the pressure exercised on them by the hierarchy of the enterprise has been the main cause of their distaste for their work. It is true that many of them confine themselves to specific complaints regarding the inefficiency of their superiors, either on technical or on psychological grounds; but it is obvious that the expressed condemnation of individuals on such a scale is tantamount to a condemnation of the system which these individuals represent.

Resentment against superiors in the enterprise is not identical with the worker's social resentment against the capitalist, or with his resentment against the employer as an "exploiter." Characteristically, it is primarily directed against the immediate chief, the foreman, himself a wage earner, once described as a man who "crawls on his belly before the boss while trampling on those who are placed under his direction." This is analogous to what we find in army life where the private usually hates the sergeant much more cordially than he hates the divisional commander. In many instances we are told in so many words in the reports that the higher members of the managerial staff and the actual employer are not such bad fellows after all; no doubt because they have shown themselves comparatively indifferent about trifling matters, and because they are usually better educated than the foreman and less rough and surly in their manners. We find, too, that the dislike of chiefs is especially strong in public enterprises in which, although they are not run for profit, bureaucratization and militarization give the hierarchical system an especially despotic character.

It is to be noted that not one of the writers ventures to declare that production could be properly carried on without some kind of disciplinary subordination of the worker. The supposition that reasonably intelligent workers hold the opposite view is confuted by the touching enthusiasm with which the reports extol the advantages of having a "good" chief, by which is meant one who is efficient, just, and animated with good will. But, we are told, the master must be in very truth a master, that is to say a man who is

---

*From *Joy in Work* (London, 1929), pp. 200–204. Translated from the German by Eden and Cedar Paul. Copyright by George Allen & Unwin, Ltd. Used by permission.

really the workman's superior in respect of craft knowledge or skill, and is at the same time fully competent to lead and to train men. Close examination shows that what the writers are really objecting to is some specific and unfavourable manifestation of hierarchical control, such as: *a.* parasitic bureaucracy; *b.* disciplinary authority exercised by persons who have not a corresponding responsibility for the technical organisation of the work; *c.* speeding-up or spying by foremen under the piecework system; *d.* incompetence. We always find that the ultimate cause of resentment against the disciplinary hierarchy, and especially against its lower-grade instruments, arises because it embodies, apart from the control technically necessary for the guidance of labour, also motives of private gain, on the one hand, and motives of social dominance, on the other. The latter cause of dissatisfaction is the more important of the two, as we see from the example of public enterprises, where discontent for this reason is widespread. Even in private capitalist enterprises, the fact that the chiefs represent the profit-making interests of the employer confronts the workers in the form of a mortifying hierarchy of social power. This superior power is based upon the propertyless condition of the worker, and on his dependence on the employer's will for his chances of gaining a livelihood. Its customary method of expression is the assertion of a claim to enhanced prestige on the part of all who exercise this disciplinary authority, and such a claim is usually made with especial crudeness and roughness by those who themselves stand on the lowest rungs of the hierarchical ladder. The nearer one in authority over workers himself stands to the workers in respect of origin, education, occupational capacity, and level of earnings, the more violently self-assertive will be the manifestations of his will-to-power, the more insistent will he be in the display of his authority, and the more sharply, therefore, will he come into conflict with the worker's sense of self-esteem.

This feeling of self-esteem is based on a sense of justice which on principle challenges the presupposition of the employer's authority. For social reasons, which are familiar enough, the worker regards it as unjust and immoral that he should be so completely dependent on the employer's will. This feeling of injustice becomes intensified where the claim to authority most directly and most frequently conflicts with the worker's own voluntary impulses, namely, where the worker comes into contact with the foreman. When a State is hated or despised by its subjects, the policeman rather than the cabinet minister has to bear the brunt of this unpopularity, for he stands in a twofold respect nearer to the common people. His local duties compel him to interfere frequently in the daily life of his neighbours; and his own humble origin deprives his authority of the prestige of distance. The minister of State, who issues the orders, inspires a far more genuine respect than does the poor devil in uniform who has to carry them out, himself usually underpaid, and subjected to a rigid discipline.

The worst feature of workshop discipline is that the disciplinary authority is exercised by a person or by a series of persons who also have to undertake technical and organizational guidance of the work. The mingling of productive discipline with social subordination is what poisons the present hierarchical system of enterprise.

It will be recalled that in Chapter 4 we dealt with the relations between individual needs and the needs of the organization, seeing the possibilities of both conflict and complementary interactions between these respective levels of needs.

We now turn to another kind of relationship between the individual and his employing organization. We ask two general questions: (1) To what extent can each member of the organization be expected to be competent and therefore able to exercise some individual judgment and initiative in carrying out his assigned responsibilities? (2) To what extent does efficiency in carrying out the business of the organization demand that each of its members displays unswerving compliance with all directives and orders governing working behavior and forego the exercise of judgment and initiative?

Attention is now fixed on the survival needs of the organization and we are concerned with the issue of whether this survival is enhanced only by strict compliance with expectations regarding working behavior, or whether it is even better achieved by combining general compliance with specific opportunities for individual judgment and initiative. This issue is a central and continuing concern in all modern organizations. The problem arises in all industrial societies, and in all organizations that carry out their business.

Bendix casts the following discussion largely in terms of governmental administration. He contrasts democratic with authoritarian social organization and shows how the solution of the compliance-initiative problems is different in each. He shows that all large-scale organizations, grounded in either a democratic or authoritarian social philosophy must solve the compliance-initiative problem in some fashion. It is worth repeating his general conclusion: "We cannot profit from the efficiency of large-scale organizations unless we succeed in making the initiative of the individual one of our principles of organization."

---

## ADMINISTRATIVE COMPLIANCE AND INITIATIVE

*Reinhard Bendix**

The analysis of large-scale organization in the modern world will be deficient, as long as it makes *either* the formal organizational structure *or* the informal human relations within that

*From "Bureaucracy: The Problem and Its Setting," *American Sociological Review,* 12:502–507 (Oct. 1947). Copyright by the American Sociological Society. Used by permission.

structure the vantage point of its observations. The historical approach conceives modern organization in industry or government in terms of a contrast to earlier forms. Consequently, it stresses the *greater* rationality of modern organization. The managerial approach, on the other hand, focuses its attention on the as yet unmanaged aspects of human relations, which have "asserted" themselves in all organizations. The tacit assumption is made that thorough study will show us how these "remaining human irrationalities" may become manageable. But this assumption is unwarranted in so far as the division of labor and the work relations requisite to the productive (or the administrative) process necessitate precisely those human irrationalities which management is now seeking to remove.

It is apparent that neither of these approaches has a sufficient theoretical basis. This shortcoming is not overcome by the observation that the studies of "rationalization" overlook the human factor, and vice versa. Instead, it is necessary to show in what manner all large-scale organizations require for their success a "proper" *irrational* foundation. In this respect the basic problem of all large-scale organizations is the same. Such organizations depend for their effectiveness on a clearly understood hierarchy of authority. Yet, they would break down if every official would follow all regulations to the letter and consult his superior whenever these rules do not provide sufficient guidance. Such "typically bureaucratic" behavior would interfere with the functioning of the organization at every point. All organizations depend, on the other hand, on the ability and the willingness of their employees to act on their own initiative, whenever that is called for. Yet it would be clearly incompatible with their effective operation, if every official conducted the business assigned to him in accordance with his independent judgment. It is consequently imperative that the employees of all ranks in industry and government strike a balance between compliance and initiative, that they temper

their adherence to formal rules by a judicious exercise of independent judgment and that they fit their initiative into the framework of formal regulation. Both the effective exercise of power or the effective organization of production depend in some measure on this mixture of compliance with authority and the creative exercise of initiative. All large-scale organizations face the problem of finding formal and informal ways, by which such a balance may be facilitated.

This balance between compliance and initiative is likely to vary with cultural and institutional differences. The contrast between business and government is perhaps the most obvious case in point. Initiative is concerned with market chances in business, but with political chances in government. Compliance in business is a matter of managerial arrangement based on a wage contract. Compliance in government involves, in addition, the special legal liabilities and disabilities of the civil servant, which concern the spirit of his work, not only its performance. Business is relatively free from being bound by precedent, it is not encumbered by the anticipation of checks other than failure of the venture itself. These obvious differences have their basis in the conditions under which in each instance the formal hierarchy of authority allows—more or less unwittingly—for an exercise of independent judgment.

In stating the problem in this manner we may have a clue to the systematic analysis and differentiation of large-scale organizations, which goes beyond the obvious contrast of government and business.[1] Attitudes to-

[1] In the study of business organizations it has always been assumed that they are essentially similar in countries of comparable economic structure. Certainly, the similarity

ward risk-taking, toward authority, and toward the public, as well as the institutional conditions of the "working climate" differ from industry to industry and from government to government. These and other variables affect the relationship of the individual employee to the organizational hierarchy; they modify the manner in which he functions within the organization and in which he sees its overall purpose. It may be useful to illustrate these points by contrasting the ideal types of democratic and authoritarian administration.[2]

*Authoritarian* administration is characterized by the fact that the official is both obedient and arbitrary. His strict compliance with the orders of his superior is not tempered (as it is under democratic conditions) by responsiveness to public demands. Reliance is placed on the feeling of loyalty, which the official demonstrates by his unquestioning support of the prevailing order of authority. Such loyalty implies a difference in status between officialdom and the public and in this manner "testifies" to the reliability of the authoritarian official. In bringing his orders nearer execution this loyalty of the subordinate finds its counterpart in the fact that he must now become a superior in his own right. In doing so he acts as a "leader" to whose guidance the people should submit without question. To be sure his authority is limited, but the official nevertheless confronts his public as

the representative of higher authority rather than as a "public employee."

The official in the middle and the lower ranks of the service is in some respects similar to the officer. . . . Even without uniform there is a strong feeling of comradeship and a feeling of solidarity against civilians. . . . The subordination of lower to higher ranks in the officialdom is similar to relations in the army and it is tolerable only when it is compensated for by a feeling of special status of the officials as against the public. . . . Officials in the middle and lower ranks still represent the superior power and wisdom of the state towards a public to whom the larger meaning of public administration is indifferent or incomprehensible. Indeed, the official will tend to regard the importance of his administrative section the more highly the less he is able to comprehend the real overall significance of his own work.[3]

In this as in all systems of administration much is left to the discretionary exercise of authority. It lies in the spirit of "authoritarian discretion" that a successful maintenance of authority is in the end more important than its possible abuse. In case of failure the official is punished, not so much for an abuse of his authority, but for his "demonstrably disloyal" (i.e., unsuccessful) exercise of it. Such methods of administration lead in the extreme case to continuous suspicion downwards and the attempt to evade responsibility on the part of subordinates. There is a telling description of this in Walter L. Dorn's analysis of Prussian bureaucracy under Frederick the Great:

___

of technical and administrative problems in large-scale industries makes this view plausible. Yet there is reason to believe that this assumption is misleading. Cf. the interesting essay by Hermann Levy, *Volkscharakter und Wirtschaft* (Leipzig: B. G. Tuebner, 1926).

[2] Although this contrast uses only illustrations from Government Administration it applies equally well in my opinion to other types of large-scale organizations.

___

[3] Ottoheinz von der Gablentz and Carl Mennicke, *Deutsche Berufskunde* (Leipzig: Bibliographisches Institut, 1930), pp. 428–29. (My translation.)

Frederick the Great cherished the inveterate belief that his officials were bent on deceiving him. . . . This distrust became an integral part of the bureaucratic system. Unreserved confidence he reposed in none of his ministers. He kept them in a perpetual state of uncertainty as to what he thought of their honesty and capacity. . . . He frequently struck upon the expedient of committing the task of reporting on any particular piece of business to two or three different officials, none of whom was aware that others were engaged in the same mission. When he did not wholly trust an official he charged an underling with secret supervision. To control his ministers he regularly corresponded with the presidents of the provincial chambers, and to assure himself of the veracity of the latter he often dealt with the individual members of the provincial chambers. By this continuous correspondence with officials and their subordinates, by controlling ministers through their subalterns and subordinates through their equals, the king tapped extraordinary sources of information which, besides the ordinary channels of information . . . , acquainted him with everything he seriously desired to know.[4]

Obviously, this system of authoritarian supervision has since become impractical with the growing complexity of administration in a modern state. Modern dictatorships have instituted instead elaborate administrative organizations for the systematic supervision of the political loyalty of the people and all government employees. A modern police system can employ the most advanced techniques in its closely calculated control over large populations.[5] Although these techniques have freed authoritarian supervision from the limitations of centralizing power in one person, they cannot escape from the necessity of forever duplicating their supervisory checks, because in this system no one spy can be trusted.

In *democratic* administration officials are given commands of greater latitude than under authoritarian conditions, and their execution of these commands is subject to a rather diffuse supervision. The democratic official is ideally expected to be obedient to his superior, but he does not thereby express his loyalty to the people's mandate. On the other hand, he is to exercise his authority in the spirit of service, not of mastery. The democratic administrator stands, therefore, in an ambivalent relationship to his superior and his subordinate. His compliance, his orders, and his initiative are tempered by a sense of direct, if imponderable, accountability to the people. In this respect, superior and subordinate are equals before the public, although they are unequal within the administrative hierarchy. This peculiar characteristic of democratic administration is well illustrated by the problems encountered in law enforcement:

The policeman may observe a multitude of violations, some relating to laws and ordinances which were never intended by the enactors to be enforced, others involving minor regulations of public order. . . . Their very number

---

[4]Walter L. Dorn, "The Prussian Bureaucracy in the 18th Century," *Political Science Quarterly*, XLVI (September, 1931), 421–22. For a modern parallel see Alexander Barmine, *One Who Survived* (New York: G. P. Putnam, 1945), pp. 196–233, 237–45. A comparable situation in business is discussed in "The Stewardship of Sewell Avery," *Fortune*, XXXIII (May, 1946), 111–13, 179–86.

[5]This point is especially emphasized by E. Kohn-Bramstedt, *Dictatorship and Political Police* (London: Kegan Paul, 1945), pp. 2–6, 95–117, 137–56.

and variety are such that their requirements are largely unknown to the people to whom they apply. Hence violations are extremely common. . . .

The policeman's art, then, consists in applying and enforcing a multitude of laws and ordinances in such degree or proportion and in such manner that the greatest degree of social protection will be secured. The degree of enforcement and the method of application will vary with each neighborhood and community. There are no set rules, nor even general guides to policy, in this regard. Each policeman must, in a sense, determine the standard which is to be set in the area for which he is responsible. . . . Thus he is a policy-forming police administrator in miniature, who operates beyond the scope of the usual devices of popular control. He makes and unmakes the fortunes of governmental executives and administrators, though rarely falling under the direct influence of the popular will. The only control to which he is subject is the discipline of his superiors.[6]

And yet, his superiors are dependent for their success on the wisdom with which this policeman in his law enforcement practices will respond to the *indirect influences* of the community.

In exercising such discretion in his direct contact with the public the democratic administrator is ideally as concerned with administering a policy as he is with the execution of a command. (Indeed, he is always contributing to a policy, whether he knows it or not.) Yet, this policy continues to be subject to a multiplicity of influences to which the administrator must remain sensitive. (Shifts in policy under

authoritarian conditions always take the form of new orders from above.) This implies that the democratic official does his duty in the continuous anticipation of checks on his authority, both from his superior *and* from his "public" (which includes legislatures, pressure groups, affected individuals, etc.). He is trained in considering his office as a mandate of responsibilities, which are subject to more or less continuous modification. Yet, his mandate is nevertheless of a general character, it is meant to be an integral part of a scheme of policies in process of reformulation. He *must,* therefore, seek to redefine his function in this scheme on the presupposition that some rational policy emerges from the "conflict of interests" and in the belief that—whatever the policy —this "conflict" itself is a basic and worthwhile feature of the democratic process.

The authoritarian administrator is, on the other hand, more immune, his work is less directly subject to "pressures" from outside the official hierarchy. Under authoritarian conditions obedience and loyalty are synonymous, since each administrative superior is ideally the only source of command, the representative of the regime, and the source of its policy formulation. For each subordinate, policy emanates from the top and is unaffected by the administrator's direct contact with the public. The role of each official in the execution of over-all policy is, consequently, a matter of intra-administrative discussion and adjustment. And because each subordinate administrator is in this sense remote from the public, responsibility for policy determination is more clearly confined to the top administrators and is by the same token less affected by public opinion. It fol-

---

[6] Bruce Smith, *Police Systems in the United States* (New York: Harper & Brothers, 1940), p. 20.

lows from these considerations that an administration will be the more democratic, the more its officials are directly affected by the "antagonism of influences"[7] and the more they are, therefore, drawn into participating, more or less directly, in the processes of policy formation.

The preceding confrontation of two ideal types of bureaucracy may serve both to dispel some misconception and to focus attention on the major area of inquiry in this field. Both forms of administration may function efficiently. This is the case under authoritarian conditions when the *esprit de corps* of the administrative group is high, its loyalty to the regime intact and in harmony with public attitude, and its resultant feeling of security a good foundation for the exercise of individual initiative by the administrator within this framework. It is the case under democratic conditions, when the spirit of public service among administrators is well developed, their responsiveness to public demands kept within limits by the public's restraint in pressing for individual privileges and by the administration's success in achieving consistent policy formulations which represent genuine compromises of the various conflicting groups.

Both forms of bureaucracy may also develop the pathology of large-scale organizations. Authoritarian bureaucracy can become a clique ridden by suspicion. Its primary concern with self-preservation results in the alienation of the public, a growing inability to operate efficiently, and the duplication of functions, which a more or less developed internal spy-system necessitates. Democratic administration may deteriorate, on the other hand, because the frustrations of administrative work deter qualified men and because suspicion of any authority goes so far as to make effective policy formulation and execution impossible.

The temptation is strong to summarize the difference between democratic and authoritarian administration by reference to Mannheim's distinction between functional and substantial rationality. . . . Authoritarian officials would be thought of as efficient in the use of administrative techniques without proper comprehension of their role in the over-all policy decided on by the Dictator (functional rationality). Democratic officials would combine, on the other hand, administrative inefficiency with an understanding of the basic policies which they are called upon to implement (substantial rationality).[8] This application of Mannheim's distinction does not aid us, however, in our analysis of large-scale organizations. Mannheim himself would point out that *all* subordinate administrators suffer from the special incapacity which exclusive attention to the techniques of implementation entails. Democratic and authoritarian officials share in the ability of comprehending the political program which "governs" their actions. Besides, Mannheim's distinction suffers from overstating its case.[9] It is impossible to run any large-scale organization without

---

[7]John Stuart Mill, "Representative Government," in *Utilitarianism, Liberty and Representative Government* (London: E. P. Dutton & Co., Inc., 1910), p. 201.

[8]This distinction has been used to characterize Nazi administration. See E. Kohn-Bramstedt, *op cit.,* 2–6 and John H. Herz, "German Administration under the Nazi Regime," *American Political Science Review,* XL (August, 1946), 684–86.

[9]Karl Mannheim, *Man and Society in an Age of Reconstruction* (New York: Harcourt, Brace, 1941), pp. 51–60. This is not to deny, of course, that Mannheim has pointed to a constant source of friction. The distinc-

some provision for fitting the specialized technician into the larger framework of operation. It is, however, not
possible to direct his every action;
some reliance must, therefore, be
placed on his own over-all comprehension of his function and on the initiative which he develops in implementing this comprehension by cooperative
action. Thus, both democratic and authoritarian officials must grapple with
the problem of overcoming the
"trained incapacity" (Veblen) of the
administrative technician to see the
larger policy framework. Both will
tend to use the rationalizations of their
respective political philosophies, for
instance, as guidance in all cases in
which they need but cannot obtain a
knowledge of basic policies.[10]

Democratic and authoritarian administrations differ, therefore, in terms
of their respective institutions and
culture patterns, not because one is
representative and inefficient, while
the other is efficient but arbitrary. The

tion goes back to Karl Marx, *Capital* (New
York: Modern Library, 1936), pp. 361–65,
395–99.

[10]The behavioristic importance of political philosophies in a study of administrative
conduct has not so far been sufficiently considered. See in this respect John M. Gaus,
Leonard D. White, and Marshall E. Dimock,
*The Frontiers of Public Administration*
(Chicago: University of Chicago Press,
1936).

distinction between these two types of
administration is an outgrowth of "historical experience" and present circumstances. As such, it affects the
manner of the administrative technician, who combines obedience and efficiency with the initiative that is essential to the success of large-scale
organization. It is not useful, therefore, to consider these organizations
from the point of view *either* of their
"rationalization" *or* of their "human
irrationalities." The problem of bureaucracy lies rather in the manner
in which technical and administrative
rationality are combined with the exercise of individual initiative in the
accomplishment of a common task.
Men have combined their efforts in
large-scale organizations throughout
history. Their success today will depend on whether or not they can combine the efficiency of modern organization with a flexibility which allows
the individual in that organization to
use his imagination and to apply his
convictions, rather than do his job in
a routine way. It is not only a question
of preserving freedom against the en-
croachments of bureaucracy. Rather,
we cannot profit from the efficiency of
large-scale organizations unless we
succeed in making the initiative of the
individual one of our principles of
organization.

# 18

# Control

If all of the systems of interaction within organizations that we have considered up to now were perfectly operative, there would be no need for control. Every individual and group within an organization would find a place and develop an organizationally appropriate mode of behavior that would contribute to the co-operative and coordinated group endeavor. This is obviously not the case.

Control within an organization has two major dimensions: we can conceive of control as the process of developing systems of standards for the guidance of organization behavior; we can view control as a system for enforcing standards of organization behavior. We will consider both of these dimensions.

There are many systems for guiding behavior in organizations. They range from the specific (and public) procedures manuals and job descriptions to the private, but nonetheless real, informal group codes. We are all aware of the great variety of such systems. Perhaps we are not always conscious of the fact that a system of standards for behavior is a means to an end, not an end in itself. This is one of the major points made by Roethlisberger in the first selection of this chapter. Indeed, over-elaboration and the use of inappropriate control systems are two roots of bureaucratic pathology, as we will discover in the last two portions of this chapter.

**INTRODUCTION**

There is a significant gap between the idea of control systems and the manner in which they are carried out. People officially involved in controlling others or

421

measuring others' performances spend much time working out adaptations to those subject to control. The selection Kubly provides is a nice description of how these adaptations are made between a quality inspector and a foreman whose output is being controlled.

There is a widespread knowledge that workers evade control procedures and restrict output. What is not so well known is that all levels of management may respond evasively to controls imposed upon their action.

The nature of these evasions is examined in Dubin's article dealing with executives and managers and in Jasinski's article dealing with the behavior of foremen.

In summary, we are viewing control in organizations as (1) a means for telling members what is expected from them and (2) a means for ensuring that they do what is expected. We remain sensitive to the fact that inadequate or wrong systems of control may fail to achieve either of these objectives.

---

## THE ADMINISTRATOR'S CONTROL FUNCTIONS

*Fritz J. Roethlisberger**

Maybe we can begin to see it [distinction between purpose and method] more clearly if we compare medical education and business education as they exist today. In medicine not only the skills required but also the class of phenomena to which they relate, excluding for the moment those relating to mental illness, can be much more clearly formulated than they can in business. In medicine, as in business, a number of measuring devices exist which tell the physician something about the internal environment of his patient. However, no physician conceives that by measuring blood pressure or taking a basal metabolism he can cure his patient or influence his patient's behavior. Measurement as-

sists him in making his diagnosis; it does not cure the patient. A number of laboratory technicians do not make up a medical practitioner.

A parallel can be drawn in business. These particular logics, of which we have spoken, help the administrator in diagnosing the situation. Only in this sense are they controls; they provide checks by means of which certain functions of the total enterprise can be evaluated in terms of economic objective. For example, the figures of the cost accountant provide the administrator with a useful tool for diagnosing what may be wrong. The figures in themselves cannot cure the business. Cost control, quality control, production control, measuring the performance of workers, salesmen, foremen—all these are also diagnostic aids to the administrator. They do not in and by themselves do the administra-

*Reprinted by permission of the publishers from Fritz J. Roethlisberger, *Management and Morale* (Cambridge, Mass.: Harvard University Press), 1941, pp. 151–155.

tor's job; they merely aid him in doing a better job in the same sense that a stethoscope and a thermometer assist the physician in making more adequate diagnoses. In other words, all these specialist logics do not make up an administrator.

But then the analogy breaks down, partly because of the more complex events and situations the administrator is trying to control. On the one hand, he is trying to control the attainment of the economic objective of the enterprise; on the other hand, he is trying to control concrete human behavior in the cooperative situation, which is the only means through which ultimately the common objective can be attained. This makes the administrator's problem exceedingly difficult. To try to use the same mechanism to achieve both kinds of control may be disastrous because the factors determining the attainment of the economic objective may not be of the same order and involve the same class of phenomena as those determining the cooperative situation. The physician in ordinary practice is sometimes up against the same problem, particularly when he has to secure the cooperation of the patient in following a treatment which involves a drastic change in his ways of life. The class of phenomena with which the physician is dealing then ceases to be organic.

When measuring the performance of a worker, a salesman, or a foreman, what is being controlled? Does the measurement of a person's performance necessarily control or improve it? What is the connection between a standard in terms of which a person's performance can be measured and that person's performance? Putting the question in these forms, it is clear that a standard is merely one more factor in a person's environment to which he

responds; and it is well to remember that his response may take different forms. If the standard has social sanction, it may operate on particular individuals with particular personal situations as an incentive to do better work.

In our so-called competitive culture it is assumed that we all want to do better than our fellow men. Give us a standard and we break our necks trying to do better than the next person. But some of us do not react that way. A standard may also act as a deterrent to good work, as any experienced teacher knows. How often, as teachers, have we tried to tell our conscientious and worried students to forget about grades, that they are really not important, and with what results! In the eyes of some students, our function is to grade them, not teach them. As a result, how many academics finally come to accept the grading system as a necessary evil! How do we correct this situation? By keeping the grading system relatively simple and by adding to it occasionally a grain of salt? Or by trying to create bigger and better grading systems? There are tendencies in both directions, but let us not linger on this painful subject so near to home, but talk more in general.

It is well to remember that the items are infinite in terms of which people can be differentiated. People can be classified by the length of the nose, by the color of the eyes, by the kind of clothes they wear. Some of these classifications are more useful than others, depending upon the purpose for which the classification is to be used. In any informal social group, formal organization, or community, people are likely to be differentiated in terms of items expressing the social values of these social systems. Any noticeable similarity or difference in terms of age, sex, occupation, can become the basis of social classification.

This process also goes on in business and industry. Employees, supervisors, and executives are being evaluated in terms of the tasks and duties they perform, in terms of the amount and the quality of work they do. They are also being evaluated by their fellow associates as contributors to group effort.

In any large business organization, there are at least two major evaluational systems in terms of which each contributor is being judged. In the case of one, he is evaluated in terms of certain measurable abstractions and standards relating to performance and efficiency. In the case of the other, he is being evaluated in terms of certain socially accepted codes and norms of conduct. The first evaluation tells him where he theoretically stands in the eyes of management; the second tells him where he stands in the eyes of his fellow associates. These two evaluations of a person may not coincide. He may be judged a poor worker in terms of his output record, and he may be judged a "regular fellow" by his fellow workers. We do not mean to imply that these two evaluational systems always lead to opposing judgments, that is, that regular fellows are always "inefficient" and cannot be "efficient." The only implication is that the factors determining technical efficiency are not of the same order as those determining a regular fellow. In the second evaluation, cooperative phenomena cannot be conveniently ignored.

There is no question that business organizations want regular fellows who are efficient. But how do they go about doing this? And what relation have their standards of performance to the formation and maintenance of regular fellows and efficient workers? It can be seen that these standards help in the direction of efficiency when the cooperative situation can be assumed as being satisfactory; that is, when it can be taken for granted that the individual and the group of which he is a member are working together as a team, that the standard is operating as an incentive, and that the supervisor applies the standard with "discretion" and "good judgment" in order to secure the cooperation of his group in attaining the economic objective. But what if the person is a member of a small group whose informal organization is at variance with the economic objective of the company? And what if the supervisor does not apply the standard with "discretion," "common sense," and "good judgment"? It is clear that in cases where the cooperative situation cannot be taken for granted, the standard ceases to control behavior in the desired direction. In such a case, "control" can be exercised only by understanding the cooperative phenomena involved; and for this other skills are required.

---

The following statement provides a summary of the steps involved in developing a single control system. This is a general scheme describing the basic features of any control system.

It is obvious that each specific control system will have its parts made appropriate to the behavior being controlled.

---

## A THEORY OF NON-FINANCIAL CONTROLS IN SMALL ENTERPRISES

### Dale Henning*

Control is the process of bringing about conformity of performance with planned action. Planning on the other hand is the process of predetermining a course of action. Control is vitally related to planning; neither can stand alone. Plans require some kind of follow-up, otherwise their objectives will not likely be achieved. Control, in turn, can be meaningful only in the presence of some purposeful predetermined course of action.

It is sometimes argued that smaller enterprises should refrain from the use of controls on the grounds that controls lead to conformity, lack of originality, rigidity, and repetition. Control *can* mean these things, but it need not.

Change comes about in two ways; it is either planned or fortuitous. If the businessman wishes to be master of his own fate, planned action is to be preferred over unplanned action. To the extent that this is true, control becomes desirable and necessary— otherwise plans become little more than statements of hope.

#### THE CONTROL SUB-PROCESSES

Control plans are componential— they are component parts of some larger, broader plan. Their objectives are always the same, to bring about conformity of a plan's implementation with the intent of the planners. The principal components (sub-processes) of a control plan are as follows:

#### Establishing Standards

A standard is a criterion against which actual results or performance are measured, compared, and evaluated. Examples of standards are: ten absences per employee per year, dimensional tolerances of one inch plus or minus .01 inch, or output of 200 units per day.

#### Measurement of Performance

"Measuring" is the determination of the results that have occurred as plans are being implemented. Measurement may take place with reference to a standard, or in the absence of any standard at all. Examples of measuring activities are: counting how many units an employee produces in a day, determining how many pay increases were granted, performing a chemical analysis on raw materials, etc. Measurements sometimes are made by persons whose performance is being controlled. Unless care is taken, this practice can result in critical losses of control.

#### Comparison of Performance With Standard

Comparison is the activity that determines differences between performance and standards. Comparison does

*Reprinted by permission from Dale Henning, "Non-Financial Controls in Smaller Enterprises" (Seattle: University of Washington Bureau of Business Research, 1964), pp. 6–7.

not involve evaluation but merely the determination of differences between performance and standard. The following is an example of a comparison activity: a clerk merely determines the number of employee absences per year and compares this with the maximum allowable number of absences, reporting the discrepancy between these two figures to her superior for action.

## Appraisal of Performance

Appraisal is the placement of values upon performance and upon differences between performance and the standard. Performance which exactly meets the standard is presumed to be acceptable and good. Performance which exceeds the standard contributes more to the enterprise than has been called for. Performance which fails to meet standard contributes less than was expected and, in the absence of mitigating circumstances is considered to be unacceptable. This determination of "goodness" and "badness" is the appraisal sub-process.

Comparison and appraisal are usually performed by the same person and concurrently.

The appraisal sub-process includes a determination of the causes of deviations from standard and of the effects of deviations from standard. A consideration of both of these phenomena is necessary in order to determine the desirability or undesirability of a given deviation from standard. The appraiser is interested in (1) the cause of the deviation, whether it is temporary or permanent, increasing or diminishing, (2) the effect of the deviation, (3) the size of the deviation, and (4) the implications the appraisal has for modification of the standard.

## Making Exceptions

Very closely related to the appraisal activity are the decisions which allow performance which does not meet the standards to be accepted in spite of the discrepancy. Examples are: allowing a product which just barely exceeds dimensional tolerances to pass inspection, not following prescribed disciplinary procedures for employee infraction of rules, continuing to employ a production worker whose performance has failed to meet minimum volume requirements. Where large numbers of exceptions are made, the administrator has cause to question the adequacy of the standards used.

## Making Aggregative Appraisals

Aggregative appraisals differ from appraisals of individual performance in that they are designed to answer general questions such as "How are we doing over-all; how many units met, exceeded, and failed to meet our standards over the past year?" The purpose of aggregative appraisals, in addition to answering questions about over-all performance, is to determine the adequacy of the standards that have been applied.

Aggregative appraisals are done less frequently than are individual appraisals. Determining if an employee has met his daily output quota represents a measurement and appraisal of an individual phenomenon. An aggregative appraisal would occur if an executive were to determine on an over-all basis how many employees met, exceeded, or failed to meet standards during the year, the magnitude by which standards were exceeded or performance failed to measure up, etc.

## SEQUENCE OF EVENTS
## IN THE CONTROL PROCESS

The control process begins with the establishment of a control plan designed to bring about conformance of a major plan's implementation with the intent of the planners. The next step involves the actual implementation, or carrying out, of the major plan. Next, the measurement of performance occurs. After this a comparison with the standard is made, and an evaluation or appraisal of the performance follows. If there are no differences between performance and standard, no changes are necessary. If, however, performance differs from standard, one of three things will happen:

1. If the deviation is considered to be acceptable or uncontrollable, no change in performance, standards, or major plan will take place and the flow of activity is uninterrupted, with more performance, measurement, comparison, and appraisal following.

2. If, however, the deviation is considered to be acceptable but nonetheless a change in standards or future performance is desired, a corrective sub-plan will be designed to change performance, or a modification of the control plan itself will be undertaken.

3. If the deviations are considered to be unacceptable and the performance is rejected, one of three things will happen: (a) a corrective sub-plan will be designed to affect future performances; (b) a change in the control plan or standards will be undertaken; (c) a change in the action or goals of the major plan will be undertaken.

---

It is often difficult to grasp the magnitude of controls in the typical business firm. Reck in the following discussion points out that a large electrical manufacturing company estimated that there were more than two million standards that applied to its operations. The author then goes on to examine the number of control systems in a simple operation and shows how this demands a vast number of controls in the eleven basic decisions employed for the production of this item.

---

## RULES, STANDARDS, AND RATIONALITY

*Dickson Reck*[*]

Control is the process of checking results against substantive standards

[*]Reprinted by permission from Dickson Reck, "The Role of Company Standards in Industrial Administration," *Advanced Management*, 19:21–23 (April, 1954).

and feeding back the comparisons to executives for appropriate action. When such reports reveal errors resulting from inadequate performance of operations, sanctions are applied to operating personnel, and when they reveal errors attributable to inadequate standards the information is relayed to the decision-making personnel, who re-examine the standards, make new decisions, and revise the standards. In this way control operates to feed back information on errors and to reactivate the administrative cycle so that a closer approximation to the best solution is found and applied to operations. Standards are essential for control since they provide the models for measuring performance and reporting errors.

The standards used for formally established control by supervisors can be only a small number of the total required to guide a company's operations. One large electrical manufacturing company, for example, estimates that the number of standards applied to its operations exceeds two million. Obviously only a small portion of these, selected because the operations they measure are strategic, can profitably be used for supervisory control. Control, however, is also exercised informally by all subordinates when they apply detailed standards to operations. Each standard is used by someone—an executive, a supervisor, or an operating worker—to guide and control the performance of some operation; otherwise the standard serves no purpose and can be profitably eliminated.

The process of decision-making begins with the most general objective —usually, in private businesses, profit maximization in the long run—and moves through successive levels at which standards are progressively more detailed. The standard arrived at by a decision at each level is linked to its objective, which is a standard arrived at by a decision at the next *higher* level, and in turn is the objective to which are linked the standards arrived at by decisions at the next

*lower* level. By this process the linkage of standards reaches down and branches out in the organizational structure, ending in a very large number of detailed standards—more than two million in the case of the electrical manufacturing concern previously mentioned—which guide the myriad of detailed operations in all departments of the firm. It is only after these final detailed operations of the company have been guided by the final and most detailed standards in the hierarchy that any degree of achievement of the general objective of the company is attained.[1]

Coordinating is the process of harmonizing operations so they all contribute to a common objective. The hierarchy of standards with its ramifications comprises an integrated system which serves the vital function of establishing and maintaining coordination of the firm's operations. To the degree that each standard in the system is well articulated with those at higher and lower levels, the final operations will be in harmony.

An example will help to clarify this concept of a system of standards. For an imaginary electrical manufacturing company, there are listed in Table 1, in rough order of their generality, some of the important decisions and their corresponding standards which guide the performance of the research, engineering, and production functions required to manufacture a single item of the company's product line, in this case an electric switch. Eleven standards, or types of standards, are shown in the hierarchy, but these include many thousands of detailed standards.

---

[1] This concept parallels that of a hierarchy of decisions; see, for example, Chester I. Barnard, *The Functions of the Executive* (Cambridge, Harvard University Press, 1951), pp. 196–197.

**Table 1**

Some Important Decisions and Standards in the System Coordinating the Production of an Electrical Switch in a Hypothetical Electrical Manufacturing Company

| Decisions | Standards |
|---|---|
| 1. To form a corporation with the objective of maximizing profit from the investment of capital in a manufacturing enterprise. | 1. Oral or written agreement of the promoters. |
| 2. To engage in the manufacture and sale of electrical equipment. | 2. Purpose clause of the corporate charter. |
| 3. To manufacture a particular line of low voltage electrical equipment. | 3. The company's catalog and sales data sheets defining the product line. |
| 4. To manufacture a particular type of switch included in the product line, to be called catalog number 38,372, which will perform as well as or better than competitive switches. | 4. Prototype model of proposed catalog number 38,372, developed by the research department. |
| 5. To manufacture 38,372 following a particular detailed design involving a multitude of decisions covering design details for the final assembly, each sub-assembly, each manufactured part, and each purchased material and part. | 5. Complete detailed engineering design drawings, bills of material, and supplementary written specifications for the final assembly, each sub-assembly, each manufactured part, and each purchased material and part. |
| 6. To invest in tools to manufacture catalog number 38,372. | 6. Standards for equipment, tools, dies, and fixtures for the final assembly, each sub-assembly, and each manufactured part. |
| 7. To produce certain quantities of 38,372 to meet forecasted demands. | 7. Standard order quantities for the final assembly, each sub-assembly, each manufactured part, and each purchased material and part. |
| 8. To use certain production methods for the final assembly, each sub-assembly, and each manufactured part of 38,372. | 8. Standard operation sheets showing the tools and routing to be used for producing the final assembly, each sub-assembly, and each manufactured part of 38,372. |
| 9. To install certain inspection procedures to control the production of 38,372. | 9. Standard methods of sampling and inspection. |
| 10. To produce the final assembly, each sub-assembly, and each part within certain times. | 10. Standard times for each operation for producing the final assembly, each sub-assembly, and each part. |
| 11. To produce the final assembly, each sub-assembly, and each part at certain costs. | 11. Standard costs for the final assembly, each sub-assembly, and each part. |

It would be possible to construct similar schematic representations of all the hierarchies of standards required for performing all the other functions involved in manufacturing and selling this single item, for example, the sales, purchasing, finance, and personnel functions. If these hierarchies were combined the resulting composite system would include many thousands of standards, and only after each of them had been applied in directing and controlling operations would the company realize its objective of making a profit from the sales of this one switch item.

If the product line of the company included 1,000 items of switching equipment, 1,000 similar systems of standards would exist. The general standards in all the systems would be identical down to and including the product line, and a large proportion of the detailed standards, those related to common technical terms, parts, and common sales programs, for example, would be common to a substantial number of the systems. If the 1,000 systems are thought of as being interconnected by their common standards, there emerges the concept of a single system of standards.

The coordinating function of such a system of standards is not difficult to visualize. If the production of a single part which enters the assembly of the switch in the example above is to make its expected contribution to the profits of the company, at least the following standards must be carefully coordinated: the detailed design standards for the part; the detailed design standards for the sub-assembly of which it is a part; the purchase and inspection standards for the material from which the part is made; the standards for the speeds and accuracy of the equipment and for the tools and fixtures by which the part is made; the production operation standards; the standard times for the operations; the standard costs for the part; the personnel standards for selecting the operators; the wage rates; and the inspection standards for the finished part. If the part is sold as a repair part, standard product data, standard prices, standard terms of sale, and standard customer classifications provided to salesmen would also be included. Only if all these

standards are harmonious will profits, so far as this part influences them, be maximized. . . .

### DO STANDARDS STRAITJACKET OPERATIONS AND HOLD BACK PROGRESS?

There is no question but that inadequate and poorly devised systems of standards do straitjacket operations and hold back progress. Since standards are an integral part of administration, however, there is no choice of whether or not to use them. It is not standards per se, but the failure to arrive at adequate standards which straitjackets operations. The corrective is to improve the process by which decisions are made so that the standards are right. Similarly, it is not standards per se, but the failure to revise them which retards progress. The corrective is to adopt a procedure by which standards are reviewed and changed whenever change is economical so that operations progress from the level defined by current standards to the new level made possible by research and defined by new standards.

Far from stultifying operations, adequate standards developed by effective procedures are the principal means of reducing solved problems to routine, and freeing personnel for working on the unsolved problems which, when solved, permit the firm to progress. Well-designed standards liberate initiative.

---

The next account of a food-processing operation deals with the interaction between an inspector, or checker, and a foreman whose work is being inspected. You will note that the purpose of the inspection, which is to maintain quality and quantity standards, is achieved through the individual adaptation of foremen and inspectors.

For the same type of operation one inspector may work out a satisfactory relationship with a foreman on one basis while the same operation may be monitored in a different fashion by a fellow inspector working with another foreman. One of the conclusions is that ultimately the human beings who make control systems effective still work out very human adaptations with those whose behavior is being controlled.

At the end of the line of a control system stands a man who must make the controls work by getting other men to respond affirmatively to them. When men control men, the human factor is still an important link between the standards set and their successful attainment.

## THE INSPECTORS AND THE FOREMAN

*Harold E. Kubly**

We have just seen that the checkers believe they work through the foremen with the possible exception of those few instances where it would be bothersome to the foremen to do so. Moreover, we have learned that the checkers go out of their way to inform the foremen when they have suggested to the workers that they take a specific action. The reason for this behavior is that the checkers have been trained not to assume any of the functions of the foremen.

Normally the interactions between checkers and foremen involve the passing of information. For instance, I observed that upon completion of the over-inspection of a tagged lot of packaged products, the checker telephoned the foreman to give him the final results.

On critical operations the foreman wants to learn from the checkers as

soon as possible how the workers are doing. Take the case of preparing certain ingredients for further processing. In view of the importance of this operation and because of his desire to achieve the material efficiency standards, the foreman is anxious to learn about the findings of the checker who samples the material as it moves down the conveyor. When the operation seems to be out of control, he asks the checkers to take more frequent samples and report to him. If the checker finds evidence of careless work, he tells the foreman at once rather than wait for a formal report to sift down to him.

It is normal for a foreman to ask a checker to keep an eye on some aspect of an operation that seems to be out of control. For example, if a report indicates that the packages leaving a department are significantly overweight, the foreman will naturally ask the checker to make more frequent weight checks. But it is also likely that the checker himself will already have decided that this operation is worthy of

*Reprinted by permission from Harold E. Kubly, *The Inspectors and the Foreman* (Madison, Wisconsin: Bureau of Business Research and Service, The University of Wisconsin, 1966), pp. 32–34.

close watching. Once the source of trouble has been found and corrected, the checker can reduce the frequency of inspection.

We can generalize that if everything is going smoothly in a department the contacts between the checkers and the foreman are routine and rather infrequent. But if something is out of control, the contacts, initiated by either party, become numerous. . . .

Normally the foreman considers the checker a source of information about the results his workers are achieving, about the condition of some ingredients, and occasionally about processes, and about the quality of the packages. Ideally these are the chief functions of the checker. Unfortunately not all foremen realize how to utilize the services of the checkers in these ways, but the good ones do. Properly used, the checker can be a real help to a foreman in running his department.

In no case did I observe a checker ordering a foreman to do something or even suggesting seriously that he do something. It would have been interesting to observe such an event, particularly in the case of several rather contentious foremen. At the same time I did hear checkers passing information to foremen and rather implying that the foreman ought to give one step in a process a bit of attention. But it was always done in such a way that the decision rested with the foreman.

I asked several checkers what they would do if they observed a deviation from a recipe and called it to the attention of the foreman who then did nothing about it. This, they said, would be most unusual, but each stated that he would notify his supervisor. Presumably the supervisor would investigate the deviation and confer either with the production supervisor or with the foreman. If the foreman acted, that closed the incident. But an

order to correct the deviation would reach the foreman from his boss, although the checker set in motion the chain of events leading to the order. All of this is consistent with orthodox management theory.

The above description of the interactions between checkers and foremen may suggest that the foremen give orders to the checkers. This is not so, although the distinction between asking the checker for information and ordering him to inspect a sample to get that information may be difficult to define.

I did get the impression that a few foremen tried to dominate the checkers in their departments and that their requests, often strongly expressed, were in effect orders. This is not surprising since foremen enjoy much greater status than do the checkers and occupy a higher level on the organization chart. Further, the foremen usually have years of experience behind them while the checkers may be novices.

In those situations where a foreman seems to dominate the checker, I was reminded of those cases where the checker gave orders and made suggestions to workers. Perhaps there is a similarity in that the checker, like the workers, accepted orders and suggestions that are reasonable and beneficial to all parties. But at no time did I observe or hear of a foreman ordering a checker to pass a lot that the checker judged to be substandard. In short, the foremen never interfered with the checkers carrying out their duties as guardians of quality.

Some foremen apparently permit an aspiring and ambitious checker to encroach on their prerogatives gradually. I did not observe this, but I heard that it had taken place in several departments earlier.

What happened was something like

this: a foreman allows a checker to verify the scales and order the workers to correct any that are not properly counter-weighted. Later he permits the checker to give orders to the workers on some other seemingly unimportant operation. This goes on until the checker is in effect an assistant foreman from whom the workers expect to get some orders. This can happen only when the foreman is weak to begin with.

By and large the relationship between the checkers and the foremen seems to be one of mutual helpfulness. We must not let exceptions to this general rule warp our judgment. Those difficulties that arise have their roots in a failure to understand what the checker's function is. This may lead to mutual suspicion. A foreman may look upon the checker, not as a helper, but as a snooper. The checker, on the other hand, may consider the foreman as someone who is trying to slip something past him.

---

For executives and managers the controls tend to be directed at measurement of results. The consequence is that those in a position to produce results may also be in a position to produce the appearance of results as well. The evasion of controls by managers and executives involves making the record of results look like the standard of expectation that has been set.

There is more, however, to the manner in which executives may influence or modify the control systems applicable to them. Executives are an important part of the communications system of their own organization and may therefore influence the standards applying to themselves or use their opportunities for communication to make invidious comparisons between their own performance and that of their colleagues.

---

## CONTROL EVASION AT THE MANAGERIAL LEVEL

*Robert Dubin**

In general, the expected or planned-for outcomes of organizational behavior have to be policed to ensure some correspondence between performance and plan. It is in this sense that we shall examine formal controls of behavior in organizations. . . .

In a pioneering study Argyris examined the impact of budget controls on those being controlled.[1] He gave repeated examples of short-run compliance with control standards that had either short- or long-run cost consequences for the organization. He reported instances of people who worked under fixed quotas of output, with some opportunity to select items to be worked on, choosing easy, rapidly completed jobs as fillers toward the

*Reprinted by permission from Chris Argyris, *et al.*, *Social Science Approaches to Business Behavior* (Homewood, Ill.: The Dorsey Press, 1962), pp. 42–47.

[1] C. Argyris, *The Impact of Budgets on People* (New York: Controllership Institute, 1952).

end of the period in order to meet a quota. . . . Blau reported the same behavior among law-enforcement case analysts, who worked with an established case load of eight per month and who picked easy, fast cases toward the end of each month if they anticipated falling short of their quotas.[2] Jasinski reported a similar adaptation by foremen of "bleeding the line" in line production by sucking all work in progress through the measuring point (using augmented crews), in order to meet a production quota, but losing efficiency in the succeeding period until the line was refilled with work in progress.[3]

An even more seriously distorting adaptive response to controls is reported by Blau, who pointed out that government employment-service interviewers were appraised by the number of interviews completed, resulting in their maximizing the number of interviews and not spending adequate time in finding jobs for clients (the obvious purpose of the interviews in the first place). This is a translation of means into ends, an apparently common response to output controls.

Perhaps the potentially most costly adaptation to controls is their deliberate evasion (on the assumption that the purposes of the controls were initially praiseworthy). Jasinski reported instances of "making out with the pencil" as a means for giving the paper appearance of meeting expected standards, without actually doing so. Dalton reported a comparable instance of evasion where local plant officials, through blandishments of, and subsequent conspiracy with, the central-

office representative were able to evade cost-control checks imposed by the central office.[4]

Remember we are here, in each instance, citing data dealing with *managerial* adaptation to controls and not that of rank-and-file workers. The phenomena of "banking" work to smooth out dips in individual output, of restriction of output, of "making with the pencil," and of outright cheating (a system-control firm recently advertised in *The Wall Street Journal* that employee fraud perpetrated on American business firms in 1961 was estimated to reach 1.5 billion dollars) have been too well documented at the worker level to need further elaboration here. What may be less comfortable for business executives to face openly is the reality that adaptive and evasive behavior is also characteristic of managers and executives.[5]

That the phenomenon of managerial adaptation to controls is not culture-bound is revealed by Granick, who pointed out that high rewards and glory attended the Soviet plant manager who set a new production record, so that there was pressure to do this at the expense of operating repairs and protective maintenance.[6] This resulted in lower output in the subsequent period while the delayed main-

---

[2] P. Blau, *Dynamics of Bureaucracy* (Chicago: University of Chicago Press, 1955).

[3] F. J. Jasinski, "Use and Misuse of Efficiency Controls," *Harvard Business Review*, 34:105–112, July–August, 1956.

[4] M. Dalton, "Managing the Managers," *Human Organization*, 14:4–10, Fall, 1955.

[5] This is highlighted by the recent price-fixing conspiracy practices among the giant electrical-goods firms when top managers asserted their "clean hands" by contending that subordinates' law-breaking was hidden from their knowledge. This is an open admission, if true, that the controls on legal pricing policies were so inadequate in all the companies that lower executives could knowingly violate the law without fear of detection by their superiors.

[6] D. Granick, *Management of the Industrial Firm in the U.S.S.R.* (New York: Columbia University Press, 1954).

tenance was undertaken, but the manager had received his payoff for the over-quota output of the earlier period. Berliner noted the phenomenon of "storming" production toward the end of a quota period in Soviet industry to meet output standards, again at the expense of maintenance and balanced output.[7] Apparently, the adaptation of management men to the controls imposed on their output is independent of the larger social value systems in which they live. Indeed, one could even argue further that the nature of productive systems, requiring some predictability of output, will generate controls over output that are universal in their effects, regardless of the social system in which they are used. The gulf between values held and actual behavior is rather ironically revealed in Berliner's quote of Bulganin, who boasted that heads rolled each year in the management of the Soviet coal industry because managers did not meet quotas (a hard-boiled efficiency outlook for a top political leader in a welfare state), whereas it is less certain that American executives respond so sternly to the failures to meet quotas by their own subordinates (a remarkably welfare state-ish outlook for production-minded executives who proclaim their idolatry of efficiency). In any event, it seems highly probable that the severity of penalties incurred for failure to meet control standards will generate a proportional adaptive effort to make a face showing of compliance, regardless of the other costs involved to the organization.

The fear of criticism by bosses seems to be a central feature of man-agerial response to controls on their behavior. Jaques' long-term study of the managers of an English factory revealed that one of the strongest conventions among the divisional managers was never to criticize each other in front of their mutual boss but that criticism was not thereby suppressed, since it moved upward by skipping levels of management as it moved.[8] Furthermore, he found that the service and advisory specialists reported to the top executive criticisms of operating managers when they demanded wrong services or rejected offered advice. Dalton has reported similar behavior by line executives that tended to impeach the competence of staff specialists through critical appraisal of them to top management.

Apparently the lines of functional specialization to be found in a firm provide natural but "hidden" channels of criticism flowing to top management, which encourage "ratting" on other functional specialists or at least deriding their performances to top executives.

We really do not have any published evidence that a secondary adaptation among managers to criticizing, or being criticized, is coalition and mutual protection against any effective criticism reaching top management through nonformal channels. We do have some reports (Ulrich, Booz, and Lawrence[9] and Dalton, among others) that have pointed out that members of management tend to withhold information that would be useful to their superiors. This might con-

---

[7]J. Berliner, "A Problem in Soviet Business Management," *Administrative Science Quarterly*, 1:87–101, June, 1956.

[8]Elliott Jaques, *The Changing Culture of a Factory* (New York: Dryden Press, 1952).

[9]D. N. Ulrich, D. R. Booz, and P. R. Lawrence, *Management Behavior and Foreman Attitude: A Case Study* (Cambridge: Harvard Graduate School of Business Administration, 1950).

ceivably be indirect evidence of "deals" that monitor the flow of adverse information upward. The only study that reveals the nature of these deals is one of Navy disbursing officers, made by Turner.[10] He pointed out that there were services and/or goods in scarce supply and needed, resulting in reciprocal trades of goods and services that paid off about equally in both directions over a period of time. Presumably, very important trading chits in such reciprocity could be critical reports that it would be considered desirable to withhold from top management.

There is one more aspect of control that we shall consider—dealing with a technical feature of communication and order giving. The field of communications research has produced the analysis of messages and message units. Out of this have come some important findings about what the sociologist calls "definition of the situation." For example, Frick and Sumby, in studying the ability of military pilot trainees to complete control-tower messages, given initial clues, demonstrated that the estimated redundancy of such messages was approximately 96 per cent.[11] They attribute most of the redundancy of the message units to the fact that each pilot perceived

the situational context of the message, including the appropriate pilot procedural responses, so that each respondent was able to "define the situation" and predict the message content with very small cues. Such studies tell us a good deal inferentially about the possible unspoken and unmentioned aspects of orders, directives, and control standards. For those who are habituated to a situation and who share all significant participants' "definition of the situation," it takes little in the way of cueing to "get the message." It is the very habituation to the situational context that makes for high redundancy in communication and therefore leads to maximum communication with minimum interaction. In the context of control, minimum effort can be invested in control activities and in adaptations to them, because of the efficiency that a common definition of the situation gives to controlling methods.

It is remarkable to note that among managers and executives—the personnel of organizations whose position demands commitment to organization goals—there exists a strong tendency to meet formal criteria of performance, even if, in so doing, high but hidden costs are generated. It may be pertinent to suggest that specialists in control systems, engineers and accountants particularly, might find additional sources of efficiency in eliminating some of the costs of managerial adaptation to controls that evade their spirit but conform to their letter.

[10]R. Turner, "The Navy Disbursing Officer as a Bureaucrat," *American Sociological Review,* 12:342–348, June, 1947.

[11]F. C. Frick and W. H. Sumby, "Control Tower Language," *Journal of the Acoustical Society of America,* 24:595–596, November, 1952.

---

It is one of the most critical features of a control system that it places the greatest amount of pressure upon those most immediately involved in getting results. Where the results are production, the point of critical pressure and reaction is the production foreman.

The following account provides a wide range of illustrations of how production control standards may produce results that are at least as costly as the mistakes the control system was designed to eliminate.

## USE AND MISUSE OF EFFICIENCY CONTROLS

*Frank J. Jasinski**

While, as will be seen, it is dangerous for management to rely on any one single index of efficiency, the controls that cause most of the trouble are those based on or derived from the concept that the efficiency of an operator or department can be determined by measuring the time actually spent to complete an item against a predetermined or "standard" time. This concept, of course, dates back to the 1920's and 1930's, when it came into great vogue as a formal system in industry. Any system that equates efficiency with quantity of output and compares output records for set, short-run time periods ends up with much the same effect.

As might be supposed, in recent years many companies have found additional and often better ways to compute efficiency. For example, among the factors now widely considered are quality, tool costs, inventory levels, and production schedules. However, the development of newer and more sensitive controls does not mean that the old approach has been abandoned. More important in terms of practical consequence is the fact that most operating people still feel that production time provides the best and most decisive way to measure efficiency. This holds true of the worker on the bench, of the foreman, of the second-line supervisor, and apparently of many an executive even higher up in the production department.

In one way or another, then, the behavior of people on the job is conditioned by their almost single-minded observance of just two variables—pieces produced and man-hours expended. But in seeking to make efficiency, measured this way, *look* good, many workers and managers act in a manner that serves to impair *real* efficiency.

### Defensive Behavior

How can controls boomerang in this way?

The answer must be found by watching the behavior of people whose efficiency is judged—or misjudged—on the basis of these quick, simple indexes that never were designed to tell the whole story or reveal the whole picture. People who must pass these rigid tests quickly acquire a pattern of behavior that has but one objective—to make their scores look better, even though this may mean the

*Reprinted by permission as an excerpt from Frank J. Jasinski, "Use and Misuse of Efficiency Controls," *Harvard Business Review*, 34:105–112 (July-August, 1956).

438

sacrifice of other less tangible advantages and of longer run gains for the business as a whole.

The failure of management to see and rectify its mistakes more quickly can probably be traced to the veneration which most businessmen have for figures. In the words of the old saw, "Figures don't lie." Maybe they don't lie, but that does not mean they are capable of dictating action without the aid of judgment or careful weighing of information gleaned from varied sources.

## CASE HISTORIES

Let us first look at a large company that measured efficiency daily and monthly for each department by the following in the plant rule-of-thumb calculations:

In each department, a daily efficiency rating was computed, based on the "time value" of completed units transferred to finished stores compared with the number of hours spent "on production" during the day of transfer. Efficiency was reported daily and accumulated to the end of the month. Thus each department earned 12 efficiency ratings each year.

In this company, the plant manager accepted the monthly efficiency figures as indicative of every department's accomplishments or progress. He placed a high value on this figure and called his subordinates to task whenever the monthly efficiency figure was low, or whenever it fell significantly under the figure of the preceding month.

### Wasted Time

When efficiency as measured by this index dropped, top supervisory personnel rushed to find out why, and lower supervisory personnel employed their wits in preparing iron-clad excuses. For example, the company's production superintendent found it necessary to compile figures to "prove" that departments with low ratings were not as inefficient as they appeared. . . .

Even where subordinate supervisors could offer what appeared to be legitimate reasons for precipitous declines in their efficiency, company "brass" devoted much time to looking for additional explanations. For example, one foreman described the following experience:

"Once we ran out of forgings for one of the two parts I make, and so we ran the other part. Then we got the late forgings in, and they wanted them done in a hurry. I had to put the parts I had been working on aside and set up the new job. By the time we got the machines changed over and got the first piece through, the end of the month came. My efficiency dropped 20 points.

*"Boy, you should have seen the brass pile in here—men four and five levels above me in management.* They spent almost the whole month in my department. If a man stopped to talk to someone, they stepped right up and told him to go back to work. The thing was, I had had the original parts which I had been working on lying on the floor—partly done. I could have finished them easily by the end of the month and got a 90%– 92% efficiency. But with the changeover, I had to leave them unfinished."

Needless to say, the managerial energy and time used up in this seemingly fruitless exploration of a problem already sufficiently explained had to be subtracted from the sum of energy and time available for working on other, perhaps more pressing, issues.

That the company had plenty of more serious problems will be seen as soon as we look a little further into the behavior of lower management in this situation. Production jams, high costs, low morale, and some dishonesty were present, all traceable in part to the emphasis placed on efficiency ratings.

## Production Jams

Because management in this company paid so much attention to the end-of-month efficiency ratings, department supervisors left no stone unturned to get as many units into finished stores as possible. They even resorted to such expensive and disruptive processes as "bleeding the line"—that is, stopping operations near the start of the cycle and shifting labor to final operations in order to complete more units by the deadline. This process is summarized by what another foreman said:

"For the last two weeks of the month we're driving hell out of the men. We have to get pieces out, and we're always jammed up at the end of the month. . . . What actually happens is that in the beginning of the month I have to put all of my men at the beginning of the line to get pieces going for the month's production. This is because we cleaned out the department in the previous month. Then, during the last two weeks I have to put all of the men at the end of the line to finish up the pieces.

"What we should be doing is to have each man work on his machine. At the end of the month we should have a piece in each machine—not cleaned out the way we are. That way we could keep a steady flow all month and not have to rush at the end of the month."

The irregular work flow resulting from this process of bleeding the line in one department generated still more scheduling jams in departments to which the work piece went later. . . .

## Higher Maintenance Costs

Just as anxiety to earn a high efficiency rating led formen to "bleed the line" and "drive hell out of the men," so it prompted them to "run a machine right to the ground at the end of the month, trying to get pieces out." . . .

## "Fudging" Figures

A more subtle but not less deleterious result of the quest for steady, high efficiency ratings was figure fudging by the top supervisors. Some of these men, anxious to equalize efficiencies among departments in their charge, did so by transferring personnel "on paper" from departments with relatively low efficiencies to those with relatively high ratings. This move had a leveling result when the ratio of "man-hours" to "time value per piece in finished stores" was computed.

If this practice tended to protect the weak, it also tended to penalize the more successful foremen by forcing them to "carry" their less efficient peers.

Some foremen also suffered a sense of moral affront at what they regarded as less than complete honesty. . . .

## Low Morale

This combination of falsehood and impaired morale is also found in another case history, where it was perhaps the outstanding problem caused by a system of efficiency ratings.

This case involved a plant where machine repair, processing, tooling, and service from the cribs was not fully adequate. Management, however, tended to disregard these factors and pressed for high efficiencies regardless. One foreman stated:

"Top management just won't take any excuses at all when it comes to efficiency. They just want you to keep up your efficiency, and they don't want any alibis."

A few workers, who were confronted with time losses which management refused to acknowledge, falsified their time tickets. Many other workers simply became resigned to the situation and turned in low efficiencies. Foremen, recognizing the factors leading to low output, did not care to press operators for higher production.

Management became convinced that most operators were falsifying their records and, more important, that foremen were too lax with their employees. It fired a few foremen and middle supervisors and made a few drastic organizational changes. Morale among hourly employees and supervisors was low because of management's pressure, on the one hand, for increased efficiency, and management's failure, on the other hand, to recognize and to act on inadequate service from supporting departments. As another foreman said:

"It does seem in this shop as if too much is put on the foreman without giving him the help he needs. Take in my case: I have to push for everything I get. I keep pushing the inspector to get the pieces out so that we can meet the schedule. I chase up tools and mater-

ials personally, and I am the one who has to keep pushing maintenance, tool repair, and the equipment. It seems to me that in a well-run shop all of these other departments should be made just as responsible for getting production out as the production people themselves. . . . It shouldn't have to be the way it is."

## Impaired Recruitment

Still another case history illustrates how worker recruitment can be impaired by the unwise application of efficiency ratings ill-adapted to meet unusual requirements.

In this company, top management became aware that the number of production workers was inadequate to meet current output schedules. Because experienced operators were difficult to find, new untrained laborers were hired. These were to be carried for a certain length of time at no charge to production; only when the period of training was over would the new employees become a full charge on their departments.

To meet the shortage of manpower on production, management shortened training time considerably and transferred the trainees to the production rolls. This manipulation brought the paper figure of manpower available closer to that required for scheduled production and removed potential criticism of the managers who knew they would be held responsible if there were too apparent a discrepancy between the two.

Unfortunately, when this plan was evolved, the duration of the training time needed for the work was not given full recognition, and the trainees were unable to produce enough to translate this paper improvement into reality.

As a result, foremen who were faced with a full charge for half-trained employees reacted by keeping only the exceptional men, firing the rest even though they were badly needed. . . .

The labor recruitment problem in this company was further aggravated by the fact that many trainees, pushed for efficiency, left even before the training period was over. Indeed, of all trainees who left the company in a seven-month period, 53% left before the second month had elapsed. Once news of the situation at the plant had leaked through the community, it became difficult for the personnel department to recruit replacements.

## Management Friction

As might be expected, the above situation provoked ill feeling between people in production and personnel. A member of the personnel department was bitterly critical of the treatment of trainees, especially in the light of the tight labor market. . . .

The problem of friction is illustrated by still another case history. In this situation the trouble started when the accounting department prepared a graph showing that in-process inventory was steadily increasing in relation to sales. Acting on this information, the plant manager's assistant decided to reduce work-in-process by not replacing employees lost through attrition. Since fewer workers would produce fewer pieces and thus reduce inventory, the action would bring the "in-process to sales" graph into balance.

This action, designed to improve an accountant's graph, overlooked the fact that plant sales were growing and orders on the books were piling up unfilled.

## Higher Unit Costs

In addition to slowing up deliveries and aggravating friction, the actions in the case just described raised the per-unit costs on output. As production fell further and further behind schedule, angry customers had to be appeased by pushing through particular orders. Split lots became the rule rather than the exception, and costs were boosted by the extra setup time. People at the lower supervisory levels could see that expenses must be rising and why. One of them reported:

"We have to break a job down because some other job is a rush job, and we have to reset the job afterward. But time standards only allow us a certain percentage of time for one setup based on the job as a whole. As a result we lose time and can't make our efficiency—especially when we make as little as five pieces at a time. . . . This business of 50 pieces here, and 50 pieces there, break up a machine, set it up, break it up—you lose a lot of efficiency.

"You've got to have stuff on the floor. It's like working capital—and you've got to have working capital. If you cut down on inventory, you increase your costs— every part becomes a special job, and you pay premiums on special treatment."

## Lowered Quality

Finally, it is possible to show that poor quality and high costs often go hand in hand, both together being caused by the efforts of production personnel to make their efficiency ratings look better.

These problems in conjunction were observed in a manufacturing division where plant efficiency was measured by the number of work pieces passing a certain point on the production line. Plant managers in the division pressed for getting pieces past this critical point, even if they were defective and would have to be reworked later on. Indeed, the division manager was seriously considering a plan whereby certain operations would purposely be left undone until after the "payoff" point, so that his plant efficiencies would "look good."

As a result of these production methods, costs per item were higher, and products were patched up. Hourly operators could not feel they had done a job well, so their morale was low. All employees were affected by the knowledge that management had adopted the doubtful expedient of trying to put quality back into a product where it was originally lacking.

In another corporation, where plant efficiency was measured by low costs, a plant manager spoke of the danger to quality in the following manner:

"Suppose we get rolling along fairly well. All of a sudden, one day, one manager jumps ten points ahead of the rest in the division. We get a delegation from the main office wanting to know why we're so far behind. What they should find out is why *he* is ten points ahead— and what it will mean for the future. But, of course, we don't want to be behind so we fall back on the rules of the game —you have to follow the rules to stay in the game. We start cutting corners to bring our percentage up—but at a sacrifice that nobody considers.

"Not only do we pay premium time to the people in the repair area, but the workers in the shop learn 'let-it-go' habits. We're putting out patched-up products—products which never can be fixed up right. This patched-up quality is going to hurt in five or six years."

# 19

# Leadership and
# Productivity

Administrative action in business organizations, as in most work organizations, is ultimately directed at building and sustaining output. People work to produce something. Whether they work well or poorly will influence how much they can produce. There arises a nice problem of determining how much difference the leadership action and climate make in the output of those being led. It would seem that this is such an obvious question that many would have sought to answer it. The research findings are, however, skimpy and inconclusive. In this chapter we will bring together a good sample of the known facts about how leaders affect the working output of their followers.

It would be comforting if we could be certain that leadership does make a difference in how effectively people work. Then we could attribute the successes of man's productivity to the human relations of the work situation. We could improve poor output by providing more effective leadership. The facts are not adequate enough to let us reach these conclusions. There are two basic reasons for this:

1. We know that productivity in all realms depends upon the materials and equipment employed. Indeed, we can go further and conclude that materials and equipment *probably* account for most of the long-term increases of productivity. Therefore, the most obvious conclusion we can reach is that leadership probably does not have much positive influence in getting people to work harder or "put out" more.

2. The second reason we cannot readily conclude

**INTRODUCTION**

443

that leadership makes a positive difference in output is the fact that human beings do as much to get into each other's way as they do to facilitate each other's actions. This may simply mean that a very important part of the function of leadership is to clear away roadblocks—human and material—that keep people from being productive. It may very well turn out that effective leaders play the part of the football blocking back who runs interference for the ball carrier.

If we put these two sets of ideas together, they add up to the conclusions that (1) it may be the things we work with and not the will to work that counts, and (2) the human environment is an important part of what we work with and leaders need to keep this part of the working situation from messing up the way we work.

Now neither of these ideas have really been tested to determine their direct effect on output. Much of the reasoning about providing autonomy to individuals as an aid to their productivity at least hints at the idea that leaders can straighten out the human messes in which work is embedded to facilitate productivity. We saw, for example, in Chapter 9 that scientists demand great autonomy and resent the normal exercise of organizational authority—for them the human mess their leaders can straighten out is the pinch of organizational authority. We saw in Chapter 18 that very legitimate systems designed with a worthy purpose in mind turned sour in their application and generated not only poor production but even working behavior that had negative consequences for output—certainly part of the human mess surrounding work that perceptive leaders could well eliminate, or at least minimize. So there is pretty good circumstantial evidence that

leadership may function in an important way to make the environment of work less messy and interfering.

Most technologists and students of mechanization and automation believe firmly that what man works with, and not his personal contribution, is the important source of increased productivity. Without really having a counter to this perfectly reasonable conclusion, we still observe that the same technology may produce considerable variability in output between different companies and even between different departments within the same company. We saw, for example, in Chapter 2 that American and English steel plants with comparable technologies had significantly different outputs and accompanying differences in the structure of their management. Perhaps here is a clue that suggests that leadership does make a difference in the way in which the structure of an organization is designed and in the way in which investment is made in human resources.

This chapter seeks some light on the question of how much we know about the influence of leadership on productivity. Because the answers are so tentative, the chapter is especially designed to raise this crucial question so that every executive, or future executive, who reads this will not soon forget that he has to answer this question many times for himself in the course of his working career.

One final word about the relationship between this chapter and Chapter 16, where we were concerned with features of leadership about which there is some general agreement. These functions of leadership stand by themselves whether or not it ultimately turns out that leaders are also essential in determining the level of productivity.

The first selection is a general statement that points out what is meant by productivity, what some of the sources of it are, and how we go about measuring it. In an effective way this very simple statement puts into perspective the idea of industrial productivity so that it can be properly understood. You will note that this viewpoint of the management of one of America's outstanding giant corporations places great stress on the importance of technology and the organizing leadership of executives and specialists as principal sources of increased productivity.

## WHAT PRODUCTIVITY IS

### General Electric Relations Services*

Productivity is the efficiency with which goods and services are produced —that is, the ratio of the output of goods and services to the input of resources. When we think or speak of *productivity increases,* too few of us are clear as to which of several kinds we have in mind in the particular instance, such as:

1. Increases in productivity—*by the economy as a whole.* This concept deals with the efficiency with which the nation produces its goods and services. The increase in productivity for the economy as a whole, of course, reflects the average performance of all enterprises—those that are advancing, those standing still, and those declining or failing. . . .

2. Increases in productive efficiency *by a company*—that is, across the whole company and from all sources. The bulk of the increases in productive efficiency comes from technological advances, creative innovation in products, and attendant progress in products, materials, facilities and methods, and in organization of the work. It is the responsibility of individual managers to plan, organize, and integrate these many different factors —as well as employee skill, care, and effort—to increase the over-all productive efficiency of the business. In today's economy, professional specialists through their innovations and creative ideas bear a substantial part of the responsibility for economic progress, along with all others who contribute to increasing the efficiency of business operations by using its resources more effectively. This process is the driving force that brings progress and better living to all concerned. . . .

3. Increases in contributions by the individual worker—that is, from his own inner resources of skill, care, and effort, and not from the arm-lengthening designs, facilities, methods, and ideas supplied him by investors through managers and professional specialists. . . .

Productivity is usually spoken of in terms of output per man-hour. But, while productivity is commonly *mea-*

*Reprinted by permission from General Electric Relations Services, "Productivity," *Relations News Letter*: 1–7 (August 1, 1960).

*sured* in terms of the number of man-hours of input, it is the *other factors of input which are the dynamic determinants of productivity growth.* These include the inputs of capital, innovation, technical proficiency, materials, managerial knowhow, and a host of other factors. Thus, it must be kept firmly in mind that productivity is actually output *from all sources*—even though it is *stated* in terms of output per man-hour.

### THE DIFFICULTY OF MEASURING PRODUCTIVITY

The complexity of factors which result in productivity increases and decreases—with some of these factors tangible or visible at the moment while the results of other factors can not be known for some time—make the measurement of productivity an extremely difficult and often questionable process. Yet we have to do the best we can.

We are all familiar with the difficulty of measuring the contributions from the inner resources of the individual worker on a particular job. We come to grips with that problem every day, and we know the best we can do is simply to keep improving the approximations so that they will more nearly approach, even if they never attain, the desired accuracy.

In the case of a highly diversified company like General Electric, the problems of meaningful measurement are compounded by the substantial differences among the company's various product lines. The custom-made products with a high labor content in our own plants and those of our suppliers—and with not enough repetition to permit rapid technological advances in equipment and methods—have not been able to achieve the same cost im-

provements as have the mass-produced products. . . .

When it comes to measuring productivity for the economy as a whole, the difficulties are only further multiplied, of course, by the size of the measurement-taking and data-gathering task. The productivity changes—as figured from the data supplied—are so highly variable from year to year as to make it improbable that any *short-term* calculations can be valid as indicating the current situation or predicting any *long-term* trend.

There are two important efforts to do what is possible in indicating trends in the over-all productivity of the country—(1) the index issued by the Bureau of Labor Statistics and (2) the "Total Factor Productivity" index approach.

The BLS measure of productivity—expressed in terms of "output per man-hour" but meaning output *from all resources* per man-hour worked—was developed to get a broad, over-all picture of such national problems as labor displacement, labor cost, and technology. In order to get a simple measurement factor, BLS divides total output by man-hours of input based on a combination of actual data and estimates. While the BLS measurements have some value for observing broad aspects of the national economy, in the words of the Bureau, "They should not be regarded as precision instruments" (BLS *Bulletin* #100, p. 308).

The fact that employee man-hours are used in computing the BLS productivity index should not cause one to conclude erroneously that the BLS concept measures the contributions of *employees.* The Bureau of Labor Statistics *itself* makes this conclusion very clear in the following statement:

"Although the measure relates output to man-hours it should not be interpreted

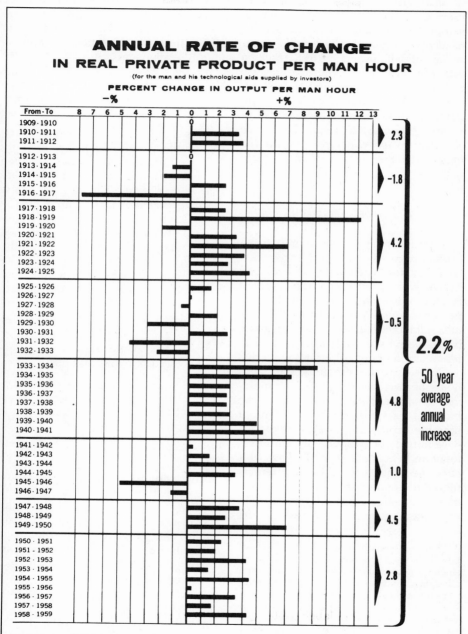

# ANNUAL RATE OF CHANGE
## IN REAL PRIVATE PRODUCT PER MAN HOUR
(for the man and his technological aids supplied by investors)

### PERCENT CHANGE IN OUTPUT PER MAN HOUR

-%          +%

*Sources:* U. S. Congress, Joint Economic Committee, *Productivity Prices and Incomes,* U. S. Govt. Print. Off. (1957), Table 5, p. 91; U. S. Dept. of Labor, BLS Bulletin #1249, Table 1, p. 5 and supplementary press release June 28, 1960.

to represent the unique contribution of labor to production. . . . Thus gains in output per man-hour cannot be ascribed to any one factor, but reflect the interaction of all factors" (BLS *Bulletin* #1249, p. 1).

*The chart, based on the BLS concept, demonstrates that short-term measurements of productivity may have little significance when compared with the long-range average of slightly more than 2%.*[1]

## A BROADER APPROACH

A second major effort at measuring productivity is the concept called "Total Factor Productivity." Developed by Dr. John Kendrick, of the National Bureau of Economic Research, this approach lessens the chance of public misunderstanding which so often arises if productivity is confusingly stated in terms of man-hours of input.

Dr. Kendrick combines the man-hours of input with a presumed measure of other resources used by the business, as indicated by an index of tangible capital employed—a dynamic determinant of productivity improvement and economic growth. Thus, this *combined* measure of input attempts more adequately to reflect management's use of more productive capital equipment, improved materials, and

higher levels of technical proficiency along with any contributions from employee skills and cooperation and any effects from the other tangible and intangible influences . . . .

## THE RECORD OF PRODUCTIVITY CHANGE

It is significant that a 40-year charting of the Total Factor Productivity indicates an annual average change for our economy of not much more than 2 per cent. The figures below indicate that, when measured by the Total Factor concept, productivity increases, particularly during the last few years, have been disappointing, as compared with the promise held by the post-war and Korean period from 1948 to 1953 when the appropriate total factor productivity index increased by 2.7 per cent on the average.

AVERAGE ANNUAL INCREASES IN TOTAL FACTORY PRODUCTIVITY 1919–1959

| 1919–1959 | 1948–1959 | 1948–1953 | 1953–1957 | 1957–1959 |
|-----------|-----------|-----------|-----------|-----------|
| 2.1% | 2.2% | 2.7% | 1.9% | 1.9% |

Source: John W. Kendrick, National Bureau of Economic Research.

There are other methods of measuring productivity. But no methods—including the two discussed in detail above—are exact, or thoroughly reliable. This is particularly true when attempts are made to apply such measures to the productivity of individual companies or industries, where sharp changes in inventories, in product mix, in employment patterns, in rate of plant capacity employed, and the like too often make for current indexes with little broad significance.

---

[1]Note particularly how fallacious it would be to draw conclusions based solely on a single year's estimate. For example, some have drawn attention to the 4% productivity increase estimated for 1958–1959. But, as the Bureau of Labor Statistics itself announced in a June 28, 1960, press release: "A higher than average gain is to be expected in a recovery year following a recession."

The term *supervisor* is used in the following selection to mean the supervision of all levels of a business firm. Thus, a president would be considered the supervisor for a group of vice presidents just as much as a foreman would supervise the workers under him.

This analysis sets forth a variety of goals being sought in the relations between leaders and those being led. It is necessary to take this approach since the leadership-productivity linkage is almost invariably viewed as having some intervening variable involved. You will therefore have to keep constantly in mind a simple formula comparable to the following:

leadership ⟶ morale ⟶ productivity.

The middle or intervening term may also be "shared goals," "autonomy," "participation," "rewards," or "group cohesiveness." In each instance, the intervening variable is measured against some measure of leadership behavior. However, it is then assumed, without

direct measurement in almost all instances, that positive values of the intervening variables are associated with positive high values of the productivity variable. This assumed second-step relationship without its empirical demonstration is what makes it so difficult to establish a direct and verified connection between leadership behavior and the productivity of those being led.

This chapter concludes our consideration of administrative action directed at the internal affairs of the business firm. These six chapters provide a framework for understanding *how* the executive and administrator behaves in order to get his job done. The preceding analysis of administrative relationships pointed out *why* an executive behaved as he did. It is appropriate that we conclude these nine chapters with a challenge to you to understand that an important but by no means settled issue is whether or not leadership behavior makes much difference in work output.

## SUPERVISION AND PRODUCTIVITY

*Robert Dubin**

What difference does the style or quality of supervision make for the productivity of those being supervised?

### SOME VIEWPOINTS

The question asked is a simple one. In the past it has evoked simple answers.

The proponents of *scientific management* have demonstrated that work simplification and rationalization improves productivity. Insofar as the supervisor simplifies and rationalizes the work of his subordinates, he presumably affects their output favorably.

The exponents of *welfare capitalism* concluded that humane treatment of subordinates improves their devotion

*Abridged with modifications from Robert Dubin *et al., Leadership and Productivity* (San Francisco: Chandler Publishing Co., 1966), pp. 1–2, 18–30, 39–50.

to the organization employing them, and that this increased commitment conduces to higher output. This theme finds its contemporary echo in the welfare-state view of workers and the conditions of their well-being under which they increase work effort on behalf of the enterprise. The supervisor presumably is a key figure in according humane treatment to subordinates and is therefore crucial in building and sustaining high-level productivity.

At a more advanced stage of capitalism, it has been urged by devotees of *group dynamics* that participation in decisions about their own welfare and working circumstances enhances commitment, and through that enhancement, the productivity of subordinates. The *socialist theory* of worker motivation reaches the same substantial conclusion that participation—representative participation—in the management of an industrial enterprise increases commitment to the collective undertaking and by this means also increases productivity. Clearly, in both of these views, the most immediate point of decision-sharing with subordinates is in the daily contact with supervisors so that the supervisor is one key figure in the productivity equation.

Employing a model of economic man, *incentive systems* are designed under capitalism and socialism to pay off workers in accordance with their output, on the assumption that worker self-interest in the value of the payoff overrides all other considerations. In the effort to maximize payoff the worker will monitor his own efforts to achieve high output levels in seeking high-level payoffs. The industrial rate-buster and the Stakhanovite socialist worker are archetypical economic men. But even economic man needs some supervision, at least to have constantly called to his attention the still-to-be-

attained payoffs available. Thus, supervision does play a role in keeping attention focused upon the payoff rewards of individual effort and productivity.

Each of the major orientations just reviewed concerning the functions of supervisors in affecting productivity derives from a theory of organization. However the linkage between the individual worker and his work organization is formulated, a supervisor mediates the linkage. The supervisor is a leader of an organized group in an organization whose efforts are directed toward achieving organizational goals.

## SUPERVISORS AND GROUP ATMOSPHERES

The question put at the beginning of this chapter implies this one: What atmospheres created by supervisors affect productivity of their subordinates?

This problem has been approached polemically and with relatively inadequate research. It is useful to begin with a statement of one view of the supervisor's role in creating a working group atmosphere.

Maier observed: "We are entering a period in work relations where mental cruelty is becoming an appropriate charge in a grievance committee meeting as it is in the divorce court." Specifically, self-determination of behavior is more acceptable than determination by others: "It is apparent that a person accepts his own decisions more often than he does another's. Group decisions are more readily accepted, but may sacrifice quality." Nevertheless, "When production is a matter of coordination of group activity, it can be increased by stimulating the group to decide on a goal. In such cases the goal set should be unanimously approved. . . . Group decision thus becomes an extremely important factor in determining the performance of a team of workers."[1]

Maier's thinking starts with the mental well-being or psychic comfort of the worker and concludes that somehow or other this is positively related to production. The argument is a very tenuous one and it may be accurate. However, the evidence is meager and when marshaled gives weak support to the conclusion. Participation in decisions about own behavior does not necessarily lead to maximizing own behavior to achieve organizational objectives, with a payoff in mental comfort. . . .

Drucker[2] has pointed out that the trend in modern industrial work emphasizes individual jobs as well as group or team jobs. He noted that many maintenance jobs are individual jobs and that these will increase in number with increasing automation of industry. Furthermore, many sales jobs are individual jobs, and these will also increase in number as secondary economic activity provides an increasing proportion of employment opportunities. An important corrective to current emphasis on the "groupness" of industrial work is to realize that there are now and will probably be an increasing proportion of all jobs which will *not* be performed in groups but will be performed individually and outside of group contexts. For individual jobs, the group theory of motivation simply will not apply and new studies will be necessary to find out how the lone worker can be moved to a high level of productivity and sustained there as

a member of a modern work organization. . . .

A more analytical reading of the group-dynamics literature was presented by Arensberg and Tootel, who drew the following conclusion: "It is worthwhile reiterating the discovery of the 'interactionists' that this process of manager-worker interaction, and the gain in productivity it brings about, seems to have *very delicate and narrow limits*."[3] Their summary is worthy of note:

Indeed, present evidence suggests that the release of productivity is not so much limited by human capacity or by "diminishing returns" of maximization, as older efficiency doctrines have it, as it is dependent upon some "feedback" between worker initiative and managerial facilitation. The next advance in our understanding will come when we work out the empirical characteristics of this process.[4]

### SHARED GOALS

Perhaps the best single piece of empirical evidence bearing on the issue of a shared goal as the stimulus to high-level group effort is found in the celebrated "Robbers' Cave Experiment."[5] Two groups of boys in a boy's camp achieved fusion in the solution of a common problem, after they had been deliberately placed in antago-

[1]Norman R. F. Maier, *Psychology in Industry* (2nd ed.; Boston: Houghton Mifflin Company, 1955), pp. 137, 141, 151–152.

[2]Peter Drucker, *The Practice of Management* (New York: Harper and Bros., 1954).

[3]Conrad M. Arensberg and Geoffrey Tootel, "Plant Sociology: Real Discoveries and New Problems," in Mirra Komarovsky (ed.), *Common Frontiers in the Social Sciences* (Glencoe: The Free Press, 1957), p. 316.

[4]*Ibid.*, p. 317.

[5]Muzafer Sherif, *Intergroup Conflict and Cooperation: The Robbers' Cave Experiment* (Norman, Okla.: University Book Exchange, 1961).

nism to each other, only when they realized that the continuous flow of behavior in each group depended on overcoming this mutual problem. The groups were driven into each other's arms and into cooperation by the need jointly to solve a problem bigger than each could handle separately. Thus, fusion was achieved between two antagonistic groups in overcoming a common obstacle.\

It is worth emphasizing that there is a difference between (1) maintaining steady states in a social system and (2) the reaction of the social system to blockages or obstacles against the normal flow of activities. Empirical evidence does indicate that "fusion" can develop among diverse groups in overcoming obstacles that they face in common. Such evidence appears in Sherif's studies and in the earlier studies of Kurt Lewin, who examined the problems of group decision to achieve eating-habit changes under wartime shortages of food.[6] Sociologists have long called attention to the fact that national unity and social cohesion are usually the products either of acute crises in the social system or of attack from outside. In wars and other major social crises, many intrasocietal differences are set aside in favor of overcoming the obstacles confronting the society as a whole. Fires, floods, and other disasters in industrial establishments automatically override differences between union and management as they work together to overcome the obstacle and restore the plant to productive effectiveness. In a mine disaster, a union and its members, normally struggling against management, may temporarily set aside antagonisms

in the common concern to save the men trapped underground. All these instances bear on the fact that "fusion" of groups with different goals can be achieved when they are simultaneously confronted with a common obstacle that halts the normal flow of behavior in the groups.

The maintenance of a steady state like high productivity, and the accompanying values necessary to sustain it, has not been shown to be the product of the "fusion" of diverse goals and values of the groups involved. Even the neglected and important research of Blake and Mouton[7] has dealt only with problem solving but not with steady-state maintenance.

It is not the purpose here to assert that maintenance of a steady state of high output is impossible, or that it may not be the product of a "fusion" of diverse group values. There is, however, no present empirical evidence to show that the fusion of group values is what sustains steady states in social systems. It is time to devote attention to actual measurement and analysis of this connection. . . .

## MULTIPLE GOALS OF SUPERVISION

Supervisors are not solely oriented toward building and maintaining the productive level of those supervised. Indeed, as theorists like Maier have indicated, the mental health or psychic well-being of workers may be a coordinate goal of the efforts of supervision, along with productivity. Beside

---

[6]Kurt Lewin, *Field Theory in Social Science* (Dorwin Cartwright, ed., New York: Harper and Bros., 1951).

[7]Some of which is summarized in Robert R. Blake and Jane S. Mouton, "Competition, Communication, and Conformity," and "Conformity, Resistance and Conversion," both in I. A. Berg and B. M. Bass (eds.), *Conformity and Deviation* (New York: Harper and Bros., 1961).

the notion of psychic well-being can be set those of morale, of loyalty, of commitment to organization, as other goals toward which supervisory practices may be directed. These all relate to the connection between employee and organization. In addition, there is an extremely large body of studies and theory dealing with such goals of supervision as maintenance of safety, reduction of employee turnover, minimization of employee grievances, reduction of scrap and other losses, quality control, and plant and equipment maintenance.

It is notable that in pursuit of this incomplete list of goals toward which supervisory behavior is directed a vast range of activities is to be found, many of which are independent of each other. The supervisor's jobs are many and varied, and it should not be at all surprising to find numerous empirical situations in which the supervisor is little, if at all, concerned with people or with productivity. Certainly, under circumstances of complete machine pacing, for example, the variability in productivity that can be attributed to supervisory practices is probably extremely small.

Morale, feelings of well-being, attitudes toward the company, acceptance or non-acceptance of supervisors, cohesiveness of the work group, employee turnover, or grievance incidence rates are in and of themselves important subjects for study and analysis. Because, however, the major test applied by operating management to any innovations in supervisory practices is the influence these may have on productivity, the authors of studies relating supervisory practices to other outcomes often gratuitously conclude that their results support the belief that productivity will also be positively affected. It is important to keep in mind that the various goals toward which supervisory practices are directed are not necessarily interrelated.

## Worker Morale As A Goal

A number of studies of supervisory behavior concern its influence on morale of workers. Almost invariably the author will conclude that if the supervisor's behavior can raise morale, then there are probably associated increases in productivity. The study may clearly demonstrate that morale does vary according to the behavior of supervisors, but the conclusion that morale change in turn influences productivity remains unsupported. Indeed, Dubin[8] has pointed out that high morale in a work group may be the basis for successful sabotage of management's productivity goals, and Seashore[9] has shown that high-cohesion work groups may deviate from production norms on *both* the high and the low sides. Since Seashore's data also show that high-cohesion work groups tend to be high-morale groups, his findings support Dubin's conclusion.

As part of the Yale study of automobile assembly-line workers, Turner[10] showed that the attitudes of workers toward the job itself and toward their own foremen were independent. In particular, Turner found that if the job was of primary impor-

---

[8]Robert Dubin, *The World of Work* (Englewood Cliffs, N. J.: Prentice-Hall, Inc., 1958), especially Chapter 12.

[9]Stanley E. Seashore, *Group Cohesiveness in the Industrial Work Group* (Ann Arbor: Institute for Social Research, University of Michigan, 1954).

[10]Arthur N. Turner, "Foreman, Job, and Company," *Human Relations* 10:99–112, 1957.

tance to the workers, then the foreman and his behavior made relatively
little difference in their orientation
toward the organization. "It was as if
the nature of the job and the nature
of supervision, as perceived by workers, were almost separate influences on
workers' over-all attitudes."[11]

Kahn, one of the principal investigators in the Michigan researches,
concluded the survey of the Michigan
studies of supervisors and workers as
follows: "None of the major indices
of satisfaction (job, supervision, company, etc.) proved either to relate to
productivity or to mediate significantly between productivity and such
independent variables as role differentiation, delegation, or employee
orientation."[12]

Turning directly to evidence on
morale, Kahn stated the following:

This research, . . . did not provide positive evidence on the matter of morale in
relation to productivity. . . . Indices of
worker satisfaction were developed by
means of factor analysis, which showed
four well-defined dimensions of satisfaction: satisfaction with supervision, with
the job itself, with the company as a
whole, and with the extrinsic rewards of
money, mobility, etc. None of these indices was significantly related to productivity.

In line with a statement already made
in this chapter, Kahn stated: "The
notion that supervision (among other
things) determines satisfaction, which
in turn determines productivity, has
been considerably discredited in our
eyes."[13]

Likert[14] has presented some other
Michigan data which show that productivity increases with supervisor's
pressure for more output (Figure 1).
Morale also increases up to about the
mid range of supervisory pressure for
output, after which it declines, just as
sharply as it increased. Thus, even the
data used by one of the strongest exponents of worker autonomy shows
that pressure *does* produce more productivity and even increases morale
through a portion of the range of increasing supervisory pressure. This
observation suggests that social systems respond to leadership pressures
in "putting the heat on" and holding
subordinates to high expectations. In
an organized production situation,
workers expect to be asked to produce
and be held to reasonable levels of
output. Furthermore, if the supervisory pressure is not excessive workers'
morale goes up with increasing pressure!

## Worker Autonomy As A Goal

Management literature is replete
with a theme that worker autonomy
is a viable goal for supervisory practices. Generally the worker autonomy
sought is one best described as the
condition wherein workers require
little supervision. Sometimes autonomy
is specified as the condition requiring
minimum "close supervision." The
definition of autonomy is almost always in the supervisor-worker context.
On its face, worker autonomy should
be an acceptable condition for many
workers, and it is obviously an aid

[11]*Ibid.*, p. 111.
[12]Robert L. Kahn, "The Prediction of
Productivity," *Journal of Social Issues*, 12:
44, 1956.
[13]*Ibid.*, from pp. 46 and 47.

[14]Rensis Likert, "Developing Patterns in
Management," in American Management
Association, *Strengthening Management for
the New Technology* (New York: The
Association, 1955).

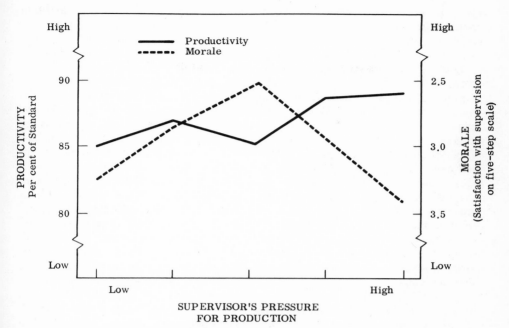

FIGURE 1. The Relation of Productivity and Morale to Supervisor's Pressure for Production. Redrawn from Rensis. Likert, "Developing Patterns in Management."

to supervisors since it reduces their burden.

Kahn,[15] in summarizing the human-relations research program at the University of Michigan, showed that in the studies of clerical and railroad workers the high-productivity groups were supervised in a general fashion rather than in a close or detailed one. This demonstration was the beginning of the repeated emphasis in the Michigan studies, castigating close and detailed supervision and pleading for worker autonomy as one of the important requisites for high output. The idea has persisted to the present and is given renewed emphasis by Likert.[16] But the study of British industry by

Argyle, Gardner, and Ciofi[17] did not demonstrate autonomy as a central variable in productivity. These data have never been incorporated into the thinking of the Michigan group.

Perhaps these disparate findings can be reconciled by noting that both railroad and clerical workers, the samples from which the Michigan group drew its conclusions, are involved in unit- or batch-production systems. Woodward's studies of technology and management show that the ratio of supervisors to workers is very low in such systems. A correlate of this low ratio is that the responsi-

[15]Robert L. Kahn, *op. cit.*

[16]In his widely acclaimed book, *New Patterns of Management* (New York: McGraw-Hill Book Company, 1961).

[17]Michael Argyle, Godfrey Gardner, and Frank Ciofi, "The Measurement of Supervisory Methods," *Human Relations*, 10:295–313, 1957, and by the same authors, "Supervisory Methods Related to Productivity, Absenteeism, and Labour Turnover," *Human Relations*, 11:23–40, 1958.

bility of individual workers may be maximal in such systems. A further correlate is that workers in unit-production technologies will produce most when given only general supervision. This relation is to be attributed to the technology rather than to a general principle that all work situations demand maximum autonomy for workers.

The study by Argyle, Gardner, and Ciofi was based on 90 foremen in eight British factories manufacturing electric motors and switchgear. These factories would all probably be classified as employing large-batch or quasi-mass production, with basic technological features different from those in the routine clerical work in a large insurance company and in the railroad gangs studied by the Michigan group. The British study revealed that the only dimension of supervisory behavior which bore a significant relationship to measured output of the departments supervised was punitive or nonpunitive correction by the foreman of worker mistakes and errors. When general supervision was combined with nonpunitive behavior and democratic relations with employees, these three dimensions of supervisor behavior were positively and significantly correlated with output, but together they accounted only for 18 per cent of the variance in output.

Likert reproduced the results of one of his earliest studies in *New Patterns of Management* in which he compared the difference between superior and mediocre life-insurance agencies. The data show that an attitude of cooperation with his sales agents by the agency manager was found more often among managers of agencies judged superior in performance. The descriptions of the managers were based on agents' evaluations. Furthermore, these same successful managers gave considerably more autonomy to their agents than the less successful managers.

It is not surprising, in view of these results secured when he made one of his first studies of managerial behavior, that Likert would conclude that considerate, nondirective leadership characteristics symbolize modern industrial statesmanship. However, it is obvious that selling life insurance is a classical unit-production process, a one-customer-one-sale situation. Each sale is a unit by itself, typically taking place away from the office and therefore removed from the point of supervision. It would seem evident that the technology associated with selling life insurance would make autonomy of sales agents an important condition of success.

Evidence is by no means conclusive in support of the contention that worker autonomy is essential for high individual productivity. Indeed, when worker autonomy (of which general supervision instead of close supervision is the foreman facet) is combined with two other dimensions of supervisory behavior found significant in combination in the English factories, the combination still accounts for less than one-fifth of the variance in productivity. Further, there is reason to believe that worker autonomy may be relevant to batch- or unit-production technologies, but probably not to mass-production technologies and almost certainly not to continuous-process technologies. . . .

## Worker Participation As A Goal

A particularly important study in the analysis of supervisory practices was that by French and Coch,[18] in which the effects of employee participation in a decision affecting them were measured. It was concluded that those who participated in decisions regarding work changes ultimately reached somewhat higher levels of output than a comparable group of workers who were told to change their methods of work. This study has been the cornerstone of theory concluding that worker participation is desirable for efficiency reasons and improvement of output levels.

Wickert[19] studied employee turnover and feelings of ego involvement in the day-to-day operations of telephone operators and female service representatives in the Michigan Bell Telephone Company. About 700 women were studied. The principal finding was that those who stayed with the company had a greater feeling of involvement in the day-to-day operations of the company than those who left. Specifically, those who stayed tended to say (1) they had a chance to make decisions on the job, and (2) they felt they were making an important individual contribution to the success of the company. It will be noted that telephone operators and service representatives are all involved in unit production, since they each have to depend upon someone initiating a call or a service request before they go into action. Under these circumstances of technology a material degree of autonomy is probably essential in maintaining levels of output. A chance to make decisions on the job and contri-

bute to company success are measures of participation. It might be concluded, however, that these aspects of participation in work are mediated by the need for autonomy that comes from the technology employed.

In Rice's study of the Indian weaving shed,[20] a comparison was made of production before and after a change in the organization of the work. The individual workers in the experimental weaving groups revised the production process from what had previously been a confused and relatively unstructured one. The data demonstrate that the subsequent steady state of output was markedly and significantly higher after the workers reorganized the work themselves. Furthermore, the rate of cloth damage in the weaving mill was lower than before reorganization of production.

Several comments need to be made about this study. The self-organizing productive groups increased their efficiency by about 18 per cent if we take the before-reorganization figures as the base. This improvement tends to give the impression, as Rice suggests, that the self-organization of work is one means for increasing efficiency considerably. But a disturbing feature of this situation also must be taken into account. The original structuring of the work situation, which continued to obtain in the nonexperimental groups in the same company, was one in which there were confused task and worker relationships, and no perceptible internal work-group structure. Thus the base from which change was measured in this study may be an instance of industrial "anarchy," or near anarchy,

[18]Lester Coch and John R. P. French, Jr., "Overcoming Resistance to Change," *Human Relations,* 1:512–532, 1948.

[19]F. R. Wickert, "Turnover and Employee's Feelings of Ego-Involvement," *Personnel Psychology,* 4:185–197, 1951.

[20]A. K. Rice, "Productivity and Social Organization in an Indian Weaving Shed," *Human Relations,* 6:297–329, 1953.

in which the designs of the production processes themselves were scarcely adequate.

Under these circumstances, any attention to the *organization* of work, whether management-initiated or worker-initiated, undoubtedly would have produced significant increases in productivity. Weaving, being a continuous-process production technology over short time spans, would require high structure for adequate performance. In the light of Fleishman's results it seems probable that structuring itself is what may have improved productivity in the Indian weaving shed, not worker participation. It may not, therefore, be desirable or warranted to draw the conclusion that high autonomy and participation in decisions by the Indian weavers are what really produced higher output.

Likert, in an early paper,[21] made the point that:

Available research findings indicate, therefore, that when . . . the amount of participation used is less than or very much greater than expected, an unfavorable reaction is likely to be evoked. Substantially greater amounts of participation than expected appear to exceed the skill of the subordinate to cope with it and produce a negative reaction because of the threatening nature of the situation to the subordinate. The available theory and research findings suggest that the best results obtain when the amount of participation used is somewhat greater than expected by the subordinate, but still within their capacity to respond to it effectively.

Likert had made this point as early as

1952, but it is a point that is rarely given attention by those who urge participative management as the be-all and end-all of supervisory practice.

Likert clearly argued for an optimal rather than a maximal level of participation of subordinates in decision-making relative to their own destinies. That is, there is a curvilinear relation between worker participation and such consequences as output. . . .

The general conclusion that emerges is that employee participation is probably not linearly related but rather curvilinearly related to aspects of working behavior. Likert has pointed out that his own researches have indicated that supervisory behavior in excess of normal expectations will not be favorably accepted by subordinates. This disfavor may be particularly likely if the supervisor invites participation beyond the subordinate's normal level of acceptance. This conclusion recalls Barnard's "zone of indifference," in which reactions of the subordinate become significant only if the supervisor exceeds the tolerance limits customarily adopted by the subordinate.[22]

## Rewarding Workers As A Goal

One of the important functions of supervisors is that of rewarding subordinates. In modern industrial firms the immediate supervisor has relatively little connection with monetary rewards, except perhaps to recommend promotions and pay increases. There remains, however, a range of nonfinancial rewards that each supervisor can monitor in influencing his

---

[21]Rensis Likert, "Effective Supervision: An Adaptive and Relative Process," *op. cit.*, p. 329.

[22]Chester I. Barnard, *The Functions of the Executive* (Cambridge, Mass.: Harvard University Press, 1938).

subordinates. Surprisingly little research has been directed at finding out what effects such rewards have.

In the interesting study by Zaleznik, Christensen, and Roethlisberger,[23] fifty industrial workers were analyzed to determine the influences of social factors on productivity. Among the major findings was the fact that individuals with high status and high status congruence (agreement between self-conception and other's perception that they are properly placed in a social system) tended to produce at the normal or expected levels of output more than they tended to deviate from "on-line" output. On the other hand, of individuals with low status and low status congruence twice as many were deviant in output as were "on-line."

In analyzing status by itself it was found that the high-status people were average in productivity and "on-line" more than they deviated, while the low-status people deviated more than they were "on-line" in output. However, when status congruence was examined by itself the relationship turned out to be nonsignificant between that and level of productivity.

The study showed that when both management and the peer group rewarded the workers, more of them produced "on-line" than were deviant by a ratio of eight to three. Similarly when management did not reward the worker but the group did, more produced "on-line" by the ratio of six to three. However, when management rewarded the individual and the group did not, or when neither rewarded, then the preponderance was deviancy

[23] Abe Zaleznik, Charles R. Christensen, and Fritz J. Roethlisberger, *The Motivation, Productivity, and Satisfaction of Workers* (Cambridge, Mass.: Harvard University Press, 1958).

by the individual from the "on-line" expectations of output. When management alone rewarded the worker, he tended to produce below norm. When neither rewarded the worker, however, he tended to produce above average.

Another way of examining the influences of the social factors on productivity is to look at the character of group membership and its impact on productivity. Those who were regular members of a group tended to produce in the ratio of fourteen at the expected average to six "off-line." Those who were perceived by the group as being deviant individuals were predominantly "off-line" in output in the ratio of ten to three who were "on-line," while isolates from the group tended to produce "off-line" in the ratio of nine to three who were "on-line." Thus, being a deviant or isolate from the work group meant that the individual would not produce at the expected norm of output. It is interesting to note that those who were deviants from the work group tended to produce higher than the norm, while those who were isolates from the work group tended to produce below standard.

These results, suggestive as they are, must be approached cautiously since the numbers on which they are based are small, there being only forty-five workers in the total sample for whom full data were available. The conclusions can be treated as suggesting the following speculations.

It seems that individual productivity is influenced by (1) the location of an individual in a social group, (2) the status accorded to him by those in his social environment, and (3) the sources of social rewards coming to him. The smallness of the sample precludes any cross tabulations to isolate the impact of rewards vs. social position when these factors are considered simultaneously.

What seems especially notable is that individual productivity varies with social factors in the work situation that may not be within the influence range of the supervisor. Indeed, strange as it may seem, insofar as supervisors manipulate non-financial rewards without parallel rewards coming from the peer work group, the worker response may be output lower than the norm! This finding is significant for reinforcement theorists in the realm of industrial incentives. Complicating the reinforcement theorist's problem even further is the finding that nonreward produces output higher than normal! Maybe if we really want high productivity, the social payoffs with which we reward industrial workers should be withheld!

The study just analyzed calls attention to the importance of the working peer group as a source of reward and reinforcement of individual behavior. This importance turns attention to the characteristics of peer groups. Among those features studied that bear on productivity is peer-group cohesiveness.

Seashore's study[24] of group cohesiveness in the industrial work group showed (Figure 2) that among low-productivity groups, worker-perceived pressure for productivity decreased as the group cohesiveness increased. When the condition of maximum group cohesiveness was approached the perceived degree of pressure for productivity went up markedly. This tendency contrasted with that in groups of high productivity, which perceived a declining degree of pres-

sure for productivity as group cohesiveness increased.

For the low-productivity group, management pressure for productivity was perceived only if the group was highly cohesive. Thus, one of the consequences of cohesiveness in low-productivity groups is to provide the opportunity for supportive rebellion against management. This conclusion is further supported by the general summing up by Seashore: "High cohesive groups differ more frequently and in greater amount than low cohesive groups from the plant norms of productivity. These deviations are toward both high and lower productivity."[25]

## CONCLUSION

Supervision does make some difference in productivity. Supervisory practices also affect other aspects of work. The details of these conclusions depart significantly from current views, and are both unique and surprising.

1. Supervisory behavior affects the productivity of individuals by being appropriate to the work setting. One key to describing the characteristics of work settings is to know the nature of the technologies employed. The descriptive task has just begun but the results are promising. By drawing simple distinctions between unit- and mass-production technologies and viewing continuous production as another type of technology, supervisory styles are found appropriate to each technological type. The more a production process resembles a unit or batch technology, the greater is the probability that worker autonomy and its supervisory counterpart—general

---

[24]Stanley E. Seashore, *op. cit.*

[25]*Ibid.*, p. 98.

rather than close supervision—will be appropriate. The more a technology resembles a continuous-production system the more appropriate will close supervision be.

2. This first proposition leads directly to the second. There is no "one best" method of supervision. As in all human systems, there is variability in the systems of supervision of industrial and commercial work. Several styles of supervision are effective, but they are individually successful only in relation to appropriate work settings. Variety in supervisory behaviors may no longer be considered a challenge to choose the "one best" for all settings, but rather as a challenge to understand where each does or does not work.

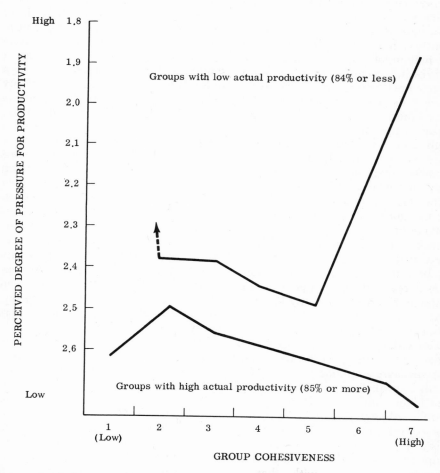

FIGURE 2. Relationship between Group Cohesiveness and Perceived Degree of Pressure for Productivity. The measure of perceived degree of pressure for productivity is based on response to the question, "How hard do you usually have to work in order to get your work done?" A high numerical score represents relatively low pressure. (Redrawn from Stanley Seashore, *Group Cohesiveness in the Industrial Work Group,* cited in footnote 9.)

3. As far as empirical data take us, it seems clear that the influence of supervisory behavior on *productivity* is small. The studies are few in number, however, and not adequately designed to measure magnitude of influence of supervision on productivity.

4. Supervision of industrial and commercial work has many functions. The variety of areas in which supervisors act is the consequence of their having numerous functional contributions to make. For a given situation supervision may have relatively little to do with individual productivity, and yet supervisors, because they perform many other functions, may retain importance in work organizations. Executives must therefore constantly face the difficult problem of organizational design and the choice of operating goals for supervisors. If, for example, top management wants workers to be happy this goal may be attained by appropriate supervisory behavior.

5. The goals of supervision and the behavior of supervisors are independent of each other in one sense and linked in another. A variety of goals may be assigned to supervisors, and those selected do not appear to be limited or determined by any features of organizational structure or process. Thus, consideration of workers may be emphasized in unit production, in mass production, or in process production if top management chooses consideration as a goal. Supervisory practices in each technological system will be different although directed toward the same goal. It is in this sense that the goals of supervision and the behaviors of supervisors are independent of each other.

On the other hand, goals and behaviors are linked through technology since behaviors necessary to achieve a particular goal must be appropriate to the operating situation. For example, consideration of workers in unit-production technologies may exhibit itself by providing workers with maximum opportunities to pace their own work, while in continuous-production technologies the same consideration may be most appropriately expressed as detailed concern with safety or physical comfort of the worker.

6. It is now possible to take a sophisticated view of the impact of supervision on working behaviors. Most analysts up to this time have assumed that whatever the linkage, it tended to be a linear one. That is, a unit change in a particular supervisory behavior was assumed to produce a corresponding change in worker response throughout the range of supervisory action. This view is simply false. Many behaviors have thresholds above which the behavior is responded to by others, but below which the behaviors produce little or no effect. Thresholds were revealed, for example, in the relationship between supervisory consideration and worker responses in terms of grievances and absenteeism. This phenomenon was also discovered in the relation between opportunity to participate in decisions and worker responses to the opportunity.

7. A supervisory practice in the low range may have one effect on worker response, but in the high range may produce exactly the opposite effect. This disparity was exhibited in the consequence of supervisory pressure for worker morale. At least in some demonstrable instances the relationship between supervisory behavior and worker response is nonlinear and may even be parabolic. Evidence supports the contention that if a little bit of a supervisory behavior may be good, a lot may be very bad indeed.

This optimization notion is sometimes overlooked in the theory and practice of personnel administration.

8. An important technological trend is making for a fundamental shift in industry from the management of people to the management of things. The detailed study of continuous-process manufacture showed the highest ratio of managers to other workers for any type of technology. It has been inferred that this high ratio reflects the need for supervisor surveillance of high-speed production processes to insure that product runs are error-free, since large numbers of defects can be produced by the time the process is halted to correct an error. As supervisors supervise machines more and people less, they will become increasingly responsible for production. Supervisory controls will not be controls on speed of output, since output will be machine- or process-paced. The supervisors will be largely concerned with controlling quality, and the operating contingencies that influence the go-no-go performance of the production process.

9. Knowledge of leadership and supervision as they affect working behavior is almost exclusively the result of studying American industrial practices. A few important English studies have been cited here, and additional studies dealing with other national economies are scattered through the literature.[26] Culture does make a dif-

ference in supervisory practices. It follows, then, that caution is necessary in applying present knowledge to cultural settings different from those in which the knowledge was gained. Generalizations may work universally, but then again they may not. We have no *a priori* reason for guessing which of these two outcomes will obtain.

10. All the studies of human relations and supervision tell little about how much productivity is affected by individual supervisory practices. Only one study attempted to tease out the answer to this question and it suggested that not more than one-fifth of the variance in productivity can be accounted for by a combination of three supervisory practices. The Western Electric and other researches showed that fellow workers influence the individual's output. Advances in technology produce steady increases in man-hour productivity. There has never been a proper analysis of variance to assay the relative importance of simultaneous factors affecting individual output. It is certainly time to turn empirical attention to just this kind of problem.

---

[26]I cite just two studies conducted in Scandinavian countries which have been scarcely noticed by American scholars although both are significant contributions. K. Raino, *Leadership Qualities: A Theoretical Inquiry and an Experimental Study of Foremen* (Helsinki: Annales Academiae Scientiarum Fennicae, Series B, Vol. 95.1, 1955); Uno Remitz, *Professional Satisfaction among Swedish Bank Employees* (Copenhagen: Munksgaard, 1960).

# part 6

# INTERNAL AND EXTERNAL ENVIRONMENT

There are several aspects of the environment of organizations deserving special attention. Viewing the internal situation of organizations we have selected two environmental features that have unique and pervasive influence on the human relations of administration. These are the technologies used in getting work done, and the fictional beliefs that help give sensible order to the inevitable inconsistencies which all organizations exhibit.

From the larger society as environment, we select for attention the influence that productive institutions have in introducing social change (especially in the values of the society), and the corresponding responsibilities that administrators have to society in general as well as for their own moral behavior in particular.

We are viewing "environment" here as containing the broad social forces over which no single person or organization has direct control. This is the same sense in which the economist holds that under perfect competition no single competitor can affect the market regardless of how extreme his own strategies are. For our purposes, this view of environment is useful because it directs the administrator's attention to features of his operating world which he has to take into account without necessarily being able to control (by **OVERVIEW** changing in a desired direction, by "holding constant," or by eliminating).

It is somewhat arbitrary to separate internal from external environment since the line separating the two is often indistinct. For example, the automation of production processes is moving ahead everywhere in the economy. No single organization is any longer free to ignore automation or even "corner the market on it" because the theoretical knowledge on which it is based and the technical equipment for carrying it out are freely available throughout society. On the other hand, when automation is employed in changing existing production methods, these changes take place, and their most immediate impacts are felt, inside the organization (although subsequent displacement of workers', changes in productive levels, and their social consequences, are felt again in the outside environment we call the larger society). We choose to view technology as a feature of the internal environment of an organization only on the arbitrary grounds that it is here that the basic decisions about it are taken, and it is inside the organization that the first visible consequences are observable.

With this analysis of the environments of organizations we close the volume. We have successively examined the nature of organizations and the characteristics of their administrative personnel, the fundamental administrative relationships, and their applications in administrative action.

It is fitting to end with a consideration of the environment surrounding the administrator, for he is both its product and its molder. Administrators of organizations are as inevitable as death and taxes. The business of any society could not be carried out save for its productive organizations and their administrative personnel. The particular wealth of a society and the well-being of its citizens are, at any given point in time, significant products of the corps of executives who govern the destinies of the society's organizations. It is hoped that this volume may contribute in some small measure to the effectiveness of those administrators who seek insight into the human relations of their tasks.

# 20

# Technology

There are a number of ways in which we can analyze the relationships between technology and human relations in a sociological framework. We can first examine the impact of technology upon society as a whole. Secondly, we can consider the impacts of technological changes upon business organizations. Most of this chapter is devoted to the second approach. In the first article, by Merton, some cursory attention is given to the interconnections between technological change and society as a whole. This is by no means an exhaustive treatment, nor is it intended to be.

There are two major phases of the technology of any work: (a) the tools, instruments, machines, and technical formulas whose employment is necessary to its performance; and (b) the body of ideas which express the goals of the work, its functional importance, and the rationale of the methods employed. Technology, then, is composed of the tools used and the specialized ideas needed in getting particular kinds of work done.

**INTRODUCTION**

In general, we have no difficulty in understanding that tools and machines are components of technology. It may not be quite so clear that technical *ideas* are also parts of technology for they guide technical behavior. For example, an inventory specialist can argue the merits of, and make a decision about using either a FIFO (first-in-first-out) or a LIFO (last-in-first-out) system of inventory management. Each system has its logical justification and its special advantages for given situations or types of goods. We would expect the inventory specialist to have mastered the ideas underlying each type of system, and to know how to apply the ideas in carrying out his responsibilities. These technical ideas are, indeed, a part of the technology and help to define the entire realm with which we are concerned when we examine the consequences of technology for human relations in organizations.

Turning now to the impact of technology on business organizations, we will examine four principal issues: (1) the pace at which technological change is introduced into the economy; (2) the relationships between technology and production; (3) the effects of automation on the demand for skills; and (4) the manner in which technology may produce results irrespective of human willingness. These are only selected aspects of the total impact of technology on modern industry. They do represent, however, those consequences of modern industrial technology that are particularly important as part of the environment of business decision-making.

The most recent examination of the impact of technology on business operations was undertaken by a national commission appointed by the President of the United States. In the

following discussion, a brief portion of the final report of this commission is presented in which consideration is given to the rate at which technological innovations are introduced into the economy. A general knowledge of the time lag between invention and application is important for every business executive because it can affect his decisions regarding strategies of competition. The businessman who is first to adopt an invention has pretty good reason to believe that his competitors will take about five years to follow suit.

While there is no good theory about why a time lag of somewhere between ten and fifteen years exists between invention and initial commercial application, or why commercial development takes somewhere between five and eight years, it seems clear that these time lags have positive consequences for the society as a whole. It is during the incubation period and the subsequent period of commercial development that social adjustments can be made to the new technological development. These time lags, in other words, provide an opportunity to plan for the consequences of the new development and thereby make their impact less disruptive.

## THE PACE OF TECHNOLOGICAL CHANGE

*National Commission on Technology,
Automation, and Economic Progress* *

The most inclusive useful index of productivity is output per man-hour in the whole private economy. In the 35

*Reprinted from National Commission on Technology, Automation, and Economic Progress, *Technology and the American Econo-*

years before the end of the Second World War, output per man-hour in the private economy rose at a trend rate of 2 percent a year. But this pe-

*my* (Washington, D. C.: U. S. Government Printing Office, February, 1966), pp. 2–5.

riod includes the depression decade of the 1930's. Between 1947 and 1965 productivity in the private economy rose at a trend rate of about 3.2 percent a year. If agriculture is excluded, the contrast is less sharp, with the rate of increase 2 percent a year before the war and 2.5 percent after ( see Figure 1).[1]

Some attempts have been made to refine a measure of the effects of technological change by allowing for the influence of better educated workers and increasing capital investment. The results are necessarily imprecise, and

If this increase in the rate of productivity growth does not square with the assumption that a veritable technological revolution has occurred, the increase itself is nevertheless substantial. Growth at 2 percent a year doubles in 36 years; growth at 2.5 percent a year doubles in 28 years; growth at 3 percent a year doubles in about 24 years. The notion that the product of an hour of work can double in 24 years —not much more than half a working lifetime—is quite enough to justify the feeling of continuous change that is so much a part of the contemporary en-

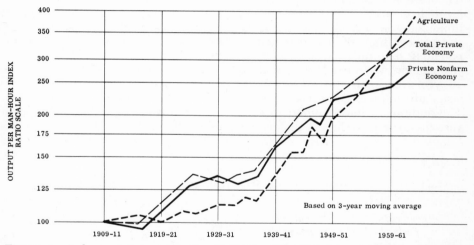

FIGURE 1. Indexes of Output Per Man-Hour; Total Private, Farm, and Private Nonfarm Economy, 1909–65. Source: Compiled from information provided by the U. S. Department of Commerce and Bureau of Labor Statistics, U. S. Department of Labor.

show, as would be expected, that not all the gain in productivity can be attributed to changing technology. They do suggest, however, some acceleration in the rate of progress and give a picture consistent with the simpler index of output per man-hour.

[1]We give the figure without agriculture not to suggest that agricultural productivity does not matter, but only to isolate the productivity trend in "industry." For manufacturing alone, the postwar rate of productivity gain was 2.6 percent per year.

vironment. The time scale has indeed shrunk visibly.

One other important aspect of innovation is at least partially amenable to measurement. The economic impact of a scientific or engineering discovery begins not when the discovery is first made, not even when it is first commercially introduced, but only later when the resulting new product or new process receives widespread commercial acceptance. The process of development and diffusion through industry takes time—some times a long time. The steam locomotive and the diesel coexisted for at least 30 years; the DC-3 introduced in the 1930's is still flying. Studies made for the Commission confirm the common belief that things happen faster nowadays: the lag between discovery and commercial application has shortened. It is nevertheless still substantial.

Lynn concluded from an examination of a limited sample of 20 major technological innovations during the last 60 to 70 years that every step in the process of technological development had accelerated. The typical time between a technical discovery and recognition of its commercial potential had fallen from about 30 years before the First World War to 16 years between the wars, and 9 years after the Second World War. The additional time required to convert these basic technical discoveries

to initial commercial application had decreased from about 7 years to about 5 years (see Table 1). The rate at which new technologies diffused throughout the economy after their introduction had speeded up considerably between the early part of the century and the interwar period, with only slight further acceleration after 1945. Technological innovations with consumer applications were developed and diffused nearly twice as fast as those with industrial applications. The implied shrinking of the time scale is quite consistent with the productivity figures already given.

Mansfield's findings were based upon a survey of 12 important technical innovations in 4 major industries. He found only a slight and unclear tendency for innovations to spread more rapidly than in the past, but his estimates of the amount of time involved are not very different from Lynn's. Mansfield calculates the

**Table 1**

AVERAGE RATE OF DEVELOPMENT OF SELECTED TECHNOLOGICAL INNOVATIONS[1]

| *Factors Influencing the Rate of Technological Development* | Mean Lapsed Time (Years) | | |
|---|---|---|---|
| | *Incubation Period*[2] | *Commercial Development*[3] | *Total Development* |
| Time Period | | | |
| Early 20th century (1885–1919) | 30 | 7 | 37 |
| Post-World War I (1920–44) | 16 | 8 | 24 |
| Post-World War II (1945–64) | 9 | 5 | 14 |
| Type of Market Application | | | |
| Consumer | 13 | 7 | 20 |
| Industrial | 28 | 6 | 34 |
| Source of Development Funds | | | |
| Private industry | 24 | 7 | 31 |
| Federal government | 12 | 7 | 19 |

[1]Based on study of 20 major innovations whose commercial developments started in the period 1885—1950.

[2]Begins with basic discovery and establishment of technical feasibility, and ends when commercial development begins.

[3]Begins with recognition of commercial potential and the commitment of development funds to reach a reasonably well-defined commercial objective, and ends when the innovation is introduced as a commercial product or process.

Source: Frank Lynn, *An Investigation of the Rate of Development and Diffusion of Technology in Our Modern Industrial Society.*

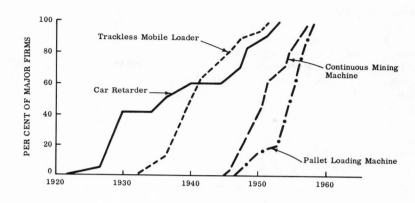

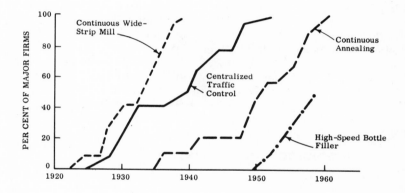

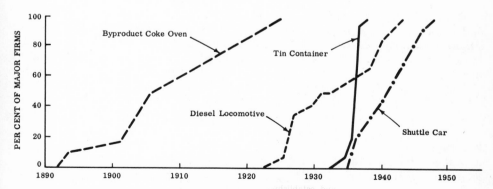

FIGURE 2.    Rate of Diffusion of Selected Technological Innovations (Percent of Firms Adopting Innovations, 1890–1958. Earliest date shown for each innovation is the year in which a firm first introduced the innovation, regardless of the scale on which it did so.) Source: Edwin Mansfield, "Diffusion of Technological Change," *Reviews of Data on Research and Development,* National Science Foundation, October, 1961.

average time lag between invention and innovation in his sample at about 14 years, with another 1 to 15 years before one-half the firms in an industry had imitated the innovation. The diffusion rate of each innovation studied is shown in Figure 2.

No small number of case studies can be conclusive; but there is certainly evidence of a faster rate of technological development. The process, however, is still a fairly long one. Our studies suggest that major technological discoveries may wait as long as 14 years before they reach commercial application even on a small scale, and perhaps another 5 years before their impact on the economy becomes large. It seems safe to conclude that most major technological discoveries which will have a significant economic impact within the next decade are already at least in a readily identifiable stage of commercial development.

---

When we get down into the factory it is important to have some notion as to how technology influences the actual design of jobs. In the following selection three different kinds of technological consequences for job design are examined: (1) specialization of work; (2) subdivision of work; and (3) the development of wholly new work tasks. Each of these methods for utilizing technology for designing jobs has its human consequences. Some of these consequences are listed and discussed.

---

## TECHNOLOGY AND PRODUCTION

### Robert Dubin*

The technology of modern industry and commerce is the most important single determinate of who does what kind of work, when, and in what manner.

There is widespread respect for the genius of Americans in developing modern industrial technology. Indeed, our technology of production is so generally acclaimed that we tend to accept it, almost without analysis for its meaning and consequences, as a permanent feature of the American industrial environment. This reaction to technology is also probably found in industrialized Europe where modern methods of production have a respectably long history.

We will examine the human consequences of modern technology. Our first focus of attention will be on the methods by which modern technology is incorporated into actual production processes, establishing the industrial division of labor. Then we will examine some human consequences for people at work of the requirements imposed by technology and production processes.

*Abridged with modifications from Robert Dubin, *The World of Work* (Englewood Cliffs, N. J.: Prentice-Hall, Inc., 1958), Chapter 10.

## SPECIALIZATION OF WORK

Specialization within a given technology, or within a given industry, is grounded in high demand for the output. If the demand is sufficiently steady for a product or service, it is then possible to employ specialists continuously to perform individual tasks in a cooperative effort. When, for example, the demand for automobiles is great enough, tool-makers can devote themselves exclusively to their operation; die-makers have enough work to spend full time making and repairing dies; and a host of specialized machine operators can produce parts that are put together by other operators called assemblers, into the finished automobile. If, however, only one or several automobiles were produced by each company at a time, there is a high probability that only those would be employed who were all-around workers, capable of doing any of the operations, and usually performing them in the manufacture of a single vehicle. The industrial and commercial division of labor, as it works out in the specialization of tasks, is the product of a continuous demand for products.

From the standpoint of the individuals involved in technological specialization of functions, there are a number of consequences. First, there is a growth of groups of specialists with specific vocational or occupational outlooks. The designation of areas of work, like tool- and die-maker, machinist, or set-up man, provides labels for permanent and lifetime careers. Technological specialization leads to the development of technical careers, professional and semi-professional pursuits.

A second consequence of technological specialization is that the degree of expertness in the specialty may be enhanced. To be able to concentrate fully on being a die-maker may lead to a higher degree of skill than might otherwise be achieved. If a worker had to make and repair dies, make and repair tools, and also be a general machinist, there is every reason to believe that his degree of skill would not be as great in the die-making part of his performance. Intense concentration on a specialty may improve skill. To the individual there may be a great deal of satisfaction in highly expert performance.

A third consequence of technical specialization is paradoxical in character. It seems obvious that each specialist would recognize his dependence on other specialists in their joint contribution to the ultimate product. Yet it tends to be true that each specialist views his particular operations with undue narrowness. This has often been referred to as the "trained incapacity" of the specialist to perceive or understand the operations and theory that underly other specialties tying in with his own. The specialist displays a narrowness and provincialism of outlook. This creates important problems in coordinating the division of labor among specialists incapable of understanding each other.

A fourth consequence of extreme specialization of tasks is to limit the ability of the general citizen of the society to designate social standing or class position in terms of occupational titles. When this development occurs, there is a strong likelihood that recognition of class position by fellow citizens comes increasingly to be the result of industrial rather than occupational attachment. Or class position may be assigned according to very broad occupational categories like "white collar" and "blue collar."

In general, specialized tasks tend to retain a wholeness and integrated character that make them complete in themselves. The tasks that a specialist performs tend to have a beginning and end that are recognizable, and that define the limits of his operations. Furthermore, his activities may be highly complex and entail a great deal of knowledge and training to accomplish them successfully. Finally, there is an exclusiveness that attaches to the performance of specialized work making it improbable in the absence of a given individual that anybody but a comparable specialist will undertake to perform his tasks. This is partly out of recognition of the difficulty of a specialized task, and partly out of recognition of the exclusive jurisdiction that the specialist has over such tasks.

## SUBDIVISION OF WORK

Subdivision of work is based on quite different grounds than specialization. Where specialization leads to more intensive development of skill and ability, subdivision leads to a limitation of skills and ability.

The general drive to subdivide work is based on the character of labor supply, and the relative lack of trained personnel in mass labor markets. Employing large numbers of people and training them rapidly for tasks that might change in short periods of time necessitate having simple tasks for which the training time is rather short, a matter often of hours and usually not more than a day or two. Subdivided tasks are relatively simple, and therefore can be learned rapidly.

The basic objective of work subdivision is to break a job down into its simple component parts and distri-

bute these task parts to individuals who perform them exclusively.

### Method of Work Subdivision

Subdivision of work is based on the general assumption that all tasks can be divided into objective, component parts. These parts of tasks are identified as physical or bodily movements. The totality of movements are then analyzed for possibilities of improvement by changing the kind of movements, or their grouping.

When task activities are grouped together in some organized fashion, it is usually discovered that the new groupings of activities can each be performed by different persons in sequential operations. The other alternative is to have each of the new groupings of activities performed by the same person, but in a new and preferred sequence. When the total task is broken up into groups of activities performed by different persons in sequential operations, we have work subdivision. This is the fundamental feature of all continuous production lines. . . .

Work subdivision satisfies the requirements for minimum schooling time in training a relatively unskilled or ill-trained work force. At the same time, it permits reduction of operating costs, since it is assumed that subdivision increases the total output of the individual. The amount of time lost in changing from one activity to another is minimized if the worker does not need to change. Thus, the subdivision of work minimizes lost motion or lost time.

The subdivision method rests, first of all, on the notion that tasks can be rationally described, and each of their parts carefully delineated. Work subdivision also depends on the assumption that more complex operations can be transformed into mechanical or machine activities, thereby relieving the operator from the need for concern with them. Indeed, examination of subdivided tasks in industry reveals the degree to which it is really a product of technology and machines that largely replace the uniquely human attributes of choice and decision. The engineer who subdivides tasks in the process of rationalizing the production scheme is dependent, by and large, on the cash investment he can make in machinery and tools to replace human skill, choice, and decision.

The engineer looks upon the human being as being capable of controlled movements and intellectual judgments. An important motivation in designing subdivided tasks is to make the most continuous use of these human faculties. A task that might require simultaneous use of both hands and both feet may not represent a rational task only because it is a difficult physical feat to accomplish. For the engineer, the integrity of the individual as a human being is judged largely on the basis of potential conflict in demands on the simultaneous exercise of human faculties. So long as the engineer cannot anticipate such conflict, he is satisfied that the tasks which he has built into the subdivision of work are perfectly compatible with the human being as a physiological mechanism. It is this physiological compatibility that is the touchstone for the engineer in designing operating tasks, using the subdivision method.

## Method of Work Integration

Work integration is a necessary and obvious corollary of work subdivision.

Subdividing tasks is breaking down a larger task complex that has been previously performed as a whole task by single individuals. In the process of subdivision, it becomes necessary to re-establish the unity that had formerly been achieved by having one person do a variety of different things in serial order. This is the problem of work integration.

It would not be economical, for example, to bore a hole in pieces of metal and then store the pieces until such time as they move to another operation where threads are cut in the hole. The need for multiple handling and storage of the items suggests the desirability of having the bored pieces of metal move promptly to a threading operation, and having the two activities occur immediately in serial order.

We see, then, that in subdividing tasks the engineer is faced with the simultaneous need of putting the subdivided work steps back together in some kind of integrated whole. This leads directly to linear production methods in which subdivided activities are placed in order along a production line and are performed one right after another in a continuous and ever-flowing sequence.

Integration of subdivided work requires that the amount of time each task takes should be roughly comparable to the time spent on all other tasks. There are variations in this general principle of timing, but the principle is simple in its basic dimensions. If a manufactured item is to flow continuously along a production line, then each stop should be neither longer nor shorter than any other stop. Once the line is filled with moving items in various stages of manufacture, each individual will be performing a task which takes just as much time as all other tasks on the line. It is obvious, of course, that some variations can be introduced in this scheme. But all variations take into account the multiples of operating time required at any given work station. . . .

Division of labor may result from establishing fundamentally new technologies. A machine may replace another to produce similar items, but the kind of skill required to operate the new machine may shift significantly. For example, when the Linotype replaced hand typesetting, the printers who set type by hand had to learn an entirely new technology in order to qualify as Linotype operators. The Linotype really required new skills that had not previously existed. At the same time, the use of Linotypes did not wholly supplant handsetting, for in many cases the larger "display" type is still set by hand.

It is one of the fundamental characteristics of the new Industrial Revolution through which we are presently going that it gives rise to the invention of many new skills that had not previously existed. We are destined to see the rapid obsolescence of many skills and their replacement by newly created ones.

*Types of New Work Tasks*

There are two types of new work tasks: (A) where the development of a technology creates an entirely new set of tasks not previously performed, and (B) where the development of technology substitutes new operations in fulfilling the same production functions.

Much of modern technology involves the creation of entirely new tasks not previously performed. Generally there are limitations on the extent to which old methods and old forms of production can be improved and perfected. The basic advances in industrial technology come as a consequence of new inventions and processes completely supplanting the old. . . .

The general motivation for introducing entirely new technologies is the desire to apply the rapidly growing body of scientific knowledge. The context of these motivations is a general notion of progress. It is not specifically related to a given operation, product, or factory. The impetus for basic technological innovation is seldom derived directly from operating problems. It has its roots in the attitudes of the society to experiment, to be imaginative in the creation of new technologies. Developments on the frontier of science are used to create new products and to revolutionize the manufacture of old products. This point is important to note. It is clear that the obsolescence of a skill as a consequence of entirely new technologies may be exceedingly important to the individual whose skill is abandoned, and he may react personally to the situation. The reason for his being thrown upon the industrial scrapheap is not the consequence of the malice of management, or the desire to hurt him personally.

The development of new technologies can be seen, for example, in the metals field, where the newer metals like aluminum and magnesium, requiring quite different technologies in their production, have been developed to a high degree and are seriously competing with the older and more common metals like iron and copper and their alloys. At the time of this writing a new solid fuel has just been announced. It will replace petroleum products for jet and missile propulsion. The fuel is made from borax, and although manufacturing details are secret, it is safe to assume that the production technology is unique.

The second general form that creation of work tasks takes is the replacement of old tasks by entirely new ones that fulfill the same functions. In simpler cases like clerical work, for example, the hand posting of ledgers may be supplanted by machine posting, and this in turn may be succeeded by a punch card system which is designed on an entirely different principle. The hand-poster, the machine-poster and the punchcard operator really do quite different activities, and for all intents and purposes are performing quite different tasks. Yet their functions are identical—to keep a set of ledgers, important in the conduct of the business. Often the changes in tasks created by technical developments are very great, and the old operators may not be really competent to undertake the new tasks.

The major human consequences of new tasks are to make obsolete and obsolescent certain skills, creating new jobs at the same time. In individual instances, the worker whose job is no longer necessary may face very severe readjustments in order to find another job. At the same time, those seeking work may find a real opportunity to develop a career in the new tasks that have been developed out of new technologies.

---

There have been many wild claims that automation would revolutionize the labor force by eliminating many existing jobs and skills and requiring wholly new jobs for which the past experience of displaced workers simply would not qualify them. These dire consequences have not been realized in the more than ten years during which automation has been widely adopted in American industry. It is therefore useful to secure a balanced view of what does happen to skill levels under conditions of industrial automation.

Here again we are dealing with a consequence of technology that is an important feature of the environment of business decision-making. The decision to automate a productive process must be accompanied by personnel decisions relating to securing an adequate labor force capable of operating with the new technology. The following discussion sets forth some of the guidelines for examining this problem of decision.

---

## AUTOMATION'S EFFECT ON SKILL LEVELS

### Richard C. Wilcock*

Turning now to the area of hiring practices and training, there seems to be some confusion among the experts as to the effect of automation on skill levels and training needs. James Bright, after several years of field work, has concluded that there is a popular misconception about skill shortages in automated factories and the inability to use the old work force without extensive retraining. The user of automation, he points out, generally can utilize the same work force with relatively few additions of specially trained maintenance men, engineers, and technicians.[1] Diebold agrees that this may be true in a particular factory but that "the spread of automation [in general] will call for training and retraining on a much broader scale."[2]

To the extent that there is a consensus, it is that many unskilled jobs will be eliminated, particularly in materials handling, that many automated jobs will require less over-all skill than had been needed in the jobs replaced,

and that for the economy as a whole there will be a substantially increased demand for many kinds of scientists, engineers, technicians, and skilled maintenance and repairmen. Thus, while many factory workers will not require extensive training or retraining, the over-all skill and educational requirements in the economy can be expected to rise steadily. Drucker speaks of a large manufacturing firm which today hires 300 college graduates a year but thinks it may require 7,000 college graduates a year after it is automated.[3]

These college graduates and others like them will receive specialized training in the firms that hire them. Labor force trends will also contribute to the need for training within industry. Of the almost 16 million who will be added to the labor force between 1958 and 1970, according to BLS projections over 4 million will be women over 35 and 7 million will be young workers under 25. Since there will be a relative shortage of male workers between the ages of 30 and 45 in the next few years, many of these women and young people will presumably be needed in jobs that will require specialized training. One of the results, with great social and economic implications, may very well be a substantial upgrading in the skill levels and utilization of women and of minority groups.

---

*Reprinted by permission of The Pennsylvania State University from Richard C. Wilcock, "Fast-Changing Technology—Its Impact on Labor Problems," *The Pennsylvania Business Survey* (December 1959), pp. 5–7.

[1] James R. Bright, "Does Automation Raise Skill Requirements?" *Harvard Business Review*, Vol. 36, No. 4, July–August 1958, pp. 85–98.

[2] John Diebold, *Automation: Its Impact on Business and Labor* (Washington: National Planning Association, May, 1959), Pamphlet No. 106, p. 37. *Editor's Note:* The difference between Bright and Diebold may reflect a difference of opinion as to just what constitutes "automation."

---

[3] Peter F. Drucker, "America's Next Twenty Years: II. The Promise of Automation," *Harper's Magazine,* April 1955.

## GREATER NEED FOR HIGHER EDUCATIONAL LEVELS

Educational requirements are changing most of all for managers and administrators. The proportion of highly educated individuals in management has been growing rapidly and this trend will undoubtedly continue. The science (and art) of management will be based increasingly upon the efficient and sophisticated application of advanced methods of human and machine organization. Many large companies have already accepted much of the responsibility for educating their management and potential management. The phenomenal growth of schools of business administration (including some company-operated schools) also illustrates the demand for educated managers.

## ATTITUDES TOWARD WORK

The need for a higher level of education extends all the way down the line and many workers are aware of this. In a study of attitudes toward company and occupation of several samples of skilled and semiskilled manual workers (a study I have conducted in cooperation with Gladys L. Palmer of the University of Pennsylvania's Wharton School, and which is now being prepared for publication) there were frequent comments on limited opportunities resulting from lack of education. In a company making electric meters, for example, a number of the tool and die makers felt that chances of advancement to foreman, tool designer, or other higher-level jobs were limited, because these jobs were going to college graduates.

One tool and die maker said he would be better suited for his occupation if he had had more education; he had graduated from high school. Another said a good tool and die maker needs the equivalent of college mathematics.

Many of the skilled workers in the sample and some of the semi-skilled workers regretted not having gone to college and believed they would have gone if they had had their present knowledge and were starting over again. A power company lineman said he would want to go into the same field, and added, "I would follow it all the way through. . . . I would try to get college and up. I have plans now to take this International Correspondence School engineering course [but] it's going to be pretty much of a gamble because I really don't have too much of a background. . . ." A tool and die maker, when asked why he was taking a radio-television correspondence course, said, ". . . sometimes you can eliminate a lot of this mechanical means through electronics. I mean, through a radio tube, or a timing switch, or such as that, you can eliminate a lot . . . do it through micro switches. It would apply directly to tool and die work. . . . More or less for automation."

Studies like this show that workers are concerned about technological change and about job security in the face of change. One of the linemen followed his father into utilities because, "Dad never missed a day during the depression." Another lineman took a pay cut to leave the coal mines and get a utility job. A maintenance machinist commented on one operator running a larger number of machines and felt he was fortunate to be on "the repair end of it."

## CHANGES IN NATURE OF JOBS

Automation is bringing many changes in the nature of work, particularly for those on automated jobs. In a study of automobile workers, one worker said, "On my old job, I controlled the machine. On my present job, the machine controls me." Another said, "I pushed a wrong button and stuff flew all over." Fortunately, he was not in a ballistic missile center. The worker continued, "I was lucky but it cost the company $13,000 to fix the machine."[4] This worker was concerned about the pressure on him and the concentration required by his job. Several writers have commented on the tension and perceptual fatigue of automated jobs. Walker quotes a steel-worker, "I'd rather have to work hard for eight hours, than have to be tense for eight hours, doing nothing with my muscles the way I do now." Another worker in the same plant said, "On this new mill your muscles don't get tired but you keep on thinking even when you go home."[5]

Faunce describes the worker on the automated line as "alienated in the sense that he no longer has control over the machine and the work pace,"[6] but Karsh speaks of "less trivialization" and

---

[4]William A. Faunce, "Automation and the Automobile Worker," *Social Problems,* Vol. 6, No. 1, Summer 1958, pp. 72, 73.
[5]Charles R. Walker, "Case History of a Steel Mill," in Society for Applied Anthropology, *Man and Automation* (The Technology Project, Yale University, 1956).
[6]Faunce, *op. cit.*, p. 72.

"a need for highly trained technical personnel who are able to see the process as a whole, and who can conceive of the factory . . . as the unit of production."[7]

Karsh mentions also, however, as a symbol of things to come, the British union which has requested "lonesome pay" for workers on automated processes.[8]

The emphasis on mental rather than manual effort, however, may assume increasing importance as the American labor force becomes more highly educated. Manual jobs are less satisfying to those whose minds have been highly trained. College and high school graduates, for the most part, want jobs that will make use of their mental faculties. The changes taking place in the occupational structure will make this possible for a growing proportion of the population.[9] Hopefully, then, we can expect the labor market to utilize an ever-increasing amount of trained talent. Education, in turn, will have to be counted on to teach people how to enjoy themselves during the increased amount of leisure that technology will provide and, also, how to consume a steadily increasing per capita output.[10]

---

[7]Bernard Karsh, "Work and Automation," in Jacobson, *op. cit.*, p. 390.
[8]*Ibid.*, p. 388.
[9]See the discussion of this point by Peter F. Drucker, *Landmarks of Tomorrow* (New York: Harper, 1959), pp. 120–123.
[10]For an imaginative discussion of work and leisure see David Riesman and Warner Bloomberg, Jr., "Work and Leisure: Fusion or Polarity?" in Conrad M. Arensberg and others, *Research in Industrial Human Relations* (New York: Harper, 1957), pp. 69–85.

---

There follows a remarkable study that has important implications for us. It reports a situation in which a high level of competitive productivity was maintained in an industrial plant *in spite of* low morale.

This study brings our analysis of the impact of technology on human relations in the plant to a mature conclusion. It suggests that because of conditions of production, and because of the nature of an industry, enforced collaboration of workers is built into the work situation. Thus, collaboration, at least under the circumstances here set forth, is not dependent upon willing acceptance of authority. Morale was low in the plant. Turnover was exceedingly high.

Collaboration of workers is not even the product of an intensive control system that enforces it, as it is in the situation of slave labor or in a totalitarian organization. There was little in the way of formal controls in this plant. The really effective controls were informal in character.

To repeat again, here is a situation in which the technological structure of the work situation, the economic position of the industry, and the condition of the labor market interlaced to produce a built-in, but unwilling, collaboration of workers in the work processes.

The words of the authors, Goode and Fowler, are worth repeating: "There is no simple relationship between harmony, morale, and production; between informal relations and worker harmony; or between formal structural patterns and worker reactions."

---

## TECHNOLOGY, COLLABORATION, AND MORALE

*William J. Goode* and *Irving Fowler**

Within the larger structural pattern of economic action there is a social structure of lesser magnitude within the factory itself. The latter may not effectively dovetail with the former, although there are several possible social structures which can do so. Informal action may, in turn, fail to serve the explicit goals of this smaller structure, and indeed a number of observers have devoted some attention to the ways by which the informal behavior of workers may actually frustrate in part the formal structure of a given plant.[1]

Nevertheless, the possibility exists that the informal behavior of a group of workers may conform to these formal demands, and that this may be the case even where there is disharmony or low morale within the social group. It is suggested that this situation may occur if the following conditions are met: (a) the goals are simple and are clearly defined; (b) the skills for attaining those goals are well known and possessed by the individuals in the group; (c) the functional roles are made clear; and (d) the ex-

*From "Incentive Factors in a Low Morale Plant," *American Sociological Review,* 14:619–624 (Oct. 1949). Copyright by the American Sociological Society. Used by permission.

[1] The best known examples are to be found in the earlier work of the Mayo school.

ternal pressures toward conformity are strong.

The position of the small feeder plant in modern industry is often such as to approximate these conditions. This type of plant has only an external resemblance to the beginnings of industry in the nineteenth century, and in terms of numerical importance is becoming an increasingly larger proportion of the small plants in our economy.[2]

The external similarities of the modern small plant to the ideal-typical small plant in the literature of economics are obvious. Both were presumably begun by an entrepreneur who has amassed capital, often risking his own. He has some technical ability, a considerable amount of capitalistic enterprise, and frequently has absorbed much of the capitalistic ethic described in textbooks. Further, the number of workers is small, and he knows each of them by first name. The workers see each other daily, and they joke among themselves and with the owner. At times, the latter may step in and work with the production group, as supervisor or laborer.

---

[2]The Committee for Economic Development cites the following figures: of 3,317,000 business units in the country in 1939, some 3,265,000 had fewer than fifty employees. This is about 95 per cent of the total number of firms. See *Meeting the Special Problems of Small Business* (New York: Committee for Economic Development, June, 1947), Ch. I, "The Place of Small Business in Our Economy," pp. 9–21. These figures differ little from those found in the numerous reports of the Smaller War Plants Corporation. See particularly, John M. Blair, Harrison F. Houghton, Matther Rose, *et al.*, "Economic Concentration and World War II," *Report of the Smaller War Plant Corporation to the Special Committee to Study Problems of American Small Business*, 79th Congress, 2nd Session, Document No. 206, July 14, 1946 (Washington: Government Printing Office, 1946), pp. 4–25. Many of the

However, the economic context of such a plant is different from that of its nineteenth century predecessor. It has arisen as part of the modern physical decentralization of industry. This decentralization is not alone an attempt to avoid high wages. Physical centralization was an historic answer to the fact that technical knowledge, skills, and markets were themselves concentrated. The cliché that physically centralized production is necessarily more economical derives from a failure to see that varying dispersal patterns are more or less efficient, depending on which of the production variables is less subject to manipulation.

Correlative with this physical decentralization is a financial decentralization of a specific kind. The prime example is the automobile industry, although it is likely to be exhibited in other mass assembly industries, and of course many examples may be found in agriculture. This financial decentralization may be described briefly: A small plant, organized independently or with the aid of a parent company, is a contractor or feeder plant for the parent company. All its production goes to the parent company, and is tailored specifically to the needs of the latter. It has no choice over the products, and naturally has little opportunity to gear its production to a broader market. It is, thus, dependent on a larger organization which fosters competition and consequent price cutting and which does not concern itself with the labor relations of the small plant or its wage policies.[3]

---

data cited above are taken from the monographs produced by the Temporary National Economic Committee.

[3]Similarities to sweatshops and to the earlier "putting out" phase of the Industrial Revolution are clear.

It is seen that this feeder plant structure is different from the textbook picture of the small plant in the past. However, its spread to many regions, and its increase within existing industrial areas, indicate a need for analyzing the resultant social relationships in such a plant, in particular their orientation toward saving, speedup, and "stretchout."

White Company is one of some 80 electroplating plants in the city of Detroit, nickel and chrome plating automobile parts. Its workers, nonunion, number from 15 to 50, depending on fluctuations in the automobile industry. Begun since the war, it is now financially successful against strong competition.

This plant was studied in three observational shifts covering the entire working day, by as many researchers. One of the investigators had previously worked for a period of three months as a semi-skilled laborer in the plant, before the study began. During this period he made extensive diary observations at the end of each work day. Nine months later, the three observers entered the plant under management auspices, explaining to the workers what was being done. The observers made systematic notes of social processes within the plant. In addition, personal interviews were arranged, sociometric diagrams were drawn, and a modified morale test was given at two separate points in the period of observation. The managerial group was interviewed both formally and informally, and production and personal records were studied intensively. Interviews with the entrepreneurs laid the basis for a description of the plant's history.[4] The

investigation continued over a period of four months.

In spite of technical and personnel changes since the original participant observer's diary observation, it was soon clear that essentially the same patterns of social relationships continued as before. This plant did not use semi-automatic electroplating equipment, although such machinery is found in electroplating plants with a larger capital investment. Nevertheless, the production level of such plants is only about 12 per cent to 14 per cent higher than for White Company.[5] Few personnel records were kept. There was a standard policy of firing anyone who showed any interest in unionism. Hiring and training practices were not formalized and the number of workers varied widely from day to day, depending upon immediate contracts. There was practically no job training. No more than a few minutes were spent in pointing out workers' duties and in introductions to co-workers. Workers exhibited considerable animosity towards the own-

---

[4]These data will be published in a separate study. They are summarized in: Irving Fow-

ler, *A Small Feeder Plant: Its Structure and Social Relations* (M.A. Thesis, Wayne University, 1949).

[5]Although there is no standard work unit in the industry, and each small plant attempts to keep secret its production records, the managers of these small plants claim to know with some accuracy the output of each electro-plating shop. The above estimate was made by the technical director of a major plating supply company. An executive of the National Association of Metal Finishers made a similar estimate, concluding that nonunion shops had a higher output than union shops. A semi-automatic plating machine could run approximately 100 racks through a tank in one hour, about 1,600 pieces in one work day. White Company can turn out about 1,400 pieces when there are sufficient orders, without such equipment. White Company's increasing solvency in a highly competitive industry is also of relevance here.

ers as well as the production manager. In addition, clearly evident clique formations divided the workers into small groups, usually with only a grudging acceptance of one another. In spite of some suspicion that the observers were hired by management, workers soon made explicit their grievances and their personal troubles.

An unformalized but clear system of cost cutting was evidenced in two main areas. One of these was constituted by five explicit managerial practices, all of them effective answers to the pressures inherent in the position of the plant in the economic structure. The other main area lay in the character of speedup and stretchout induced by the informal social structure of the workers themselves.

The character of these managerial practices sets the stage for the social relations within the plant, in which internal and external pressures toward work combined to push production upward in spite of low morale and social disharmonies. They would be called "poor" policies by many, but the savings from these measures are obvious.

1. *Repairs* were neglected, and workers were expected to make up for this mechanical ineffectiveness.

2. *Personal equipment* was not quickly replaced, forcing the workers to take special care of safety equipment.

3. Many *safety practices* were neglected, such as measures of protection against acids and high temperatures.

4. *Hiring and training* were fitted with a situation of high turnover, so that new workers were given little training, and fired if they did not quickly learn to turn out a standard amount of production. The new worker received a beginner's wage long after he had learned to produce at a standard rate.

5. *Over-all wages* were so low that the most highly paid workers received only average union wages for the industry. In addition, the workers did not receive the usual union fringe concessions: vacations with pay, paid holidays, rest periods, etc.[6]

As to wage pattern:

The comparison of wage rates is based on the two following sources. First, the rates of average workers in a "typical" union plant in January, 1948: These rates were for 52 forty-hour weeks per year.[7] Second, the wage rates of White Company's most highly paid workers, its "key" personnel: The computed rates were those for June, 1948, and were for an indeterminate number of forty-hour weeks per year. These rates were pieced together from the company's crude pay-

WAGE RATES IN A TYPICAL UNION PLANT AND IN WHITE COMPANY

| Labor Class | Average rate per hour for workers in Union Plant, January, 1948 | Rate for "key" workers, White Company, June, 1948 | |
|---|---|---|---|
| Polisher and Buffer (days) | $1.545 | $1.50 | (lower) |
| Polisher and Buffer (piece) | 1.775 | | |
| Plating Leader .... | 1.595 | 1.45 | (lower) |
| Shift Leader ...... | 1.495 | | |
| Operator ......... | 1.345 | 1.40 | (higher) |
| Racker (male) .. | 1.145 | 1.25 | (higher) |
| Racker (female) | 1.145 | 1.10 | (lower) |
| Inspector ......... | 1.245 | 1.20 | (lower) |
| Packer ............. | 1.195 | | |
| Trucker ........... | 1.215 | 1.25 | (higher) |

[6]As to the cost of the "fringe concessions," see Richard C. Smyth, "Economic Fringe Demands of Unions," *Personnel*, Vol. 24, No. 4 (1948), 243–256.

[7]See Table entitled "Wage Increases" in an article "Electroplating Costs Have Increased Since 1940," *National Plating News* (May, 1948), Vol. 2, No. 5, 1–3.

roll records. The earlier (and lower) wage rates in January, 1948, were never carefully examined. But they indicate that many of the workers gained increases of five to ten cents about that time through individual bargaining. If these earlier rates were compared with the "typical" union plant, the contrast would have been the more striking.

These practices, important in themselves, also helped to structure social relations in the plant. The resultant was a set of informal social pressures which pushed toward high production at all times.[8] These social pressures represented an interaction between the type of worker hired and a social structure channeled in the direction of "stretchout" and speedup.

The types of workers may be grouped into two main social categories, (1) *high turnover personnel,* and (2) *key* workers. (1) The high turnover personnel in turn may be divided into several groups. The first of these can be characterized as *part-time* workers, some of whom were students seeking temporary employment. Other part-time workers were friends or relatives who worked briefly in order to help key personnel or to tide themselves over a period of unemployment elsewhere. A second group of *high turnover* personnel were experienced workers from other companies who used the plant while they were on strike or layoff. In addition, there was a third group, just entering the labor market. It will be immediately noted that all of these high turnover workers would or could adjust to personnel policies which might incite considerable resentment in larger, unionized plants over a longer period. Even the experienced workers in this category, nearly all union members, did not overtly object, since their future employment and plans lay with other plants elsewhere. It may also be noted that this was true whether one considers wages or working conditions.

However, it must be obvious that the selection of such workers could not constitute a working force in itself. Any social group selects, but it must also socialize.[9] By a process of *adult* socialization not sufficiently described in the literature, these people must be made a part of the work organization. This function was mainly performed by the group called *key personnel.* Key personnel in this plant seemed to be extremely heterogeneous. However, closer analysis revealed a number of common characteristics. First of all, most of them were in a poor competitive position. Several of the women needed jobs desperately in order to help dependent males. Other workers had various physical defects which would prevent or hinder their employment at a large plant with less flexible hiring practices. Second, many of them had been with the plant since its beginning. Third, all of them had been tested by repeated managerial demands for extra, over-time, or holiday work and had met this challenge. Fourth, almost all of them could per-

---

[8]See, for comparison, *Aspects sociaux de la nationalisation,* B.I.T. (Geneva, 1931), no. 5, p. 347. Also, E. Sachsenberg, "Psychologie der Arbeit am Laufenden Band," *Maschinenbau* (1925), p. 538. Further, George Friedmann, "Esquisse d'une psychosociologie du travail à la chaine," *Journal de Psychologie Normale et Pathologique* (Jan.–March, 1948), pp. 127–144. Also, the studies by Fox, Scott, Lombard, and Mayo should again be mentioned, as demonstrating how informal social groupings may guarantee the fulfillment of managerial demands.

[9]"Socialize," not "train," since we refer to the acquisition of the group values, not merely the industrial skills. Such acquisition is only partly cognitive, and its basis is habitual emotional reaction.

form nearly every task and could substitute for an absent worker without great difficulty. Fifth, it was they who made the decision as to the acceptability of any workers into the informal group activities.[10]

The position of the plant in the economic structure imposed strains toward high production, and management attempted to push the workers toward this end, substituting labor for capital equipment. The selective characteristics of these workers suggest the type of informal work process which developed. It should be noted that although informal social relations can be pleasant to the worker, if in a small plant they are *not* so, there is then no room for escape without quitting the job. Informal practices of speedup and stretchout were followed even without explicit suggestions by foremen. In each such case, one or more key workers would initiate a work pace which the high turnover group had to follow. Those who did not follow such a pace were exposed to reprimand by word, gesture, or look from their co-workers. If they continued this lack of cooperation, informal pressures on the foremen by the key workers would eventually cause their discharge. If a worker was absent, it was understood without any necessity for explanation that each man would have to contribute more to the work process during that day. Because of the timing aspects of electroplating, frequent bottlenecks occurred. However, these bottlenecks did not necessarily mean delays in production. They rather meant that at such times the key workers would attack the bottleneck with increased energy and,

with the spontaneously induced help of the high turnover personnel, would erase the difficulty. If this in turn produced a piling up of units at a later phase of the plating process, then the key personnel utilized the same practices and again the bottleneck was relieved.

It must be understood that these key personnel accepted the definition of management in such *actional* terms, but not internally. One must speak here of alternatives. The alternative to compliance with high production demands was discharge; and in the case of a number of workers, employment elsewhere would be difficult. The status and power of the key personnel were higher than those of the high turnover personnel, and of course they obtained some recognition from owners and foremen. Expressions of resentment against management were, then, fairly common; and from time to time a given worker would utilize one of several techniques for evading the speedup.[11] He might, for example, spend a considerable amount of time in the washroom, or delay his return to work from lunch, or indulge in horseplay. At times he might refuse to cooperate in relieving a bottleneck. All such practices, however, were temporary and unsystematic. Even when the workers felt that management had no interest in them as people, there was little choice as to alternatives. The constant appearance of foreman and production manager, frequently working side by side with the production

---

[10]There were five such workers, thus making up from one-third to one-tenth of the total working group.

[11]This may be called "antagonistic cooperation." Such cooperation may occur: (a) When individuals cooperate for a group goal, to be achieved only by working together, as for example, army draftees; or (b) When *each* individual knows his personal goal can be attained only in this way, the classical example being that of shipwrecked passengers.

personnel, offered little chance for escape.

Thus, a particular type of small plant, increasing in numbers, is found in an economic structure demanding high production. The reaction of the personnel in this particular plant is not the only possible one. However, the reaction fitted well the pressures of that position.

Further, it is clear that major structural components apparently necessary to effective action in the face of disharmony or low morale are to be observed here: (a) clearly defined, simple goals; (b) skills are well known and are possessed by the group; (c) functional roles are made clear; and (d) pressures toward conformity are strong from outside the group itself.[12]

---

[12]Military leaders also utilize these components in the common technique of making the *group* responsible for the cooperation of *individuals.*

As a consequence, a selection process put into key positions those individuals who fitted the structural demands. These key workers helped to indoctrinate or weed out the new workers. And the informal relationships which developed were such as to maintain pressures toward high production in the face of considerable animosity toward the owners and among the workers themselves.

It is thus seen that there is no simple relationship between harmony, morale, and production; between informal relationships and worker harmony; or between formal structural patterns and worker reactions. The shaping of research by certain value orientations has left a number of areas still undefined and in need of considerable empirical investigation. The feeder plant is one definable type of small plant, increasing in number, which lends itself to the study of these relationships.

# 21

# Organization Fictions

Barnard's *Education for Executives*, in Chapter 1, ends with the suggestion that everyone in an organization, but particularly the executive, has to have some methods for dealing with the unknown. That is one of the functions of this chapter. We want to examine some of the ways in which approaches to the unknown in the environment of organizations become institutionalized.

This is one of the several areas of administration that have been neglected by students of the subject. In this chapter, therefore, we are as much concerned with stimulating an interest in a neglected area as with setting forth a set of substantive conclusions and principles.

In the following selection, the late, great philosopher, Morris R. Cohen, first establishes the role of fictions as part of hypotheses in scientific research. The real is predicted in the hypothesis. Until the hypothesis is verified, it may contain elements of fiction. It should not be difficult to extend this notion one step further, to the situation of decision-making and planning in organization activities. Fictions may play a very important positive role in business in a fashion analogous to their positive role in science.

Cohen also shows the relationships between fictions and ceremony. He develops, in addition, the way in which the symbolic leader is viewed from a fictional standpoint. This recalls the discussion of organization office in Chapter 6.

This chapter rounds out our consideration of the human relations of administration. We have progressed

**INTRODUCTION**

to the point where we can deal realistically with certain kinds of nonlogical behavior. We can relate it to an organization structure. We can see how the use of fictions of certain types is a form of nonlogical behavior that nevertheless functions positively to sustain an organized group. In short, with our background of insight into organizations, we can view nonlogical behavior as an integral part of organization behavior, and not the perverse product of ignorant individuals.

It is a matter of some importance that we "locate" a source for nonlogical behavior in the environment of an organization. Otherwise we may come to assume that it is only in the heads of individuals that we can locate such phenomena. The fictions of an organization are matters of collective agreement among its members. The fictions are therefore located in the environment of the organization, in the interaction and agreement among its participants. Furthermore, and this is a point made in the first selection, the fictions, which are not real, serve to facilitate and guide behavior, which is very real. Thus, we establish in one area an important manner in which logical and non-logical are positively linked.

---

### FICTIONS

#### Morris R. Cohen*

The processes of abstraction and classification have been called neglective fictions because the class "man" does not exist and only individuals do. But it cannot be denied that such statements as "John is a man" can have significance only if the predicate denotes something really common to a number of individuals. Even an artificial classification of governments such as Aristotle's cannot be called fictional merely because particular governments do not conform to it. For existing governments may be mixed forms or combinations of the elements of monarchy, aristocracy, and democracy and their perversions, and the classifi-

*From "Fictions," *Encyclopaedia of the Social Sciences* (New York, 1931), Vol. III, 226–228. Copyright by The Macmillan Company. Used by permission.

cation helps us to recognize the significant elements of such mixed forms. Although certain elements always occur in conjunction with others and never in isolation, this is no argument against their reality. The fact that no one can be a brother or a creditor without being other things is no argument against the reality of the fraternal or the credit relation. Science must abstract some elements and neglect others because not all things that exist together are relevant to each other. Hence there is no fiction in talking about purely economic motives if we remember, as Adam Smith surely did, that in actual life these are associated with other motives.

If the reality of abstractions is recognized, then there is nothing fictional (in the sense of false) about perfectly straight or circular lines, perfectly free bodies, frictionless engines, and other entities which seem imaginary and indeed are known to be impossible of separate existence. For the relation of distance between things exists in nature where the things are and is independent of the thickness of cord or chain by which it is measured; while there exist no free bodies (i.e., bodies not acted upon by any forces), all existing bodies do move in such a way that we can detect the part played by inertia and can tell what would happen if all other forces ceased to act. Similarly, while no actual engine is frictionless, we can compute from certain data the part that friction plays in the total work of any engine. It is not true that "artificial" lines of latitude or longitude are fictional merely because such lines are not actually marked on the earth. They do represent certain actual geometric relations. No map is ever a perfect picture of the country it represents. It must neglect all except a very few traits. But it may be perfectly accurate or truthful within the required limits. Another way of looking at neglective fictions such as perfectly rigid bodies, perfect distribution and the like is to view them as ideal limits. No one thing in nature corresponds to them, but classes of things do differ in degrees of rigidity or homogeneity and there is no falsity in using the limit as a real characteristic of a series.

If there is no inherent falsification in abstraction, there is none in proper scientific "construction" out of such elements. Examples of such constructions are the typical vertebrate animal, the typical river valley, the manor or factory as an economic unit and the ideal of a government by law. Much abuse has been heaped on the "social contract" as a fiction. If asserted as a

historical fact it is clearly a myth. But thinkers like Hobbes have not advanced it as a historical fact. To them it is rather a logical device for analyzing actual complex social processes. If we apply the term "state of nature" to human conduct apart from the influence of laws, we can regard our actual social relations as those of a state of nature modified in certain ways analogous to the way our conduct is modified by contract. The analogy is helpful only to the limited extent to which it is true.

In its search for the truth science must formulate some anticipation of what it expects to find. Such anticipation is clearly not fictional even if it turns out to be false, provided it has been held as a hypothesis to be tested. In trying to visualize the unknown the imagination must clothe it with attributes analogous to the known. Thus electricity was first conceived as a fluid, then as lines or tubes of force, and is now viewed as a current of mutually repellent "electrons." Thus also the mind was viewed by British associationist psychologists as an associated group of "mental states" and by William James as a "stream of consciousness." Each of these, like the various mechanical models of the ether or of various unknown physical processes, suggests verifiable analogies and thus directs research. If these directions prove false, the analogy has acted like a false hypothesis. But the term fiction may properly be applied to certain imaginary and unverifiable entities that vivify our conceptions but are strictly irrelevant to the truth or falsity of our conclusions. Thus Helmholz' and Poincaré's one or two dimensional beings, Maxwell's "sorting demon" and similar entities in social science are really metaphors to express abtract relations. Where one of these figures is used any one of an infinity of others could be substituted, just as according to Poincaré's proof wherever a mechanical model is used an infinity of others is possible. If these metaphors are taken literally we have the myths of which popular science is full.

It must be recognized, however, that metaphors are not always invented to vivify discourse. They are often the way in which creative minds perceive things, so that the explicit recognition that metaphors are implicit analogies comes later as a result of reflection or analysis. Although undiscriminating, such primitive perception is likely to be most vivid and its apt expression may become current coin, so that it becomes difficult if not impossible to discriminate between metaphor and literal truth. As the essence of science is the search for truth, it seeks to eliminate irrelevant fictions through the use of technical terms or symbols that denote the abstract relations studied and nothing else. But as no human terms can adequately express (although they can point to or adumbrate) the unknown, science is engaged in an endless process of self-correction and revision of its language. Such a process is irksome to popular discourse and to the social sciences that employ such discourse. Language itself is a prolific source of mythology.

The foregoing analysis of metaphors will clarify the role of fictions in the primitive mind. It is a pseudo-rationalism to explain primitive animism as the result of an explicit analogy, of attributing souls to inanimate objects because they sometimes move like animated ones. Human perception is vague in its beginnings and such discrimination as that between one's own "papa" and other "papas" comes later. Thus when a child kicks a chair against which he stumbles he does not personify the chair on the basis of an analogy. His reaction is at first directly organic, and only later does he learn to discriminate between the chair and those who are to be punished. Now if primitive perception is intellectually indiscriminating, it is also organically and emotionally vivid. When such metaphoric expressions get established by usage they lose their vividness, but like other habitual practices they are difficult to change. Also words as all symbols absorb the emotional value of the things they symbolize, just as the flag or the scroll of the law becomes sacred apart from that which it denotes.

This points the way to an understanding of the fictional element in ceremonial expressions. Just as the ritual of social life demands certain forms of dress or certain steps or gestures regardless of convenience, so it demands certain accredited expressions regardless of their literal truth. Thus the rules of courtesy among the Chinese and others require the host to say always that his house is mean and that his guest is distinguished and confers an honor. Even those who do not take such expressions literally may be offended at any departure from the social mode. The role of ceremonial expressions in the outer forms of make believe is as important in social life generally as in the games of children and primitive man. The social life of a country like England may be viewed as a game that requires among other things that people should speak of His Majesty's army, navy, and treasury (although the debt is "national") or that the actual leaders of the government should speak of "advising" the king when the latter has in fact no choice but to obey. Similarly, it is the fashion to speak of the United States as a democracy where the law is the will of the people made by its representatives, even though few know what laws are being made or have much control over those who make them.

These considerations will illumine the nature of fictions as they appear in the field of their greatest development: the law. Here fictions appear clearly as assertions that contain an element admittedly false but convenient and even indispensable to bring about certain desired results. Although fictions border on myths which are genuinely believed and on pious frauds which are intended to deceive in aid of good causes, they can be distinguished from them. Thus when a court asserts that for the purposes of a given suit the high seas are situated in a given parish in London, no one believes the assertion to be literally true and no one is deceived. But the fiction makes it possible for the court to acquire jurisdiction and helps the parties to settle their case in a convenient court. The Roman jurists explained such fictions by means of the Greek philosophic distinction between convention and nature. In the nineteenth century Jhering called attention to the element of implicit analogy in them. An adopted child is like a natural child in his rights and the rights of a Roman citizen in captivity may be treated as if he were away on state business. So in our own law when a deed or mortgage is recorded a really innocent purchaser is said to have had notice and is not allowed to prove the contrary. For this really means that the act of recording makes the rights of all purchasers (innocent or not) alike, so that the fact of actual ignorance is irrelevant.

Why, however, does not the law use accurate expressions instead of asserting as a fact that which need not be so? Why assert that a corporation *is* a person, instead of saying that a certain group of rights and duties are analogous to some extent to those of a natural person? Why say that the United States embassy in China and an American boat at sea are on American soil, when we mean to assert that certain legal relations are to be determined by the law of the United States? The answer is partly that the practical convenience of brevity outweighs the theoretic gain of greater accuracy. But more important is the fact that all times, and not merely (as Maine would have it) in "primitive" society where legislatures are not functioning, the law must grow by assimilating new situations to the old, and in moments of innovation we cling all the more to old linguistic forms. The latter minister to the general feeling of security especially where the prevailing myth or make believe is that the judge merely declares the law and cannot change or extend it. That we can obey the law even when making it grow is more than the legal profession itself can often grasp.

From the point of view of social policy fictions are, like eloquence, important in giving emotional drive to propositions that we wish to see accepted. They can be used, as indicated above, to soften the shock of innovation or to keep up a pleasant veneration for truths which have been abandoned, as when new allegoric or psychologic meaning is given to old theologic dogmas that we no longer believe. But if fictions sometimes facilitate change they often hinder it by cultivating undue regard for the past. If the social interest in truth were to prevail, we should in our educational and social policies encourage greater regard for literal accuracy even when it hurts national pride and social sensibilities. But no one has seriously suggested penalizing rhetoric and poetic eloquence in the discussion of social issues. The interest in truth is in fact not as great as in the preservation of cherished beliefs, even though the latter involves feelings which while temporarily pleasant prove ultimately to be illusions.

---

In the following selection a systematic treatment of organization fictions is attempted. You will observe that this presentation builds upon Professor Cohen's analysis. It is first of all suggested that there are different types of fictions. The functions that fictions perform in organizations are then examined. It seems reasonably clear that all organizations have their fictions in at least some areas. Because fictions are contrasted with truth, we are at first inclined to view the existence of fictions as imperfections of organizations. The following selection should make clear that this is a limited view of organization fictions. Such fictions do have positive values.

---

## ORGANIZATION FICTIONS

*Robert Dubin*

The study of formal organizations has taken the direction of emphasizing their rational mode of administration. Great stress has been placed upon the rational, impersonal, and technically efficient characteristics of the bureaucratic form of administration.

In this paper we shall deal with organization fictions. This is a neglected area of study of formal organizations from a sociological point of view. Yet the analysis of the types and functions of organization fictions provides us with one bridge between the logical and the nonlogical, the rational and the sentimental, the certain and the uncertain, the formal and the informal, which are categories of behavior universally found in formal organizations.

It should be evident that the emphasis on the rationality of the bureaucratic form of administration implies that modern bureaucracy leaves little room for the operation of sentimental or nonlogical forms of behavior. It is implied that there is always a strain within the organization to eliminate the uncertain and circumscribe the informal.

From this kind of analysis of formal organizations we get the strong impression that conscious and deliberate behavior is the basic mode of action on the part of members of organizations. Conscious and deliberate action requires a known and relatively stable framework within which decisions are made and behavior is carried out. This framework is composed of the policies, rules, regulations, procedures, and sanctions that make up and enforce the sum of the organizationally approved behavior. The status system of the organization provides another framework for orienting action within the organization. Finally, the systems of informal groups and informal interaction provide still another set of criteria affecting action of organization members.

In relation to each of these three general frameworks, standards of behavior are developed. However—and this is the crucial point—there are "missing links" in each of these frameworks. It is precisely in relation to this fact that organization fictions play a central role. Each system of organization behavior (formal, status, and informal) is never complete and wholly prescribed. It is never fully rounded out and completely systematized.

Furthermore, these systems are dynamic. They undergo change and modification by virtue of changes in the organization of which they are an integral part. In their very nature, these systems of behavior standards can never be wholly prescribed. Yet each individual member of the organization has to be able to operate *as if* his behavior were truly oriented to a body of fixed standards. Where voids exist in the standards, as they inevitably must in a dynamic formal organization, there is a strain toward creating guides for behavior that will fill the voids. These creations are the *organization fictions.*

A fiction is defined as "the act of feigning or imagining that which does not exist or is not true." Organization fictions are those fictions that are necessary in order that action within the formal organization may proceed. They are relevant specifically to the formal organization of which they are a part. They may or may not be transferable to similar or identical organizations. The context of their meaning is the specific business, government

bureau, fraternal organization, school, club, political party unit, or other kind of organization unit. In the same industry, for example, each separate business firm has its own special organization fictions.

It is worth while to draw one further distinction before analyzing the types and functions of organization fictions. Organization fictions are group-oriented. They are not the private fictions of a single individual. Thus, the paranoid executive may operate in a private world filled with his special brand of fictions. His executive behavior will undoubtedly be related to these private fictions. But these fictions become organization fictions only when his fellow executives share them and operate in the organization as if the fictions were true.

### TYPES OF ORGANIZATION FICTIONS

We can delineate two basic types of organization fictions. These types are distinguished from each other by the fact that the first deals with the unknown while the second deals with the known. We can further subdivide the first general type into three subtypes, and the second general type into two subtypes.

1. *Fictions About the Unknown.* There is a general category of organization fictions that deals with the unknown or the unknowable.[1] These fictions provide an immediate substitute for facts that are necessary but unobtainable. The facts for which the fictions can substitute are necessary as a basis for immediate action in the organization or for planning future

---

[1] See in this connection the first chapter of this book, at the end of which emphasis is placed upon learning how to handle the unknown and unknowable.

action. Hence, it is imperative that some kind of knowledge be available as a basis for rational action.

A. *Fictions about the unknown past.* Often present or future action is dependent upon knowledge of what happened in the past. When past events are not directly recorded, the facts about them tend to be lost. Yet these facts might be highly pertinent if they were only known. In place of the missing facts, assumptions are made that only have a *probability* of being true. These assumptions are the fictions about the unknown past. In general, they can never be verified because of inability to recapture the past.

There are many organizational examples of fictions about the unknown past. To cite but one, it is a common belief, shared by some business executives, that workers used to be more willing to work hard than they are now. This fiction (and it is that because we have no records or other data to prove the point) can be the basis for management evaluation of union demands in collective bargaining. Based upon such a fiction, most union demands would be viewed as striving to get more pay for less work. This fiction about the unknown past provides the basis for determining present action and for interpreting the present environment.

B. *Fictions about the unknown present.* Most organizational situations demanding action or decision are limited by practical considerations. Time may be important; money may be equally important, so that a delay in decision may be costly. Under such circumstances, all the facts pertinent to the decision or action cannot be made available within the limitations of the situation. These facts may be potentially discoverable but must be passed by because of limited time or resources. To take the place of the unknown present, convenient fictions are used.

An example of a fiction about the unknown present is the situation in which a union demands a flat wage increase with the argument that all industry is enjoying high profits. Here, the union conclusion may be based upon lack of knowledge about the company's particular financial position. Using syllogistic reasoning—"Industry is profitable, this company is part of industry, therefore, it is profitable"—the union develops the fiction of this firm's ability to pay as a basis for collective bargaining demands.

C. *Fictions about the unknown future.* The future, of course, is unknowable. More or less accurate predictions can be made about it based upon past experience. In the very nature of anticipating the future, important kinds of information are not accessible. Yet something has to take the place of the missing information. The fictions about the unknown future do this.

An example of such a fiction is the sometimes used rationalization of paternalism in personnel relations. The executive adopts a paternalistic program in anticipation of reactions of personal loyalty and gratitude on the part of his personnel. The anticipated reaction is the fiction that confuses individual gratitude with group response to the subtle domination of paternalism. When the good deeds of the executive are met with resentment by the recipients, the executive feels hurt and disturbed. The fictional response he anticipated has failed to materialize.

2. *Fictions About the Known.* There is another general category of organization fictions that has to do with the known. These fictions provide a means

for making acceptable or useful to the organization situations that might otherwise be harmful.

A. *Fictions that disguise the truth.* There are organization situations whose true character is known. The truth, however, is disturbing, so by a kind of silent agreement among members of the organization, this truth is clothed with a fiction. For example, an executive may be incapable of filling his job adequately. He also happens to be son of the owner of the company. There is likely to grow up around him a relationship with the other members of the firm in which people behave toward him to his face as though he were competent in his office. The organization is less likely to be harmed if all those who have official relations with the executive behave toward him as though he were capable, regardless of their private opinion of him. Thus, the truth is disguised in a convenient organization fiction.

B. *Fictions that emphasize the false.* There is only a rather subtle difference between this kind of fiction and the previous type. Fictions that emphasize the false are characterized by a more deep-seated reluctance to face up to the truth and are more aggressively oriented toward hiding the truth. An example is the instance of a food-processing company that makes a great show of cleanliness and hygienic conditions for the benefit of the food inspector's periodic visits, and, in its advertising, for the benefit of its consuming public. It would probably lead to censure to call the situation of only periodic cleanliness to the attention of the company officials, who may themselves be unaware of the extent of the fiction of cleanliness. In fact, they would prefer to believe that the plant is clean and up to standard and might even be genuinely shocked to find it otherwise. It relieves them of the burden of having to face up to the problem if they can operate with the fiction of cleanliness, especially if it is validated by the inspector's report.

These types of organization fictions indicate the range of ways in which the unknown and the truth may be fictionalized to serve the purposes of the organization. We may now turn to a consideration of the function of fictions in organizations. If we admit their existence, we must be interested in the roles they play in organizations.

## FUNCTION OF FICTIONS

There are six general functions performed by organization fictions. We will examine them individually.

1. *Fictions facilitate organization action.* In the previous selection, Cohen indicated how certain legal fictions permit the legal process to operate where it otherwise would have no jurisdiction. There are many situations in which the truth *prevents* action necessary to the daily functioning of an organization. But fictions that modify the truth may also facilitate action within the group. The example of the incompetent executive, cited above, illustrates the point. If members of his staff behaved toward him in the light of his true capabilities, the organization would soon founder in indecision or there would be a major shift in the authority structure of the organization to shunt the incompetent to one side.

2. *Fictions facilitate organization change.* It is often possible to make a change in an organization by fictionalizing the basis for the change. For example, a personnel department may be set up in a firm with the ostensible

purpose of helping, in staff fashion, the line administrators. In fact, the real purpose for establishing the new department may be to take the personnel functions away from the line executives. The first, or fictional, purpose is set forth to secure acceptance of the change, and the second objective is hoped for when the change is accomplished. The point to emphasize is that organizations are dynamic and need the device of organization fictions to make growth and change possible with a minimum of resistance.

3. *Fictions can paralyze organization action.* The reverse of the point cited above is the situation where fictions prevent action within the organization. Thus, fictions operate as one form of social control within the organization. For example, the knowledge that authority to punish violators of organization rules exists in the organization may operate effectively to prevent such violations. The fiction of absolute authority to punish may be an effective social control. In a real situation of rule-violation, the fiction comes to be tested against the actual treatment of the violator. If there is wide divergence between what is expected and what actually happens, the authority may be modified thereby. In general, the anticipation of the future consequences of action may prevent the proposed course of action, an instance of fictions dealing with the future.

4. *Fictions organize the future.* The pressure in organizations to anticipate and plan for the future is great. In business firms this is built into the very technology of the operations in the form of inventory, production, and marketing anticipations. Hence, when there are indeterminate elements in the future, as there must necessarily be, fictions take the place of the un-

certainties as a basis for making decisions.

5. *Fictions support organization offices.* Fictions play an important role in supporting respect for the occupant of an organization office. Fictions surround the technical, status, decision-making, and authority aspects of every organization office, where they play the role of glossing over any discrepancies between the requirements of an office and the personal peculiarities of the office-holder. Thus, a college diploma in engineering may be taken as the measure of a man's technical competence to be a mechanical engineer in a company, when in fact, the individual is not adequately trained to fill his assigned job. The diploma is indeed a fictional validation of competence under such circumstances.

The importance of sustaining organization office can hardly be overemphasized. It gives the officeholder time to learn his official position and to adjust to it. It permits the organizational members who contact the officeholder to behave toward him in officially meaningful ways, even though there are obvious discrepancies between his actual and officially prescribed behavior. In this respect, the fictions of organization are part of the cement that holds the organization together.

6. *Fictions support the entire organization structure.* Fictions can serve to legitimize the authority structure of the organization in the eyes of its members. Charismatic authority is an excellent case in point. (See Chapter 12 for a discussion of this type of authority.) Fictions can also provide the ideological goals and purposes necessary to an organization. For example, the claim to making the best product in a field will not be judged against the accuracy of the assertion provided

the members of the firm believe it is true and act under the inspiration of the belief. The fiction of superiority, or largest size, or exclusiveness, or what not, is important in motivating members toward greater effort on behalf of the organization.

## SUMMARY

We have seen that organization fictions play important roles in permitting organizations to function effectively. Indeed, we can conclude that there is no organization so rationally organized and staffed, and so completely in possession of the facts necessary to operate, that it can function without fictions. Fictions are real and necessary.

This suggests at once that we can be misled if we believe that bureaucratic administration is wholly rational. There are areas in which the rational combines with the fictional to make the organization work. It would also be a mistake to assume that there is always pressure in a bureaucratic administration to narrow the area of organization fictions and broaden the area of factual bases for operations. If our analysis of the function of fictions in organizations is accurate, there are facts and truths that are unpleasant or organizationally disturbing and have to be clothed in fictions to keep the organization on an even keel.

---

One of the preferred values of American society is that of democratic behavior among people in their personal relations. Thus, the politician is expected to shake the hands of utter strangers and kiss their babies in his quest for popular votes. The business executive is likewise expected to conform in some way with the expectation that his relations with subordinates will be democratic.

The extent to which observation of this expectation is negated by actual behavior is some measure of the degree to which the idea of democratic relations between boss and his subordinates is an organization fiction. The following selection is a complete article from *Modern Office Proce-*

*dures,* a technical business journal. It reports the prevalance of a caste system in a surveyed group of business firms. Focused on the problem of how the man who is promoted must change his relations to his former colleagues and peers, the article ends with a set of seven steps for breaking ties with former office friends.

As if anticipating that the facts of this article might be interpreted by readers as an attack on the fiction of business democracy, the editorial comment in the table of contents under the title listing for the article was as follows: "This revealing article on social discrimination in the office will startle you, and it may make you mad."

## THE OFFICE CASTE SYSTEM

*Harrison R. Johnson**

You won't find "caste" under C in any filing cabinet, but it's everywhere in the office. Rigid unwritten rules of protocol freeze office workers into castes, then reach beyond the office to affect their families. The caste system, deeply entrenched, mocks one of business's oldest legends: that a company is one big happy family. This threadbare tradition is chanted with a steady repetition. Companies say it, print it, lip-serve it, but don't believe it. They don't because they can't afford to. When companies drop the barriers of caste, it costs them money.

*Modern Office Procedures* conducted a month-long survey to find out company attitudes on caste. We wanted to know what rules they follow in prohibiting or discouraging friendships between management and employees. The survey reveals these facts:

Nearly all companies willingly have an office caste system. They make no moral judgments about its ethics. Instead, they retreat behind a shield of balance sheets and defend caste almost in terms of company survival. One executive about summed up the case for caste by saying:

"You've got to have discipline in a company. Someone has to give orders; someone has to take them. If the relation between supervisor and subordinate is fettered by friendship, the company loses." No company we con-

tacted has a written rule "Thou shalt not fraternize." But the rule is there all the same. And it is hardest on the newly promoted employee.

When we first talked to companies about the office caste system, most spokesmen fought a delaying action. They sent up evasive smoke screens, pungent with comments like: "Everyone here calls the president by his first name," or "Our executives make a special effort to know all about a clerk's family," or "We insist that department heads play softball with their employees at company picnics." Finally they came out of orbit and got down to caste. Would a department head invite a clerk and his wife over for an evening of bridge? "That's ridiculous," snapped one executive, quickly glancing at his secretary to make sure she couldn't overhear. "If we started doing that we'd have anarchy in the office." At last, caste is out in the open.

Few companies speak as bluntly about the caste system as this one does. Yet practically every company we surveyed admitted it had a caste system. Only one company sincerely dissented, and even they admitted "a difference of interests between employees on different levels would naturally reduce friendly contacts after office hours." The rest have caste and are glad of it. Caste, they say, is a good thing.

"It's essential," says one company. "Every supervisor at one time or another has to get tough with his subordinates. He has to berate for poor work, discuss salaries, even fire peo-

*From "The Office Caste System," *Modern Office Procedures,* 5:11–13 (June 1960). Used by permission.

ple. He can't do this if he's too friendly with the people under him. He compromises his ability to manage. He's not worth much to us."

A department head drew on his own experience to support this position and the economic basis for caste. "I had an accounting manager who had two close friends working for him. They were inefficient. Other workers resented them. Their sloppy work lost three customers and $40,000 of business. I told the manager to crack down. He wouldn't or couldn't, I don't know which. So I fired the two workers. And I fired the manager. He refused to learn where his job began and friendship ended."

Another highly placed executive is one of the rare ones who reflected about the caste system. "I've often wondered," he says, "if it wouldn't be a good idea to get together with the people who work for me. It's tempting to let them know what a prince of a guy they work for. But I've decided against it. I'll never get so close to a subordinate that I can't supervise him." Says another mid-management man, "I'm all for the caste system. It's the only way to run a business. If you don't keep your people at arm's length, you're in trouble."

## TOGETHERNESS BACKFIRES

Some of the companies we talked to have tried to break down the caste system with some strenuous sessions of enforced loving. One company had been adamant about it. "We came out bloody," an executive recalls. "We decided each department should have monthly parties at employees' homes. I guess we were trying to promote togetherness, but the whole idea was

filled with bad feelings. Employees felt they had to put in an appearance. They felt put upon when their turn came to be hosts. They vied for supervisors' attention. Management wives seemed to think they were holding court. We ran into petty personality fights, accusations of favoritism, severe back-biting that carried over into the office. The whole plan simply backfired on us." What did the company do? "We completely reversed our field, told management to cut off all outside friendships with subordinates. I imagine we're now the most caste-ridden company you'll talk to."

The office caste system is cruelest to the supervisor newly promoted from the ranks. Almost without exception, the companies we contacted spoke about this special dilemma. One young executive summed up the predicament: "I got together regularly with the boys in my department for cards and golf. We traded invitations at home, griped about the company, commented on the mental senility of the president. Then overnight I'm the guy who gives them orders. I have to watch everything I say. What do I do about my friends?"

His question gets a brief, sharp answer from the personnel director of a large company: "Cut 'em off. If a man cherishes his old friendships, he'd better not take the promotion." Most companies agree it's best to amputate. They say the caste system makes it easier for a new supervisor to escape the burdens of old friendships. "He might as well make the break," reports an executive, "because he's going to be discarded by the old gang anyhow. They'll feel uncomfortable and embarrassed with him."

There's comfort in caste for the new supervisor. Says one, "It's rough when you first sit down with a guy you've been working side by side with and point out his weaknesses and squeeze more work out of him. Your relation changes in that instant, and it's never the same again. The caste system is good. It puts people promptly on different levels, makes discipline easier."

But what's easier for the supervisor is harder for his wife. She too is touched by caste, often without understanding why. "My wife played bridge regularly with the wives of seven other men on my level," reports a supervisor. "Then I was promoted. I told her she'd have to drop out of the group. She flared up, said she wouldn't sacrifice her friends just because I'd been moved up." Unfortunately, companies don't agree with her. One executive speaks for a lot of companies when he says, "The wife has no choice. She can be downright dangerous if she insists on keeping close friendships with the wives of her husband's subordinates. Her friendships will rub off on him, color his judgment about the people under him, jeopardize his job."

Children don't escape caste either. "When parents drift away from former friends," a personnel man states, "kids go too. Parents don't say to them 'you're too good to play with Johnny now,' but the father's new title and income make Johnny undesirable." Isn't this vicious? "Maybe," he shrugged.

### SEVEN STEPS TO FOLLOW

Old hands at management are fairly immune to the callous dictates of caste. Says one top executive, "I accepted long ago the hard fact that the higher I rose in business, the fewer friends I'd have in the company." The

new supervisors don't have thick skins and few companies help them over the first hurdles that the caste system imposes. "When I was promoted," recalls a supervisor, "the company said I should break away from the people under me. I'd worked with them a long time and it didn't seem right to cut them off abruptly. But no one told me how to do it."

This is common, our survey shows. Here's one set of steps to follow—based on the composite experience of many management men—to bow out gently:

1. Make the break gradually. If a supervisor snaps the cord too fast, he'll build resentment.
2. Find logical excuses for not joining the group at coffee breaks or lunch.
3. Miss the department bowling or card sessions, occasionally at first, then more frequently.
4. Accept invitations at first to subordinates' homes, but reciprocate only with group invitations. Then don't accept at all.
5. Give employees the chance to pull away from the supervisor. A gradual withdrawal from department activities by the supervisor lets them do it painlessly.
6. Give wives more time to pull away from friendships with her husband's subordinates. "They don't understand the protocol of office organization" a department head says, "because they aren't exposed to it daily." Let them make the transition more slowly.
7. Reduce all contact eventually to office hours. But at all times be friendly and helpful to everyone in the department impartially.

# 22

# Organization and Society

In this final chapter we turn specifically to consider the environment external to the organization, and the orientations of executives to it. We can broadly characterize that external environment as the larger society. Usually this is dealt with under some such title as "industry and society."[1]

We have selected some major problems among the many with which we could deal. These problems are of particular importance to the executive for they (1) tell him why he has to take into account the larger society, (2) what it is he has to take into account, and (3) the attitudes and values that contemporary executives have taken toward society and their relations to it.

We shall proceed by asking: What is there in the environment of an organization that generates a sense of social responsibility among its leaders? The first three selections all suggest important answers, ranging from the impact of public opinion to the stresses created by conflicting external demands upon the organization.

*INTRODUCTION*

We then follow with a detailed analysis of the ways in which businessmen have formulated their sense of social responsibility. This is a sober and fair presentation of what has happened to the climate of leadership thinking in the business world.

Finally, a neglected aspect of the relation between

---

[1]See, for example, an excellent recent work in this area by W. H. Form and D. C. Miller, *Industry, Labor, and Community* (New York: Harper & Brothers, 1960).

an institution and the larger society is examined. It is suggested in the last selection that the question of influence is a two-way street. While it is true that the larger society has ways of generating a broadly responsible outlook among the leaders of its private organizations, it also seems to be true that the thinking of these leaders may feed back on the society to change some of its values. Thus, organizational leaders have a special sense in which they must cast up their accounts to the larger society: they are both influenced by, and influence it.

We start this chapter with a broad question. Why are the organizations of society thrust into the limelight so that their leaders are compelled to assume some degree of social responsibility to large segments of society? In the current era, schoolmen and the schools have been spotlighted; so have union organizations and their leaders. For more than three decades, commercial and industrial organizations have had to respond to strong pressures demanding some recognition of their links with, and impacts on the larger society.

Where are these pressures generated that make organizational leaders take cognizance of their social responsibilities, whether or not they feel any inner moral compulsion to do so? In the first selection it is suggested that public opinion is focused on special areas at any given time. When the public turns its attentions to particular institutions, the leaders of the organizations who carry out the institutional purposes are forced to take their stand and declare their obligations to the society. Thus, public opinion turns out to be a strong force leading to the development of social responsibility among organizational leaders.

It is also suggested that once in the focus of public attention, an institution is likely to undergo rapid change in many of its aspects in addition to the change in orientation of organization leaders toward their social responsibilities. Thus, public opinion has the specific effect of generating an orientation of social responsibility, and a more general effect of increasing the rate of social change, when focused on a particular institutional setting.

---

## PUBLIC OPINION AND INSTITUTIONAL CHANGE

*Robert Dubin**

One of the key problems in understanding the nature of social institu-

*From "Industrial Research and the Discipline of Sociology," *Proceedings of the 11th Annual Meeting,* Industrial Relations Research Association (Madison: The Association, 1959), pp. 163–167. Used by permission.

tions is understanding their interrelationships. Our most enlightening literature here comes from the field of social anthropology where the interrelations among institutions of a culture is one of the primary foci of attention. Theory deriving from this source tends, in general, to give us a picture of simpler societies organized around a central institution like family, kinship, or moiety with the secondary institutions being coordinated with, but subordinated to, the central institution.

When we come to a modern industrial society our descriptive literature seems to make clear that institutions tend to become highly specialized in their functions and to be bounded and distinguished by functional isolation from other institutions. The general mechanism that makes this distinctiveness of institutions possible is the growth of formal organizations, each performing a specialized institutional function. Thus the school system and schools developed to carry on education, the factory system and individual firms developed to carry on economic functions, and government bureaus proliferate at all levels to carry out political functions. . . .

Our present view of an institution is essentially one of aggregates of organizations carrying on similar functions within an institutional boundary. This gives rise to what may be a surface over-emphasis on the distinctiveness of institutions and a corresponding inattention to their interrelationships as distinct from the present way of emphasizing their discreet characteristics.

Schools educate the populace and business firms employ the citizens of the society to produce goods and services. These are distinctive institutional realms. Furthermore, they each have unique types of formal organizations to carry on the institutional functions: schools for education, business firms for production. An examination of the literature of industrial training at all levels reveals immediately that there is a very large volume, indeed probably a much larger volume than we

currently suspect, of education being performed in business firms.[1] Thus the education-production distinction is not, in fact, clear-cut as the evidence of training and education carried on in industry confirms. Furthermore, this is not a reciprocal sharing of institutional functions. Business firms are in education but very few schools engage in production.

What conclusions can we draw from examples of interinstitutional penetration taken from the industrial relations field? They may be summarized as follows: (1) Institutions are not unitary in the functions they perform. This is in accord with existing sociological theory. (2) The functions shared between institutions are selective. Institutions overlap for only a portion of their functions. (3) Functions may shift between institutions. As a consequence of automation, for example, many leaders in the industrial sphere are re-thinking training problems and considering the possibility that retraining displaced workers as well as training a new labor force to work with automation should be returned to the schools, if for no other reason than the costs involved. (4) The expansion of functions in a given institution appears to take place at a very conscious level. The whole industrial training movement is a self-conscious development with its own educational goals and body of educational doctrine governing methods of instruction and learning. (5) There appears to be a hierarchy of institutions in the focus of community atten-

---

[1] An attempt to survey the dimensions of industrial training is H. F. Clark and H. S. Sloan, *Classrooms in the Factories: An Account of Educational Activities Conducted by American Industry* (Rutherford, N. J.: Institute of Research, Fairleigh Dickinson University, 1958).

tion at any given period of time. Some institutions are emphasized over others in the public's opinion. This hierarchy of institutions may not be grounded in a rational weighting of their relative functional importance. Institutional proponents, for example, may claim functional importance to command public attention, as schoolmen are now doing by elevating education to the level of a weapon in the cold war.

The concept of a hierarchy of institutions in a public view may become important in giving us a theoretical basis for determining which aspects of culture are lagging and which leading in social change at a given time. Ogburn introduced the concept of "cultural lag" as a way of describing the unevenness with which culture changes, illustrating the idea with changes in a given institution followed at a later date by necessary changes in other institutions.[2] It seems obvious that a parallel concept of "cultural lead," focusing on those elements of institutions that are in the vanguard of social change, may be important to understand cultural lag.

The concept of "cultural lead" begins to suggest for us why particular elements of culture change so that others have to adjust to them. I am here suggesting that a prime requisite is public attention to a given institution. On the basis of such public attention justifications are developed whereby scarce resources can be allocated to undertakings not hitherto considered important enough to command those resources. The Manhattan project and its subsequent development of the atom bomb is a case in point. The advent of automation as a wholly self-conscious development is

another illustration; so are concerns with executive loyalty, the organization man, and right-to-work legislation.

The productive institutions, industry and business, have been in the public attention for two decades. The Roosevelt revolution focused public attention on the productive institution, and our enduring social legislation was directly or indirectly concerned with the functions or outcomes of this institution. What is equally important is that those who guide the destiny of the productive institution, industrialists, corporate decision makers, and union leaders, have had to respond willy-nilly to the spotlighted position of that institution. The change was dramatic for them. The earlier conception of the industrial institution was that it was largely a privatized affair. This was given theoretical justification in a *laissez faire* policy which had the primary consequence of keeping public attention unfocused on the productive institution. If the best business decisions were private decisions and effective control of them was maintained by the market mechanism of competition, then public opinion and public attention were irrelevant to institutional functioning.

In the history of the United States this was further facilitated by other kinds of issues that captured public attention. These institutional problems included integration of millions of immigrants into the society, filling the vast geography of the country by expanding settlement westward, and meeting the challenge of exploitation offered by the fabulous natural resources available.

The great depression focused attention on the production institution as it ground to a paralysis. Industrialists

[2]William F. Ogburn, *Social Change* (New York: Viking Press, 1922).

generally reacted with a conservative stance, inveighing against this public attention by hoping for the return of obscurity in the public view. It is only on the contemporary scene that the leaders of business and industry have come to recognize the semi-permanent position of public attention which the productive institution now occupies. This has led to a great deal of soul-searching, and attempts at formulating the responsibilities of institutional leadership.[3] Whatever else one may say of President Eisenhower's two administrations, it seems very clear that one of their great functions has been to confirm the fact that the productive institution will remain in the public view. By virtue of this, industry is in the position of leadership with respect to institutional development and social change.

If we can characterize the Roosevelt revolution as having elevated the productive institution to the level of public consciousness, then we can also characterize the Eisenhower revolution as having effectively destroyed the opportunity to retreat back to a private and unmolested position among the institutions of our society. In short, the Eisenhower revolution has destroyed the conservative stance of industrialists. The decision-makers of industry now have to assume the position of leadership in guiding the

destiny of the productive institution because the spotlight of public attention will not move away from this institution. The simple conservative position that says, "leave us alone," is no longer viable. In the hierarchy of American institutions the productive institution now has a pre-eminent position. Those who make decisions about all aspects of the production of goods and services are, indeed, the new men of power because public opinion now accords to the productive institution the role of leadership in social change.

What I have just said about the analysis of the interpenetration of institutions can now be summarized. Our theory of institutional interdependencies and institutional change has been largely grounded in an implicit rational position. We have assumed that there is a best way for social functions to fit together and that institutional arrangements undergo transformation in a teleological sense while moving toward the best means of social arrangements. I think we may now perceive the possibility that public attention and public opinion play an important role in selecting out those institutions which display cultural lead in the society. When public attention is focused on an institution, and the behaviors it catches up, then this institution may move forward more rapidly in its development of functions than other institutions. It seems to me the role of public attention to institutional arrangements has not been accorded adequate importance when we focus on the problem of interinstitutional balance. "Cultural lead" may be the consequence of public attention, and "cultural lag" the consequence of public inattention.

---

[3]*Fortune* magazine has been one of the principal proponents of the new leadership responsibilities of American management. Such books as H. R. Bowen, *Social Responsibilities of the Businessman* (New York: Harper & Brothers, 1953), and its companion volume, M. W. Childs and Douglass Cater, *Ethics in a Business Society* (New York: Harper & Brothers, 1954) are serious attempts to cast up the accounts of business leadership, particularly as it affects the entire society.

Chamberlain, in the next selection, points up the central fact that all organizations face intervention by external groups. This is a fact of life characteristic of the environment of any organization.

What differentiates a cooperative from an antagonistic reaction to this intervention is the degree to which values are shared by organization leaders and those who intervene. Where there is some sharing there is likely to be a minimum of antagonism. Where there is apparently little sharing, then the typical reaction is that of antagonism to the intervention.

This problem is common to all kinds of organizations. Business leaders were largely opposed to the leadership of the late President Roosevelt because it was felt that he directed governmental action antagonistically against business. Labor leaders called the Taft-Hartley revisions of the Wagner Act a "slave-labor bill" and castigated its legislative proponents for their antagonism to organized labor. Public school administrators and teachers have resented the demands of educated citizens that the schools "tighten up" their educational standards because it was sometimes feared that such criticism might reduce schoolman control over education.

The fact of outside intervention in organizations seems indisputable. The reactions to it are highly colored by the perceptions of whether this is friendly or hostile intervention.

---

## THE MANAGER'S "STRUCTURE OF LIVING" AND OUTSIDE INTERVENTION

*Neil W. Chamberlain**

Other forms of intervention in managerial decisions may be presented but these [cited in the next sentence] are sufficient to establish the point of present interest—namely, that collective bargaining with unions is not the only means by which management shares its authority. By bargaining with other collectivities, and by responding to the influences of strategically situated "outside" groups of financial houses, suppliers, customers, competitors, and trade associations, it is likewise sharing authority. The proce-

dures may be less formal, the results less openly arrived at, the relationships more traditional. Nevertheless, it is clear that the unions are breaking no new paths in seeking to participate in the determination of corporate policy. Since this is so, the question arises why there has been more widespread managerial opposition to granting the unions a voice in business decisions than there has been to the intervention of other pressure groups.

Basically . . . the answer to the question of why management has more willingly accepted outside intervention other than that from unions lies in the fact that, except primarily for the unions, outside interveners have

*From *The Union Challenge to Management Control* (New York: 1948), from pp. 69, 71, 72. Copyright by Harper & Brothers. Used by permission.

shared with management the same social and economic beliefs, the same goals, the same philosophy, the same legal responsibilities. In short, management and such outside pressure groups have a common structure of living. Business is part and parcel of this structure of living. Banking houses, suppliers, customers, and competitors are all themselves business corporations faced with the same kinds of problems as the businesses with which they deal, and meeting them in the same manner. Trade associations are merely such corporations in collaboration. Sharing authority with such groups might mean a loss of personal power (though in some instances it means an actual expansion in power, an enlargement of the area within which authority is exercised). It involves no violation of the system of authority itself, however, or of the business framework. It constitutes no threat to the social position of the managers. It is, in fact, part of "the game." To win at the game may therefore be accepted merely as evidence of ability, commanding respect and providing example for emulation, so long as one observes the codes and rules. The significant fact is that man-

agers have been more willing to accept outside intervention when brought by those who are themselves "in business." To sum it up briefly, they understand each other.

To this structure of living of the managers, the unions, however, pose a threat. They seem to endanger the organizational framework and the system of authority throughout the corporation. Their philosophy has idealistic values foreign to the predominantly realistic outlook of businessmen. They challenge the accepted codes and rules. They substitute for the legal responsibilities of the managers political responsibilities of their own. Their program is revolutionary insofar as it seeks not merely a shifting of authority within the existing system but modification of the system itself. How common it is to hear the managerial condemnation that the methods and objectives of the unions "won't work" in a competitive business society.

It is this challenge to the way of life of the managers that provides them with their sterner attitude to the intervention of unions than to the intervention of other business groups.

---

In an attempt to understand more readily the belief systems of businessmen, Bowen surveyed the public utterances and writings of a broad cross-section of leading business leaders. From this was distilled the essence of what these businessmen took to be their responsibilities as executives.

The report makes enlightening read-

ing. It suggests that there are broadly based values among business executives that bespeak a strong sense of social responsibility. The goals of individual businesses have undergone significant modification since the era of the "robber barons." It is now considered to be good business to be good citizens.

---

## SOCIAL RESPONSIBILITIES OF BUSINESSMEN

### *Howard R. Bowen**

There is no doubt of an increasing awareness on the part of businessmen that they have important obligations to society. The concept of "stewardship" is, of course, an old one, and many businessmen have been thinking in this direction. Only within the past few years, however, have large numbers of business leaders publicly acknowledged and actively preached the doctrine that they are servants of society and that management merely in the interests (narrowly defined) of stockholders is not the sole end of their duties. Indeed, discussion of the "social responsibilities of business" has become not only acceptable in leading business circles, but even fashionable. Many heads of major corporations have made eloquent and apparently sincere expressions of the obligations of business to society at large,[1] introducing a positive and constructive note into the social thinking of businessmen.

Prior to World War II, much of their social thinking had been reflected in attacks on the New Deal and on organized labor, with strong feelings of persecution and bitter resentment against the authors of new restrictions. During the war, however, the success of American business in meeting productive requirements was so spectacular that public attitudes toward business notably changed. And with continuing postwar prosperity, businessmen regained, in large measure, the respect of the community and their own self-confidence. No longer have they been so deeply troubled by the persecution complex which had colored their thoughts and actions in the years before the war.

Nevertheless, the experience of the thirties, combined with worldwide tendencies toward social control and socialization of business, has led businessmen to think deeply about the conditions which must be met if the private-enterprise system is to continue as the basic economic organization of this country. They have seen clearly that private enterprise would be accepted and could continue only if it demonstrably served society better than any alternative system. Passionately sincere in their belief that

---

*From Howard R. Bowen, *Social Responsibilities of the Businessman* (New York: Harper & Brothers, 1953). Used by permission.

[1] In 1946, businessmen were polled by *Fortune* magazine regarding their social responsibilities. The following are two of the questions asked and the replies (*Fortune*, March, 1946, pp. 197–98):

"A few years ago it was frequently said that businessmen ought to acquire a 'social consciousness.' What was usually meant was that businessmen were responsible for the consequences of their actions in a sphere somewhat wider than that covered by their profit-and-loss statements. Do you think that

businessmen should recognize such responsibilities and do their best to fulfill them?

"Yes, 93.5 per cent; no, 1.6 per cent; depends, 4.7 per cent; don't know, 0.2 per cent.

"About what proportion of the businessmen you know would you rate as having a 'social consciousness' of this sort?

"None, 0.4 per cent; less than 10 per cent, 11.8 per cent; about a quarter, 22.2 per cent; about a half, 29.2 per cent; about three-quarters, 26.7 per cent; all, 3.0 per cent; don't know, 6.7 per cent."

the private enterprise system is superior to alternatives, their problem has been to consider how business should be conducted if it is to serve society well, and how to demonstrate that business does in fact serve society well. From this line of thinking emerged the new emphasis of businessmen upon their social responsibilities. . . .

I shall summarize the verbal statements of top executives in large corporations toward their responsibilities to society. In doing so, frankly, I shall not attempt to present all of the many views held by various businessmen or to indicate the proportion of businessmen who hold any particular view. I am not offering a business opinion poll based upon a scientifically selected sample. My purpose, rather, is to describe the thinking of a large and growing group of businessmen who are actively and articulately concerned about their role in society. The summary is based partly upon speeches, articles, annual reports, official testimony, and many other public pronouncements in which businessmen have professed their social ideals.[2] (The number of such documents runs into hundreds, perhaps thousands.) And it is based partly also upon numerous personal contacts with businessmen.

An analysis of this kind is open to criticism on the ground that it is impossible to distinguish the propaganda, the pious declarations, and the rationalizations of businessmen from their genuine beliefs as expressed in their policies and actions. This criticism is plausible, but not wholly valid. The expressed views of businessmen

are often reasonably consistent with their evolving policies and actions, and there is much evidence of sincere soul-searching and of attempts to think through the difficult problems of how to achieve a satisfying economic life for the masses of the people within the framework of private enterprise. No one would deny, however, that businessmen, like the rest of us, fall short of their professed ideals.

## THE BUSINESSMAN'S ECONOMICS

A first step in understanding the businessman's conception of his social responsibilities is to examine his economic ideas. The businessman is an eloquent spokesman in our society for abundant production. In his view, it is axiomatic that the primary aim of economic life is an ever-higher standard of living; and, if we are to achieve this aim, that we must produce more and more and more.

Most of the businessman's economic ideas flow from his concern for production. For example, he almost uniformly opposes any measures or attitudes which conflict with productive efficiency. He believes strongly in research as a way of developing better methods, new products, and ultimately a higher standard of living. He is interested in high labor productivity and is concerned about any tendencies toward reduced output on the part of workers.

The businessman favors strong incentives toward higher productivity. He believes that profits provide the greatest and most dependable incentive to businessmen; that the prospect and possibility of "reasonable" returns on capital are essential as incentives to the maintenance and advancement of production. He believes also that

---

[2]A list of some of the businessmen whose published statements have been consulted is presented in Appendix B [of source volume].

profits are necessary as a source of capital for expansion. He would have workers at all levels paid according to their net productive contributions, not only as incentive to high productivity but also as a matter of simple justice. He believes also that there should be widespread opportunities for people to get ahead on the basis of demonstrated abilities.

The businessman's belief that production is the sole source of our high standard of living and that growing production is a prerequisite to economic progress also leads him to the view that the interests of the various classes of society—particularly those of laborers and capitalists—are fundamentally in harmony and mutual dependence rather than in conflict. Since higher real wages can be obtained, as he sees it, only through greater production, labor has as much interest as capital in promoting higher output. The businessman, therefore, is distressed when he finds that labor sometimes focuses its attention on the division of the output between capital and labor rather than on the total amount of the output to be divided. The businessman feels that his concept of the identity of interest between labor and capital is so important, and the concept of conflicting interest so fallacious, that he makes a great effort to "educate" his workers and the general public in these ideas.

When the objection is raised that the real wages of workers *are* related not only to the size of the pie but also to the manner in which it is divided, the businessman answers that "tools" are indispensable to production and that the effectiveness of labor is related to the kind and quantity of tools it has to work with. In order to provide the tools, capitalists must have an adequate incentive in the form of a good return. Morever, a large part of the necessary capital derives directly from profits as they are plowed back into the business or reinvested by stockholders. Therefore, any attempt to raise wages at the expense of profits is likely to slow up the growth of production and, in the long run, to hurt labor both in terms of real wages and in terms of employment opportunities.

As part of his interest in growing production, the businessman believes that business must aggressively create the demands for an expanding output by means of advertising and other sales-promotion techniques. Business is not to wait supinely for demand to keep up with the possible rate of production progress, but is to prod it continuously. At the same time, business must sell its products at the lowest possible prices consistent with "reasonable" returns on capital. Only in this way will the fruits of technological advance be passed on to consumers and a growing market be assured.

The businessman believes in free enterprise on the ground that it provides the motivation, permits the flexibility, and mobilizes the imaginative energies required for a dynamic and progressive economy. By the same token, he believes in the efficacy of competition as a control on the individual enterprise. He also believes in free consumer choice. It is the job of business to produce products that will have consumer acceptance. He does not concern himself much with the kind of choices made by consumers, except in the market for his own product. He is content to let the consumer exercise his sovereignty and to adjust production accordingly. Consumer acceptance, therefore, becomes one of the tests of business success. The existence of a profit is an indication *prima facie* that the business has succeeded in producing something which consumers want and value. Free enterprise and free consumer choice are not only economically sound but absolutely indispensable to political freedom.

## GENERAL VIEWS ON SOCIAL RESPONSIBILITY

In keeping with the businessman's production-oriented economics, he regards his primary responsibility to be the achievement of ever-expanding production. This calls for operating efficiency, research, incentives to worker productivity, growth of capital, aggressive sales promotion, and low prices. In achieving the goal of increasing production, the businessman regards the making of a profit as his first and foremost duty. To him, a business that fails to make an adequate profit is a house of cards. It cannot grow or provide more jobs or pay higher wages. In the long run, it cannot even survive. It offers no stability or security or opportunity for its workers and investors. It cannot meet its broader obligations to society. It is a failure from all points of view. If a business is to make a profit, and thus to avoid failure, it must produce goods that are attractive in quality and price, and it must produce them efficiently and at low cost. These are the primary responsibilities of businessmen, and, indeed, the primary conditions of being in business at all. Only then is a business in a position to consider its other responsibilities to society.

Having laid down this general principle, a considerable number of businessmen express the view that the directors of a corporation are trustees, not alone for stockholders or owners, but also for workers, suppliers, con-

sumers, the immediate community, and the general public. According to this view, the board of directors should serve as a mediator, equitably balancing the legitimate interests of the several principal beneficiaries of corporate activity. The duty of the directors is to see that the interests of each group are fully recognized and protected. As early as 1929, Owen D. Young, then chairman of General Electric Company, expressed this view.[3]

Similar statements of this general idea have multiplied in recent years to the extent that this has become a widely prevalent theme in the thinking of American business leaders. One of the more thoughtful and complete statements of this idea was made by the late Lewis Brown, chairman of Johns-Manville Corporation, who said:

In the evolution of a complex industrial society the social responsibility of management has broadened correspondingly. Management no longer represents, as it once did, merely the *single interest* of ownership; increasingly it functions on the basis of a *trusteeship* which endeavors to maintain, between four basic interlocking groups, a proper balance of equity. Today the executive head of every business is accountable not only to his stockholders, but to the members of his working organization, to his customers, and to the public.[4]

In a similar vein, Clarence Francis, chairman of General Foods Corporation, has said:

Today, most managements, in fact, operate as trustees in recognition of the

[3] Quoted in John H. Sears, *The New Place of the Stockholder* (New York, Harper & Brothers, 1929), pp. 209–10.
[4] Quoted by Bronson Batchelor in *The New Outlook in Business* (New York, Harper & Brothers, 1940).

claims of employees, investors, consumers, and government. The task is to keep these forces in balance and to see that each gets a fair share of industry's rewards.[5]

The same note has recently been sounded by Beardsley Ruml, who also has interesting suggestions for its further implementation. Mr. Ruml referred to business as a system of private government of stockholders, suppliers, customers, and employees.[6]

These statements of leading businessmen—and many more such statements could be exhibited—clearly suggest the emergence of a kind of managerial thinking in which social responsibility is a fundamental ingredient. Once the *sine qua non* of a reasonable profit has been attained, then, according to these views, it becomes the duty of corporate directors and managers to conduct their enterprises with concern for all the interests affected. The function of management is one of mediation among these interests—to insure that each gets a square deal and that the interests of no one party are unduly sacrificed to those of others.

This theory of managerial responsibility assumes (1) that businessmen have considerable latitude in determining their prices, costs, and operating decisions; and (2) that within the limits of this latitude, product prices, wages, salaries, prices paid to suppliers, dividends, reinvested earnings, and operating decisions should be set so that the interests of all parties may

be equitably balanced. In this context, the businessman's vocabulary contains many phrases such as "low price for a product of good quality," "fair wages," "reasonable return to investors," and "sound growth of the company." So far as can be determined, the businessman seldom considers the precise meaning of these phrases. It is doubtful that many businessmen could supply criteria for determining when prices are or are not low; when wages are or are not fair; when the return to investors is or is not reasonable; etc. Nevertheless, the businessman thinks of these magnitudes as being determinable in part through business decisions rather than through the impersonal forces of the market, and he thinks of them as having ethical connotations which extend far beyond the narrow principle of profit maximization.

In line with this thinking, an increasing number of businessmen are beginning to regard management as a profession having underlying ethical principles and social responsibilities similar to the learned professions of medicine or law.[7]

[5]Address at Annual Conference of Harvard Business School Alumni Association, June 12, 1948.

[6]"Corporate Management as a Locus of Power," Address to Conference on the Social Meaning of Legal Concepts, New York University School of Law, April 3, 1951.

[7]These ideas are thoughtfully expressed by Frank W. Abrams, chairman of the Standard Oil Company (New Jersey): "I would like especially to impress upon you my own feeling that business management in the United States is well on its way toward achieving many of the characteristics of a profession. It is recognizing the kind of responsibility to the community as a whole which all professions must see and acknowledge. The profession of medicine, without its observance of the Hippocratic Oath, would not have the integrity and standing which it enjoys. The profession of teaching, without the magnificent roster of great teachers and devoted men and women who have set an example to the world by their devotion to the idea of education, would not today have so fully won the confidence and respect of the world. The legal profession, without a history of public service, would

## ALTRUISM VERSUS SELF-INTEREST

The protestations of businessmen regarding their responsibilities as trustees for the several interests affected by business operations do not necessarily derive from altruism. This is not to suggest that these ideas are advanced thoughtlessly or insincerely. They are advanced primarily because of a conviction that if business fails demonstrably to serve the interests of consumers, workers, and the general public it will be inviting repudiation in the form of deteriorated public relations, increased public control, and even socialization.[8]

not in any true sense be a profession today. It is my belief that technical education and training are not enough, if business managers are to have true professional competence. A clear sense of responsibility to and integration with the public welfare is a prerequisite to successful business management in today's complex world."—"What Top Management Expects of Collegiate Education," *Proceedings of the Golden Anniversary Convocation of the School of Commerce, Accounts, and Finance* (New York University, 1950).

[8]This thought has been ably expressed by Mr. Frank W. Pierce, director of the Standard Oil Company (New Jersey): "It is becoming clear that in our modern society top management has the opportunity—in fact, I should say the duty—to act as a balance wheel in relation to three groups of interests —the interests of owners, of employees, and of the public, all of whom have a stake in the output of industry. Management can best represent the interests of ownership by acting fairly and wisely with respect to the claims of employees and public as well. It is a difficult but vital role. It seems to me only too obvious that the very survival of private enterprise requires that private enterprise act to maintain a productive and equitable relation among these three elements: the individual's right to, and the social necessity for, profits; the economic and human aspirations of all workers; and the public's demand for an abundance of goods at low cost. The alternative is plainly intensified industrial conflict followed by increased government

Some businessmen have frankly suggested that the unfriendly public attitudes toward business and the resulting vulnerability of the free-enterprise system are due to abuses on the part of businessmen in the past, or to an excessively narrow preoccupation with the interests of stockholders.[9]

The important point which more and more businessmen are seeing is that the climate of public opinion and of political forces within which business is operating today is drastically

regulation forced by an impatient public." —"Developing Tomorrow's Business Leaders," an address before the Cincinnati Chapter of the Society for the Advancement of Management, December 6, 1945.

Senator Ralph E. Flanders, who was for years a leading businessman, has also expressed this idea: "In this age of management, in which the manager enjoys power, material reward, and a feeling of satisfaction in exercising his experience and abilities, the preservation of his position must be to him and to his class a matter of serious consideration. That preservation can only come as a result of the sensitiveness of the members of the management class to their responsibilities as trustees for stockholders, for suppliers, for employees, and for their customers. Fortunately, the tradition on which this class has been developed is on the whole favorable to this sensitiveness. . . . As for myself, I do not believe that this recognition of the general interest involves the neglect of the private interest. I hold the opposite view and have a very simple reason. The private interest is involved in the public interest. If the public interest is not served, the private interest ends in disaster. What we are faced with here is the distinction between short-range private interests and long-range private interests. As we grow in experience and intelligence, we see farther and farther into our long-range interests, and, except as we do this, our short-range interests will lead us into disaster."—*The Function of Management in American Life* (Graduate School of Business, Stanford University, 1948), pp. 8, 9, 51.

[9]Mr. Morris Sayre, president of the Corn Products Refining Company, has said: "Let's be frank about it. If our predecessors in man-

different from that of fifty or even twenty-five years ago. The experience at home of depression, war, and inflation, and the observation abroad of socialism and communism, have changed the criteria by which the operations of private business are judged. In Holmes' words, "Man's mind once stretched to a new idea never returns to its former dimensions."

The day of plunder, human exploitation, and financial chicanery by private businessmen has largely passed. And the day when profit maximization was the sole criterion of business success is rapidly fading. We are entering an era when private business will be judged solely in terms of its demonstrable contribution to the general welfare. Leading thinkers among businessmen understand this clearly. For them, therefore, the acceptance of obligations to workers, consumers, and the general public is a condition for survival of the free-enterprise system. Hence, even if the interests of stock-

holders be taken as the sole aim of business, concern for broader social objectives becomes obligatory for management.

That the businessman's concern for his social responsibilities is rooted in self-interest does not in any sense detract from the credit that should be his for recognizing and acting upon his obligations. As history has shown repeatedly, it is all too easy for a social class to ignore changes in the world about it and to fail to adjust its outlook and its social functions accordingly.[10] If American businessmen prove to be adaptable to changing conditions and changing concepts of their social role, they should receive the highest commendation, even though such adaptation is entirely consistent with their own long-run interests. Moreover, the fact that socially constructive business behavior often is, or can be made to be, consistent with self-interest means that such behavior is more dependable than it would be if it were based upon altruism or even upon legal controls. Also, it is not necessarily a valid criticism of these new concepts of social responsibility that businessmen do not always in practice live up to their professed concern for the social interest.

---

agement, two or three generations ago, had devoted a mere modicum of their time to some individual soul-searching about their motives, about their good faith, about the responsibilities they owe to the people—we wouldn't be facing some of the tough problems we face today. . . . An active social conscience . . . and individual recognition of social responsibilities will compel us, as individuals, to test *every* managerial practice, measure *every* policy by a simple yardstick. Not 'What does it mean for me,' but rather 'What will this mean to my *workers* as *people*, to my *customers*, to my *suppliers*, to my *stockholders*, to the *community* in which my plant is located, to my *government*, to the *industry* of which I am a part, to the *economy* as a whole?' These tests, honestly made, of *every* individual managerial action, policy, and practice, will be evidence of true social consciousness."—"We Owe It to America," an address before the Congress of American Industry, December 3, 1948.

[10]In an address before a business group, Walter Lippmann has said that if any businessman "imagines that consideration of public policy can be treated lightly, improvised without prolonged study and consultation and self-examination, or settled by saying the hell with the New Deal, the hell with the labor unions, the hell with the Russians, the hell with the British, the hell with all foreigners, politicians, professors, theorists who do not have to meet a payroll, they are talking and acting exactly like all other governing classes who throughout history were on their way down and on their way out."—"Why an Inferiority Complex in Business Leaders?" *Commercial and Financial Chronicle* (November 29, 1945), p. 2606.

Businessmen are human. Like any of us, they sometimes engage in behavior that does not conform to their highest ideals. And not all of them are in agreement on ideals. But the fact that their ideals and their conception of their social role are changing is of the greatest significance, even though performance does not measure up in every case.

The changing viewpoint of businessmen is a vivid example of the power of public value and attitudes over economic life. The changing values and attitudes of the public have persuaded businessmen, in a decisive way, to reconsider their social role and the aims of their activity. This illustrates the strength of moral sanctions and suggests the method by which religious and other ethically motivated groups may exert a powerful impact upon economic life.

---

There has been widespread interest in recent years concerning the distribution of power among those who determine local community affairs. The phrase "the power structure" is generally used to designate a kind of conspiratorial elite which is presumed to run local affairs for its private gain. It is not uncommon that "the power structure" is characterized as a group of self-seeking, reactionary, business-associated leaders.

Where so much heat surrounds an issue, it is especially desirable to have an objective research appraisal of the situation. Following is a report of a local community power structure analysis. William H. Form, the senior author, has made a number of studies of local communities and their power structure. This particular report is concerned with Lansing, Michigan, in which a General Motors automobile plant is located. It is worthwhile emphasizing one of the conclusions the authors draw: "Both community and labor influentials agree that, although businessmen dominate community decision-making, they are interested, hard-working citizens who act openly and responsibly for the good of the community."

We have already seen how the force of public opinion and the attitudes of senior business executives are creating a climate within which businessmen are responding constructively to the positions of social leadership which they occupy. The study of Form and Sauer confirms both the fact of continued leadership in local community affairs and a responsible exercising of this function by the local business executives.

## LOCAL BUSINESS AND LABOR LEADERSHIP

### *William H. Form* and *Warren L. Sauer**

Social scientists have observed several trends in the local community which may have relevance for the structure of community power. Big business has been said to be relinquishing positions of power and influence to other groups because it feels that the local community is no longer the most important locus of decision making.[1] Moreover, an alleged effect of big businessmen and top managers moving to the suburbs has been a decline in their interest in the affairs of the central city and a gradual shifting of controls to minority groups, which are being welded together by labor leaders who have begun to develop genuine community consciousness.[2] The latter presumably are not only filling a power vacuum but are launching a coordinated attack on surviving business controls in all institutional sectors.[3] Already labor presumably controls some institutions such as government, welfare, and recreation. Some students would deny this laboristic profile of community power and insist that *many* groups, including organized labor, share power which is no longer monopolized by one interest group.[4] They believe that, in a pluralistic society, power shifts from one bloc to another according to the specific issues at hand.[5] . . .

### RESEARCH PROBLEMS

The position taken in this study was that the vaunted increase in labor union power in the local community derives from an erroneous projection

*Reprinted by permission from William H. Form and Warren L. Sauer, "Labor and Community Influentials: A Comparative Study of Participation and Imagery," Industrial and Labor Relations Review 17:3–19, October, 1963.*

[1] Robert O. Schulze and Leonard Blumberg, "The Determination of Local Power Elites," *The American Journal of Sociology,* Vol. 63, November 1957, pp. 291–296. An opposing view is taken by Floyd Hunter, *Community Power Structure* and *Top Leadership U.S.A.* (Chapel Hill: University of North Carolina Press, 1953 and 1959, respectively); and C. Wright Mills, *The Power Elite* (New York: Oxford University Press, 1956), chaps. 2, 3.

[2] See James McKee, "Status and Power in the Industrial Community," *The American Journal of Sociology,* Vol. 58, January 1953, pp. 364–370; C. W. M. Hart, "Industrial Relation Research and Theory," *Canadian Journal of Economics and Political Science,* Vol. 15, February 1949, pp. 53–73; Donald E. Wray, "The Community and Labor-Management Relations," *Labor-Management Relations in Illini City* (Champaign: Institute of Labor and Industrial Relations, 1953); W. L. Warner *et al., Democracy in Jonesville* (New York: Harper and Brothers, 1949).

[3] See J. B. S. Hardman and Maurice Neufeld, *The House of Labor* (New York: Prentice-Hall, Inc., 1951); and William H. Form, "Organized Labor's Place in the Community Structure," *Industrial and Labor Relations Review,* Vol. 12, July 1959, pp. 526–539.

[4] See Daniel Bell, "America's Un-Marxist Revolution" *Commentary,* Vol. 7, March 1949, pp. 207–215; and David Riesman, *The Lonely Crowd* (New Haven: Yale University Press, 1951).

[5] See, for example, Robert A. Dahl, "A Critique of the Ruling Elite Model," *The American Political Science Review,* Vol. 52, June 1958, pp. 463–469; Bell, *op. cit.;* Riesman, *op. cit.;* and others.

of its power on the national scene to the local community, and an equally erroneous assumption that increased bargaining strength in local plants results automatically in increased political and social power in the community. It was, therefore, hypothesized that "the business community" still plays a dominating role in decision making in the community as a whole and in its institutions. Despite protests by the business community that labor "is taking over," and despite labor's increasing confidence in its own power, the hypothesis was that there would be general consensus that business still dominates, if it does not monopolize, local decision making. Moreover, despite the semantics of conflict commonly found in national economic and political bargaining,[6] it was further hypothesized that labor and other influentials would perceive the local decision-making process to

be essentially cooperative. That is, the community arena would be generally considered as a place to cooperate, even if conflict is expected over national economic and political issues. Thus we predicted that both white-collar and labor influentials would identify the same local projects and issues and agree on the need for cooperation to resolve them. Since business historically has dominated local decision making, labor was expected to agree with business identification of local issues and projects. . . .

## BACKGROUNDS OF INFLUENCE

Table 1 presents data on some of the background characteristics of the influentials. Most of the community influentials were born in small midwestern cities somewhat more than fifty years ago. Three-quarters had fathers in white-collar occupations, and the majority were businessmen or professionals. Over four-fifths of the respondents attended college and most of them majored in economics. After

[6] See "The Language of Labor," *Fortune,* Vol. 44, September 1951, p. 256; Edward H. Chamberlain, *et al., Labor Unions and Public Policy* (Washington: American Enterprise Association, 1958).

**Table 1**

BACKGROUND CHARACTERISTICS OF COMMUNITY AND LABOR UNION INFLUENTIALS

| Characteristics | Labor (N=39) | Community (N=39) |
|---|---|---|
| Median age, years | 48 | 58 |
| Education | | |
| Eight years or less | 36% | — |
| Some high school | 43% | 16% |
| Some college | 21% | 84% |
| Median years lived in community | 27 | 38 |
| Median number of present community organizational affiliations | 3.3 | 13.0* |
| Median number of past community organizational affiliations | 3.0 | 6.9* |
| Median years tenure in present office | 14† | 19‡ |
| Mean number of votes received as "key influential" by "peer" influentials | 22 | 20 |

*Represent officerships.
†Tenure as a union official.
‡Tenure in present company, 29 years.

entering the labor force they changed jobs two or three times before locating with their present company at about the age of thirty. Within ten years they occupied the highest position within the organization. Upon arrival in the community they became immediately and continuously involved in its organizational life. They became a genuine collectivity because most of them joined the same organizations, held the top positions in them, and acquired common financial interests.[7]

Table 1 also summarizes some of the chief characteristics of the labor influentials. Twelve of them were district, regional, or international officers, twenty held high offices in their locals, and seven held minor local offices. The typical labor influentials were born about fifty years ago in small villages or cities in the midwest. After obtaining some high school education they came to the city in search of employment. They displayed very little mobility, staying in the same community, job, and industry. Most of them joined the union when first given the opportunity and soon after became officers. As they became increasingly involved with union activities, they shifted their affiliations away from "private" associations (Elks and Odd Fellows) to "public" organizations (Community Chest and the like) as union representatives. In the past they constituted an intimate and cohesive

group, but today their contacts are largely limited to official union functions.

In terms of social backgrounds, the community panel had a decisive advantage over the labor leaders in community influence. They were reared in families in which it was the custom to participate in community affairs; they had received superior education, had become deeply and widely committed to community participation earlier in their careers than the labor leaders, and had become a more cohesive self-conscious group bound by economic, social, and political ties.

## PRESENT POSITION OF BUSINESS AND LABOR IN THE COMMUNITY

Although businessmen historically have had dominant influence in community affairs, organized labor—especially since World War II—set out to increase its share of that influence. The official policy of the UAW since World War II has been to encourage its members to become involved extensively in local community affairs, become politically aggressive, and to obtain representation in the total range of voluntary community organizations.[8] An attempt was made to estimate labor's success in reaching its goals by (a) ascertaining its representation in community agencies, (b) finding the proportion of union leaders among community influentials, and (c) estimating labor's power in community projects and issues.

An intensive analysis was first made of the occupational composition of the boards of all of the major community

---

[7]Twenty-three have known business ties with each other. See Donald A. Clelland, "Economic Dominants in a Middle-Sized City," unpublished M.A. thesis, Michigan State University, 1960. For a further description of the group, see William H. Form and Warren L. Sauer, "Community Influentials in a Middle-Sized City" (Ann Arbor: Institute of Community Development and Labor and Industrial Relations Center, Michigan State University, 1960), pp. 1–10.

[8]See Leo Perlis, "Unions and Community Services: The CIO Community Services Program," in Hardman and Neufeld, *op. cit.*, pp. 333–340.

agencies since World War II. Table 2 reveals that organized labor and manual workers had less than 10 percent of the officers in all institutional sectors. Businessmen alone, or with professionals, constituted the vast majority of officers in community organizations. A ranking of labor's institu-

they expressed varying degrees of anti-union attitudes in the interviews. "Key" influentials were the ten men receiving the highest number of votes as leaders from the influentials themselves. Neither the union officials nor the "neutrals" were among the key influentials selected.

**Table 2**

OCCUPATIONAL BACKGROUNDS OF MEMBERS OF
SELECTED COMMUNITY ORGANIZATIONS, IN PERCENTAGES

| Occupational Level | Elected City Officials 1945–57 | Appointive City Commissions 1945–57 | Board of Education 1945–57 | Welfare Board 1953 | Community Influentials 1958 | Labor Force* 1958 |
|---|---|---|---|---|---|---|
| Professionals | 17 | 16 | 24 | 43 | 20 | 12 |
| Proprietors | 25 | 28 | 62 | 32 | 54 | 3 |
| Mgrs. & officials | 10 | 14 | 9 | 6 | 20 | 3 |
| Govt. officials | 17 | 19† | — | 2 | 3 | 1 |
| Sales & office clerks | 19 | 10 | — | 4 | — | 29 |
| Manual workers | 6 | 8‡ | — | 4 | — | 51 |
| Union officials | 3 | 1 | 6 | 3 | 3 | — |
| Not ascertained | 3 | 4 | — | 6 | — | 1 |
| Totals | 100 | 100 | 100 | 100 | 100 | 100 |
| Number of Cases | 185 | 515 | 34 | 609 | 39 | 39,212 |

*Resident in Lansing.
†Three percent are professionals.
‡Largely firemen and policemen.

tional influence from high to low is estimated as follows: welfare, political party, board of education, city government, religion, and mass communication.[9] Labor's primary achievement since the war was to get some representation in areas where it was previously lacking.

Among the thirty-nine community influentials were two union officials, the ex-presidents of the local AFL and CIO. A clergyman and an insurance agent could sometimes be expected to be neutral or prolabor. The remaining influentials were all Republicans, and

[9] The method of establishing the relative influence of labor in each institutional sector is amplified in Form, *op. cit.*

The third area of influence considered was the role of influentials in community decision making. They were asked to reconstruct in detail their activities in connection with local projects or issues in which they had participated during the last ten years. The interview was organized to obtain data on the initiation pattern of the project or issue, the sequence of involvement of various persons and agencies, and the sanctions or facilities which were used to reach given ends.

About two-thirds of the respondents gave answers which included the following fourteen community issues: hospital expansion, parking bond, payroll tax, downtown development, annexation, metropolitan planning, Sunday shopping, bus subsidy, fluoridation, city charter revision, location of city hall, airport improvement, street extension, and Tricounty planning. Ten of these were listed by the community influentials and six by labor; only two issues were mentioned by both. Labor gave descriptions of fewer issues and these descriptions were less detailed than those provided by the community influentials. Labor admittedly did not initiate any of the projects, but mentioned the involvement of business and government in all the issues it mentioned. Labor did not claim that its influence was decisive in any issue and indicated that the threat of non-participation, especially in fund raising, was its main sanctioning technique.

The community influentials indicated that they had initiated two-thirds of the issues and had involved government officials in all of them. In addition, they had approached labor union officials to work with them on two of the issues. According to their own analysis, the community influentials exercised decisive influence on all but two of the issues, by dominating the flow of communications, occupying strategic offices, and providing the necessary services, personnel, or finances.

## ASSESSMENTS OF POWER

A major objective of the research was to determine whether the perceptions which the labor and community influentials had of local power arrangements corresponded with the situation outlined above. Both panels were asked to: (a) estimate their personal effectiveness and that of their associates in determining policies in organizations in which they participated; (b) identify individuals and organizations which initiated, executed, or vetoed community projects; and (c) make a blanket comparison of the relative power of business and labor in community decision making. . . .

Table 3 shows how both sets of influentials ranked the top ten. The two groups overlapped on six choices and differed on four choices. Labor's selections included four businessmen, two labor leaders, two educators, the mayor (an ex-businessman), and one clergyman, and omitted a lawyer and three businessmen. The community respondents selected seven businessmen, two educators, and the mayor, omitting the two labor leaders, the Catholic Bishop, and a realtor. The comparison of the two lists supports a consistent trend found in the interviewing. Although both groups perceived business as more powerful, labor consistently attributed more influence to itself than the others were willing to grant it. Moreover, labor's top choice manifested a strong tendency toward a wider institutional representation and a smaller representation of businessmen than that given by the community influentials.

This pattern revealed itself in the ranking of the powerful organizations in the city. Over half of the community influentials listed business organizations such as the Chamber of Commerce, the local newspaper (Republican), and the General Motors plant as the most powerful voices in community affairs. Three-tenths selected organized labor, and fewer chose other organizations such as the service clubs, churches, and PTA. This general picture of business dominance was confirmed by the labor influentials, except that they included organized labor more often than the community in-

**Table 3**

THE KEY INFLUENTIALS AND THE MOST POWERFUL ORGANIZATIONS IN
COMMUNITY AFFAIRS AS INDICATED BY LABOR AND COMMUNITY INFLUENTIALS

|  | Community Influentials Votes | Labor Influentials Votes |
|---|---|---|
| Occupations of Top Ten Key Community Influentials |  |  |
| Newspaper publisher | 26 | 28 |
| Mayor | 16 | 27 |
| Catholic Bishop | 21 | 21 |
| Superintendent of public schools | — | 22 |
| President of Labor Council | — | 19 |
| Manager of automobile plant | 32 | 18 |
| University president | 29 | 17 |
| Realtor | — | 16 |
| Union subregional director | — | 13 |
| Retired department store manager | 21 | 11 |
| Manager of metal manufacturing plant | 14 | — |
| Executive of auto-parts concern | 13 | — |
| Lawyer | 13 | — |
| Banker | 13 | — |
|  |  |  |
| Most Powerful Organizations |  |  |
| Chamber of Commerce | 29 | 28 |
| Organized labor | 15 | 28 |
| Newspaper | 22 | 10 |
| Board of realtors | 7 | 10 |
| Service clubs | 17 | 6 |
| Churches | 10 | 6 |
| General Motors auto plant | 20 | 7 |
| Downtown Businessmen's Association | — | 5 |
| Community Chest | — | 3 |
| City Council | — | 2 |
| Parent-Teachers Association | 7 | — |

fluentials. Thus seven-tenths of them indicated that both the Chamber of Commerce and organized labor were the most influential local organizations. The newspaper, board of realtors, the GM plant, and business organizations were mentioned much less frequently, while the City Council and churches were mentioned by only a few.

Finally, both sets of influentials were asked to make a blanket comparison between the relative power of business and labor in local affairs.

General consensus was indicated by the fact that nine-tenths of the community influentials and three-quarters of the labor influentials agreed that business was stronger than labor....

## CONCLUSIONS

The following conclusions are subject to the limitations of a case study and limitations of using influentials as the major source of data concerning community power. They are, therefore, limited to cases where the balance between labor and business is similar to the Lansing situation. Unfortunately, relevant systematic evidence is not available for many cities. Compared to other middle-sized industrial communities in the United States, Lansing probably represents a situation where labor is relatively strong. Yet our data indicate that the influential persons do not see business relinquishing its formal or informal controls over local decision making. Influential businessmen still constitute a "community" in the sociological meaning of the term, and they maintain their interest in local affairs. They have so institutionalized their control that they do not see the need to intervene often in local affairs to maintain control. This situation is most clearly evident in the governmental and educational arenas where the business community defines, initiates, and implements all major community projects.[10] Despite twenty years of effort, labor influentials agree that they have not basically altered the local power situation. Neither they nor the community influentials support the pluralistic view that representatives in the various institutional sectors exert dominant influence in decisions involving their institutions.

The research question was posed whether influential persons view local decision makers as acting according to an oligarchic or responsible model of control. Both community and labor influentials agreed that, although busi-

nessmen dominate community decision making, they are interested, hardworking citizens who act openly and responsibly for the good of the community. While labor's estimate of its own strength in local affairs was higher than that accorded them by community influentials, it did not claim credit for successful projects, nor did it fight others to increase its power. For both groups the community represented a cooperative arena which excluded the intervention of economic and political conflicts in the nation, state, and local plants.

Labor faced a problem of legitimatizing its community participation in a situation where it had neither an independent ideology nor a clear-cut community program. While it saw itself as slightly more responsible, less selfish, and more consumer-oriented than business, it did not disagree with business' goals for the community. Labor's rationale for opposing traditional controls was articulated in terms of values of democratic participation. It wanted decision makers to operate more publicly and to consult members of other groups. In short, labor wanted pluralistic representation and consultation, but not partisan politics.

As in many smaller communities, business control in Lansing is viewed by most groups as part of the natural and traditional order which needs no legitimation.[11] Therefore, business ideology finds expression in the operations of many community organizations. Labor, then, is faced with the problem of gaining respect in a traditional order, which it does not reject, but which does not grant it sufficient

[10]Of course, it would be an oversimplification to conclude that all such business activity is for selfish economic reasons. See Peter H. Rossi, "Theory Research and Practice in Community Organization," in *Social Science and Community Action*, Charles R. Adrian, ed. (East Lansing, Mich.: Institute of Community Development, Michigan State University, 1960), pp. 22–23.

[11]Not unlike the situation described in Arthur J. Vidick and Joseph Bensman, *Small Town in Mass Society* (Garden City, N. Y.: Doubleday & Company, Inc., 1960).

status. Indeed, labor is in a vulnerable position if it rejects the local control system or insists on sponsoring new community goals. Since it does not suffer from a sense of persecution and does not have distinctive community goals, it cannot point to local achievements and gain greater status and power from achievement.

A significant change in the local reputations of business and labor probably cannot be achieved without a transitional period of conflict.[12] In the

United States the alteration of local power arrangements tends to be found in those communities which have sufficient ethnic and other types of economic and social heterogeneity to base a meaningful struggle for control. Studies of community power in other nations suggest that existence of more than one ideology is a necessary condition for a changing power relationship between business and labor.[13]

---

[12]See James A. Coleman, *Community Conflict* (Glencoe, Ill.: The Free Press, 1957), p. 21.

[13]See the studies of Bristol, England, C. Juarez, Mexico, and other cities reported in Form and Miller, *Industry, Labor, and Community* (New York: Harper and Brothers, 1960), pp. 552–612.

---

We conclude the chapter by considering some of the impacts of industry and commerce on society. When an institution becomes central to the functioning of a society, it is held that some of the goals and values characterizing that institution will "seep out" to the larger society.

While we tend, from the previous selections, to gain a sense that organizations are molded by their environments, we are here called back to recognize that important institutional segments of society (and the organizations in these sectors) also mold society. This is illustrated in the follow-

ing selection by pointing to several broad social values that seem to have their genesis in the industrial institution.

If we characterize ours as an urban-industrial society, then we should not be surprised if its value system is derived from the logics and practices of industrial life. Whether or not they are conscious of their role as molders of the larger social values, business executives actually perform this function because of the centrality to our society of the organizations they direct.

---

## INDUSTRY AND SOCIAL VALUES

### Robert Dubin*

The productive institutions have generated significant values that are now working themselves out in the

larger society. I will discuss two central values of the industrial institution because they are substantially inter-

---

*From "Industrial Research and the Discipline of Sociology," *Proceedings of the 11th Annual Meeting,* Industrial Relations Research Association (Madison: The Association, 1959), pp. 167–172. Used by permission.

esting, and because their analysis reveals the interaction of values and behavior in our society. The two central industrial values are *persistence,* and *interdependence.*

In classic analyses of the rise of capitalism, Weber and Tawney saw developments in other institutions, notably the rise of the Protestant ethic, as independent variables affecting the industrial institution.[1] In our mature capitalism it becomes significant to inquire whether the productive institution has generated significant values and systems of behavior that are now working themselves out in the larger society. I think it has.

Industry has moved from the position of being a dependent variable in the social fabric, dependent on developments in other institutions, to the position where it is now an independent variable in the society, influencing, if not determining, the character and structure of other institutions. There is a centrality to the industrial institutions in the operation of the whole society not previously accorded to it by social analysts. It can be argued, of course, that Marx and others gave the industrial institution its pre-eminent position as an independent variable in social change, and that therefore the centrality of industry is really nothing new. What I am more concerned in emphasizing is the fact that the industrial institution has had pervasive effects not only on its own development (which is the Marxian position) but also on the daily round of life of all citizens in an industrial society. The emerging values surrounding industrial work have generated new values

surrounding the lives of industrial workers. The discipline of working in a factory or office has changed the behaviors of peoples in their communities and the rhythm of their community life.

The problem of productive work, at least in our society, is no longer that of subsistence and has not been for several generations. This is the affluent society in Galbraith's terms and its major problem is persistence, not subsistence. The dynamism of modern industry now seems to rest on full resource utilization, not profit-making alone. This means growth at least in proportion to the increase in resources (population, power, raw materials, markets, etc.) and preferably at a greater rate made possible by higher levels of consumption. Persistence is an underlying industrial value from which derives the motive power to make big business bigger, small businesses large, expand markets to world spheres, put two cars in every garage, etc.

If persistence is a fundamental industrial value, then we have to inquire, as sociologists, how it works its way out into the larger society. In the consumer spheres it leads to the development of credit policies permitting present consumption with delayed payments, the stimulation of consumer demands based on style changes rather than utilitarian considerations, and a widely held assumption that because the economic and social system are now so inextricably related, every effort must be made, through government or other agencies, persistently to keep the economy on an even keel or preferably on an up-grade. The quiet revolution of government monetary and credit manipulations and the more drastic pump-priming through increased governmental expenditures for

---

[1]Max Weber, *The Protestant Ethic and the Spirit of Capitalism* (New York: Charles Scribner's Sons, 1930); and R. H. Tawney, *Religion and the Rise of Capitalism* (New York: Penguin Books, 1947).

public works can be seen not so much as the triumph of a liberal economic policy as more nearly the consequences of the industrial value system; the persistence value of the industrial system permeating the larger social system. It is notable that many "industrial statesmen," among managers and labor leaders, are the most active proponents of devices to insure the persistence of the industrial dynamic. It is no longer meaningful to label such industrialists with classic tags like liberal or conservative. They are, perforce, industrialists *sui generis* who apply the values of productive institutions to the larger society.

An emerging American value of tremendous significance for industry, originating in the industrial institution but also permeating the whole society, is this value of societal success displacing the value of individual success. I say displacing advisedly. The measure of individual success is no longer only the accumulation of personal wealth exhibited through conspicuous consumption. An additional test is that of contribution to the persistence of a high level economy.

A second value related to that of persistence of a high level economy is the growing belief in the interdependence of the institutions making up the social fabric. This belief in the inevitable interdependence of industry, government, family, religious, military, and recreation institutions, to mention only the more obvious, has had the effect of focusing on institutional interdependencies as a major concern of policy makers in all walks of life. For example, it does make a difference to industrialists who will employ them as workers whether Negroes get adequate education, making it both possible and logical for industrialists to accept integration in schools as well as in their plants. It

makes a great deal of difference to labor unions whether their members have adequate medical facilities for themselves and family members since this is an area in which a direct payoff can be made to members through collective bargaining. Employers recognize the interconnections between family health and living, on the one hand, and work, on the other hand, and have not been entirely reluctant to accept and support health and welfare and similar fringe benefits in collective bargaining.

I have illustrated two underlying values of our industrial institution. Both derive from habituation to business operations and are logically congruent with them. To put it most colorfully we can summarize these values as follows: A factory is no damn good if it isn't running; and whether it runs or not depends on conditions exterior to it. These are direct restatements of the *persistence* value and the *interdependence* value oriented towards the production institution.

Here now is the analytical problem. How do values come into being? How do they become stabilized within a given institution? What are the mechanisms by which they extend beyond the given institutional setting into others? These are clearly subjects for sociological analysis. The data of industry suggests a very fruitful body of knowledge which, if analyzed, will give us new insights into theoretical explanation of the phenomenon of values. Outside of such classic studies as Weber's and Tawney's and such excellent historical studies of changing norms as Bendix's and Wyllie's, we do not have adequate theory to handle the problem of values.[2]

---

[2]Reinhard Bendix, *Work and Authority in Industry* (New York: John Wiley and Sons, 1956); and Irvin G. Wyllie, *The Self-Made*

Before trying to predict what such theory might look like, let us consider some specific examples of consequences of these values. The current concerns with individual freedom within the organizational straightjackets of company and union take on new meaning in the light of these values. The persistence value for either organization places in the hands of management and union leadership decisions made for and on behalf of the continuity of organization. Mr. Whyte's "organization man" is so because the continued persistence of the organization is a value higher than that of individualism. The dictatorship of unions over the working destinies of their members is similarly viewed as a legitimate pursuit of organization as over against individual goals. The organization man and the union member as organization automaton are the logical consequences of the value of persistence. Furthermore, these two outcomes are buttressed by the interdependence value. For the business organization the team and team player who knows his place, his specialty, and his interdependence with other members of the team, is more valued than the individualist, however brilliant his potential contribution might be. The individualistic worker who may upset the solidarity of the union *vis à vis* management is a similar threat because of the dimly perceived interdependence among workers to maximize their bargaining strength. Thus it becomes possible to characterize some of the central problems of man in organization in terms of the underlying dual values which arise out of behaviors in our industrial institution.

Parkinson has satirized the persis-

tence value in modern organization, the satire being all the more trenchant because of the underlying reality it portrays.[3] Academic students have illustrated the working out of the persistence value in business organizations and in labor unions. Their studies make clear that market mechanisms of competition, however decisive they may appear to operate, are not the sufficient condition of organization survival. Among organization participants, there develops out of the logics of daily operations and the pressure of past investment of resources, a belief in the value that persistence of the organization is itself a goal.

The interdependence value is expressed everywhere about us. Labor is in politics, so is business. The military institution consumes a major share of the national product and decisions have become too important, for international relations as well as the national economy, to be left to the generals. The entire citizenry is being called to arms to support significant changes in our common schools because it affects the quality and allocation of our human resources in adult productive work. The "company wife" has become a preoccupation of at least some business concerns as an obvious bow to the interdependence between working and family life. Unions have become welfare organizations with some even attempting to embrace the entire round of life of their members. Market competition among business firms is as much concerned with increasing the total market for a product as with driving competitors out of business. The arts have become a weapon in the cold war (through cultural exchanges) as well as hand-

---

*Man in America* (New Brunswick: Rutgers University Press, 1954).

[3]C. N. Parkinson, *Parkinson's Law and Other Studies in Administration* (Boston: Houghton Mifflin Co., 1957).

maiden of the industrial designer. Philanthropy on a scale unique in world history becomes a national policy as an instrument of economics and politics through our economic aid programs to foreign governments (remember when the slogan, "a quart of milk for every Hottentot" once characterized the foolishness of national philanthropy?). We could multiply examples endlessly. The point seems clear. Interdependence is a central value of American life.

What can we conclude from these examples that tells us something about the dynamics of the origin of new values, their spread and final dominance in an institution, and in the larger society? In each of these examples it seems apparent that the behavior becomes systematized in terms of specific and uncoordinated norms guiding the behavior. There then gradually unfolds a generalization of these specific norms into a broad overarching guiding value which is logically consistent with the individual norms, and a summary of them. When these over-arching values finally become articulated, they serve the purpose of giving meaning and goals for the complex behavior systems out of which they have been derived.

Thus I would suggest that a possible theoretical formulation of the relations between values as goals for behavior, and behavior itself, is that the former grow out of the latter. Behavior, in turn, is the product of the functional logics of a given institution. It is customary to assert the success motif as a central goal of American society and to view behavior as a product of it. I am now suggesting that industrial behavior guided by the logics of industrial production has, in fact, given rise to new social goals that are at least coordinate with the individual success motif.

The dynamics of value formation may be from behavior to a rationalization of goals, rather than the more customary formulation of goals as the guides for behavior. It may be thoroughly worthwhile for sociologists seriously to address themselves to this kind of problem and perhaps even to consider the dynamics I have just outlined as the theoretical model.

# Name Index

Page numbers followed by an (S) indicate selections in this volume.

Abegglen, James C., 248
Abrams, Frank W., 513
Achminow, H., 16
Acton, Lord, 271
Adler, R. B., 7
Adrian Charles R., 523
Alderson, Wroe, 13
Ammer, Dean, 214
Arensberg, Conrad M., 103, 451, 480
Argyle, Michael, 455, 456
Argyris, Chris, 44, 46, 80(S), 83, 89, 91, 92, 93, 97, 101, 102, 179, 182, 243, 291, 433
Aristotle, 489
Avery, Sewell, 296

Bakke, E. Wight, 44, 58, 65, 79, 81, 91
Barker, R. B., 88
Barkin, Solomon, 59
Barmine, Alexander, 417
Barnard, Chester, I., 4, 5, 10, 18, 19(S), 33, 37, 183, 224, 279, 284, 285, 301, 302(S), 314, 323, 347, 348(S), 358, 383, 388, 389, 390(S), 428, 458, 488
Bass, B. M., 452
Batchelor, Bronson, 513
Bates, Fredrick L., 263

Bauer, Raymond A., 16(S)
Bavelas, Alex, 276, 381, 383
Beard, Miriam, 135
Bell, Daniel, 517
Bell, H. M., 70
Bell Telephone, 22
Bendix, Reinhard, 180, 414(S), 526
Bennis, Warren G., 96, 97, 99, 102
Bensman, Joseph, 523
Benthan, Jeremy, 279, 282
Berg, I. A., 452
Berle, A. A., Jr., 7
Berliner, J., 435
Berry, P. C., 332
Bierstedt, Robert, 272
Blair, John M., 482
Blake, Robert R., 452
Blau, Peter, 434
Blauner, Robert, 96, 102
Block, C. H., 332
Bloomberg, Warner, Jr., 480
Blumberg, Leonard, 517
Blumer, Herbert, 58
Booz, D. R., 48, 179, 435
Bossard, J. H. S., 167, 173
Bowen, Howard R., 506, 508, 509(S)
Bowie, J. A., 7
Bradford, L. P., 88, 382
Braybrooke, David, 372
Brayfield, Arthur H., 96, 102

Brenner, M., 336
Bright, James R., 478
Brown, J. A. C., 96, 102
Brown, Lewis, 512
Brown, Walter, 319
Brown, Wilfred, 218
Browne, C. G., 165
Buchanan, N. S., 136, 364
Bulganin, Nicholai, 435
Burgess, Eugene W., 38, 44
Burke, Edmund, 155
Burling, Temple, 233
Burns, Tom, 179, 180, 181, 182, 246, 329, 330(S), 332, 400(S), 404
Burtt, H. E., 46

Campbell, J. P., 333
Carey, H., 380
Carlson, Sune, 179, 182, 329
Carnegie Corporation, 19
Carnegie, Dale, 180
Cartwright, D., 273, 298
Cassell, Frank, 40
Cater, Douglass, 506
Chamberlain, Edward H., 518
Chamberlain, Neil W., 359, 507(S)
Chandler, Margaret, 119
Chapple, Elliot R., 100, 102, 182
Chenery, W. L., 359

Child, I. L., 56
Childs, M. W., 506
Chinoy, Ely, 74
Christensen, Charles R., 459
Ciofi, Frank, 455, 456
Clark, H. F., 504
Clark, James V., 93, 102
Cleeton, G. U., 169
Clelland, Donald A., 519
Coase, R. H., 43
Coates, Charles H., 47, 223, 248(S)
Coch, Lester, 457
Cohen, Morris R., 488, 489(S), 493, 496
Cole, Taylor, 161
Coleman, James A., 524
Cooley, Charles H., 104, 248
Coonley, H., 359
Cordiner, E. J., 188

Dahl, Robert A., 272, 517
Dale, Ernest R., 180
Dalton, Melville, 150, 181, 192, 202(S), 245, 434, 435
Danielson, L. E., 287
Davenport, Russell, 298
Davis, Kingsley, 196
Davis, Louis E., 100, 102
Davis, W. H., 359
Davitz, J., 336
Delaney, W., 184
deMan, Henri, 298, 411, 412(S)
Dennis, Wayne, 53
Deutsch, M., 86, 87
Dewey, John, 54, 155
Dewhurst, J. F., 167, 173
DeWitt, Nicholas, 17
Dickson, W. J., 284
Diebold, John, 478
Dill, W. R., 45
Dimock, Marshall E., 158, 159(S), 203, 358, 420
Divine, Father, 296
Dollard, John, 88
Dooher, M. J., 169
Dorn, Walter L., 416, 417
Douglas, Dean J., 221
Drake, C. A., 319
Dror, Yehezkel, 371, 372(S)
Drucker, Peter F., 183, 399, 451, 478, 480
Drury, H. B., 366
Dubin, Robert, 44(S), 53(S), 58, 63(S), 72(S), 74, 90(S), 98, 102, 106, 107, 118, 147(S), 152(S),

Dubin, Robert (*cont.*)
179(S), 180, 181, 243(S), 245, 250, 255, 271, 279(S), 294(S), 301, 317(S), 367(S), 387, 407(S), 422, 433(S), 449(S), 453, 471(S), 493(S), 503(S), 524(S)
Dunlap, John L., 98, 103
Dunnette, Marvin D., 331, 332(S), 333
Dyer, Jack L., 263

Earle, E. M., 42
Einstein, Albert, 272
Eisenhower, Dwight D., 506
Eliot, T. S., 4
Emerson, Richard M., 273
Endicott, F. S., 168
Erikson, E., 80, 81
Etzioni, Amitai, 272, 275, 285, 286(S)

Farnsworth, Paul, 103
Faunce, William A., 480
Fayol, Henri, 83, 86
Feld, Sheila, 94, 103
Ferrarrotti, Franco, 38
Flanders, Ralph E., 514
Fleishman, E. A., 46, 458
Florence, P. S., 135
Follett, Mary Parker, 83
Ford, Henry, 134
Form, William H., 315(S), 502, 516, 517(S), 519, 520, 524
Fowler, Irving, 100, 103, 481(S), 482
Fox, D., 336, 485
Fox, W. M., 179
Francis, Clarence, 512
Frank, Andrew G., 218
Freedman, L., 86, 87
French, John R. P., Jr., 95, 98, 103, 273, 381, 384, 457
Freud, Sigmund, 99
Friedmann, Georges, 84, 100, 103, 290, 485
Friedrich, Carl J., 159, 161, 282
Frick, F. C., 436
Fromm, Eric, 97
Fuller, J. F. C., 285

Galbraith, John Kenneth, 271, 525
Galenson, Walter, 102

Gandhi, Mahatma, 296
Gardner, Burleigh B., 105, 166, 203, 224, 226
Gardner, Godfrey, 455, 456
Gaus, John M., 420
General Motors Corporation, 57
Ghiselli, E. E., 165
Gillespie, J. J., 84
Gillin, John, 54
Golden, C. S., 359
Goldhammer, Herbert, 256, 257(S), 278
Goode, C. E., 166
Goode, William J., 100, 103, 481(S)
Gordon, R. A., 3, 4, 5(S), 7, 9(S), 131(S), 164, 169, 170(S), 190, 358, 360(S)
Gouldner, Alvin W., 165, 276, 277, 286
Granick, D., 434
Greenwich Employment Exchange, 157
Grey, A. P., 288
Guerin, Gerald, 94, 98, 103
Guest, Robert H., 70, 74, 94, 103, 179, 243, 244, 245, 246
Guetzkow, Harold, 179
Gulick, Luther, 161, 284

Haire, Mason, 46, 185, 243
Halpin, Andrew W., 288
Hammond, Peter B., 34(S)
Harbison, Frederick H., 37(S), 40, 44, 98, 103, 136, 137(S), 146
Hardman, J. B. S., 517, 519
Hargrave, T. H., 298
Harrell, Thomas W., 70
Harris, E. F., 46
Hart, C. W. M., 517
Hartley, E. L., 276, 380
Hartmann, Heinz, 38
Hawkes, Robert W., 34(S)
Hearle, Edward F. R., 375(S)
Hebb, D. O., 53
Heinritz, Stuart F., 215
Hemphill, J. K., 170
Henderson, L. J., 325
Henning, Dale, 425(S)
Henry, William E., 166, 249, 250
Hertzberg, Frederick, 93, 94, 101, 103
Herz, John H., 419
Hirschman, Albert O., 372

Hitler, Adolf, 296
Hobbes, Thomas, 490
Hockey, B., 288
Holmes, Oliver Wendell, 515
Homans, George C., 289, 290
Hoppock, R., 70
Houghton, Harrison F., 482
Howell, James E., 3, 5(S),
    9(S), 164, 169, 170(S)
Hughes, Everett C., 301,
    397(S)
Hughes-Jones, E. M., 91
Hull, R. L., 70
Hunt, J. McV., 88
Hunter, Floyd, 517
Hyde, Howard K., 158,
    159(S)

Ibrahim, Ibrahim A., 38

Jaastad, Kay, 333
James, William, 490
Janowitz, Morris R., 184
Jaques, Elliott, 46, 47, 181,
    245, 381, 435
Jasinski, Frank J., 245, 422,
    434, 437(S)
Jenner, William, 199
Johnson, Harrison R., 499(S)
Jones, M. R., 53
Joslyn, C. J., 135
Junker, Buford H., 34(S)

Kahn, Robert L., 59, 95, 103,
    298, 454, 455
Karsh, Bernard, 480
Kasl, Stanislov V., 98, 103
Katz, Daniel, 59, 298
Katz, R. L., 176
Kelley, Harold H., 273, 276
Kendrick, John, 448
Kennedy, Andrew M., Jr.,
    215
Kerr, Clark, 98, 103
King, Alexander, 6
Kluckholn, Clyde, 55
Köchling, Ernst, 38, 40
Kohn-Bramstedt, E., 417,
    419
Kolstad, A., 70
Komarovsky, Mirra, 451
Koontz, H., 48
Kornhauser, Arthur, 95, 98,
    103, 180, 381, 384
Korol, Alexander, 17
Krauss, Irving, 164
Krech, David, 53
Kubly, Harold, 422, 431(S)

Landes, David, 42
Landsberger, Henry A.,
    291(S)
Larrabee, Eric, 75, 289
Laski, Harold, 199
Lasswell, Harold D., 284
Lawrence, P. R., 48, 179, 435
Lazarsfeld, Paul F., 115
Leavitt, Harold J., 6, 93, 95,
    100, 103, 276
Lentz, Edith, 119, 232, 233
Levy, Hermann, 416
Levy, S., 86, 87
Lewin, G. W., 81
Lewin, Kurt, 54, 81, 88, 297,
    298, 380, 381, 452
Likert, Rensis, 59, 100, 103,
    454, 455, 456, 458
Lindblom, Charles E., 372,
    373
Lippitt, Ronald, 88, 381, 382
Lippmann, Walter, 515
Lipset, Seymour Martin, 102
Lipson, Leslie, 282
Litchfield, E. H., 34
Littler, M. C. Robert, 359
Lombard, George F. F., 107,
    108(S), 485
Lorge, I., 336, 337
Luce, R. D., 243
Lynn, Frank, 470

Maccoby, E., 276
McEwen, W. J., 10
McGregor, Douglas, 93, 95,
    103, 380, 383
Mack, Raymond W., 263
McKee, James S., 517
McMurry, R. N., 45, 46, 176
McNamara, Robert, 374
Maier, Norman R. F., 93, 94,
    98, 103, 450, 451, 452
Mandell, M. M., 169
Mann, Floyd C., 95, 103
Mannheim, Karl, 419
Mansfield, Edwin, 470, 471
March, James G., 10, 11,
    31(S)
Marcson, Simon, 218,
    219(S)
Marrow, Alfred, 381, 384
Marting, Elizabeth, 169
Marx, Karl, 420, 525
Maslow, A. H., 54, 93, 98,
    103
Mason, C. W., 169
Massarik, Fred, 379(S)
Maurer, Herrymon, 172

Mausner, Bernard, 94, 103
Maxwell, Clark, 490
May, R., 86
Mayo, Elton, 91, 107,
    108(S), 230, 231, 298,
    481, 485
Mead, George Herbert, 54,
    55, 248
Mechanic, David, 271,
    272(S)
Meissner, Martin, 324,
    342(S)
Melman, Seymour, 184
Mennicke, Carl, 416
Merriam, Charles E., 284,
    285, 358
Merton, Robert K., 93, 103,
    115, 148, 154, 155(S),
    191, 197(S), 199, 274,
    288, 467
Meyer, H. D., 165
Meyersohn, Rolf, 75
Michels, Robert, 396
Michigan Bell Telephone
    Co., 457
Michigan Survey Research
    Center, 70
Mill, John Stuart, 419
Miller, D. C., 502, 524
Miller, Frank B., 232, 233,
    291(S)
Mills, C. Wright, 517
Mills, John, 206
Montgomery Ward and
    Company, 296
Montjoie, René, 38
Moore, Wilbert E., 191,
    195(S), 196, 199, 218
Morris, Charles W., 248
Morse, Nancy C., 70
Mosca, Gaetano, 288, 396
Mouton, Jane S., 452
Mowrer, O. H., 86, 392
Myers, Charles A., 98, 103,
    136, 137(S), 146, 367

National Commission on
    Technology, Automation,
    and Economic Progress,
    468(S)
National Institute of Mental
    Health, 95
National Restaurant
    Association, 119
Neufeld, Maurice, 517, 519
Newcomb, T. M., 88, 276,
    380
Newcomer, Mabel, 5

New Jersey Bell Telephone
    Company, 19, 22
New Jersey Relief
    Administration, 19
Noland, E. William, 65
Nourse, E. G., 366

O'Donnell, Cyril, 48
Ogburn, William F., 505
Ogden, C. K., 326
Olds, James, 55, 56
Osborn, A. F., 332, 333, 335

Palmer, Gladys L., 479
Parkinson, C. N., 527
Parsons, Talcott, 54, 56, 263,
    288, 303
Pasteur, Louis, 199
Paul, Cedar, 412
Paul, Eden, 412
Pellegrin, Roland J., 47, 223,
    248(S)
Pelz, D. C., 46
Perlis, Leo, 519
Pierce, Frank W., 514
Piersol, D. T., 244
Pierson, Frank, 3
Pigors, P., 367
Poincaré, Henri, 490, 491
Ponder, Z. D., 243, 244, 246
Porter, L. W., 164, 165
Pound, Roscoe, 358
Pressel, G. L., 165

Raino, K., 463
Randle, C. W., 168, 170, 171,
    176
Raven, Bertram, 273
Reck, Dickson, 427(S)
Reder, M. W., 42
Remitz, Uno, 463
Reynolds, Lloyd G., 74
Rice, A. K., 457
Richards, I. A., 326
Richardson, F. L. W., 245
Richardson, Stephen A., 236
Riesman, David, 6, 289, 480,
    517
Robinson, Austin, 43
Roethlisberger, Fritz J., 180,
    190, 193(S), 194, 195,
    199, 222, 223(S), 243,
    284, 323, 324(S), 325(S),
    406, 421, 422(S), 459
Rogers, C. R., 81
Roosevelt, Franklin D., 296,
    506, 507

Rose, Matther, 482
Rosenberg, Bernard, 75, 289
Ross, E. A., 205
Rossi, Peter H., 523
Ruebmann, H. C., 40
Ruml, Beardsley, 513

Sachsenberg, E., 485
Sauer, Warren L., 516,
    517(S), 519
Sayles, Leonard R., 96, 100,
    102, 103, 107, 109,
    110(S), 182
Sayre, Morris, 514
Schaefer, John, 119
Scheff, Thomas J., 274
Schulze, Robert O., 517
Schumpeter, Joseph, 365
Schwartz, M. S., 287
Scott, William, 38
Sears, John H., 512
Seashore, Stanley E., 453,
    460, 461
Selekman, B. M., 367
Seligman, Daniel, 177
Selvin, H. C., 288
Selznick, Philip, 93, 103, 288,
    360, 387, 388(S), 394,
    395(S)
Shartle, Carroll L., 179, 182
Shaw, M. E., 336
Shepard, Herbert, 94, 103
Sherif, Muzafer, 189, 451
Shils, Edward A., 115(S),
    256, 257(S), 263, 278
Shister, Joseph, 74
Shore, R. P., 165
Simmel, Georg, 408, 409(S)
Simon, Herbert A., 10, 11,
    31(S), 82, 84, 93, 101,
    218, 256, 278, 279(S),
    285, 286, 288, 289, 293,
    324, 327, 328(S), 344,
    345(S)
Simpson, R. L., 245
Skinner, B. F., 53
Slichter, Sumner H., 359,
    360
Sloan, H. S., 504
Smith, Adam, 489
Smith, Bruce, 418
Smithburg, D. W., 286
Smyth, Richard C., 484
Snyderman, Barbara, 94, 103
Stagner, Ross, 185(S)
Stalker, G. M., 500(S)
Stanton, A. H., 287
Stene, E. O., 280

Stettinius, Edward R., Jr.,
    159
Stogdill, Ralph, 179, 182
Stone, Donald C., 358
Stone, Gregory P., 315(S)
Stone, Raleigh W., 359
Stephens, Richard, 263
Stouffer, Samuel A., 115
Strauss, George, 92, 93(S),
    96, 100, 103, 213, 214(S),
    218, 222, 232(S), 233
Stryker, Perrin, 166, 171
Sumby, W. H., 436
Super, Donald, 70
Sutton, F. X., 7, 12
Sykes, Gresham M., 275

Tagiuri, Renato, 165
Tannenbaum, Robert,
    355(S), 379(S), 380
Taussig, F. W., 135
Tawney, R. H., 525, 526
Taylor, D. W., 332, 333, 335,
    336
Taylor, Frederick W., 6, 72,
    83, 86
Tead, Ordway, 280
Thibaut, John, 273, 276
Thomas, W. I., 54
Thompson, James D., 10,
    34(S), 255, 262, 263(S)
Thompson, V. A., 286
Thorndike, Edward L., 70
Tootel, Geoffrey, 451
Tschirwa, Barbara, 16(S)
Tuckman, J., 336, 337
Tuden, Arthur, 34(S)
Tumin, Melvin M., 191,
    195(S), 199, 218
Turner, Arthur N., 453
Turner, Ralph, 436

Uhrbrock, R., 70
Ulrich, D. N., 48, 179, 435
United Service
    Organizations, 24
United States Steel
    Corporation, 57
Urwick, Lyndall, 161, 284

Veblen, Thorstein, 69, 155,
    191, 198, 289, 420
Vernoff, Joseph, 94, 103
Vidick, Arthur J., 523
Viteles, Morris, 59
von der Gablentz, Ottoheinz,
    326, 416
Vroom, Victor, 94, 98, 103

Walker, Charles R., 70, 74, 94, 103, 181, 245, 480
Warner, W. Lloyd, 243, 248, 517
Watt, R. J., 359
Weber, Max, 145, 146, 147, 149, 154, 155, 198, 258, 274, 288, 293, 294, 525, 526
Weinshall, Theodore D., 332, 339(S)
Weiss, R. S., 47, 181, 245
Werling, Richard, 100, 102
Whisler, Thomas L., 6, 100, 103
White, D. M., 75, 289
White, Leonard D., 279, 420

White, R. W., 80
Whitehead, A. N., 352
Whiting, J. M., 56
Whyte, William F., 73, 94, 105, 118, 119(S), 182, 232, 233, 243, 302
Whyte, William H., Jr., 6, 77, 103, 234, 527
Wickert, F. R., 457
Wilcock, Richard C., 478(S)
Wilensky, Harold W., 99, 103
Williams, L. C. S., 86, 87
Williams, Whiting, 59, 60(S), 318
Willits, Joseph H., 20

Wilson, Robert N., 233
Witte, E. E., 359
Wolf, R. B., 298
Wolff, Kurt H., 409
Woodward, Joan, 455
Worthy, J., 298, 380
Wray, Donald E., 58, 120, 517
Wyllie, Irvin G., 526

Young, Owen D., 512

Zaleznik, Abraham, 118, 459
Zander, A., 273, 298

# Subject Index

Adaptation of specialists, 220
Adaptive segregation of organizational membership, 46
Administered collectivities, 35
Administration, bureaucratic, 146; definition of, 34; functions of, 36; theories of, 34; types of, 145
Administrative personnel, personality characteristics of, 127; and self-confidence, 127
Administrative relationships, 253; and status, power, and authority, 254
Alienation from work, 96
Ambition, 398
Authoritarian administration, 416; and rationality, 419; and trained incapacity, 419
Authority, acceptance by subordinates, 283–84; allocation of, 288; and charisma, 295–96; charismatic type, 294; and communication, 330; defined, 256, 278–79; delegation of, 241; delegation to subordinates, 407; and democratic values, 297; distinguished from influence, 280; and its exercise, 282; and the expert, 285; formal nature of, 295; and the "last word," 281; of line and staff, 286; managerial, 139; and managers, 288; and manager-staff interaction, 294; of managers, 286; and rationality, 295–96; and status, 313
Authority pay, defined, 318
Authority structures, 294
Autocratic supervision, advantages and disadvantages of, 99; vs. power-equalization, 99
Automation, and alienation, 480; and education for leisure, 480; and hiring practice

Automation, and alienation (*cont.*)
and training, 478; and new personnel requirements, 478; and worker tensions, 480

Bleeding the line, 439
Brainstorming, 331ff.
Bureaucracy, causes of, 147–48; and compliance, 415; conditions for, 147; and decision-making, 134; and decision-making conservatism, 363; defined, 145; features of, 152; and features of bureaucratic office, 149; and functional specialization, 148; and impersonality, 152; levels of, 147; and morale, 161; and motivation, 151; pathologies of, 154ff.; and predictability, 152, 154; and rationality, 152; recruitment to, 151; and red tape, 161; and sanctions, 152; and specialists, 198; as a system of organization, 144; tendency to grow, 161; unresponsiveness of, 160; and waste, 144
Bureaucratic administration, 146
Bureaucratic office, 149–50
Bureaucratic power, 274
Business, and community leadership, 516ff.; formal characteristics of, 27; functions of, 10; and public opinion, 509; social responsibilities of, 509ff.; structure of, 9
Business changes and automation, 6; in education of executives, 6–8; and human relations, 6; and need for flexibility, 8; in organization, 5; in ownership, 5

Capital investment, 38
Caste system, and control, 500; in the office, 499; and relations off the job, 500; and social segregation, 499

Centrality, and power, 276
Centralization, of control, 140; of management, 45; and rules, 368
Central life interests, 91
Chain of command, 84
Change, by increments, 372–73
Charismatic authority, 294ff.; leadership, 401
Clothing, functions of, 314; as a function of expectations, 316; as an influence, 315; and mobility, 316; and occupational differences, 315
Coalitions, 276
Coercion, and productivity, 486
Command, defined, 387; specialization of, 310; and status, 309
Communication and the art of persuasion, 23; and authority, 330; and brain-storming, 332ff.; and coordination, 33; and coordination and cooperation, 328; defined, 323; and definition of the situation, 436; and delegation of authority, 383; and differences in perspectives, 329; of executives, 179, 185, 338; executive use of, 325; as expression of sentiments, 326–27; of foremen, 243, 246; and the function of gossip, 404; and the function of words, 326; and "getting through," 340–42; and information flow, 246; and internal and external transactions, 33; and language, 323; and "lost" interactions, 340; and media used, 339–41; misunderstandings in, 43; nonverbal, 342–43; and perspective differences, 324; physical barriers to, 343; and recall, 339; and role, 32; and rumor transmission, 32; self-perception of, 340; and sentiments, 324; and sharing knowledge, 328; and status protection, 331; and the use of conferences, 327; and the use of language, 32; and the use of symbols, 323; and work flow, 125
Community influentials, 518ff.; and business, 523; characteristics of, 518; and labor, 523
Compliance, and authoritarian administration, 415; and initiative, 415; of subordinates, 414
Conferences, 327
Conflict, between the individual and the organization, 80, 89; between specialists, 216; between staff and line, 203ff.; management of, 217
Conformity, as a function of control, 425; and the "organization man," 79
Consultants, management use of, 201
Contravailing power, 271
Control, 438; assumptions underlying, 85–86; and cheating, 434; and communication, 436; and conformity, 425; and control systems, 430ff.; and defensive behavior, 437; and deviance, 427; difficulties of, 85;

Control (*cont.*)
dimensions of, 421; and efficiency, 436ff.; evasion of, 433; and executives, 433; and leadership, 86; and managerial adaptation, 434; means of, 273; and motivation, 86; of "necessary" behavior, 74; of organization members, 85; and organization objectives, 422; and performance measurement, 423ff.; and personality, 86; and the "rabble hypothesis," 86; and rationality, 85; and standards, 425; system of, 421; and use of rules, 276; and waste, 438
Cooperation, and communication, 328; in organizations, 4; and shared values, 452; and status, 313
Cooptation, and adaptation to change, 395; defined, 395; and unity, 395
Coordination, and characteristics of individuals, 30; definition of, 428; and division of labor, 120; and molding organization members, 29; and standards, 430; and tension reduction, 121; of activities, 27ff.
Cultural lead, 505

Decentralization of industry, 482
Decision-making, and bureaucratic conservatism, 133, 363; circumstances of, 349; and communication, 11; conflicts in, 185; considerations in, 185; and coordination, 133, 428; defined, 379; and delegation, 10, 133, 379; and desires for personal power, 364; and determination of goals, 10; and the division of labor, 291; as a division of labor, 370; and economic considerations, 360ff.; and enlargement of alternatives, 382; environment of, 352–53; and evaluation of decision-makers, 351; and executive power, 188; by executives, 132, 182–83; and experimentation, 362; and feelings of inadequacy, 403; and the functions of trust, 403; in a group context, 366; and identification of variables, 375; and indeterminacy, 403; and influences on the decision-maker, 357; and kinds of decision, 348; and knowledge, 10; at lower levels, 133; and mathematical models, 374; and muddling through, 372; and need for actions, 350; occasions for decisions, 349ff.; and organization objectives, 352, 354ff.; and planning, 363; and policy changes, 370; programming of, 376; and the public influences, 507; and risk-taking, 24; and the rule-making process, 369; sharing with subordinates, 379; and simulation models, 377; and specification of objectives, 376ff.; stages of, 380; and standards, 428ff.; and subordinates, 355ff.; and uncertainty, 11, 25;

Decision-making (*cont.*)
and unions, 359, 507; and use of committees, 403; worker participation in, 451
Defensive behavior, 437
Delegation of authority, 241, 381, 407; conditions for its feasibility, 382; and education for participation, 384; and employee motivation, 381; and enlargement of decision-making alternatives, 382; and time availability, 383
Democratic administration, 417; and conflict of interests, 418; direct and indirect influences on, 418; and rationality, 419; and trained incapacity, 419
Democratic leadership, 389; dilemmas in, 386
Democratic values, and authority, 297
Depth in management, 40
Division of labor, and decision-making, 291, 371; and rule-making, 371; and specialization, 197

Economic management, and change, 13–15
Economic rewards, 99
Education, and chances for advancement, 479; for participation in decision-making, 384; and the requirements of automation, 478; of Soviet engineers, 17; of Soviet executives, 16; and values, 3
Education of executives, 6ff.; and development of intellectual capacities, 20; frame of reference, 19; and motivation, 18; and understanding, 20
Efficiency measurement, 437ff.; and cheating, 439; and friction, 441; and production jams, 439; and quality, 441; and waste, 438
Entrepreneurship in industrial development, 38
Environment, business, 11–13
Environment of organizations, 465–66
Executive communication and the art of persuasion, 23
Executive frame of reference, 4
Executives, behavior of, 164; careers of, 170; characteristics of modern type, 134; and decision-making, 182, 351; defined, 128; education of in USSR, 18; horizontal relations of, 181; importance of communication to, 325; influences on decisions, 357; interaction of, 181; internal training of, 177; personality characteristics of, 168; personal traits of, 165ff.; and pressures of responsibility, 250; recruitment of, 167, 171; recruitment of in USSR, 17; and remembered communications, 339; requirements for, 175; requirements for success, 167; and risk-taking, 24; self-conceptions of, 47, 249; self-perception of

Executive, behavior of, (*cont.*)
communication, 338; skills of, 171, 175; and strategic reasoning, 23; time spent talking, 179, 185; training of, 134, 171ff.; and use of consultants, 201; use of criticism, 435; use of specialists, 193, 202; use of time, 184; as viewed by subordinates, 250, 252
Experts, limitations of, 287; as viewed by managers, 289

Fictions, effects on innovation, 492; and ceremonial expression, 489; defined, 494; function of, 496; and organization action, 496; and organization change, 496; and organization environment, 489; and personification, 492; and planning, 497
Foremen, and communication, 242, 246; comparison of American and British, 39; comparison of American and German, 39; and control systems, 432; and delegation of authority, 241; domination of subordinates, 432; and giving orders, 246; and information flow, 246; and interaction with subordinates, 244; as marginal men, 223, 227, 229ff.; relations with subordinates, 227, 237, 433; relations with superiors, 224; relations with supervisors, 432; relations with other foremen, 226; relations with specialists, 225–26; relations with working supervisors, 234, 237; time spent talking, 243; and the union, 229; use of time, 246–47
Formal organization, 22; functions of, 503; and public opinion, 505; and rationality, 82
Frictions, organizational, 47; and efficiency measurement, 441; reduction of, 118, 121; types of, 42
Functional status systems, 311
Functions, departmental, 159
Functions of the business firm, 10

Gossip, 404
Government, and management, 143
Grapevine, 345ff.
Group dynamics, 450; defined, 298; and feedback, 451; and privilege pay, 298
Groups, apathetic, 110–11; conservative, 114; erratic, 111–12; family, 108; informal, 115; "natural," 108; organized, 109; primary, 115; strategic, 112; typology of, 108, 110

Hierarchical exclusiveness, 398
Hierarchy, 159
Horizontal relations, between departments, 292; of executives, 181; of foremen, 245; and work flow, 245

Human relations, 8, 19; and management, 128; as a supervisory function, 235; and trends to impersonalization, 236

Incentives, based on dissatisfactions, 65; based on satisfactions, 65; defined, 63; and financial payoffs, 68–69; as "functional equivalents" of services or rewards, 65; non-financial, 62, 69; to promote either mobility or stability, 67–68; for specialists, 221; and status, 313; worker response to, 64–65
Income, and mental health, 98
Incremental change, 372–73
Indifference, of the worker, 90; to work, 74
Individualism, forms of individual freedom, 78; historical context of, 77; and the organization, 79; and "self-development," 80; as a social value, 77
Industrial development, 38
Industrialization, and management, 137ff.
Industry, and the businessman's economics, 510; and industrial values, 527ff.; and its social influence, 524; and public opinion, 514; and social responsibility, 502, 512, 515, 524, 526; and society, 502
Inefficiency and irrationality, organizational causes of, 41
Influence, 280–81
Informal communication, and the grapevine, 345
Informal groups, and effects on formal organization, 115; functions of, 104ff.; influence on behavior, 106ff.; pervasiveness of, 104; relations to formal organization goals, 105; as a source of values and goals, 106; types of, 107
Informal power, 271ff.
Informal relations, defined, 118
Information flow, to and from foremen, 246
Innovation, and organization, 492
Interaction, of executives, 180; of foremen, 243ff.
Interdepartmental coordination, 217–18

Job design, 471
Job enlargement, 88
Job satisfaction, 70; and alienation, 96; alternatives to, 98; as a function of stability, 101; and idealization of the past, 96

Labor, and community leadership, 517ff.
Leadership, 449; and centralization and decentralization, 387; charismatic, 401; defined, 387; and dissidents, 394; and formal position, 390; and incentives, 131; and inherent democracy, 393; and institutional goals, 389; and morale, 449; and

Leadership (*cont.*)
policy, 388; political character of, 386; procedures for selecting, 393; and productivity, 444ff.; qualifications for, 392; recruitment of, 386; and responsibility, 392; and sponsorship, 397; and technology, 445; trained incapacity of, 399
Line authority, 286

Machine theory of organization, 30ff.
Management, and a balanced perspective, 8; centralization of, 45; and charismatic leadership, 401; and dependency on subordinate support, 401; and escape from isolation, 402; and favoritism, 403; and human relations, 8; as an investment, 37ff.; participation in, 381; practices of, 493ff.; professional, 160; relations with specialists, 217; as a resource, 138; and social isolation, 400; in the USSR, 16; and staff-line conflict, 211; as the ultimate authority, 400; and use of committees, 402; and use of mathematical models, 375; and work load, 184
Managerial authority, 140–41
Managers, characteristics of, 287; dependency on others, 291; professional, 135–36, 142–43; recruitment of, 287
Marginal man, the foreman, 227ff.; the supervisor, 223; the working supervisor, 235
Mathematical models, 374ff.; use of, 378
Mental health, 97–98
Mobility, 397
Motivation, and conformity, 71; defined, 53; and drives, 55; and economic rewards, 99; and emotional commitment, 57; as exchange between individual and environment, 50ff.; as a function of task requirements, 57, 73; and incentives, 55, 450; and indifference, 73–74; as internalized social definitions, 56ff.; mechanisms of, 53; and non-financial payoffs, 317; and socialist theory, 450; of specialists, 221; stability of, 58–59; and status, 307; of supervisors, 251; worker, 450
Muddling through, 371ff.

Necessary behavior, 76ff.
Need hierarchy, 93ff.
Nepotism in leadership, 399
Non-financial incentives, 62ff.
Non-formal relations, 118
Non-verbal communication, 342ff.

Organization, attachment to, 90; boundaries of, 28; charter of, 44; environment, 5, 45–46, 502ff.
Organization fictions, 488ff.

Organization man, 526–27
Organization office, 129ff.
Output per man-hour, 446ff.; as a measure of productivity, 468

Passing the buck, 197, 369
Pathology, bureaucratic, 155ff.
Payoffs, and authority pay, 318; financial, 68ff.; non-financial, 317; and power pay, 317; to specialists, 221; and status pay, 319
Performance, measurement of, 423ff.
Performance standards for workers, 100
Personality vs. organization hypothesis, 93ff.
Personal relations, 117
Pluralism, 78–79
Political aspects of leadership, 388
Power, allocation of, 263ff.; assessments of in community, 521–22; bilateral, 260; of bureaucrats, 274; and centrality, 276; concentration and diffusion of, 261; contravailing, 271; and control, 273; defined, 256, 263, 273; direct and indirect exercise of, 260; and domination, 258; and expertise, 275; forms of, 257; as a function of knowledge, 276; informal, 271ff.; and knowledge, 275; as a latent force, 256; and legitimacy, 258; perception of, 268–69; and personal characteristics, 276; and power structure defined, 263; and rank, 272; and replaceability, 275; and status differentials, 265; of subordinates, 271ff.; and use of sanctions, 259
Power-equalization, 92ff.
Power pay, 317
Power structure, 263
Primary group, 115
Privilege pay, 297
Problem solving, 334ff.; and cooperation, 452
Productivity, 443; and collaboration of workers, 481; and company efficiency, 445; and creative thinking, 445; and decentralization, 482; defined, 445; of deviants, 459; difficulty in measurement of, 446; and group cohesiveness, 460; and group dynamics, 451; influence of social factors on, 458; of labor as a function of organization, 40–41; and leadership, 443ff.; and morale, 481; and output per man-hour, 469; as output per man-hour, 446ff.; and rewards, 459; and social status, 459; and supervision, 460ff.; and technology, 443, 469; as total factor productivity, 448; and work group influences, 463
Professionalization of business, 5, 131
Professional managers, 135ff., 159
Profits, 361ff.
Programmed work, 100

Programming of decisions, dynamic, 377; linear, 376

Rabble hypothesis, 86
Rational economics, 383
Rationality, 82–83
Reciprocity, 116
Recruitment, of managers, 287; of specialists, 219; of workers, 440–41
Redesign of jobs, 101
Reign of rules, 368
Resentment of authority, 412
Rules, in bargaining, 277; and buck passing, 369; and centralization, 368; and efficiency, 368; as indirect control devices, 276; and predictability, 367
Rumor transmission, 32

Sanctions, applied to superiors, 283; and group behavior, 116; and power, 259
Scientific management, 375, 449
Scientists, 219ff.
Self-actualization, 84ff.; and apathy, 97; and freedom, 97; relative need for, 95
Self-conceptions, of executives, 47, 249; of specialists, 219ff.; of supervisors, 250ff.
Self-development, 80ff.
Span of control, 43
Specialists, adaptation to the organization, 220; and autonomy, 444; as bureaucrats, 198; clothing of, 208; conflict with line, 203ff.; conflict with other specialists, 216; and consumers, 195–96; defined, 128; and efficiency, 193; frustrations of, 205; functions of, 190, 193–94; incentives for, 220–21; integration into organization, 44; as marginal men, 218; motivation of, 221; as organization members, 191ff., 202, 213ff.; and passing the buck, 197; professional ethic of, 197; recruitment of, 219; relations with foremen, 225–26; relations with management, 217; self-conception of, 219, 221; social insulation of, 198, 207; social status of, 195, 207; and trade secrets, 196; and trained incapacity, 191, 199
Specialization, 6, 84; and chain of command, 84; of command, 310; and expertise, 473; as integrated tasks, 474; and job placement, 73; and task requirements, 73; and technology, 72–73, 473; and trained incapacity, 473
Sponsorship, 397
Staff-line conflict, 203ff.; and fear of innovations, 211; line resistance to staff influence, 208; management's role in, 212; and staff compromises, 210–11

Standards, and coordination, 430; and decision-making, 428–29; need for, 430; and rules, 367

Status, and ability, 305, 308; and authority, 312; and clothing, 314–15; and command, 309; and cooperation, 310, 313; credentials of, 306; defined, 300ff.; differentials of, 228; effects on motivation, 307; as a functional system, 302–3, 311–12; induction into, 304; as insignia of office, 311; as non-financial payoff, 317; and power and authority differentials, 265; scalar, 303; segregation by ability, 309–10; and social values, 307; sources of, 305; and status pay, 319; symbols of, 304; types of, 301; of work, 60ff.

Status pay, 319

Status protection, 331

Strategic groups, 113

Subdivision of work, 474ff.

Subordination, 406ff.; and authoritarian administration, 416; and coercion, 410; and democratic administration, 417; positive functions of, 408; and resentment, 412; and self-esteem, 413

Superordination, 409ff.

Supervision, and management of machines, 463; and morale, 453, 455; multiple goals of, 452; and productivity, 453ff.; and worker autonomy, 454

Supervisors, and the caste system, 500; and coordination of activity, 450; defined, 128; and human relations, 235; as marginal men, 222; motivations of, 251; personality characteristics of, 247; and public opinion, 503; sharing decision-making with, 451; and social responsibility, 503; and work group atmosphere, 450

Task specialization, 84

Technological innovation, 470ff.; and job security, 477ff.

Technology, American genius for, 471; and change, 467; human consequences of, 471; and ideas, 467; industrial motivation for, 476; and new work tasks, 476; and productivity, 468ff.; and specialization, 72, 473; and tools, 467

Tension, 122

Theory Y, 95

Total factor productivity, 448

Trained incapacity, 191, 199

Unions, and authority sharing with management, 507; community power of, 519ff.; influence of, 507; influence on managerial decision-making, 359; and organizational rules, 368; and the working supervisor, 239

Voluntarism, 76

Voluntary associations of executives, 47

Welfare capitalism, 449

Work, and central life interests, 91–92

Worker autonomy, 455–56

Worker participation, in decision-making, 456ff.; and motivation, 457; and zone of indifference, 458

Workers, and communication, 342ff.

Work flow, and communication, 124; and friction, 125; and horizontal relations, 245; and origination of action, 122; and social insulation, 123

Working supervisor, 222ff.; changing functions of, 232ff.; as marginal men, 235; and the new foremen, 234; and promotion opportunities, 236; and the union, 239

Zone of indifference, 284–85, 458